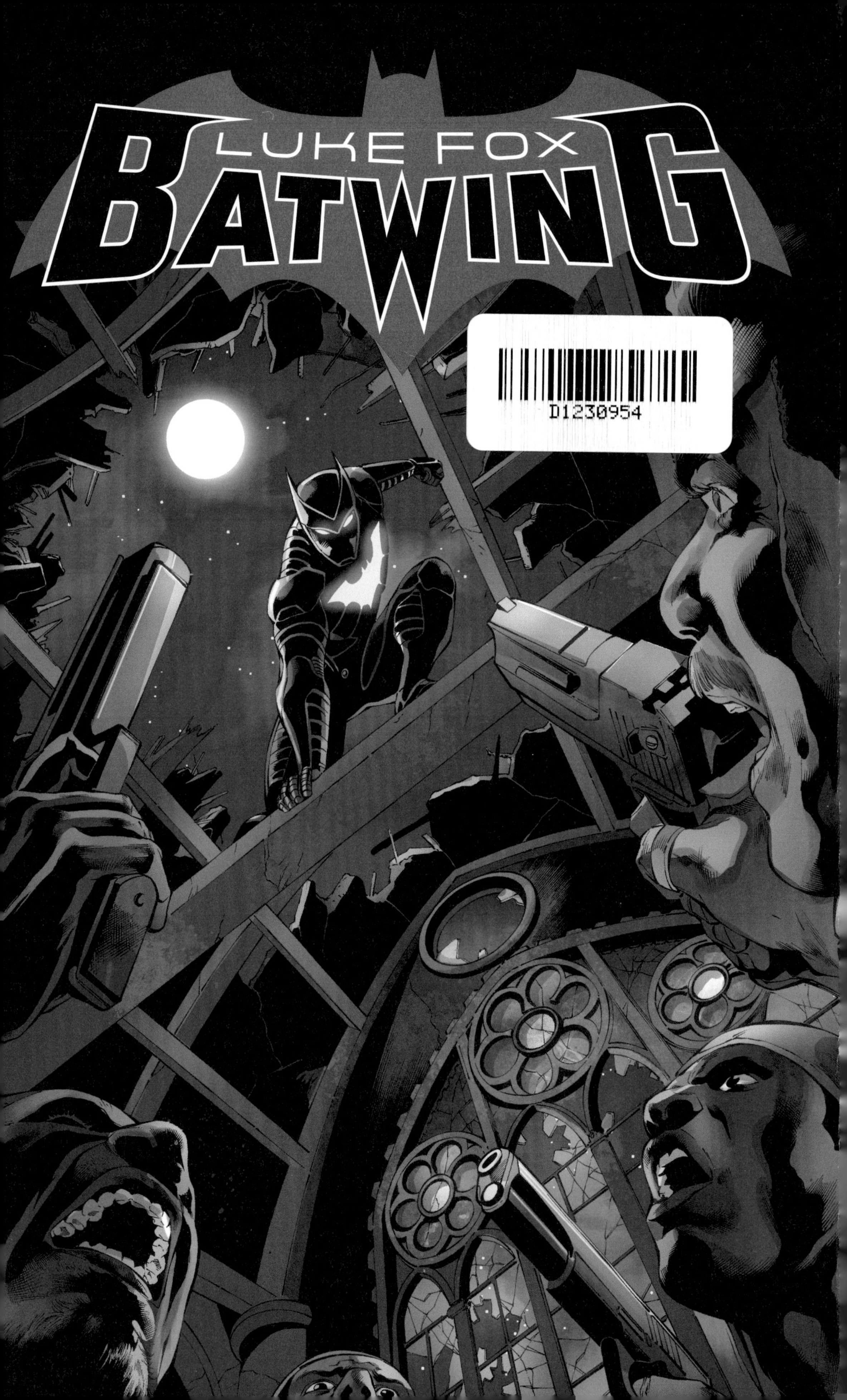
LUKE FOX
BATWING

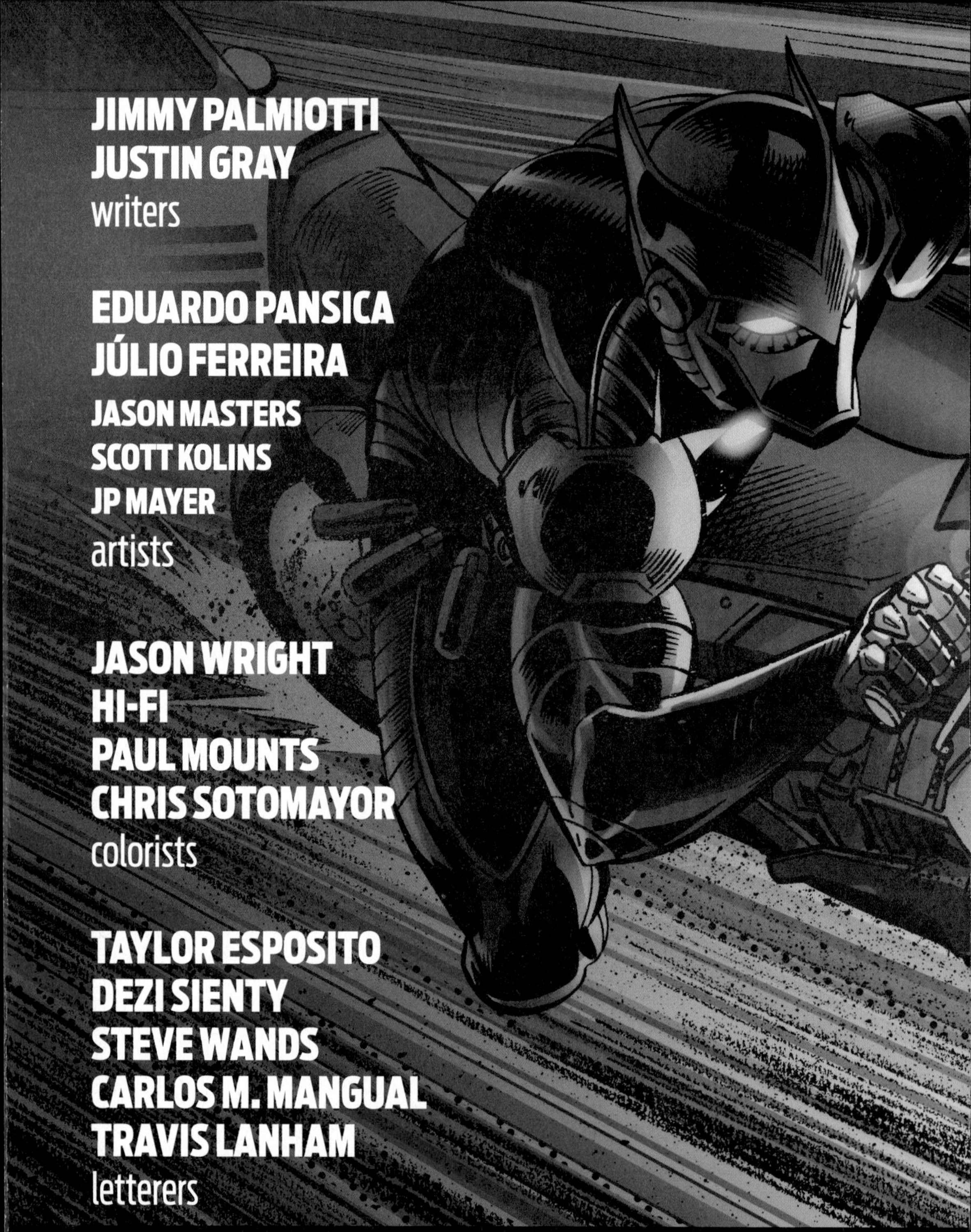

JIMMY PALMIOTTI
JUSTIN GRAY
writers

EDUARDO PANSICA
JÚLIO FERREIRA
JASON MASTERS
SCOTT KOLINS
JP MAYER
artists

JASON WRIGHT
HI-FI
PAUL MOUNTS
CHRIS SOTOMAYOR
colorists

TAYLOR ESPOSITO
DEZI SIENTY
STEVE WANDS
CARLOS M. MANGUAL
TRAVIS LANHAM
letterers

MIKE McKONE
collection cover artist

BATMAN created by
BOB KANE with **BILL FINGER**

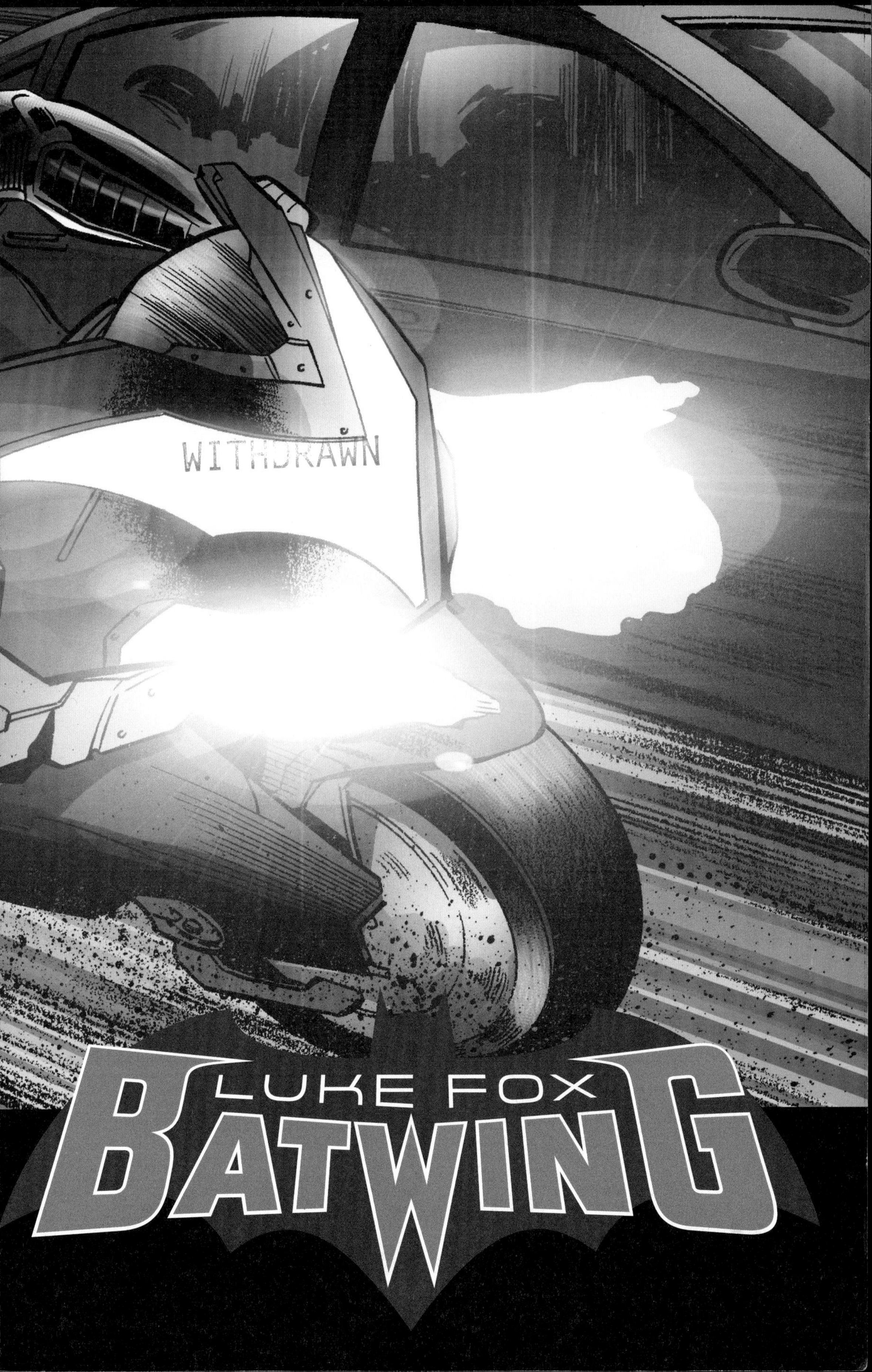

LUKE FOX BATWING

Rachel Gluckstern	Editor - Original Series
Darren Shan	Associate Editor - Original Series
Matt Humphreys	
Dave Wielgosz	Assistant Editors - Original Series
Robin Wildman	Editor - Collected Edition
Steve Cook	Design Director - Books & Publication Design
Suzannah Rowntree	Publication Production
Marie Javins	Editor-in-Chief, DC Comics
Daniel Cherry III	Senior VP - General Manager
Jim Lee	Publisher & Chief Creative Officer
Don Falletti	VP - Manufacturing Operations & Workflow Management
Lawrence Ganem	VP - Talent Services
Alison Gill	Senior VP - Manufacturing & Operations
Jeffrey Kaufman	VP - Editorial Strategy & Programming
Nick J. Napolitano	VP - Manufacturing Administration & Design
Nancy Spears	VP - Revenue

BATWING: LUKE FOX

Published by DC Comics. Compilation and all new material Copyright © 2022 DC Comics. All Rights Reserved. Originally published in single magazine form in *Batwing* 19-34, *Batwing: Futures End* 1. Copyright © 2013, 2014 DC Comics. All Rights Reserved. All characters, their distinctive likenesses, and related elements featured in this publication are trademarks of DC Comics. The stories, characters, and incidents featured in this publication are entirely fictional. DC Comics does not read or accept unsolicited submissions of ideas, stories, or artwork. DC - a WarnerMedia Company.

DC Comics, 2900 West Alameda Ave., Burbank, CA 91505
Printed by Solisco Printers, Scott, QC, Canada. 1/7/22.
First Printing. ISBN: 978-1-77951-420-2

Library of Congress
Cataloging-in-Publication
Data is available.

PEFC Certified

This product is from
sustainably managed
forests and controlled
sources

PEFC

PEFC/26-31-02   www.pefc.org

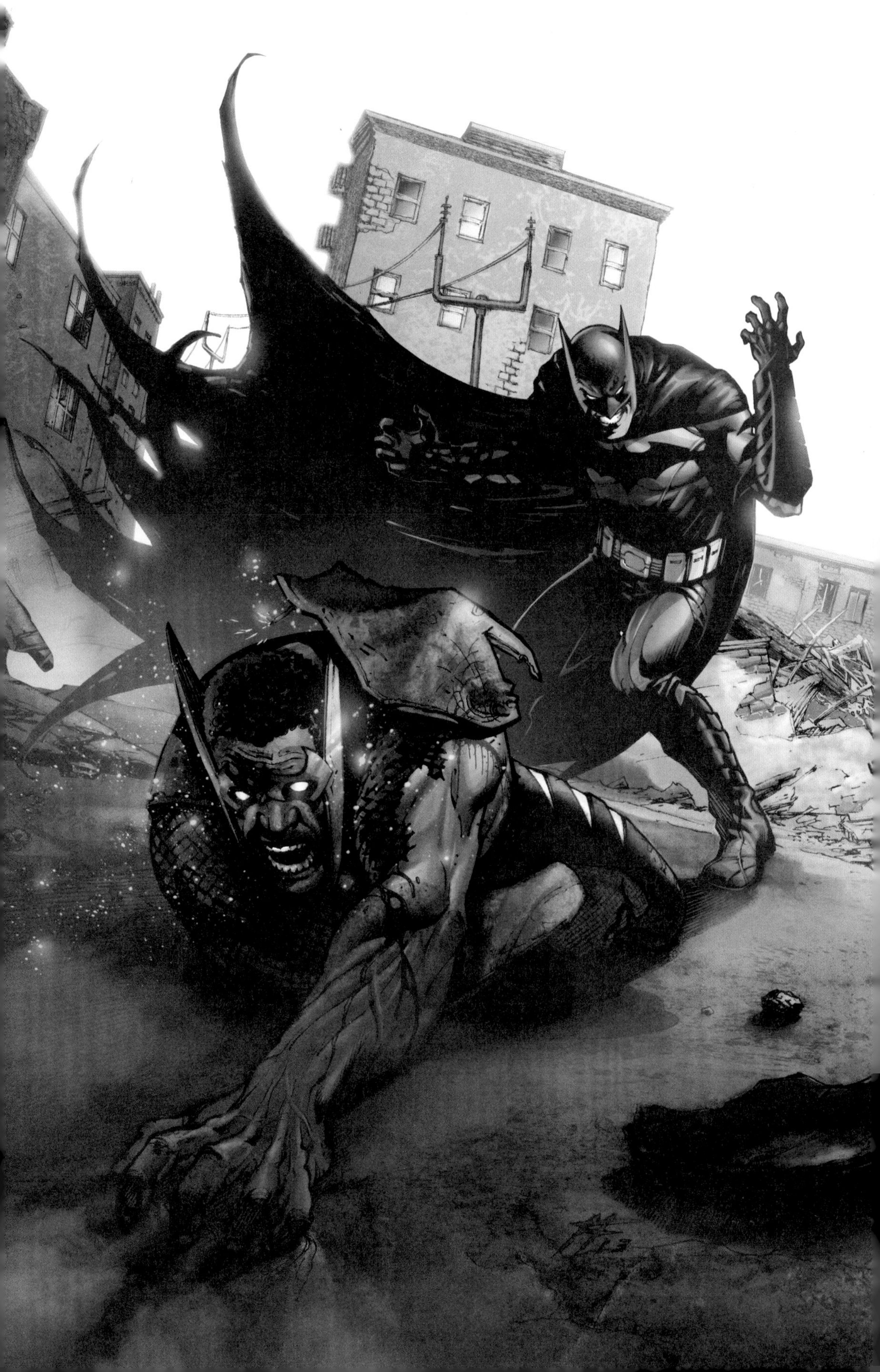

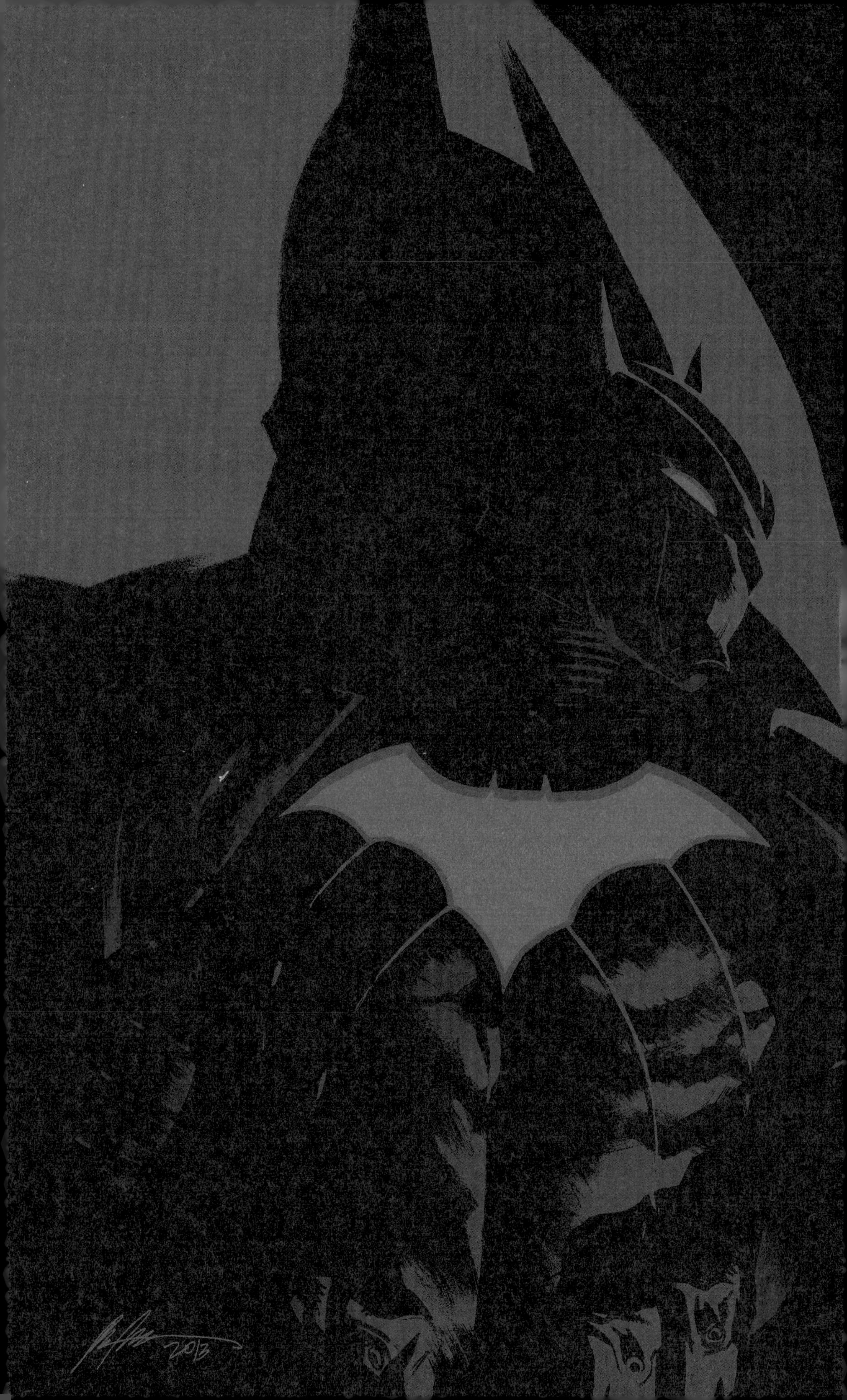

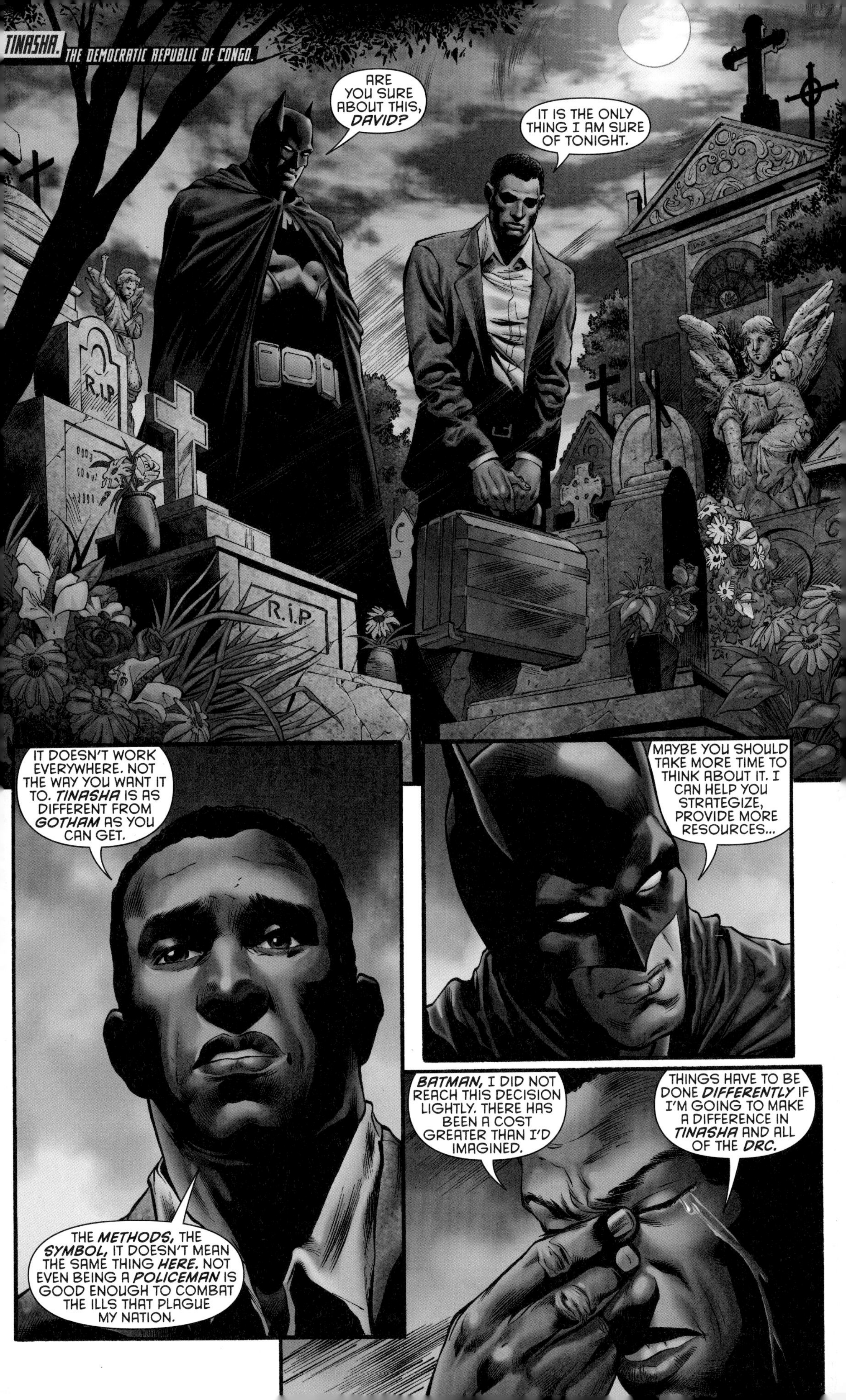
TINASHA. THE DEMOCRATIC REPUBLIC OF CONGO.
ARE YOU SURE ABOUT THIS, DAVID?
IT IS THE ONLY THING I AM SURE OF TONIGHT.
IT DOESN'T WORK EVERYWHERE. NOT THE WAY YOU WANT IT TO. TINASHA IS AS DIFFERENT FROM GOTHAM AS YOU CAN GET.
THE METHODS, THE SYMBOL, IT DOESN'T MEAN THE SAME THING HERE. NOT EVEN BEING A POLICEMAN IS GOOD ENOUGH TO COMBAT THE ILLS THAT PLAGUE MY NATION.
MAYBE YOU SHOULD TAKE MORE TIME TO THINK ABOUT IT. I CAN HELP YOU STRATEGIZE, PROVIDE MORE RESOURCES...
BATMAN, I DID NOT REACH THIS DECISION LIGHTLY. THERE HAS BEEN A COST GREATER THAN I'D IMAGINED.
THINGS HAVE TO BE DONE DIFFERENTLY IF I'M GOING TO MAKE A DIFFERENCE IN TINASHA AND ALL OF THE DRC.

A SEASON OF CHANGE

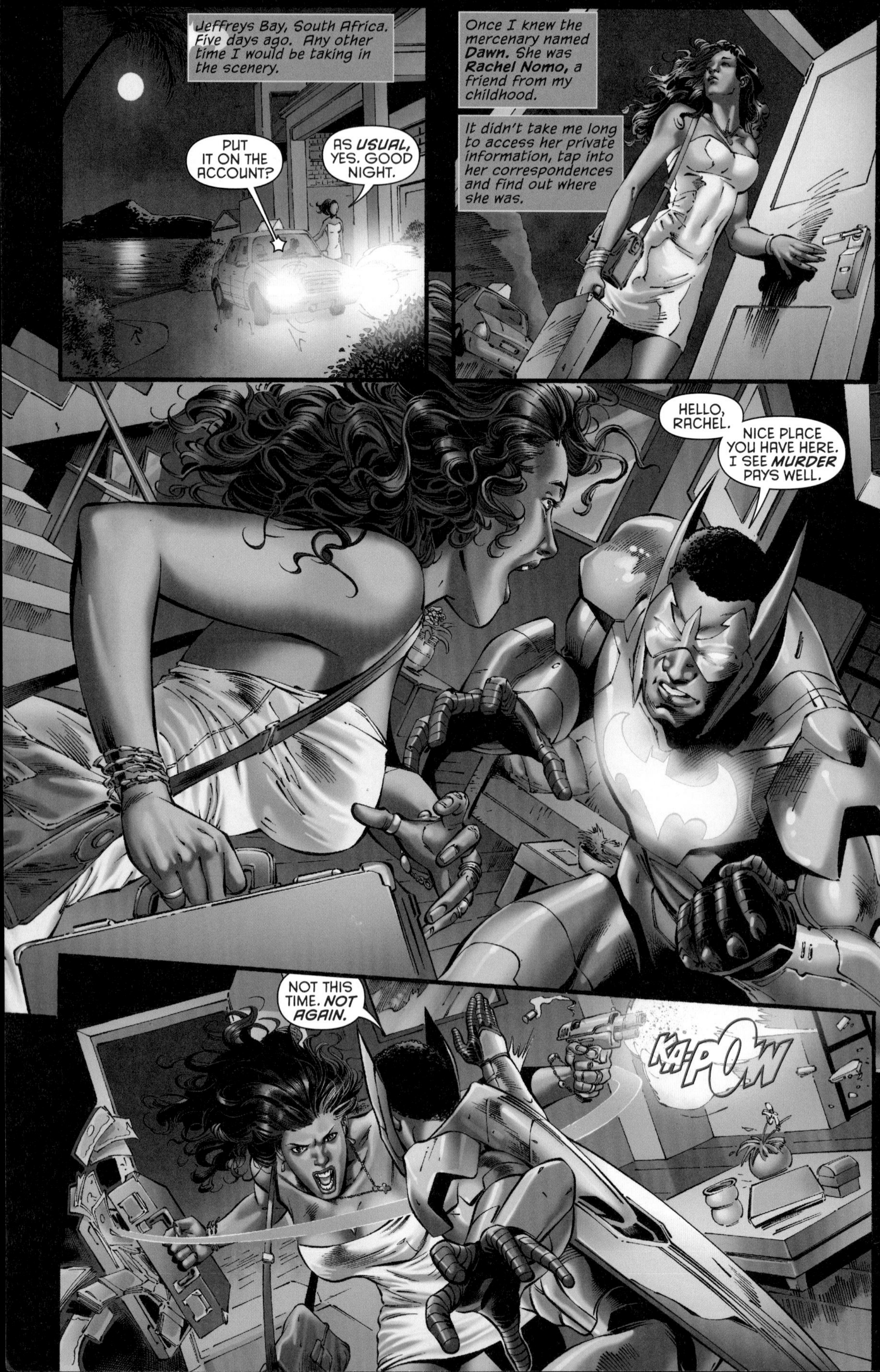

Jeffreys Bay, South Africa. Five days ago. Any other time I would be taking in the scenery.
PUT IT ON THE ACCOUNT?
AS USUAL, YES. GOOD NIGHT.
Once I knew the mercenary named Dawn. She was Rachel Nomo, a friend from my childhood.
It didn't take me long to access her private information, tap into her correspondences and find out where she was.
HELLO, RACHEL.
NICE PLACE YOU HAVE HERE. I SEE MURDER PAYS WELL.
NOT THIS TIME. NOT AGAIN.
KA-POW

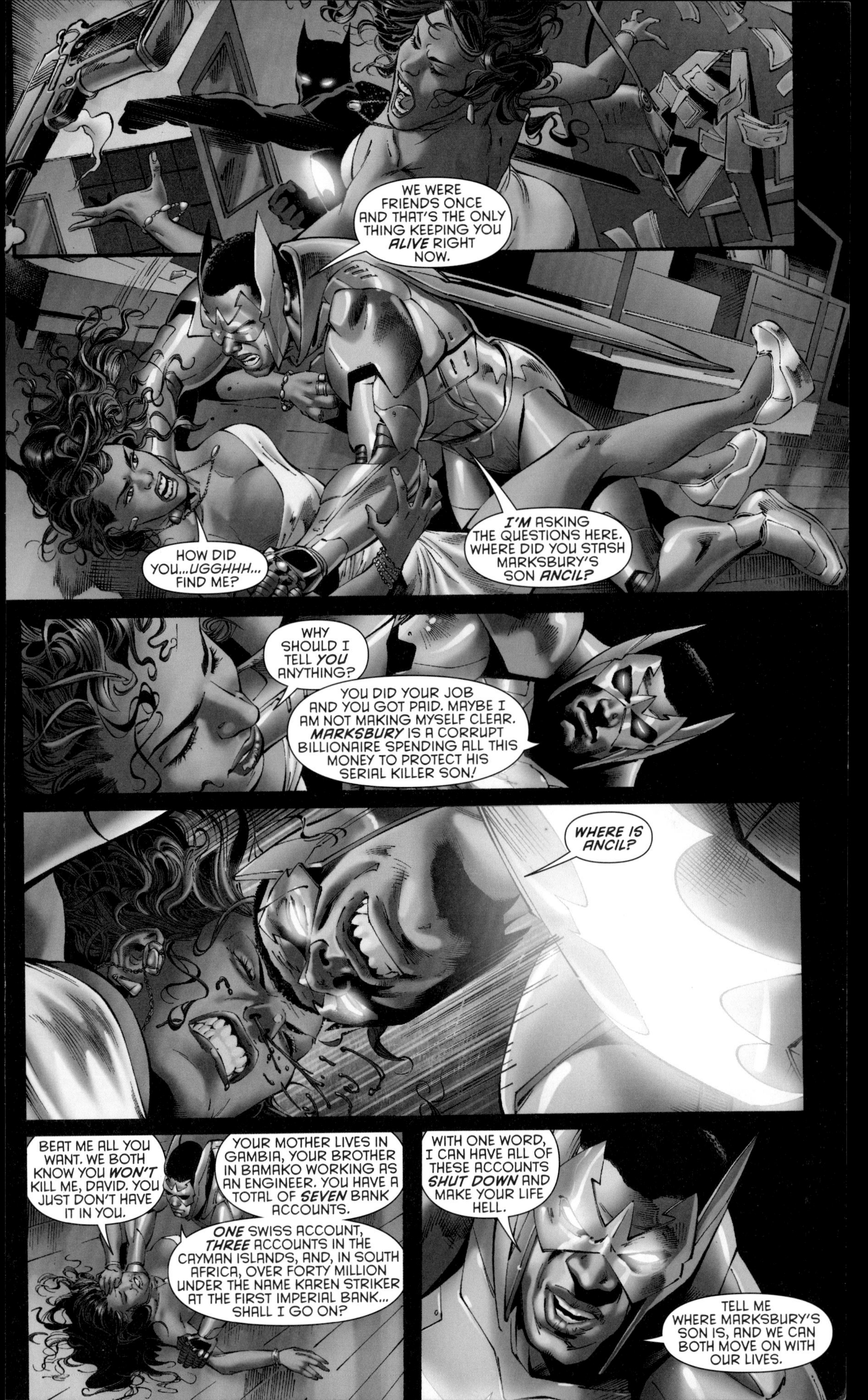

WE WERE FRIENDS ONCE AND THAT'S THE ONLY THING KEEPING YOU ALIVE RIGHT NOW.
HOW DID YOU...UGGHHH... FIND ME?
I'M ASKING THE QUESTIONS HERE. WHERE DID YOU STASH MARKSBURY'S SON ANCIL?
WHY SHOULD I TELL YOU ANYTHING?
YOU DID YOUR JOB AND YOU GOT PAID. MAYBE I AM NOT MAKING MYSELF CLEAR. MARKSBURY IS A CORRUPT BILLIONAIRE SPENDING ALL THIS MONEY TO PROTECT HIS SERIAL KILLER SON!
WHERE IS ANCIL?
BEAT ME ALL YOU WANT. WE BOTH KNOW YOU WON'T KILL ME, DAVID. YOU JUST DON'T HAVE IT IN YOU.
YOUR MOTHER LIVES IN GAMBIA, YOUR BROTHER IN BAMAKO WORKING AS AN ENGINEER. YOU HAVE A TOTAL OF SEVEN BANK ACCOUNTS.
ONE SWISS ACCOUNT, THREE ACCOUNTS IN THE CAYMAN ISLANDS, AND, IN SOUTH AFRICA, OVER FORTY MILLION UNDER THE NAME KAREN STRIKER AT THE FIRST IMPERIAL BANK... SHALL I GO ON?
WITH ONE WORD, I CAN HAVE ALL OF THESE ACCOUNTS SHUT DOWN AND MAKE YOUR LIFE HELL.
TELL ME WHERE MARKSBURY'S SON IS, AND WE CAN BOTH MOVE ON WITH OUR LIVES.

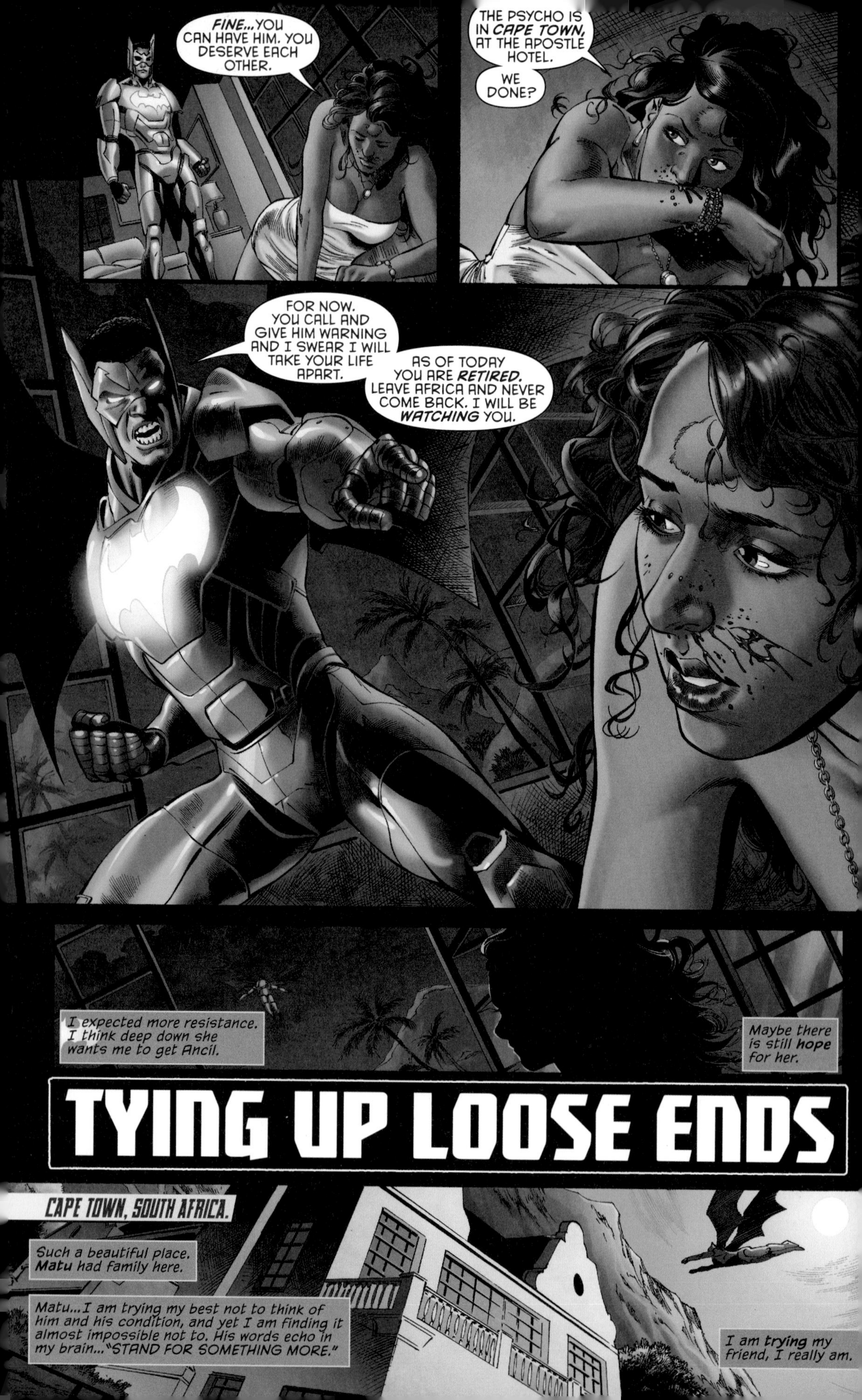

FINE...YOU CAN HAVE HIM. YOU DESERVE EACH OTHER.
THE PSYCHO IS IN CAPE TOWN, AT THE APOSTLE HOTEL.
WE DONE?
FOR NOW. YOU CALL AND GIVE HIM WARNING AND I SWEAR I WILL TAKE YOUR LIFE APART.
AS OF TODAY YOU ARE RETIRED. LEAVE AFRICA AND NEVER COME BACK. I WILL BE WATCHING YOU.
I expected more resistance. I think deep down she wants me to get Ancil.
Maybe there is still hope for her.
TYING UP LOOSE ENDS
CAPE TOWN, SOUTH AFRICA.
Such a beautiful place. Matu had family here.
Matu...I am trying my best not to think of him and his condition, and yet I am finding it almost impossible not to. His words echo in my brain..."STAND FOR SOMETHING MORE."
I am trying my friend, I really am.

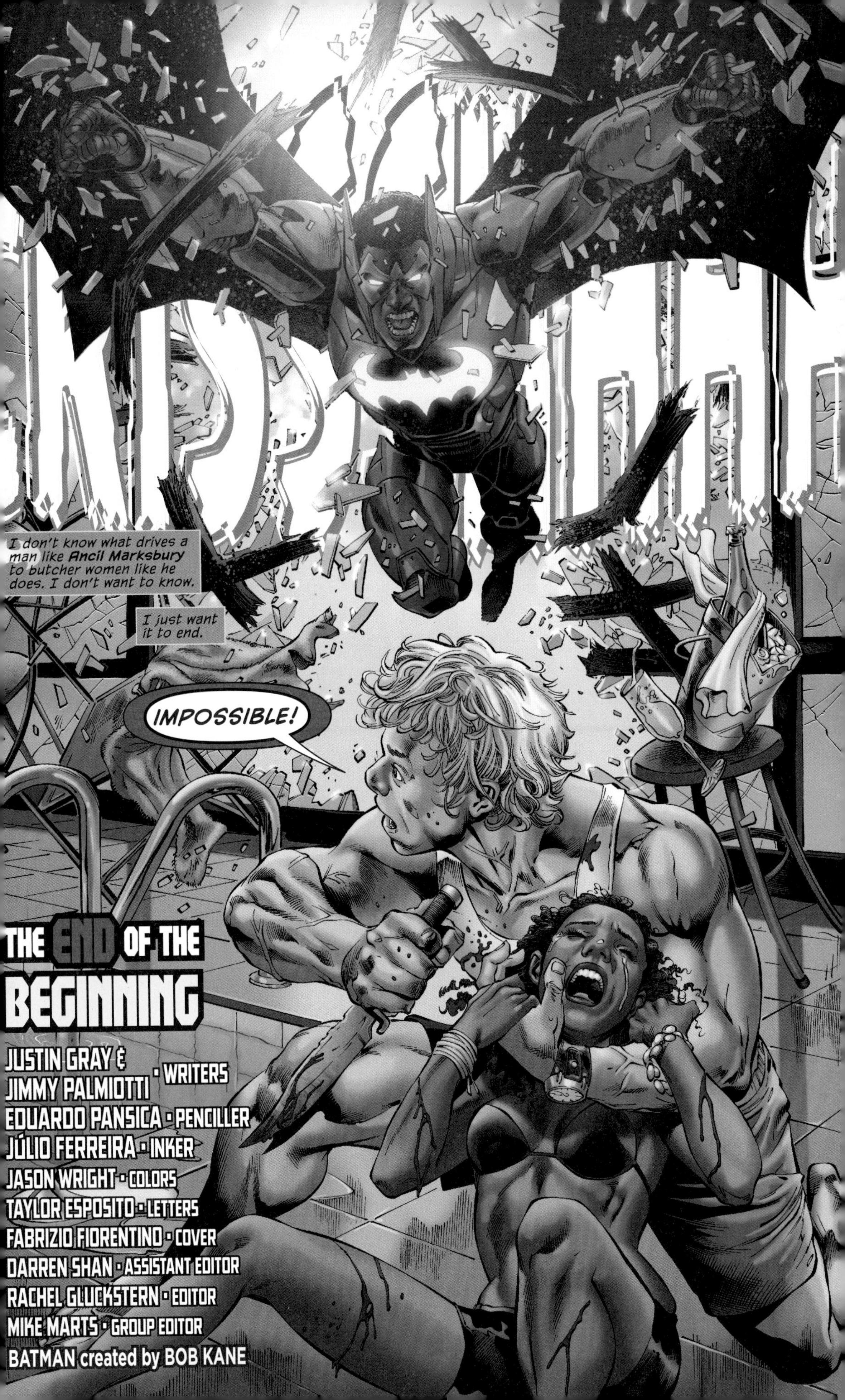
I don't know what drives a man like Ancil Marksbury to butcher women like he does. I don't want to know.
I just want it to end.
IMPOSSIBLE!
THE END OF THE BEGINNING
JUSTIN GRAY & JIMMY PALMIOTTI • WRITERS
EDUARDO PANSICA • PENCILLER
JÚLIO FERREIRA • INKER
JASON WRIGHT • COLORS
TAYLOR ESPOSITO • LETTERS
FABRIZIO FIORENTINO • COVER
DARREN SHAN • ASSISTANT EDITOR
RACHEL GLUCKSTERN • EDITOR
MIKE MARTS • GROUP EDITOR
BATMAN created by BOB KANE

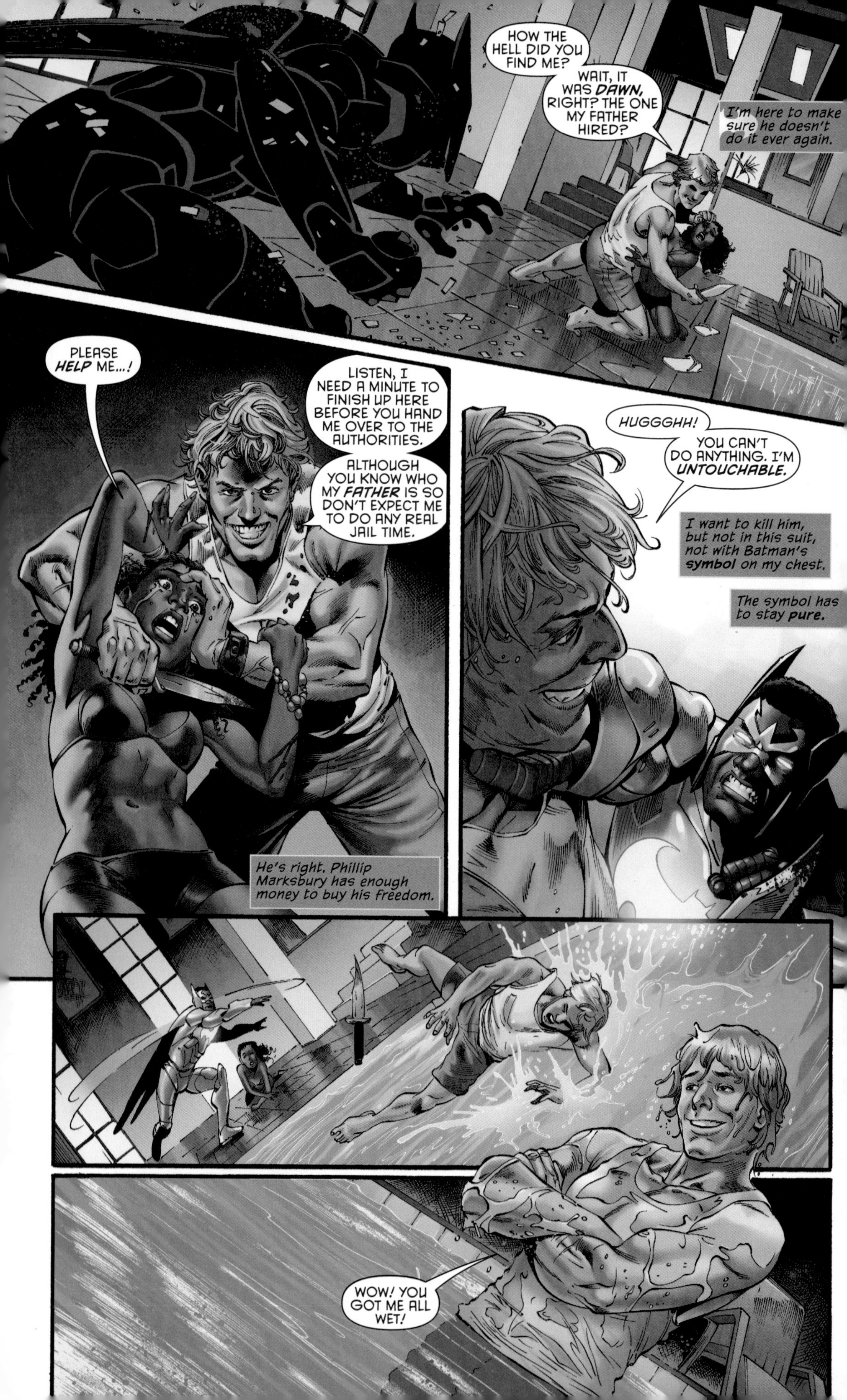
HOW THE HELL DID YOU FIND ME?
WAIT, IT WAS DAWN, RIGHT? THE ONE MY FATHER HIRED?
I'm here to make sure he doesn't do it ever again.
PLEASE HELP ME...!
LISTEN, I NEED A MINUTE TO FINISH UP HERE BEFORE YOU HAND ME OVER TO THE AUTHORITIES.
ALTHOUGH YOU KNOW WHO MY FATHER IS SO DON'T EXPECT ME TO DO ANY REAL JAIL TIME.
He's right. Phillip Marksbury has enough money to buy his freedom.
HUGGGHH!
YOU CAN'T DO ANYTHING. I'M UNTOUCHABLE.
I want to kill him, but not in this suit, not with Batman's symbol on my chest.
The symbol has to stay pure.
WOW! YOU GOT ME ALL WET!

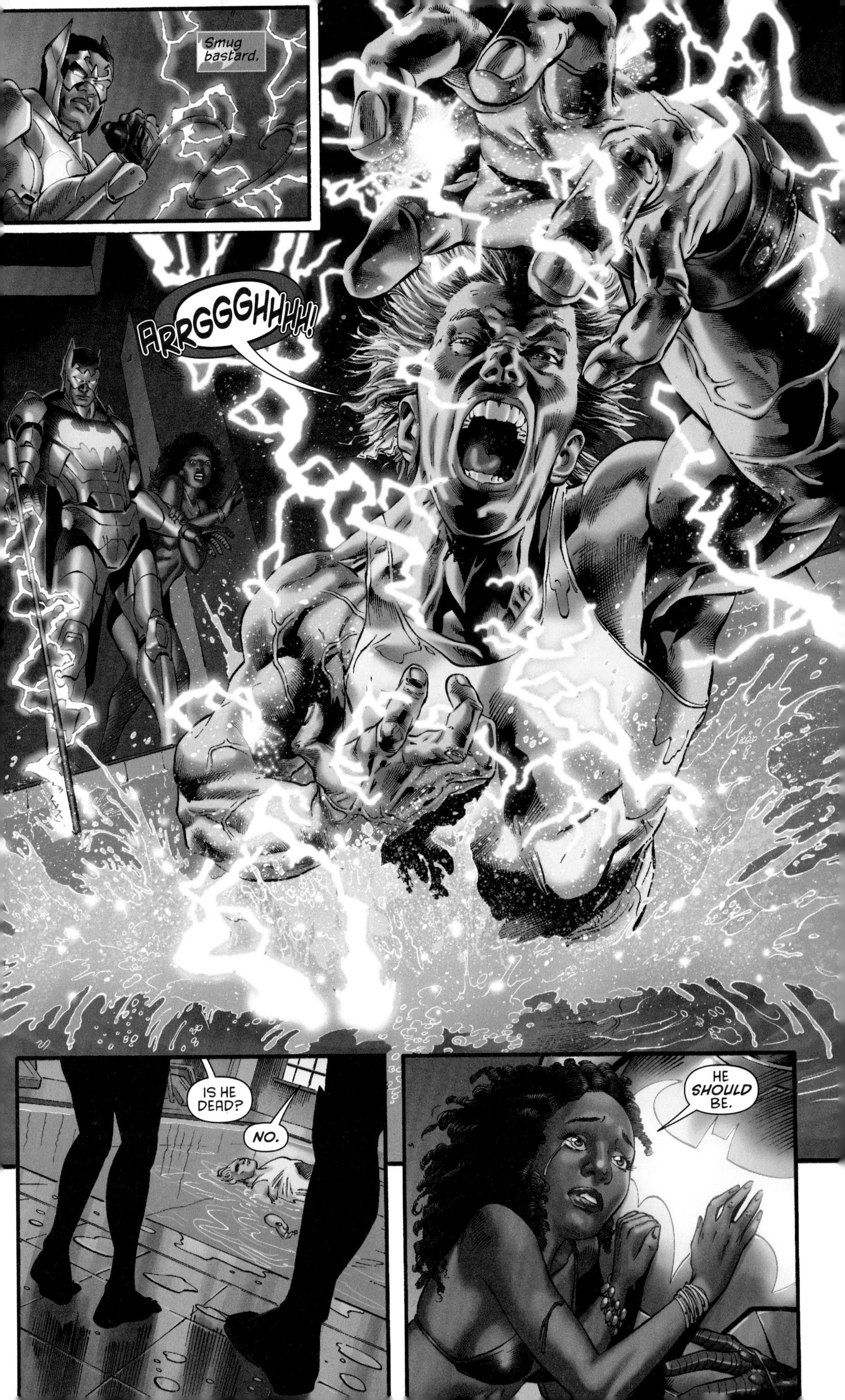
Smug bastard.
ARRGGGHHHH!
IS HE DEAD?
NO.
HE SHOULD BE.

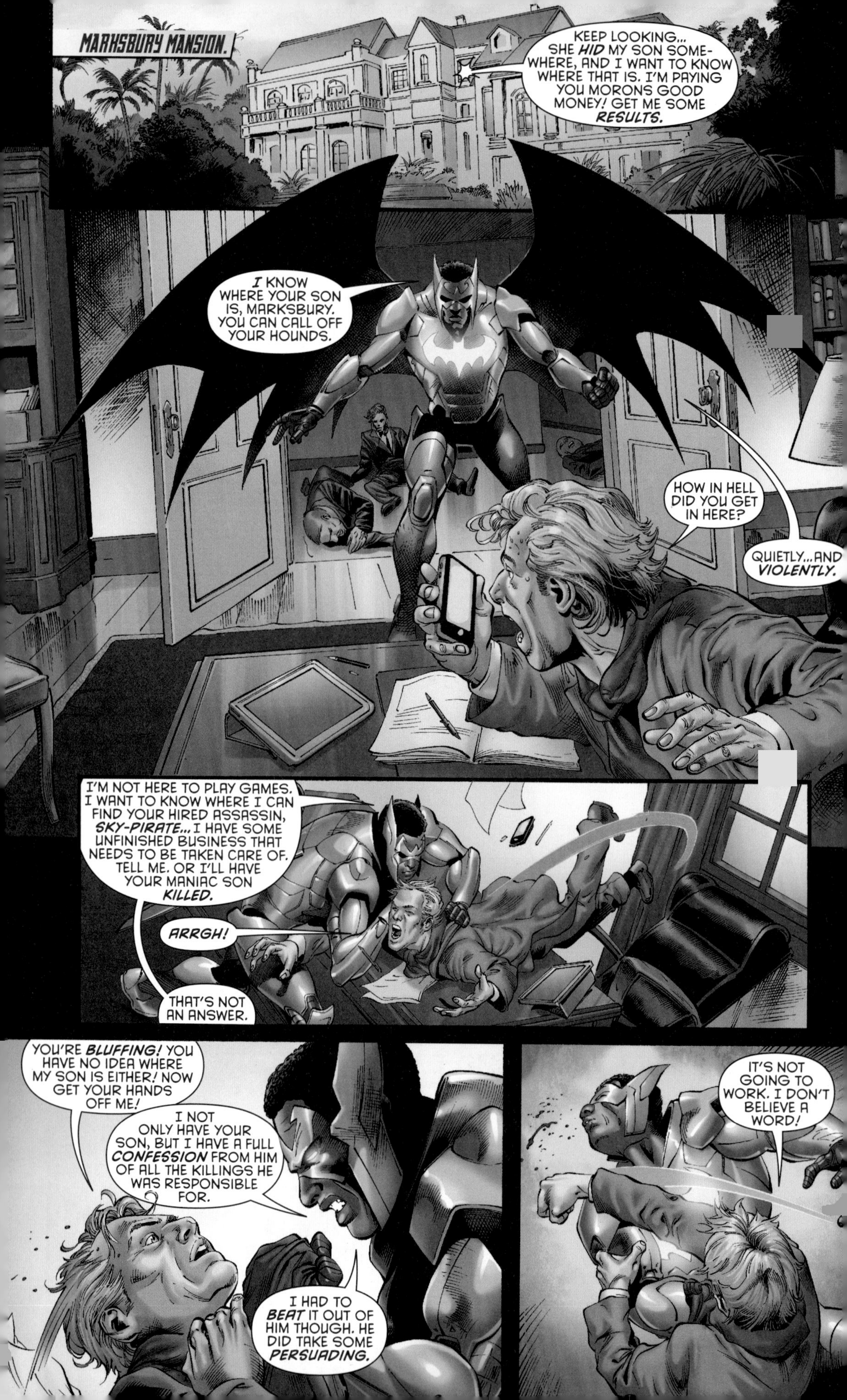
MARKSBURY MANSION.
KEEP LOOKING... SHE HID MY SON SOMEWHERE, AND I WANT TO KNOW WHERE THAT IS. I'M PAYING YOU MORONS GOOD MONEY! GET ME SOME RESULTS.
I KNOW WHERE YOUR SON IS, MARKSBURY. YOU CAN CALL OFF YOUR HOUNDS.
HOW IN HELL DID YOU GET IN HERE?
QUIETLY...AND VIOLENTLY.
I'M NOT HERE TO PLAY GAMES. I WANT TO KNOW WHERE I CAN FIND YOUR HIRED ASSASSIN, SKY-PIRATE... I HAVE SOME UNFINISHED BUSINESS THAT NEEDS TO BE TAKEN CARE OF. TELL ME. OR I'LL HAVE YOUR MANIAC SON KILLED.
ARRGH!
THAT'S NOT AN ANSWER.
YOU'RE BLUFFING! YOU HAVE NO IDEA WHERE MY SON IS EITHER! NOW GET YOUR HANDS OFF ME!
I NOT ONLY HAVE YOUR SON, BUT I HAVE A FULL CONFESSION FROM HIM OF ALL THE KILLINGS HE WAS RESPONSIBLE FOR.
I HAD TO BEAT IT OUT OF HIM THOUGH. HE DID TAKE SOME PERSUADING.
IT'S NOT GOING TO WORK. I DON'T BELIEVE A WORD!

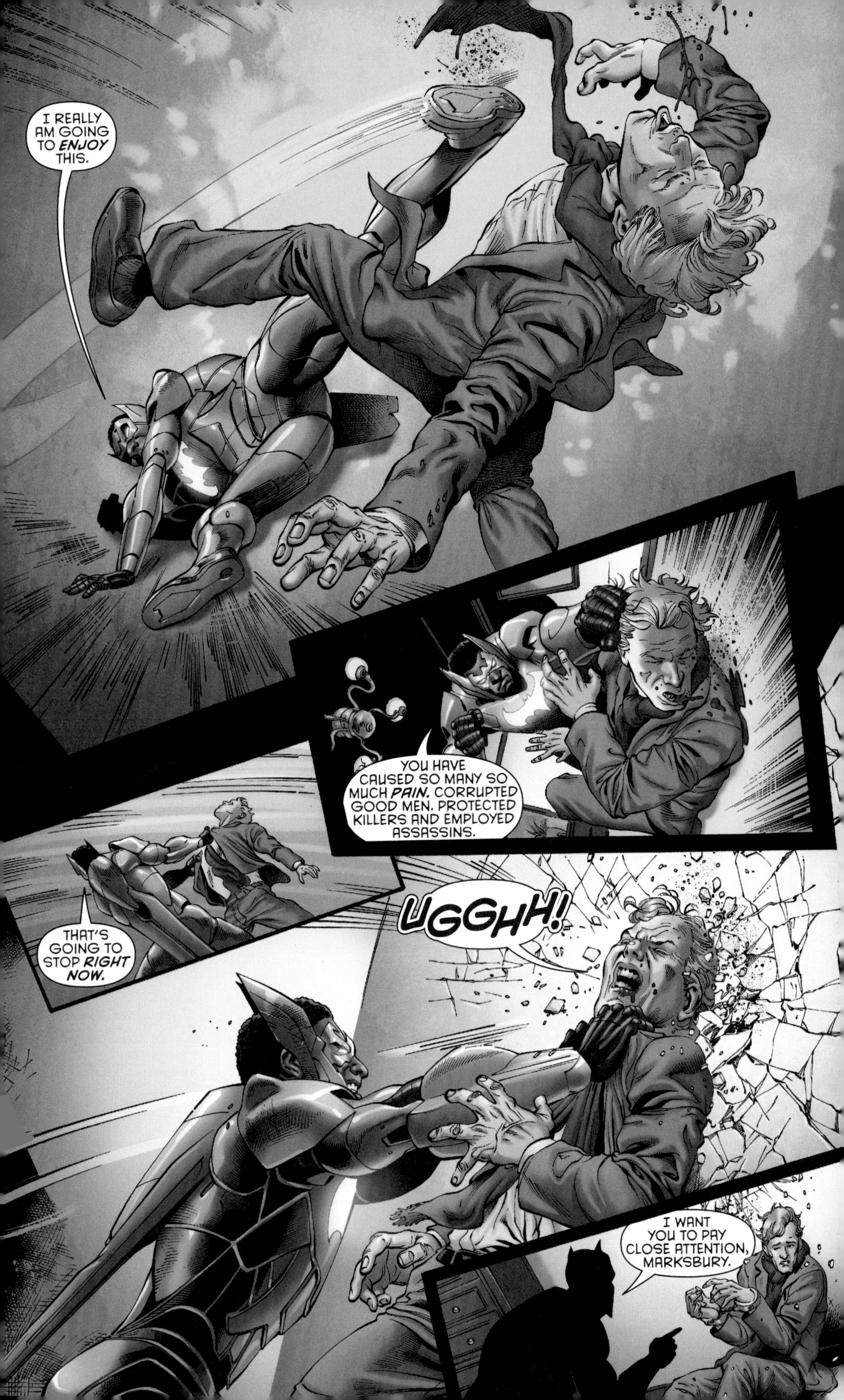
I REALLY AM GOING TO ENJOY THIS.
YOU HAVE CAUSED SO MANY SO MUCH PAIN. CORRUPTED GOOD MEN. PROTECTED KILLERS AND EMPLOYED ASSASSINS.
THAT'S GOING TO STOP RIGHT NOW.
UGGHH!
I WANT YOU TO PAY CLOSE ATTENTION, MARKSBURY.

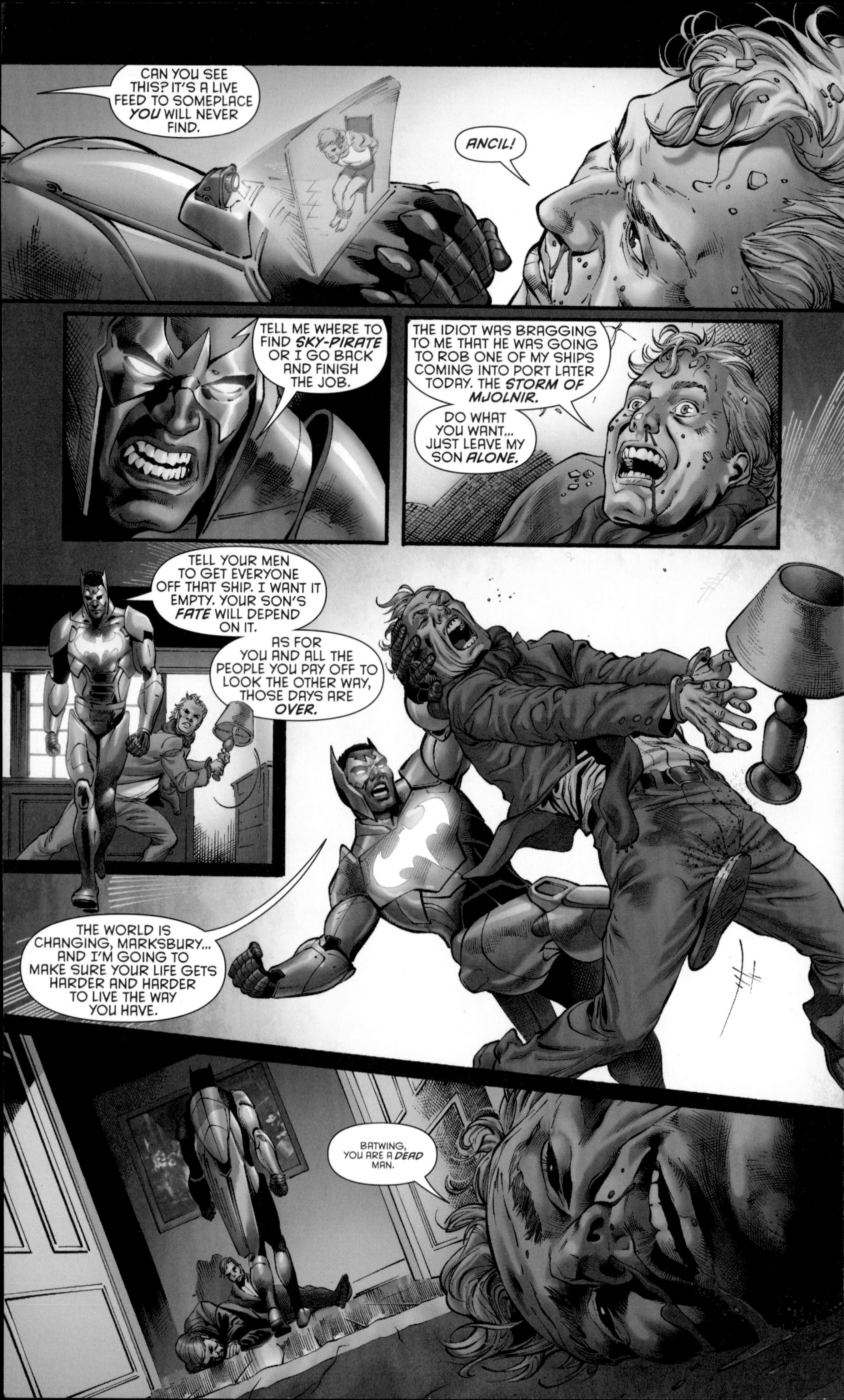
CAN YOU SEE THIS? IT'S A LIVE FEED TO SOMEPLACE YOU WILL NEVER FIND.
ANCIL!
TELL ME WHERE TO FIND SKY-PIRATE OR I GO BACK AND FINISH THE JOB.
THE IDIOT WAS BRAGGING TO ME THAT HE WAS GOING TO ROB ONE OF MY SHIPS COMING INTO PORT LATER TODAY. THE STORM OF MJOLNIR.
DO WHAT YOU WANT... JUST LEAVE MY SON ALONE.
TELL YOUR MEN TO GET EVERYONE OFF THAT SHIP. I WANT IT EMPTY. YOUR SON'S FATE WILL DEPEND ON IT.
AS FOR YOU AND ALL THE PEOPLE YOU PAY OFF TO LOOK THE OTHER WAY, THOSE DAYS ARE OVER.
THE WORLD IS CHANGING, MARKSBURY... AND I'M GOING TO MAKE SURE YOUR LIFE GETS HARDER AND HARDER TO LIVE THE WAY YOU HAVE.
BATWING, YOU ARE A DEAD MAN.

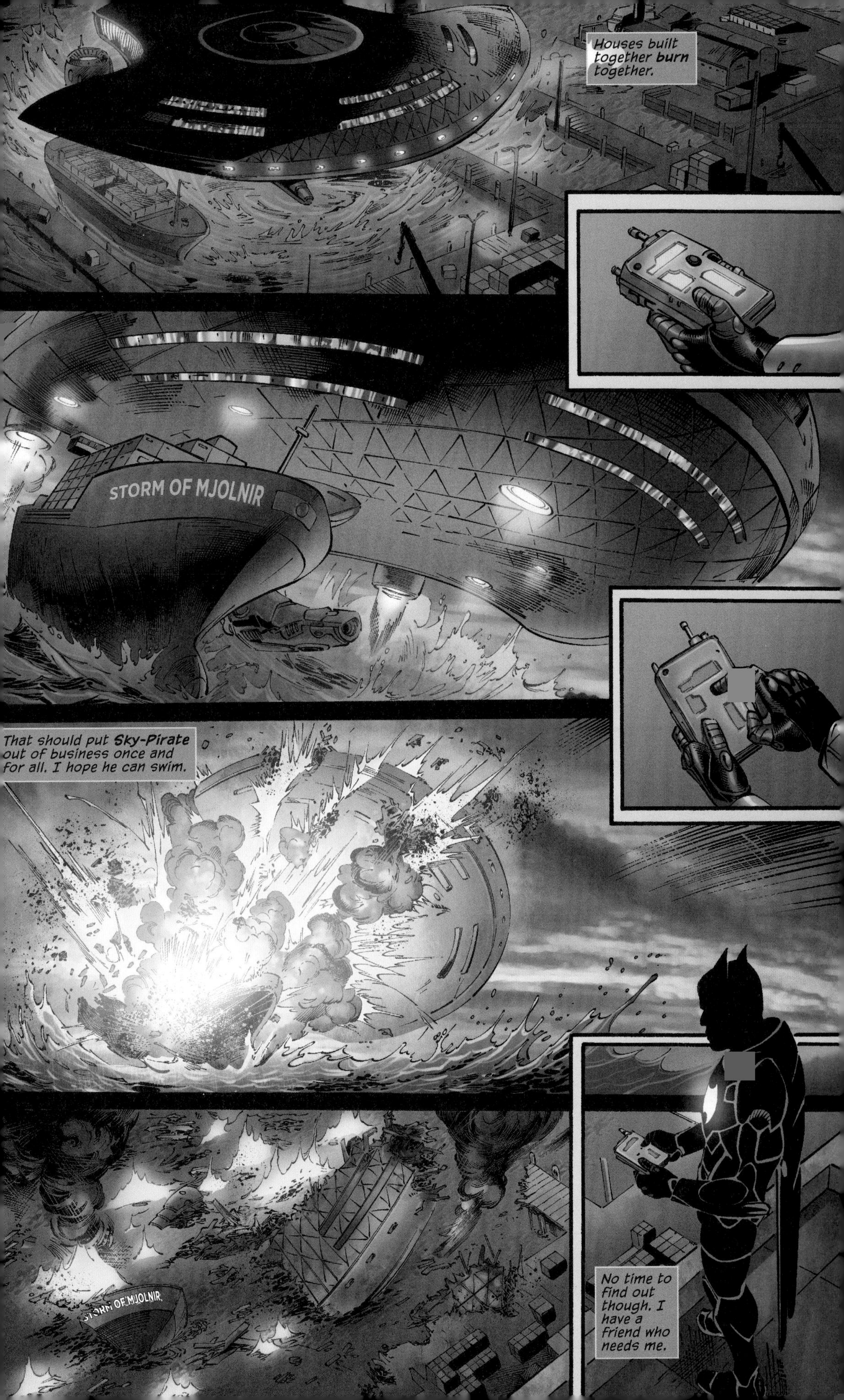
Houses built together burn together.
STORM OF MJOLNIR
That should put Sky-Pirate out of business once and for all. I hope he can swim.
STORM OF MJOLNIR
No time to find out though. I have a friend who needs me.

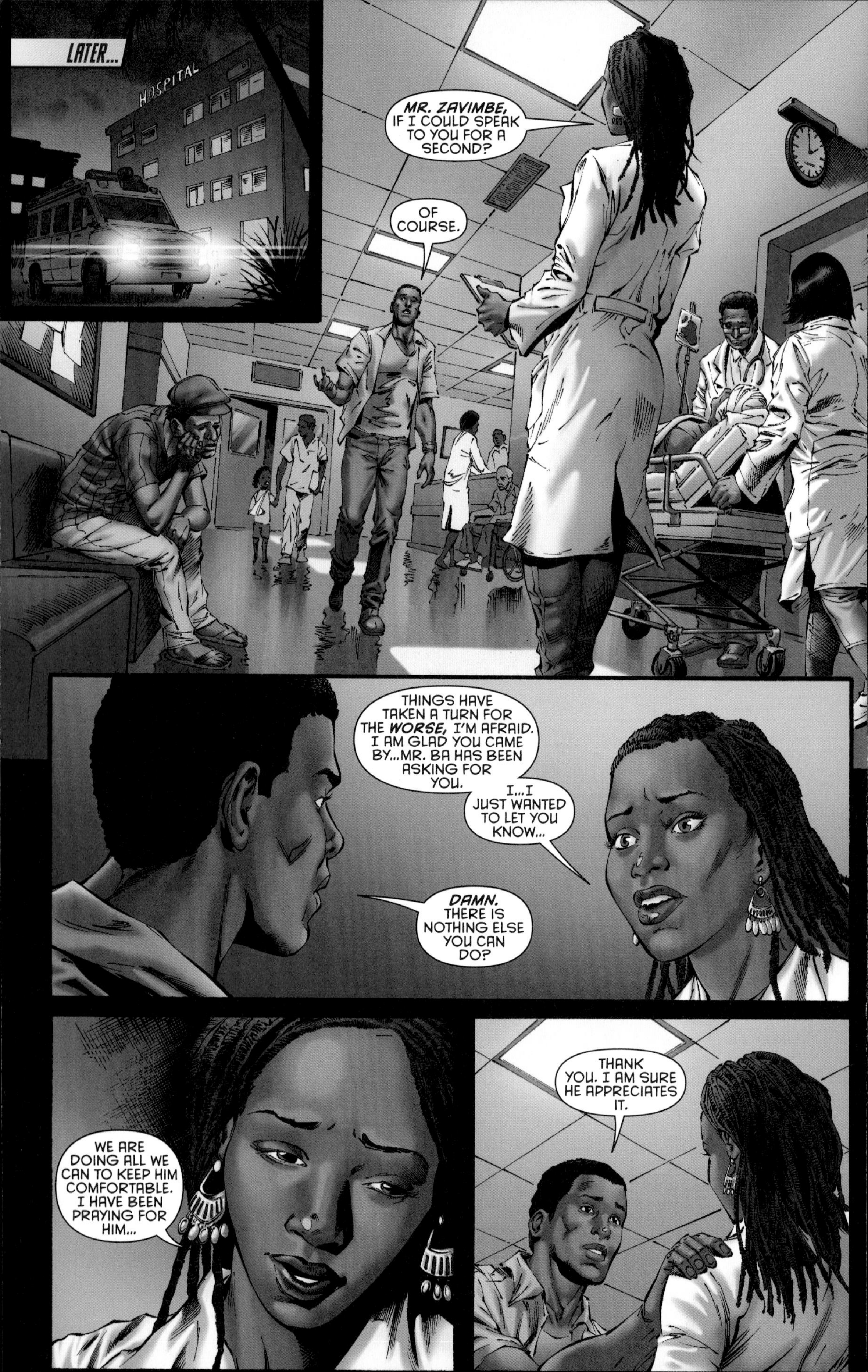
LATER...
HOSPITAL
MR. ZAVIMBE, IF I COULD SPEAK TO YOU FOR A SECOND?
OF COURSE.
THINGS HAVE TAKEN A TURN FOR THE WORSE, I'M AFRAID. I AM GLAD YOU CAME BY...MR. BA HAS BEEN ASKING FOR YOU.
I...I JUST WANTED TO LET YOU KNOW...
DAMN. THERE IS NOTHING ELSE YOU CAN DO?
WE ARE DOING ALL WE CAN TO KEEP HIM COMFORTABLE. I HAVE BEEN PRAYING FOR HIM...
THANK YOU. I AM SURE HE APPRECIATES IT.

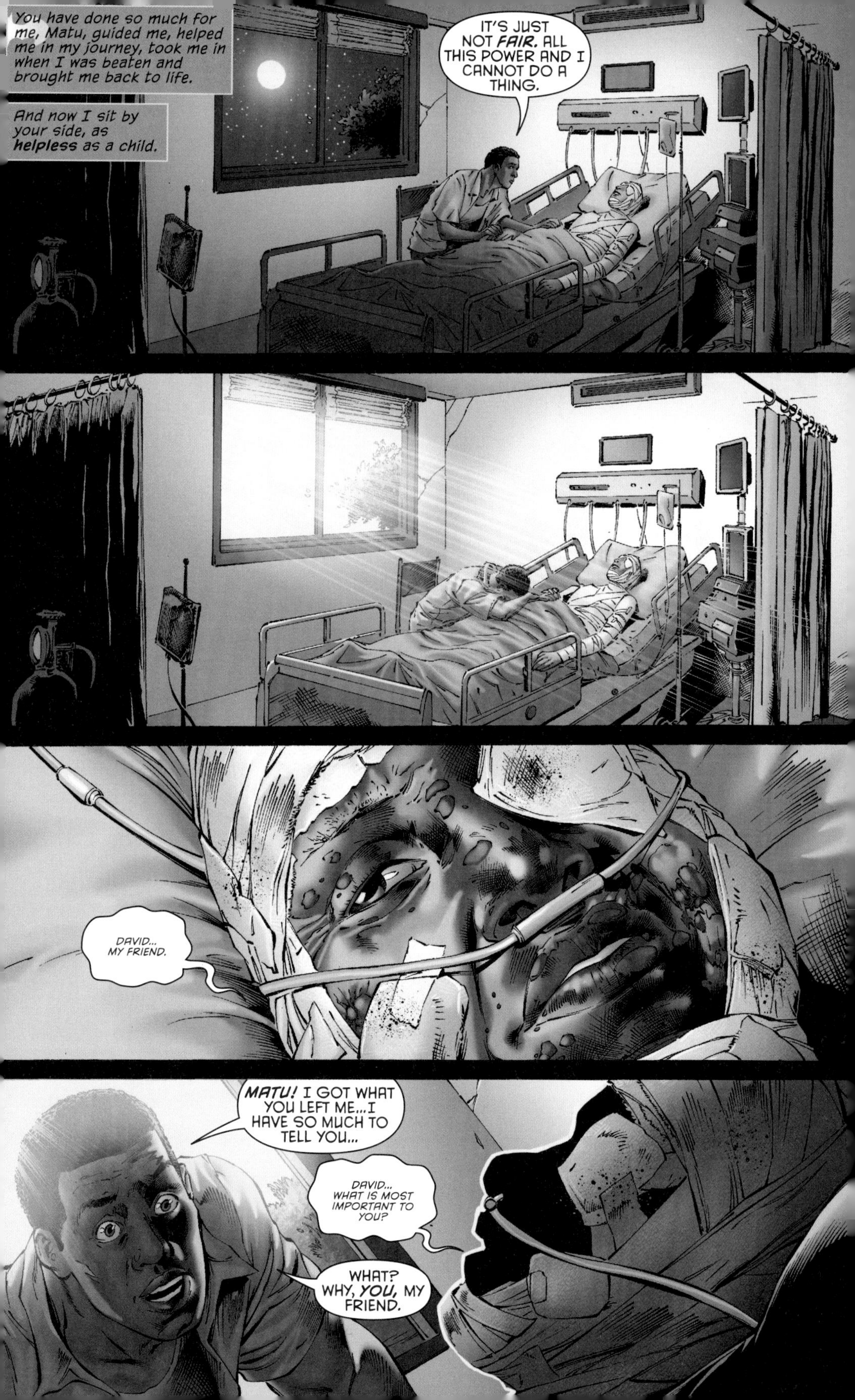
You have done so much for me, Matu, guided me, helped me in my journey, took me in when I was beaten and brought me back to life.
And now I sit by your side, as **helpless** as a child.
IT'S JUST NOT ***FAIR.*** ALL THIS POWER AND I CANNOT DO A THING.
DAVID... MY FRIEND.
MATU! I GOT WHAT YOU LEFT ME...I HAVE SO MUCH TO TELL YOU...
DAVID... WHAT IS MOST IMPORTANT TO YOU?
WHAT? WHY, ***YOU,*** MY FRIEND.

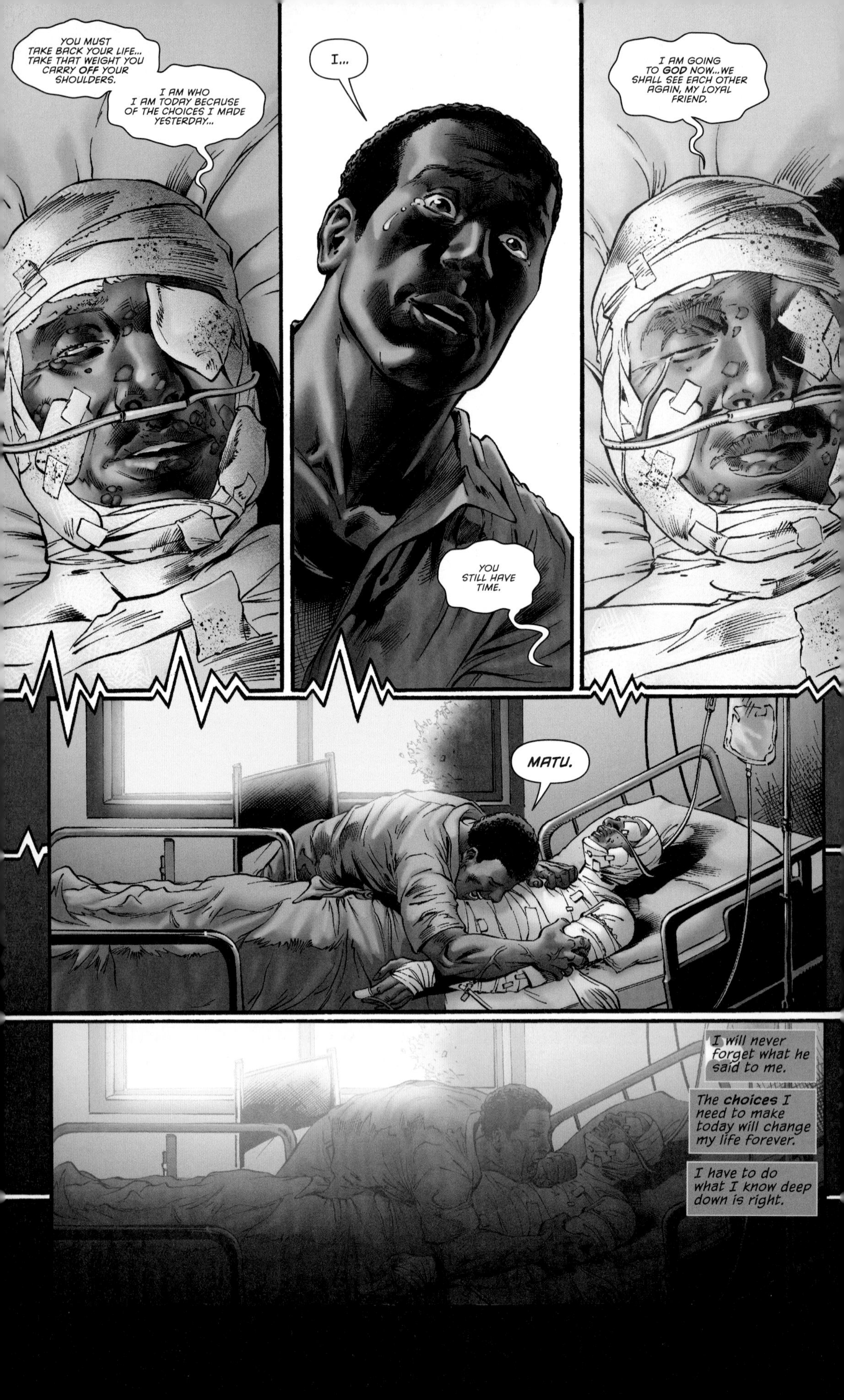

YOU MUST TAKE BACK YOUR LIFE... TAKE THAT WEIGHT YOU CARRY OFF YOUR SHOULDERS.
I AM WHO I AM TODAY BECAUSE OF THE CHOICES I MADE YESTERDAY...
I...
YOU STILL HAVE TIME.
I AM GOING TO GOD NOW...WE SHALL SEE EACH OTHER AGAIN, MY LOYAL FRIEND.
MATU.
I will never forget what he said to me.
The choices I need to make today will change my life forever.
I have to do what I know deep down is right.

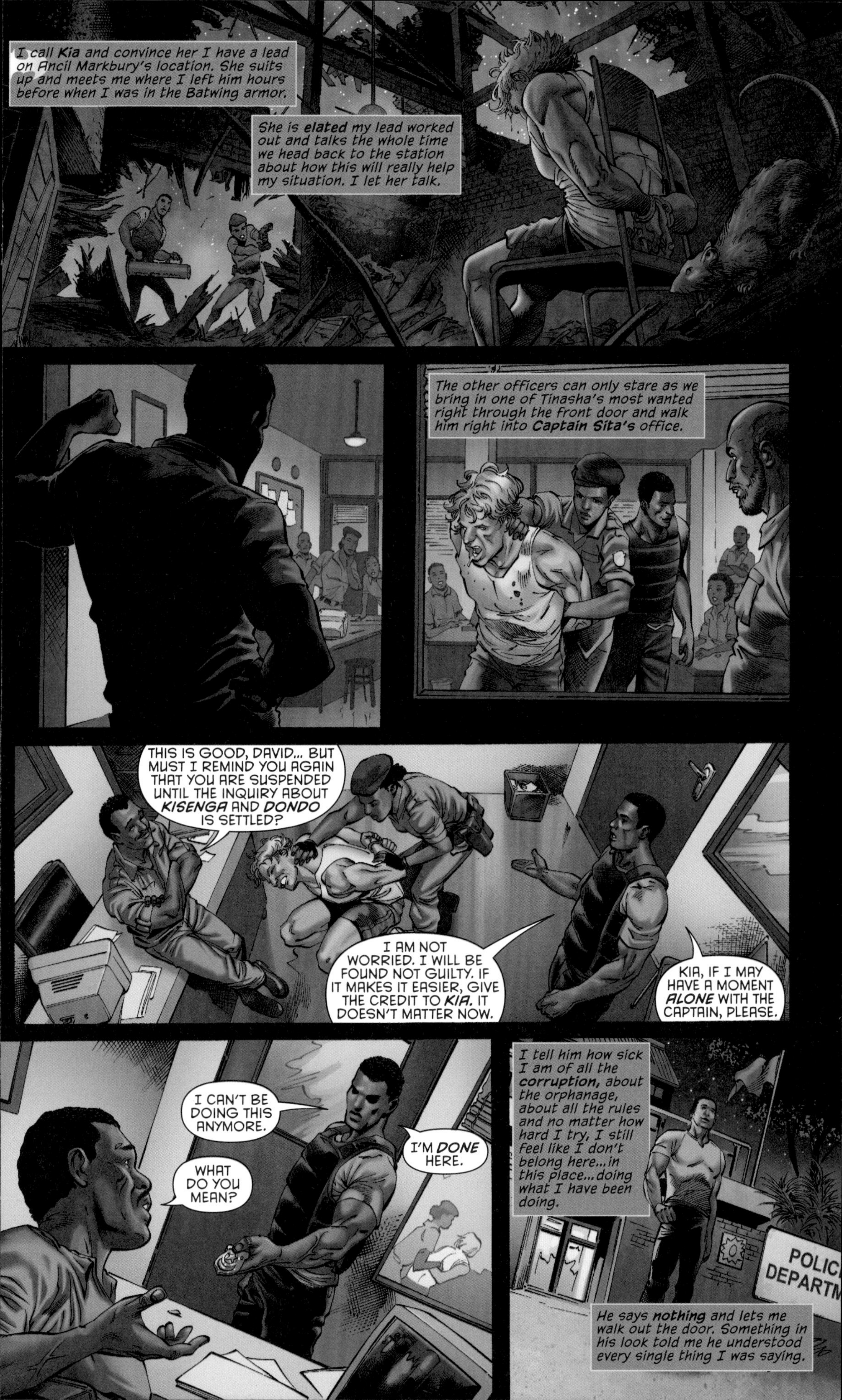

I call Kia and convince her I have a lead on Ancil Markbury's location. She suits up and meets me where I left him hours before when I was in the Batwing armor.
She is elated my lead worked out and talks the whole time we head back to the station about how this will really help my situation. I let her talk.
The other officers can only stare as we bring in one of Tinasha's most wanted right through the front door and walk him right into Captain Sita's office.
THIS IS GOOD, DAVID... BUT MUST I REMIND YOU AGAIN THAT YOU ARE SUSPENDED UNTIL THE INQUIRY ABOUT KISENGA AND DONDO IS SETTLED?
I AM NOT WORRIED. I WILL BE FOUND NOT GUILTY. IF IT MAKES IT EASIER, GIVE THE CREDIT TO KIA. IT DOESN'T MATTER NOW.
KIA, IF I MAY HAVE A MOMENT ALONE WITH THE CAPTAIN, PLEASE.
I CAN'T BE DOING THIS ANYMORE.
WHAT DO YOU MEAN?
I'M DONE HERE.
I tell him how sick I am of all the corruption, about the orphanage, about all the rules and no matter how hard I try, I still feel like I don't belong here...in this place...doing what I have been doing.
POLIC DEPARTM
He says nothing and lets me walk out the door. Something in his look told me he understood every single thing I was saying.

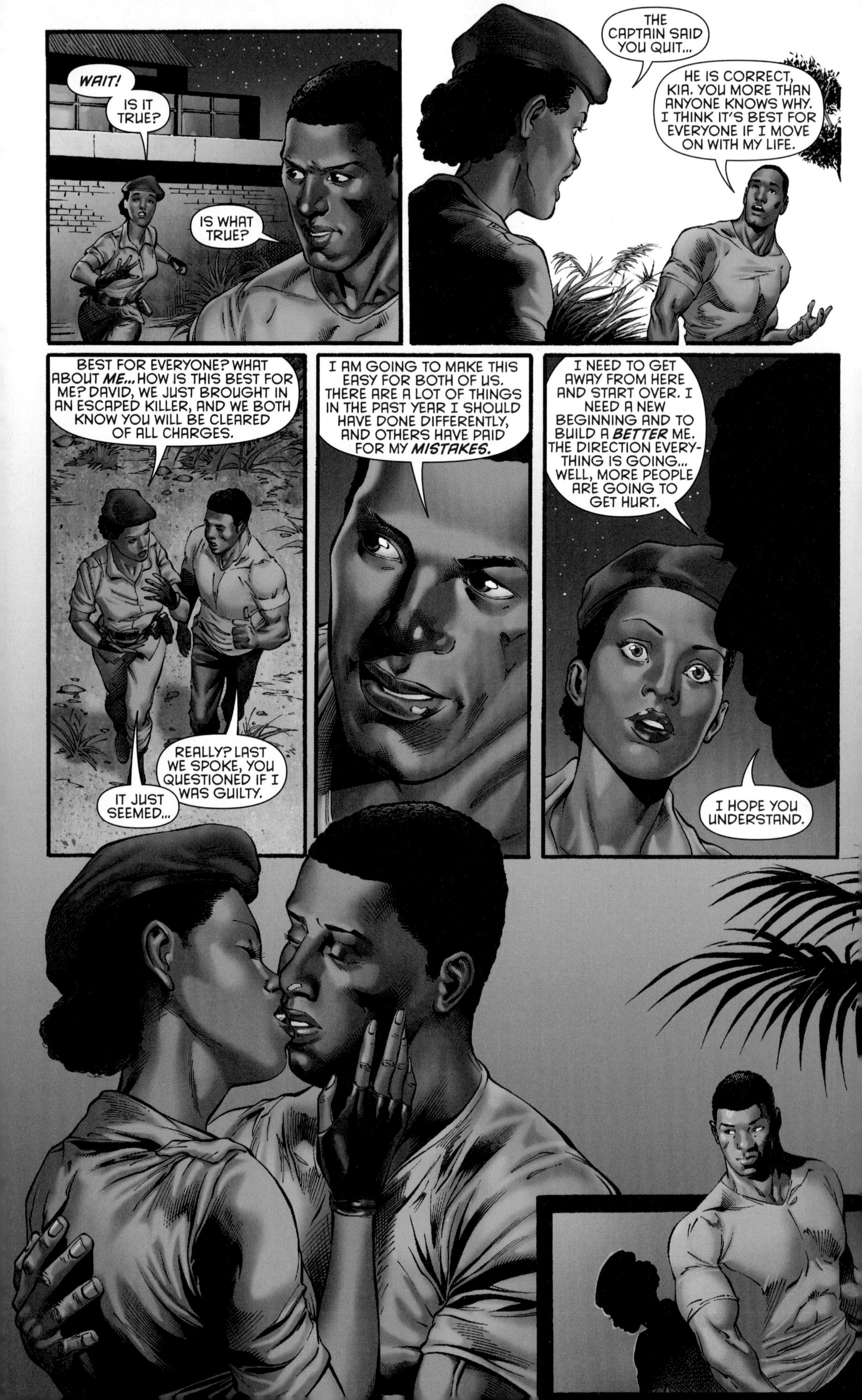
WAIT!
IS IT TRUE?
IS WHAT TRUE?
THE CAPTAIN SAID YOU QUIT...
HE IS CORRECT, KIA. YOU MORE THAN ANYONE KNOWS WHY. I THINK IT'S BEST FOR EVERYONE IF I MOVE ON WITH MY LIFE.
BEST FOR EVERYONE? WHAT ABOUT ME... HOW IS THIS BEST FOR ME? DAVID, WE JUST BROUGHT IN AN ESCAPED KILLER, AND WE BOTH KNOW YOU WILL BE CLEARED OF ALL CHARGES.
REALLY? LAST WE SPOKE, YOU QUESTIONED IF I WAS GUILTY.
IT JUST SEEMED...
I AM GOING TO MAKE THIS EASY FOR BOTH OF US. THERE ARE A LOT OF THINGS IN THE PAST YEAR I SHOULD HAVE DONE DIFFERENTLY, AND OTHERS HAVE PAID FOR MY MISTAKES.
I NEED TO GET AWAY FROM HERE AND START OVER. I NEED A NEW BEGINNING AND TO BUILD A BETTER ME. THE DIRECTION EVERY-THING IS GOING... WELL, MORE PEOPLE ARE GOING TO GET HURT.
I HOPE YOU UNDERSTAND.

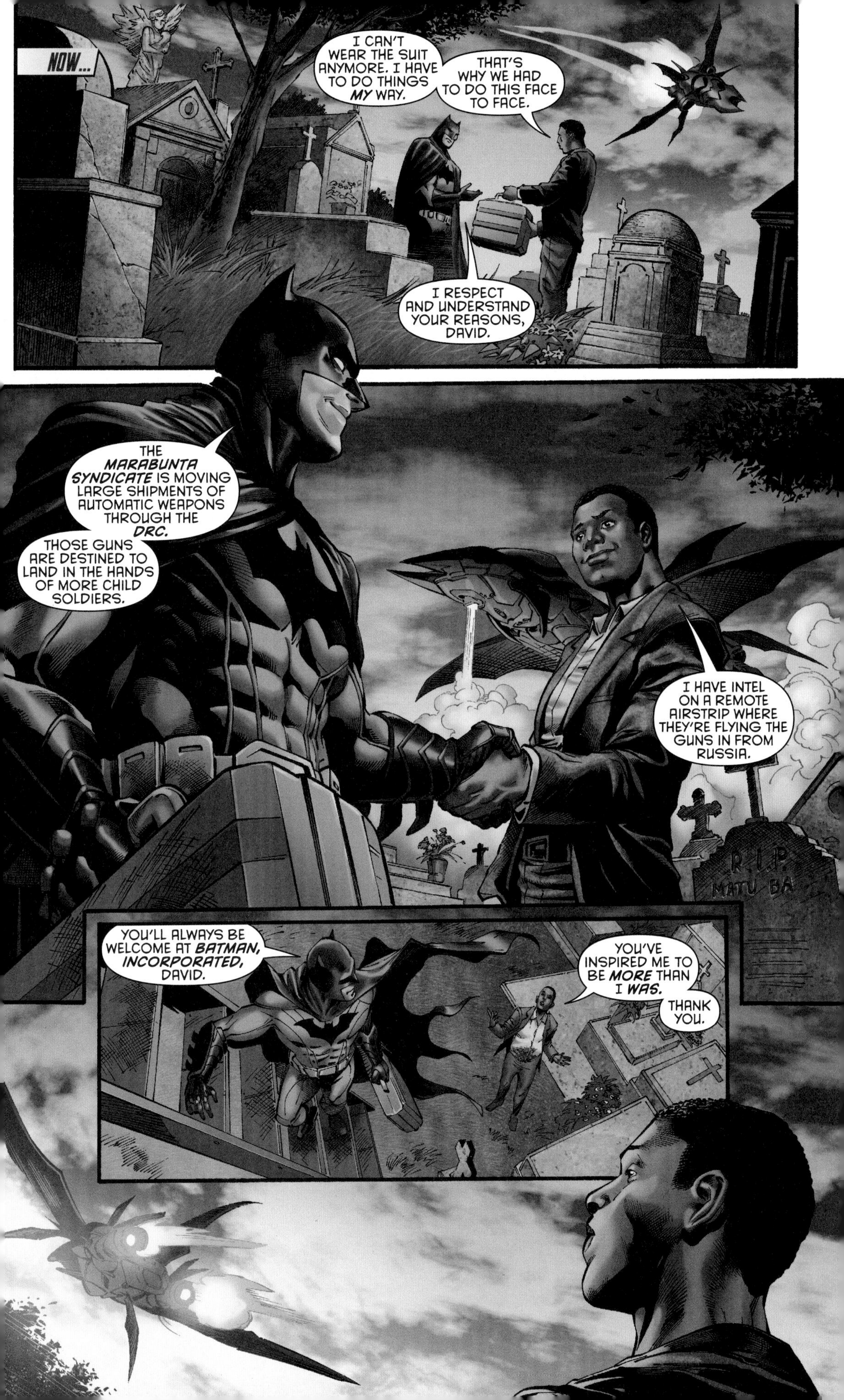
NOW...
I CAN'T WEAR THE SUIT ANYMORE. I HAVE TO DO THINGS MY WAY.
THAT'S WHY WE HAD TO DO THIS FACE TO FACE.
I RESPECT AND UNDERSTAND YOUR REASONS, DAVID.
THE MARABUNTA SYNDICATE IS MOVING LARGE SHIPMENTS OF AUTOMATIC WEAPONS THROUGH THE DRC.
THOSE GUNS ARE DESTINED TO LAND IN THE HANDS OF MORE CHILD SOLDIERS.
I HAVE INTEL ON A REMOTE AIRSTRIP WHERE THEY'RE FLYING THE GUNS IN FROM RUSSIA.
R.I.P. MATU BA
YOU'LL ALWAYS BE WELCOME AT BATMAN, INCORPORATED, DAVID.
YOU'VE INSPIRED ME TO BE MORE THAN I WAS.
THANK YOU.

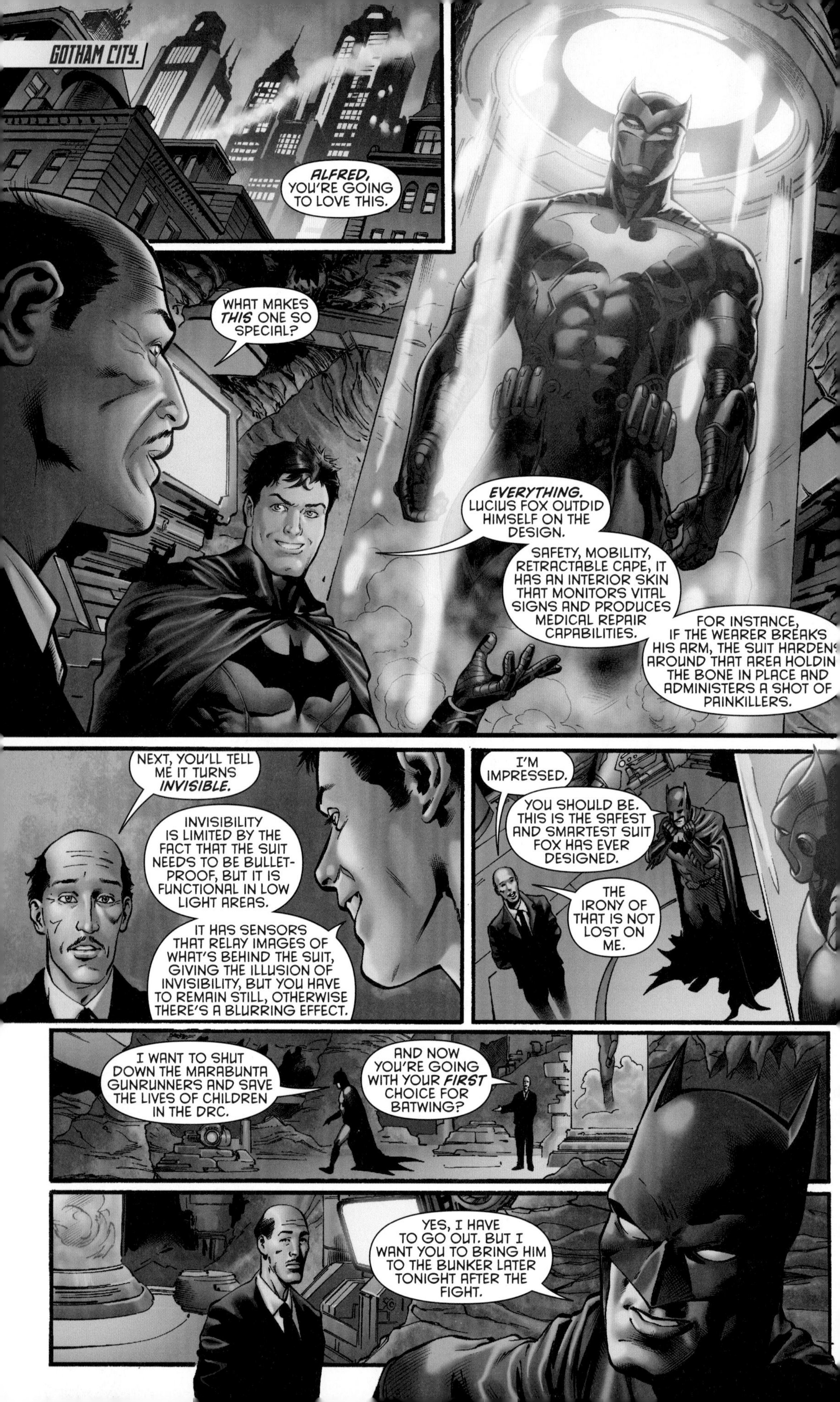
GOTHAM CITY.
ALFRED, YOU'RE GOING TO LOVE THIS.
WHAT MAKES THIS ONE SO SPECIAL?
EVERYTHING. LUCIUS FOX OUTDID HIMSELF ON THE DESIGN.
SAFETY, MOBILITY, RETRACTABLE CAPE, IT HAS AN INTERIOR SKIN THAT MONITORS VITAL SIGNS AND PRODUCES MEDICAL REPAIR CAPABILITIES.
FOR INSTANCE, IF THE WEARER BREAKS HIS ARM, THE SUIT HARDENS AROUND THAT AREA HOLDIN THE BONE IN PLACE AND ADMINISTERS A SHOT OF PAINKILLERS.
NEXT, YOU'LL TELL ME IT TURNS INVISIBLE.
INVISIBILITY IS LIMITED BY THE FACT THAT THE SUIT NEEDS TO BE BULLET-PROOF, BUT IT IS FUNCTIONAL IN LOW LIGHT AREAS.
IT HAS SENSORS THAT RELAY IMAGES OF WHAT'S BEHIND THE SUIT, GIVING THE ILLUSION OF INVISIBILITY, BUT YOU HAVE TO REMAIN STILL, OTHERWISE THERE'S A BLURRING EFFECT.
I'M IMPRESSED.
YOU SHOULD BE. THIS IS THE SAFEST AND SMARTEST SUIT FOX HAS EVER DESIGNED.
THE IRONY OF THAT IS NOT LOST ON ME.
I WANT TO SHUT DOWN THE MARABUNTA GUNRUNNERS AND SAVE THE LIVES OF CHILDREN IN THE DRC.
AND NOW YOU'RE GOING WITH YOUR FIRST CHOICE FOR BATWING?
YES, I HAVE TO GO OUT. BUT I WANT YOU TO BRING HIM TO THE BUNKER LATER TONIGHT AFTER THE FIGHT.

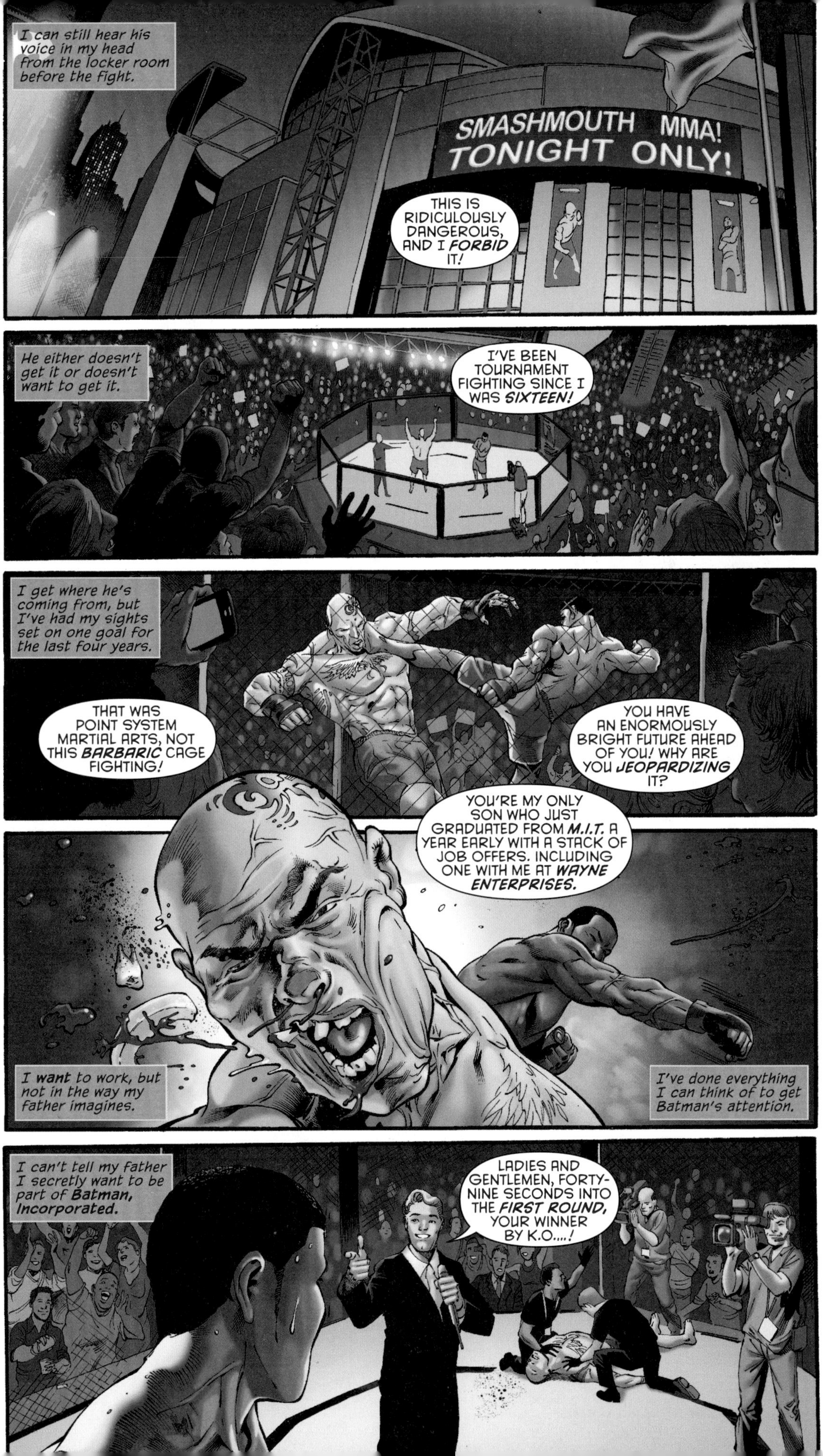
I can still hear his voice in my head from the locker room before the fight.
SMASHMOUTH MMA! TONIGHT ONLY!
THIS IS RIDICULOUSLY DANGEROUS, AND I FORBID IT!
He either doesn't get it or doesn't want to get it.
I'VE BEEN TOURNAMENT FIGHTING SINCE I WAS SIXTEEN!
I get where he's coming from, but I've had my sights set on one goal for the last four years.
THAT WAS POINT SYSTEM MARTIAL ARTS, NOT THIS BARBARIC CAGE FIGHTING!
YOU HAVE AN ENORMOUSLY BRIGHT FUTURE AHEAD OF YOU! WHY ARE YOU JEOPARDIZING IT?
YOU'RE MY ONLY SON WHO JUST GRADUATED FROM M.I.T. A YEAR EARLY WITH A STACK OF JOB OFFERS. INCLUDING ONE WITH ME AT WAYNE ENTERPRISES.
I want to work, but not in the way my father imagines.
I've done everything I can think of to get Batman's attention.
I can't tell my father I secretly want to be part of Batman, Incorporated.
LADIES AND GENTLEMEN, FORTY-NINE SECONDS INTO THE FIRST ROUND, YOUR WINNER BY K.O....!

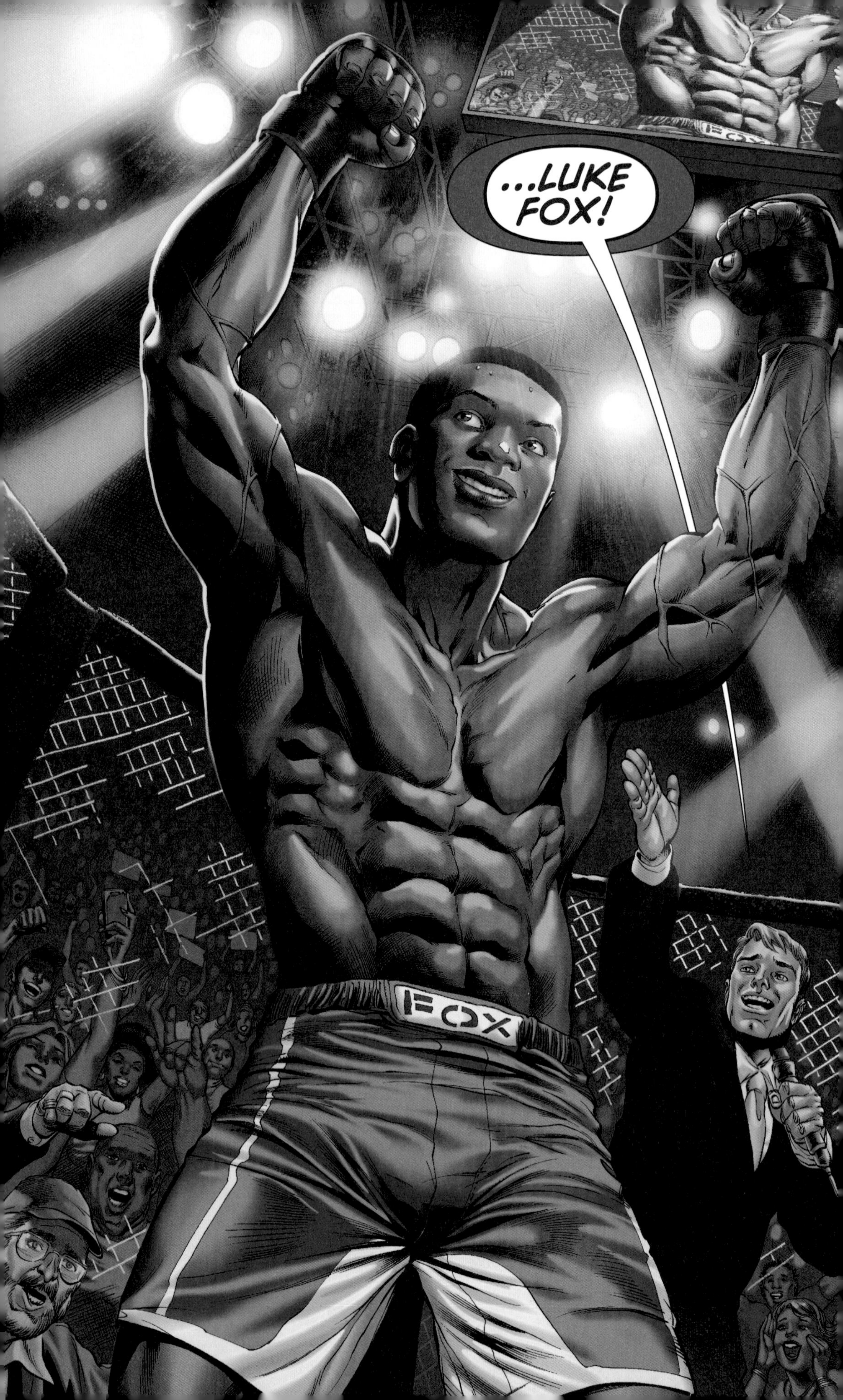
...LUKE FOX!
FOX

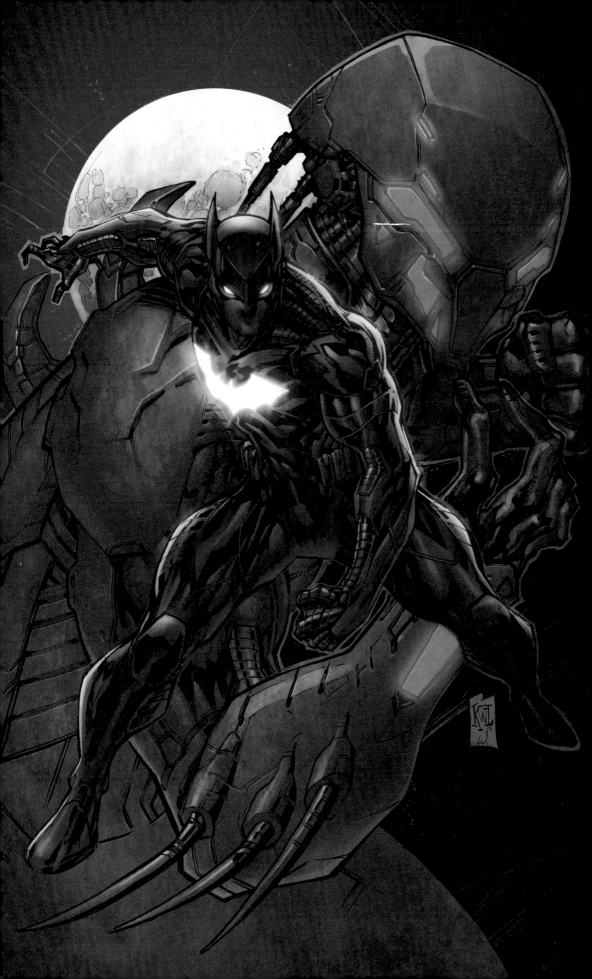

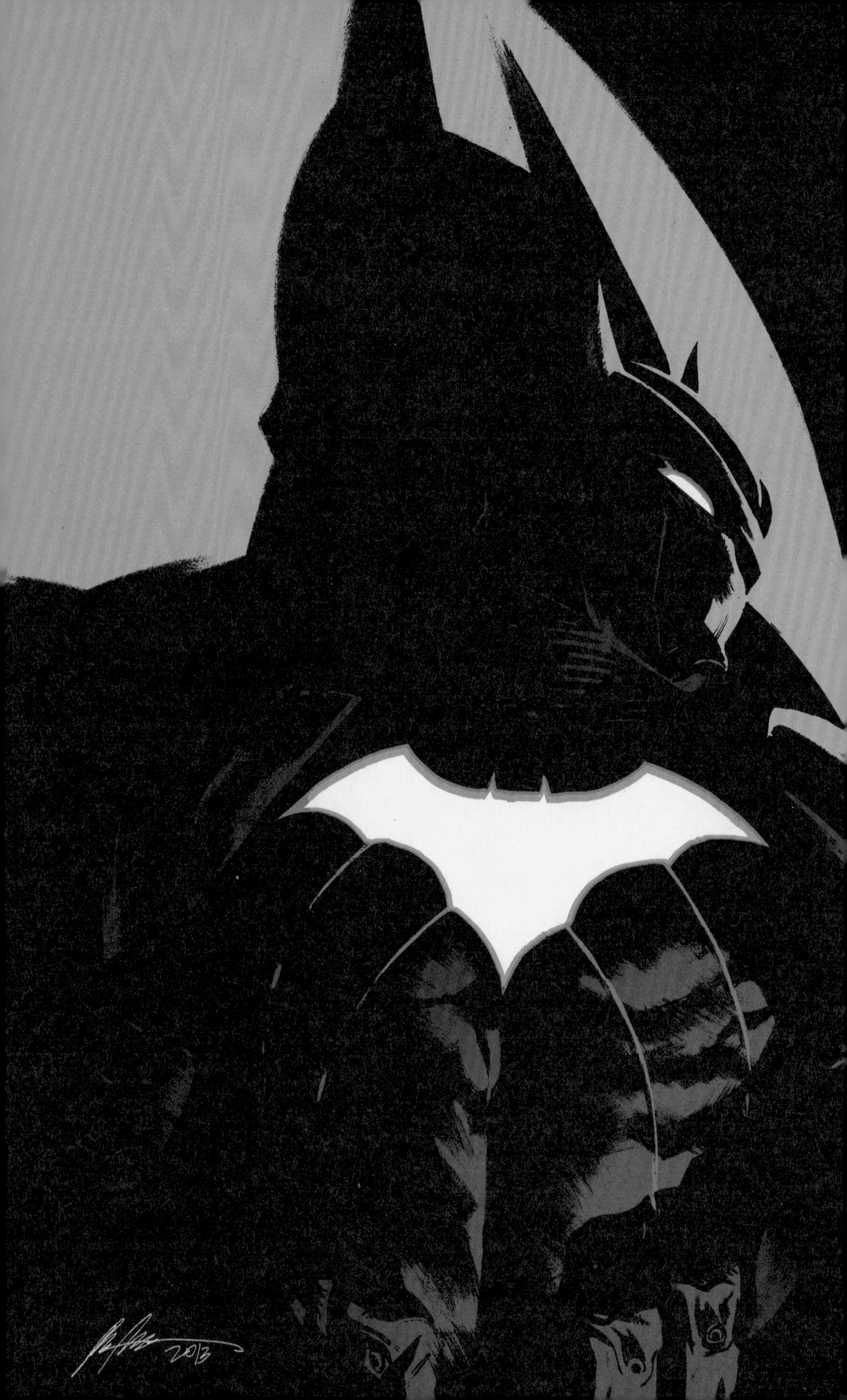
2013

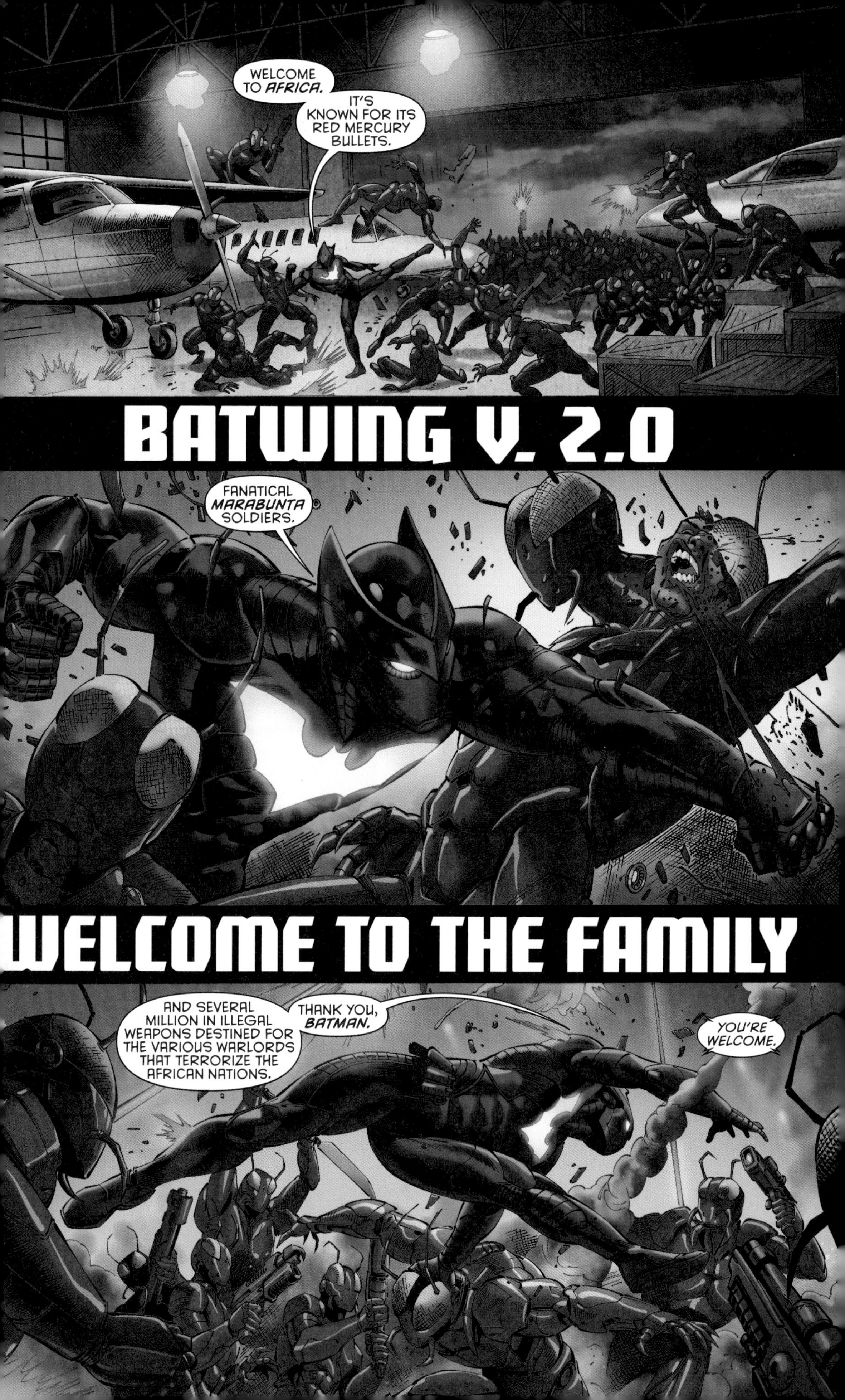
WELCOME TO AFRICA.
IT'S KNOWN FOR ITS RED MERCURY BULLETS.
BATWING V. 2.0
FANATICAL MARABUNTA SOLDIERS.
WELCOME TO THE FAMILY
AND SEVERAL MILLION IN ILLEGAL WEAPONS DESTINED FOR THE VARIOUS WARLORDS THAT TERRORIZE THE AFRICAN NATIONS.
THANK YOU, BATMAN.
YOU'RE WELCOME.

NOW FOCUS, BATWING.

YOU SAID THERE'S A CARE PACKAGE.

WHY WOULD YOU WANT ONE?

I'M MASSIVELY OUT-NUMBERED.

GET USED TO IT.

SCRIPT Jimmy Palmiotti & Justin Gray

WE NEED AN INFORMANT.

I FIGURED AS MUCH.

ART Eduardo Pansica & Júlio Ferreira

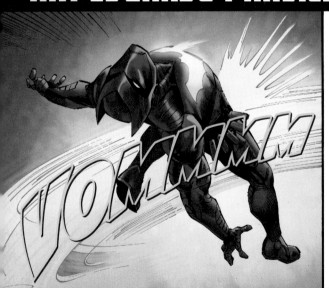

VOMMMMM

YOU SEEING THIS?

YES. IT IS EXACTLY WHAT WE WANTED.

COLOR Jason Wright   LETTERS Taylor Esposito
COVER Ken Lashley & Jason Wright   ASST. EDITOR Darren Sha[r]
EDITOR Rachel Gluckstern   GROUP EDITOR Mike Marts

DC COMICS™
PROUDLY PRESENTS:
BATWING
WE WANTED THIS?
YES. TWENTY SECONDS. TRY NOT TO DIE.
MOVE ASIDE! LADY MARABUNTA IS GONNA BLOW HIM UP!
Rewind six months, and I'm standing in a secret Bat bunker.

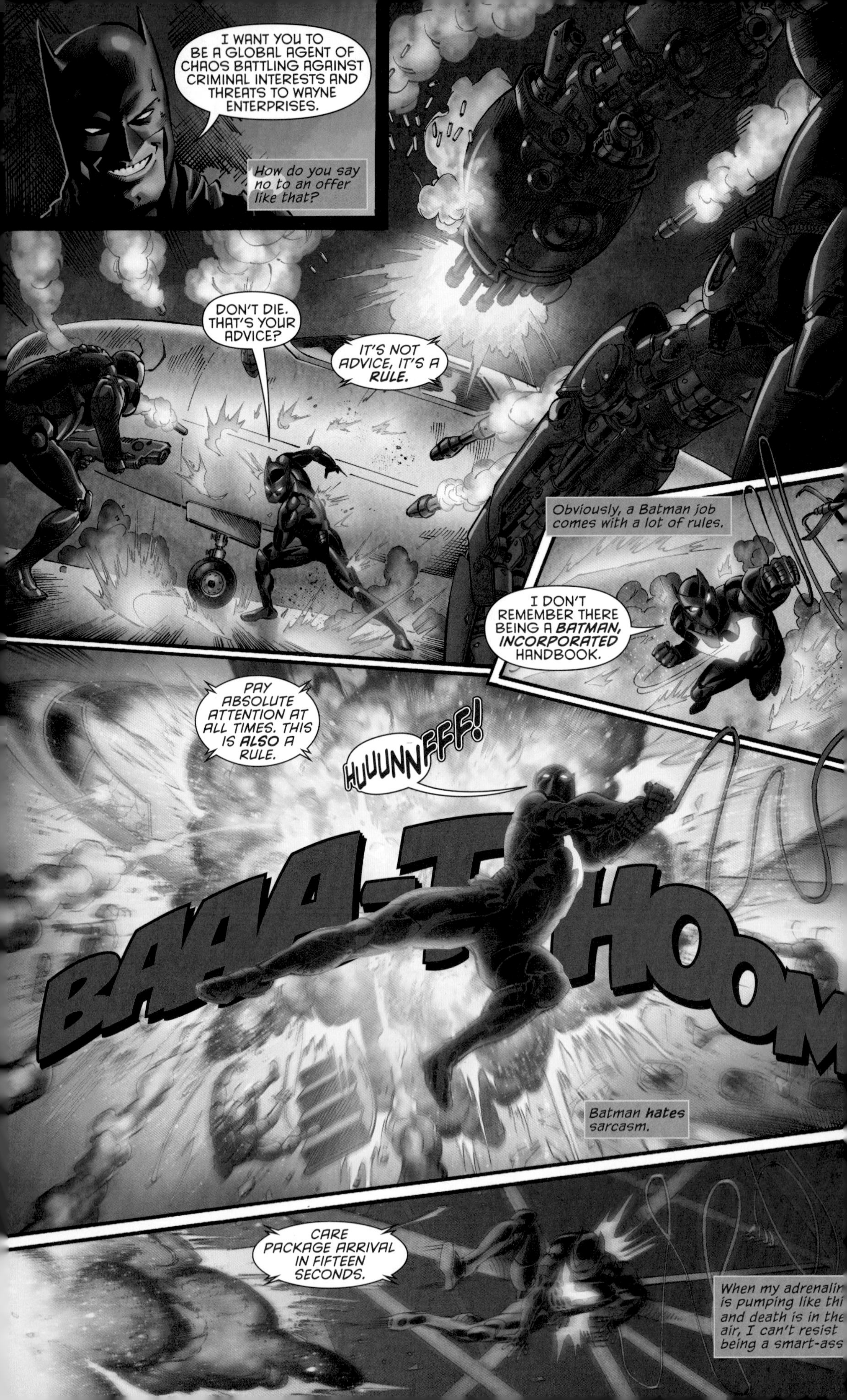
I WANT YOU TO BE A GLOBAL AGENT OF CHAOS BATTLING AGAINST CRIMINAL INTERESTS AND THREATS TO WAYNE ENTERPRISES.
How do you say no to an offer like that?
DON'T DIE. THAT'S YOUR ADVICE?
IT'S NOT ADVICE, IT'S A RULE.
Obviously, a Batman job comes with a lot of rules.
I DON'T REMEMBER THERE BEING A BATMAN, INCORPORATED HANDBOOK.
PAY ABSOLUTE ATTENTION AT ALL TIMES. THIS IS ALSO A RULE.
HUUUNNFFF!
Batman hates sarcasm.
CARE PACKAGE ARRIVAL IN FIFTEEN SECONDS.

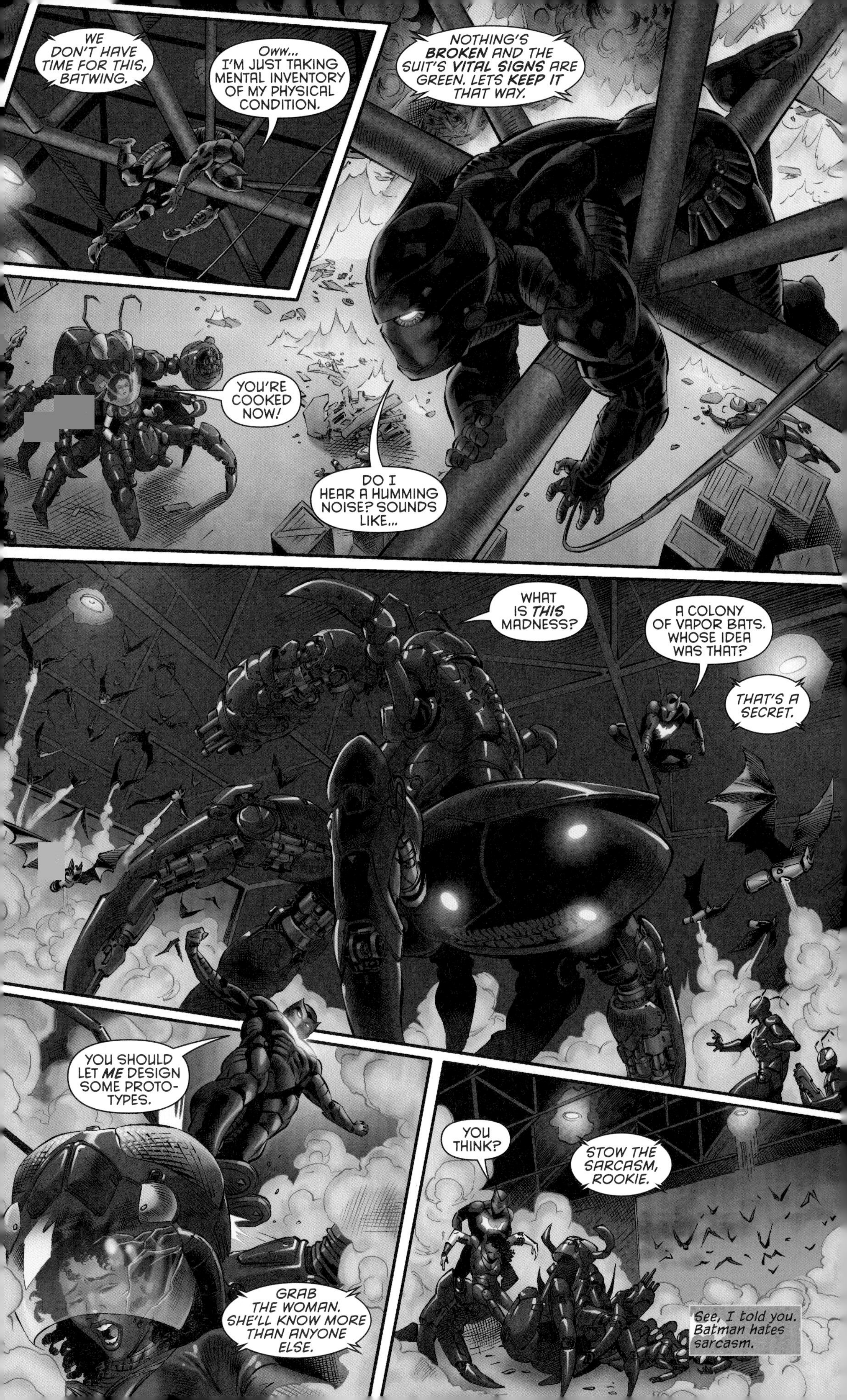
WE DON'T HAVE TIME FOR THIS, BATWING.
OWW... I'M JUST TAKING MENTAL INVENTORY OF MY PHYSICAL CONDITION.
NOTHING'S BROKEN AND THE SUIT'S VITAL SIGNS ARE GREEN. LETS KEEP IT THAT WAY.
YOU'RE COOKED NOW!
DO I HEAR A HUMMING NOISE? SOUNDS LIKE...
WHAT IS THIS MADNESS?
A COLONY OF VAPOR BATS. WHOSE IDEA WAS THAT?
THAT'S A SECRET.
YOU SHOULD LET ME DESIGN SOME PROTO-TYPES.
GRAB THE WOMAN. SHE'LL KNOW MORE THAN ANYONE ELSE.
YOU THINK?
STOW THE SARCASM, ROOKIE.
See, I told you. Batman hates sarcasm.

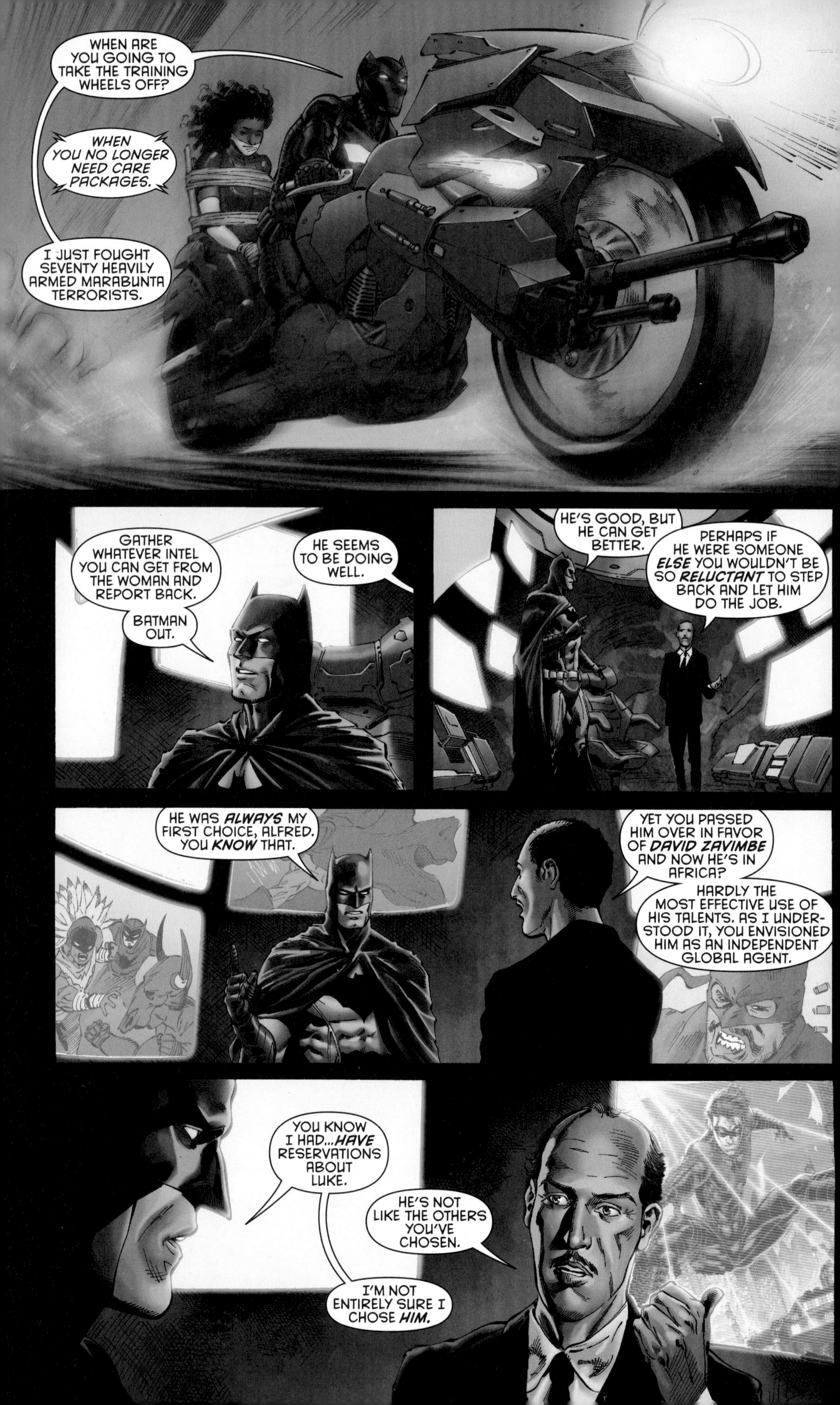

WHEN ARE YOU GOING TO TAKE THE TRAINING WHEELS OFF?
WHEN YOU NO LONGER NEED CARE PACKAGES.
I JUST FOUGHT SEVENTY HEAVILY ARMED MARABUNTA TERRORISTS.
GATHER WHATEVER INTEL YOU CAN GET FROM THE WOMAN AND REPORT BACK.
BATMAN OUT.
HE SEEMS TO BE DOING WELL.
HE'S GOOD, BUT HE CAN GET BETTER.
PERHAPS IF HE WERE SOMEONE ELSE YOU WOULDN'T BE SO RELUCTANT TO STEP BACK AND LET HIM DO THE JOB.
HE WAS ALWAYS MY FIRST CHOICE, ALFRED. YOU KNOW THAT.
YET YOU PASSED HIM OVER IN FAVOR OF DAVID ZAVIMBE AND NOW HE'S IN AFRICA?
HARDLY THE MOST EFFECTIVE USE OF HIS TALENTS. AS I UNDER-STOOD IT, YOU ENVISIONED HIM AS AN INDEPENDENT GLOBAL AGENT.
YOU KNOW I HAD...HAVE RESERVATIONS ABOUT LUKE.
HE'S NOT LIKE THE OTHERS YOU'VE CHOSEN.
I'M NOT ENTIRELY SURE I CHOSE HIM.

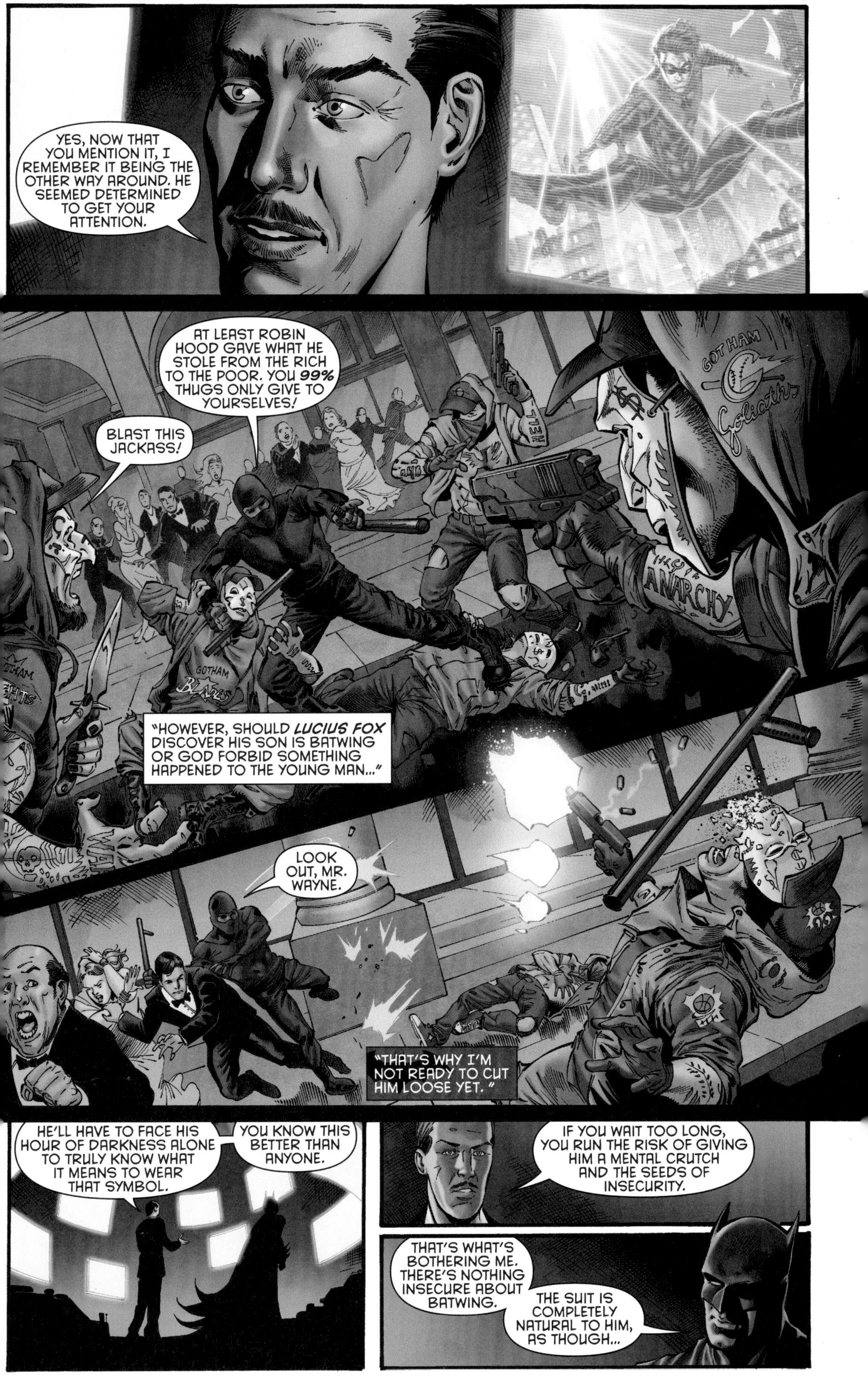

YES, NOW THAT YOU MENTION IT, I REMEMBER IT BEING THE OTHER WAY AROUND. HE SEEMED DETERMINED TO GET YOUR ATTENTION.
AT LEAST ROBIN HOOD GAVE WHAT HE STOLE FROM THE RICH TO THE POOR. YOU 99% THUGS ONLY GIVE TO YOURSELVES!
BLAST THIS JACKASS!
GOTHAM Goliaths
ANARCHY
GOTHAM BLADES
"HOWEVER, SHOULD LUCIUS FOX DISCOVER HIS SON IS BATWING OR GOD FORBID SOMETHING HAPPENED TO THE YOUNG MAN..."
LOOK OUT, MR. WAYNE.
"THAT'S WHY I'M NOT READY TO CUT HIM LOOSE YET."
HE'LL HAVE TO FACE HIS HOUR OF DARKNESS ALONE TO TRULY KNOW WHAT IT MEANS TO WEAR THAT SYMBOL.
YOU KNOW THIS BETTER THAN ANYONE.
IF YOU WAIT TOO LONG, YOU RUN THE RISK OF GIVING HIM A MENTAL CRUTCH AND THE SEEDS OF INSECURITY.
THAT'S WHAT'S BOTHERING ME. THERE'S NOTHING INSECURE ABOUT BATWING.
THE SUIT IS COMPLETELY NATURAL TO HIM, AS THOUGH...

HE WAS BORN TO WEAR IT

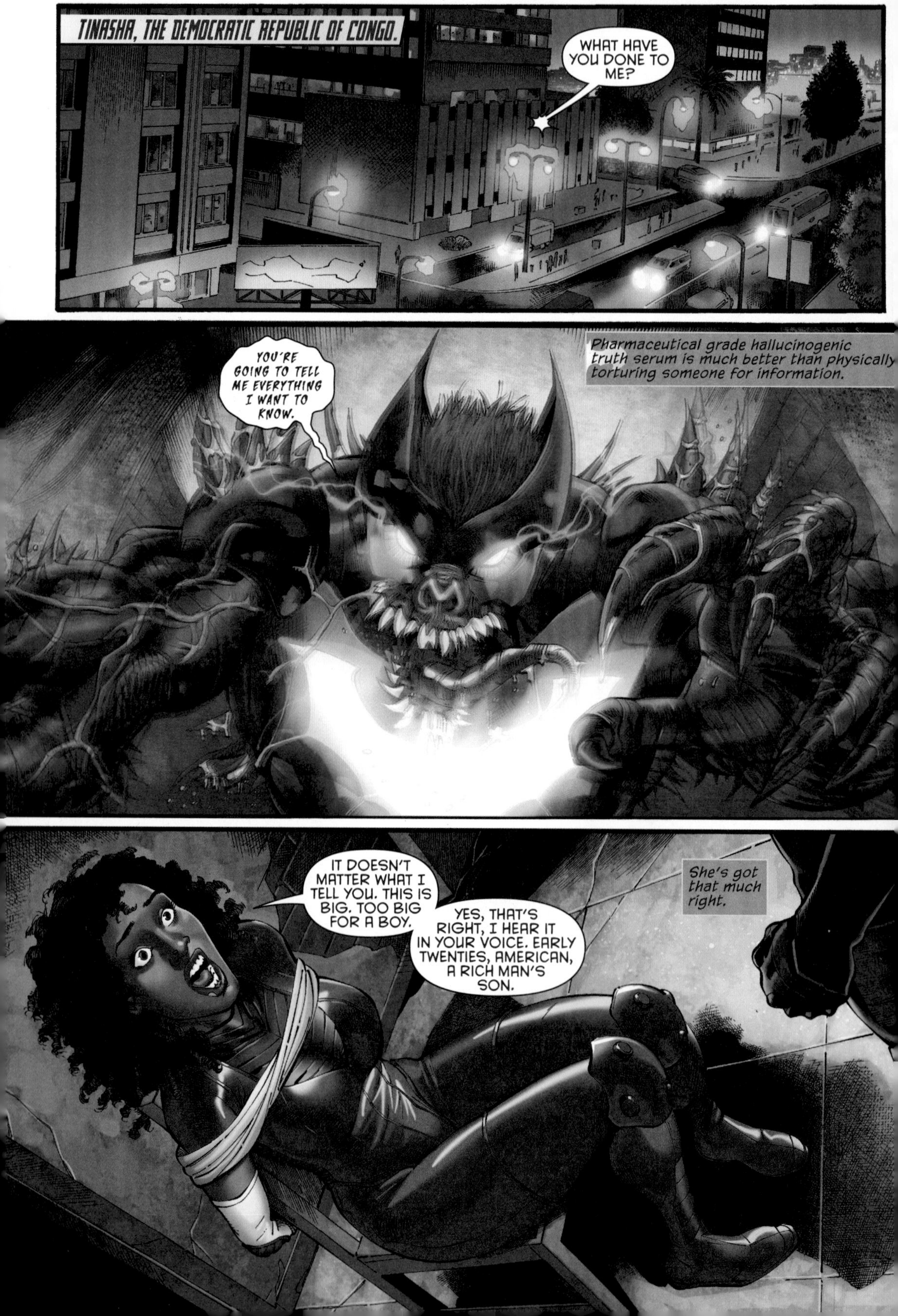

TINASHA, THE DEMOCRATIC REPUBLIC OF CONGO.
WHAT HAVE YOU DONE TO ME?
Pharmaceutical grade hallucinogenic truth serum is much better than physically torturing someone for information.
YOU'RE GOING TO TELL ME EVERYTHING I WANT TO KNOW.
IT DOESN'T MATTER WHAT I TELL YOU. THIS IS BIG. TOO BIG FOR A BOY.
YES, THAT'S RIGHT, I HEAR IT IN YOUR VOICE. EARLY TWENTIES, AMERICAN, A RICH MAN'S SON.
She's got that much right.

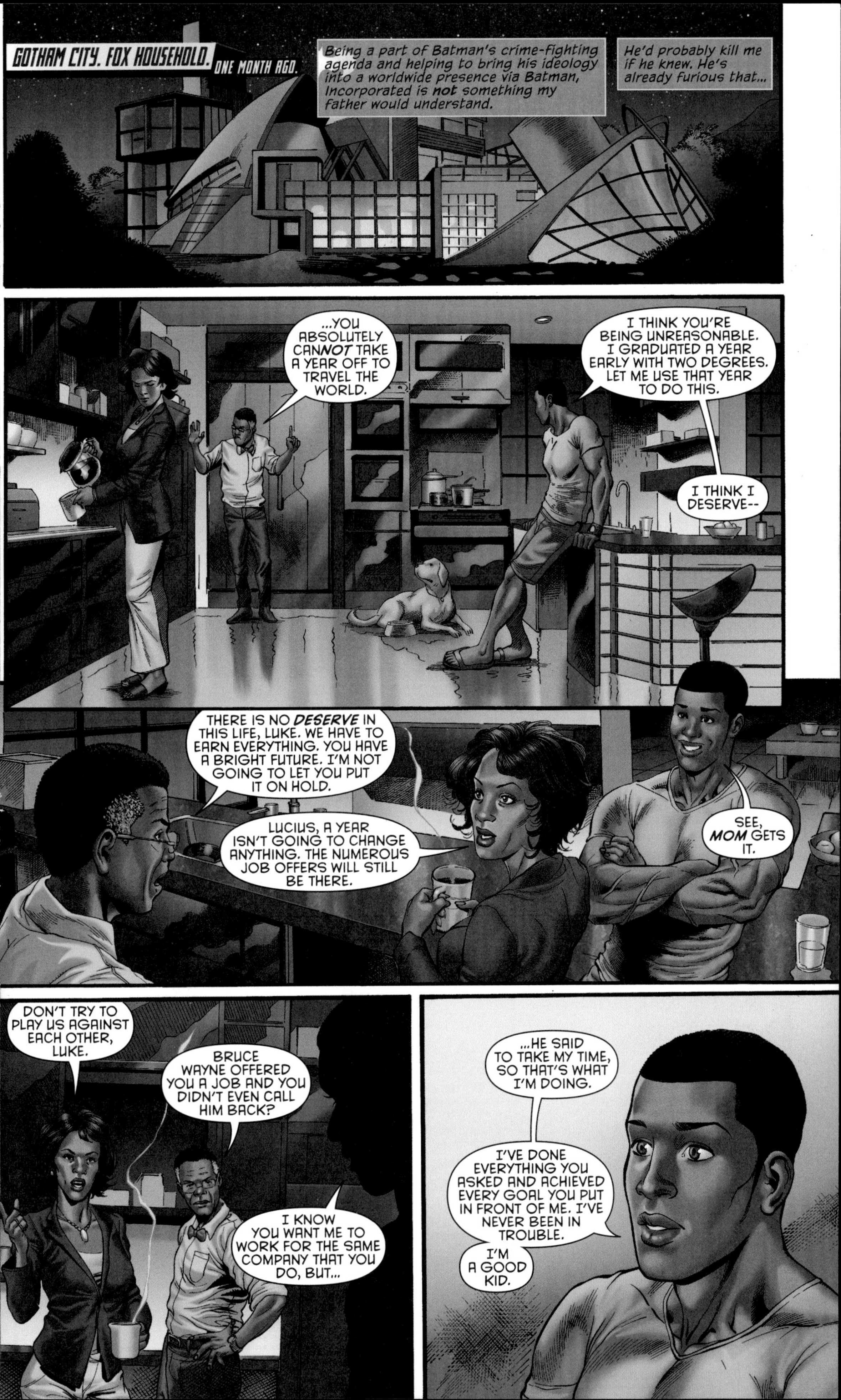
GOTHAM CITY. FOX HOUSEHOLD.
ONE MONTH AGO.
Being a part of Batman's crime-fighting agenda and helping to bring his ideology into a worldwide presence via Batman, Incorporated is not something my father would understand.
He'd probably kill me if he knew. He's already furious that...
...YOU ABSOLUTELY CANNOT TAKE A YEAR OFF TO TRAVEL THE WORLD.
I THINK YOU'RE BEING UNREASONABLE. I GRADUATED A YEAR EARLY WITH TWO DEGREES. LET ME USE THAT YEAR TO DO THIS.
I THINK I DESERVE--
THERE IS NO DESERVE IN THIS LIFE, LUKE. WE HAVE TO EARN EVERYTHING. YOU HAVE A BRIGHT FUTURE. I'M NOT GOING TO LET YOU PUT IT ON HOLD.
LUCIUS, A YEAR ISN'T GOING TO CHANGE ANYTHING. THE NUMEROUS JOB OFFERS WILL STILL BE THERE.
SEE, MOM GETS IT.
DON'T TRY TO PLAY US AGAINST EACH OTHER, LUKE.
BRUCE WAYNE OFFERED YOU A JOB AND YOU DIDN'T EVEN CALL HIM BACK?
I KNOW YOU WANT ME TO WORK FOR THE SAME COMPANY THAT YOU DO, BUT...
...HE SAID TO TAKE MY TIME, SO THAT'S WHAT I'M DOING.
I'VE DONE EVERYTHING YOU ASKED AND ACHIEVED EVERY GOAL YOU PUT IN FRONT OF ME. I'VE NEVER BEEN IN TROUBLE.
I'M A GOOD KID.

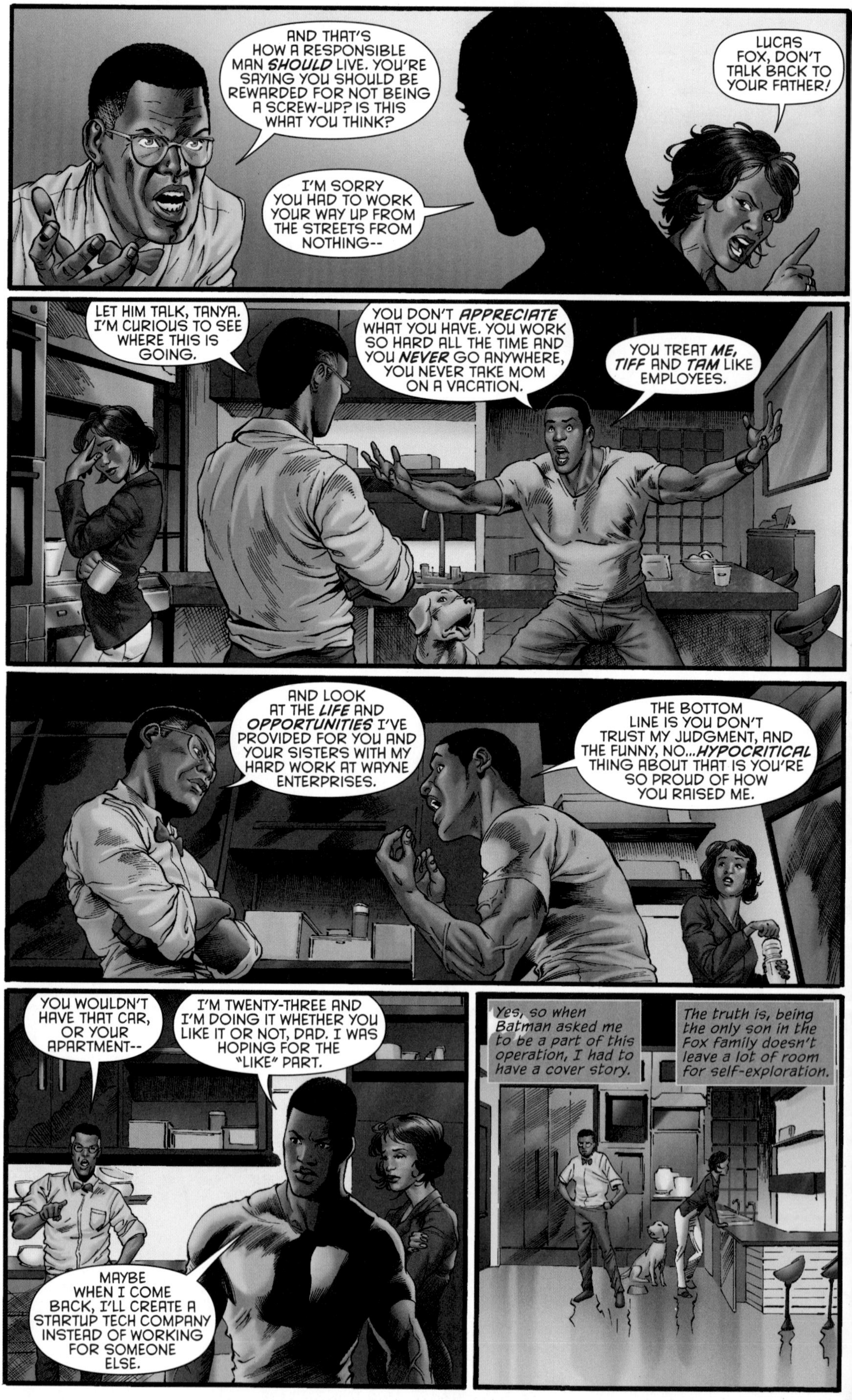
AND THAT'S HOW A RESPONSIBLE MAN SHOULD LIVE. YOU'RE SAYING YOU SHOULD BE REWARDED FOR NOT BEING A SCREW-UP? IS THIS WHAT YOU THINK?
I'M SORRY YOU HAD TO WORK YOUR WAY UP FROM THE STREETS FROM NOTHING--
LUCAS FOX, DON'T TALK BACK TO YOUR FATHER!
LET HIM TALK, TANYA. I'M CURIOUS TO SEE WHERE THIS IS GOING.
YOU DON'T APPRECIATE WHAT YOU HAVE. YOU WORK SO HARD ALL THE TIME AND YOU NEVER GO ANYWHERE, YOU NEVER TAKE MOM ON A VACATION.
YOU TREAT ME, TIFF AND TAM LIKE EMPLOYEES.
AND LOOK AT THE LIFE AND OPPORTUNITIES I'VE PROVIDED FOR YOU AND YOUR SISTERS WITH MY HARD WORK AT WAYNE ENTERPRISES.
THE BOTTOM LINE IS YOU DON'T TRUST MY JUDGMENT, AND THE FUNNY, NO...HYPOCRITICAL THING ABOUT THAT IS YOU'RE SO PROUD OF HOW YOU RAISED ME.
YOU WOULDN'T HAVE THAT CAR, OR YOUR APARTMENT--
I'M TWENTY-THREE AND I'M DOING IT WHETHER YOU LIKE IT OR NOT, DAD. I WAS HOPING FOR THE "LIKE" PART.
MAYBE WHEN I COME BACK, I'LL CREATE A STARTUP TECH COMPANY INSTEAD OF WORKING FOR SOMEONE ELSE.
Yes, so when Batman asked me to be a part of this operation, I had to have a cover story.
The truth is, being the only son in the Fox family doesn't leave a lot of room for self-exploration.

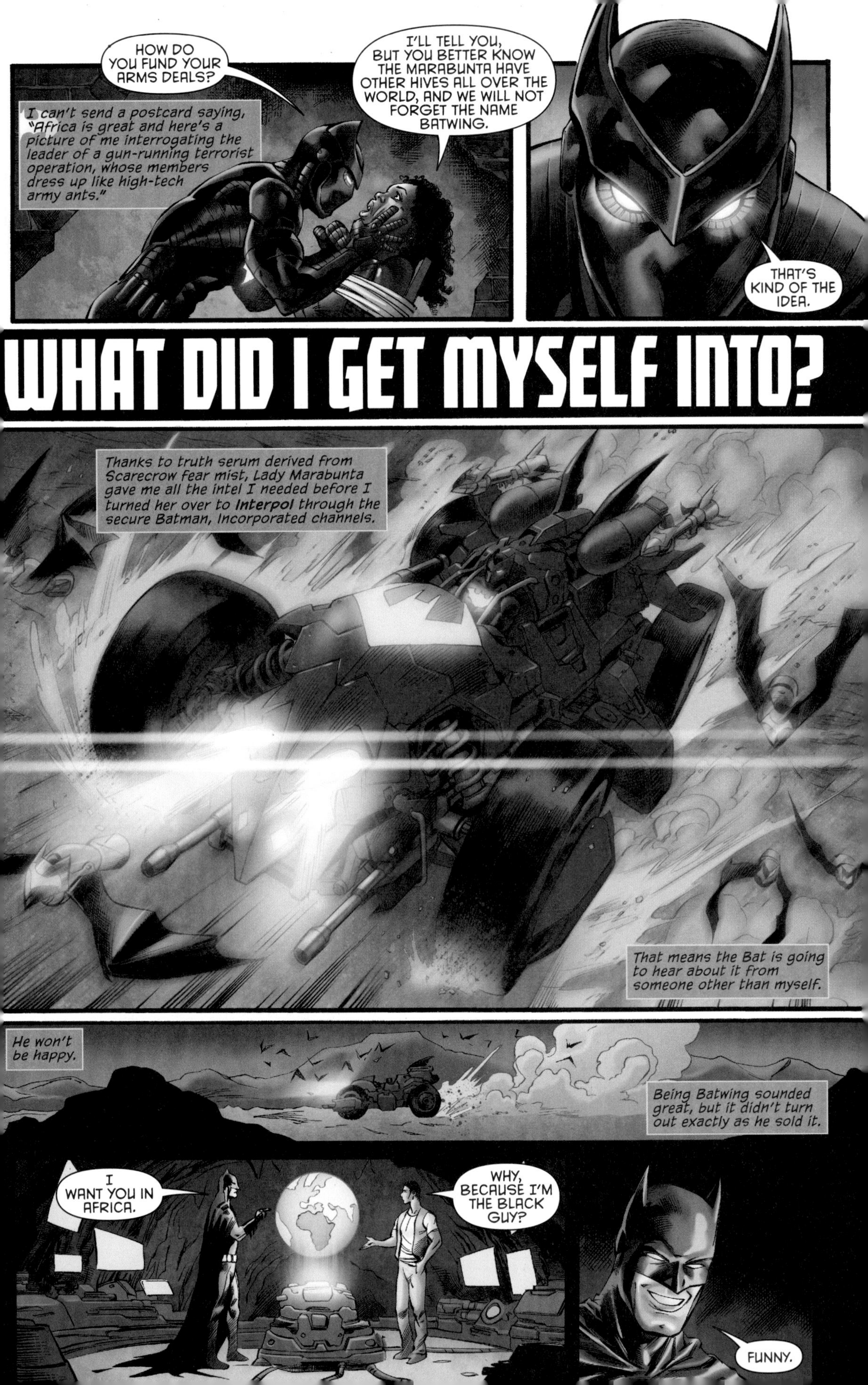
HOW DO YOU FUND YOUR ARMS DEALS?
I can't send a postcard saying, "Africa is great and here's a picture of me interrogating the leader of a gun-running terrorist operation, whose members dress up like high-tech army ants."
I'LL TELL YOU, BUT YOU BETTER KNOW THE MARABUNTA HAVE OTHER HIVES ALL OVER THE WORLD, AND WE WILL NOT FORGET THE NAME BATWING.
THAT'S KIND OF THE IDEA.
WHAT DID I GET MYSELF INTO?
Thanks to truth serum derived from Scarecrow fear mist, Lady Marabunta gave me all the intel I needed before I turned her over to Interpol through the secure Batman, Incorporated channels.
That means the Bat is going to hear about it from someone other than myself.
He won't be happy.
Being Batwing sounded great, but it didn't turn out exactly as he sold it.
I WANT YOU IN AFRICA.
WHY, BECAUSE I'M THE BLACK GUY?
FUNNY.

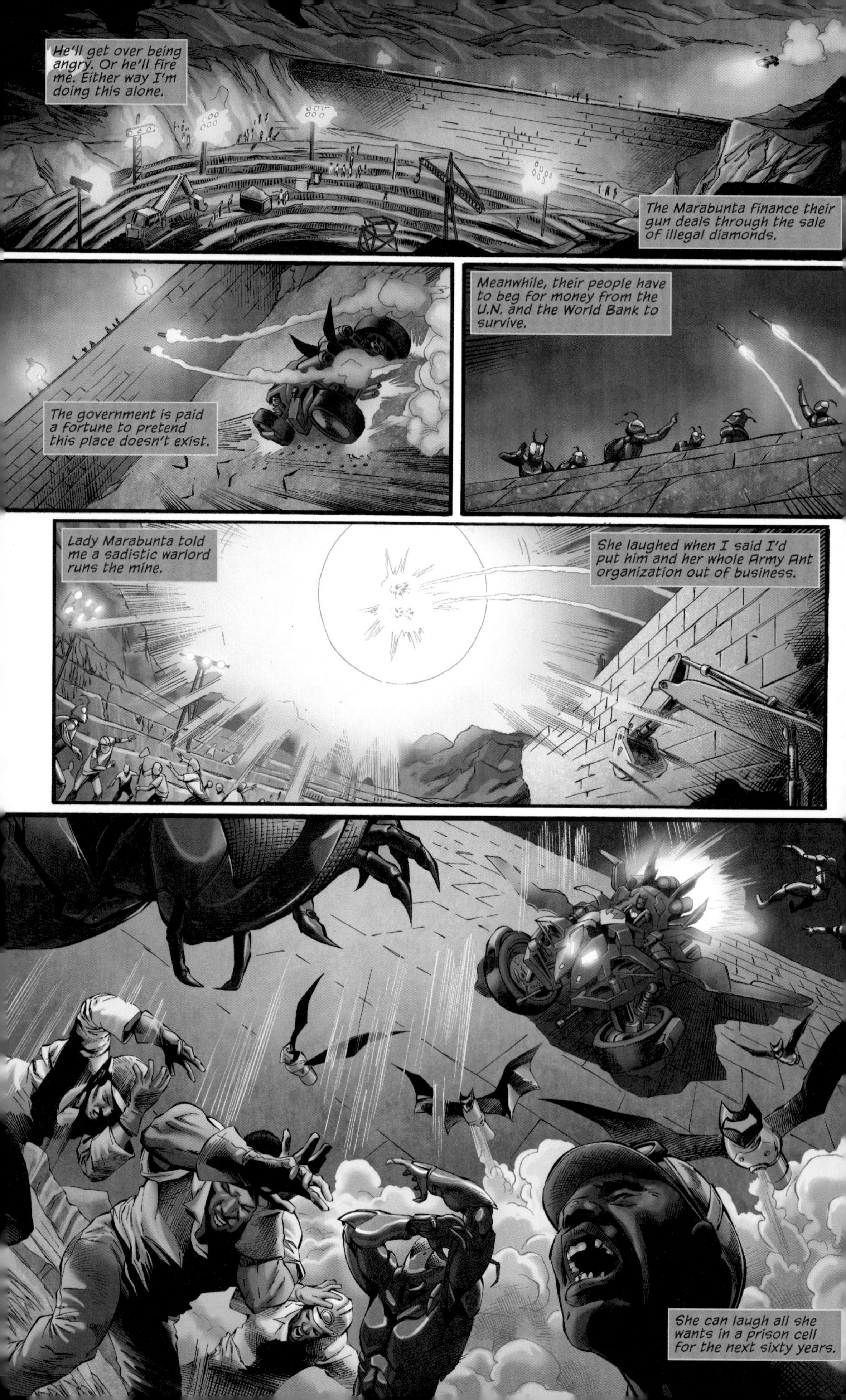
He'll get over being angry. Or he'll fire me. Either way I'm doing this alone.
The Marabunta finance their gun deals through the sale of illegal diamonds.
The government is paid a fortune to pretend this place doesn't exist.
Meanwhile, their people have to beg for money from the U.N. and the World Bank to survive.
Lady Marabunta told me a sadistic warlord runs the mine.
She laughed when I said I'd put him and her whole Army Ant organization out of business.
She can laugh all she wants in a prison cell for the next sixty years.

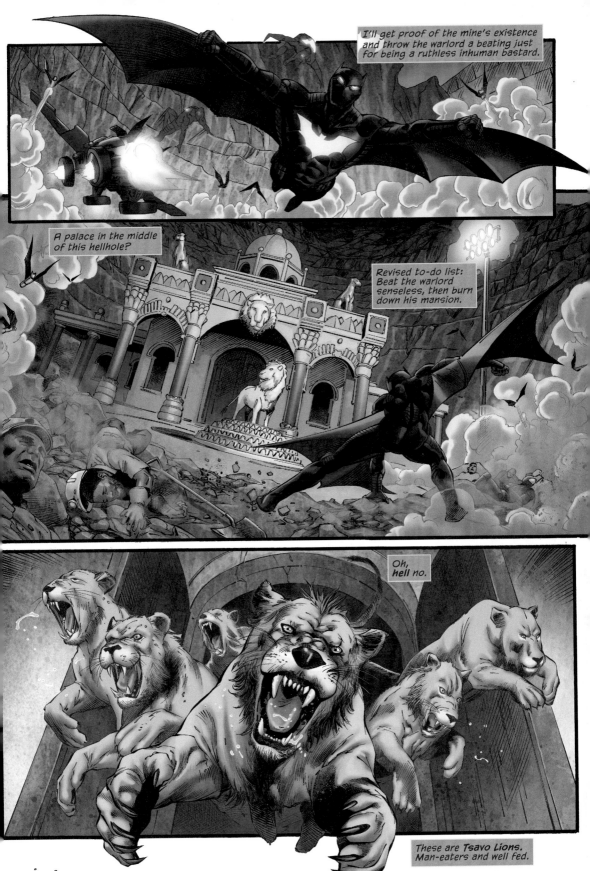

I'll get proof of the mine's existence and throw the warlord a beating just for being a ruthless inhuman bastard.

A palace in the middle of this hellhole?

Revised to-do list: Beat the warlord senseless, then burn down his mansion.

Oh, hell no.

These are *Tsavo Lions.* Man-eaters and well fed.

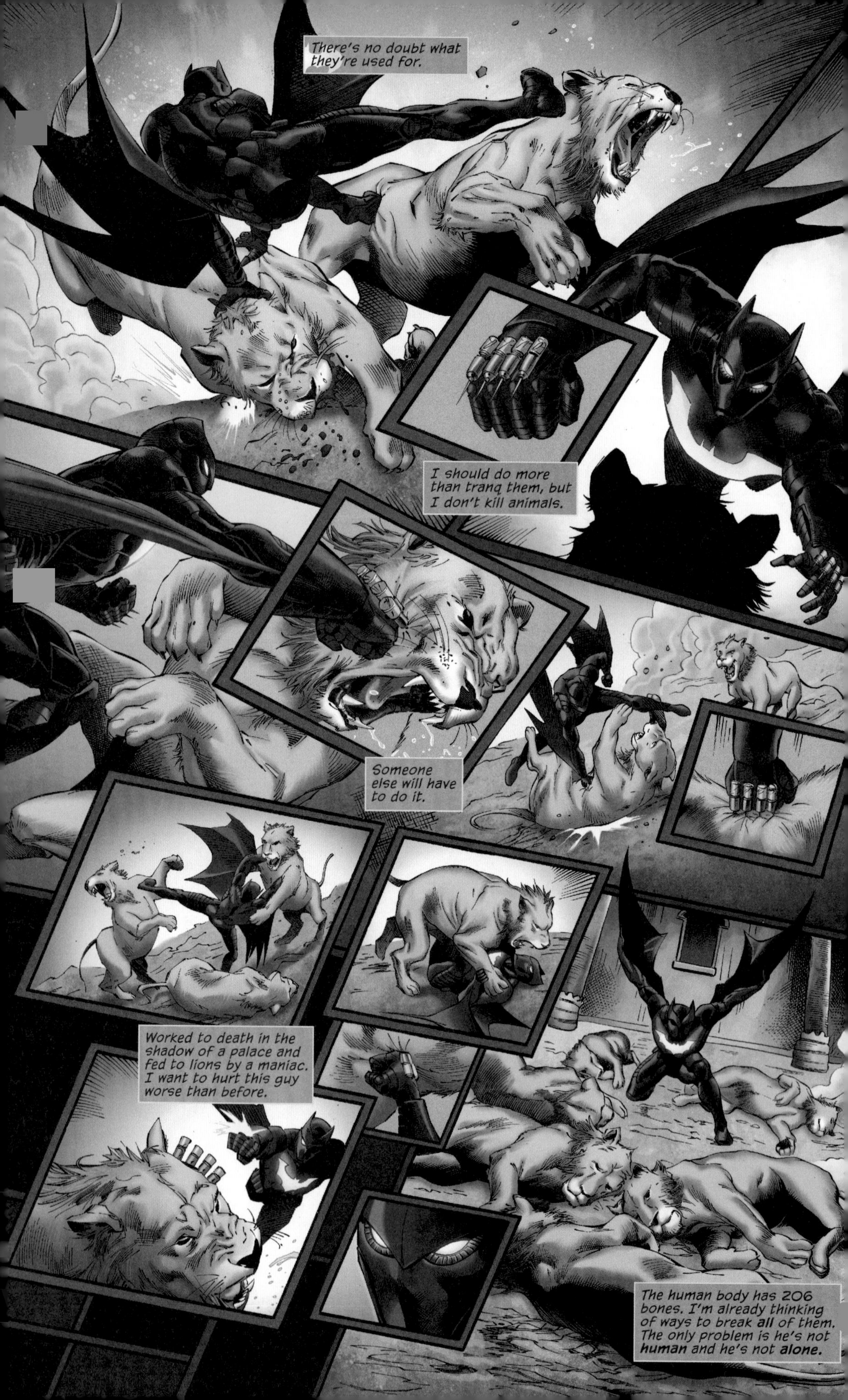
There's no doubt what they're used for.
I should do more than tranq them, but I don't kill animals.
Someone else will have to do it.
Worked to death in the shadow of a palace and fed to lions by a maniac. I want to hurt this guy worse than before.
The human body has 206 bones. I'm already thinking of ways to break **all** of them. The only problem is he's not **human** and he's not **alone.**

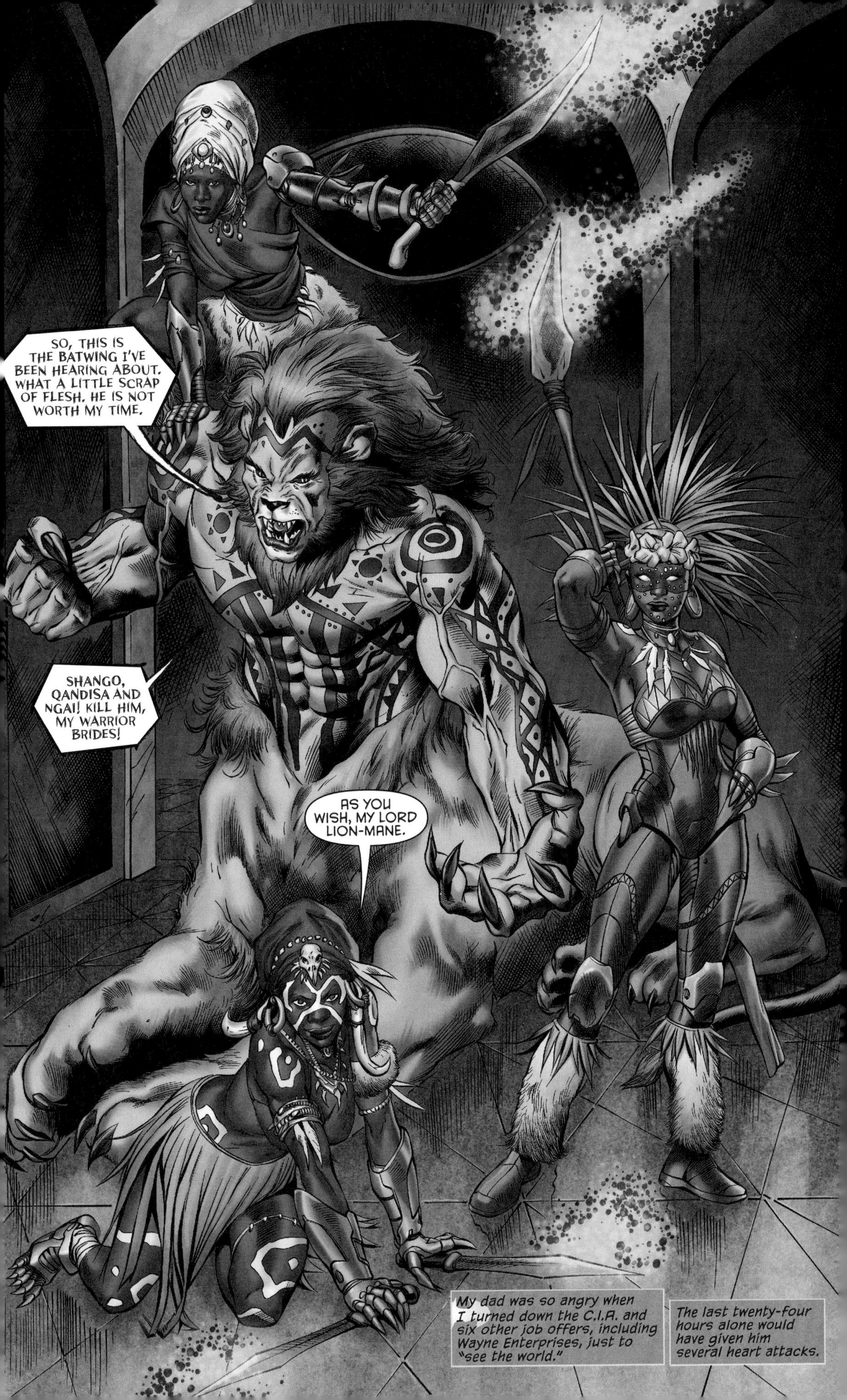

SO, THIS IS THE BATWING I'VE BEEN HEARING ABOUT. WHAT A LITTLE SCRAP OF FLESH. HE IS NOT WORTH MY TIME.
SHANGO, QANDISA AND NGAI! KILL HIM, MY WARRIOR BRIDES!
AS YOU WISH, MY LORD LION-MANE.
My dad was so angry when I turned down the C.I.A. and six other job offers, including Wayne Enterprises, just to "see the world."
The last twenty-four hours alone would have given him several heart attacks.

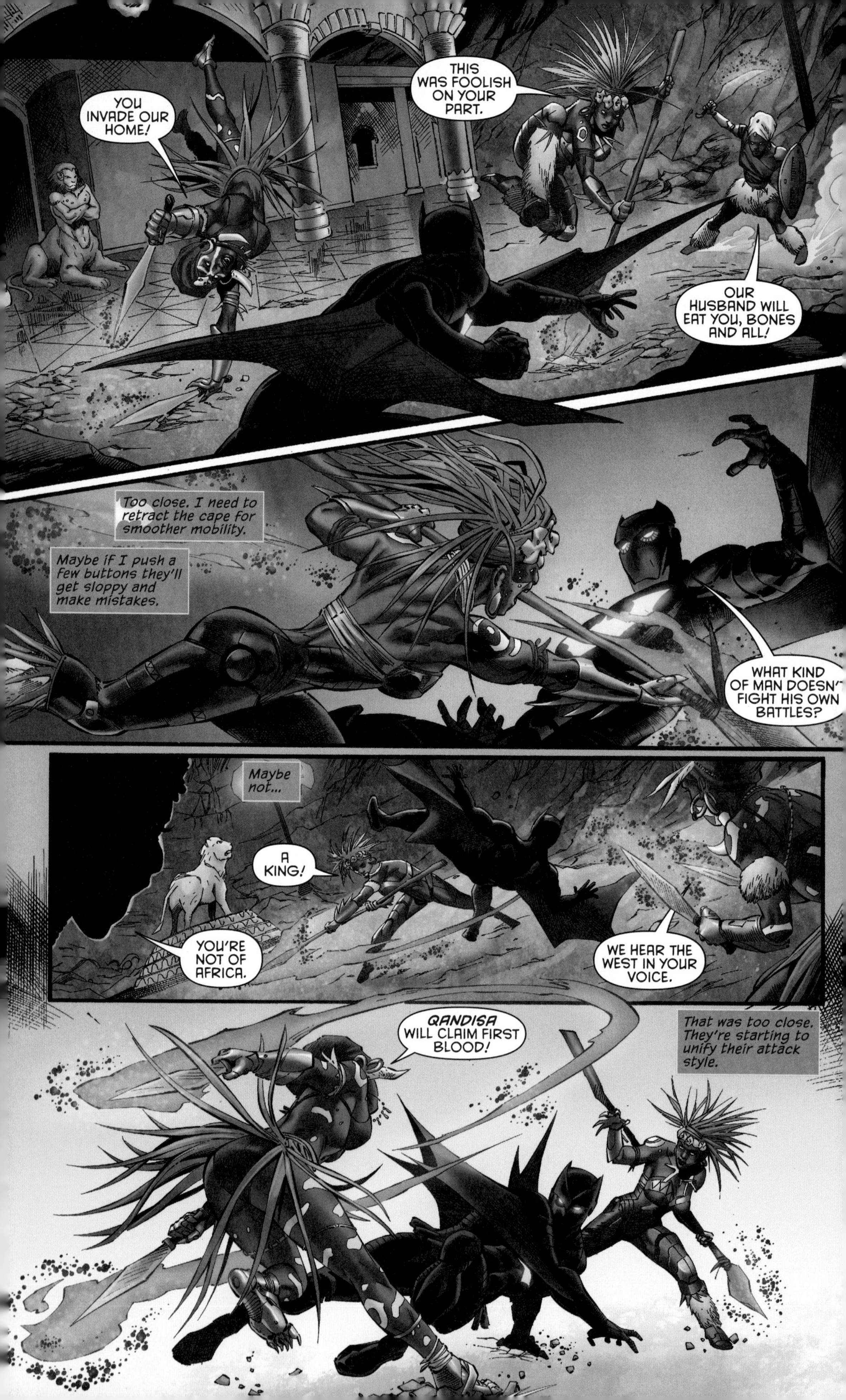
YOU INVADE OUR HOME!
THIS WAS FOOLISH ON YOUR PART.
OUR HUSBAND WILL EAT YOU, BONES AND ALL!
Too close. I need to retract the cape for smoother mobility.
Maybe if I push a few buttons they'll get sloppy and make mistakes.
WHAT KIND OF MAN DOESN'T FIGHT HIS OWN BATTLES?
Maybe not...
A KING!
YOU'RE NOT OF AFRICA.
WE HEAR THE WEST IN YOUR VOICE.
QANDISA WILL CLAIM FIRST BLOOD!
That was too close. They're starting to unify their attack style.

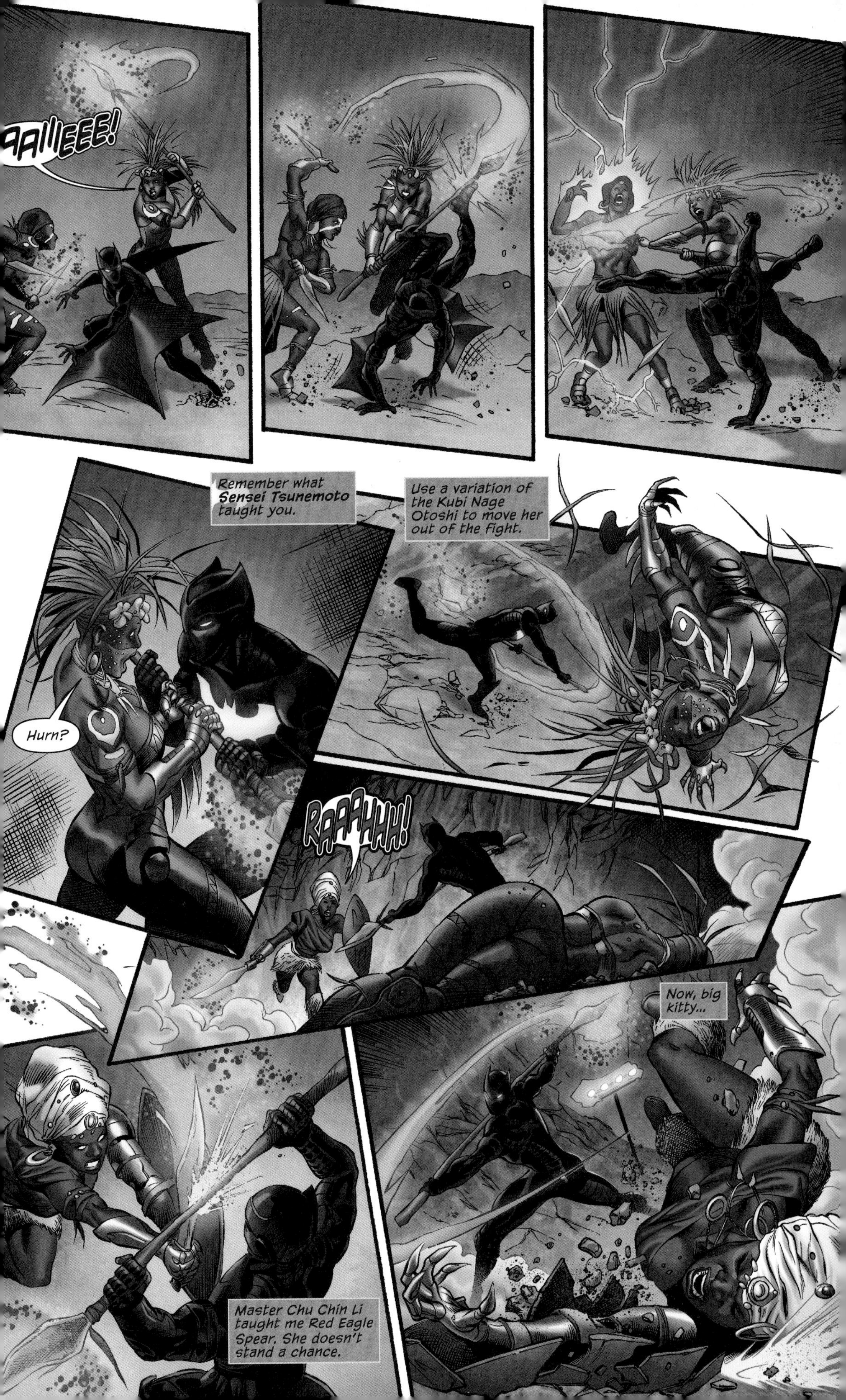
AAIIIEEE!
Remember what Sensei Tsunemoto taught you.
Hurn?
Use a variation of the Kubi Nage Otoshi to move her out of the fight.
RAAAHHH!
Master Chu Chin Li taught me Red Eagle Spear. She doesn't stand a chance.
Now, big kitty...

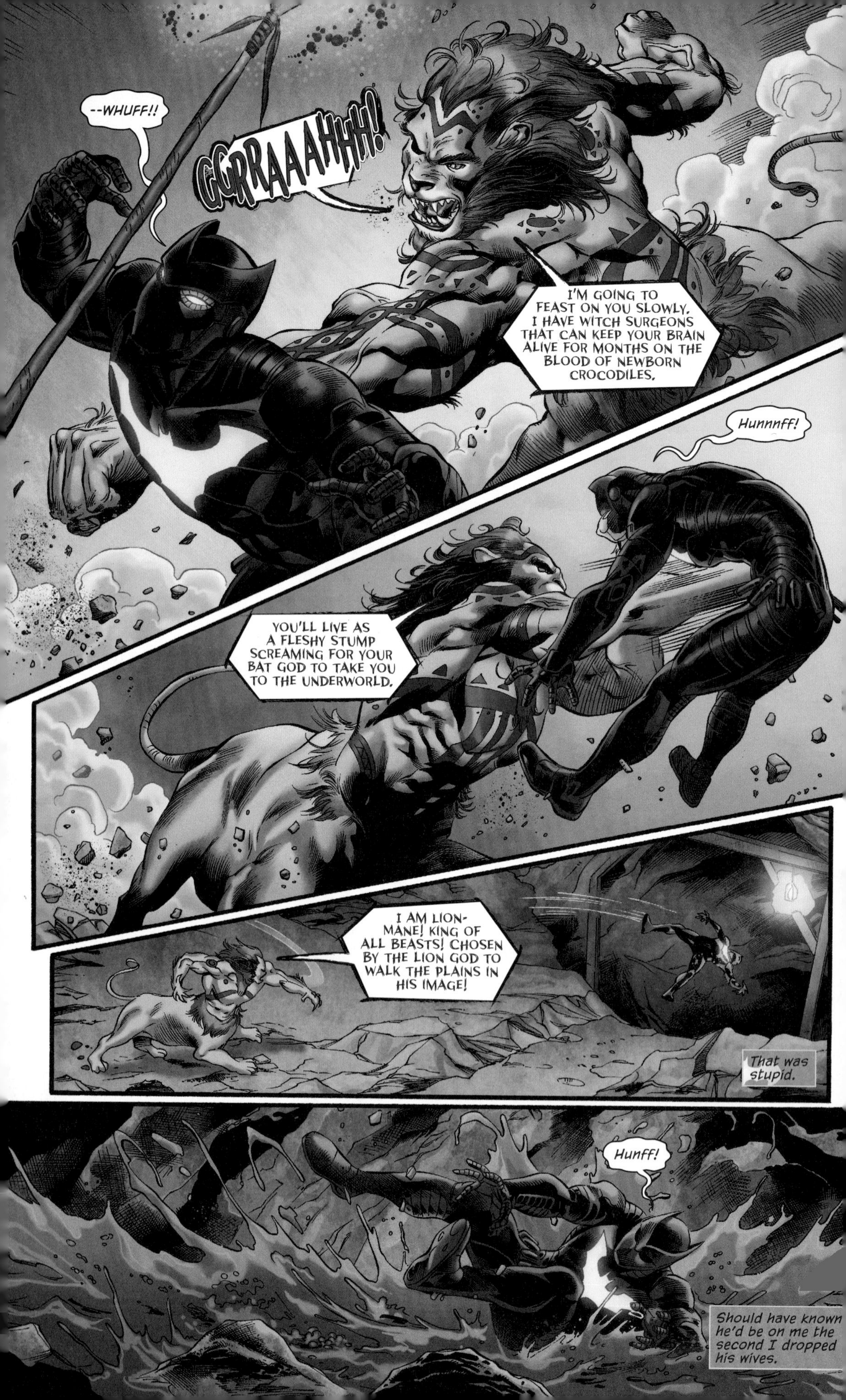
--WHUFF!!
GGRRAAAHHHH!
I'M GOING TO FEAST ON YOU SLOWLY. I HAVE WITCH SURGEONS THAT CAN KEEP YOUR BRAIN ALIVE FOR MONTHS ON THE BLOOD OF NEWBORN CROCODILES.
Hunnnff!
YOU'LL LIVE AS A FLESHY STUMP SCREAMING FOR YOUR BAT GOD TO TAKE YOU TO THE UNDERWORLD.
I AM LION-MANE! KING OF ALL BEASTS! CHOSEN BY THE LION GOD TO WALK THE PLAINS IN HIS IMAGE!
That was stupid.
Hunff!
Should have known he'd be on me the second I dropped his wives.

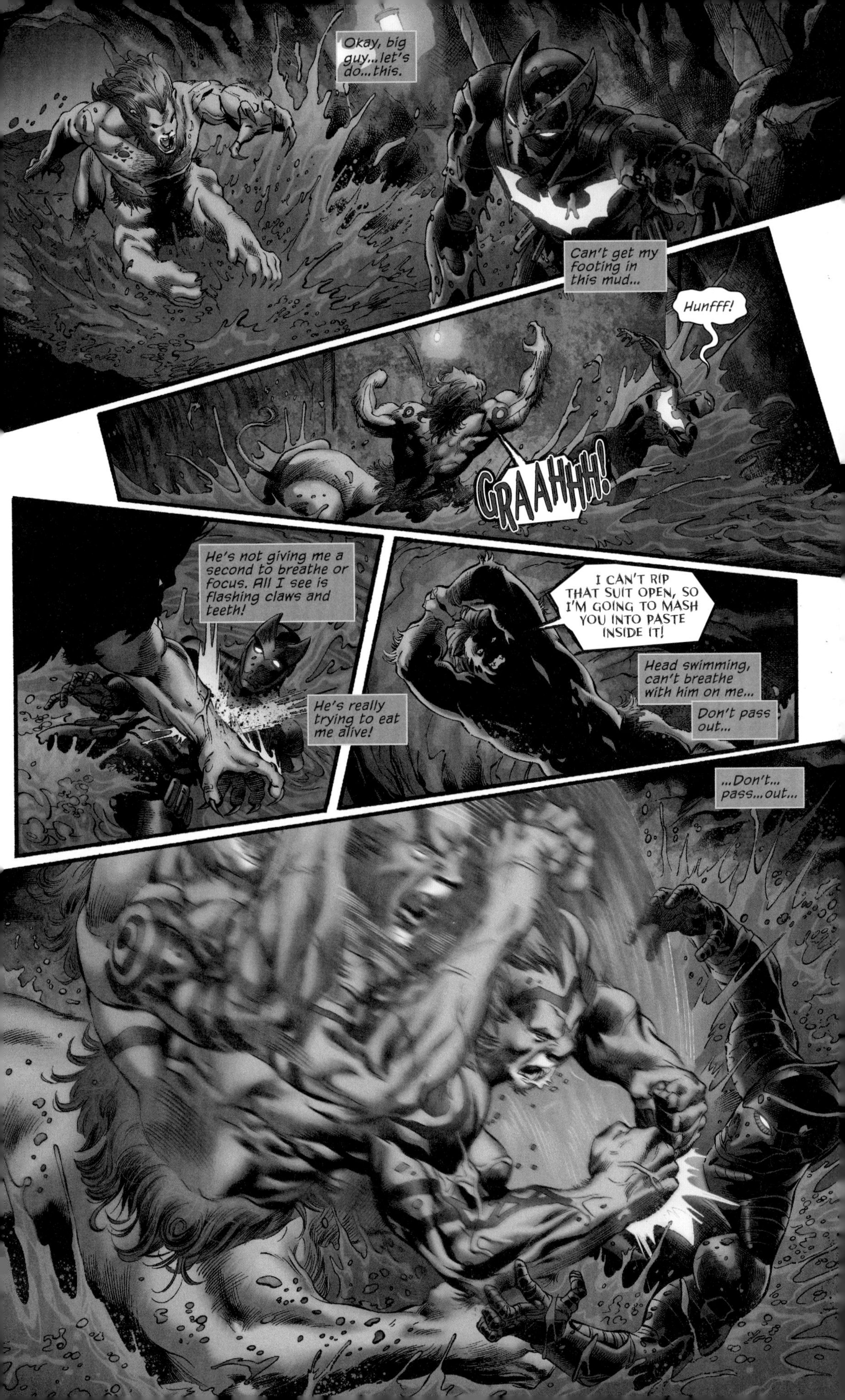
Okay, big guy...let's do...this.
Can't get my footing in this mud...
Hunfff!
GRAAHHH!
He's not giving me a second to breathe or focus. All I see is flashing claws and teeth!
He's really trying to eat me alive!
I CAN'T RIP THAT SUIT OPEN, SO I'M GOING TO MASH YOU INTO PASTE INSIDE IT!
Head swimming, can't breathe with him on me...
Don't pass out...
...Don't... pass...out...

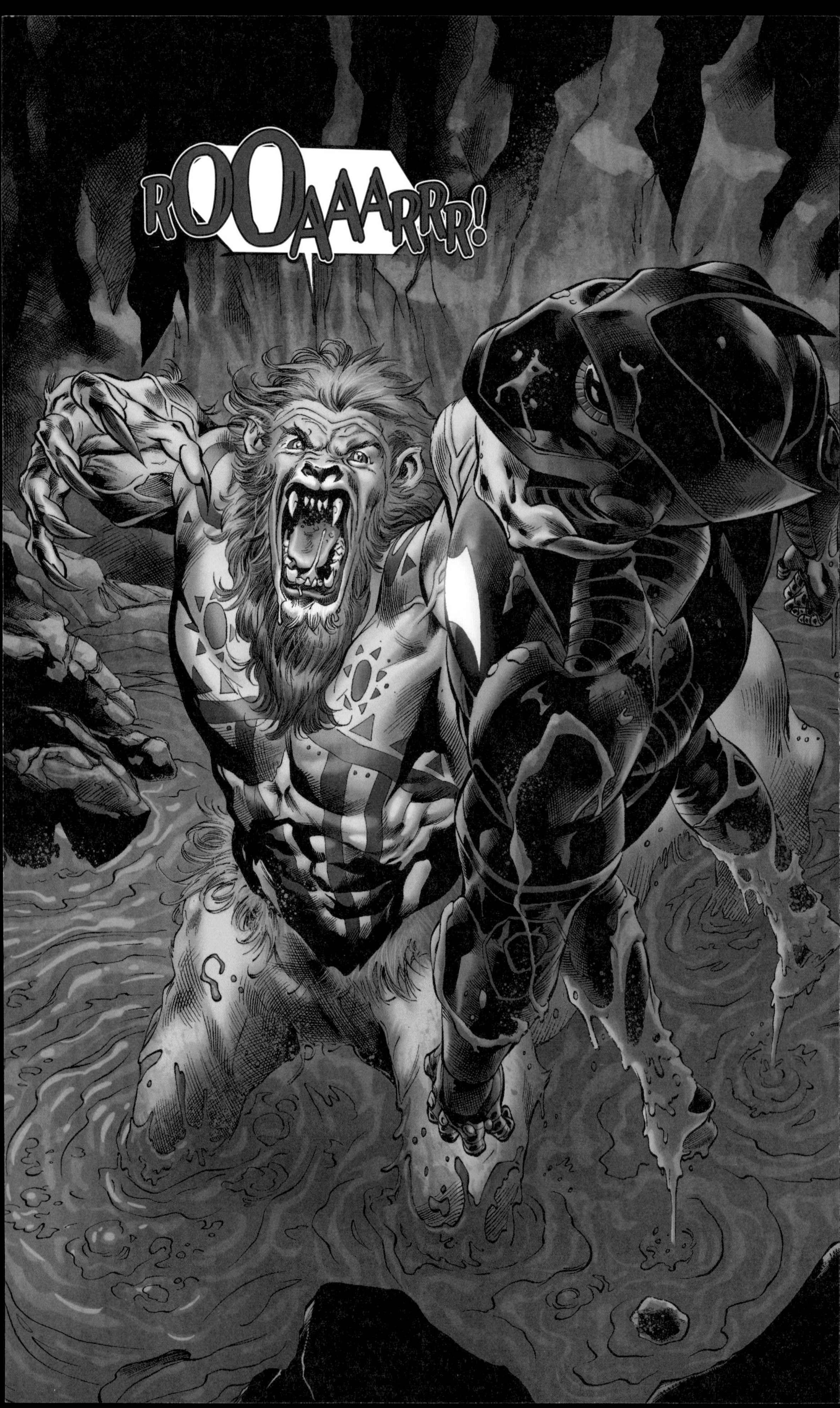
rOOAAARRRR!

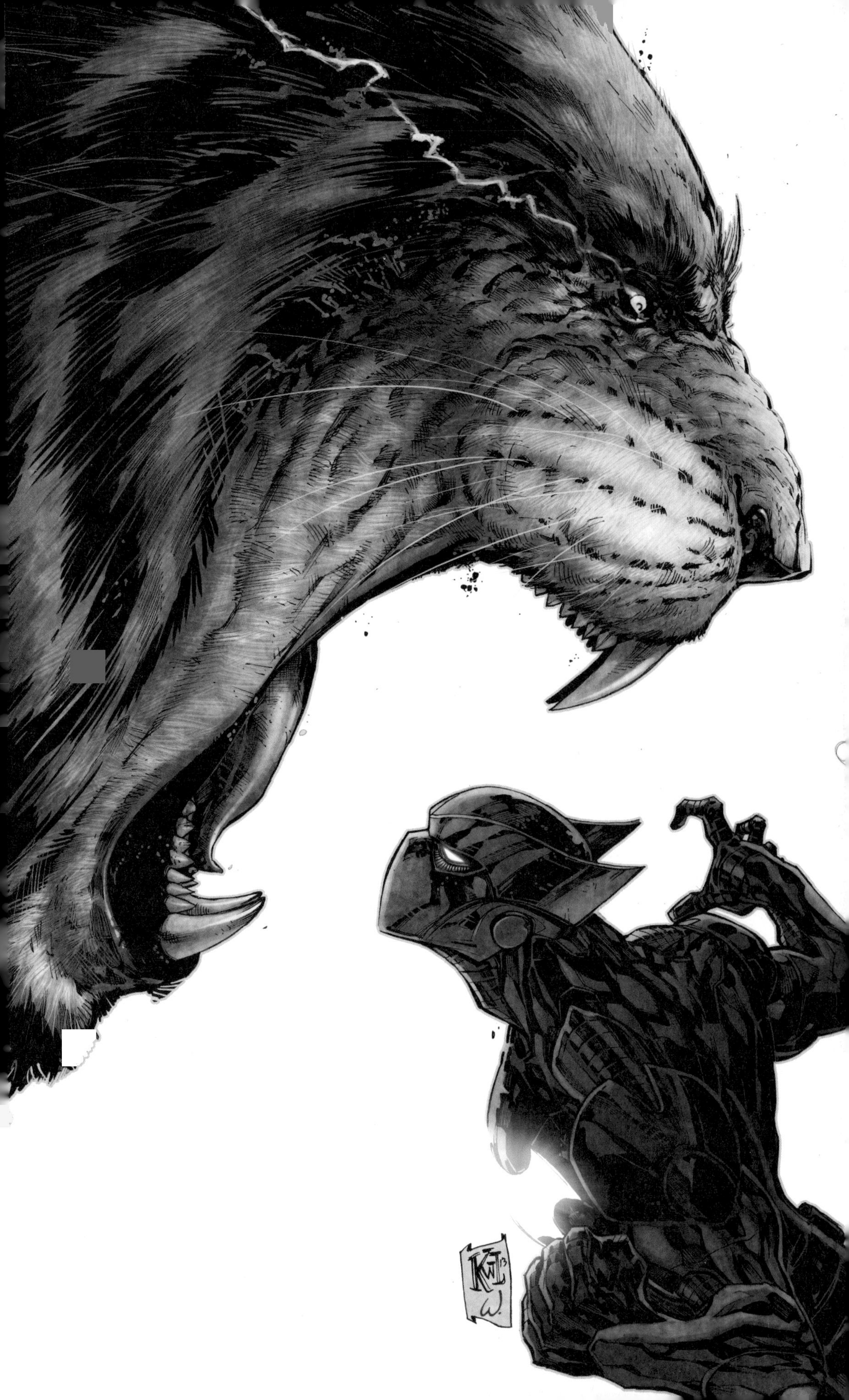

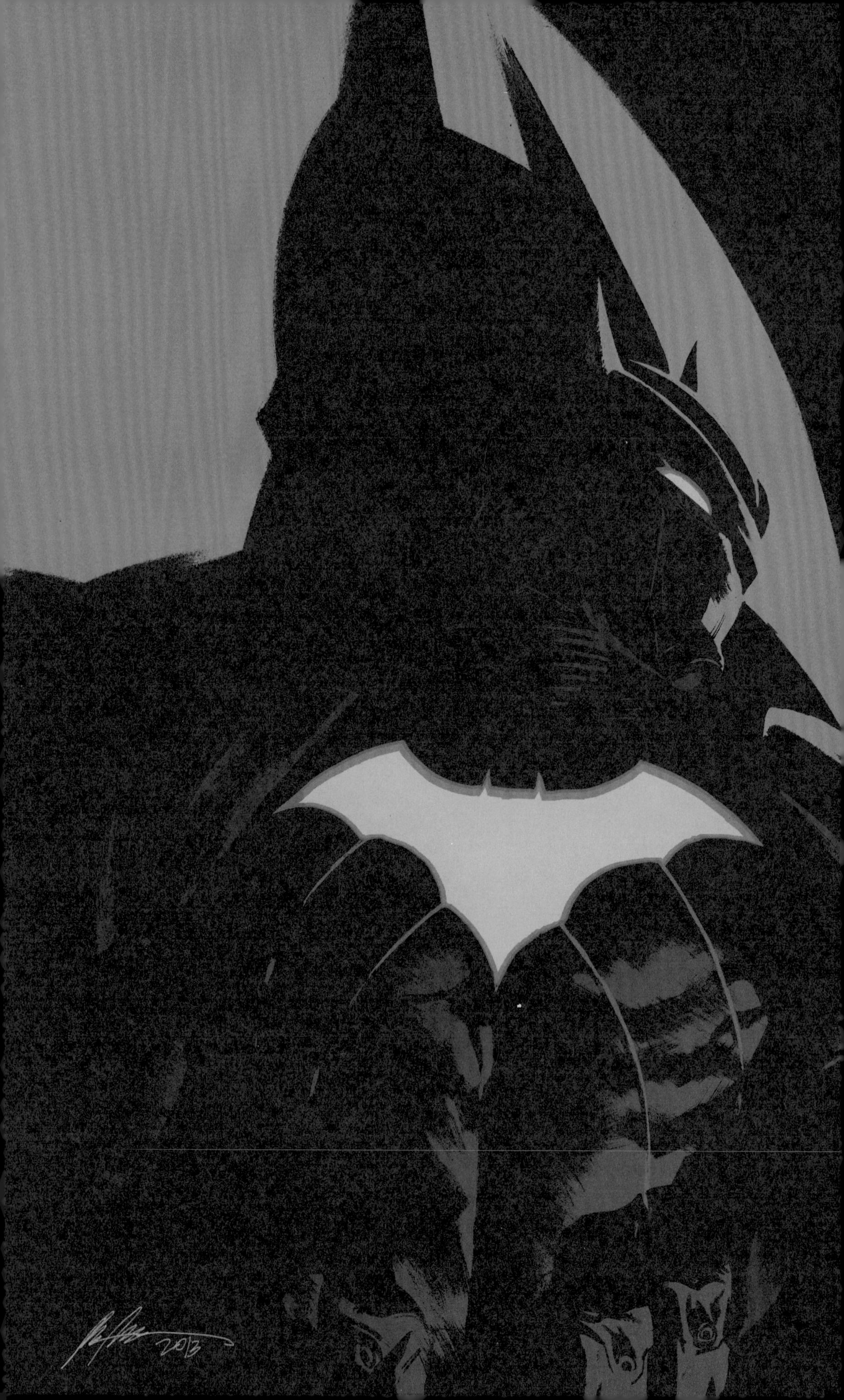

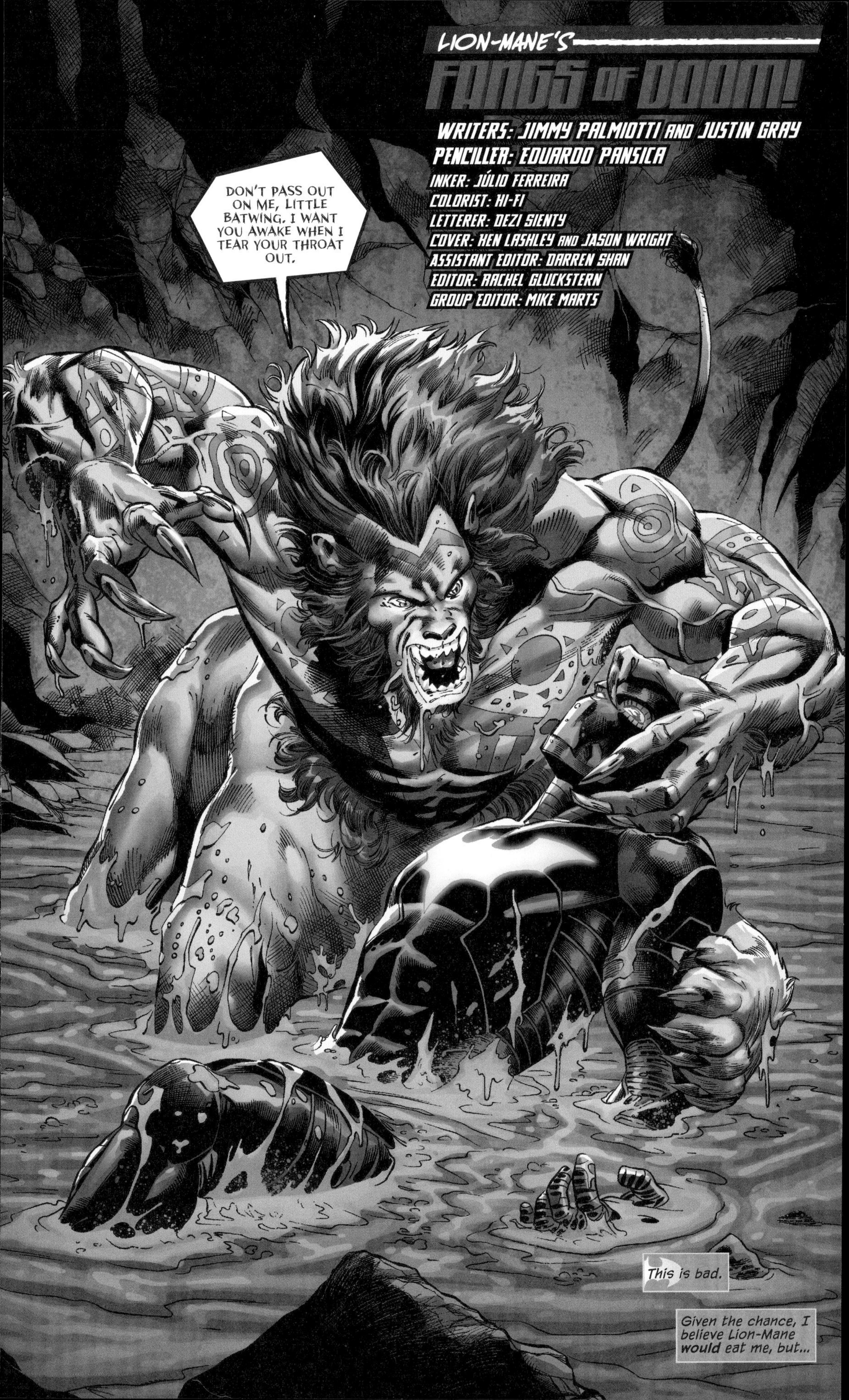
LION-MANE'S
FANGS OF DOOM!
WRITERS: JIMMY PALMIOTTI AND JUSTIN GRAY
PENCILLER: EDUARDO PANSICA
INKER: JÚLIO FERREIRA
COLORIST: HI-FI
LETTERER: DEZI SIENTY
COVER: KEN LASHLEY AND JASON WRIGHT
ASSISTANT EDITOR: DARREN SHAN
EDITOR: RACHEL GLUCKSTERN
GROUP EDITOR: MIKE MARTS
DON'T PASS OUT ON ME, LITTLE BATWING. I WANT YOU AWAKE WHEN I TEAR YOUR THROAT OUT.
This is bad.
Given the chance, I believe Lion-Mane would eat me, but...

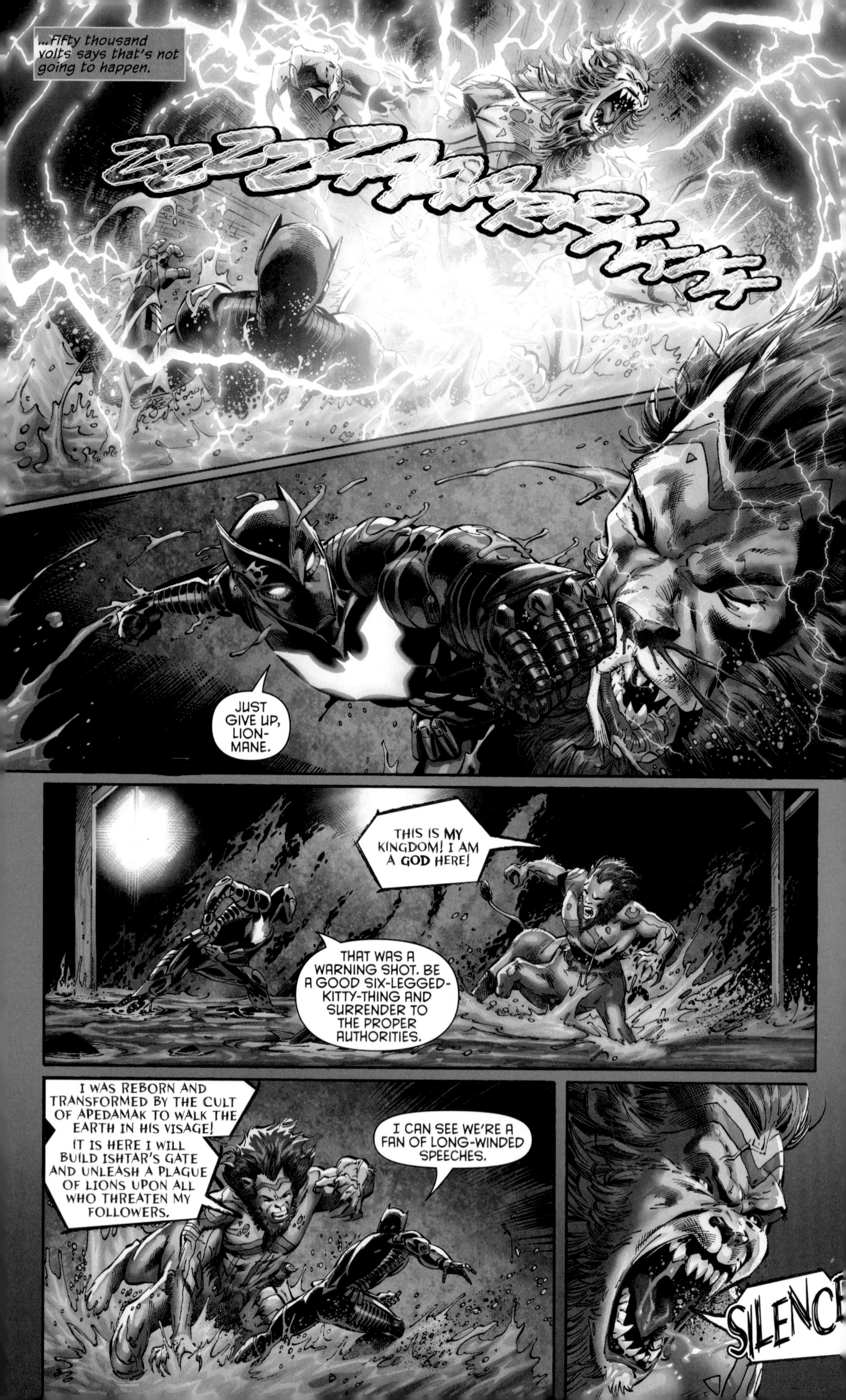

...fifty thousand volts says that's not going to happen.
ZZZZZZRRRRRRRKKKK
JUST GIVE UP, LION-MANE.
THIS IS MY KINGDOM! I AM A GOD HERE!
THAT WAS A WARNING SHOT. BE A GOOD SIX-LEGGED-KITTY-THING AND SURRENDER TO THE PROPER AUTHORITIES.
I WAS REBORN AND TRANSFORMED BY THE CULT OF APEDAMAK TO WALK THE EARTH IN HIS VISAGE!
IT IS HERE I WILL BUILD ISHTAR'S GATE AND UNLEASH A PLAGUE OF LIONS UPON ALL WHO THREATEN MY FOLLOWERS.
I CAN SEE WE'RE A FAN OF LONG-WINDED SPEECHES.
SILENCE

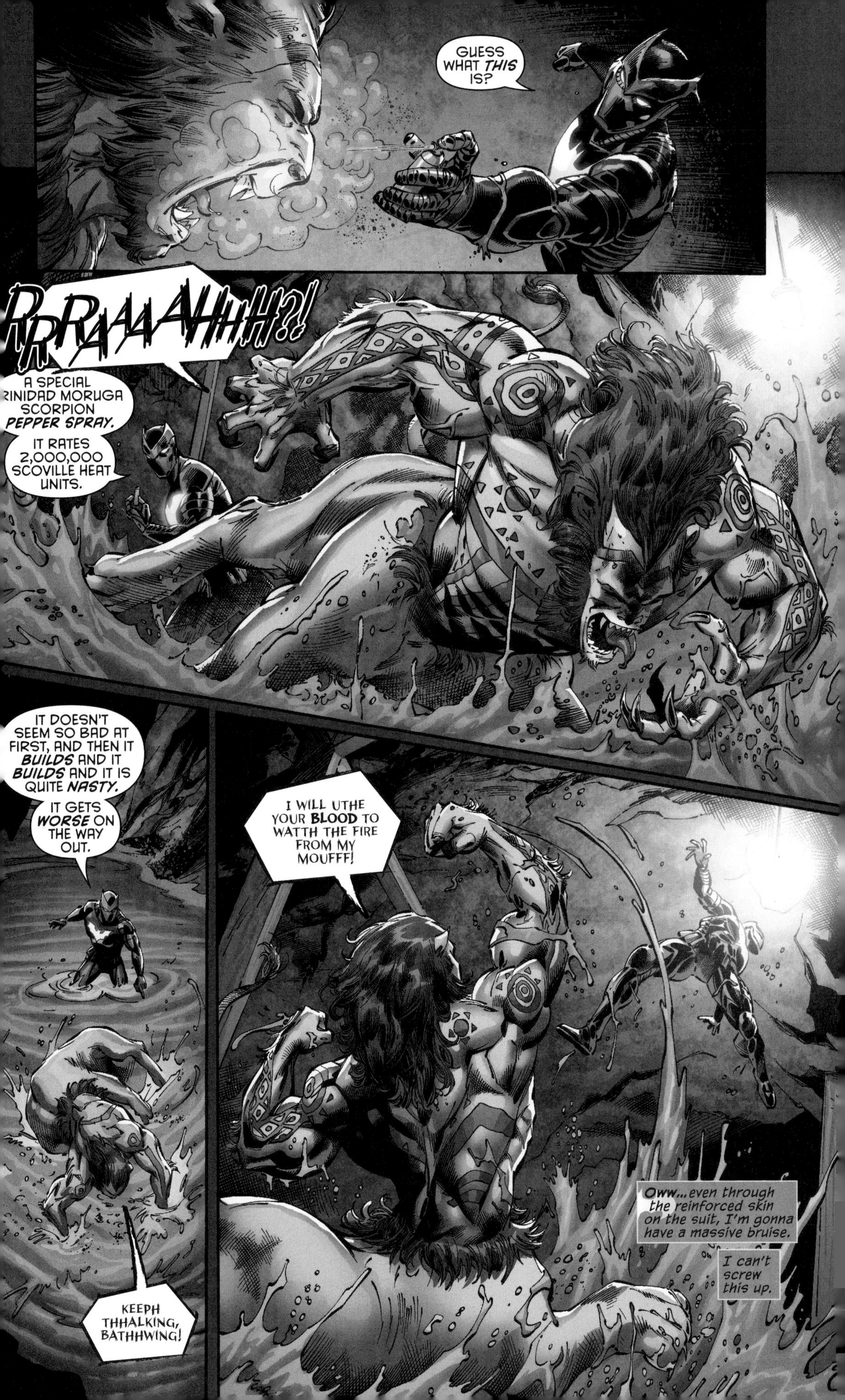
GUESS WHAT *THIS* IS?
RRRAAAAHHHH?!
A SPECIAL RINIDAD MORUGA SCORPION *PEPPER SPRAY.*
IT RATES 2,000,000 SCOVILLE HEAT UNITS.
IT DOESN'T SEEM SO BAD AT FIRST, AND THEN IT *BUILDS* AND IT *BUILDS* AND IT IS QUITE *NASTY.*
IT GETS *WORSE* ON THE WAY OUT.
KEEPH THHALKING, BATHHWING!
I WILL UTHE YOUR **BLOOD** TO WATTH THE FIRE FROM MY MOUFFF!
Oww... *even through the reinforced skin on the suit, I'm gonna have a massive bruise.*
I can't screw this up.

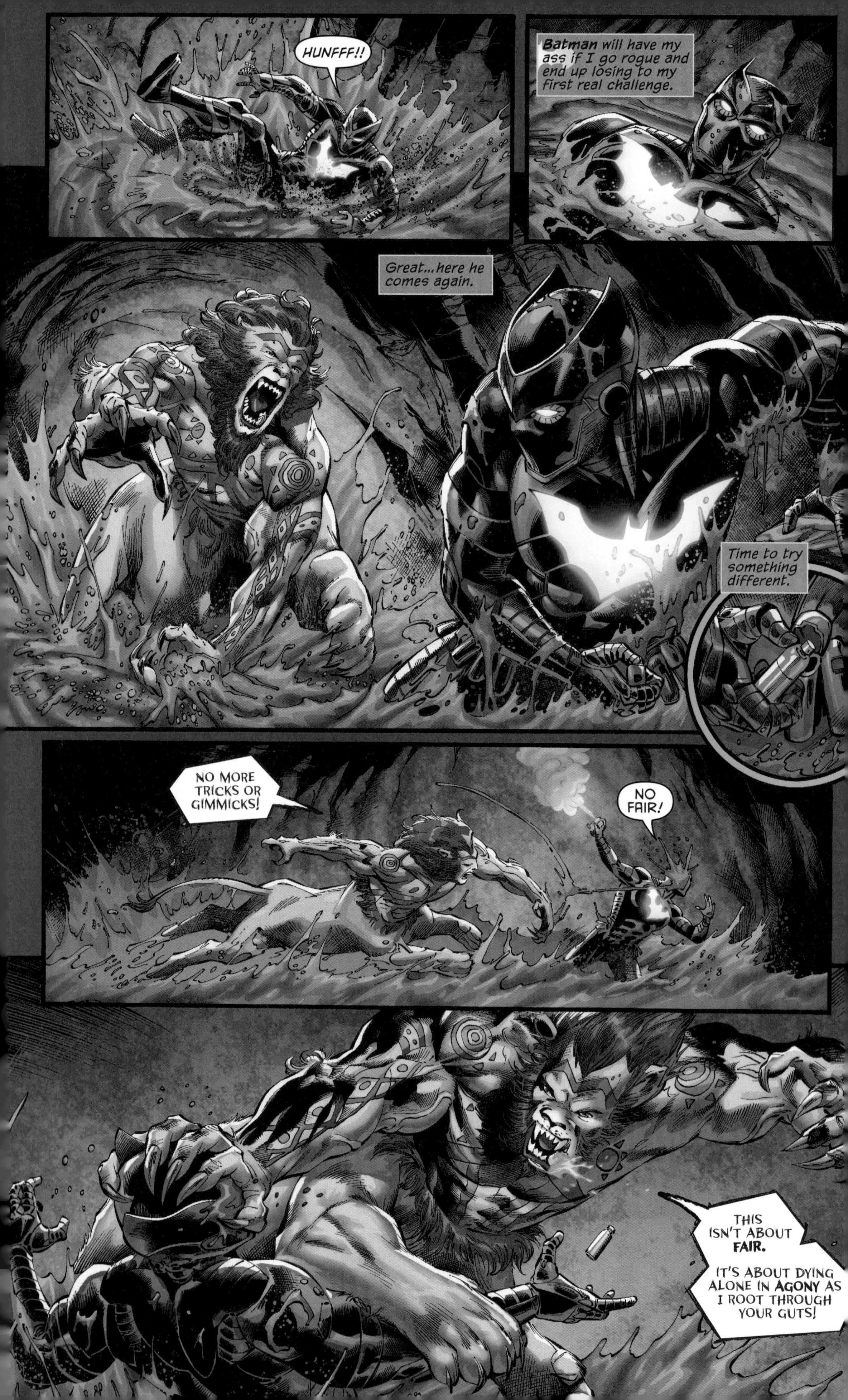
HUNFFF!!
Batman will have my ass if I go rogue and end up losing to my first real challenge.
Great...here he comes again.
Time to try something different.
NO MORE TRICKS OR GIMMICKS!
NO FAIR!
THIS ISN'T ABOUT FAIR.
IT'S ABOUT DYING ALONE IN AGONY AS I ROOT THROUGH YOUR GUTS!

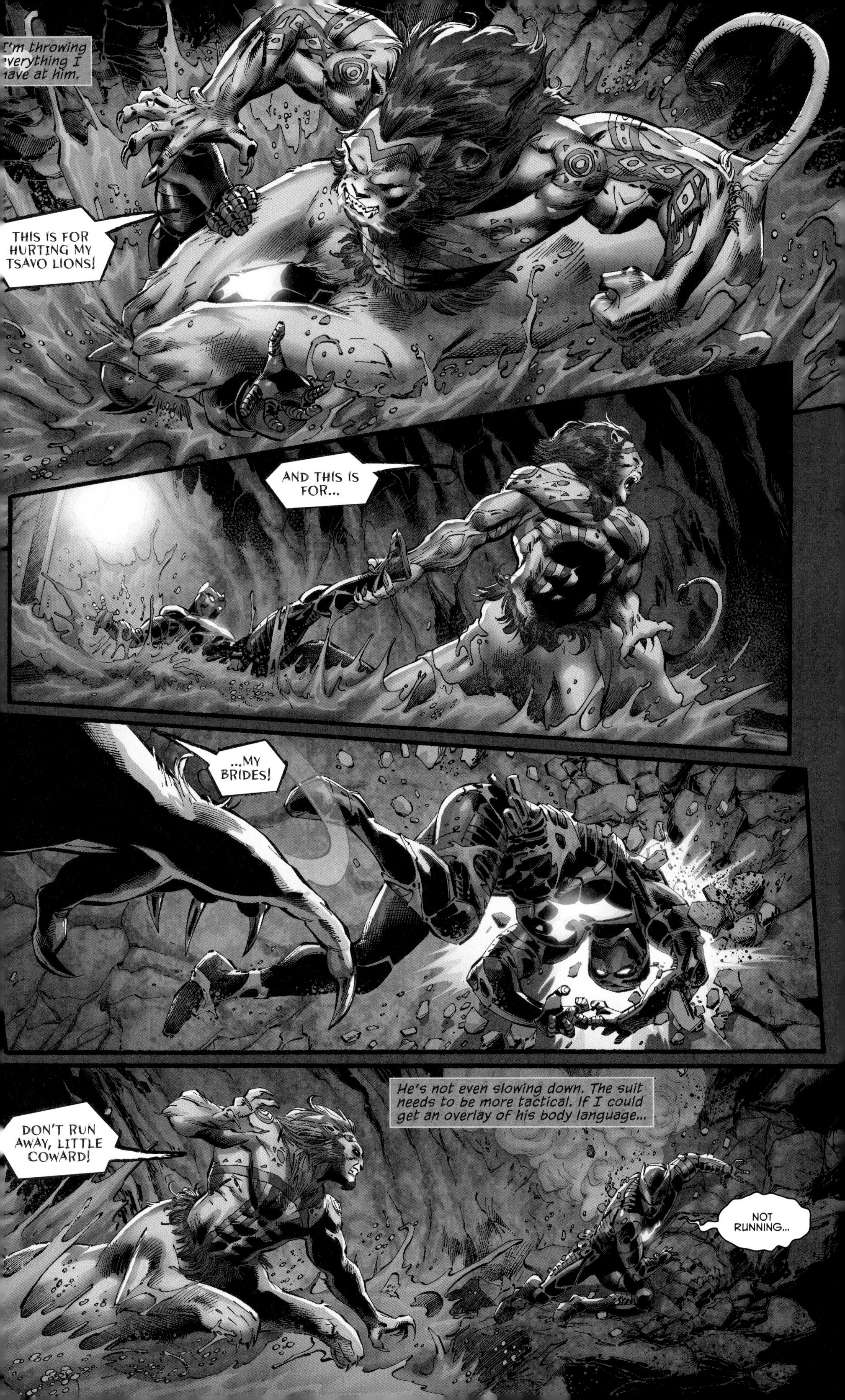
I'm throwing
everything I
have at him.
THIS IS FOR HURTING MY TSAVO LIONS!
AND THIS IS FOR...
...MY BRIDES!
He's not even slowing down. The suit needs to be more tactical. If I could get an overlay of his body language...
DON'T RUN AWAY, LITTLE COWARD!
NOT RUNNING...

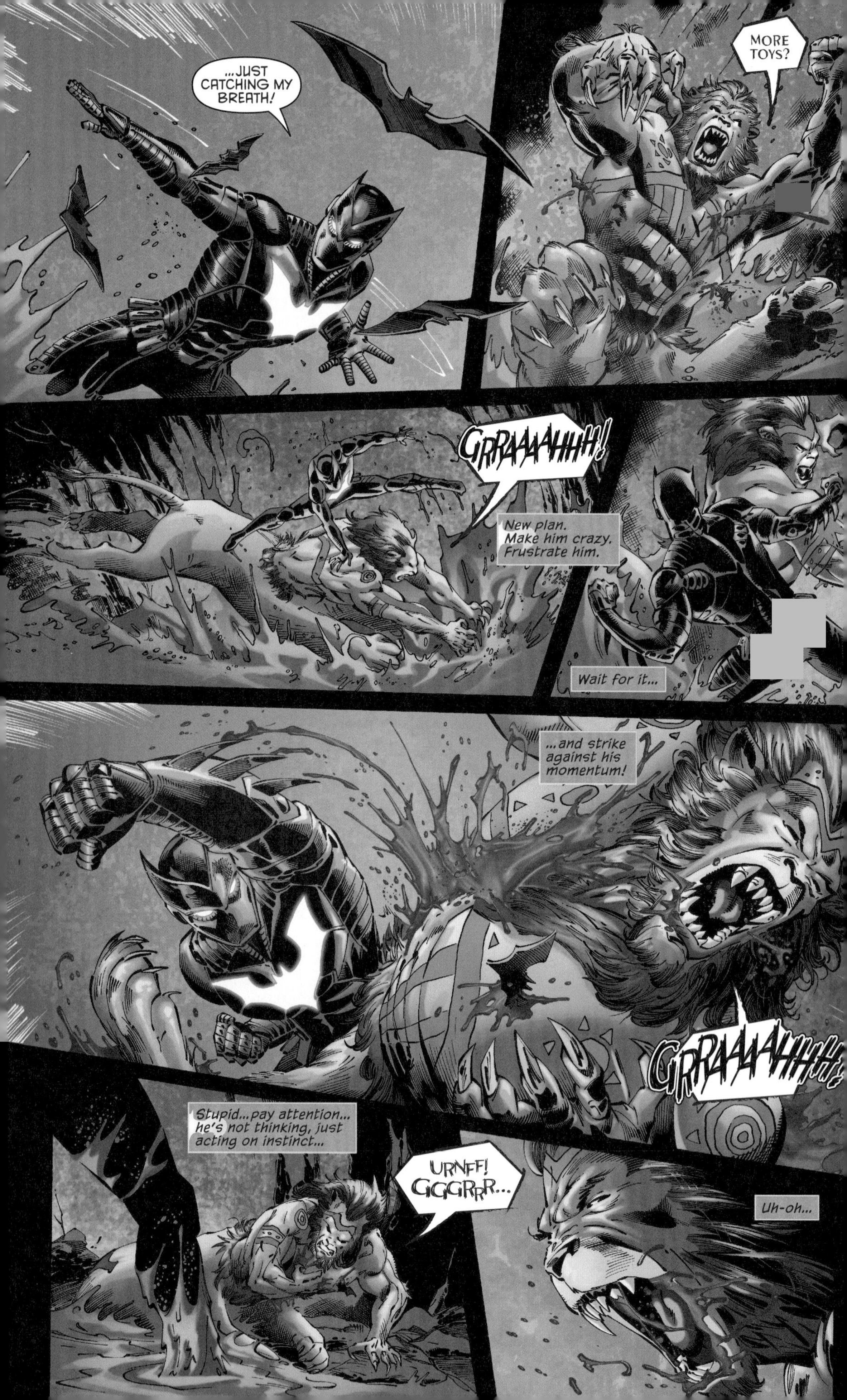
...JUST CATCHING MY BREATH!
MORE TOYS?
GRRAAAAHHHH!
New plan. Make him crazy. Frustrate him.
Wait for it...
...and strike against his momentum!
GRRAAAAHHHH!
Stupid...pay attention... he's not thinking, just acting on instinct...
URNFF! GGGRRR...
Uh-oh...

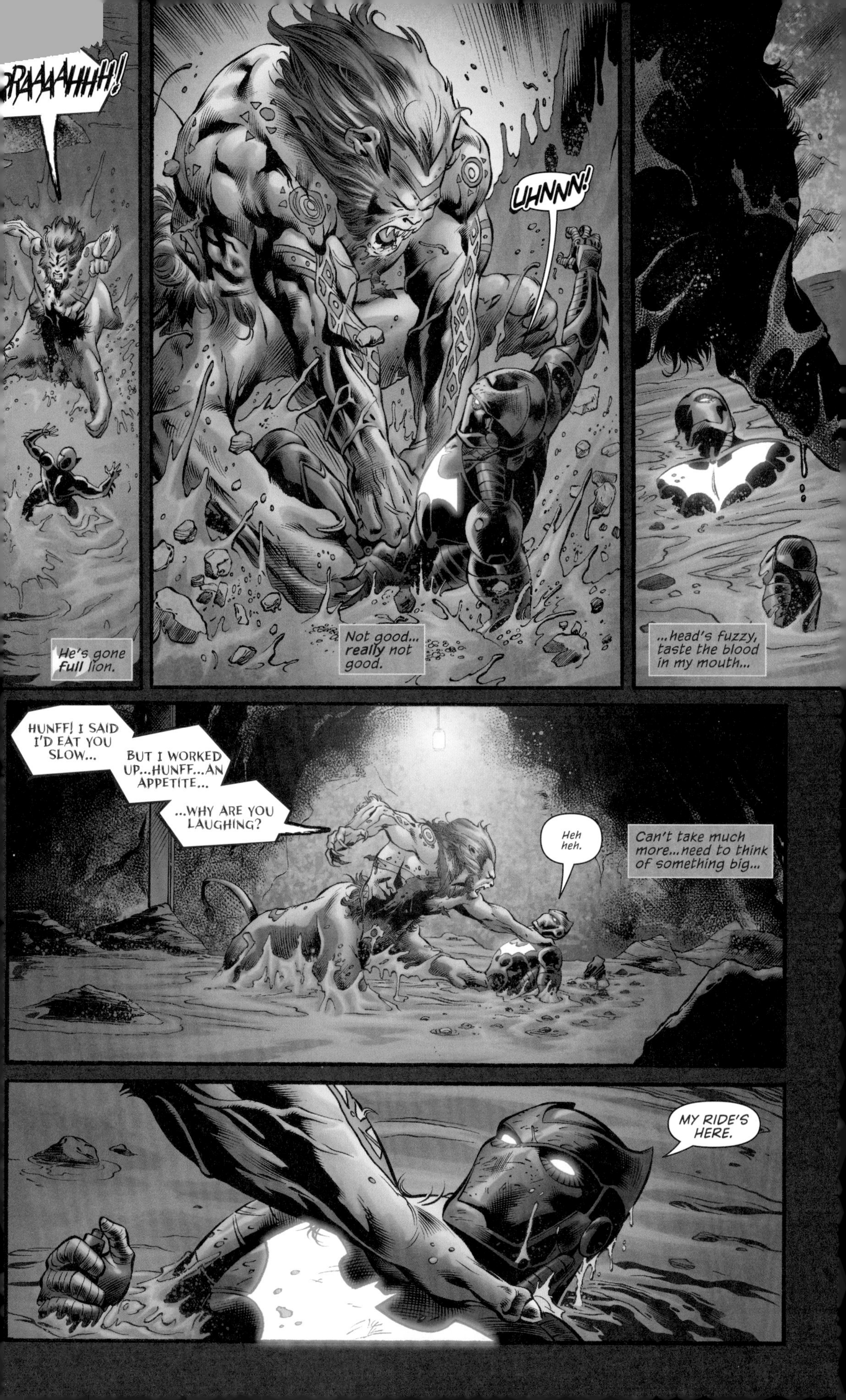
RAAAAHHH!
He's gone full lion.
UHNNN!
Not good... really not good.
...head's fuzzy, taste the blood in my mouth...
HUNFF! I SAID I'D EAT YOU SLOW...
BUT I WORKED UP...HUNFF...AN APPETITE...
...WHY ARE YOU LAUGHING?
Heh heh.
Can't take much more...need to think of something big...
MY RIDE'S HERE.

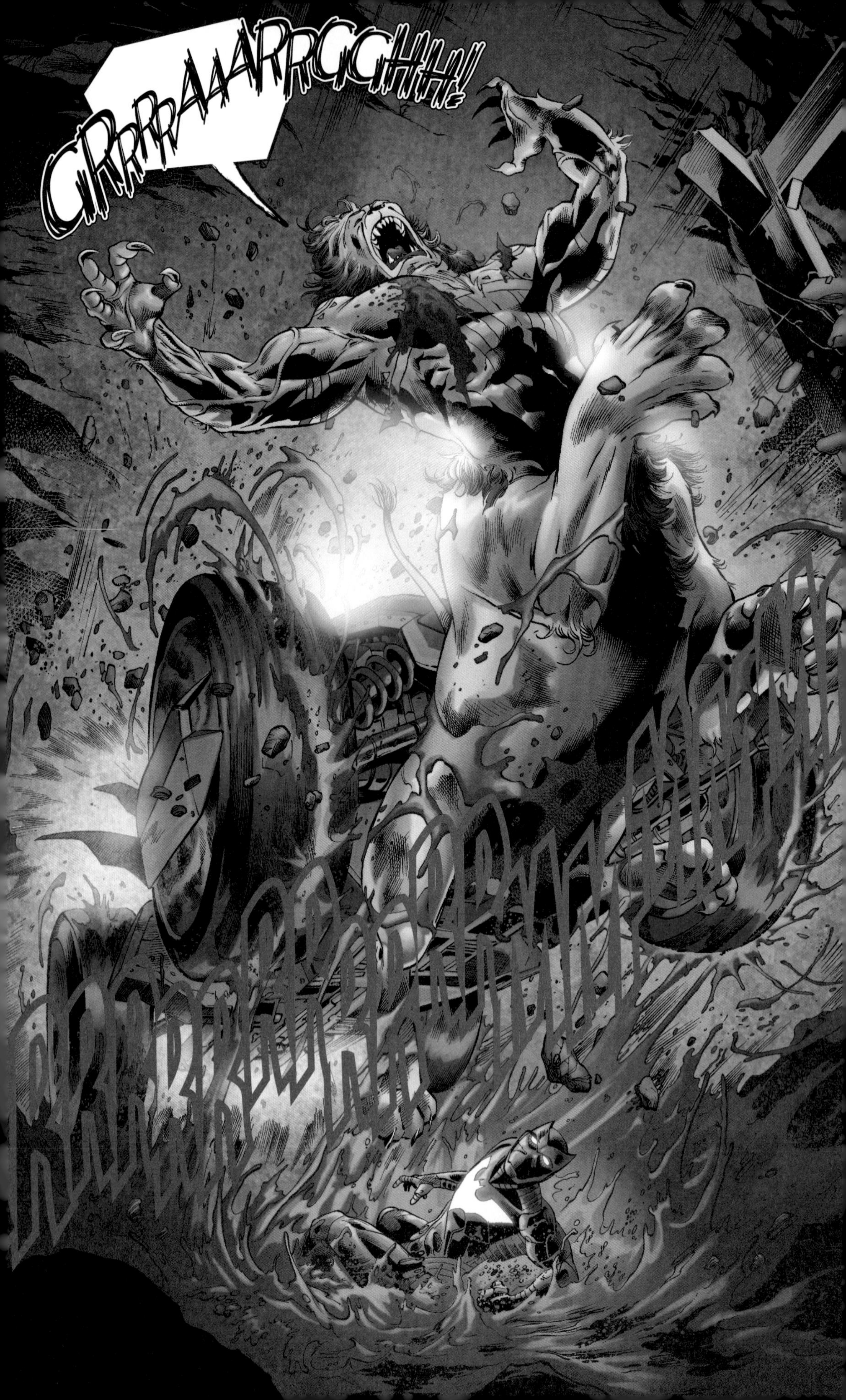
GRRRRAAARRGGHHH!!

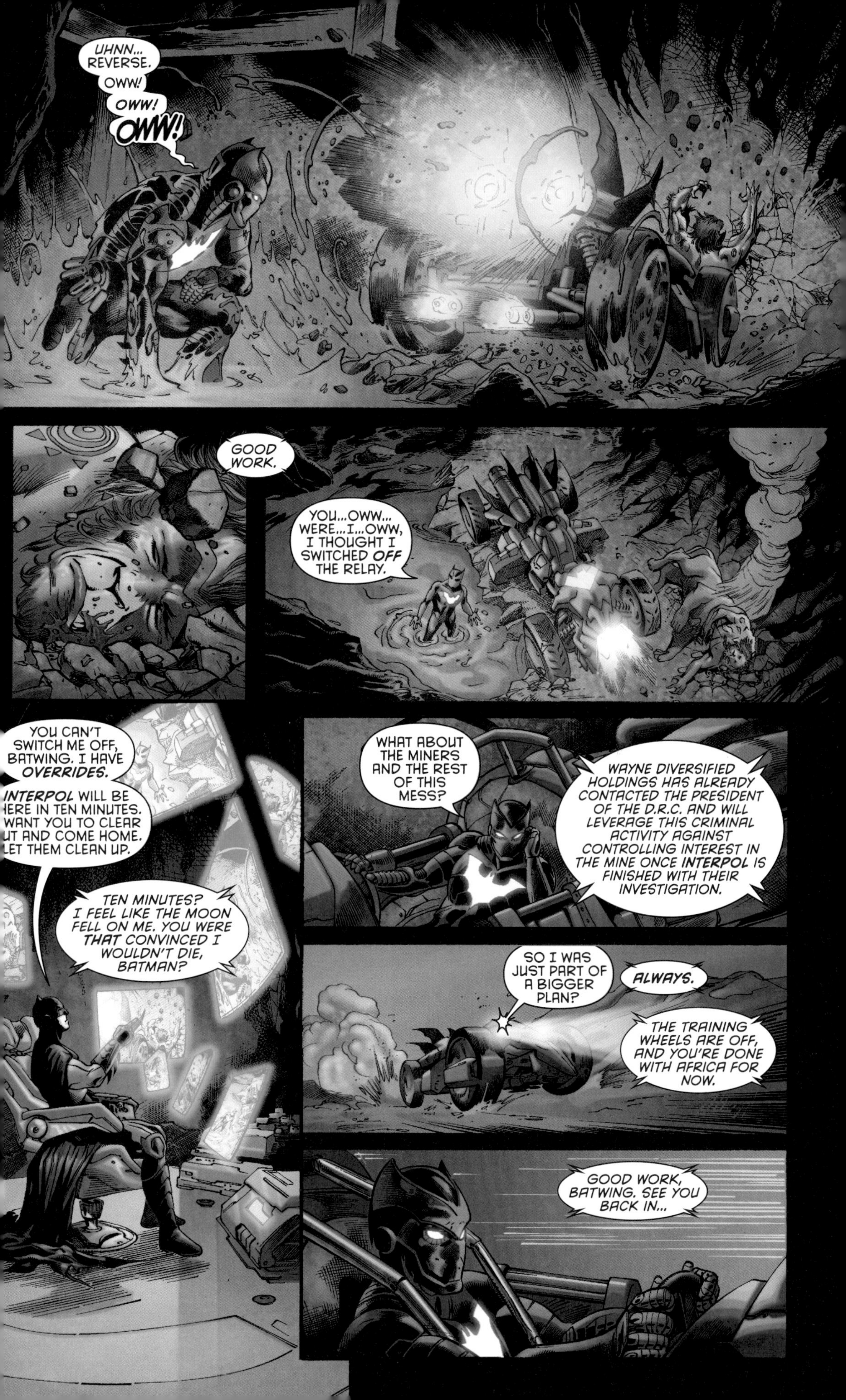

UHNN... REVERSE.
OWW!
OWW!
OWW!
GOOD WORK.
YOU...OWW... WERE...I...OWW, I THOUGHT I SWITCHED OFF THE RELAY.
YOU CAN'T SWITCH ME OFF, BATWING. I HAVE OVERRIDES.
INTERPOL WILL BE HERE IN TEN MINUTES. WANT YOU TO CLEAR UT AND COME HOME. LET THEM CLEAN UP.
TEN MINUTES? I FEEL LIKE THE MOON FELL ON ME. YOU WERE THAT CONVINCED I WOULDN'T DIE, BATMAN?
WHAT ABOUT THE MINERS AND THE REST OF THIS MESS?
WAYNE DIVERSIFIED HOLDINGS HAS ALREADY CONTACTED THE PRESIDENT OF THE D.R.C. AND WILL LEVERAGE THIS CRIMINAL ACTIVITY AGAINST CONTROLLING INTEREST IN THE MINE ONCE INTERPOL IS FINISHED WITH THEIR INVESTIGATION.
SO I WAS JUST PART OF A BIGGER PLAN?
ALWAYS.
THE TRAINING WHEELS ARE OFF, AND YOU'RE DONE WITH AFRICA FOR NOW.
GOOD WORK, BATWING. SEE YOU BACK IN...

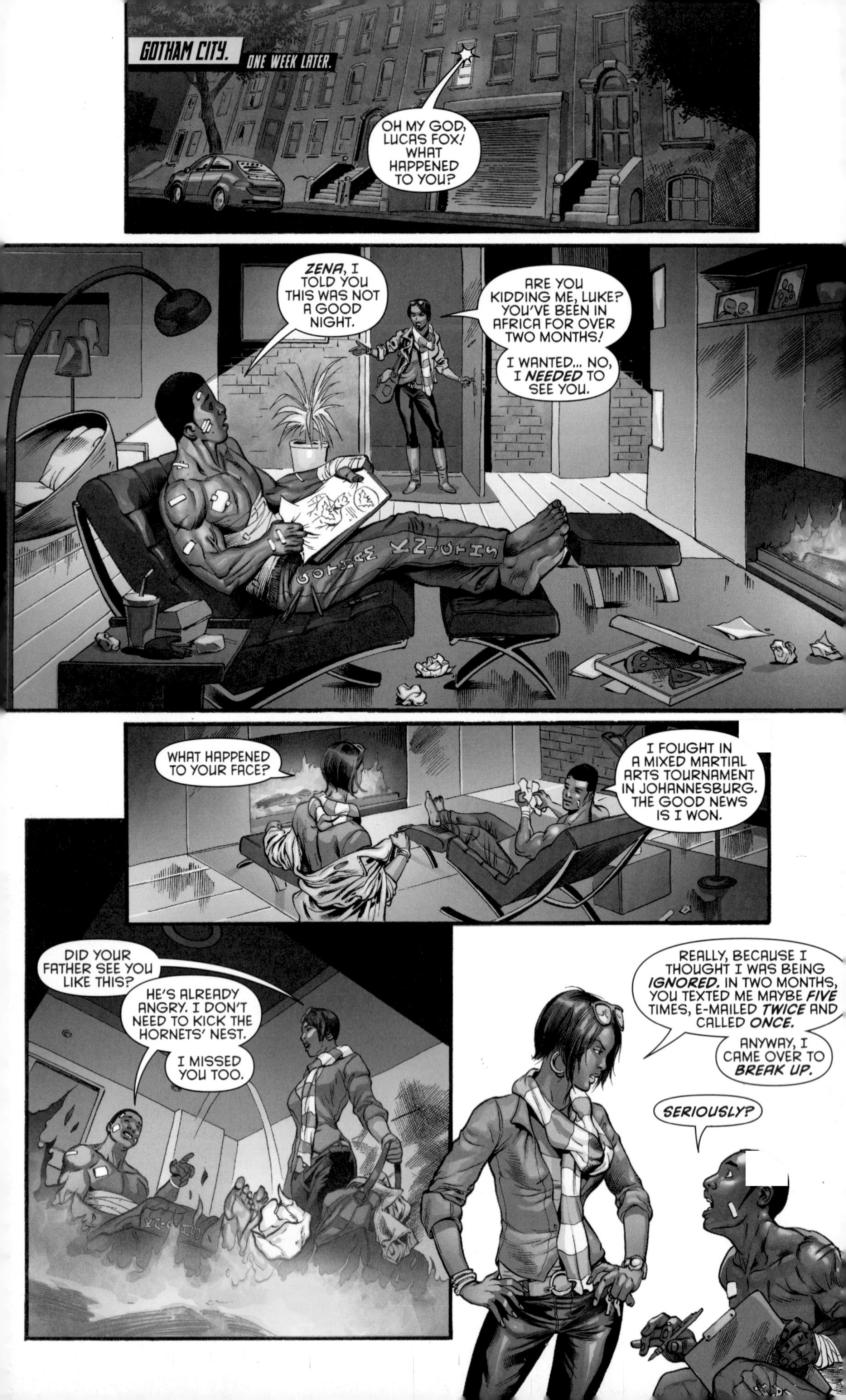
GOTHAM CITY.
ONE WEEK LATER.
OH MY GOD, LUCAS FOX! WHAT HAPPENED TO YOU?
ZENA, I TOLD YOU THIS WAS NOT A GOOD NIGHT.
ARE YOU KIDDING ME, LUKE? YOU'VE BEEN IN AFRICA FOR OVER TWO MONTHS!
I WANTED... NO, I NEEDED TO SEE YOU.
WHAT HAPPENED TO YOUR FACE?
I FOUGHT IN A MIXED MARTIAL ARTS TOURNAMENT IN JOHANNESBURG. THE GOOD NEWS IS I WON.
DID YOUR FATHER SEE YOU LIKE THIS?
HE'S ALREADY ANGRY. I DON'T NEED TO KICK THE HORNETS' NEST.
I MISSED YOU TOO.
REALLY, BECAUSE I THOUGHT I WAS BEING IGNORED. IN TWO MONTHS, YOU TEXTED ME MAYBE FIVE TIMES, E-MAILED TWICE AND CALLED ONCE.
ANYWAY, I CAME OVER TO BREAK UP.
SERIOUSLY?

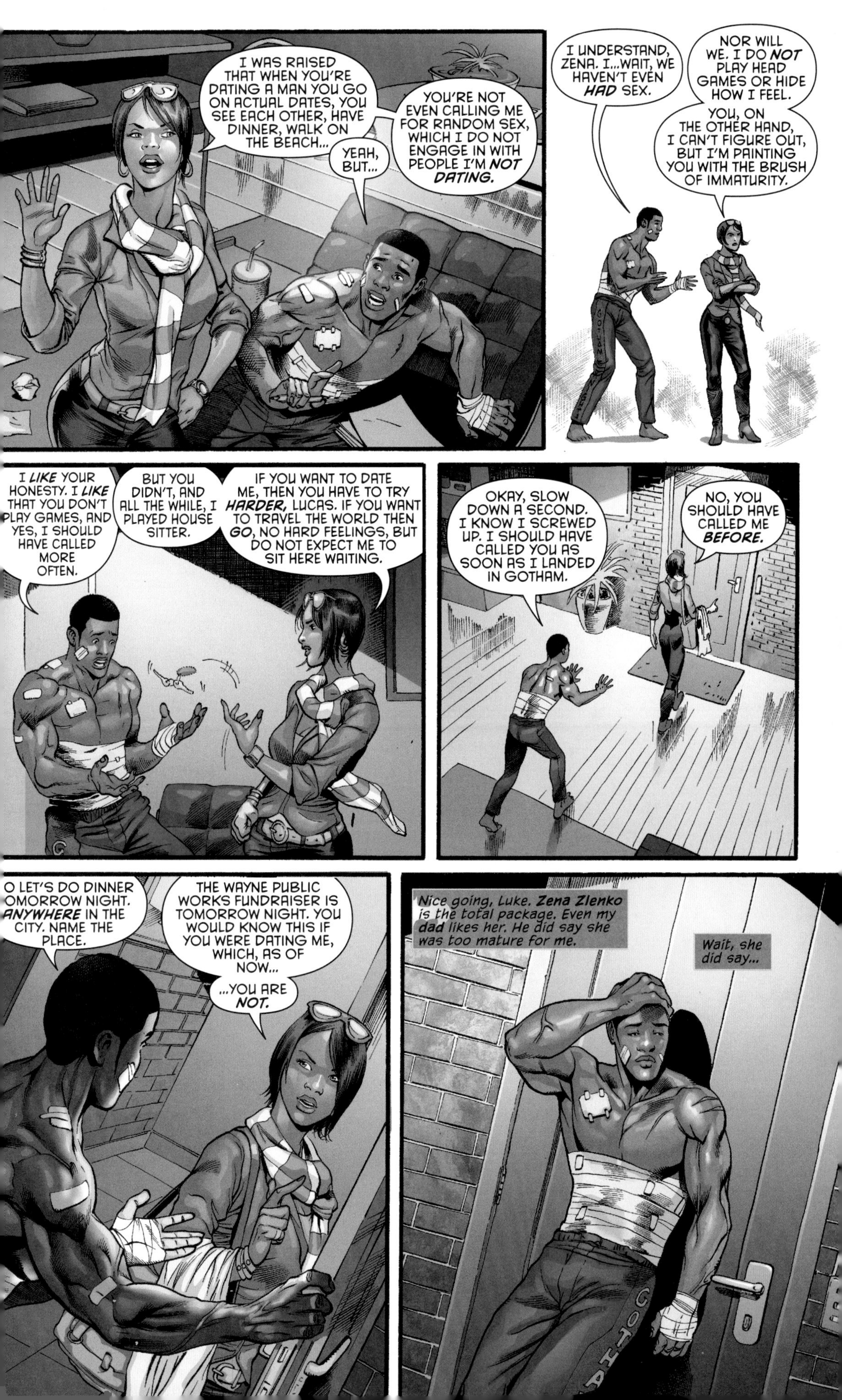
I WAS RAISED THAT WHEN YOU'RE DATING A MAN YOU GO ON ACTUAL DATES, YOU SEE EACH OTHER, HAVE DINNER, WALK ON THE BEACH...
YEAH, BUT...
YOU'RE NOT EVEN CALLING ME FOR RANDOM SEX, WHICH I DO NOT ENGAGE IN WITH PEOPLE I'M NOT DATING.
I UNDERSTAND, ZENA. I...WAIT, WE HAVEN'T EVEN HAD SEX.
NOR WILL WE. I DO NOT PLAY HEAD GAMES OR HIDE HOW I FEEL.
YOU, ON THE OTHER HAND, I CAN'T FIGURE OUT, BUT I'M PAINTING YOU WITH THE BRUSH OF IMMATURITY.
I LIKE YOUR HONESTY. I LIKE THAT YOU DON'T PLAY GAMES, AND YES, I SHOULD HAVE CALLED MORE OFTEN.
BUT YOU DIDN'T, AND ALL THE WHILE, I PLAYED HOUSE SITTER.
IF YOU WANT TO DATE ME, THEN YOU HAVE TO TRY HARDER, LUCAS. IF YOU WANT TO TRAVEL THE WORLD THEN GO, NO HARD FEELINGS, BUT DO NOT EXPECT ME TO SIT HERE WAITING.
OKAY, SLOW DOWN A SECOND. I KNOW I SCREWED UP. I SHOULD HAVE CALLED YOU AS SOON AS I LANDED IN GOTHAM.
NO, YOU SHOULD HAVE CALLED ME BEFORE.
O LET'S DO DINNER OMORROW NIGHT. ANYWHERE IN THE CITY. NAME THE PLACE.
THE WAYNE PUBLIC WORKS FUNDRAISER IS TOMORROW NIGHT. YOU WOULD KNOW THIS IF YOU WERE DATING ME, WHICH, AS OF NOW...
...YOU ARE NOT.
Nice going, Luke. Zena Zlenko is the total package. Even my dad likes her. He did say she was too mature for me.
Wait, she did say...

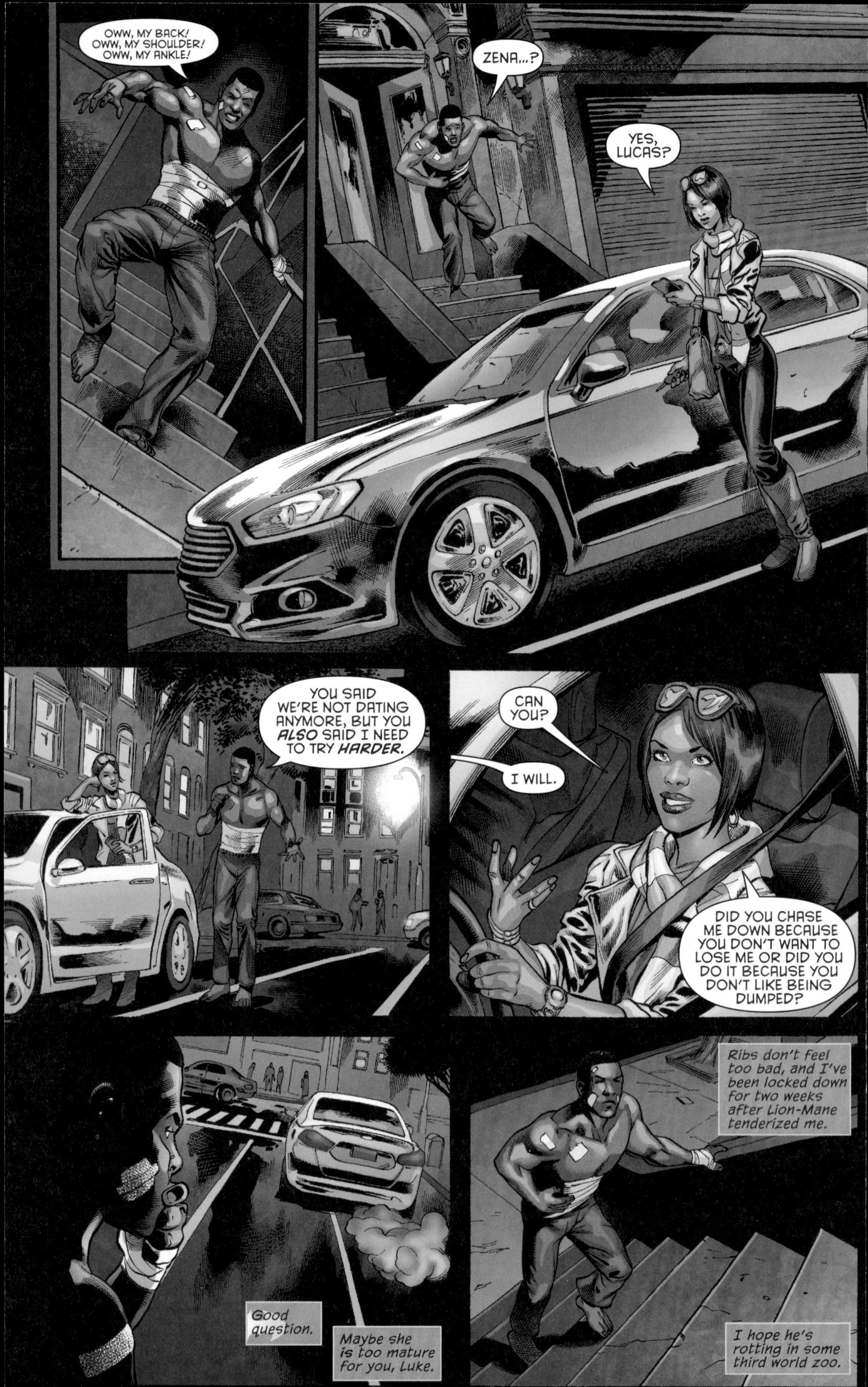

OWW, MY BACK! OWW, MY SHOULDER! OWW, MY ANKLE!
ZENA...?
YES, LUCAS?
YOU SAID WE'RE NOT DATING ANYMORE, BUT YOU ALSO SAID I NEED TO TRY HARDER.
CAN YOU?
I WILL.
DID YOU CHASE ME DOWN BECAUSE YOU DON'T WANT TO LOSE ME OR DID YOU DO IT BECAUSE YOU DON'T LIKE BEING DUMPED?
Good question.
Maybe she is too mature for you, Luke.
Ribs don't feel too bad, and I've been locked down for two weeks after Lion-Mane tenderized me.
I hope he's rotting in some third world zoo.

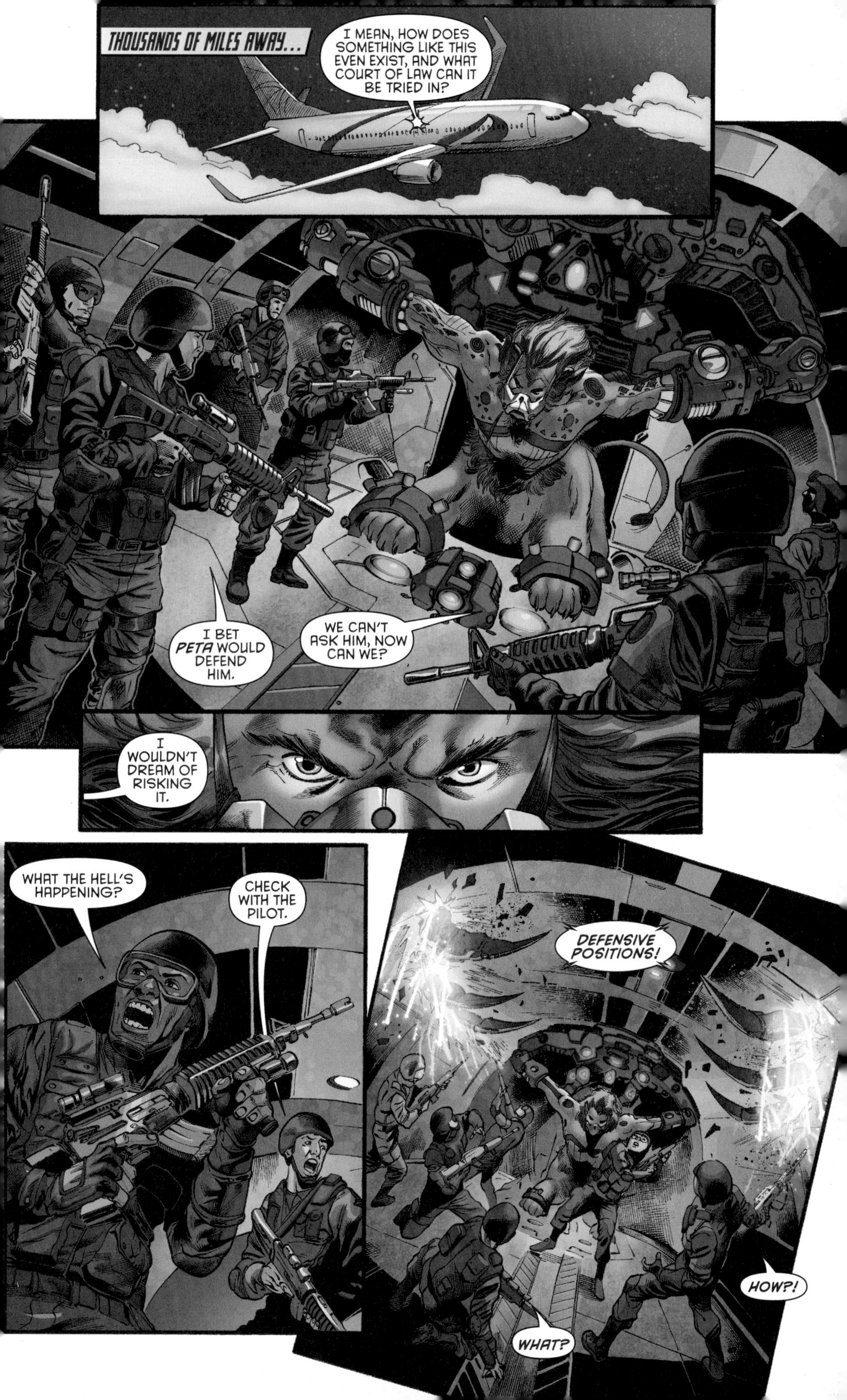
THOUSANDS OF MILES AWAY...
I MEAN, HOW DOES SOMETHING LIKE THIS EVEN EXIST, AND WHAT COURT OF LAW CAN IT BE TRIED IN?
I BET PETA WOULD DEFEND HIM.
WE CAN'T ASK HIM, NOW CAN WE?
I WOULDN'T DREAM OF RISKING IT.
WHAT THE HELL'S HAPPENING?
CHECK WITH THE PILOT.
DEFENSIVE POSITIONS!
WHAT?
HOW?!

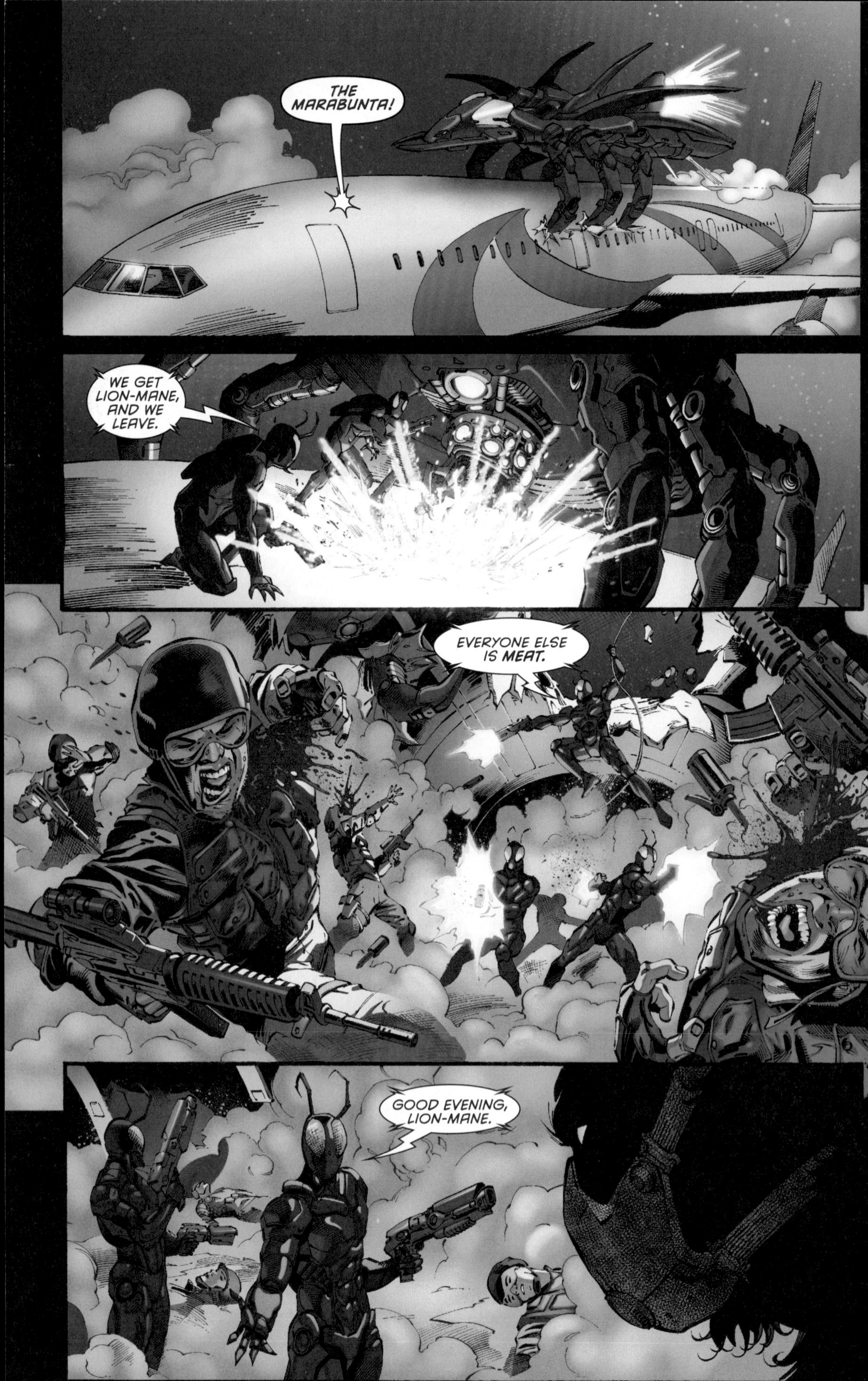
THE MARABUNTA!
WE GET LION-MANE, AND WE LEAVE.
EVERYONE ELSE IS MEAT.
GOOD EVENING, LION-MANE.

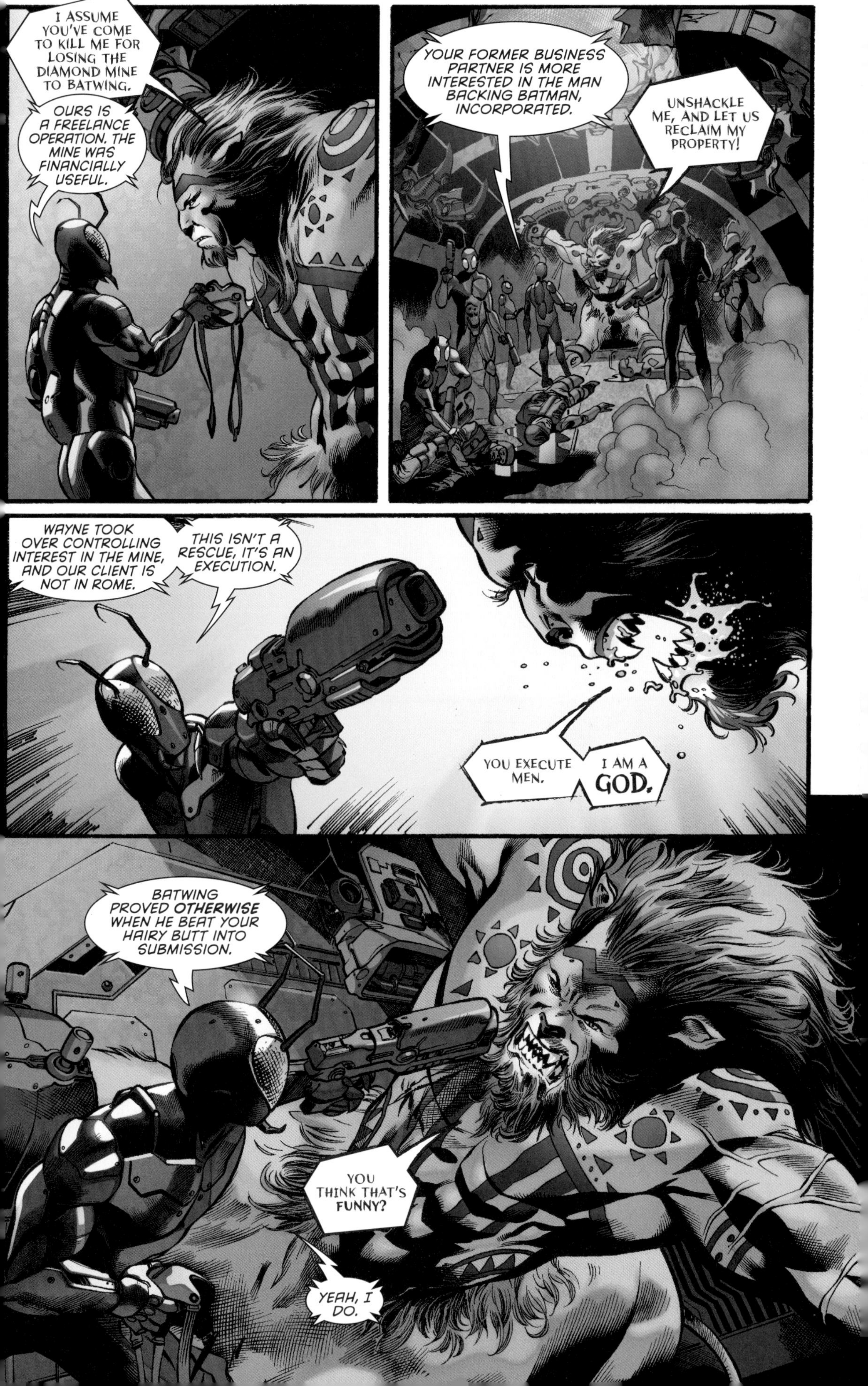
I ASSUME YOU'VE COME TO KILL ME FOR LOSING THE DIAMOND MINE TO BATWING.
OURS IS A FREELANCE OPERATION. THE MINE WAS FINANCIALLY USEFUL.
YOUR FORMER BUSINESS PARTNER IS MORE INTERESTED IN THE MAN BACKING BATMAN, INCORPORATED.
UNSHACKLE ME, AND LET US RECLAIM MY PROPERTY!
WAYNE TOOK OVER CONTROLLING INTEREST IN THE MINE, AND OUR CLIENT IS NOT IN ROME.
THIS ISN'T A RESCUE, IT'S AN EXECUTION.
YOU EXECUTE MEN.
I AM A GOD.
BATWING PROVED OTHERWISE WHEN HE BEAT YOUR HAIRY BUTT INTO SUBMISSION.
YOU THINK THAT'S FUNNY?
YEAH, I DO.

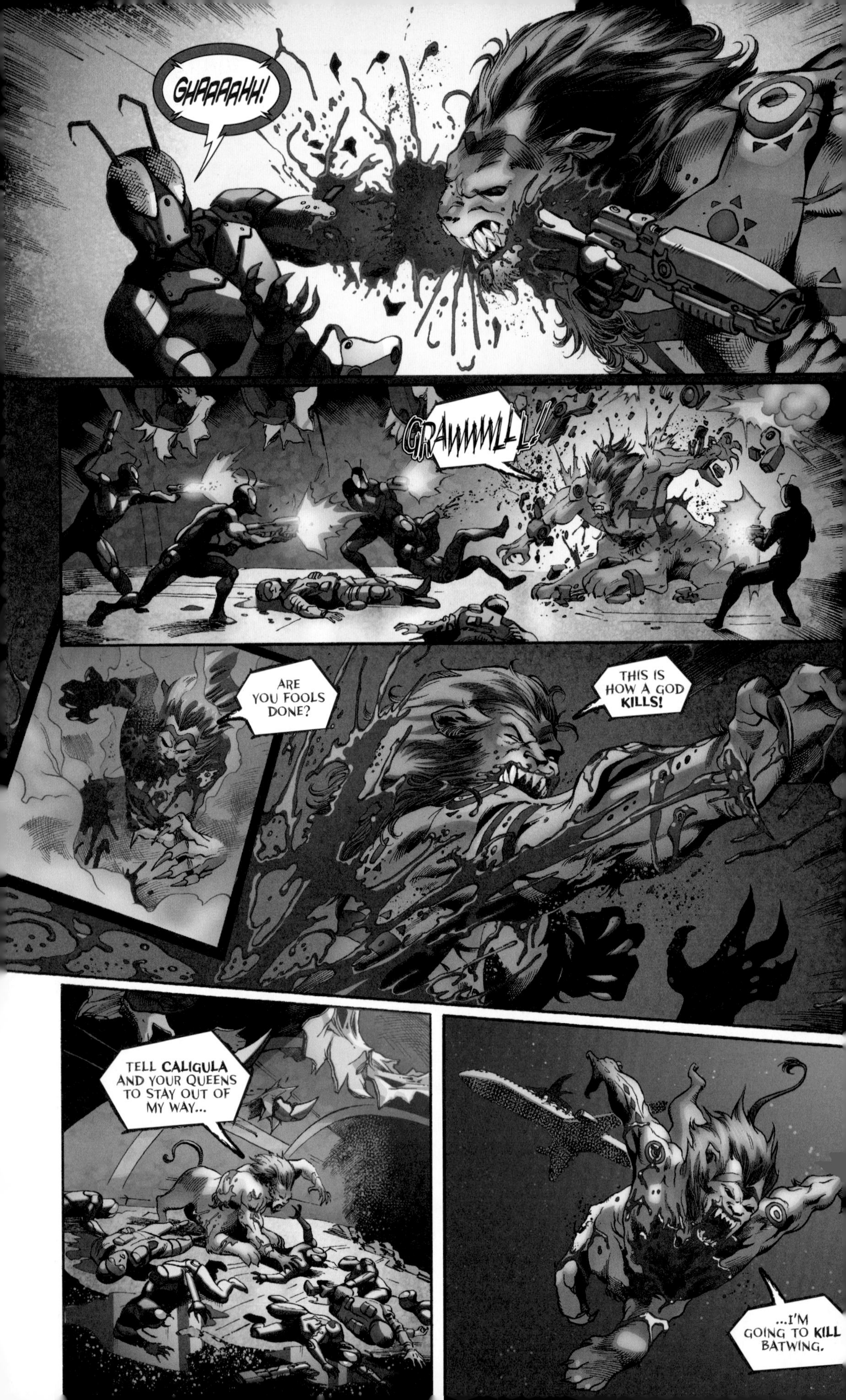
GHAAAAHH!
GRAWWWLLL!
ARE YOU FOOLS DONE?
THIS IS HOW A GOD **KILLS!**
TELL **CALIGULA** AND YOUR QUEENS TO STAY OUT OF MY WAY...
...I'M GOING TO **KILL** BATWING.

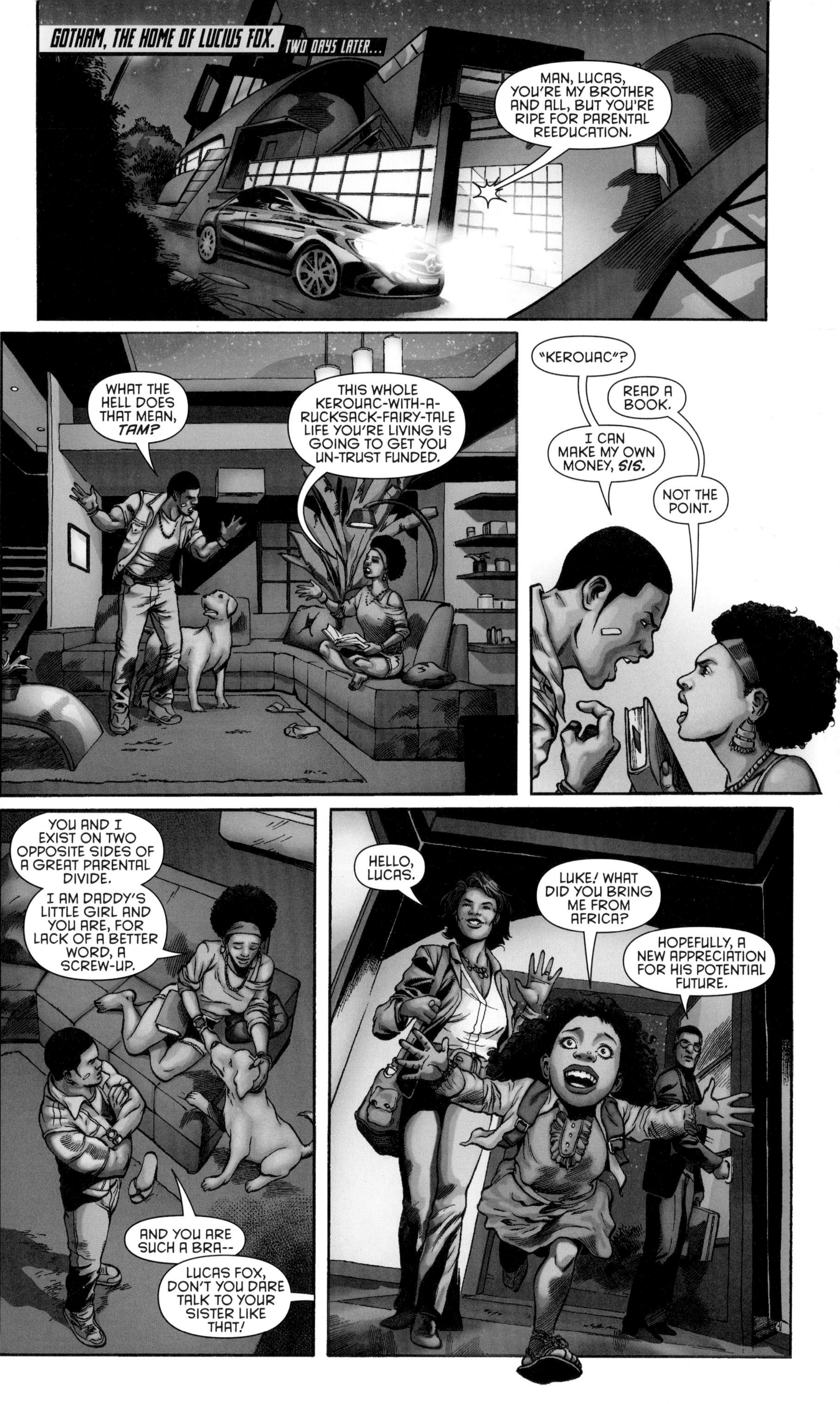
GOTHAM, THE HOME OF LUCIUS FOX.
TWO DAYS LATER...
MAN, LUCAS, YOU'RE MY BROTHER AND ALL, BUT YOU'RE RIPE FOR PARENTAL REEDUCATION.
WHAT THE HELL DOES THAT MEAN, TAM?
THIS WHOLE KEROUAC-WITH-A-RUCKSACK-FAIRY-TALE LIFE YOU'RE LIVING IS GOING TO GET YOU UN-TRUST FUNDED.
"KEROUAC"?
READ A BOOK.
I CAN MAKE MY OWN MONEY, SIS.
NOT THE POINT.
YOU AND I EXIST ON TWO OPPOSITE SIDES OF A GREAT PARENTAL DIVIDE.
I AM DADDY'S LITTLE GIRL AND YOU ARE, FOR LACK OF A BETTER WORD, A SCREW-UP.
AND YOU ARE SUCH A BRA--
LUCAS FOX, DON'T YOU DARE TALK TO YOUR SISTER LIKE THAT!
HELLO, LUCAS.
LUKE! WHAT DID YOU BRING ME FROM AFRICA?
HOPEFULLY, A NEW APPRECIATION FOR HIS POTENTIAL FUTURE.

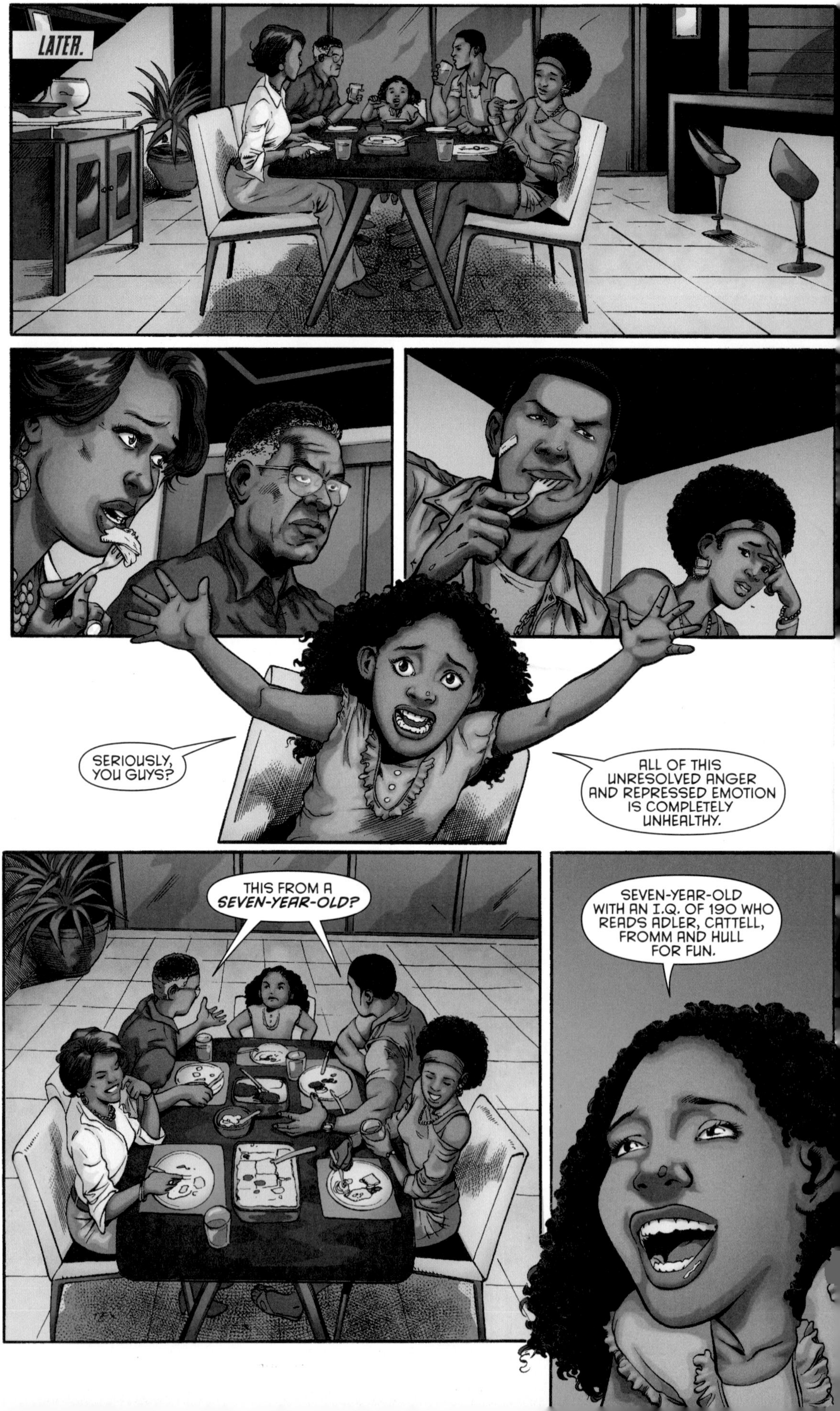
LATER.
SERIOUSLY, YOU GUYS?
ALL OF THIS UNRESOLVED ANGER AND REPRESSED EMOTION IS COMPLETELY UNHEALTHY.
THIS FROM A SEVEN-YEAR-OLD?
SEVEN-YEAR-OLD WITH AN I.Q. OF 190 WHO READS ADLER, CATTELL, FROMM AND HULL FOR FUN.

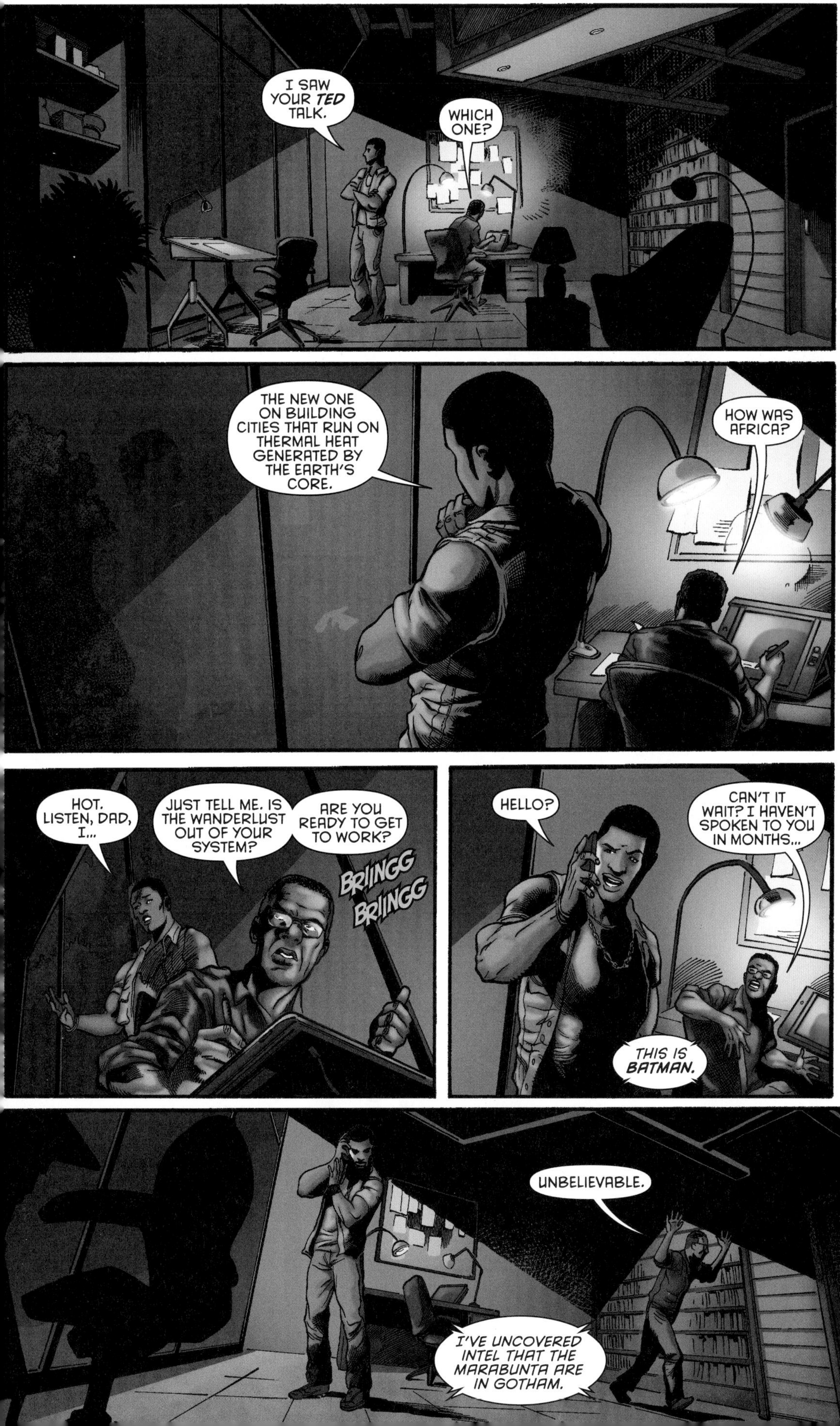
I SAW YOUR *TED* TALK.
WHICH ONE?
THE NEW ONE ON BUILDING CITIES THAT RUN ON THERMAL HEAT GENERATED BY THE EARTH'S CORE.
HOW WAS AFRICA?
HOT. LISTEN, DAD, I...
JUST TELL ME. IS THE WANDERLUST OUT OF YOUR SYSTEM?
ARE YOU READY TO GET TO WORK?
BRIINGG
BRIINGG
HELLO?
CAN'T IT WAIT? I HAVEN'T SPOKEN TO YOU IN MONTHS...
THIS IS ***BATMAN.***
UNBELIEVABLE.
I'VE UNCOVERED INTEL THAT THE MARABUNTA ARE IN GOTHAM.

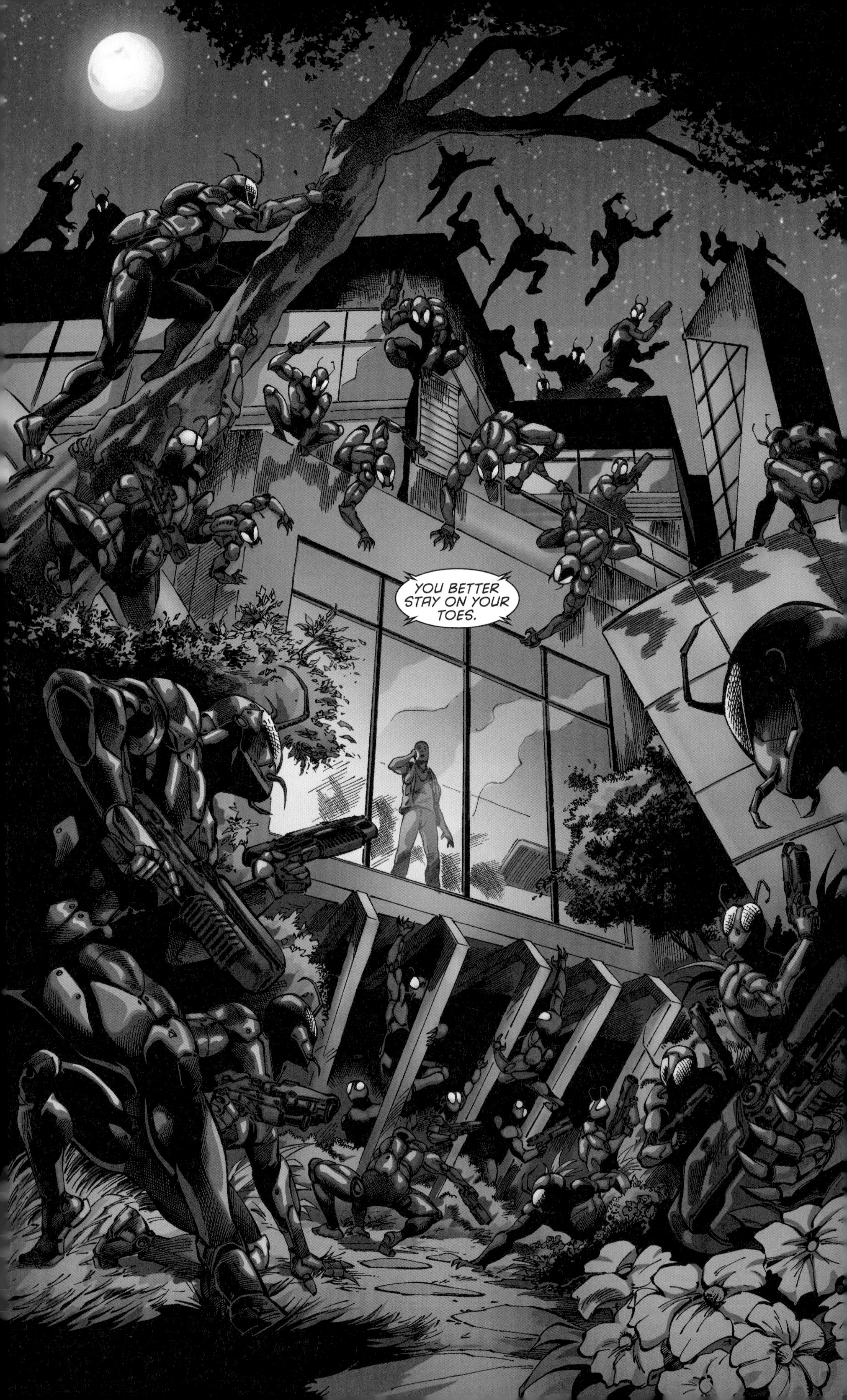
YOU BETTER STAY ON YOUR TOES.

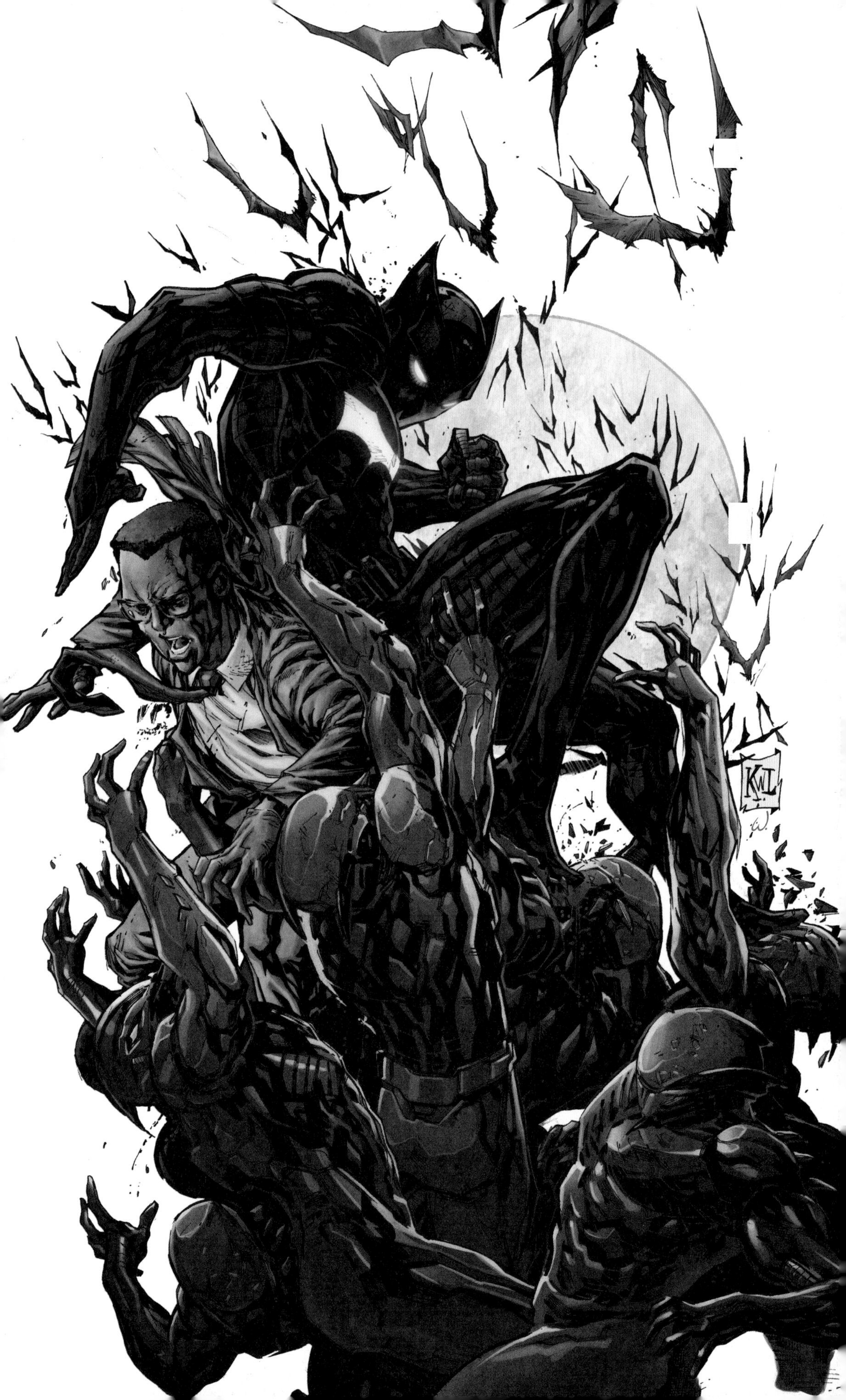

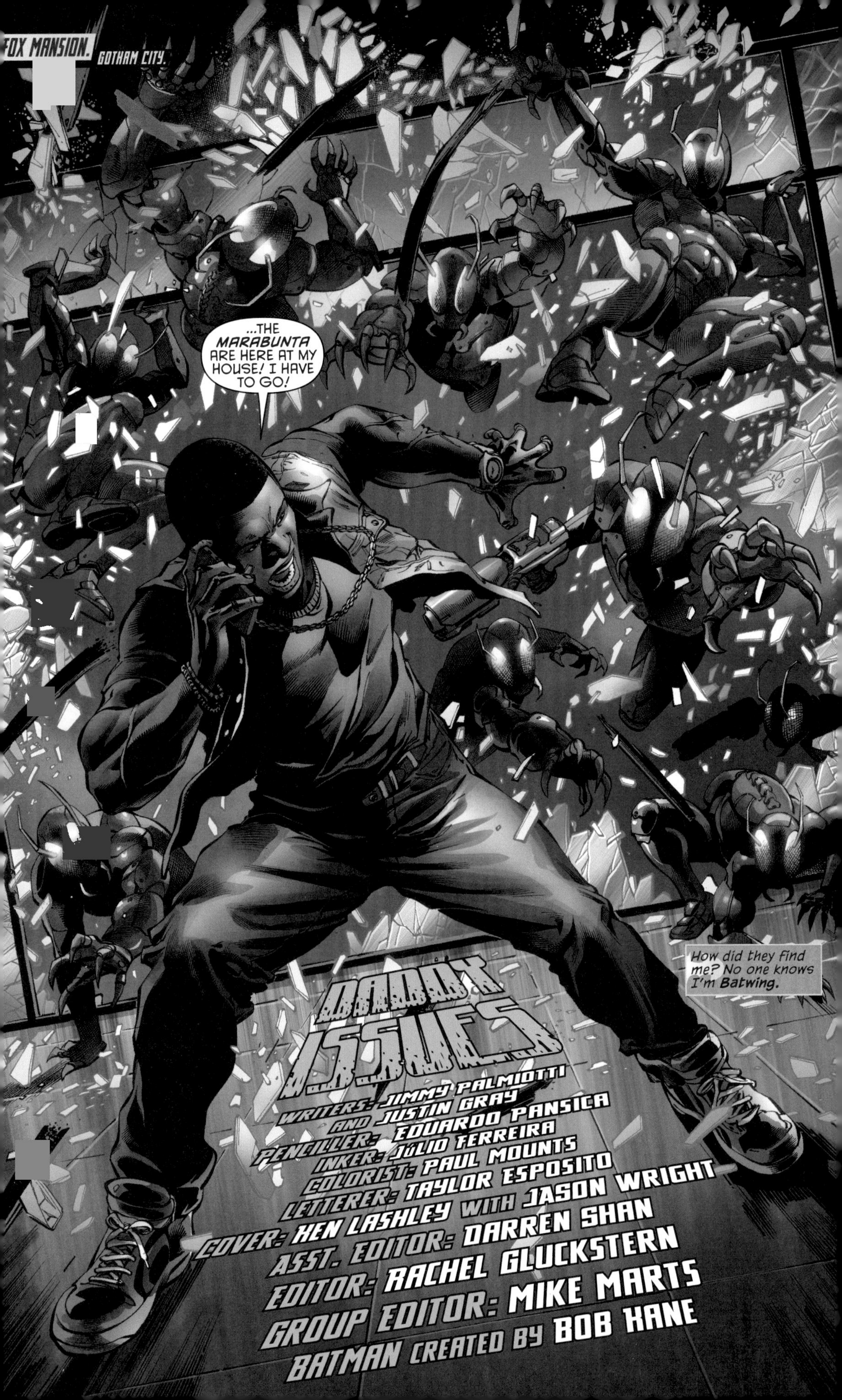
FOX MANSION. GOTHAM CITY.
...THE MARABUNTA ARE HERE AT MY HOUSE! I HAVE TO GO!
How did they find me? No one knows I'm Batwing.
DADDY ISSUES
WRITERS: JIMMY PALMIOTTI AND JUSTIN GRAY
PENCILLER: EDUARDO PANSICA
INKER: JÚLIO FERREIRA
COLORIST: PAUL MOUNTS
LETTERER: TAYLOR ESPOSITO
COVER: KEN LASHLEY WITH JASON WRIGHT
ASST. EDITOR: DARREN SHAN
EDITOR: RACHEL GLUCKSTERN
GROUP EDITOR: MIKE MARTS
BATMAN CREATED BY BOB KANE

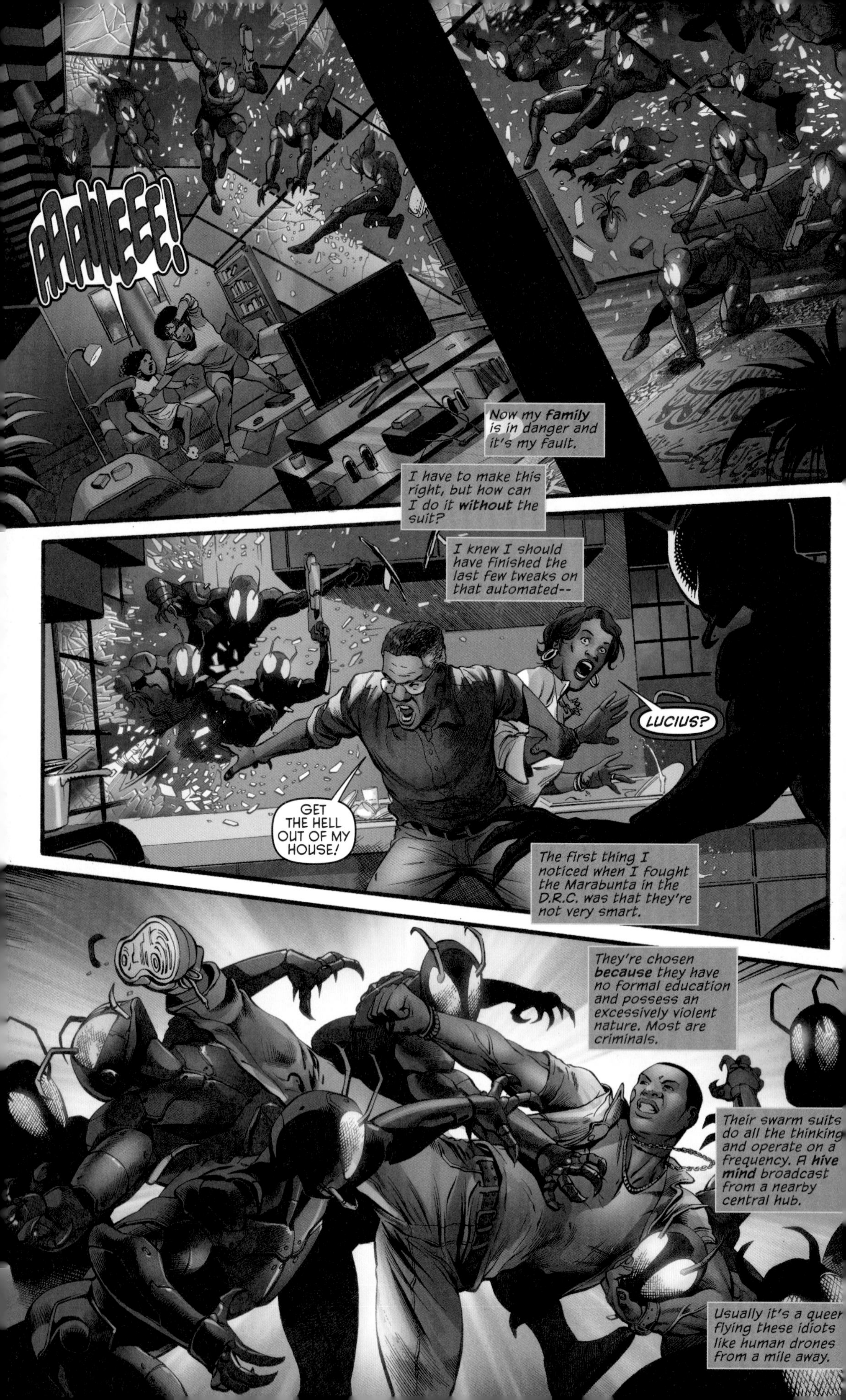

AAAIIEEE!
Now my family is in danger and it's my fault.
I have to make this right, but how can I do it without the suit?
I knew I should have finished the last few tweaks on that automated--
LUCIUS?
GET THE HELL OUT OF MY HOUSE!
The first thing I noticed when I fought the Marabunta in the D.R.C. was that they're not very smart.
They're chosen because they have no formal education and possess an excessively violent nature. Most are criminals.
Their swarm suits do all the thinking and operate on a frequency. A hive mind broadcast from a nearby central hub.
Usually it's a queen flying these idiots like human drones from a mile away.

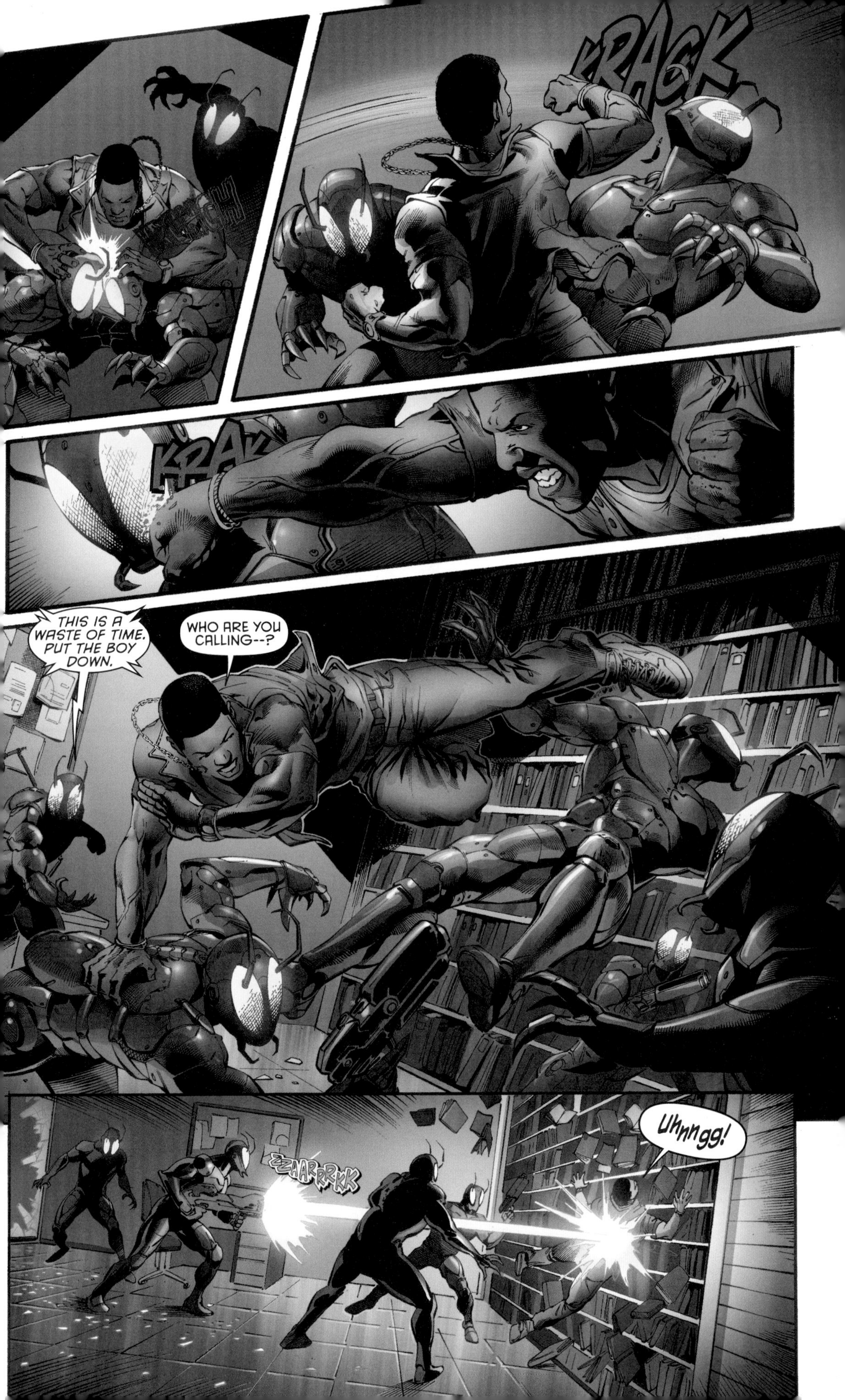
KRACK
KRAK
THIS IS A WASTE OF TIME. PUT THE BOY DOWN.
WHO ARE YOU CALLING--?
ZZAARRRKK
Uhnngg!

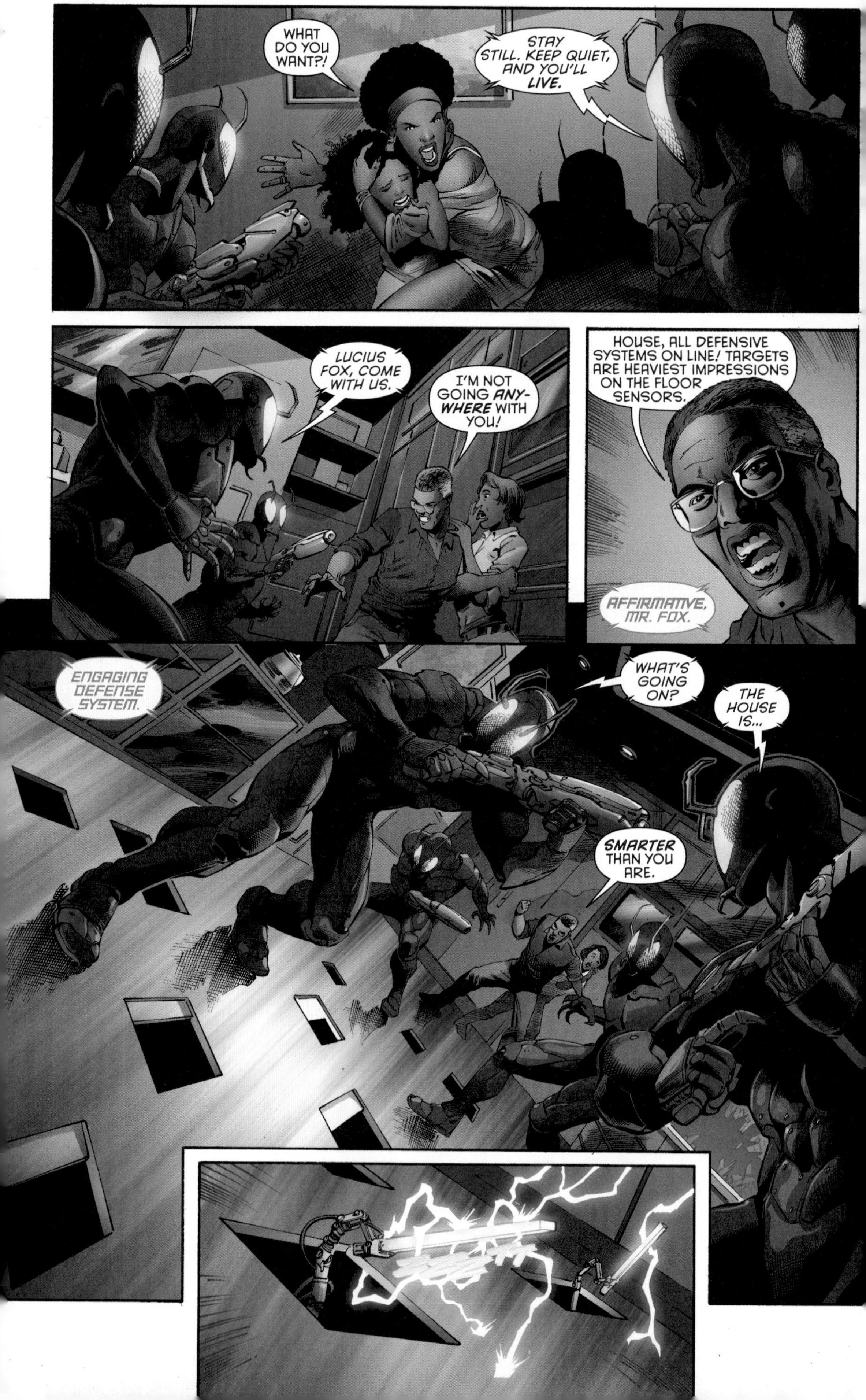
WHAT DO YOU WANT?!
STAY STILL. KEEP QUIET, AND YOU'LL LIVE.
LUCIUS FOX, COME WITH US.
I'M NOT GOING ANY-WHERE WITH YOU!
HOUSE, ALL DEFENSIVE SYSTEMS ON LINE! TARGETS ARE HEAVIEST IMPRESSIONS ON THE FLOOR SENSORS.
AFFIRMATIVE, MR. FOX.
ENGAGING DEFENSE SYSTEM.
WHAT'S GOING ON?
THE HOUSE IS...
SMARTER THAN YOU ARE.

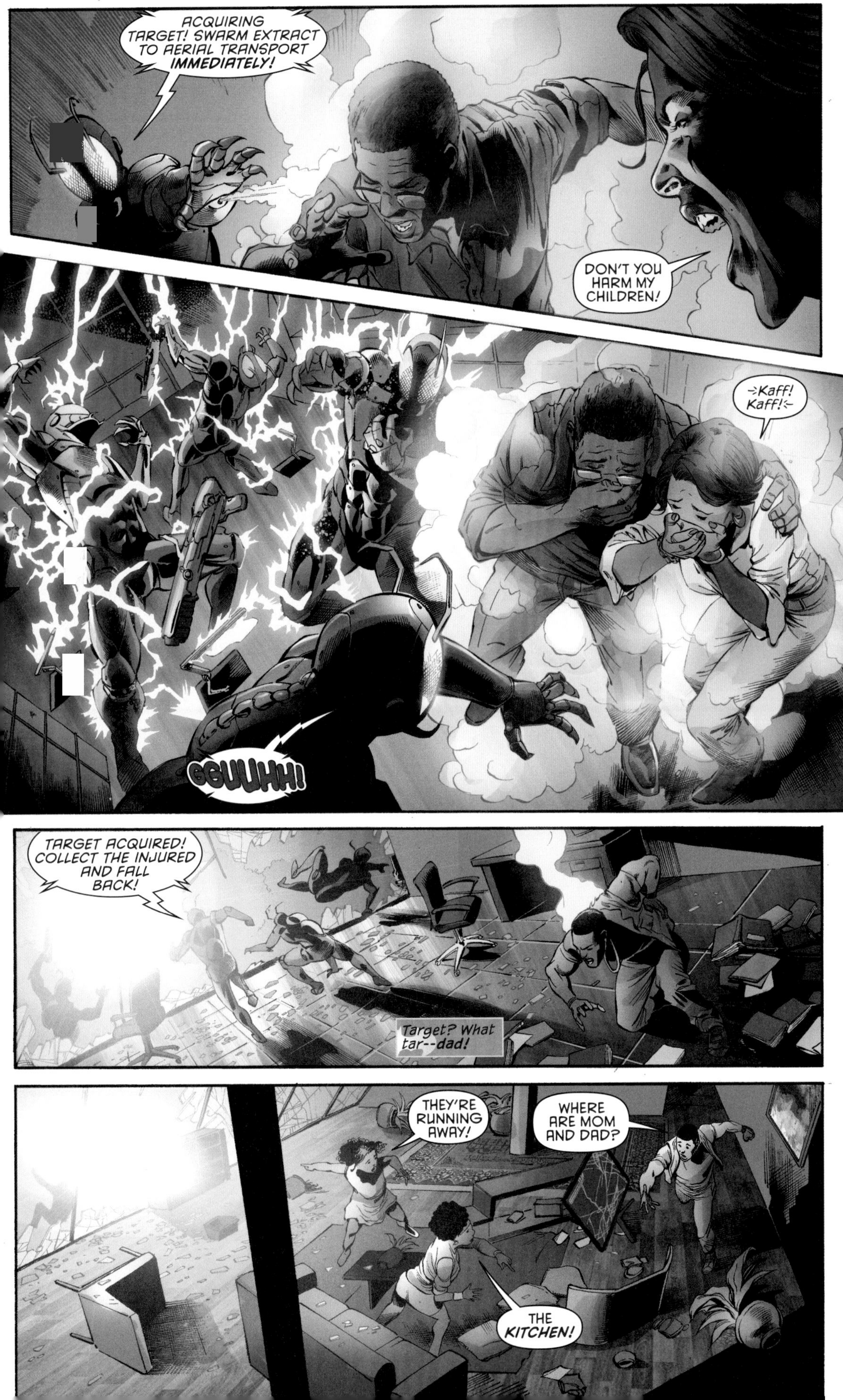
ACQUIRING TARGET! SWARM EXTRACT TO AERIAL TRANSPORT IMMEDIATELY!
DON'T YOU HARM MY CHILDREN!
-Kaff! Kaff!-
GGUUHH!
TARGET ACQUIRED! COLLECT THE INJURED AND FALL BACK!
Target? What tar--dad!
THEY'RE RUNNING AWAY!
WHERE ARE MOM AND DAD?
THE KITCHEN!

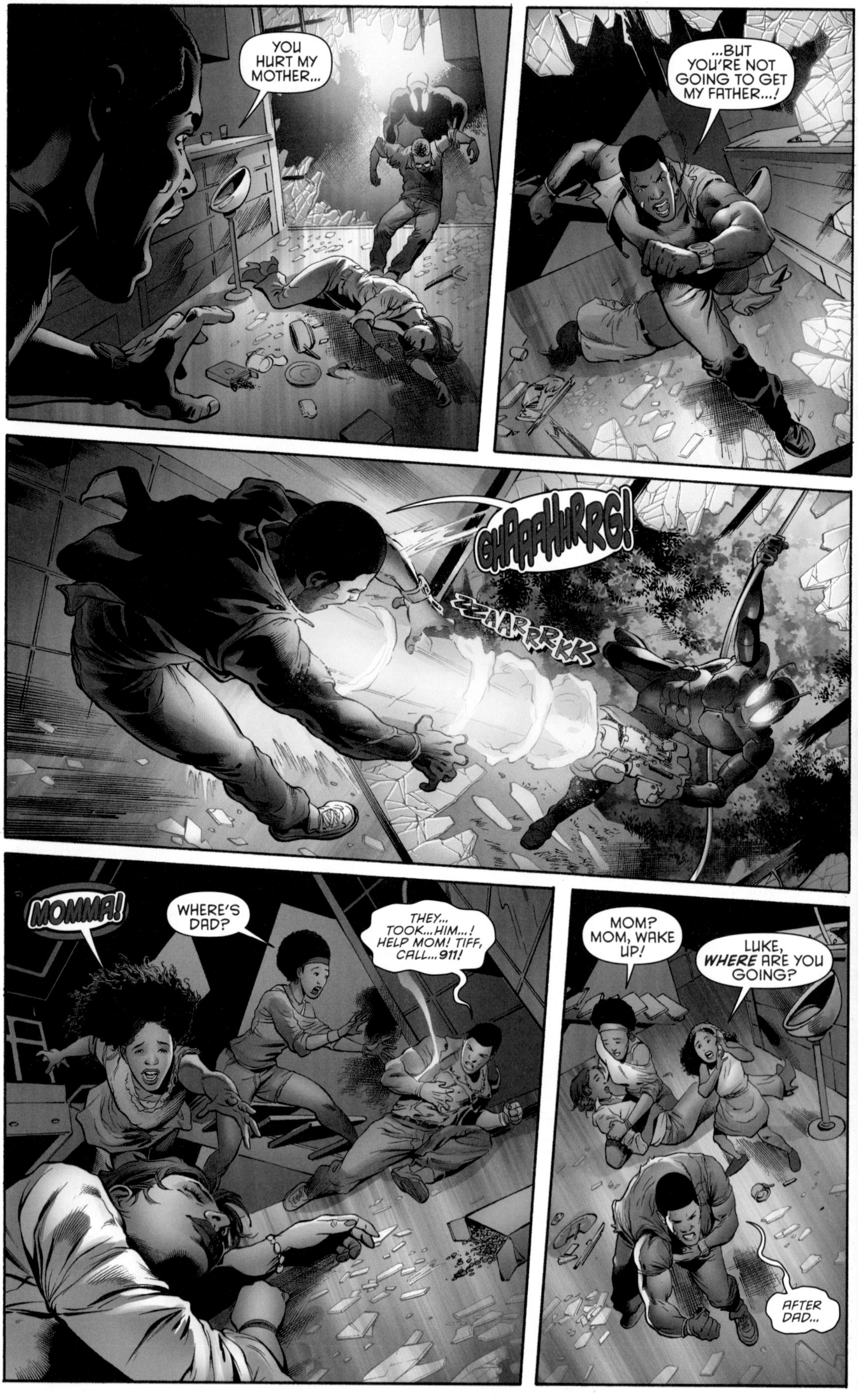

YOU HURT MY MOTHER...
...BUT YOU'RE NOT GOING TO GET MY FATHER...!
GHAAAHHRRG!
ZZAARRRKK
MOMMA!
WHERE'S DAD?
THEY... TOOK...HIM...! HELP MOM! TIFF, CALL...911!
MOM? MOM, WAKE UP!
LUKE, WHERE ARE YOU GOING?
AFTER DAD...

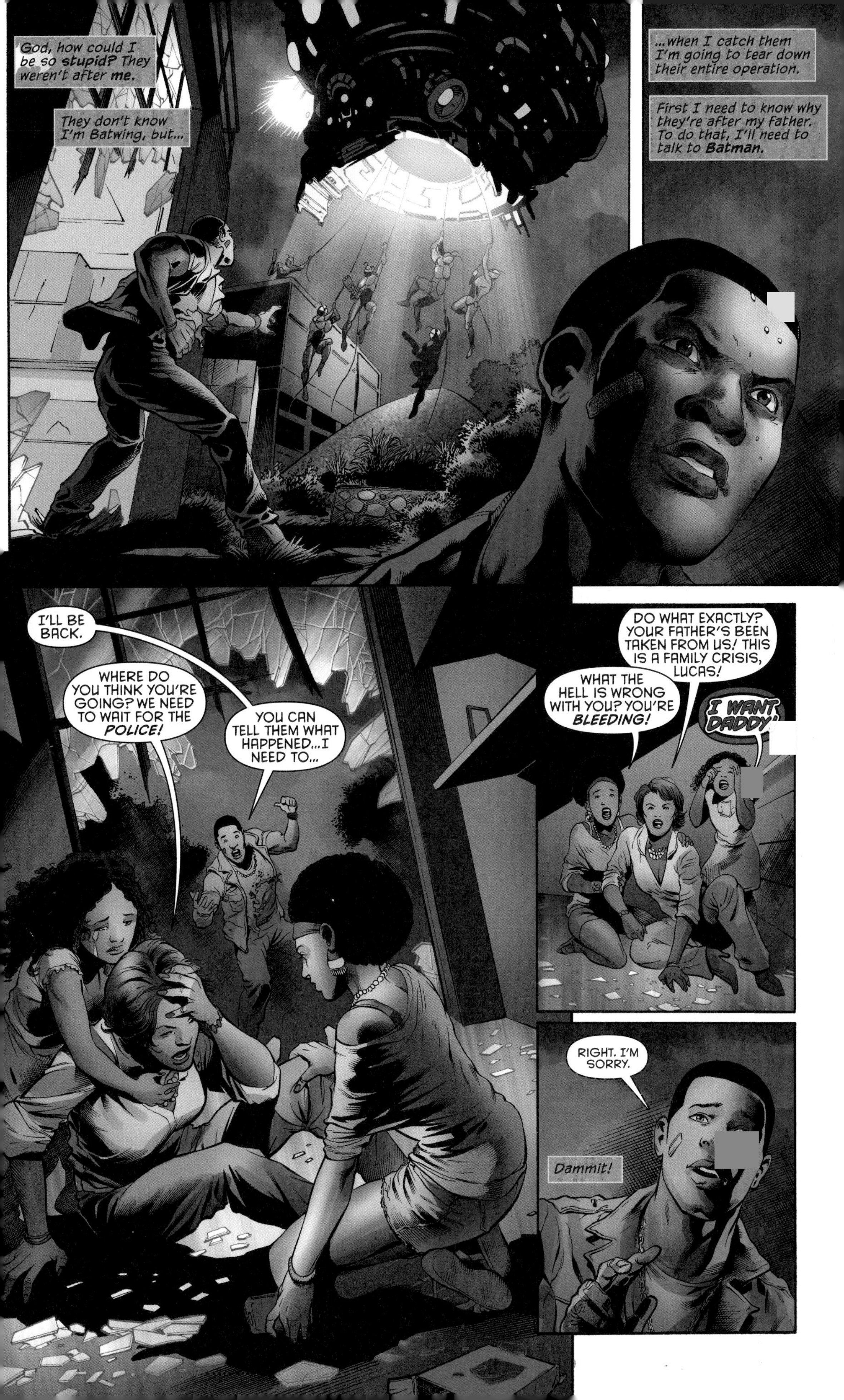

God, how could I be so **stupid?** They weren't after **me.**
They don't know I'm Batwing, but...
...when I catch them I'm going to tear down their entire operation.
First I need to know why they're after my father. To do that, I'll need to talk to **Batman.**
I'LL BE BACK.
WHERE DO YOU THINK YOU'RE GOING? WE NEED TO WAIT FOR THE ***POLICE!***
YOU CAN TELL THEM WHAT HAPPENED...I NEED TO...
DO WHAT EXACTLY? YOUR FATHER'S BEEN TAKEN FROM US! THIS IS A FAMILY CRISIS, LUCAS!
WHAT THE HELL IS WRONG WITH YOU? YOU'RE ***BLEEDING!***
I WANT DADDY!
RIGHT. I'M SORRY.
Dammit!

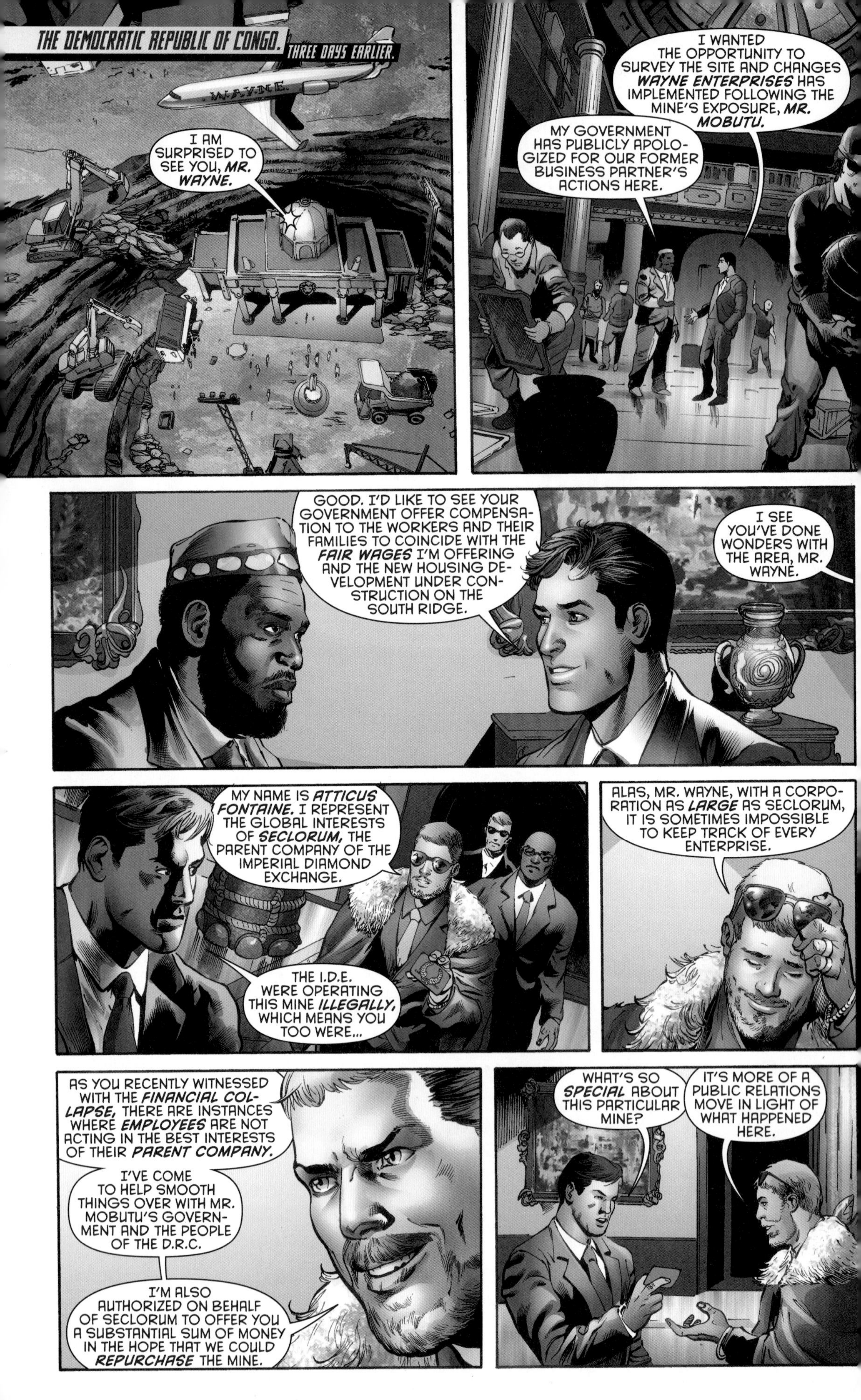
THE DEMOCRATIC REPUBLIC OF CONGO.
THREE DAYS EARLIER.
W.A.Y.N.E.
I AM SURPRISED TO SEE YOU, MR. WAYNE.
I WANTED THE OPPORTUNITY TO SURVEY THE SITE AND CHANGES WAYNE ENTERPRISES HAS IMPLEMENTED FOLLOWING THE MINE'S EXPOSURE, MR. MOBUTU.
MY GOVERNMENT HAS PUBLICLY APOLOGIZED FOR OUR FORMER BUSINESS PARTNER'S ACTIONS HERE.
GOOD. I'D LIKE TO SEE YOUR GOVERNMENT OFFER COMPENSATION TO THE WORKERS AND THEIR FAMILIES TO COINCIDE WITH THE FAIR WAGES I'M OFFERING AND THE NEW HOUSING DEVELOPMENT UNDER CONSTRUCTION ON THE SOUTH RIDGE.
I SEE YOU'VE DONE WONDERS WITH THE AREA, MR. WAYNE.
MY NAME IS ATTICUS FONTAINE. I REPRESENT THE GLOBAL INTERESTS OF SECLORUM, THE PARENT COMPANY OF THE IMPERIAL DIAMOND EXCHANGE.
THE I.D.E. WERE OPERATING THIS MINE ILLEGALLY, WHICH MEANS YOU TOO WERE...
ALAS, MR. WAYNE, WITH A CORPORATION AS LARGE AS SECLORUM, IT IS SOMETIMES IMPOSSIBLE TO KEEP TRACK OF EVERY ENTERPRISE.
AS YOU RECENTLY WITNESSED WITH THE FINANCIAL COLLAPSE, THERE ARE INSTANCES WHERE EMPLOYEES ARE NOT ACTING IN THE BEST INTERESTS OF THEIR PARENT COMPANY.
I'VE COME TO HELP SMOOTH THINGS OVER WITH MR. MOBUTU'S GOVERNMENT AND THE PEOPLE OF THE D.R.C.
I'M ALSO AUTHORIZED ON BEHALF OF SECLORUM TO OFFER YOU A SUBSTANTIAL SUM OF MONEY IN THE HOPE THAT WE COULD REPURCHASE THE MINE.
WHAT'S SO SPECIAL ABOUT THIS PARTICULAR MINE?
IT'S MORE OF A PUBLIC RELATIONS MOVE IN LIGHT OF WHAT HAPPENED HERE.

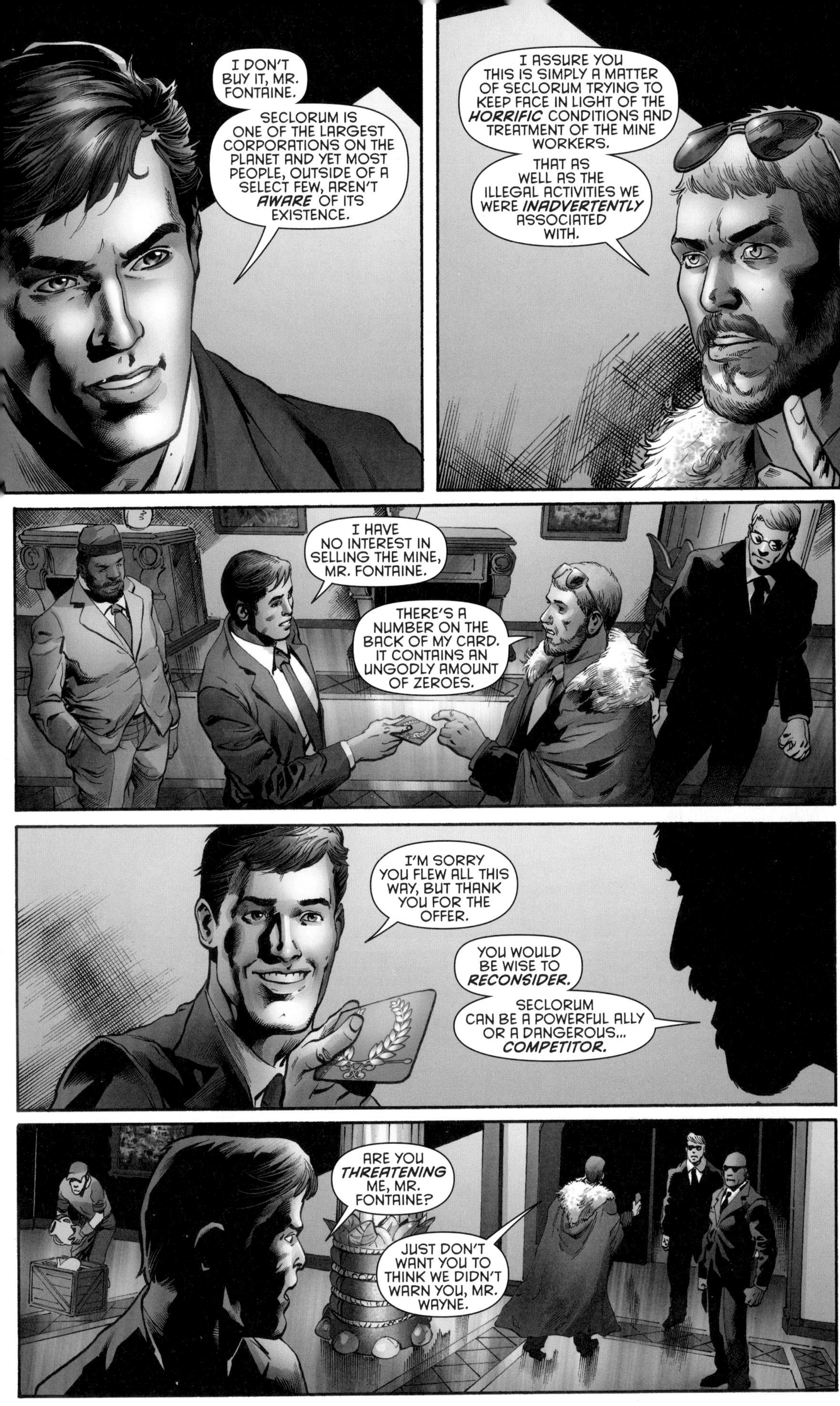
I DON'T BUY IT, MR. FONTAINE.
SECLORUM IS ONE OF THE LARGEST CORPORATIONS ON THE PLANET AND YET MOST PEOPLE, OUTSIDE OF A SELECT FEW, AREN'T AWARE OF ITS EXISTENCE.
I ASSURE YOU THIS IS SIMPLY A MATTER OF SECLORUM TRYING TO KEEP FACE IN LIGHT OF THE HORRIFIC CONDITIONS AND TREATMENT OF THE MINE WORKERS.
THAT AS WELL AS THE ILLEGAL ACTIVITIES WE WERE INADVERTENTLY ASSOCIATED WITH.
I HAVE NO INTEREST IN SELLING THE MINE, MR. FONTAINE.
THERE'S A NUMBER ON THE BACK OF MY CARD. IT CONTAINS AN UNGODLY AMOUNT OF ZEROES.
I'M SORRY YOU FLEW ALL THIS WAY, BUT THANK YOU FOR THE OFFER.
YOU WOULD BE WISE TO RECONSIDER.
SECLORUM CAN BE A POWERFUL ALLY OR A DANGEROUS... COMPETITOR.
ARE YOU THREATENING ME, MR. FONTAINE?
JUST DON'T WANT YOU TO THINK WE DIDN'T WARN YOU, MR. WAYNE.

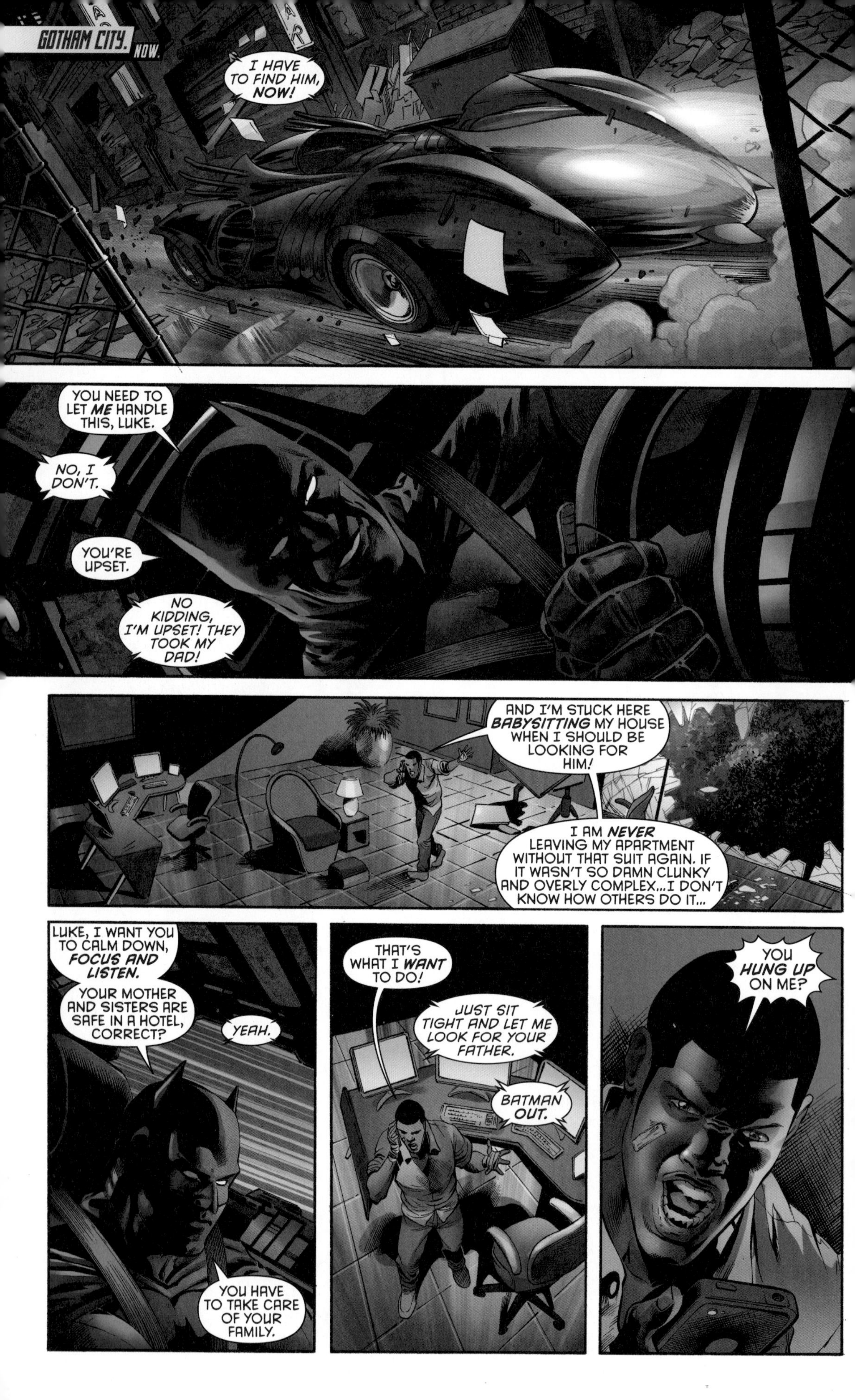
GOTHAM CITY. NOW.
I HAVE TO FIND HIM, NOW!
YOU NEED TO LET ME HANDLE THIS, LUKE.
NO, I DON'T.
YOU'RE UPSET.
NO KIDDING, I'M UPSET! THEY TOOK MY DAD!
AND I'M STUCK HERE BABYSITTING MY HOUSE WHEN I SHOULD BE LOOKING FOR HIM!
I AM NEVER LEAVING MY APARTMENT WITHOUT THAT SUIT AGAIN. IF IT WASN'T SO DAMN CLUNKY AND OVERLY COMPLEX...I DON'T KNOW HOW OTHERS DO IT...
LUKE, I WANT YOU TO CALM DOWN, FOCUS AND LISTEN.
YOUR MOTHER AND SISTERS ARE SAFE IN A HOTEL, CORRECT?
YEAH.
YOU HAVE TO TAKE CARE OF YOUR FAMILY.
THAT'S WHAT I WANT TO DO!
JUST SIT TIGHT AND LET ME LOOK FOR YOUR FATHER.
BATMAN OUT.
YOU HUNG UP ON ME?

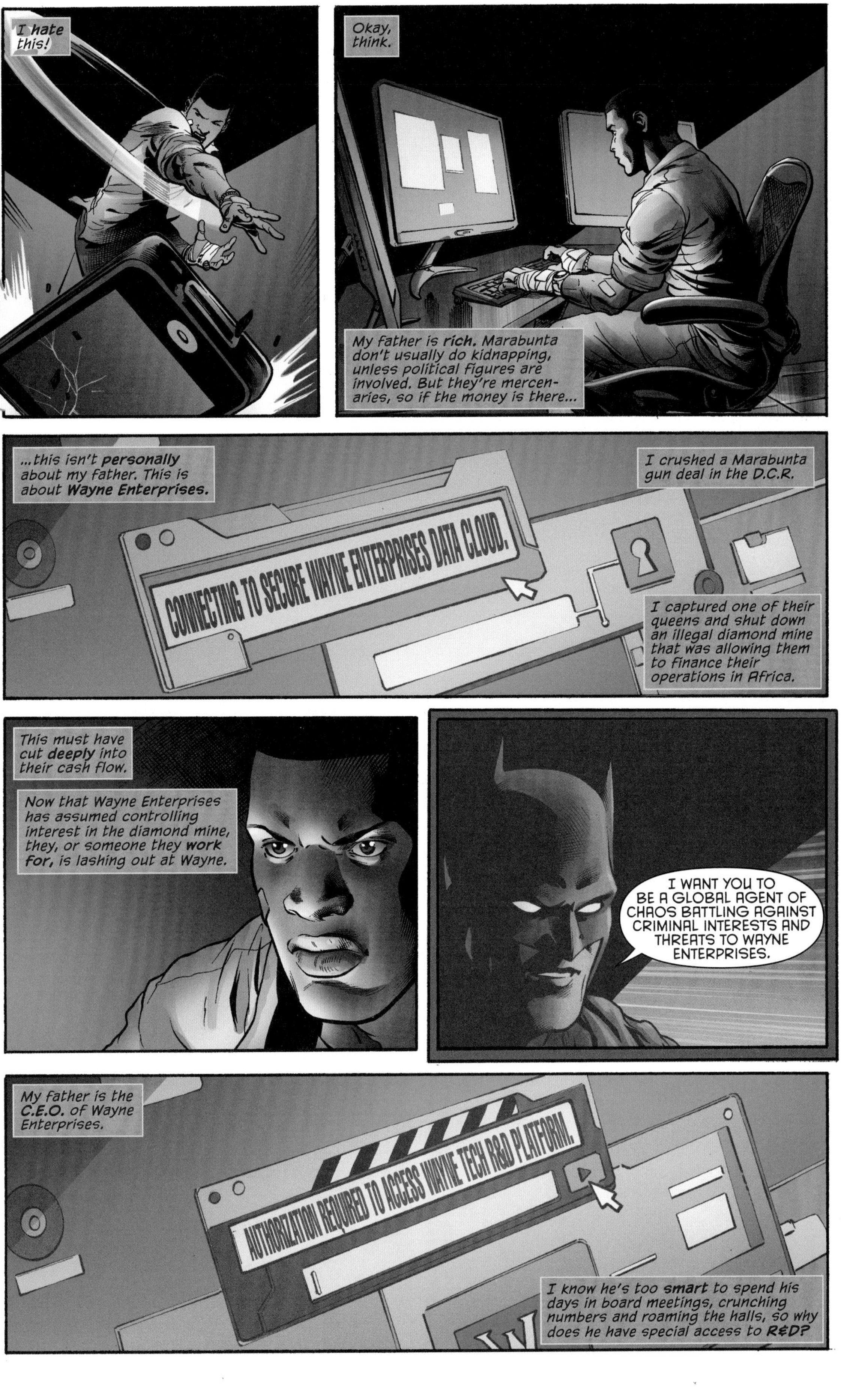
I hate this!
Okay, think.
My father is rich. Marabunta don't usually do kidnapping, unless political figures are involved. But they're mercenaries, so if the money is there...
...this isn't personally about my father. This is about Wayne Enterprises.
I crushed a Marabunta gun deal in the D.C.R.
CONNECTING TO SECURE WAYNE ENTERPRISES DATA CLOUD.
I captured one of their queens and shut down an illegal diamond mine that was allowing them to finance their operations in Africa.
This must have cut deeply into their cash flow.
Now that Wayne Enterprises has assumed controlling interest in the diamond mine, they, or someone they work for, is lashing out at Wayne.
I WANT YOU TO BE A GLOBAL AGENT OF CHAOS BATTLING AGAINST CRIMINAL INTERESTS AND THREATS TO WAYNE ENTERPRISES.
My father is the C.E.O. of Wayne Enterprises.
AUTHORIZATION REQUIRED TO ACCESS WAYNE TECH R&D PLATFORM.
I know he's too smart to spend his days in board meetings, crunching numbers and roaming the halls, so why does he have special access to R&D?

He still uses a code system for **pass-words** based on all of our birthdays.

Aaaand I'm...

...in?

It makes complete sense, and yet I'm still surprised. I thought Batman designed his own stuff.

If the Marabunta get this info, they could sell it on the open market. The damage to Wayne Enterprises and Batman would be insane.

BATPLANE

TACTICAL ARMOR

VEHICLE PROTOTYPES

SUBSET: ROBIN TACTICAL GEAR

SUIT VARIATIONS

SUBSET TACTICAL

STEALTH CUPONENTS

NON-LETHAL COMBAT GEAR

CHEMICAL AGENTS

SONICS

BATPLANE V4.7

SUBSET: NIGHTWING TACTICAL GEAR

SUBSET: BATGIRL TACTICAL GEAR

Sit tight, he says.

That's **not** gonna happen.

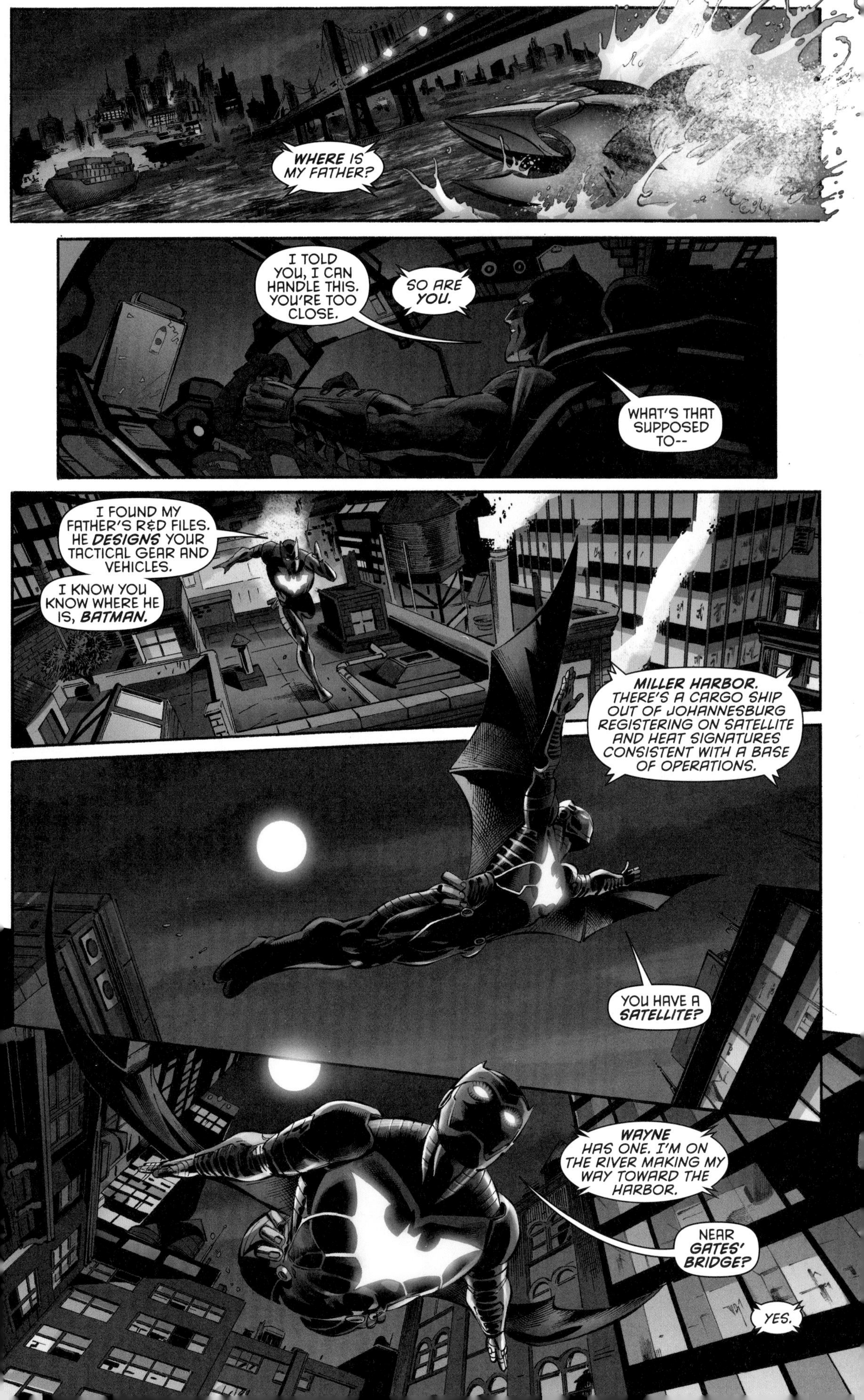

WHERE IS MY FATHER?
I TOLD YOU, I CAN HANDLE THIS. YOU'RE TOO CLOSE.
SO ARE YOU.
WHAT'S THAT SUPPOSED TO--
I FOUND MY FATHER'S R&D FILES. HE DESIGNS YOUR TACTICAL GEAR AND VEHICLES.
I KNOW YOU KNOW WHERE HE IS, BATMAN.
MILLER HARBOR. THERE'S A CARGO SHIP OUT OF JOHANNESBURG REGISTERING ON SATELLITE AND HEAT SIGNATURES CONSISTENT WITH A BASE OF OPERATIONS.
YOU HAVE A SATELLITE?
WAYNE HAS ONE. I'M ON THE RIVER MAKING MY WAY TOWARD THE HARBOR.
NEAR GATES' BRIDGE?
YES.

I'LL BE THERE IN A MINUTE. BATWING OUT.

WHAT THE... *BATMAN?!*

BAT*WING.* I NEED A LIFT.

OFFICIAL SUPERHERO CRIME FIGHTING BUSINESS. ARE YOU IN?

HELLS YEAH. WHERE ARE WE HEADED, BAT*WING?*

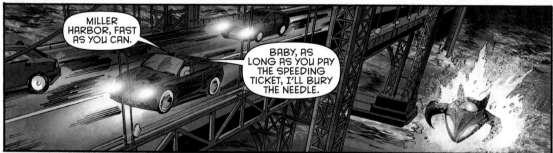

MILLER HARBOR, FAST AS YOU CAN.

BABY, AS LONG AS YOU PAY THE SPEEDING TICKET, I'LL BURY THE NEEDLE.

HANG ON. CHANGE OF PLAN. I SEE MY *RIDE.*

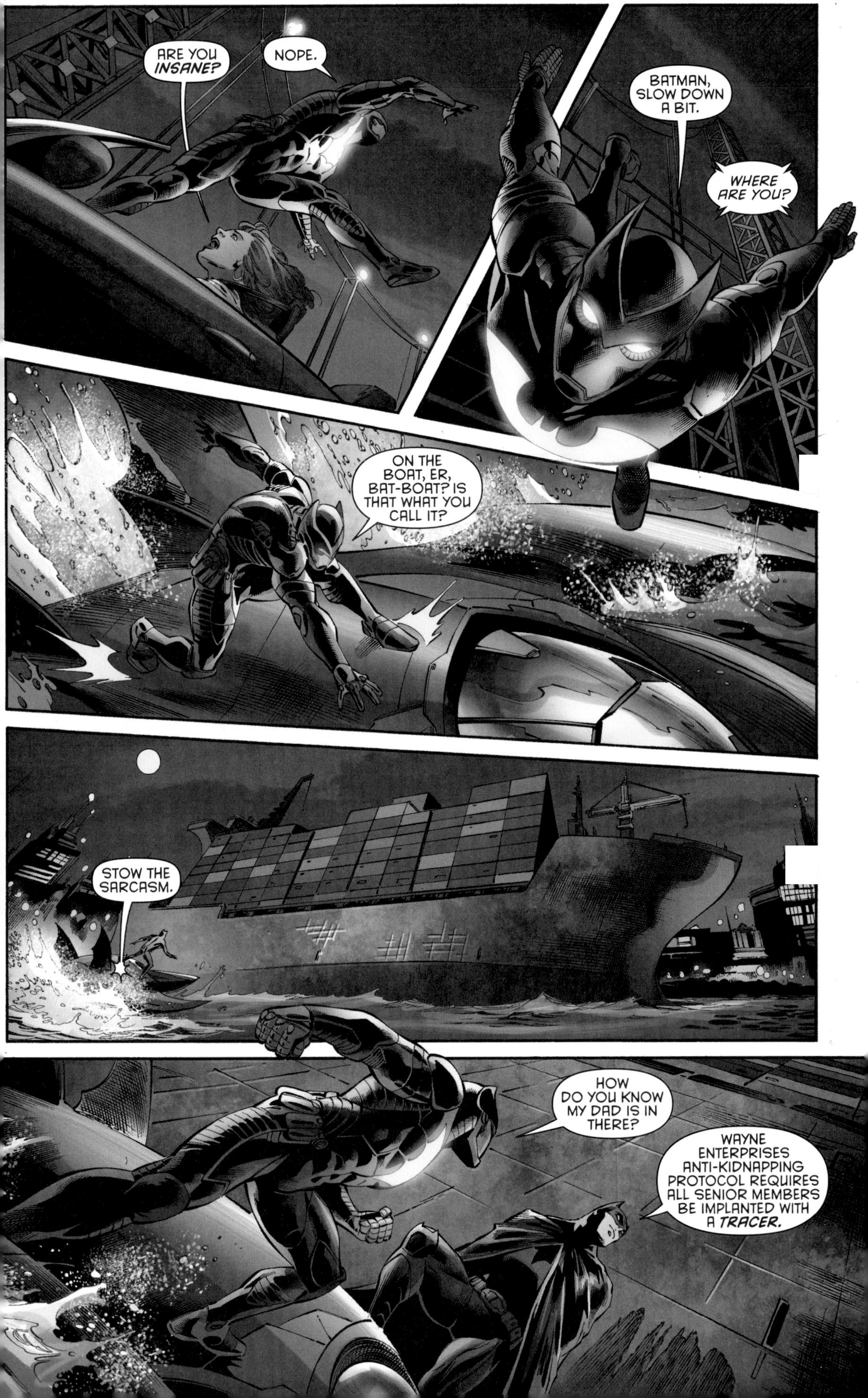
ARE YOU *INSANE?*
NOPE.
BATMAN, SLOW DOWN A BIT.
WHERE ARE YOU?
ON THE BOAT, ER, BAT-BOAT? IS THAT WHAT YOU CALL IT?
STOW THE SARCASM.
HOW DO YOU KNOW MY DAD IS IN THERE?
WAYNE ENTERPRISES ANTI-KIDNAPPING PROTOCOL REQUIRES ALL SENIOR MEMBERS BE IMPLANTED WITH A *TRACER.*

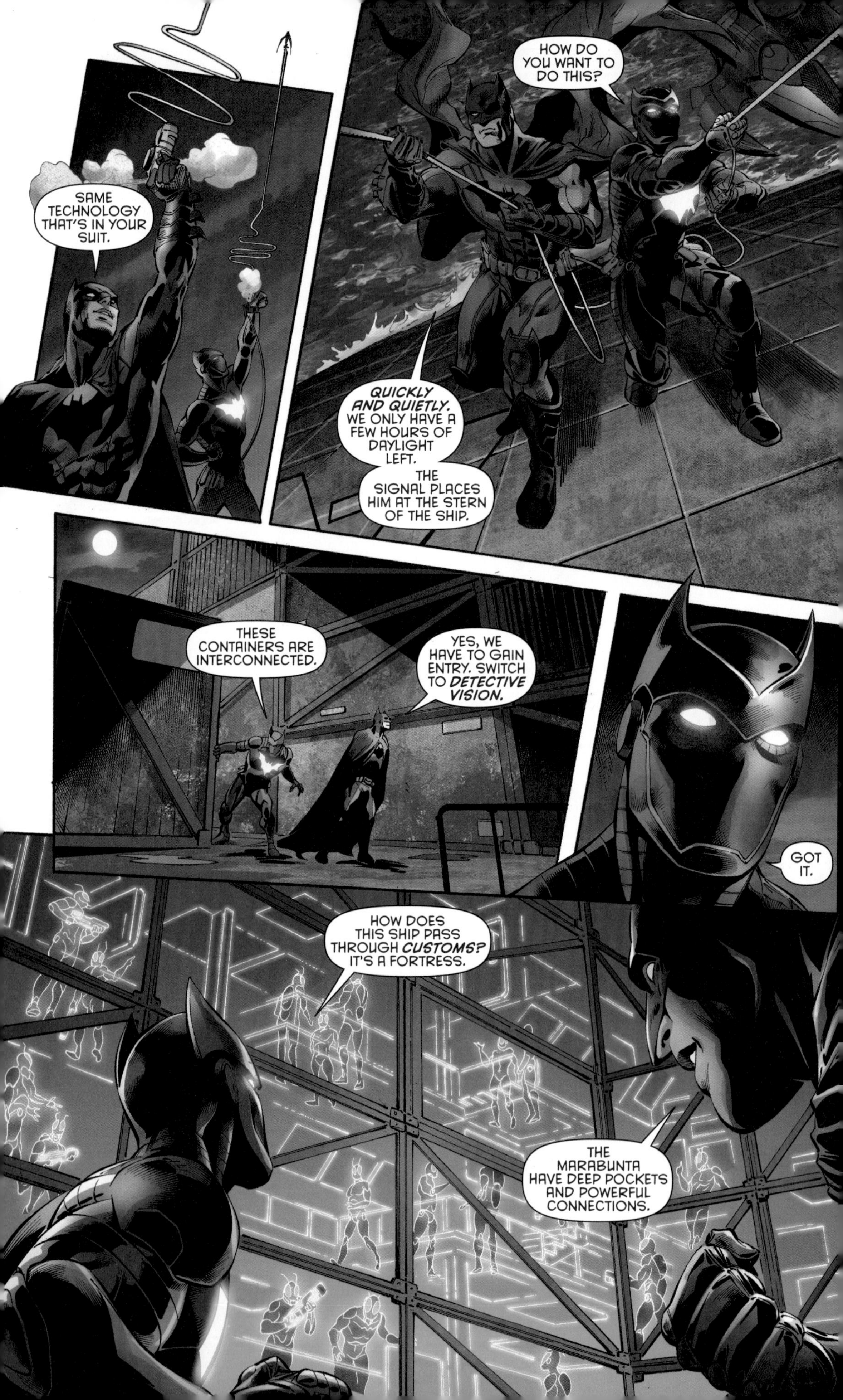
SAME TECHNOLOGY THAT'S IN YOUR SUIT.
HOW DO YOU WANT TO DO THIS?
QUICKLY AND QUIETLY. WE ONLY HAVE A FEW HOURS OF DAYLIGHT LEFT.
THE SIGNAL PLACES HIM AT THE STERN OF THE SHIP.
THESE CONTAINERS ARE INTERCONNECTED.
YES, WE HAVE TO GAIN ENTRY. SWITCH TO DETECTIVE VISION.
GOT IT.
HOW DOES THIS SHIP PASS THROUGH CUSTOMS? IT'S A FORTRESS.
THE MARABUNTA HAVE DEEP POCKETS AND POWERFUL CONNECTIONS.

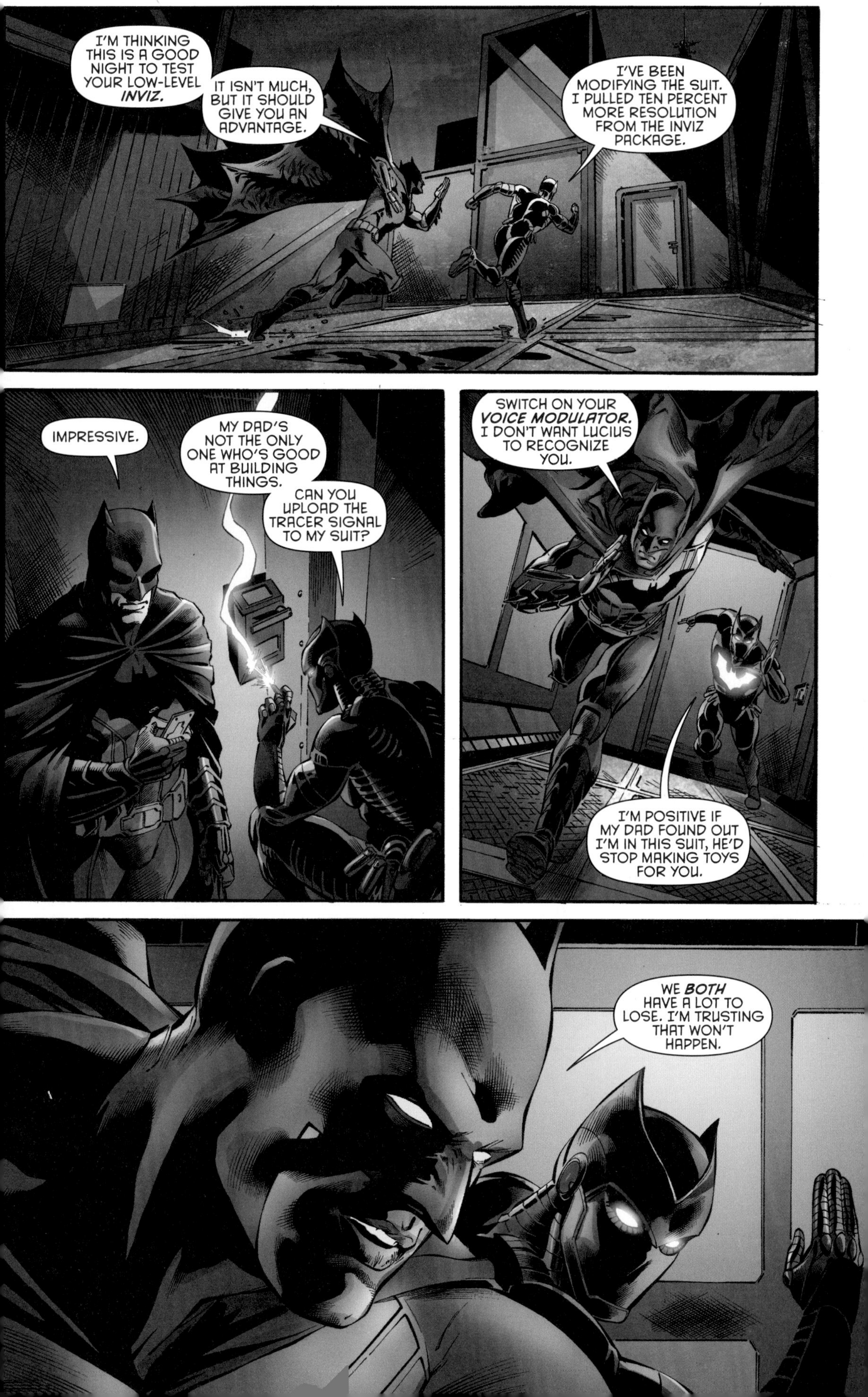
I'M THINKING THIS IS A GOOD NIGHT TO TEST YOUR LOW-LEVEL *INVIZ.*
IT ISN'T MUCH, BUT IT SHOULD GIVE YOU AN ADVANTAGE.
I'VE BEEN MODIFYING THE SUIT. I PULLED TEN PERCENT MORE RESOLUTION FROM THE INVIZ PACKAGE.
IMPRESSIVE.
MY DAD'S NOT THE ONLY ONE WHO'S GOOD AT BUILDING THINGS.
CAN YOU UPLOAD THE TRACER SIGNAL TO MY SUIT?
SWITCH ON YOUR *VOICE MODULATOR.* I DON'T WANT LUCIUS TO RECOGNIZE YOU.
I'M POSITIVE IF MY DAD FOUND OUT I'M IN THIS SUIT, HE'D STOP MAKING TOYS FOR YOU.
WE *BOTH* HAVE A LOT TO LOSE. I'M TRUSTING THAT WON'T HAPPEN.

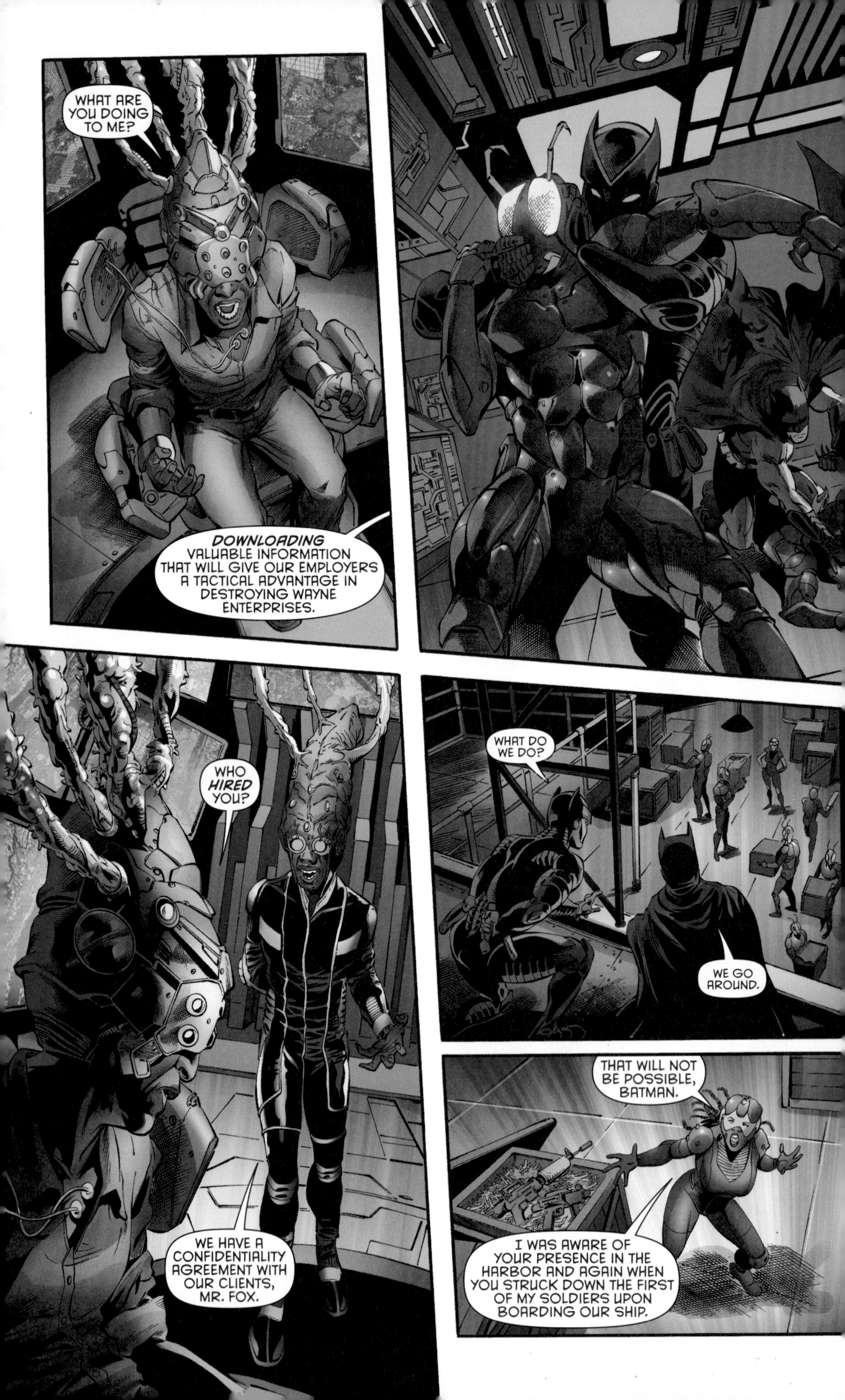
WHAT ARE YOU DOING TO ME?
DOWNLOADING VALUABLE INFORMATION THAT WILL GIVE OUR EMPLOYERS A TACTICAL ADVANTAGE IN DESTROYING WAYNE ENTERPRISES.
WHO *HIRED* YOU?
WE HAVE A CONFIDENTIALITY AGREEMENT WITH OUR CLIENTS, MR. FOX.
WHAT DO WE DO?
WE GO AROUND.
THAT WILL NOT BE POSSIBLE, BATMAN.
I WAS AWARE OF YOUR PRESENCE IN THE HARBOR AND AGAIN WHEN YOU STRUCK DOWN THE FIRST OF MY SOLDIERS UPON BOARDING OUR SHIP.

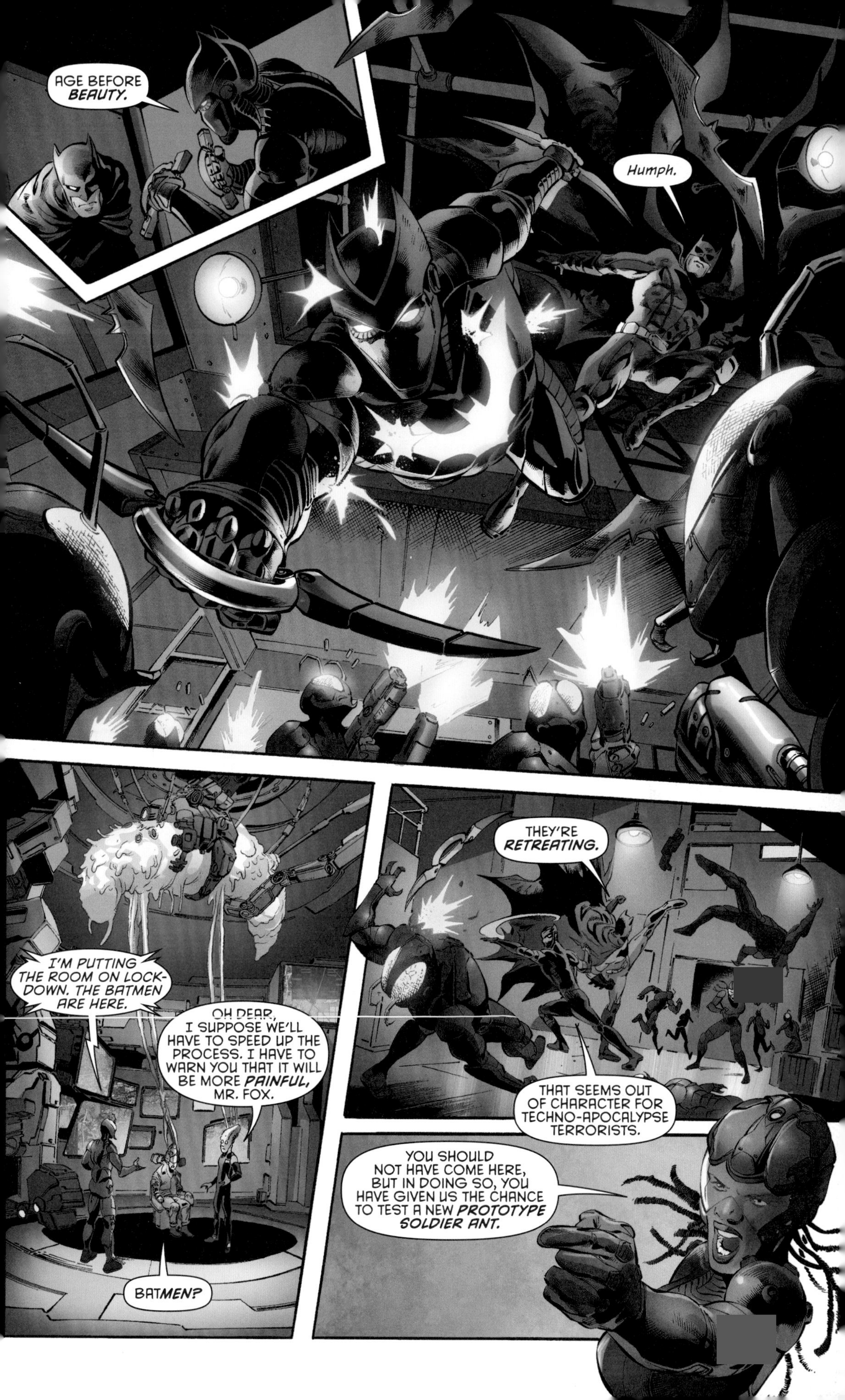
AGE BEFORE *BEAUTY.*
Humph.
I'M PUTTING THE ROOM ON LOCK-DOWN. THE BATMEN ARE HERE.
OH DEAR, I SUPPOSE WE'LL HAVE TO SPEED UP THE PROCESS. I HAVE TO WARN YOU THAT IT WILL BE MORE *PAINFUL,* MR. FOX.
BAT*MEN?*
THEY'RE *RETREATING.*
THAT SEEMS OUT OF CHARACTER FOR TECHNO-APOCALYPSE TERRORISTS.
YOU SHOULD NOT HAVE COME HERE, BUT IN DOING SO, YOU HAVE GIVEN US THE CHANCE TO TEST A NEW *PROTOTYPE SOLDIER ANT.*

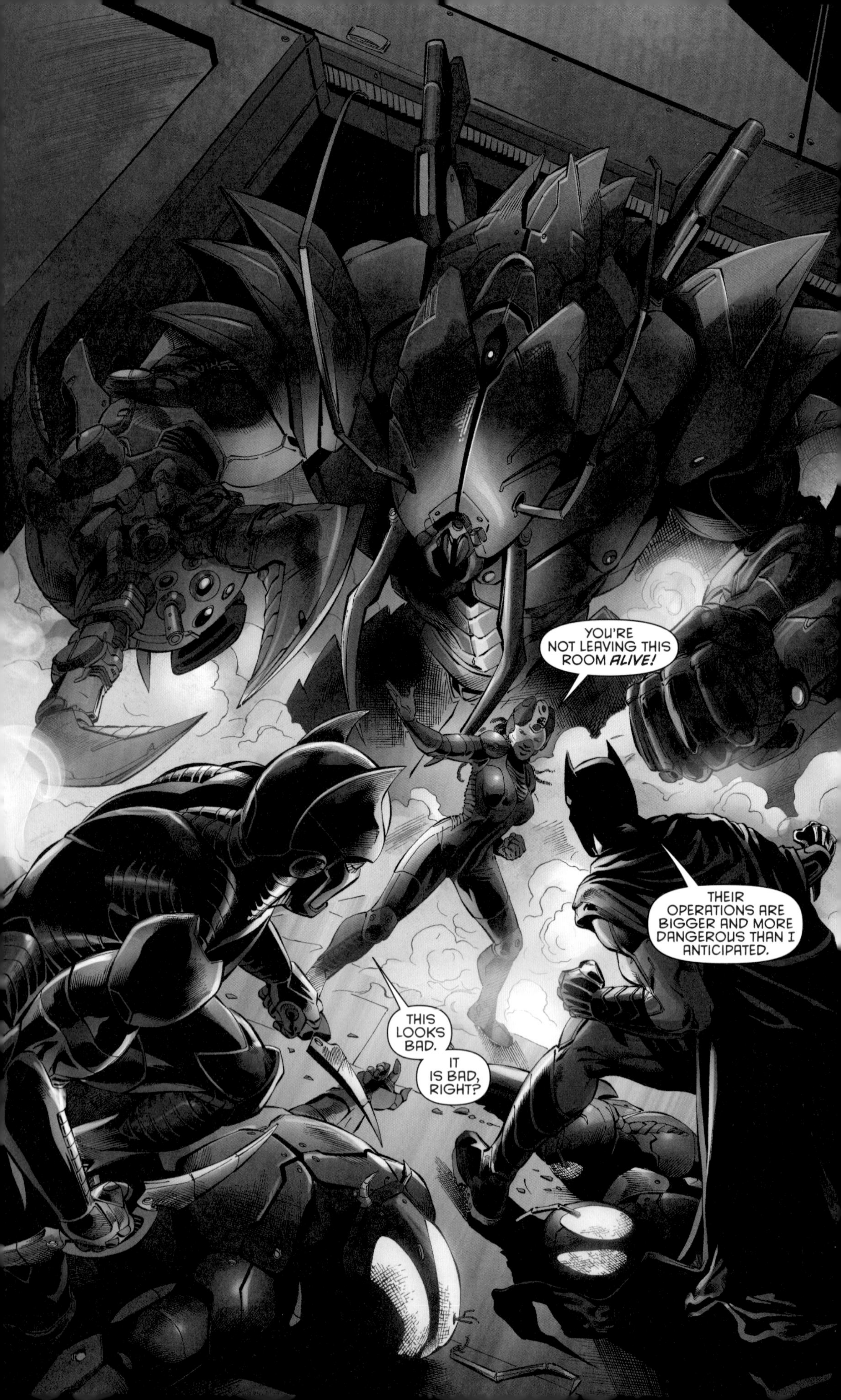
YOU'RE NOT LEAVING THIS ROOM *ALIVE!*
THEIR OPERATIONS ARE BIGGER AND MORE DANGEROUS THAN I ANTICIPATED.
THIS LOOKS BAD.
IT IS BAD, RIGHT?

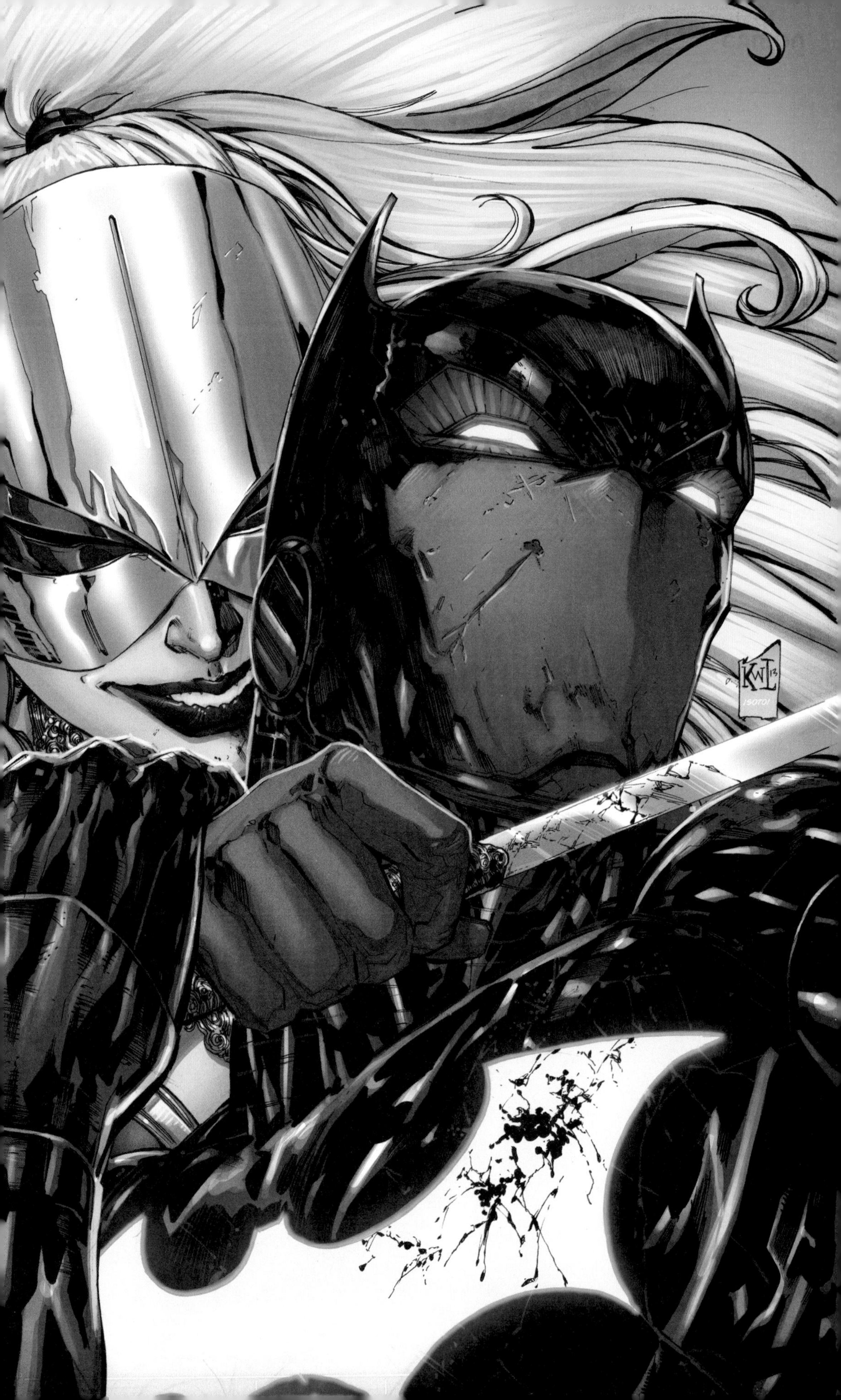

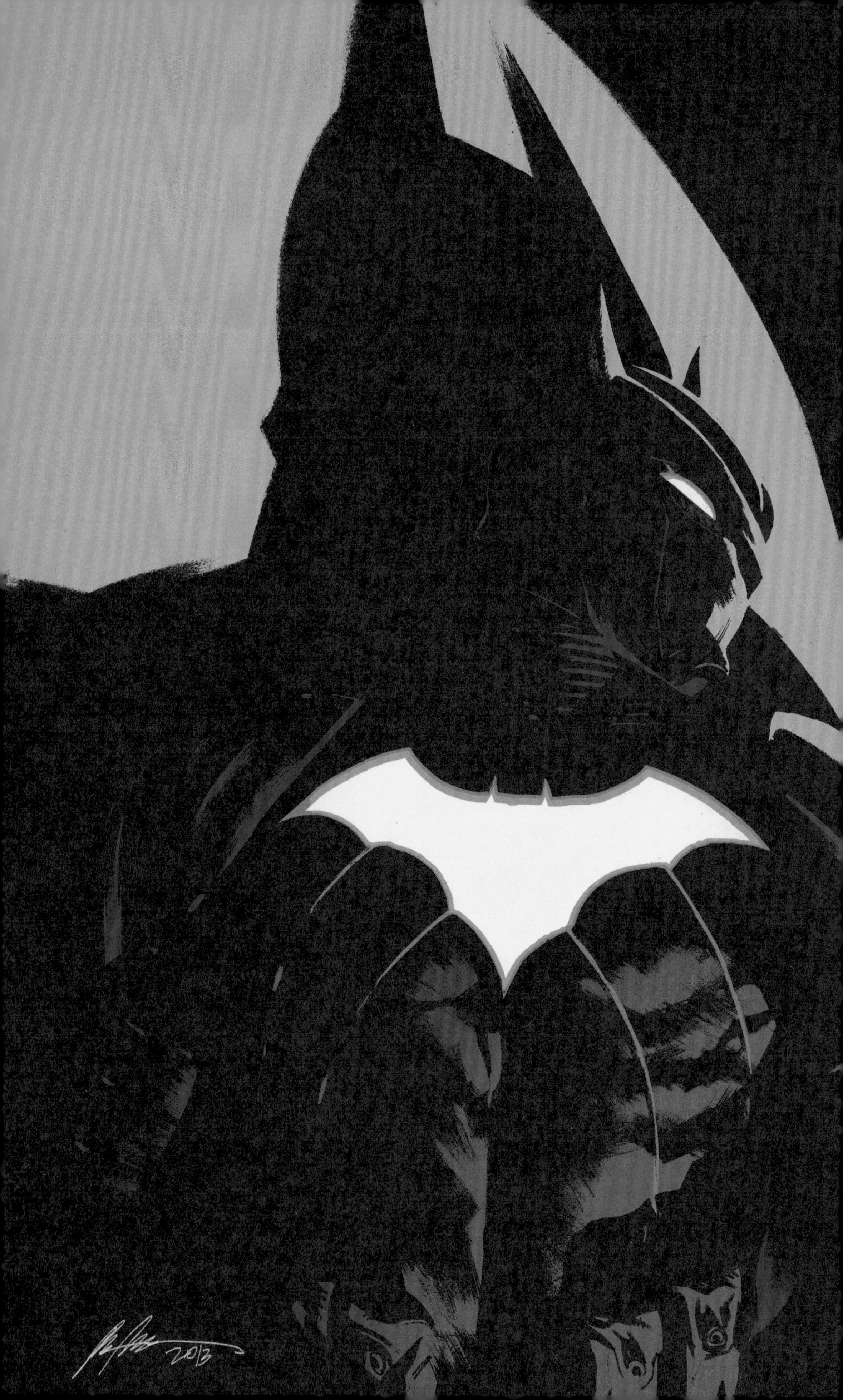
2013

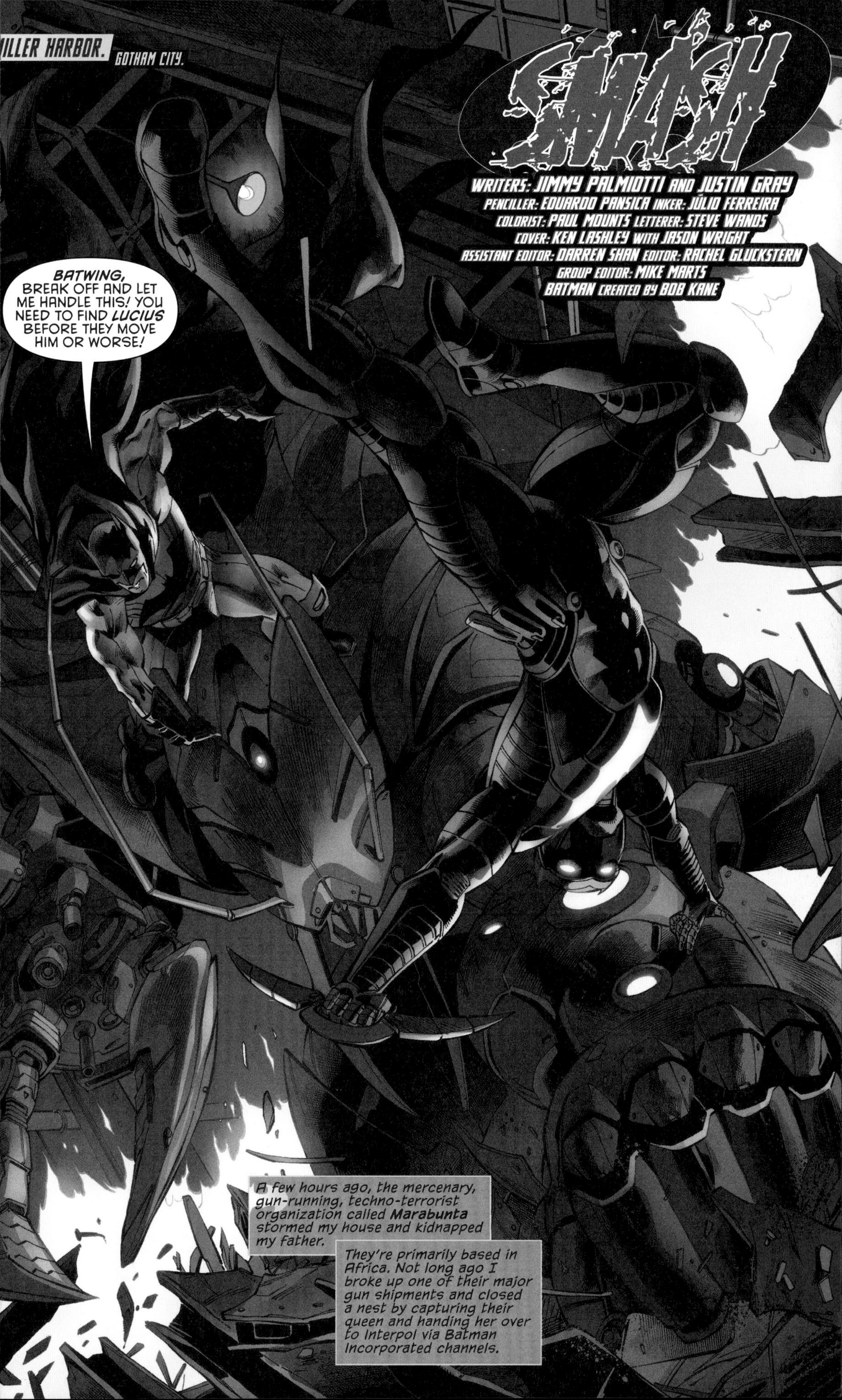

ILLER HARBOR. GOTHAM CITY.
SMASH
WRITERS: JIMMY PALMIOTTI AND JUSTIN GRAY
PENCILLER: EDUARDO PANSICA INKER: JÚLIO FERREIRA
COLORIST: PAUL MOUNTS LETTERER: STEVE WANDS
COVER: KEN LASHLEY WITH JASON WRIGHT
ASSISTANT EDITOR: DARREN SHAN EDITOR: RACHEL GLUCKSTERN
GROUP EDITOR: MIKE MARTS
BATMAN CREATED BY BOB KANE
BATWING, BREAK OFF AND LET ME HANDLE THIS! YOU NEED TO FIND LUCIUS BEFORE THEY MOVE HIM OR WORSE!
A few hours ago, the mercenary, gun-running, techno-terrorist organization called Marabunta stormed my house and kidnapped my father.
They're primarily based in Africa. Not long ago I broke up one of their major gun shipments and closed a nest by capturing their queen and handing her over to Interpol via Batman Incorporated channels.

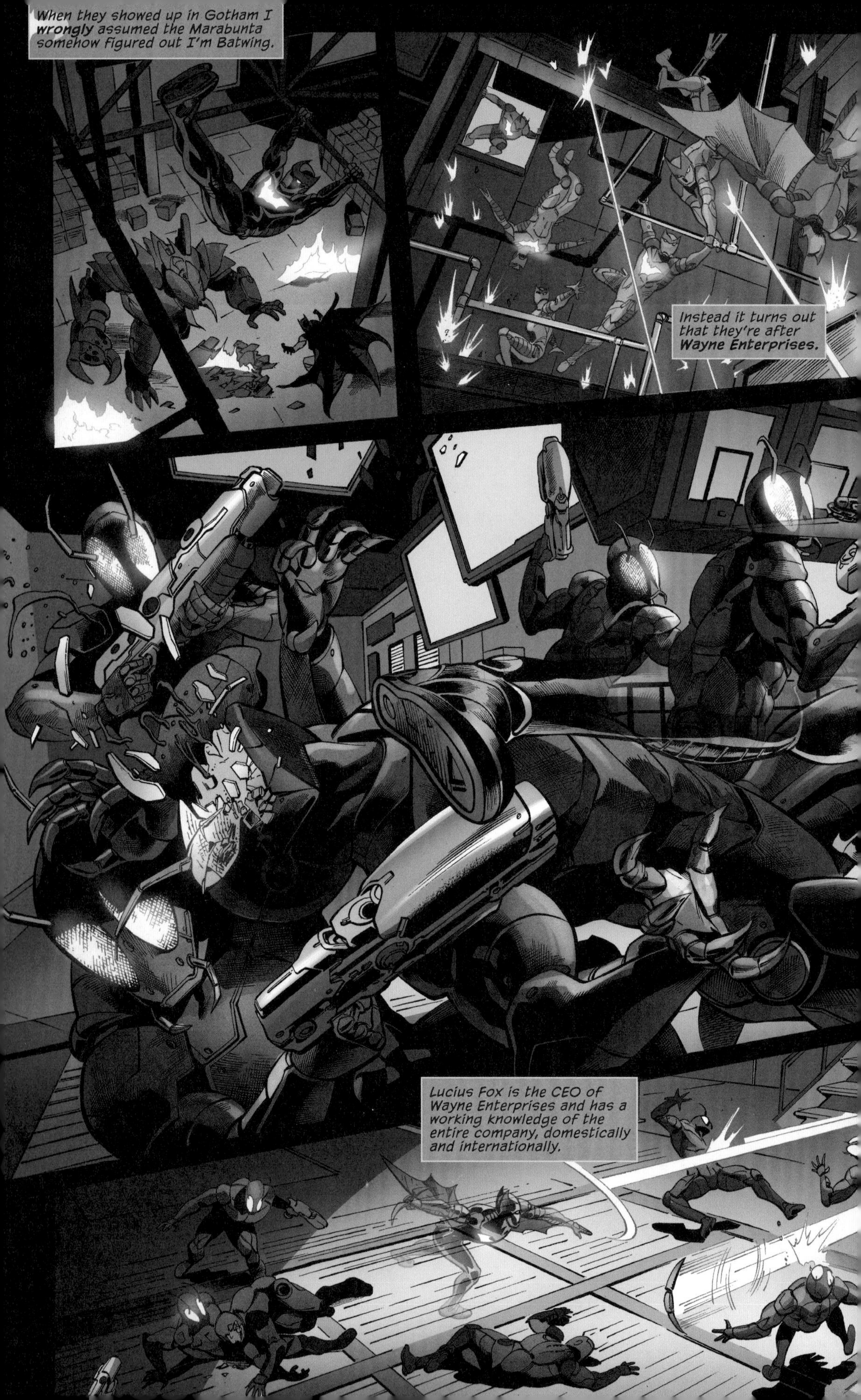
When they showed up in Gotham I **wrongly** assumed the Marabunta somehow figured out I'm Batwing.
Instead it turns out that they're after **Wayne Enterprises.**
Lucius Fox is the CEO of Wayne Enterprises and has a working knowledge of the entire company, domestically and internationally.

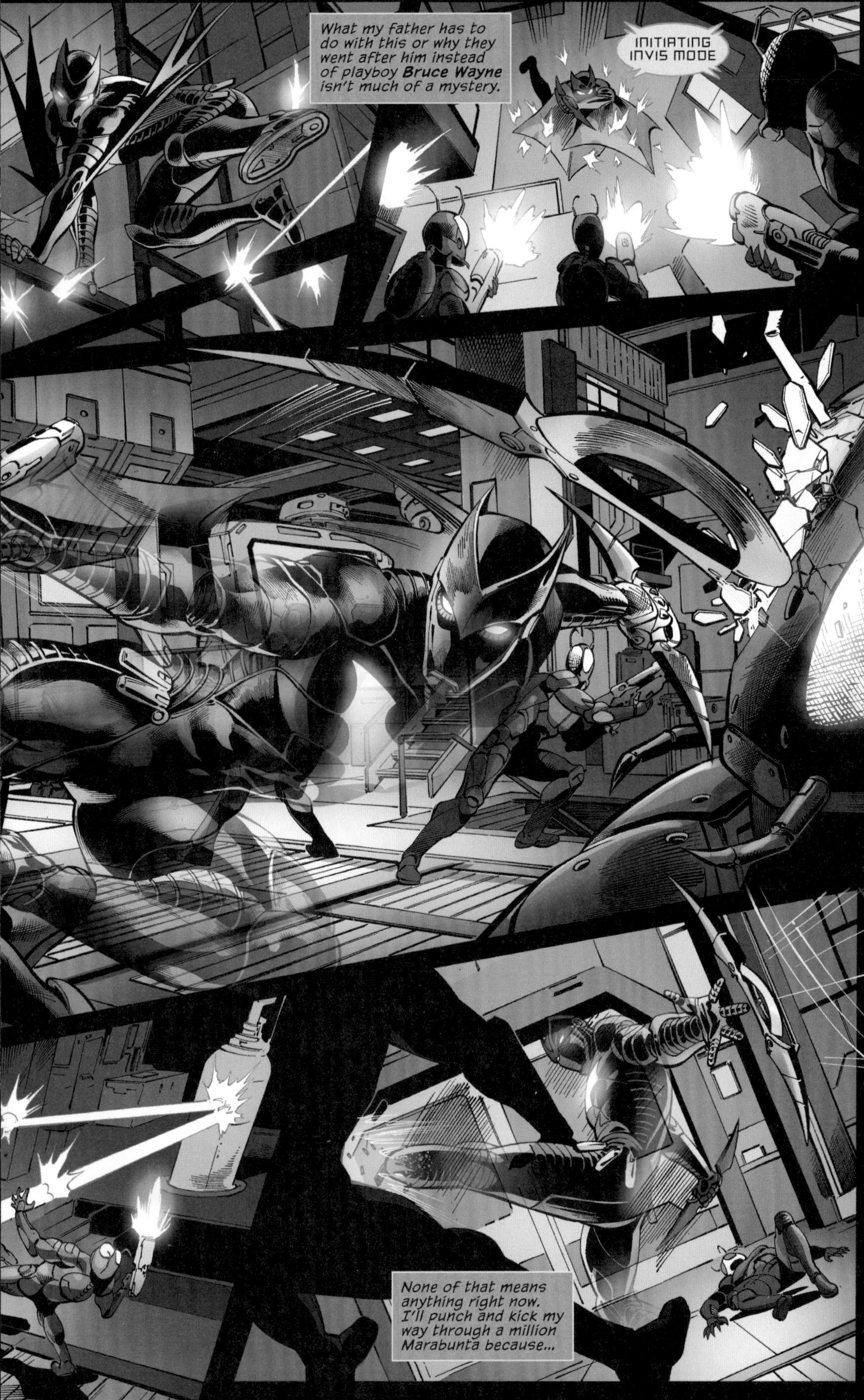
What my father has to do with this or why they went after him instead of playboy **Bruce Wayne** isn't much of a mystery.
INITIATING INVIS MODE
None of that means anything right now. I'll punch and kick my way through a million Marabunta because...

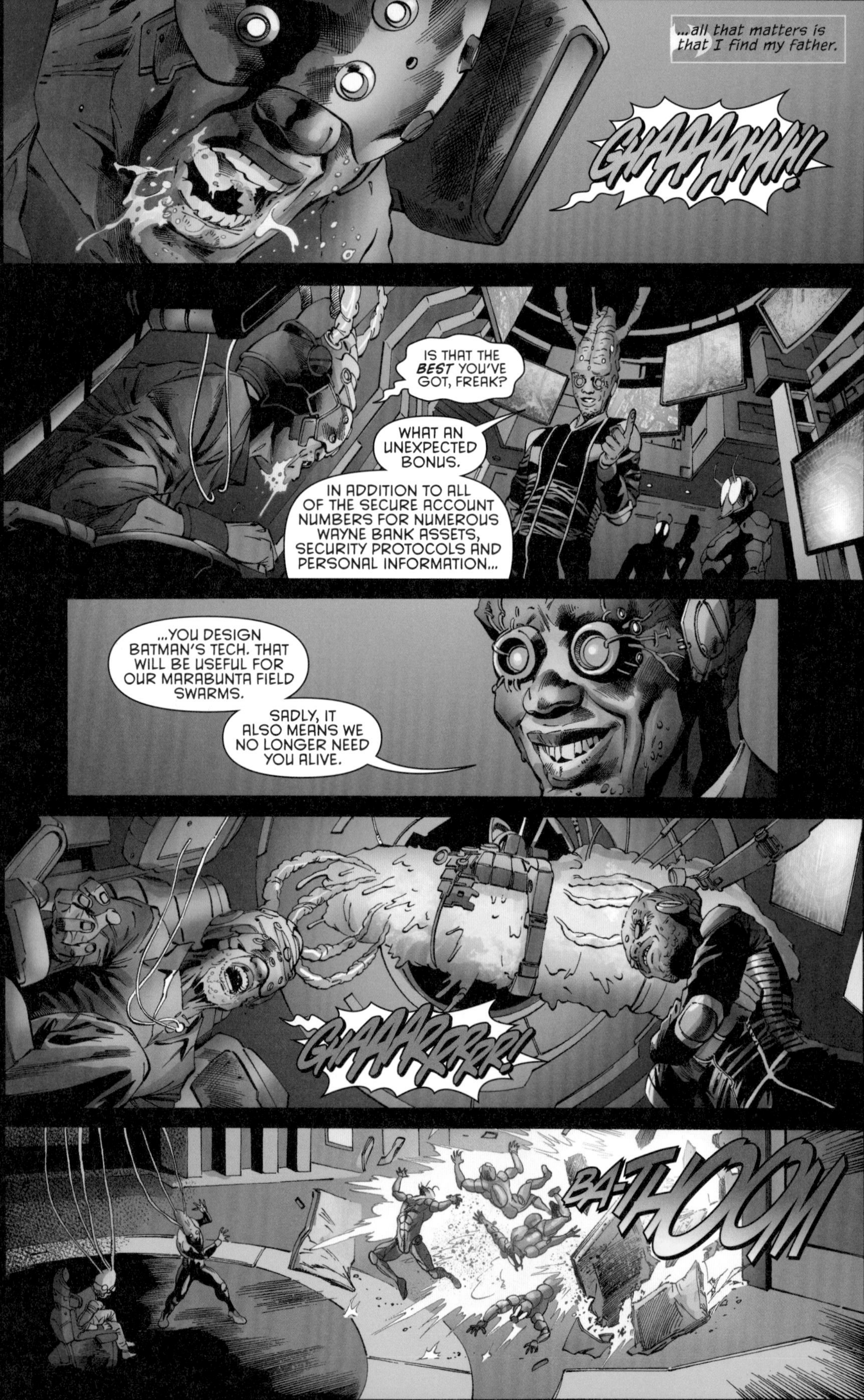
...all that matters is that I find my father.
GHAAAAHHH!
IS THAT THE BEST YOU'VE GOT, FREAK?
WHAT AN UNEXPECTED BONUS.
IN ADDITION TO ALL OF THE SECURE ACCOUNT NUMBERS FOR NUMEROUS WAYNE BANK ASSETS, SECURITY PROTOCOLS AND PERSONAL INFORMATION...
...YOU DESIGN BATMAN'S TECH. THAT WILL BE USEFUL FOR OUR MARABUNTA FIELD SWARMS.
SADLY, IT ALSO MEANS WE NO LONGER NEED YOU ALIVE.
GHAAARRRRR!
BA-THOOM

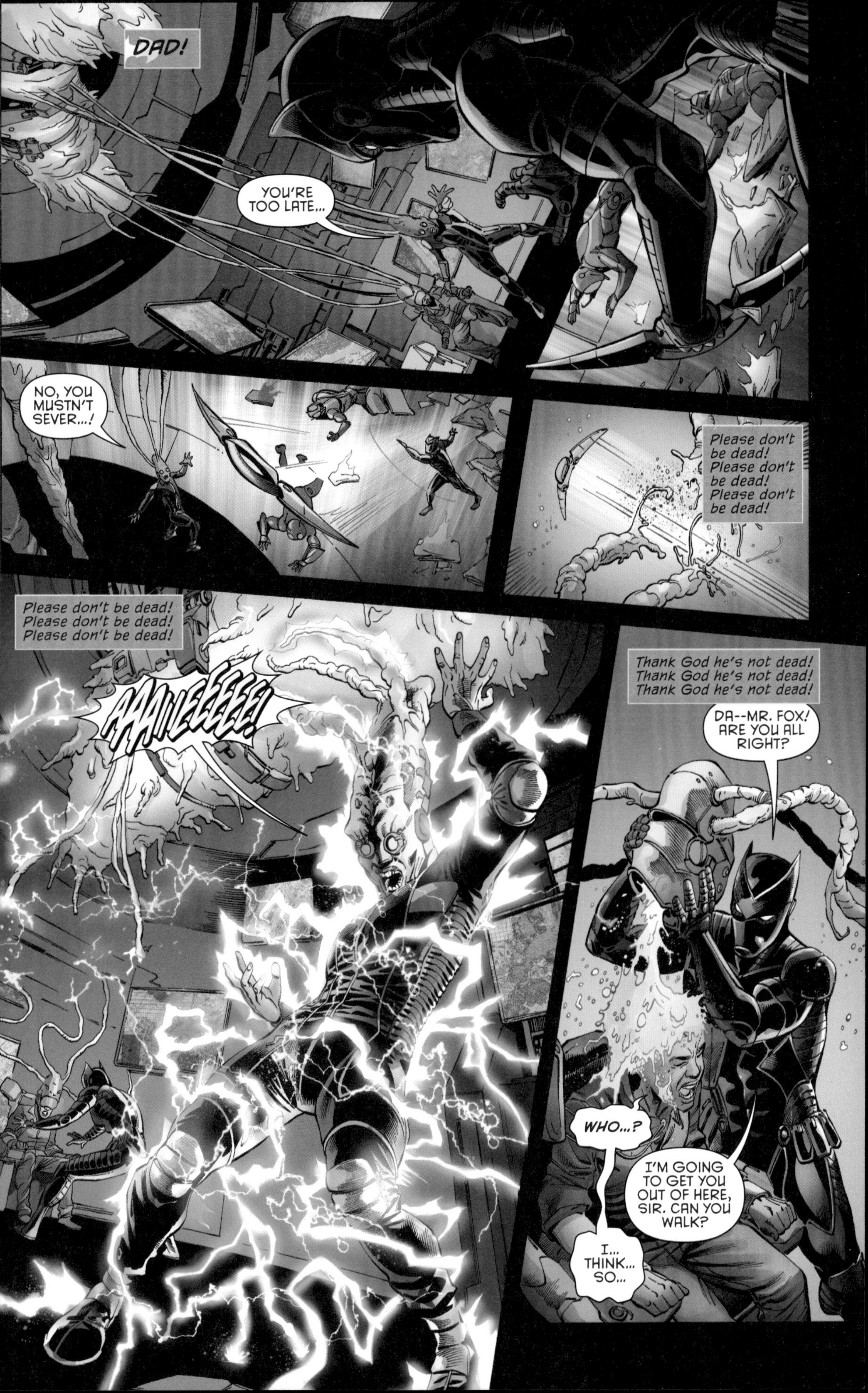
DAD!
YOU'RE TOO LATE...
NO, YOU MUSTN'T SEVER...!
Please don't be dead! Please don't be dead! Please don't be dead!
Please don't be dead! Please don't be dead! Please don't be dead!
AAAIIEEEEEE!
Thank God he's not dead! Thank God he's not dead! Thank God he's not dead!
DA--MR. FOX! ARE YOU ALL RIGHT?
WHO...?
I'M GOING TO GET YOU OUT OF HERE, SIR. CAN YOU WALK?
I... THINK... SO...

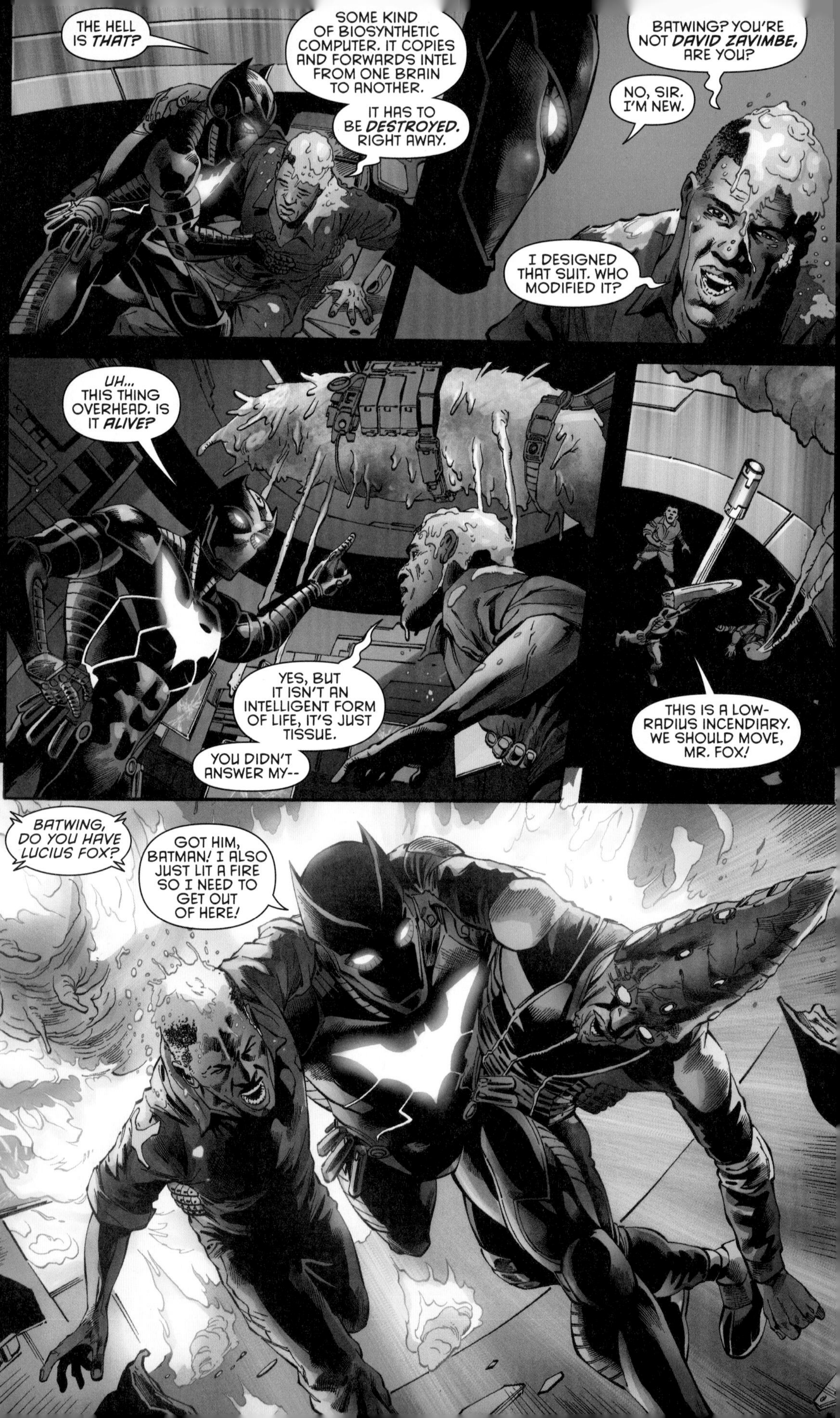
THE HELL IS *THAT?*
SOME KIND OF BIOSYNTHETIC COMPUTER. IT COPIES AND FORWARDS INTEL FROM ONE BRAIN TO ANOTHER.
IT HAS TO BE ***DESTROYED.*** RIGHT AWAY.
BATWING? YOU'RE NOT ***DAVID ZAVIMBE,*** ARE YOU?
NO, SIR. I'M NEW.
I DESIGNED THAT SUIT. WHO MODIFIED IT?
UH... THIS THING OVERHEAD. IS IT ***ALIVE?***
YES, BUT IT ISN'T AN INTELLIGENT FORM OF LIFE, IT'S JUST TISSUE.
YOU DIDN'T ANSWER MY--
THIS IS A LOW-RADIUS INCENDIARY. WE SHOULD MOVE, MR. FOX!
BATWING, DO YOU HAVE LUCIUS FOX?
GOT HIM, BATMAN! I ALSO JUST LIT A FIRE SO I NEED TO GET OUT OF HERE!

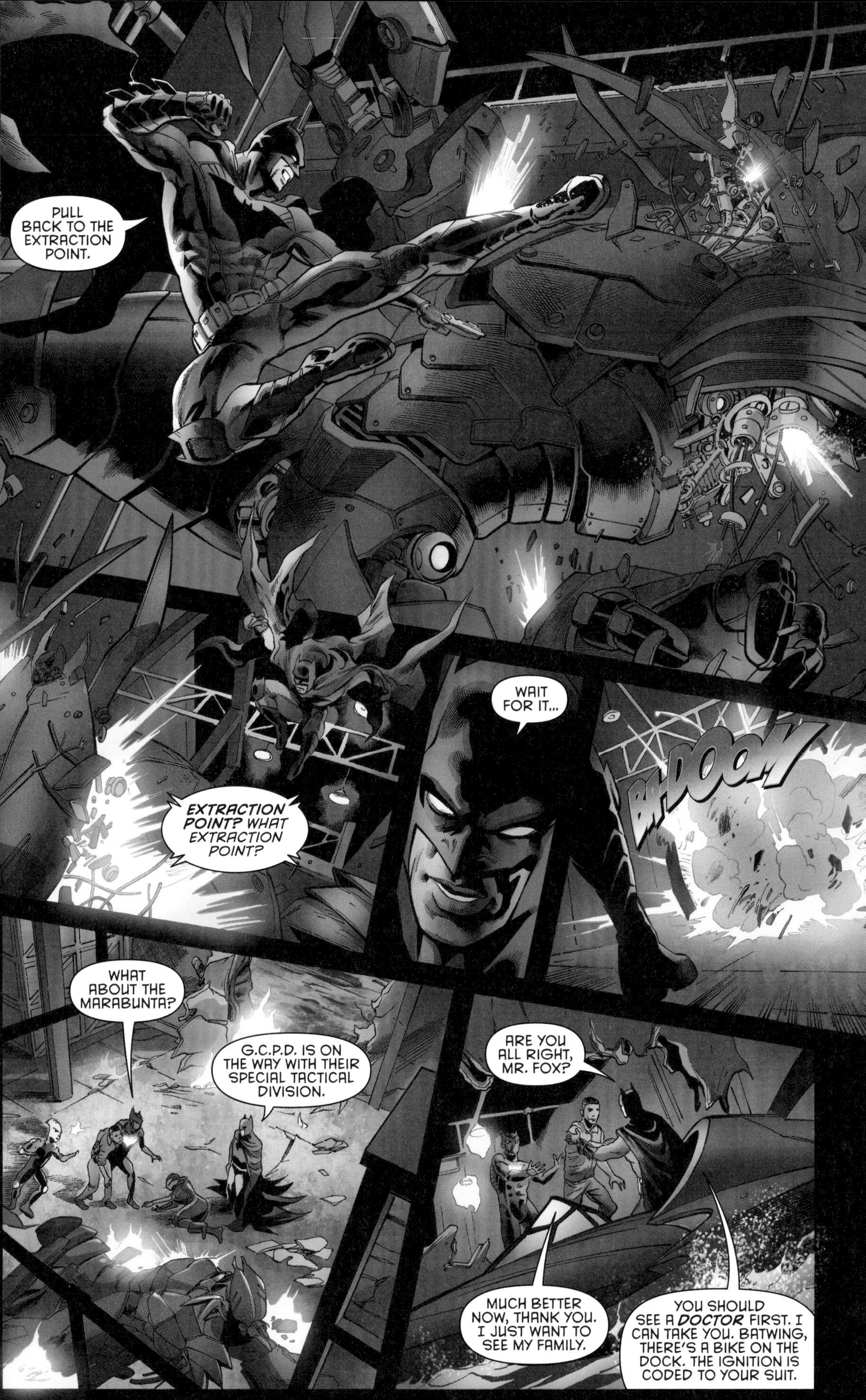
PULL BACK TO THE EXTRACTION POINT.
EXTRACTION POINT? WHAT EXTRACTION POINT?
WAIT FOR IT...
BADOOM
WHAT ABOUT THE MARABUNTA?
G.C.P.D. IS ON THE WAY WITH THEIR SPECIAL TACTICAL DIVISION.
ARE YOU ALL RIGHT, MR. FOX?
MUCH BETTER NOW, THANK YOU. I JUST WANT TO SEE MY FAMILY.
YOU SHOULD SEE A DOCTOR FIRST. I CAN TAKE YOU. BATWING, THERE'S A BIKE ON THE DOCK. THE IGNITION IS CODED TO YOUR SUIT.

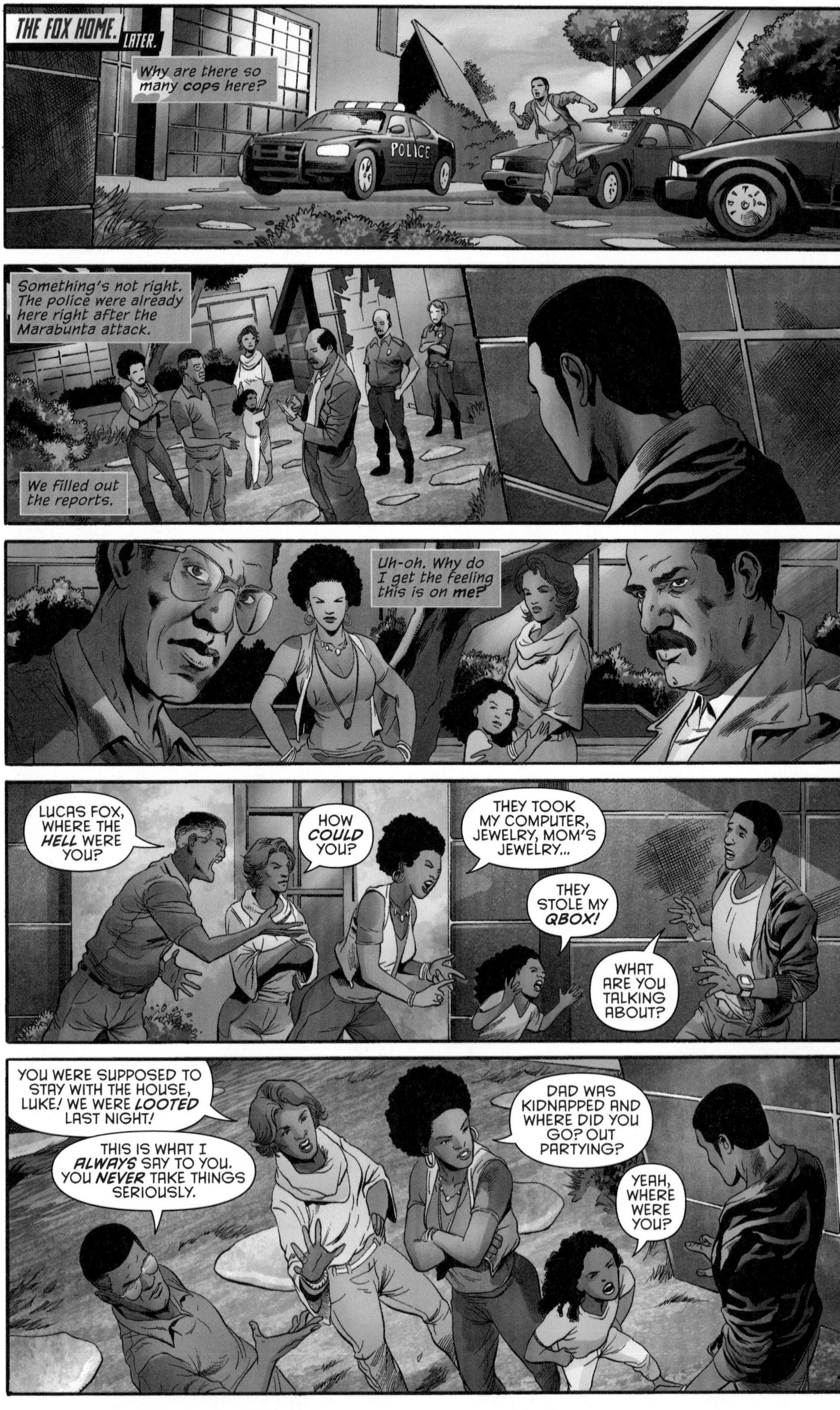

THE FOX HOME. LATER.
Why are there so many cops here?
POLICE
Something's not right. The police were already here right after the Marabunta attack.
We filled out the reports.
Uh-oh. Why do I get the feeling this is on me?
LUCAS FOX, WHERE THE HELL WERE YOU?
HOW COULD YOU?
THEY TOOK MY COMPUTER, JEWELRY, MOM'S JEWELRY...
THEY STOLE MY QBOX!
WHAT ARE YOU TALKING ABOUT?
YOU WERE SUPPOSED TO STAY WITH THE HOUSE, LUKE! WE WERE LOOTED LAST NIGHT!
THIS IS WHAT I ALWAYS SAY TO YOU. YOU NEVER TAKE THINGS SERIOUSLY.
DAD WAS KIDNAPPED AND WHERE DID YOU GO? OUT PARTYING?
YEAH, WHERE WERE YOU?

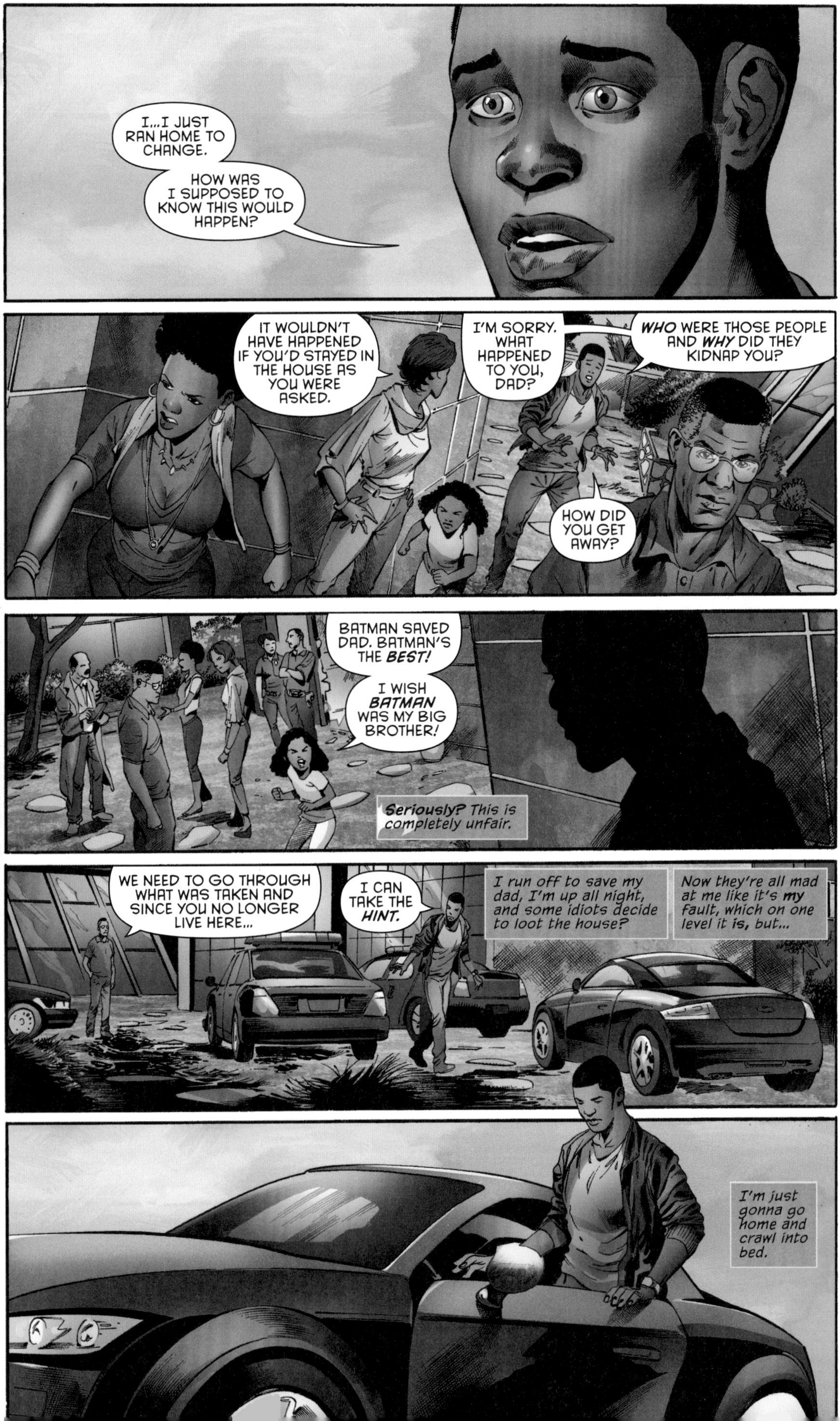
I...I JUST RAN HOME TO CHANGE.
HOW WAS I SUPPOSED TO KNOW THIS WOULD HAPPEN?
IT WOULDN'T HAVE HAPPENED IF YOU'D STAYED IN THE HOUSE AS YOU WERE ASKED.
I'M SORRY. WHAT HAPPENED TO YOU, DAD?
WHO WERE THOSE PEOPLE AND WHY DID THEY KIDNAP YOU?
HOW DID YOU GET AWAY?
BATMAN SAVED DAD. BATMAN'S THE BEST!
I WISH BATMAN WAS MY BIG BROTHER!
Seriously? This is completely unfair.
WE NEED TO GO THROUGH WHAT WAS TAKEN AND SINCE YOU NO LONGER LIVE HERE...
I CAN TAKE THE HINT.
I run off to save my dad, I'm up all night, and some idiots decide to loot the house?
Now they're all mad at me like it's my fault, which on one level it is, but...
I'm just gonna go home and crawl into bed.

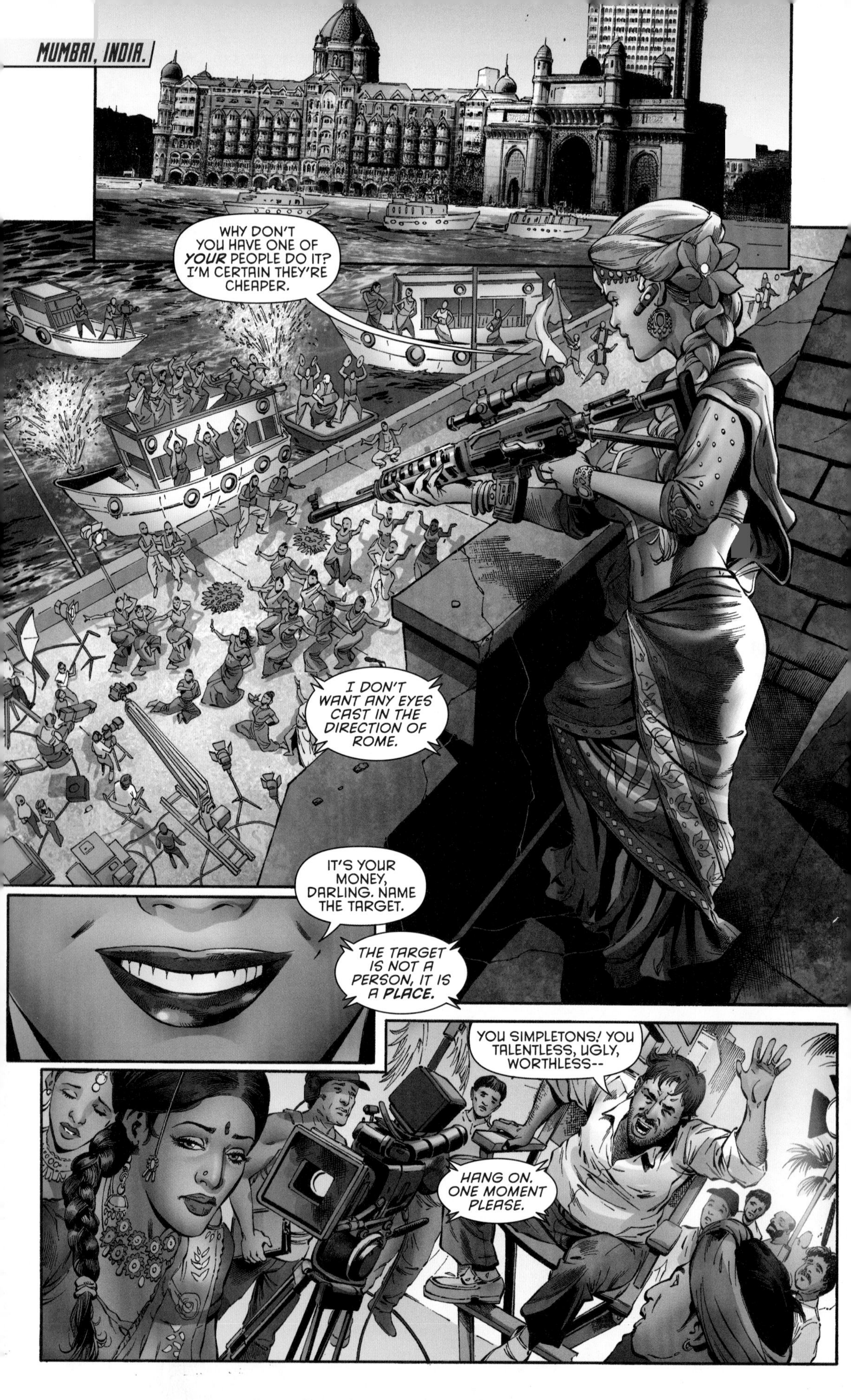
MUMBAI, INDIA.
WHY DON'T YOU HAVE ONE OF YOUR PEOPLE DO IT? I'M CERTAIN THEY'RE CHEAPER.
I DON'T WANT ANY EYES CAST IN THE DIRECTION OF ROME.
IT'S YOUR MONEY, DARLING. NAME THE TARGET.
THE TARGET IS NOT A PERSON, IT IS A PLACE.
YOU SIMPLETONS! YOU TALENTLESS, UGLY, WORTHLESS--
HANG ON. ONE MOMENT PLEASE.

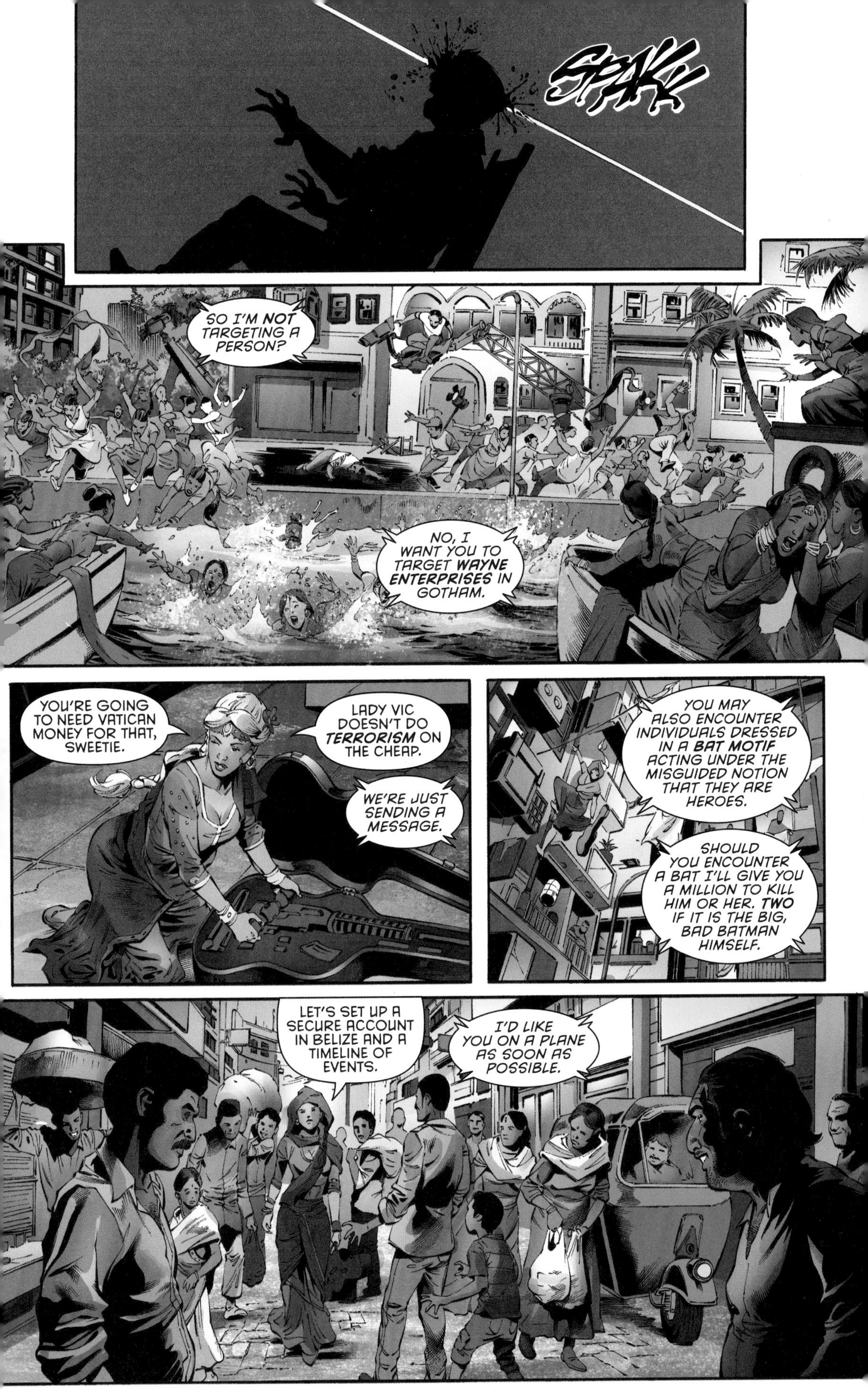
SO I'M NOT TARGETING A PERSON?
NO, I WANT YOU TO TARGET WAYNE ENTERPRISES IN GOTHAM.
YOU'RE GOING TO NEED VATICAN MONEY FOR THAT, SWEETIE.
LADY VIC DOESN'T DO TERRORISM ON THE CHEAP.
WE'RE JUST SENDING A MESSAGE.
YOU MAY ALSO ENCOUNTER INDIVIDUALS DRESSED IN A BAT MOTIF ACTING UNDER THE MISGUIDED NOTION THAT THEY ARE HEROES.
SHOULD YOU ENCOUNTER A BAT I'LL GIVE YOU A MILLION TO KILL HIM OR HER. TWO IF IT IS THE BIG, BAD BATMAN HIMSELF.
LET'S SET UP A SECURE ACCOUNT IN BELIZE AND A TIMELINE OF EVENTS.
I'D LIKE YOU ON A PLANE AS SOON AS POSSIBLE.

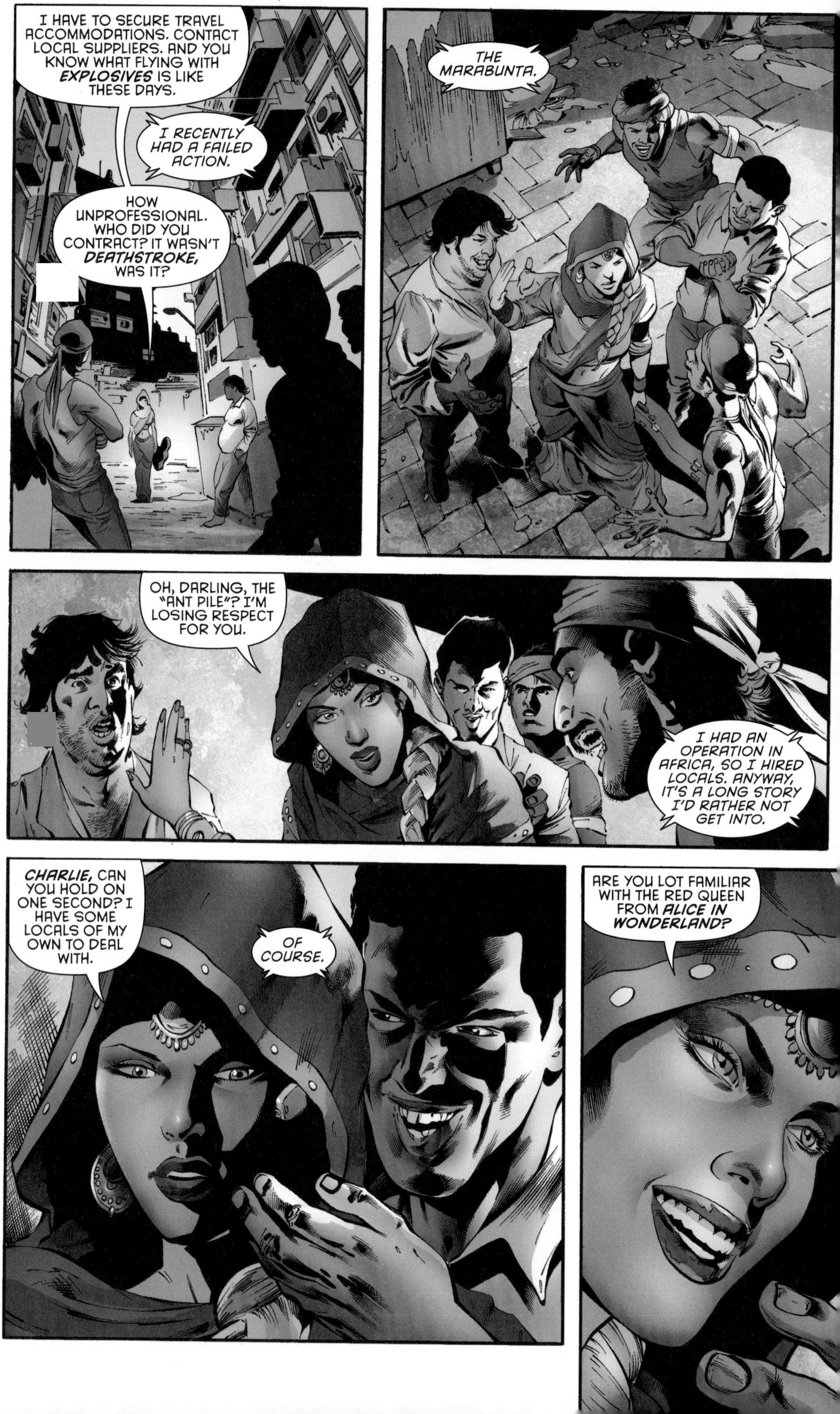
I HAVE TO SECURE TRAVEL ACCOMMODATIONS. CONTACT LOCAL SUPPLIERS. AND YOU KNOW WHAT FLYING WITH EXPLOSIVES IS LIKE THESE DAYS.
I RECENTLY HAD A FAILED ACTION.
HOW UNPROFESSIONAL. WHO DID YOU CONTRACT? IT WASN'T DEATHSTROKE, WAS IT?
THE MARABUNTA.
OH, DARLING, THE "ANT PILE"? I'M LOSING RESPECT FOR YOU.
I HAD AN OPERATION IN AFRICA, SO I HIRED LOCALS. ANYWAY, IT'S A LONG STORY I'D RATHER NOT GET INTO.
CHARLIE, CAN YOU HOLD ON ONE SECOND? I HAVE SOME LOCALS OF MY OWN TO DEAL WITH.
OF COURSE.
ARE YOU LOT FAMILIAR WITH THE RED QUEEN FROM ALICE IN WONDERLAND?

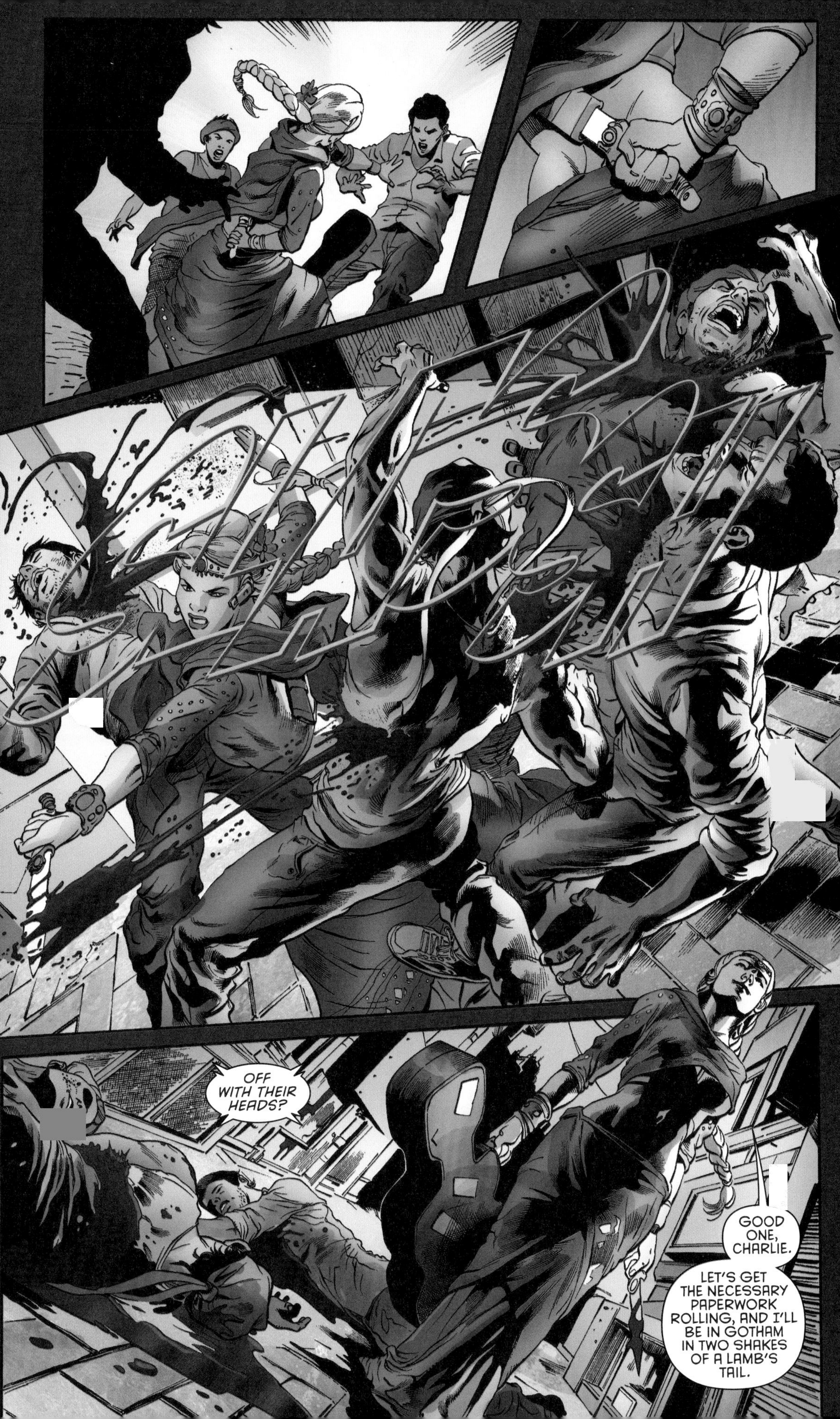

OFF WITH THEIR HEADS?
GOOD ONE, CHARLIE.
LET'S GET THE NECESSARY PAPERWORK ROLLING, AND I'LL BE IN GOTHAM IN TWO SHAKES OF A LAMB'S TAIL.

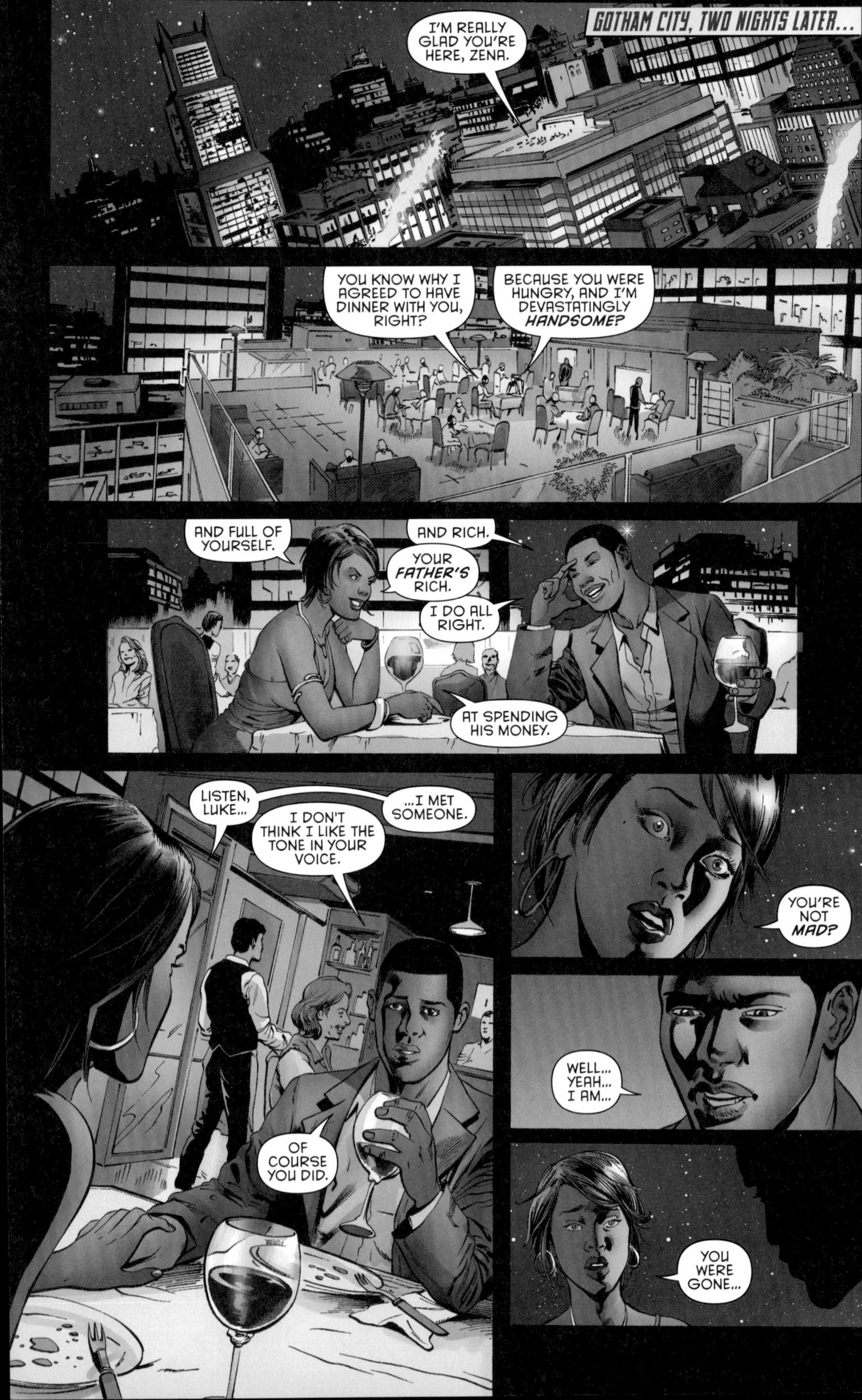

GOTHAM CITY, TWO NIGHTS LATER...
I'M REALLY GLAD YOU'RE HERE, ZENA.
YOU KNOW WHY I AGREED TO HAVE DINNER WITH YOU, RIGHT?
BECAUSE YOU WERE HUNGRY, AND I'M DEVASTATINGLY HANDSOME?
AND FULL OF YOURSELF.
AND RICH.
YOUR FATHER'S RICH.
I DO ALL RIGHT.
AT SPENDING HIS MONEY.
LISTEN, LUKE...
...I MET SOMEONE.
I DON'T THINK I LIKE THE TONE IN YOUR VOICE.
OF COURSE YOU DID.
YOU'RE NOT MAD?
WELL... YEAH... I AM...
YOU WERE GONE...

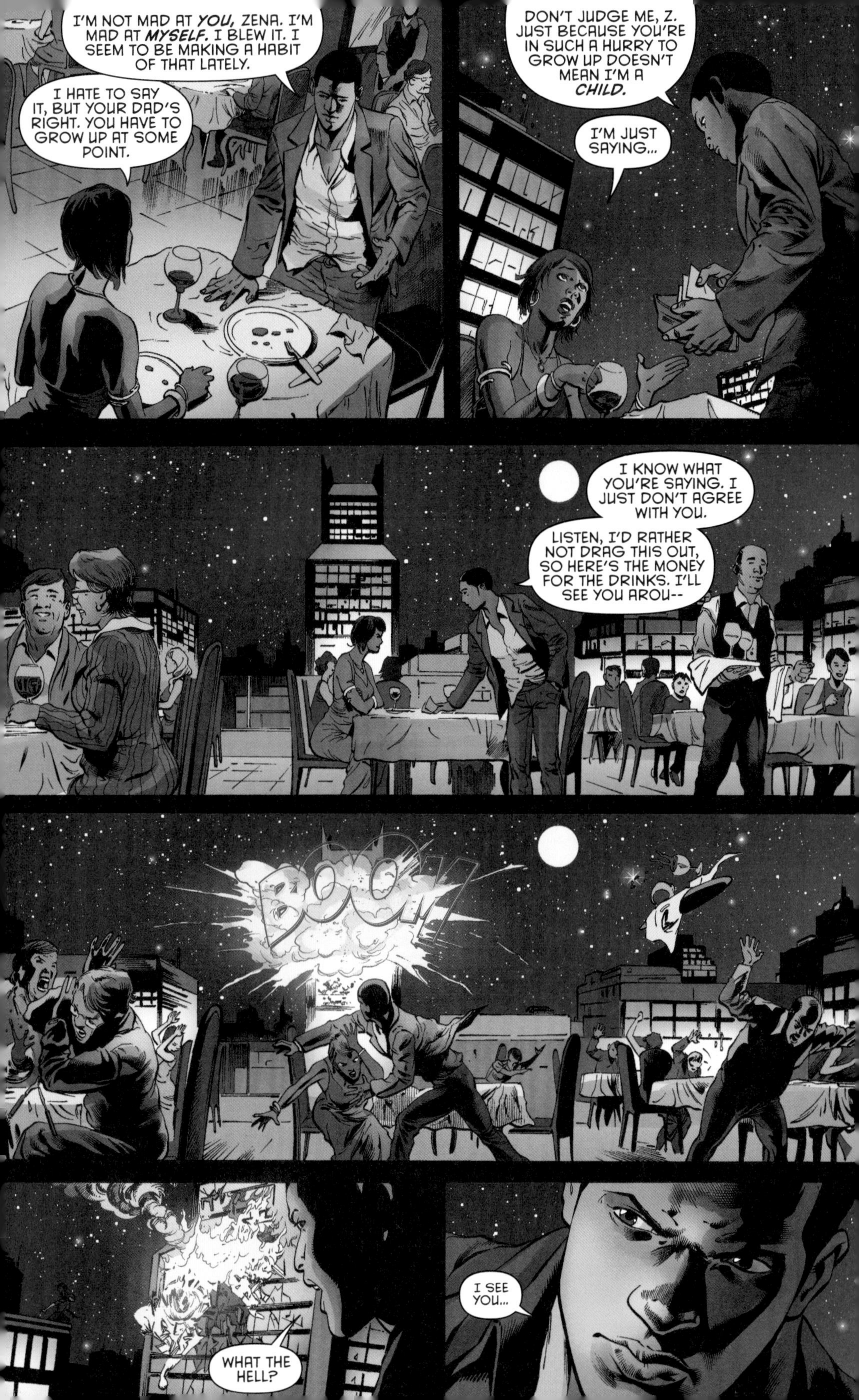
I'M NOT MAD AT *YOU,* ZENA. I'M MAD AT ***MYSELF.*** I BLEW IT. I SEEM TO BE MAKING A HABIT OF THAT LATELY.
I HATE TO SAY IT, BUT YOUR DAD'S RIGHT. YOU HAVE TO GROW UP AT SOME POINT.
DON'T JUDGE ME, Z. JUST BECAUSE YOU'RE IN SUCH A HURRY TO GROW UP DOESN'T MEAN I'M A ***CHILD.***
I'M JUST SAYING...
I KNOW WHAT YOU'RE SAYING. I JUST DON'T AGREE WITH YOU.
LISTEN, I'D RATHER NOT DRAG THIS OUT, SO HERE'S THE MONEY FOR THE DRINKS. I'LL SEE YOU AROU--
BOOM
WHAT THE HELL?
I SEE YOU...

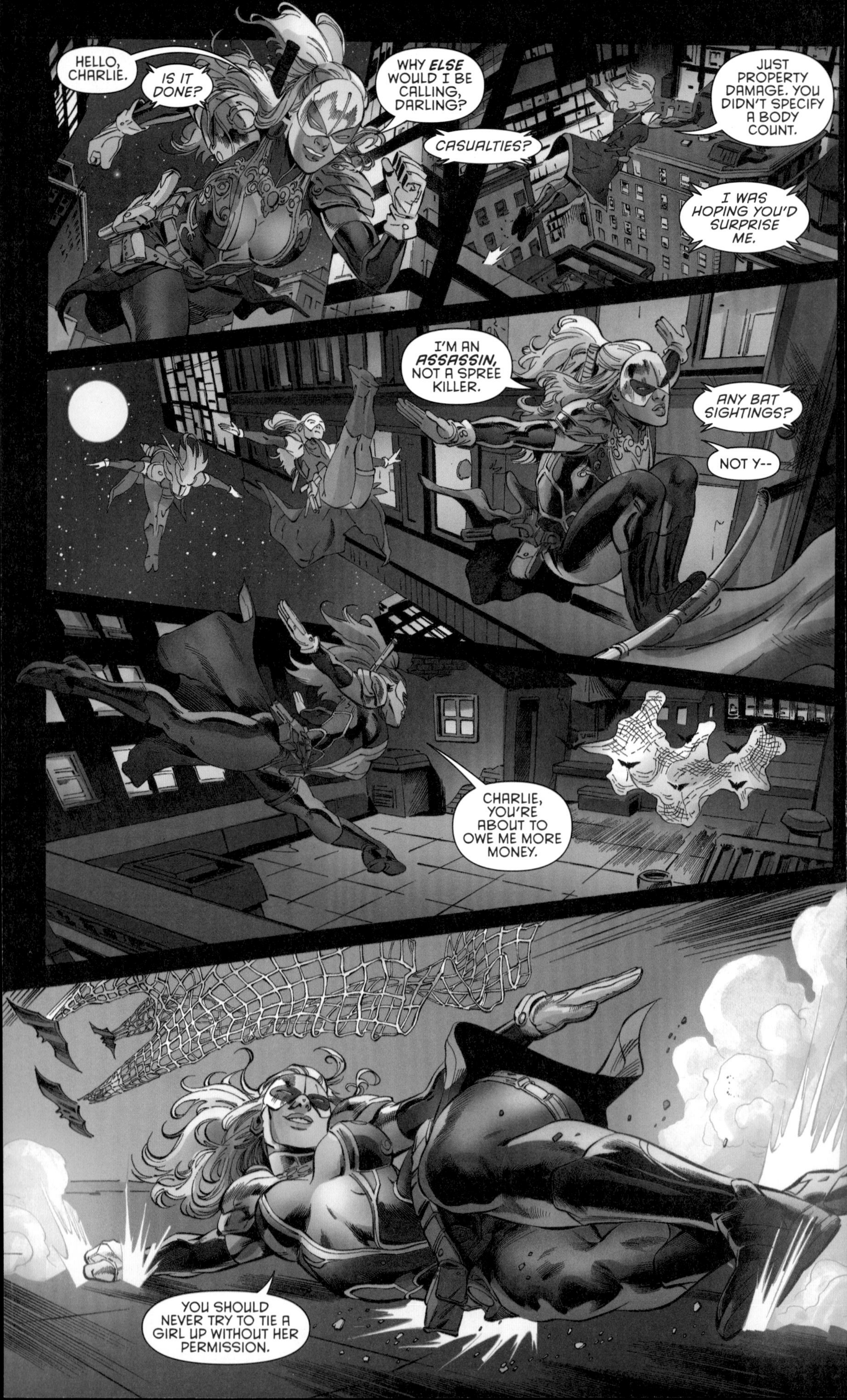
HELLO, CHARLIE.
IS IT DONE?
WHY *ELSE* WOULD I BE CALLING, DARLING?
CASUALTIES?
JUST PROPERTY DAMAGE. YOU DIDN'T SPECIFY A BODY COUNT.
I WAS HOPING YOU'D SURPRISE ME.
I'M AN *ASSASSIN,* NOT A SPREE KILLER.
ANY BAT SIGHTINGS?
NOT Y--
CHARLIE, YOU'RE ABOUT TO OWE ME MORE MONEY.
YOU SHOULD NEVER TRY TO TIE A GIRL UP WITHOUT HER PERMISSION.

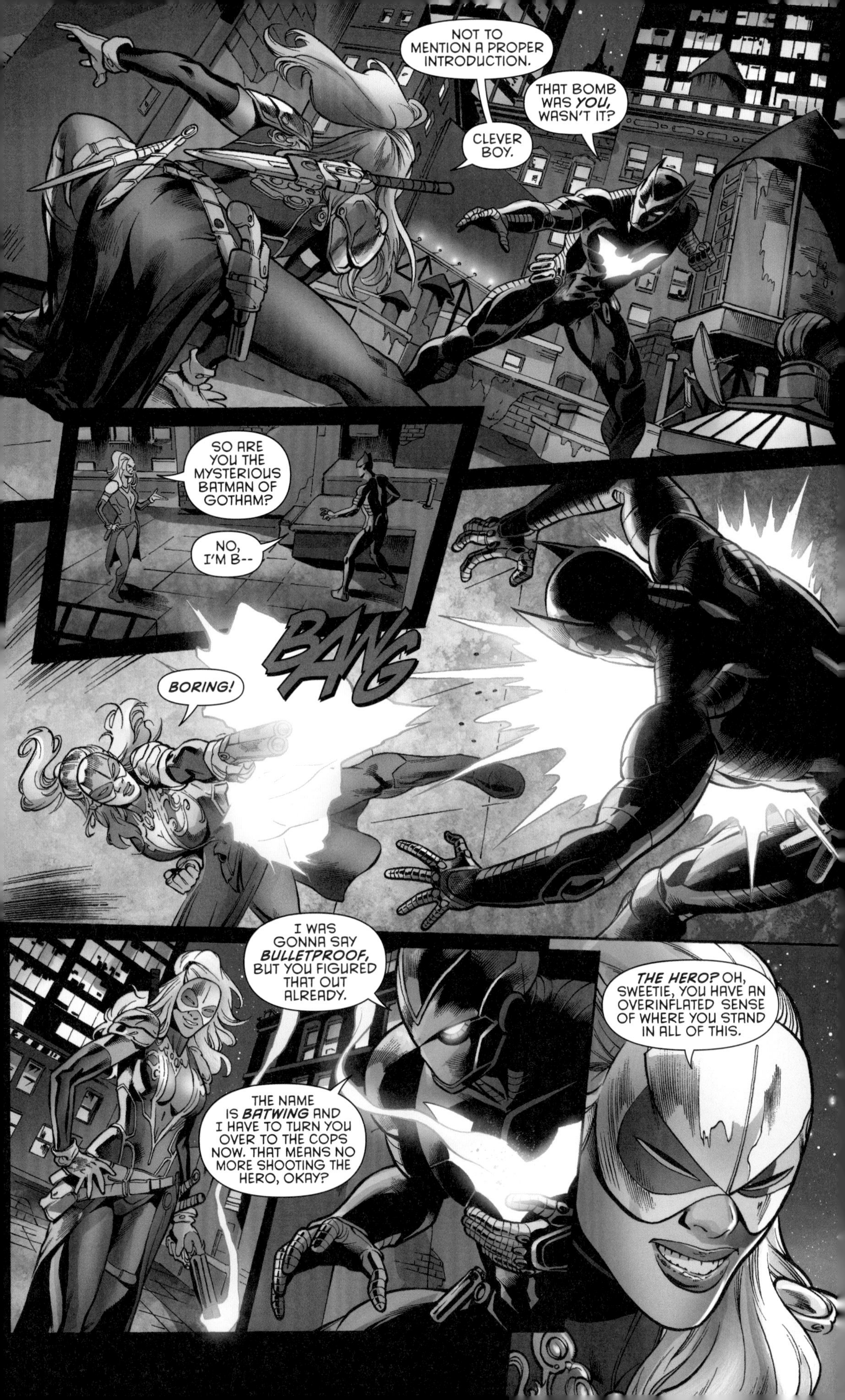
NOT TO MENTION A PROPER INTRODUCTION.
CLEVER BOY.
THAT BOMB WAS *YOU,* WASN'T IT?
SO ARE YOU THE MYSTERIOUS BATMAN OF GOTHAM?
NO, I'M B--
BANG
BORING!
I WAS GONNA SAY *BULLETPROOF,* BUT YOU FIGURED THAT OUT ALREADY.
THE NAME IS *BATWING* AND I HAVE TO TURN YOU OVER TO THE COPS NOW. THAT MEANS NO MORE SHOOTING THE HERO, OKAY?
THE HERO? OH, SWEETIE, YOU HAVE AN OVERINFLATED SENSE OF WHERE YOU STAND IN ALL OF THIS.

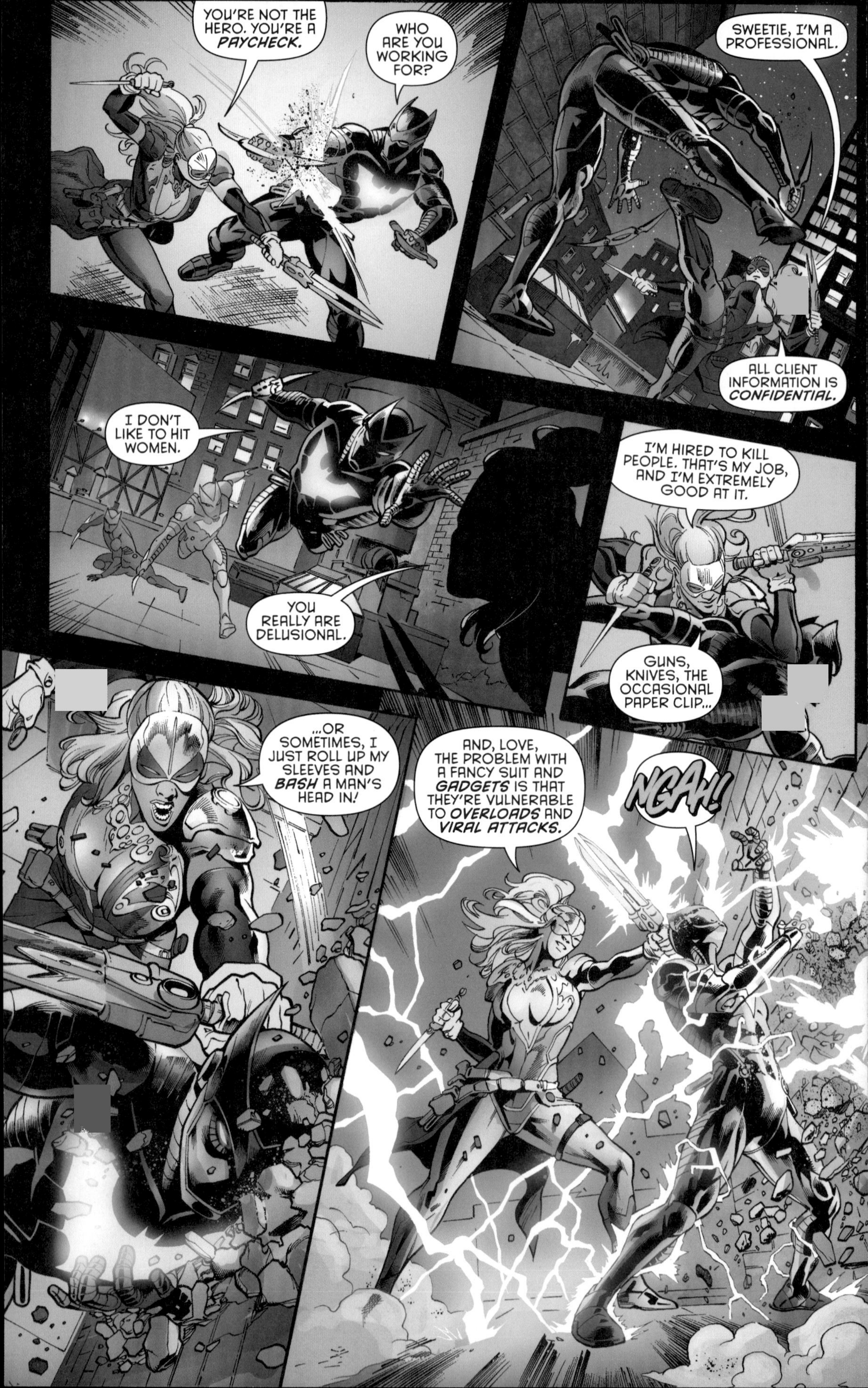
YOU'RE NOT THE HERO. YOU'RE A PAYCHECK.
WHO ARE YOU WORKING FOR?
SWEETIE, I'M A PROFESSIONAL.
ALL CLIENT INFORMATION IS CONFIDENTIAL.
I DON'T LIKE TO HIT WOMEN.
YOU REALLY ARE DELUSIONAL.
I'M HIRED TO KILL PEOPLE. THAT'S MY JOB, AND I'M EXTREMELY GOOD AT IT.
GUNS, KNIVES, THE OCCASIONAL PAPER CLIP...
...OR SOMETIMES, I JUST ROLL UP MY SLEEVES AND BASH A MAN'S HEAD IN!
AND, LOVE, THE PROBLEM WITH A FANCY SUIT AND GADGETS IS THAT THEY'RE VULNERABLE TO OVERLOADS AND VIRAL ATTACKS.
NGAH!

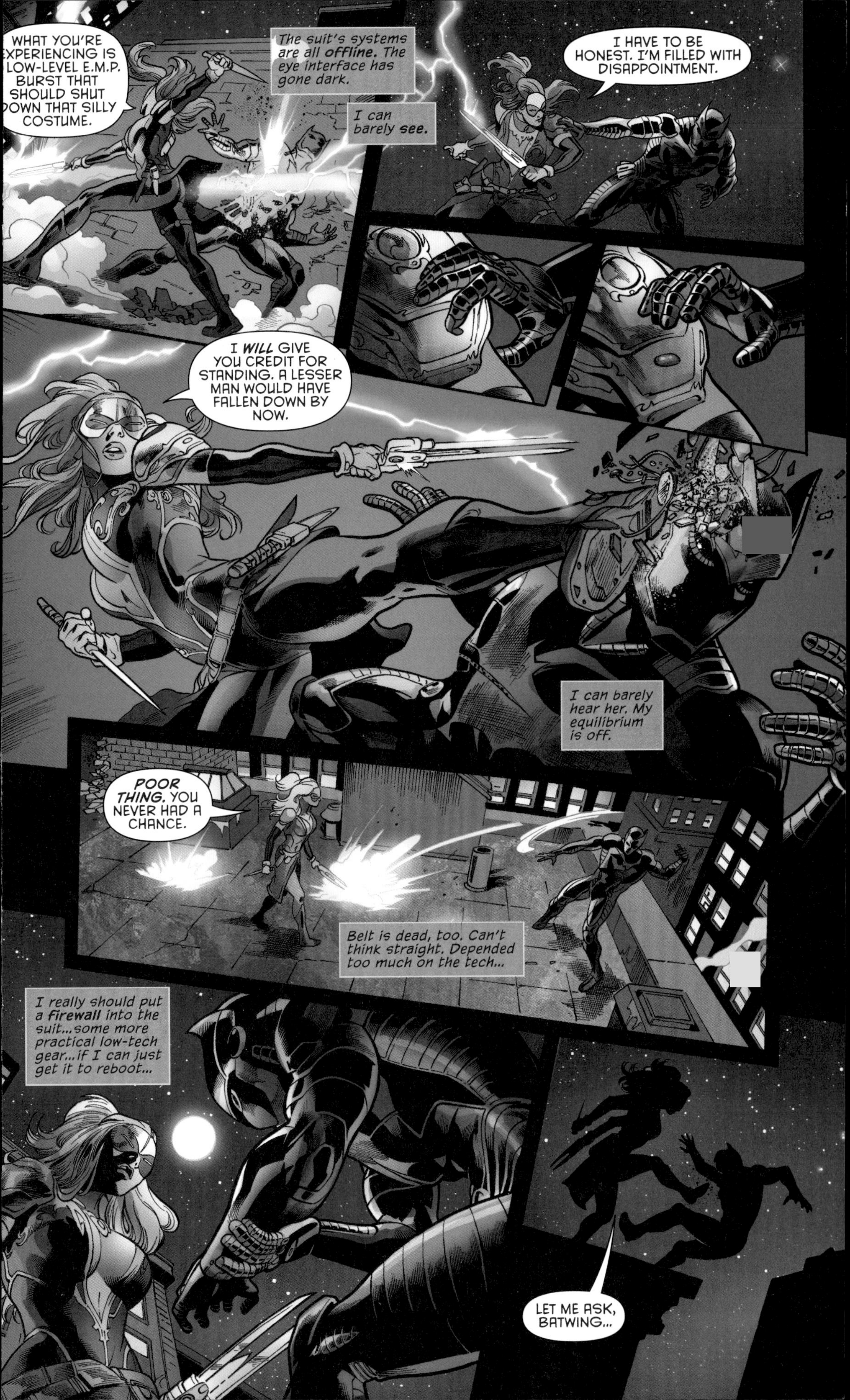

WHAT YOU'RE EXPERIENCING IS LOW-LEVEL E.M.P. BURST THAT SHOULD SHUT DOWN THAT SILLY COSTUME.
The suit's systems are all offline. The eye interface has gone dark.
I can barely see.
I HAVE TO BE HONEST. I'M FILLED WITH DISAPPOINTMENT.
I WILL GIVE YOU CREDIT FOR STANDING. A LESSER MAN WOULD HAVE FALLEN DOWN BY NOW.
I can barely hear her. My equilibrium is off.
POOR THING. YOU NEVER HAD A CHANCE.
Belt is dead, too. Can't think straight. Depended too much on the tech...
I really should put a firewall into the suit...some more practical low-tech gear...if I can just get it to reboot...
LET ME ASK, BATWING...

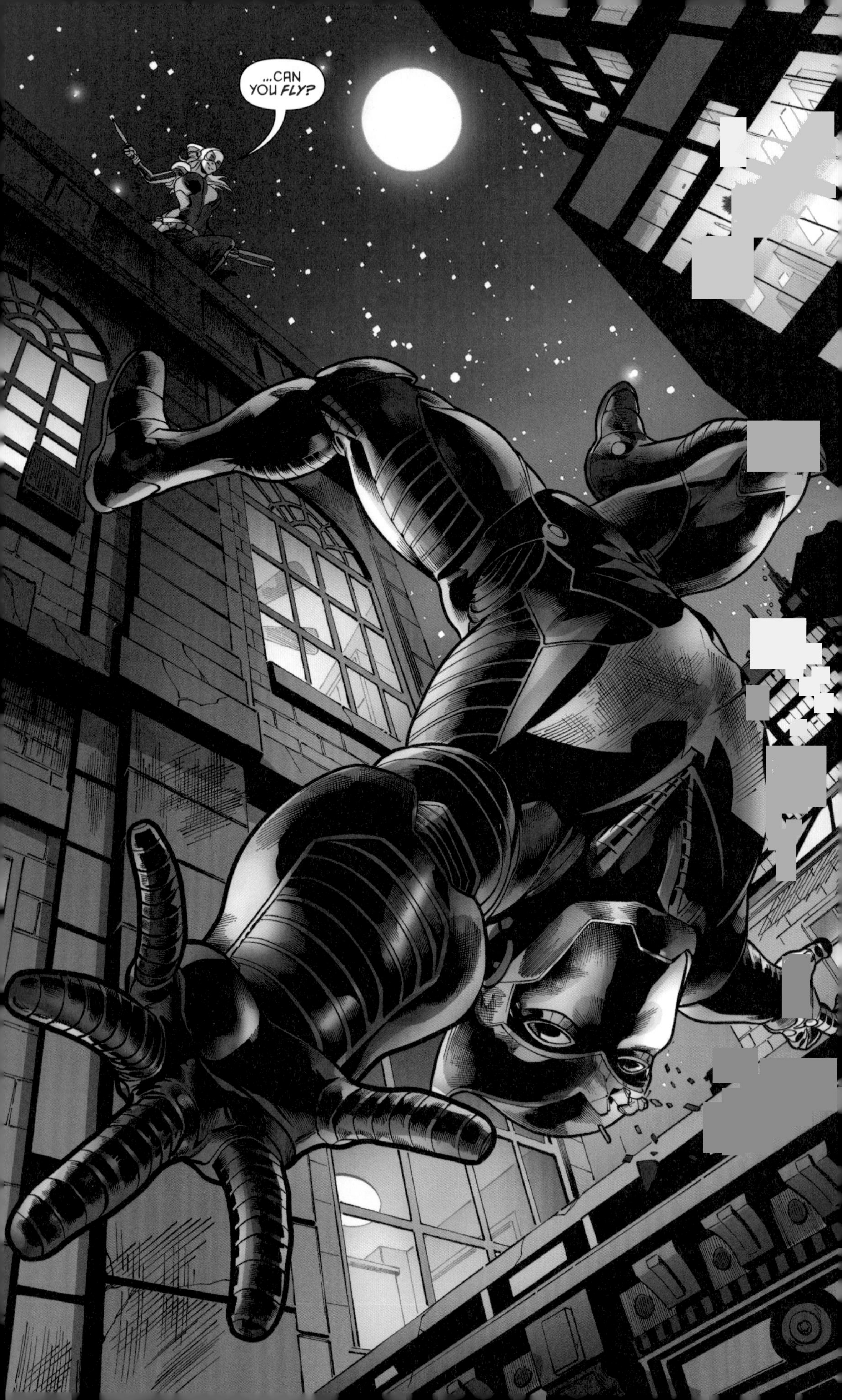
...CAN YOU FLY?

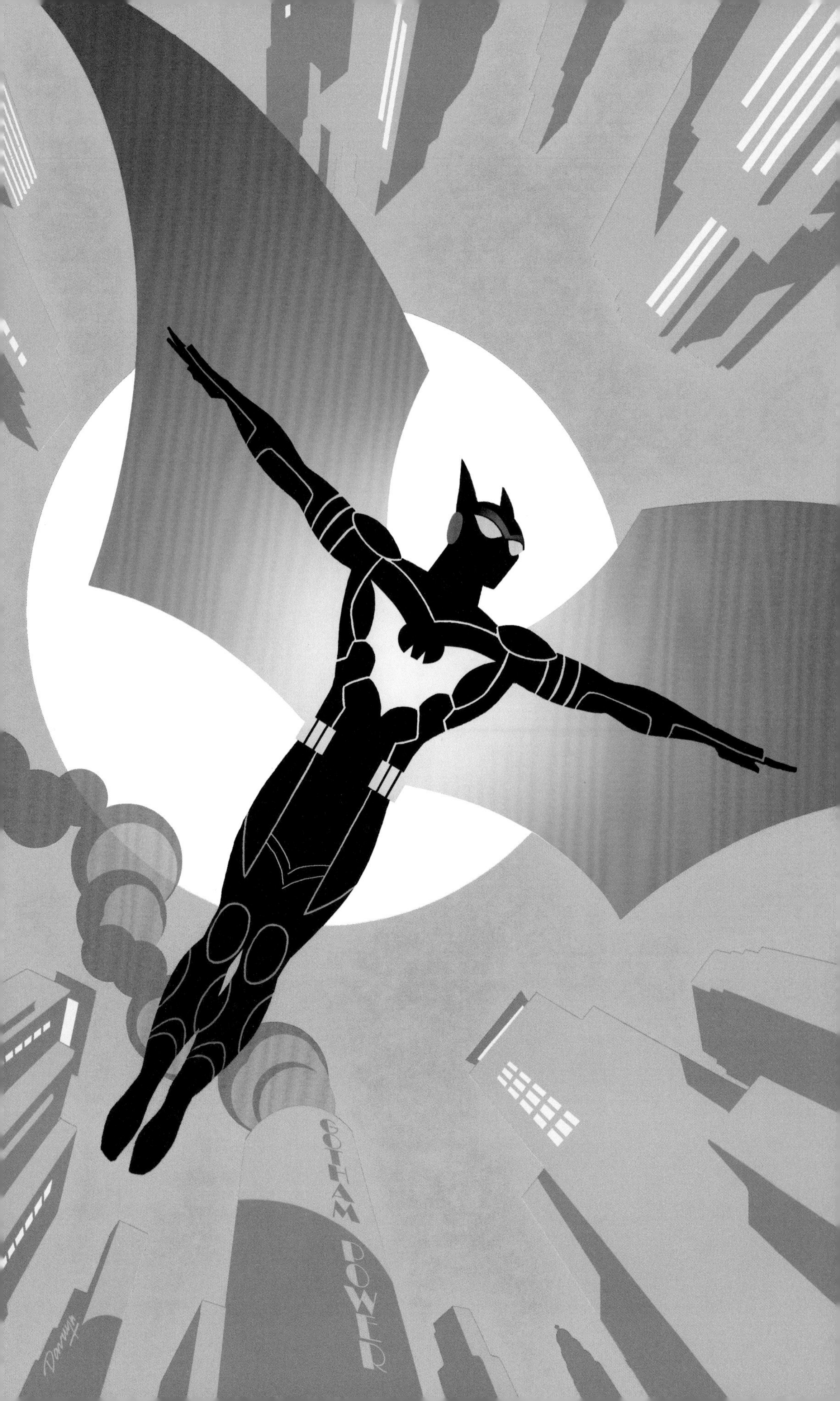
GOTHAM
POWER

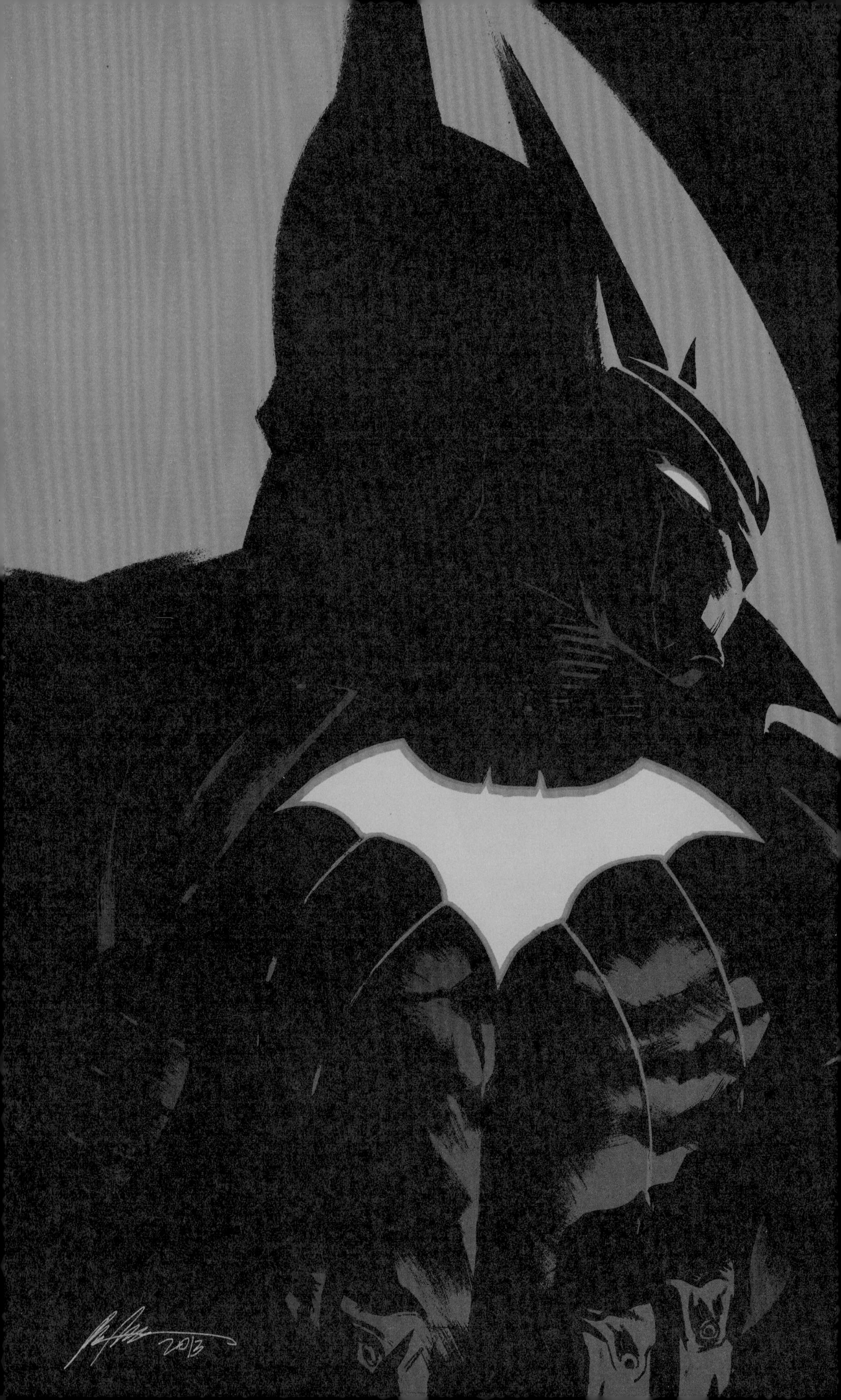

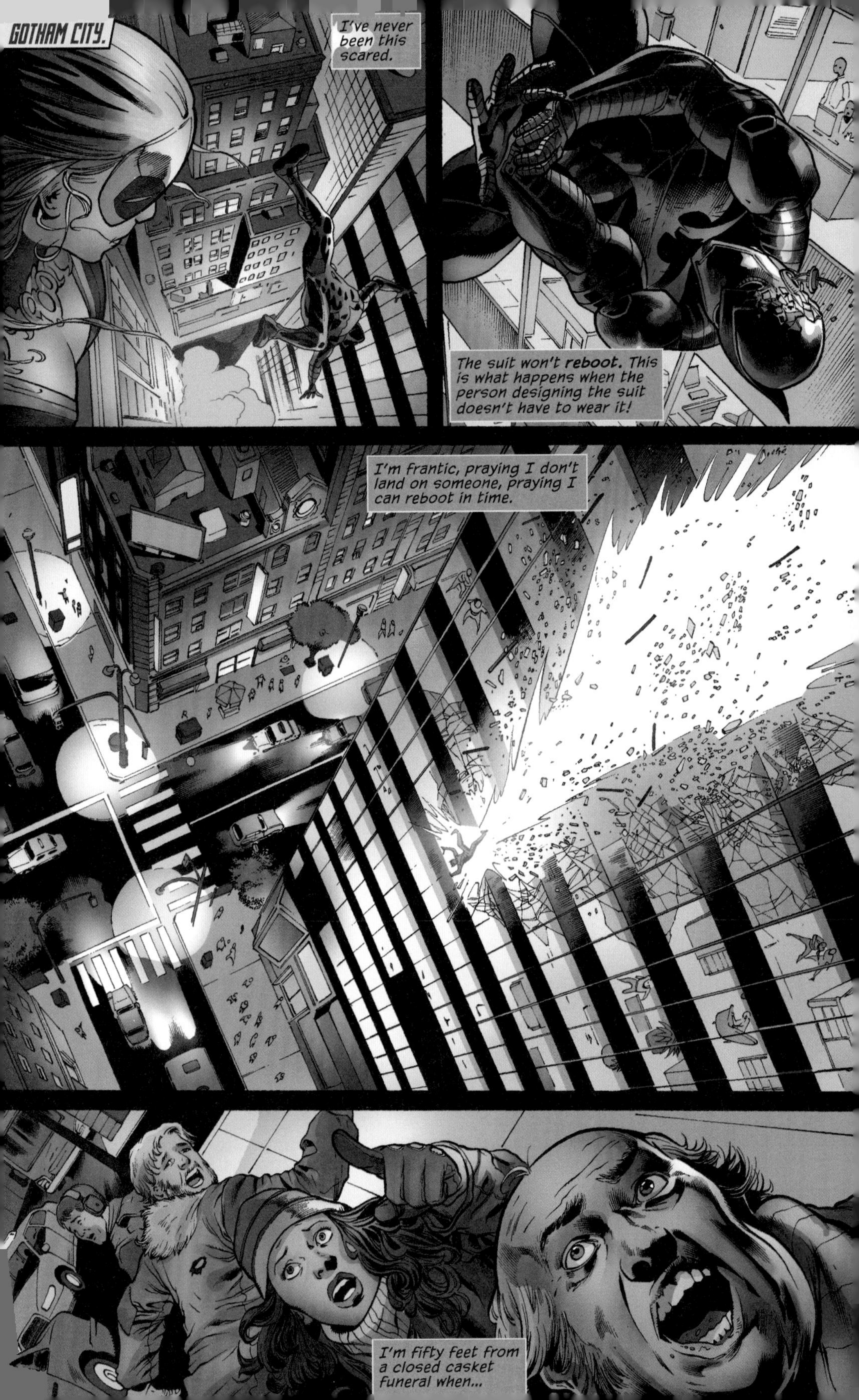
GOTHAM CITY.
I've never been this scared.
The suit won't reboot. This is what happens when the person designing the suit doesn't have to wear it!
I'm frantic, praying I don't land on someone, praying I can reboot in time.
I'm fifty feet from a closed casket funeral when...

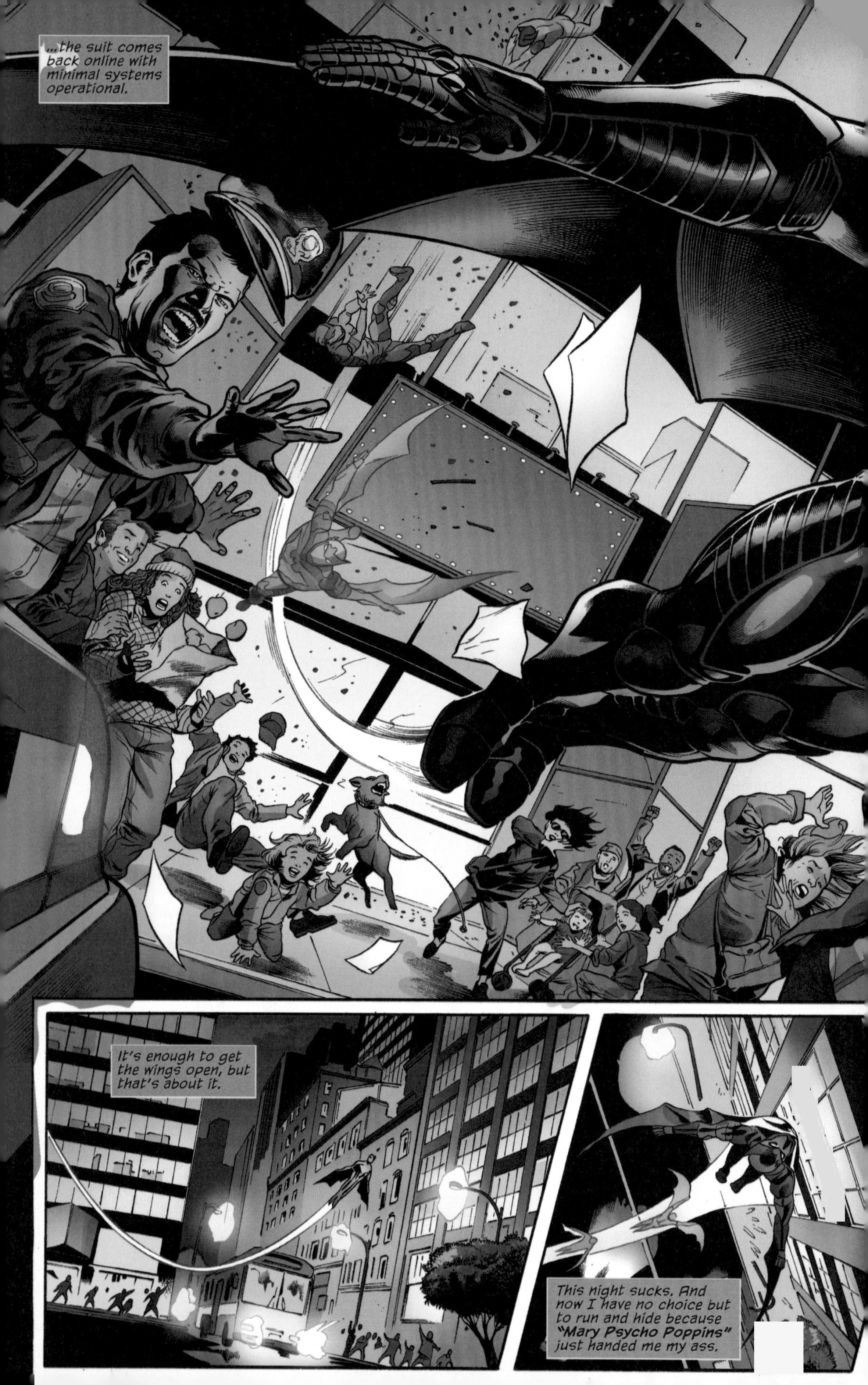
...the suit comes back online with minimal systems operational.
It's enough to get the wings open, but that's about it.
This night sucks. And now I have no choice but to run and hide because "Mary Psycho Poppins" just handed me my ass.

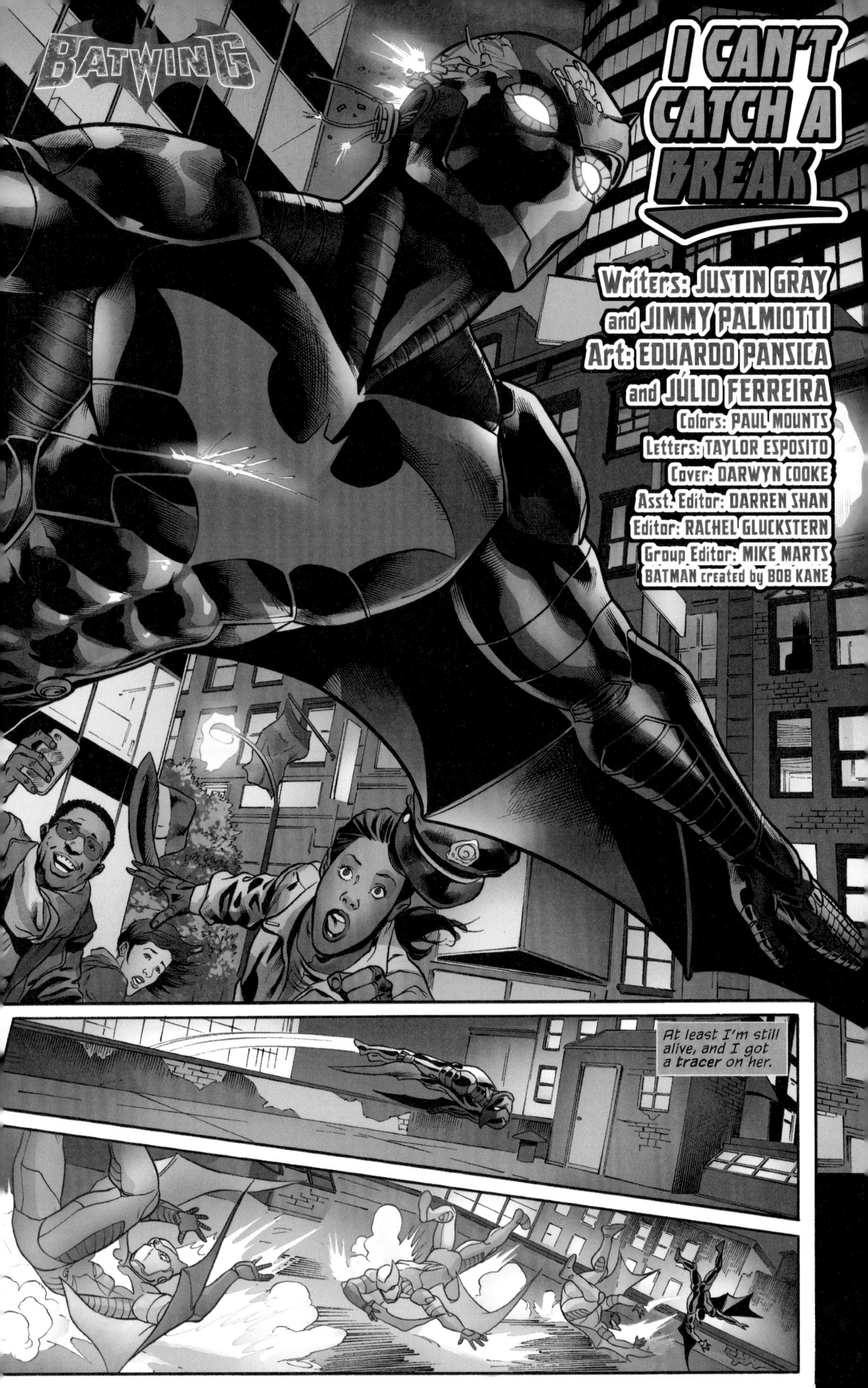
BATWING
I CAN'T CATCH A BREAK
Writers: JUSTIN GRAY and JIMMY PALMIOTTI
Art: EDUARDO PANSICA and JÚLIO FERREIRA
Colors: PAUL MOUNTS
Letters: TAYLOR ESPOSITO
Cover: DARWYN COOKE
Asst. Editor: DARREN SHAN
Editor: RACHEL GLUCKSTERN
Group Editor: MIKE MARTS
BATMAN created by BOB KANE
At least I'm still alive, and I got a tracer on her.

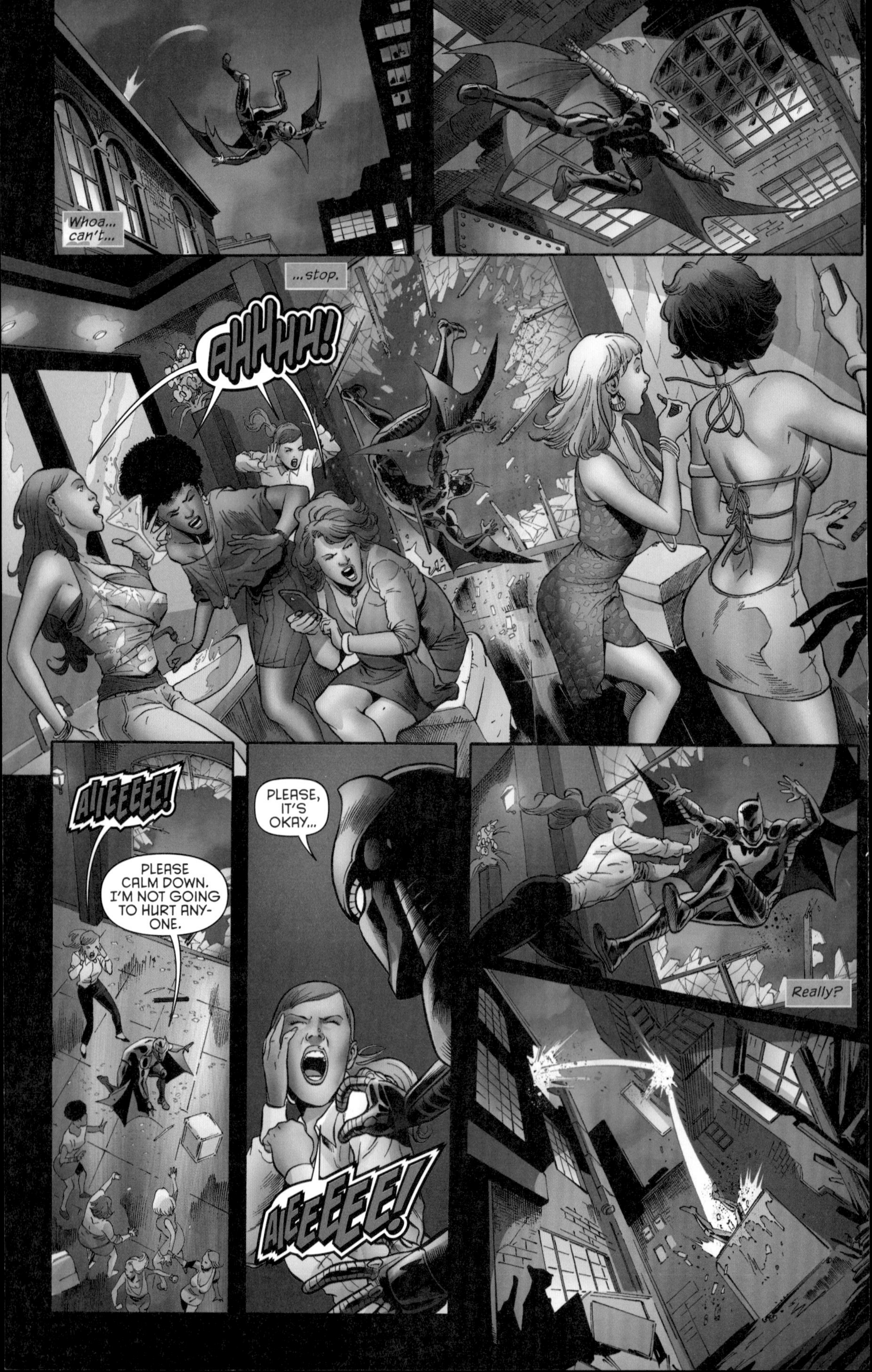
Whoa... can't...
...stop.
AHHHH!
AIIEEEEE!
PLEASE CALM DOWN. I'M NOT GOING TO HURT ANY-ONE.
PLEASE, IT'S OKAY...
AIEEEEE!
Really?

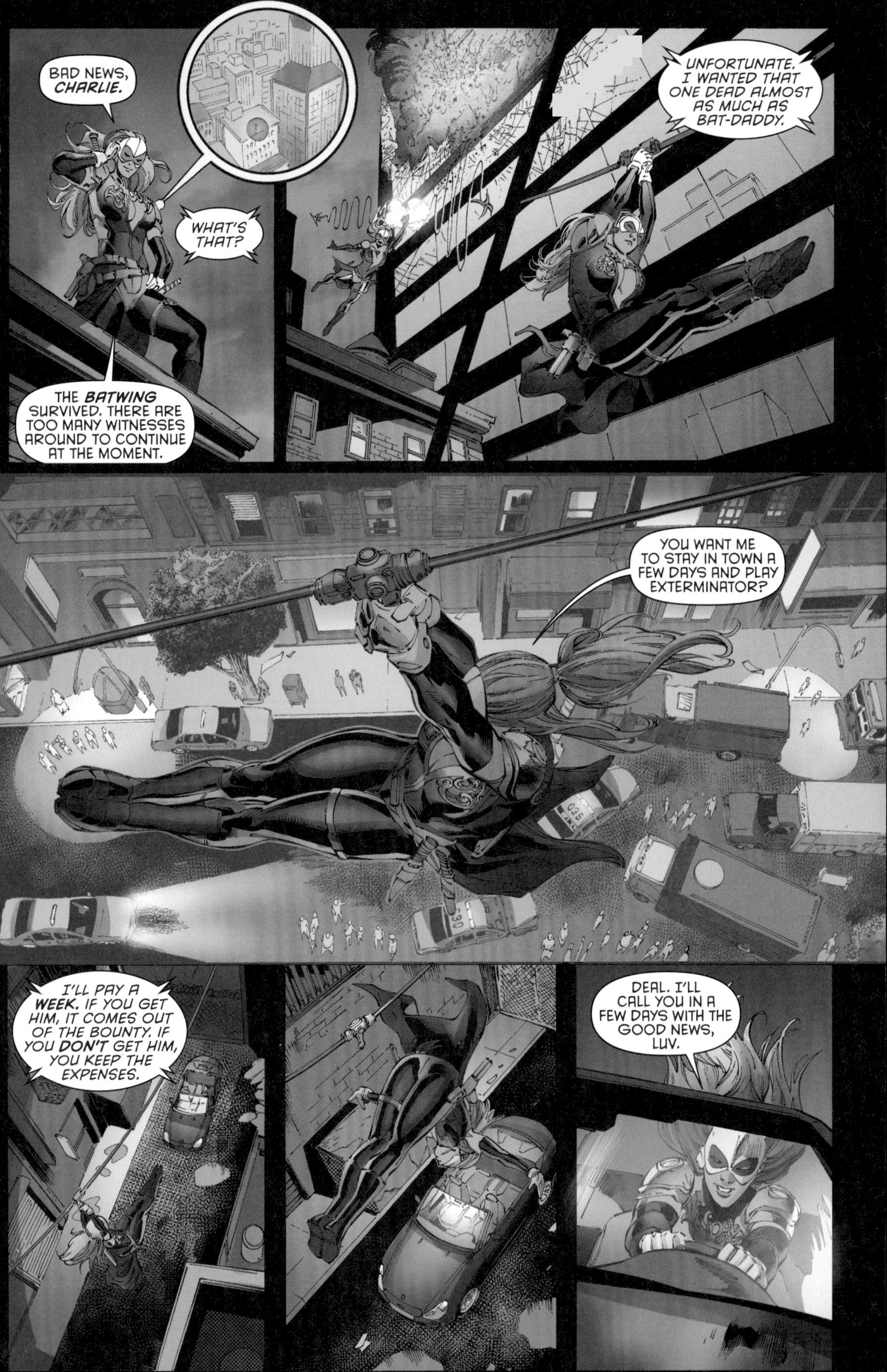
BAD NEWS, CHARLIE.
WHAT'S THAT?
THE BATWING SURVIVED. THERE ARE TOO MANY WITNESSES AROUND TO CONTINUE AT THE MOMENT.
UNFORTUNATE. I WANTED THAT ONE DEAD ALMOST AS MUCH AS BAT-DADDY.
YOU WANT ME TO STAY IN TOWN A FEW DAYS AND PLAY EXTERMINATOR?
I'LL PAY A WEEK. IF YOU GET HIM, IT COMES OUT OF THE BOUNTY. IF YOU DON'T GET HIM, YOU KEEP THE EXPENSES.
DEAL. I'LL CALL YOU IN A FEW DAYS WITH THE GOOD NEWS, LUV.

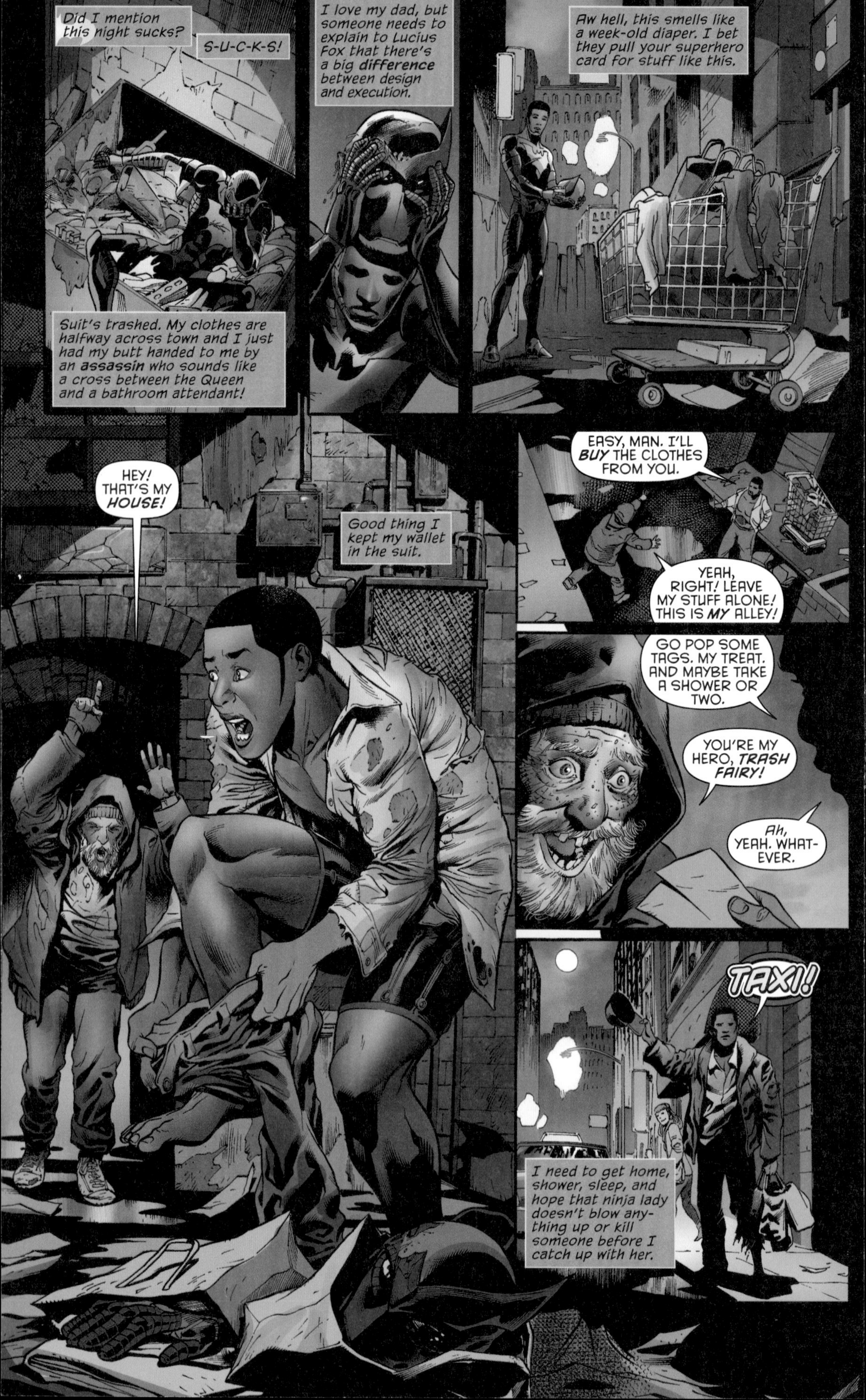
Did I mention this night sucks?
S-U-C-K-S!
Suit's trashed. My clothes are halfway across town and I just had my butt handed to me by an assassin who sounds like a cross between the Queen and a bathroom attendant!
I love my dad, but someone needs to explain to Lucius Fox that there's a big difference between design and execution.
Aw hell, this smells like a week-old diaper. I bet they pull your superhero card for stuff like this.
HEY! THAT'S MY HOUSE!
Good thing I kept my wallet in the suit.
EASY, MAN. I'LL BUY THE CLOTHES FROM YOU.
YEAH, RIGHT! LEAVE MY STUFF ALONE! THIS IS MY ALLEY!
GO POP SOME TAGS. MY TREAT. AND MAYBE TAKE A SHOWER OR TWO.
YOU'RE MY HERO, TRASH FAIRY!
Ah, YEAH. WHAT-EVER.
TAXI!
I need to get home, shower, sleep, and hope that ninja lady doesn't blow any-thing up or kill someone before I catch up with her.

TAKE A *BATH*, FREAK!

LOVE YOU, TOO.

What is Zena doing here?

I CALLED AND LEFT MESSAGES ALL NIGHT.

WAIT, YOU JUST *BROKE UP* WITH ME. NOW YOU'RE HERE WAITING FOR ME? WHAT THE HELL, Z?

IT'S MY... HE'S...MY DAD IS *DEAD*, LUKE. A MASSIVE HEART ATTACK.

I FOUND HIM WHEN I GOT HOME AND I CAN'T GO BACK AND SLEEP IN THE HOUSE.

I DIDN'T KNOW WHERE ELSE TO GO BECAUSE BECCA IS OUT OF TOWN.

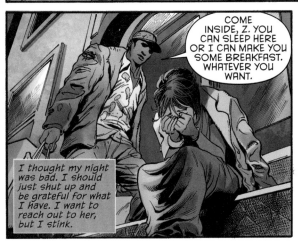

COME INSIDE, Z. YOU CAN SLEEP HERE OR I CAN MAKE YOU SOME BREAKFAST. WHATEVER YOU WANT.

I thought my night was bad. I should just shut up and be grateful for what I have. I want to reach out to her, but I stink.

THANKS...

COME ON.

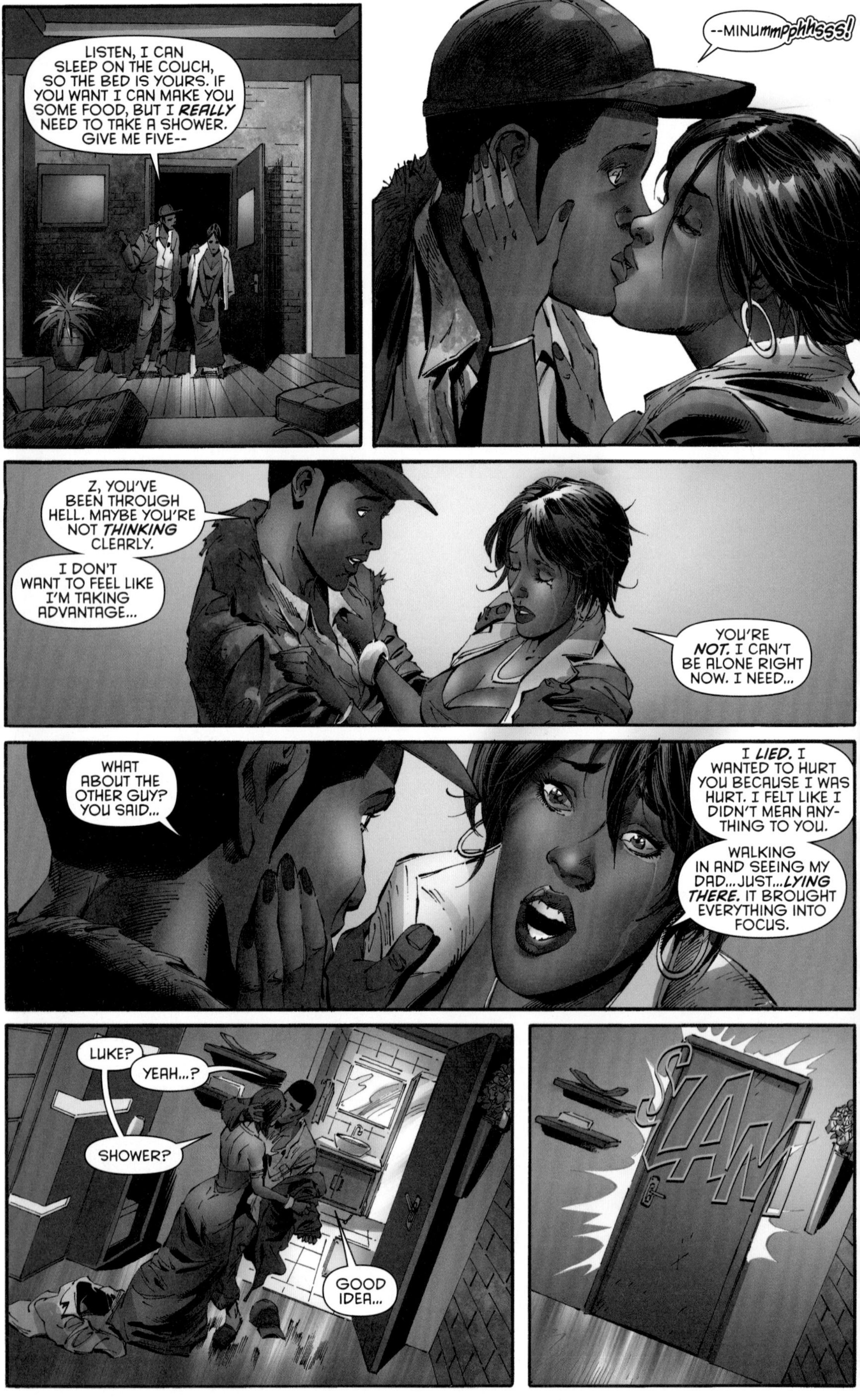
LISTEN, I CAN SLEEP ON THE COUCH, SO THE BED IS YOURS. IF YOU WANT I CAN MAKE YOU SOME FOOD, BUT I REALLY NEED TO TAKE A SHOWER. GIVE ME FIVE--
--MINUmmpphhsss!
Z, YOU'VE BEEN THROUGH HELL. MAYBE YOU'RE NOT THINKING CLEARLY.
I DON'T WANT TO FEEL LIKE I'M TAKING ADVANTAGE...
YOU'RE NOT. I CAN'T BE ALONE RIGHT NOW. I NEED...
WHAT ABOUT THE OTHER GUY? YOU SAID...
I LIED. I WANTED TO HURT YOU BECAUSE I WAS HURT. I FELT LIKE I DIDN'T MEAN ANY-THING TO YOU.
WALKING IN AND SEEING MY DAD...JUST...LYING THERE. IT BROUGHT EVERYTHING INTO FOCUS.
LUKE?
YEAH...?
SHOWER?
GOOD IDEA...
SLAM

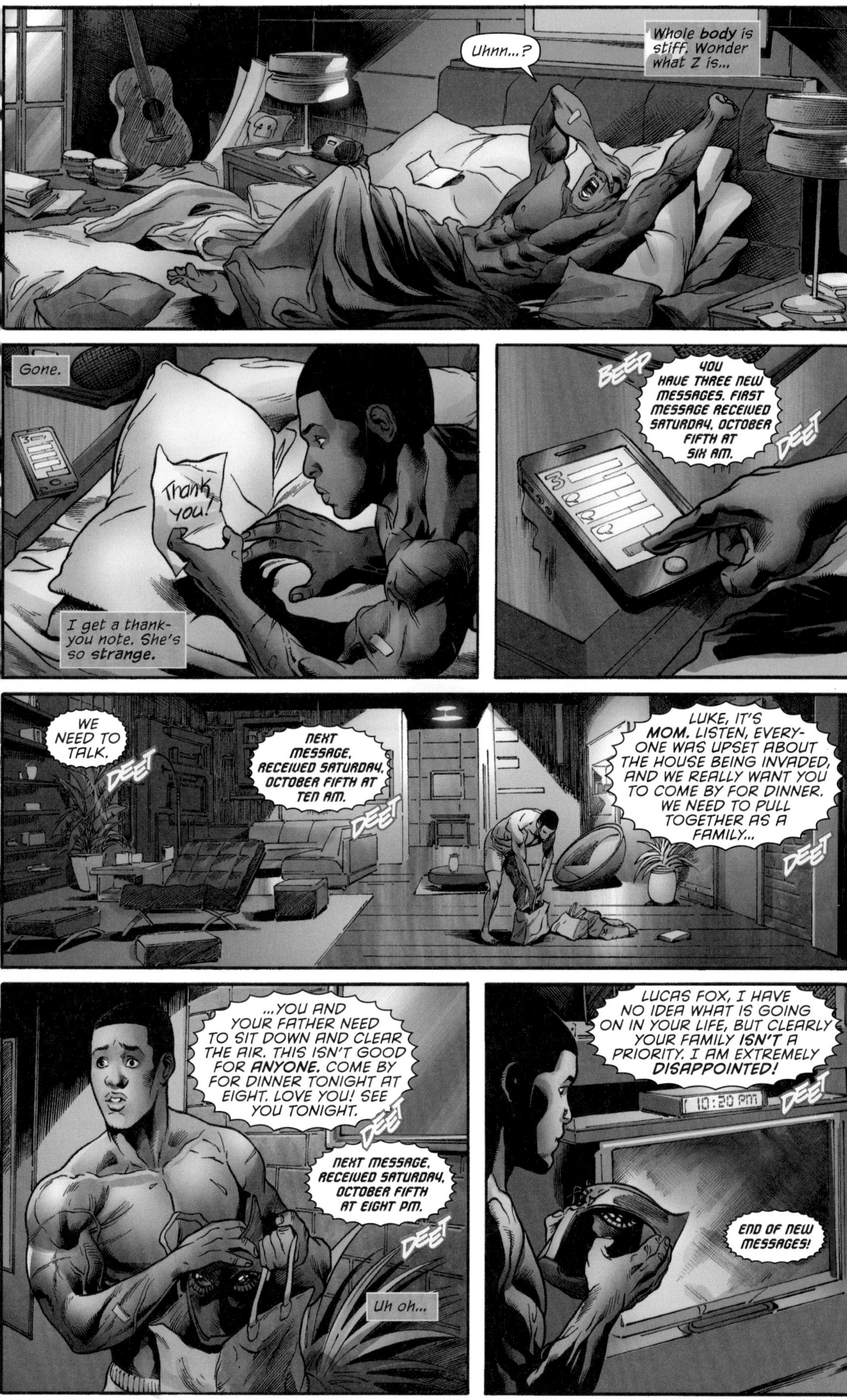
Uhnn...?
Whole body is stiff. Wonder what Z is...
Gone.
Thank you!
I get a thank-you note. She's so strange.
BEEP
YOU HAVE THREE NEW MESSAGES. FIRST MESSAGE RECEIVED SATURDAY, OCTOBER FIFTH AT SIX AM.
DEET
WE NEED TO TALK.
DEET
NEXT MESSAGE, RECEIVED SATURDAY, OCTOBER FIFTH AT TEN AM.
DEET
LUKE, IT'S MOM. LISTEN, EVERYONE WAS UPSET ABOUT THE HOUSE BEING INVADED, AND WE REALLY WANT YOU TO COME BY FOR DINNER. WE NEED TO PULL TOGETHER AS A FAMILY...
DEET
...YOU AND YOUR FATHER NEED TO SIT DOWN AND CLEAR THE AIR. THIS ISN'T GOOD FOR ANYONE. COME BY FOR DINNER TONIGHT AT EIGHT. LOVE YOU! SEE YOU TONIGHT.
DEET
NEXT MESSAGE, RECEIVED SATURDAY, OCTOBER FIFTH AT EIGHT PM.
DEET
Uh oh...
LUCAS FOX, I HAVE NO IDEA WHAT IS GOING ON IN YOUR LIFE, BUT CLEARLY YOUR FAMILY ISN'T A PRIORITY. I AM EXTREMELY DISAPPOINTED!
10:20 PM
DEET
END OF NEW MESSAGES!

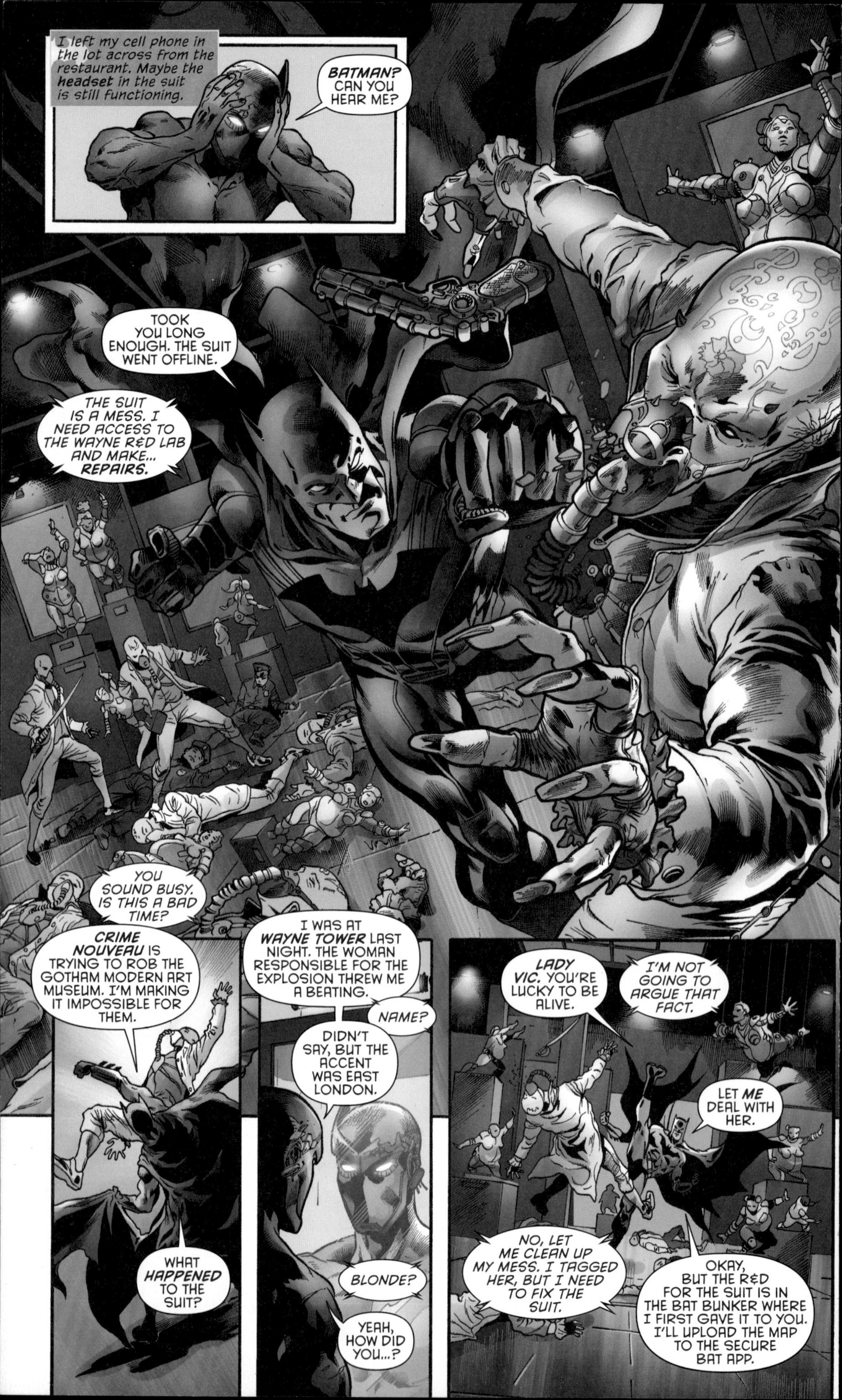
I left my cell phone in the lot across from the restaurant. Maybe the headset in the suit is still functioning.
BATMAN? CAN YOU HEAR ME?
TOOK YOU LONG ENOUGH. THE SUIT WENT OFFLINE.
THE SUIT IS A MESS. I NEED ACCESS TO THE WAYNE R&D LAB AND MAKE... REPAIRS.
YOU SOUND BUSY. IS THIS A BAD TIME?
CRIME NOUVEAU IS TRYING TO ROB THE GOTHAM MODERN ART MUSEUM. I'M MAKING IT IMPOSSIBLE FOR THEM.
WHAT HAPPENED TO THE SUIT?
I WAS AT WAYNE TOWER LAST NIGHT. THE WOMAN RESPONSIBLE FOR THE EXPLOSION THREW ME A BEATING.
NAME?
DIDN'T SAY, BUT THE ACCENT WAS EAST LONDON.
BLONDE?
YEAH, HOW DID YOU...?
LADY VIC. YOU'RE LUCKY TO BE ALIVE.
I'M NOT GOING TO ARGUE THAT FACT.
LET ME DEAL WITH HER.
NO, LET ME CLEAN UP MY MESS. I TAGGED HER, BUT I NEED TO FIX THE SUIT.
OKAY, BUT THE R&D FOR THE SUIT IS IN THE BAT BUNKER WHERE I FIRST GAVE IT TO YOU. I'LL UPLOAD THE MAP TO THE SECURE BAT APP.

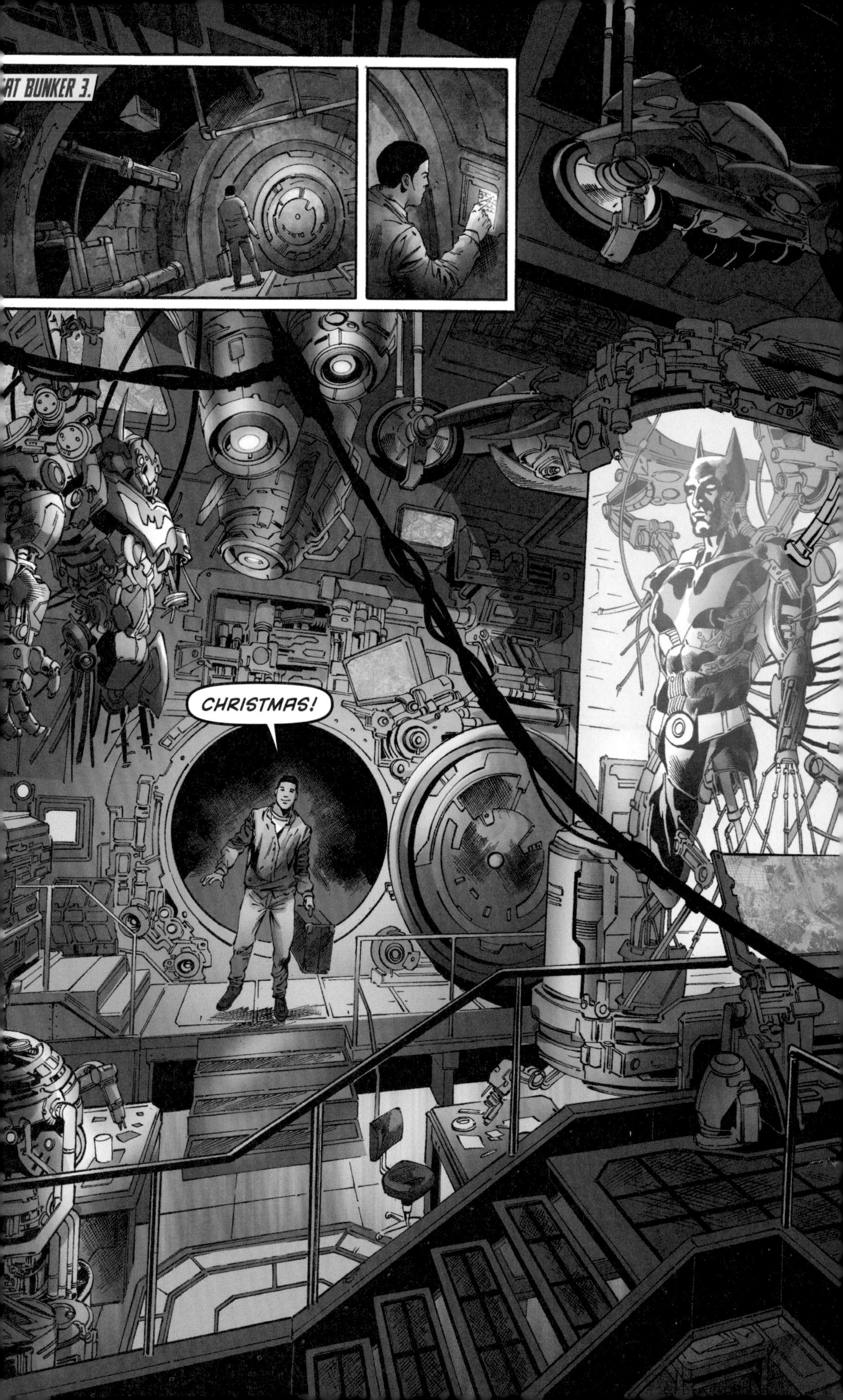
AT BUNKER 3.
CHRISTMAS!

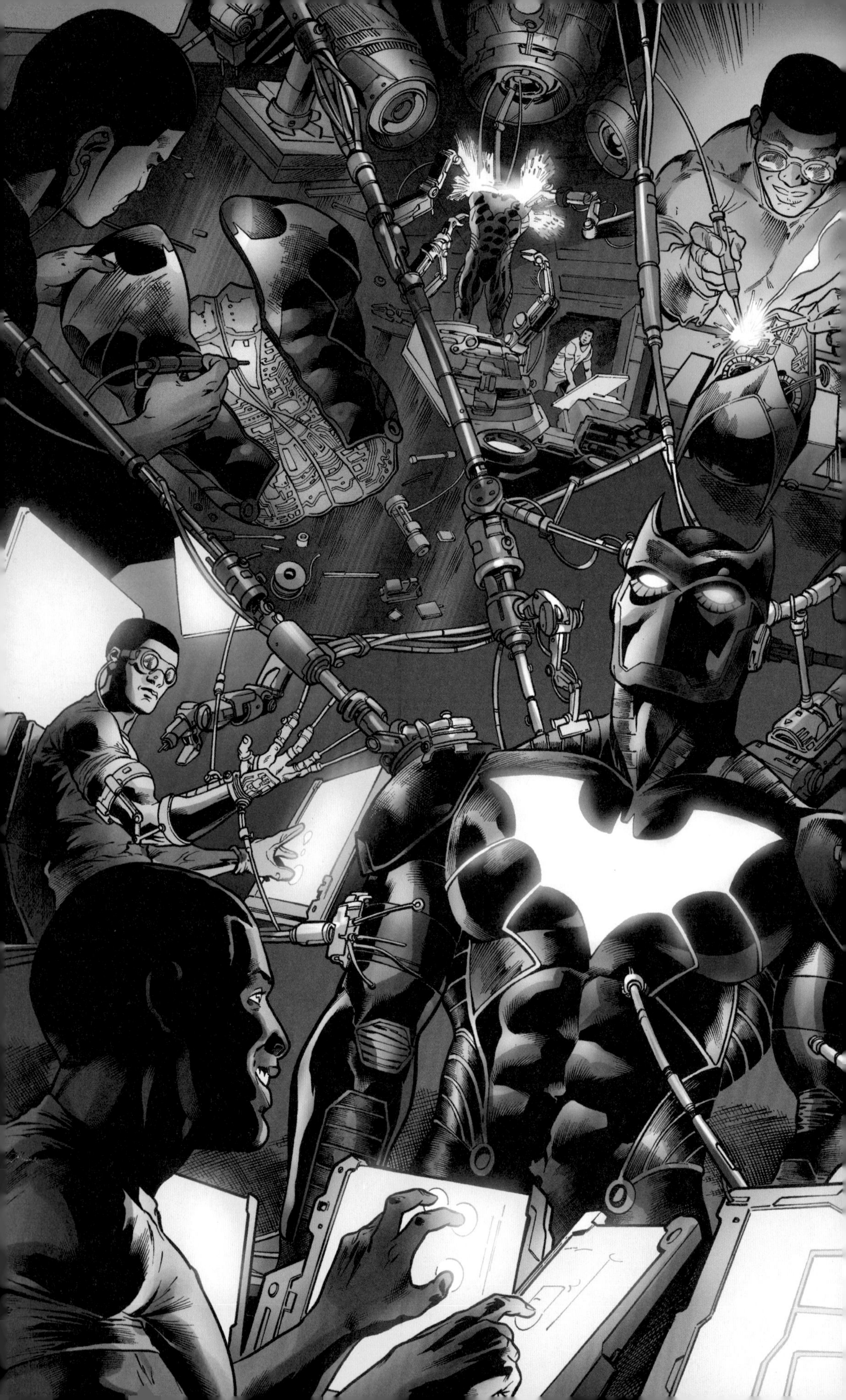

LATER. FOX MANSION.

EXCUSE ME.

LOOK WHO DECIDED TO SHOW UP.

MOM, I'M *SORRY.*

YOU SHOULD BE. I HAD YOUR FATHER CALM, REASONABLE AND READY TO TALK, AND YOU DON'T EVEN HAVE THE DECENCY TO CALL?

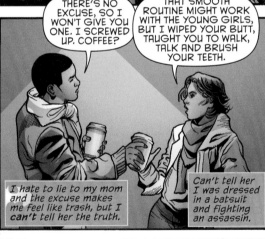

THERE'S NO EXCUSE, SO I WON'T GIVE YOU ONE. I SCREWED UP. COFFEE?

THAT SMOOTH ROUTINE MIGHT WORK WITH THE YOUNG GIRLS, BUT I WIPED YOUR BUTT, TAUGHT YOU TO WALK, TALK AND BRUSH YOUR TEETH.

I hate to lie to my mom and the excuse makes me feel like trash, but I can't tell her the truth.

Can't tell her I was dressed in a batsuit and fighting an assassin.

ZENA'S DAD DIED THE NIGHT BEFORE YOU CALLED. WE WERE UP ALL NIGHT AND BY THE TIME I WOKE UP I WAS ALREADY MORE THAN AN HOUR LATE FOR DINNER.

I NEVER EVEN SAW YOUR MESSAGES.

OH. THAT POOR GIRL.

I'M HERE NOW, SO ANYTHING YOU NEED, JUST ASK.

EVERYTHING IS UNDER CONTROL. YOU SHOULD BE WITH ZENA. I *LIKE* HER.

WE'LL SET UP ANOTHER DINNER. I PROMISE.

SURE, AND LET ME KNOW WHEN THE WAKE IS AND WHERE WE CAN SEND FLOWERS.

THANKS, MOM. LOVE YOU.

LOVE YOU TOO, SON.

I feel like such a jerk right now.

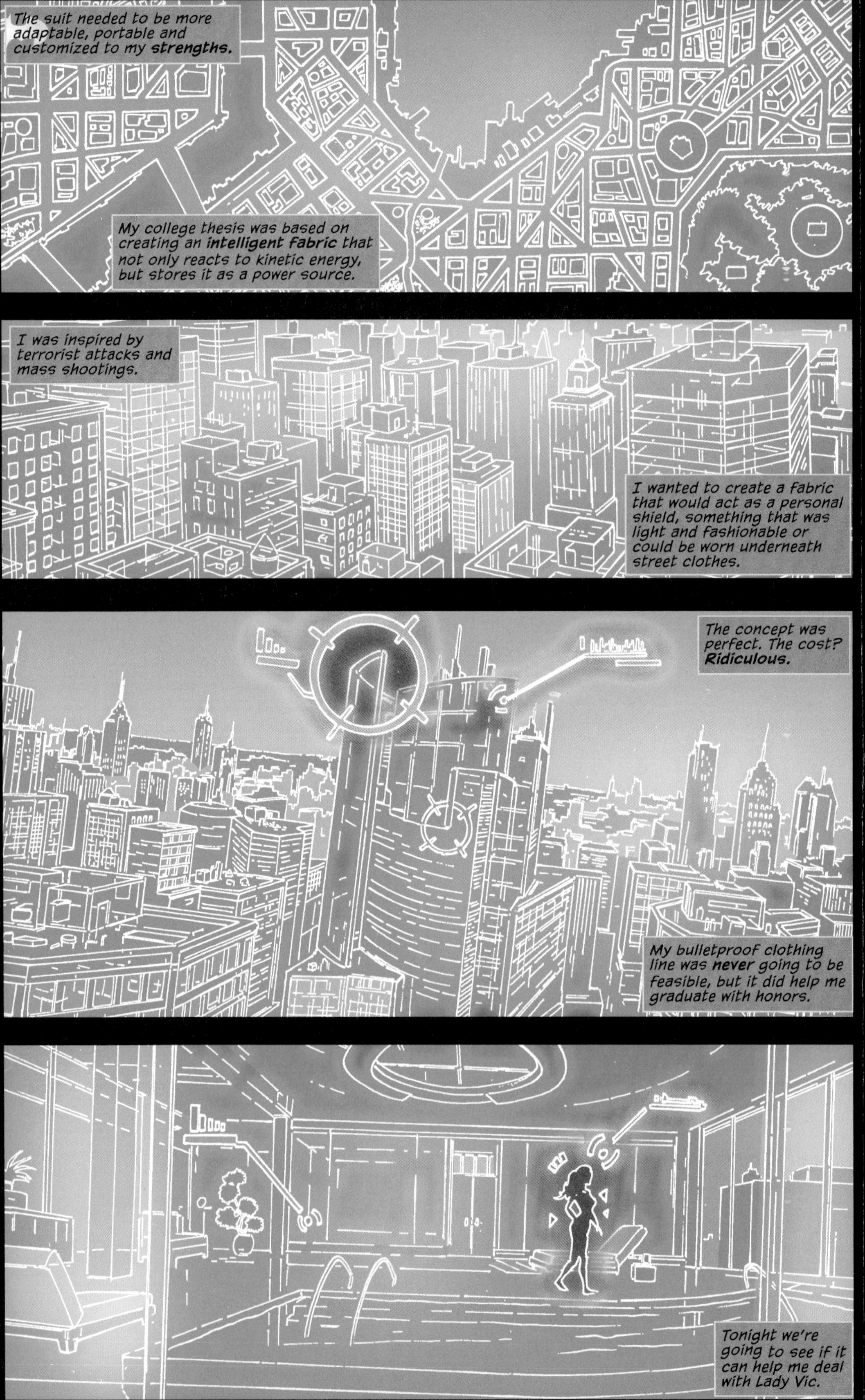

The suit needed to be more adaptable, portable and customized to my **strengths.**
My college thesis was based on creating an **intelligent fabric** that not only reacts to kinetic energy, but stores it as a power source.
I was inspired by terrorist attacks and mass shootings.
I wanted to create a fabric that would act as a personal shield, something that was light and fashionable or could be worn underneath street clothes.
The concept was perfect. The cost? **Ridiculous.**
My bulletproof clothing line was **never** going to be feasible, but it did help me graduate with honors.
Tonight we're going to see if it can help me deal with Lady Vic.

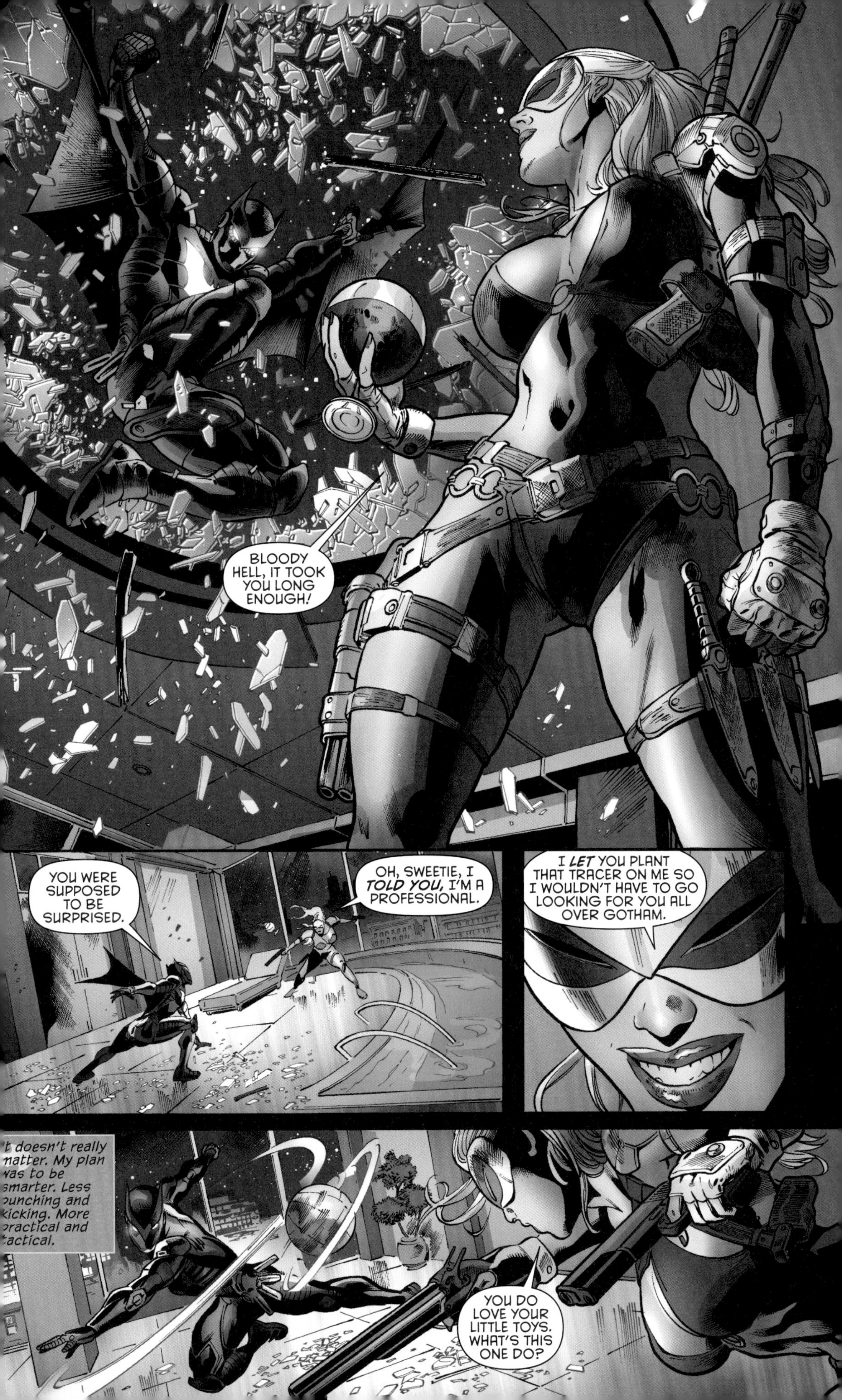
BLOODY HELL, IT TOOK YOU LONG ENOUGH!
YOU WERE SUPPOSED TO BE SURPRISED.
OH, SWEETIE, I TOLD YOU, I'M A PROFESSIONAL.
I LET YOU PLANT THAT TRACER ON ME SO I WOULDN'T HAVE TO GO LOOKING FOR YOU ALL OVER GOTHAM.
It doesn't really matter. My plan was to be smarter. Less punching and kicking. More practical and tactical.
YOU DO LOVE YOUR LITTLE TOYS. WHAT'S THIS ONE DO?

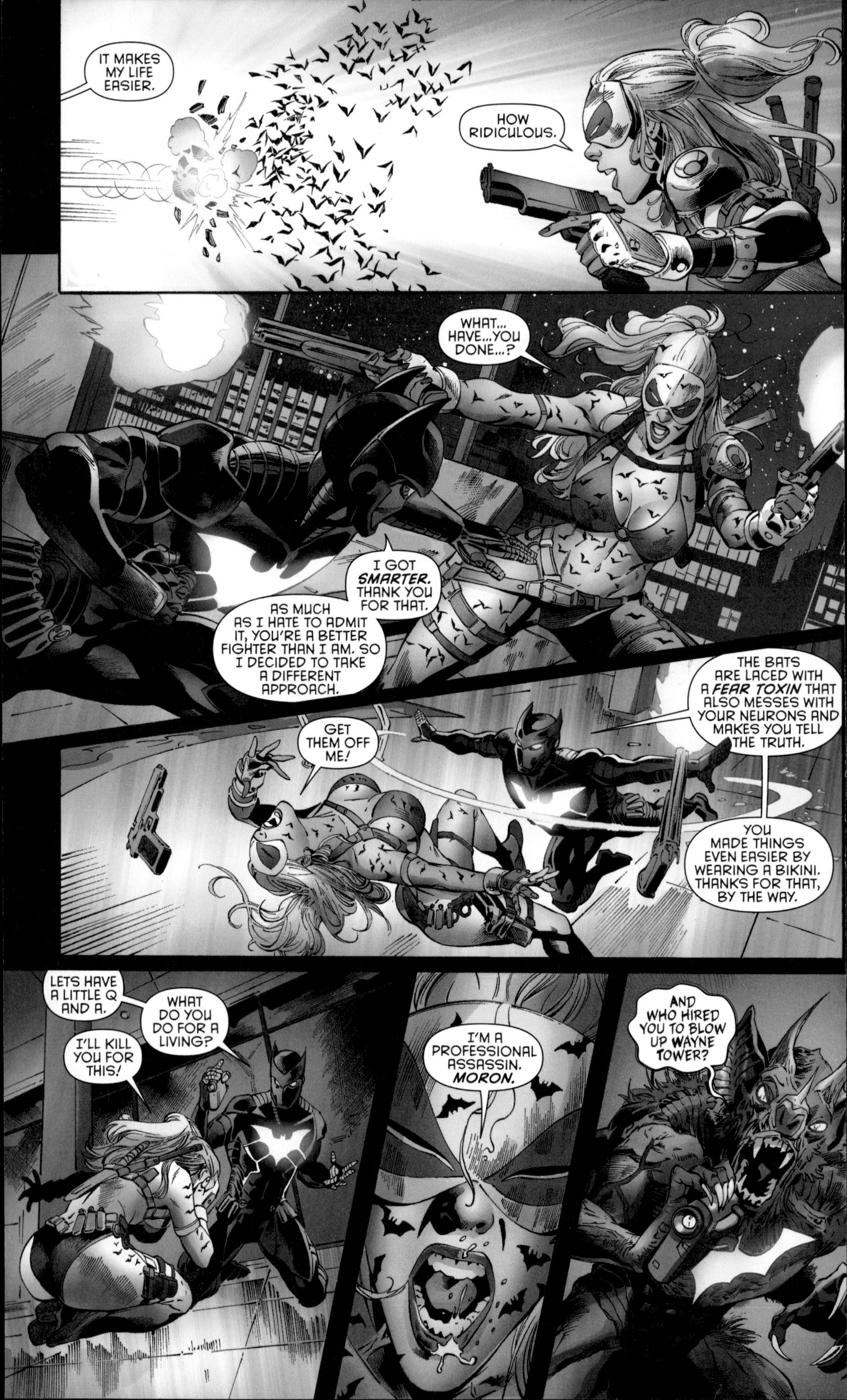
IT MAKES MY LIFE EASIER.
HOW RIDICULOUS.
WHAT... HAVE... YOU DONE...?
I GOT SMARTER. THANK YOU FOR THAT.
AS MUCH AS I HATE TO ADMIT IT, YOU'RE A BETTER FIGHTER THAN I AM. SO I DECIDED TO TAKE A DIFFERENT APPROACH.
THE BATS ARE LACED WITH A FEAR TOXIN THAT ALSO MESSES WITH YOUR NEURONS AND MAKES YOU TELL THE TRUTH.
GET THEM OFF ME!
YOU MADE THINGS EVEN EASIER BY WEARING A BIKINI. THANKS FOR THAT, BY THE WAY.
LETS HAVE A LITTLE Q AND A.
I'LL KILL YOU FOR THIS!
WHAT DO YOU DO FOR A LIVING?
I'M A PROFESSIONAL ASSASSIN. MORON.
AND WHO HIRED YOU TO BLOW UP WAYNE TOWER?

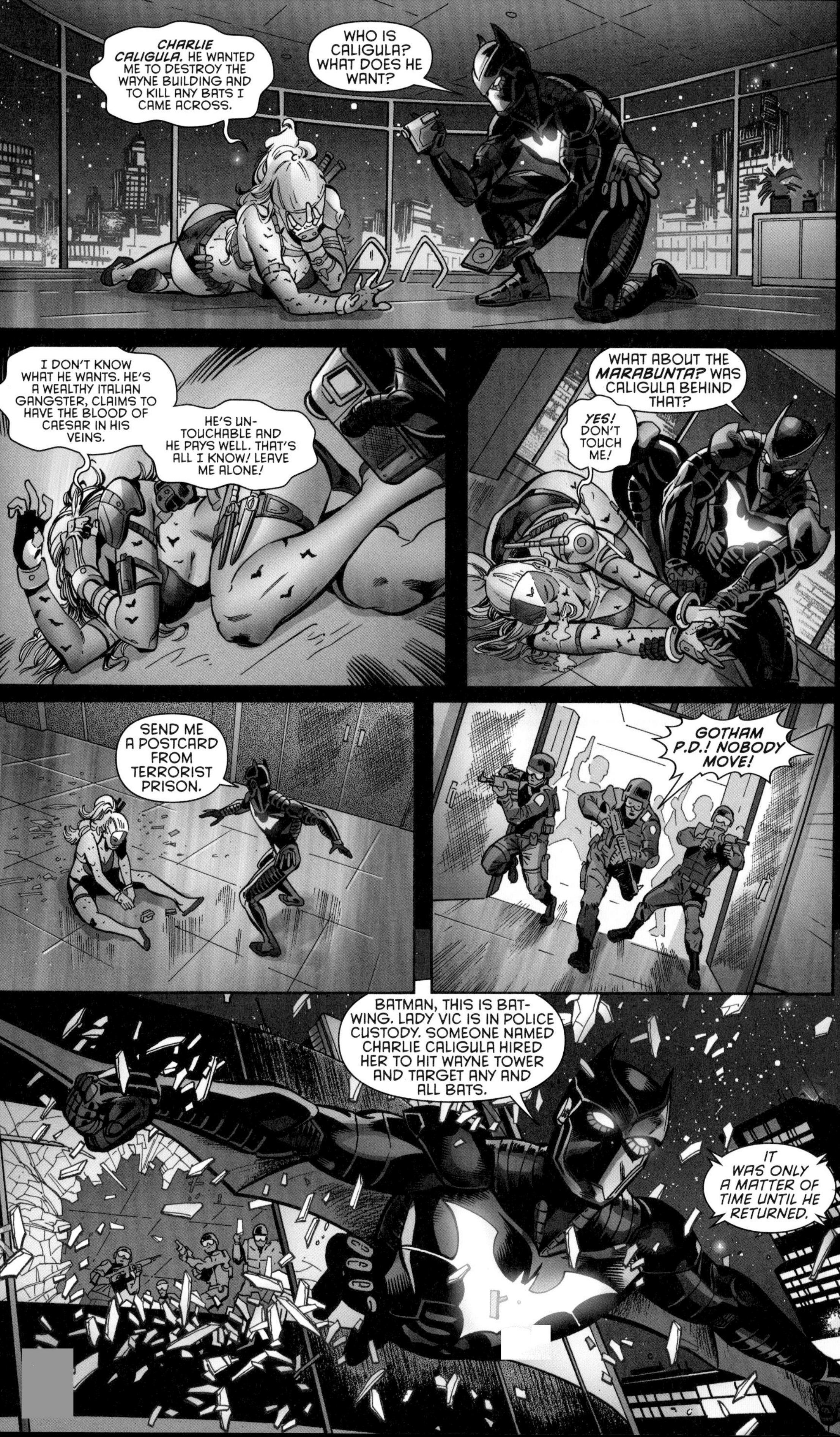
CHARLIE CALIGULA. HE WANTED ME TO DESTROY THE WAYNE BUILDING AND TO KILL ANY BATS I CAME ACROSS.
WHO IS CALIGULA? WHAT DOES HE WANT?
I DON'T KNOW WHAT HE WANTS. HE'S A WEALTHY ITALIAN GANGSTER, CLAIMS TO HAVE THE BLOOD OF CAESAR IN HIS VEINS.
HE'S UNTOUCHABLE AND HE PAYS WELL. THAT'S ALL I KNOW! LEAVE ME ALONE!
WHAT ABOUT THE MARABUNTA? WAS CALIGULA BEHIND THAT?
YES! DON'T TOUCH ME!
SEND ME A POSTCARD FROM TERRORIST PRISON.
GOTHAM P.D.! NOBODY MOVE!
BATMAN, THIS IS BATWING. LADY VIC IS IN POLICE CUSTODY. SOMEONE NAMED CHARLIE CALIGULA HIRED HER TO HIT WAYNE TOWER AND TARGET ANY AND ALL BATS.
IT WAS ONLY A MATTER OF TIME UNTIL HE RETURNED.

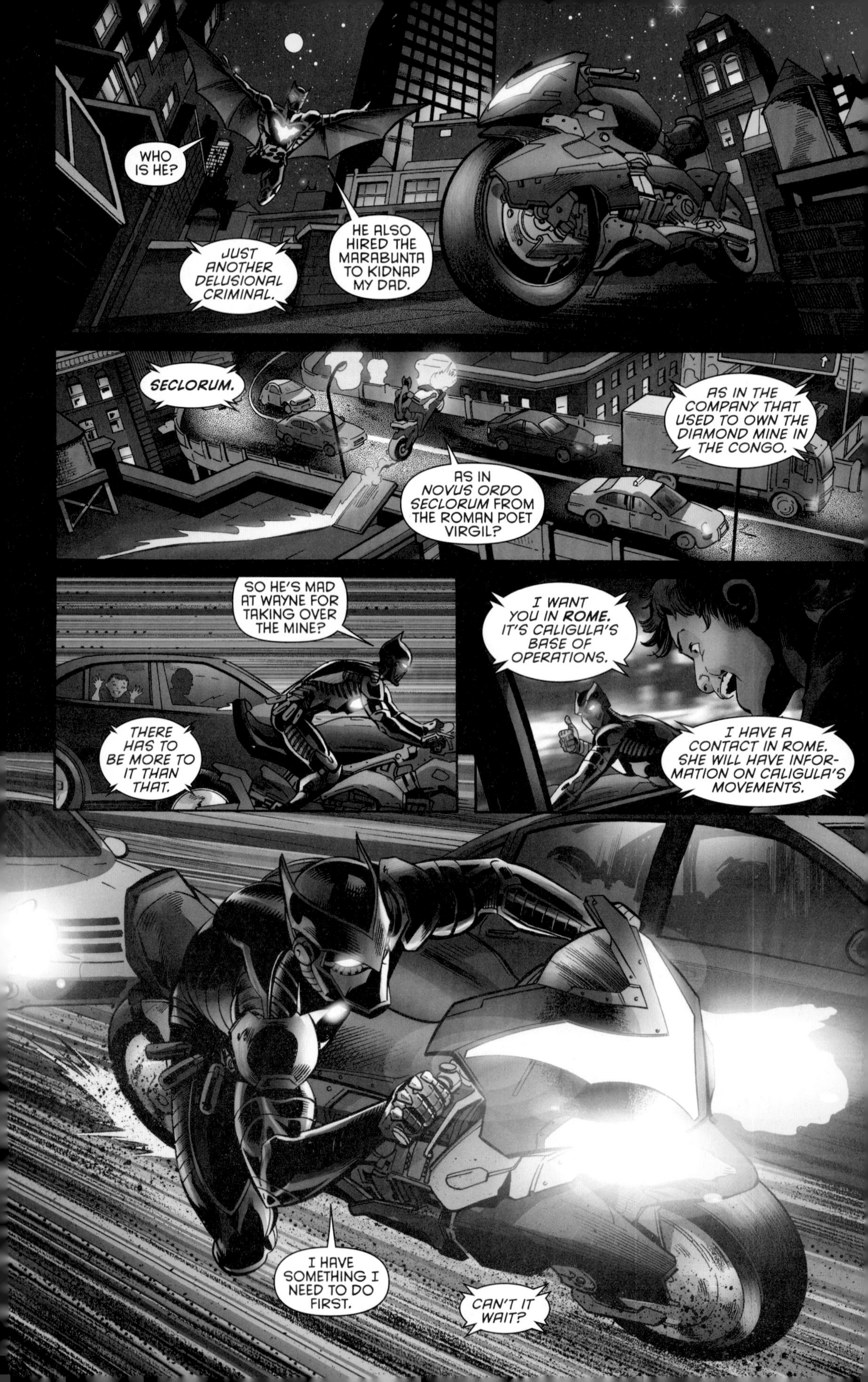
WHO IS HE?
JUST ANOTHER DELUSIONAL CRIMINAL.
HE ALSO HIRED THE MARABUNTA TO KIDNAP MY DAD.
SECLORUM.
AS IN NOVUS ORDO SECLORUM FROM THE ROMAN POET VIRGIL?
AS IN THE COMPANY THAT USED TO OWN THE DIAMOND MINE IN THE CONGO.
SO HE'S MAD AT WAYNE FOR TAKING OVER THE MINE?
THERE HAS TO BE MORE TO IT THAN THAT.
I WANT YOU IN ROME. IT'S CALIGULA'S BASE OF OPERATIONS.
I HAVE A CONTACT IN ROME. SHE WILL HAVE INFORMATION ON CALIGULA'S MOVEMENTS.
I HAVE SOMETHING I NEED TO DO FIRST.
CAN'T IT WAIT?

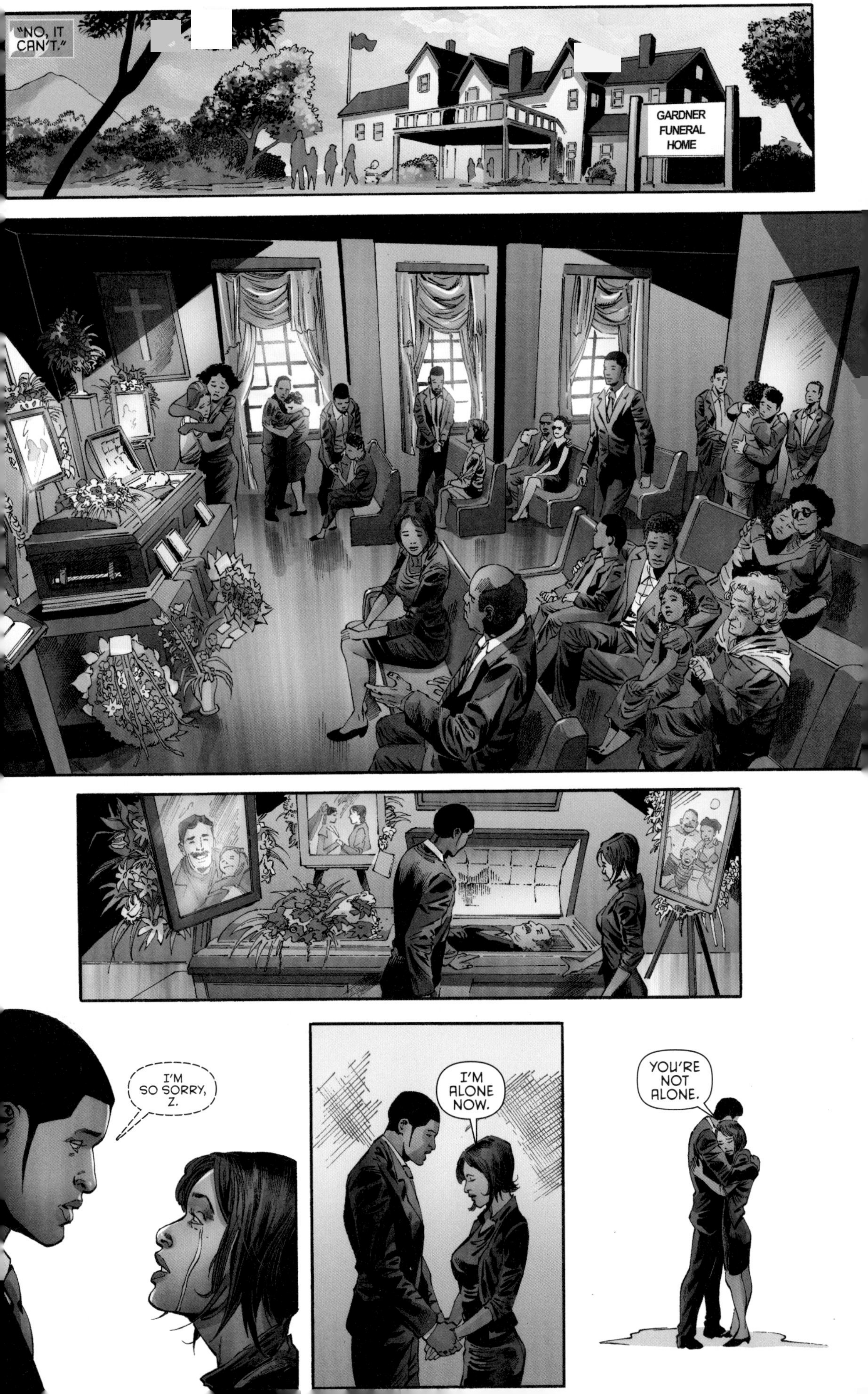
"NO, IT CAN'T."
GARDNER FUNERAL HOME
I'M SO SORRY, Z.
I'M ALONE NOW.
YOU'RE NOT ALONE.

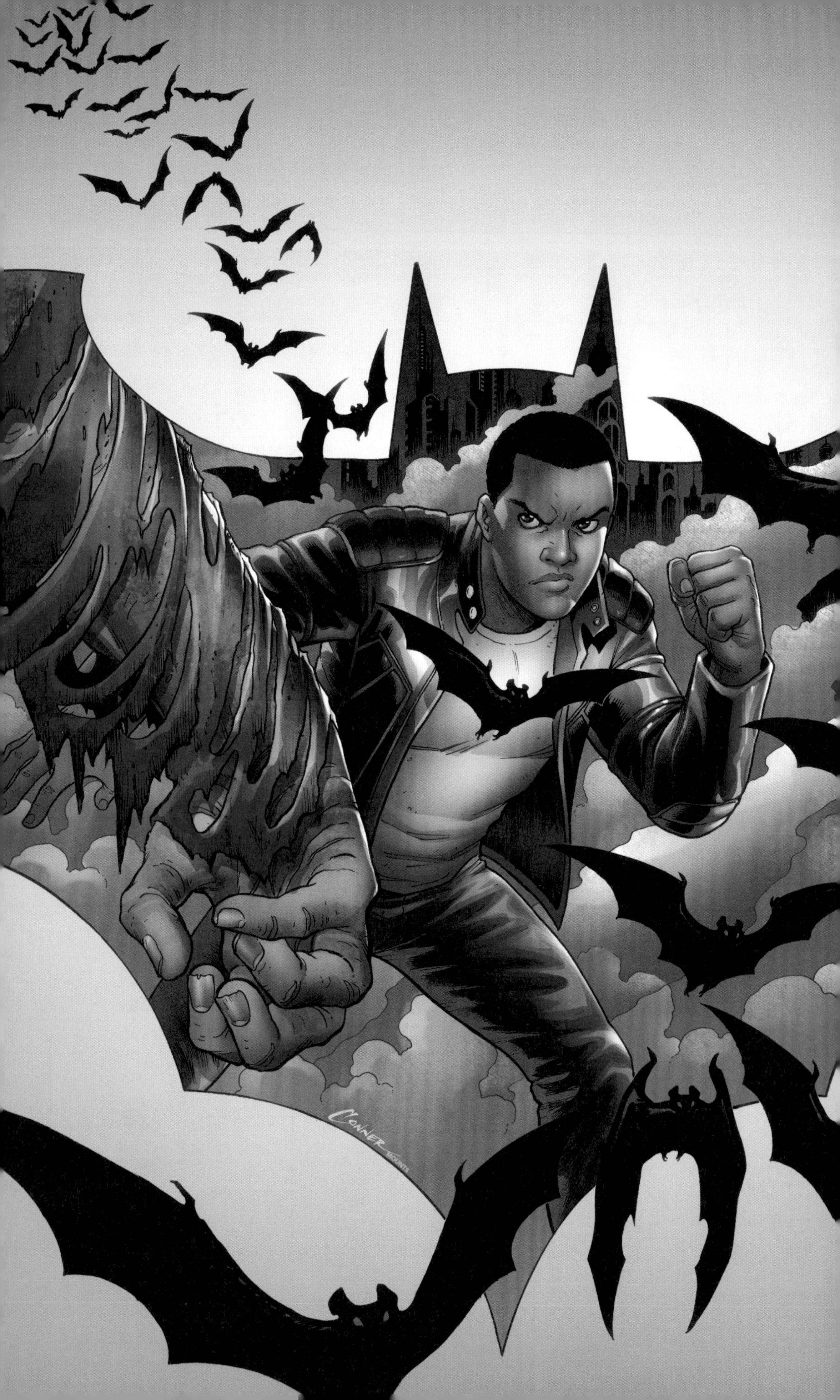
Conner
Mounts

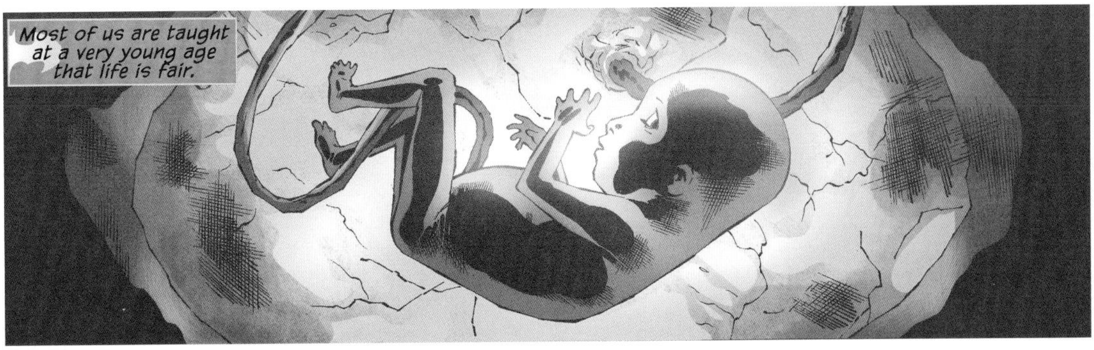
Most of us are taught at a very young age that life is fair.

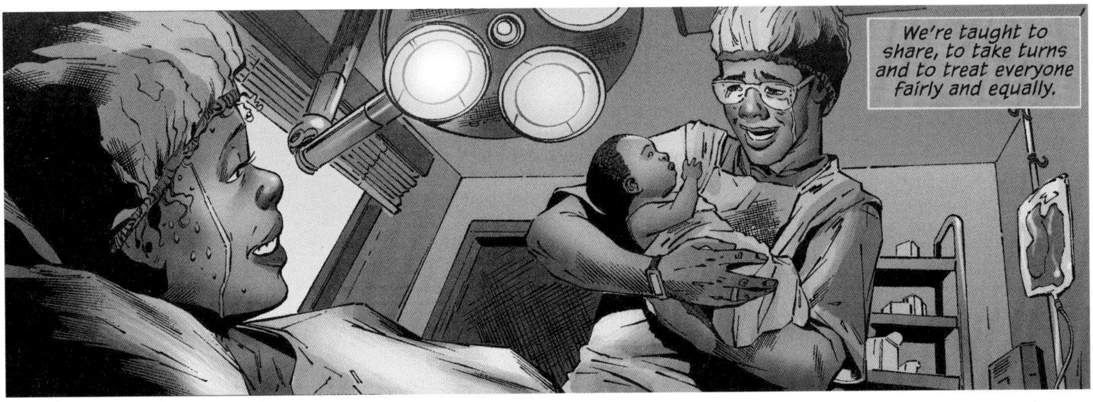
We're taught to share, to take turns and to treat everyone fairly and equally.

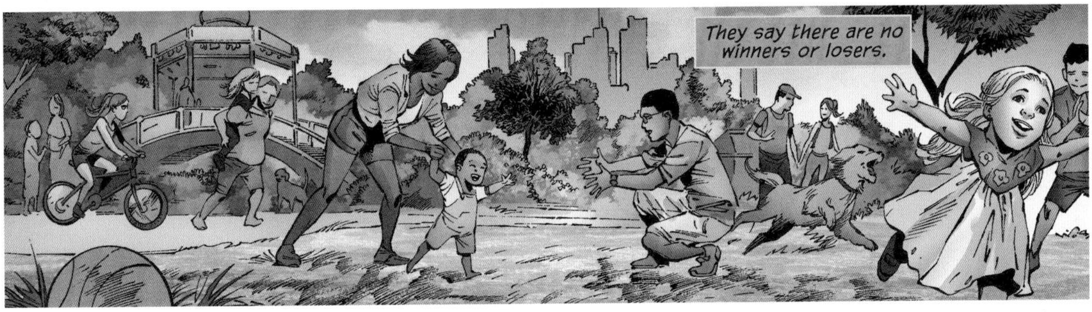
They say there are no winners or losers.

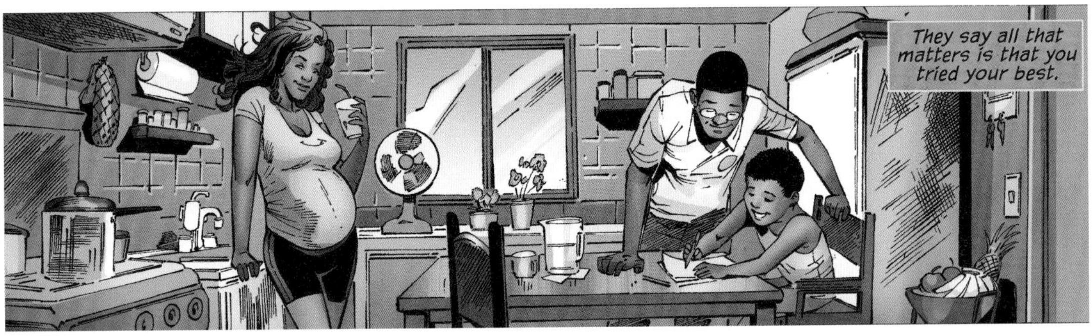
They say all that matters is that you tried your best.

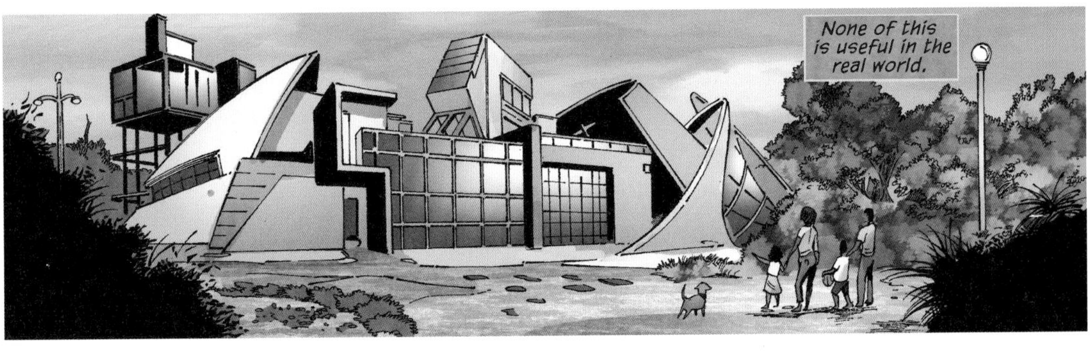
None of this is useful in the real world.

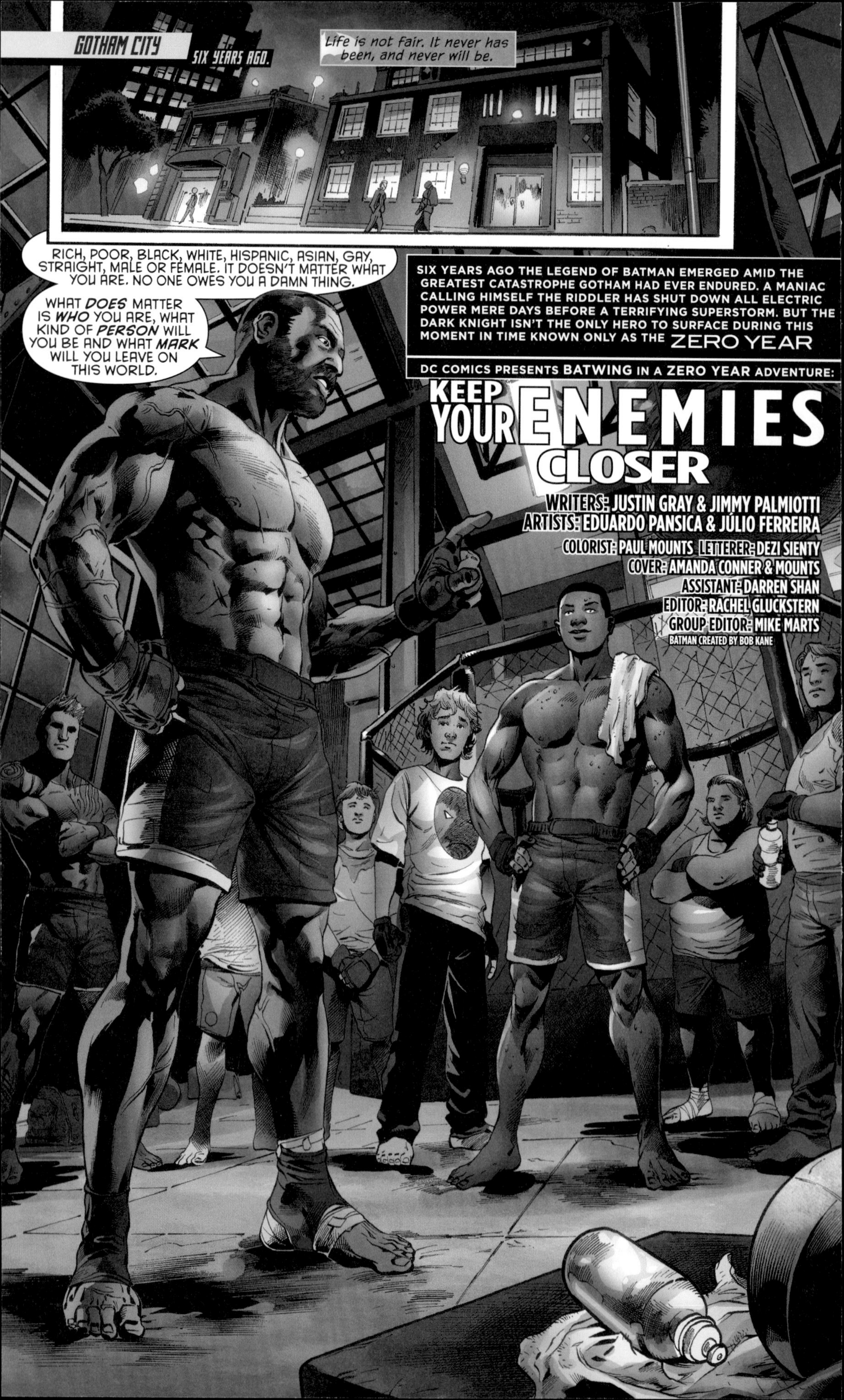

GOTHAM CITY
SIX YEARS AGO.
Life is not fair. It never has been, and never will be.
RICH, POOR, BLACK, WHITE, HISPANIC, ASIAN, GAY, STRAIGHT, MALE OR FEMALE. IT DOESN'T MATTER WHAT YOU ARE. NO ONE OWES YOU A DAMN THING.
WHAT DOES MATTER IS WHO YOU ARE, WHAT KIND OF PERSON WILL YOU BE AND WHAT MARK WILL YOU LEAVE ON THIS WORLD.
SIX YEARS AGO THE LEGEND OF BATMAN EMERGED AMID THE GREATEST CATASTROPHE GOTHAM HAD EVER ENDURED. A MANIAC CALLING HIMSELF THE RIDDLER HAS SHUT DOWN ALL ELECTRIC POWER MERE DAYS BEFORE A TERRIFYING SUPERSTORM. BUT THE DARK KNIGHT ISN'T THE ONLY HERO TO SURFACE DURING THIS MOMENT IN TIME KNOWN ONLY AS THE ZERO YEAR
DC COMICS PRESENTS BATWING IN A ZERO YEAR ADVENTURE:
KEEP YOUR ENEMIES CLOSER
WRITERS: JUSTIN GRAY & JIMMY PALMIOTTI
ARTISTS: EDUARDO PANSICA & JÚLIO FERREIRA
COLORIST: PAUL MOUNTS LETTERER: DEZI SIENTY
COVER: AMANDA CONNER & MOUNTS
ASSISTANT: DARREN SHAN
EDITOR: RACHEL GLUCKSTERN
GROUP EDITOR: MIKE MARTS
BATMAN CREATED BY BOB KANE

PAD UP AND PAIR UP. WE'RE GOING TO BE WORKING ON OUR STRIKING.

YOU GO FIRST, RUSS.

I DON'T KNOW, LUKE. THIS ISN'T REALLY MY THING.

NEITHER IS GETTING *BULLIED*, BUT DO YOUR BEST AND THIS WILL HELP YOU TAKE BACK SOME CONTROL AT STERNWOOD.

YEAH, BUT YOU'RE MY FRIEND. YOU CAN JUST TELL THEM TO LEAVE ME ALONE.

I'M NOT ALWAYS GOING TO BE THERE, MAN. YOU HAVE TO BE ABLE TO STAND UP FOR YOURSELF OR THOSE GUYS ARE GONNA FEAST ON YOU.

MY DAD SAYS THEY'RE JUST *JEALOUS* BECAUSE I'M SO MUCH *SMARTER.*

WE'RE FRIENDS, SO I'M GOING TO BE REAL WITH YOU. IT AIN'T BECAUSE YOU'RE SMART. YOU LACK CONFIDENCE, AND YOU'RE WEIRD.

THANKS. *SO* GLAD WE'RE FRIENDS.

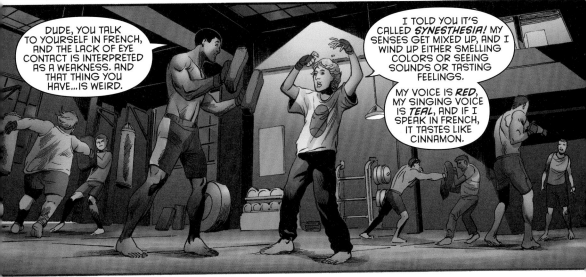

DUDE, YOU TALK TO YOURSELF IN FRENCH, AND THE LACK OF EYE CONTACT IS INTERPRETED AS A WEAKNESS. AND THAT THING YOU HAVE...IS WEIRD.

I TOLD YOU IT'S CALLED *SYNESTHESIA!* MY SENSES GET MIXED UP, AND I WIND UP EITHER SMELLING COLORS OR SEEING SOUNDS OR TASTING FEELINGS.

MY VOICE IS *RED,* MY SINGING VOICE IS *TEAL,* AND IF I SPEAK IN FRENCH, IT TASTES LIKE CINNAMON.

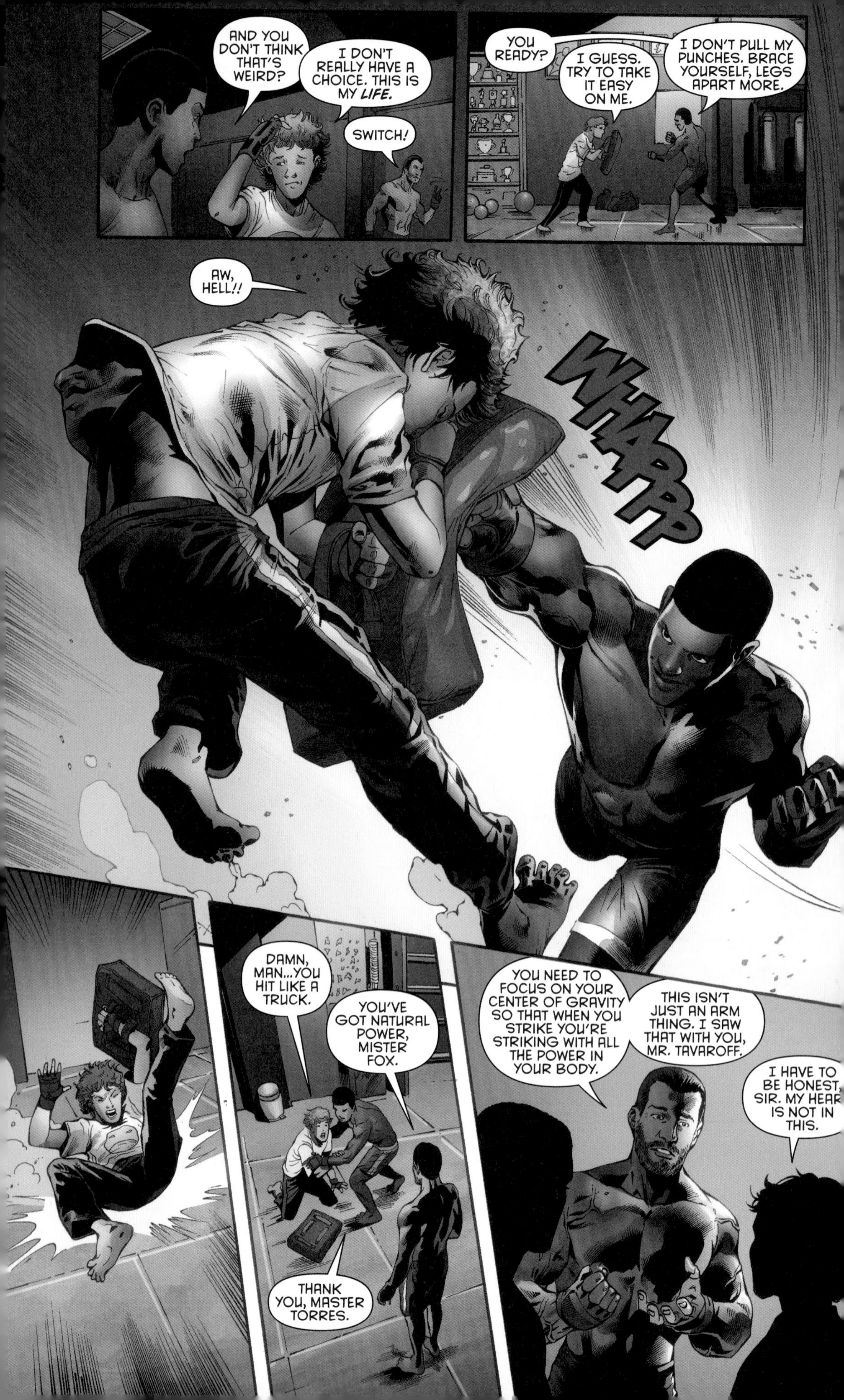
AND YOU DON'T THINK THAT'S WEIRD?
I DON'T REALLY HAVE A CHOICE. THIS IS MY *LIFE.*
SWITCH!
YOU READY?
I GUESS. TRY TO TAKE IT EASY ON ME.
I DON'T PULL MY PUNCHES. BRACE YOURSELF, LEGS APART MORE.
AW, HELL!!
WHAPP
DAMN, MAN...YOU HIT LIKE A TRUCK.
YOU'VE GOT NATURAL POWER, MISTER FOX.
THANK YOU, MASTER TORRES.
YOU NEED TO FOCUS ON YOUR CENTER OF GRAVITY SO THAT WHEN YOU STRIKE YOU'RE STRIKING WITH ALL THE POWER IN YOUR BODY.
THIS ISN'T JUST AN ARM THING. I SAW THAT WITH YOU, MR. TAVAROFF.
I HAVE TO BE HONEST, SIR. MY HEAR IS NOT IN THIS.

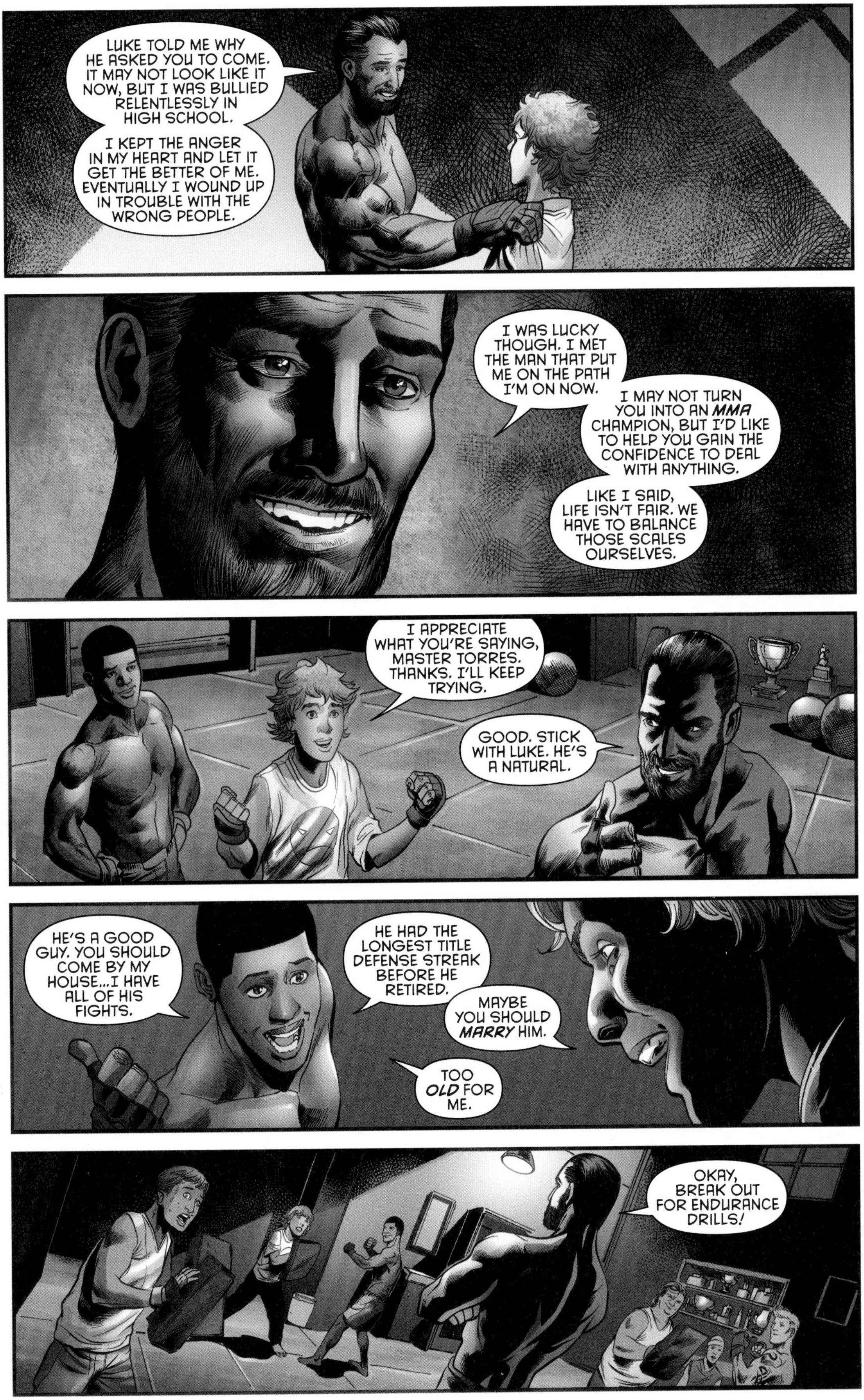

LUKE TOLD ME WHY HE ASKED YOU TO COME. IT MAY NOT LOOK LIKE IT NOW, BUT I WAS BULLIED RELENTLESSLY IN HIGH SCHOOL.
I KEPT THE ANGER IN MY HEART AND LET IT GET THE BETTER OF ME. EVENTUALLY I WOUND UP IN TROUBLE WITH THE WRONG PEOPLE.
I WAS LUCKY THOUGH. I MET THE MAN THAT PUT ME ON THE PATH I'M ON NOW.
I MAY NOT TURN YOU INTO AN MMA CHAMPION, BUT I'D LIKE TO HELP YOU GAIN THE CONFIDENCE TO DEAL WITH ANYTHING.
LIKE I SAID, LIFE ISN'T FAIR. WE HAVE TO BALANCE THOSE SCALES OURSELVES.
I APPRECIATE WHAT YOU'RE SAYING, MASTER TORRES. THANKS. I'LL KEEP TRYING.
GOOD. STICK WITH LUKE. HE'S A NATURAL.
HE'S A GOOD GUY. YOU SHOULD COME BY MY HOUSE...I HAVE ALL OF HIS FIGHTS.
HE HAD THE LONGEST TITLE DEFENSE STREAK BEFORE HE RETIRED.
MAYBE YOU SHOULD MARRY HIM.
TOO OLD FOR ME.
OKAY, BREAK OUT FOR ENDURANCE DRILLS!

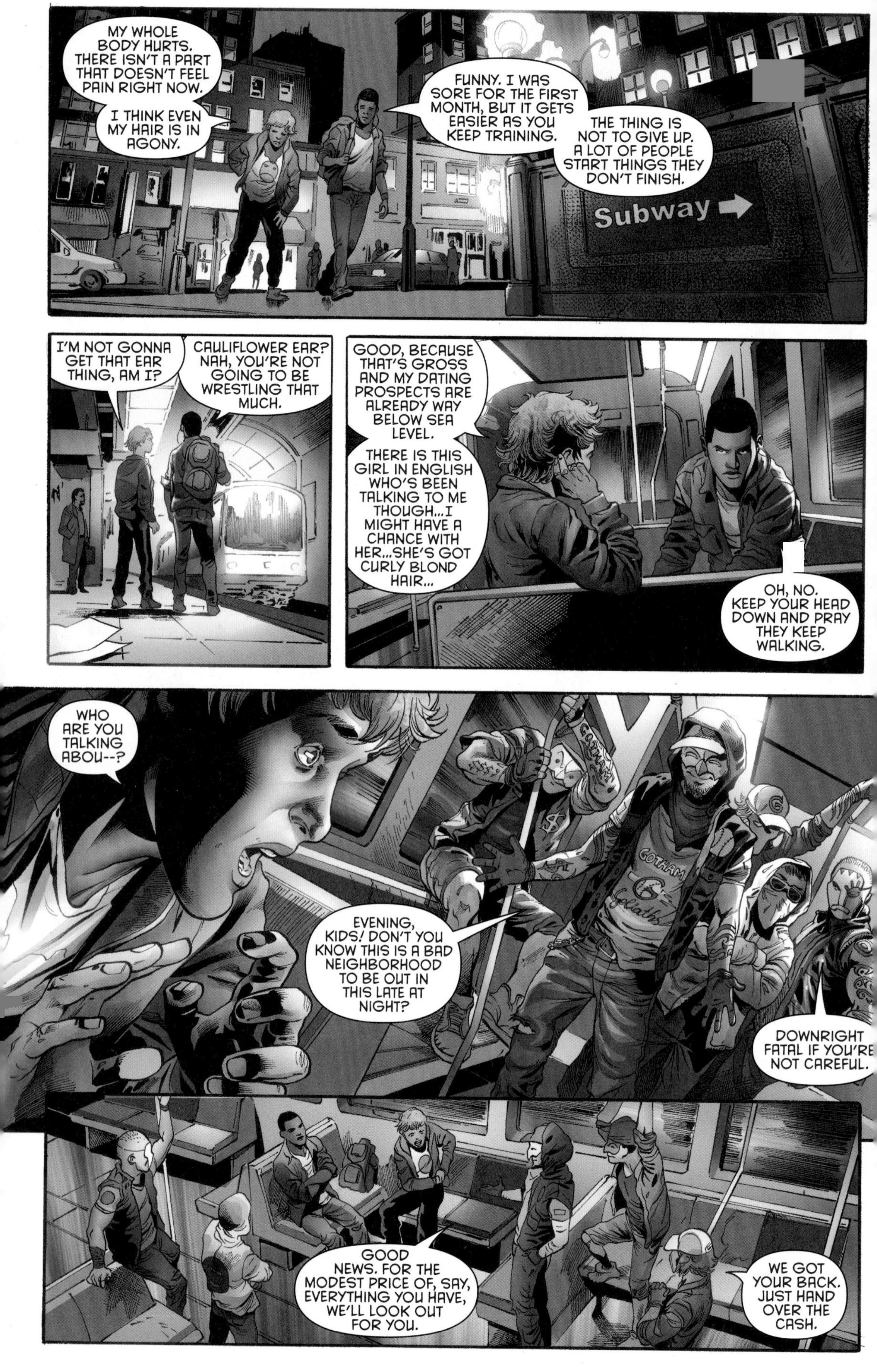

MY WHOLE BODY HURTS. THERE ISN'T A PART THAT DOESN'T FEEL PAIN RIGHT NOW.
I THINK EVEN MY HAIR IS IN AGONY.
FUNNY. I WAS SORE FOR THE FIRST MONTH, BUT IT GETS EASIER AS YOU KEEP TRAINING.
THE THING IS NOT TO GIVE UP. A LOT OF PEOPLE START THINGS THEY DON'T FINISH.
Subway
I'M NOT GONNA GET THAT EAR THING, AM I?
CAULIFLOWER EAR? NAH, YOU'RE NOT GOING TO BE WRESTLING THAT MUCH.
GOOD, BECAUSE THAT'S GROSS AND MY DATING PROSPECTS ARE ALREADY WAY BELOW SEA LEVEL.
THERE IS THIS GIRL IN ENGLISH WHO'S BEEN TALKING TO ME THOUGH...I MIGHT HAVE A CHANCE WITH HER...SHE'S GOT CURLY BLOND HAIR...
OH, NO. KEEP YOUR HEAD DOWN AND PRAY THEY KEEP WALKING.
WHO ARE YOU TALKING ABOU--?
EVENING, KIDS! DON'T YOU KNOW THIS IS A BAD NEIGHBORHOOD TO BE OUT IN THIS LATE AT NIGHT?
DOWNRIGHT FATAL IF YOU'RE NOT CAREFUL.
GOOD NEWS. FOR THE MODEST PRICE OF, SAY, EVERYTHING YOU HAVE, WE'LL LOOK OUT FOR YOU.
WE GOT YOUR BACK. JUST HAND OVER THE CASH.

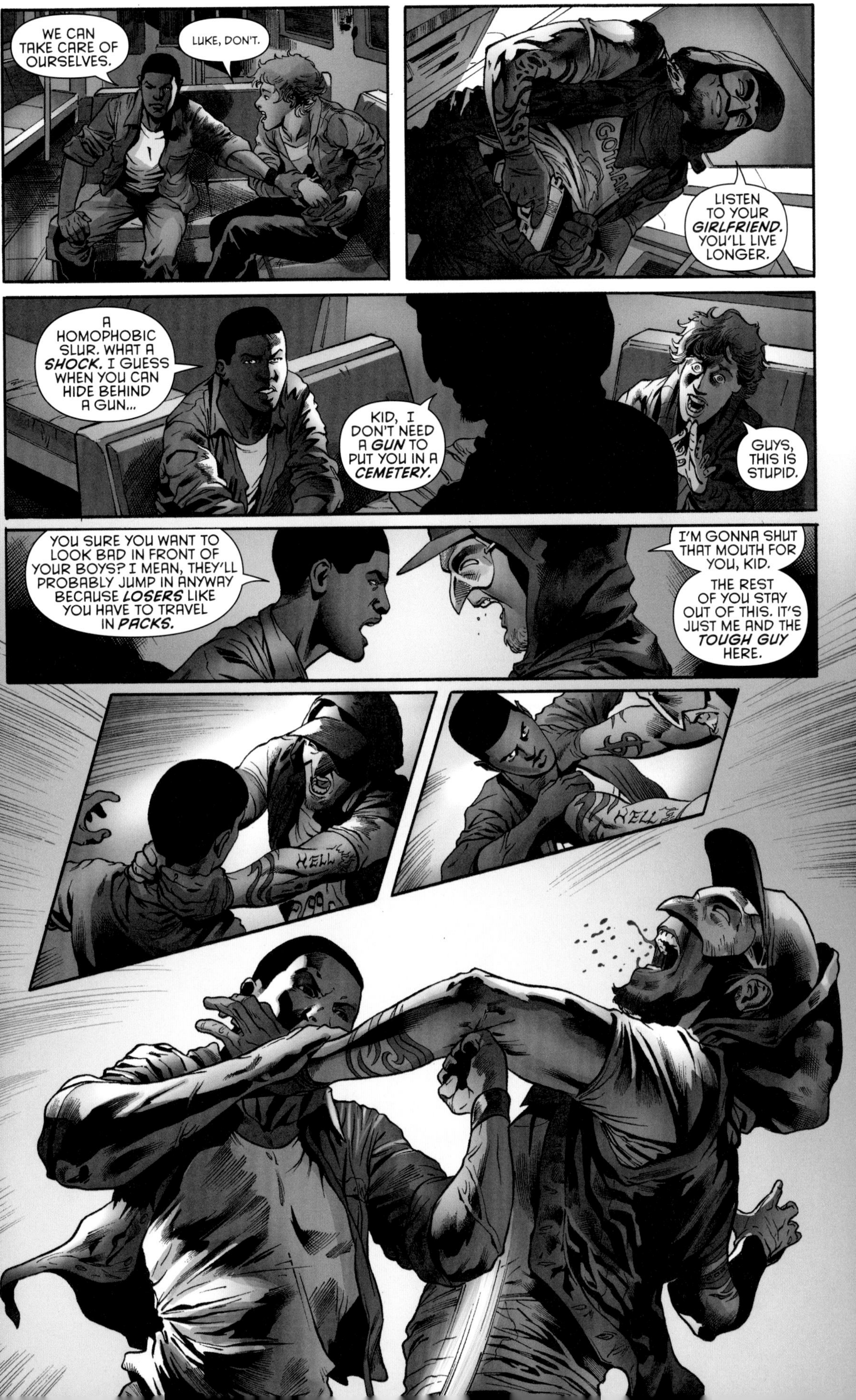
WE CAN TAKE CARE OF OURSELVES.
LUKE, DON'T.
LISTEN TO YOUR GIRLFRIEND. YOU'LL LIVE LONGER.
A HOMOPHOBIC SLUR. WHAT A SHOCK. I GUESS WHEN YOU CAN HIDE BEHIND A GUN...
KID, I DON'T NEED A GUN TO PUT YOU IN A CEMETERY.
GUYS, THIS IS STUPID.
YOU SURE YOU WANT TO LOOK BAD IN FRONT OF YOUR BOYS? I MEAN, THEY'LL PROBABLY JUMP IN ANYWAY BECAUSE LOSERS LIKE YOU HAVE TO TRAVEL IN PACKS.
I'M GONNA SHUT THAT MOUTH FOR YOU, KID.
THE REST OF YOU STAY OUT OF THIS. IT'S JUST ME AND THE TOUGH GUY HERE.

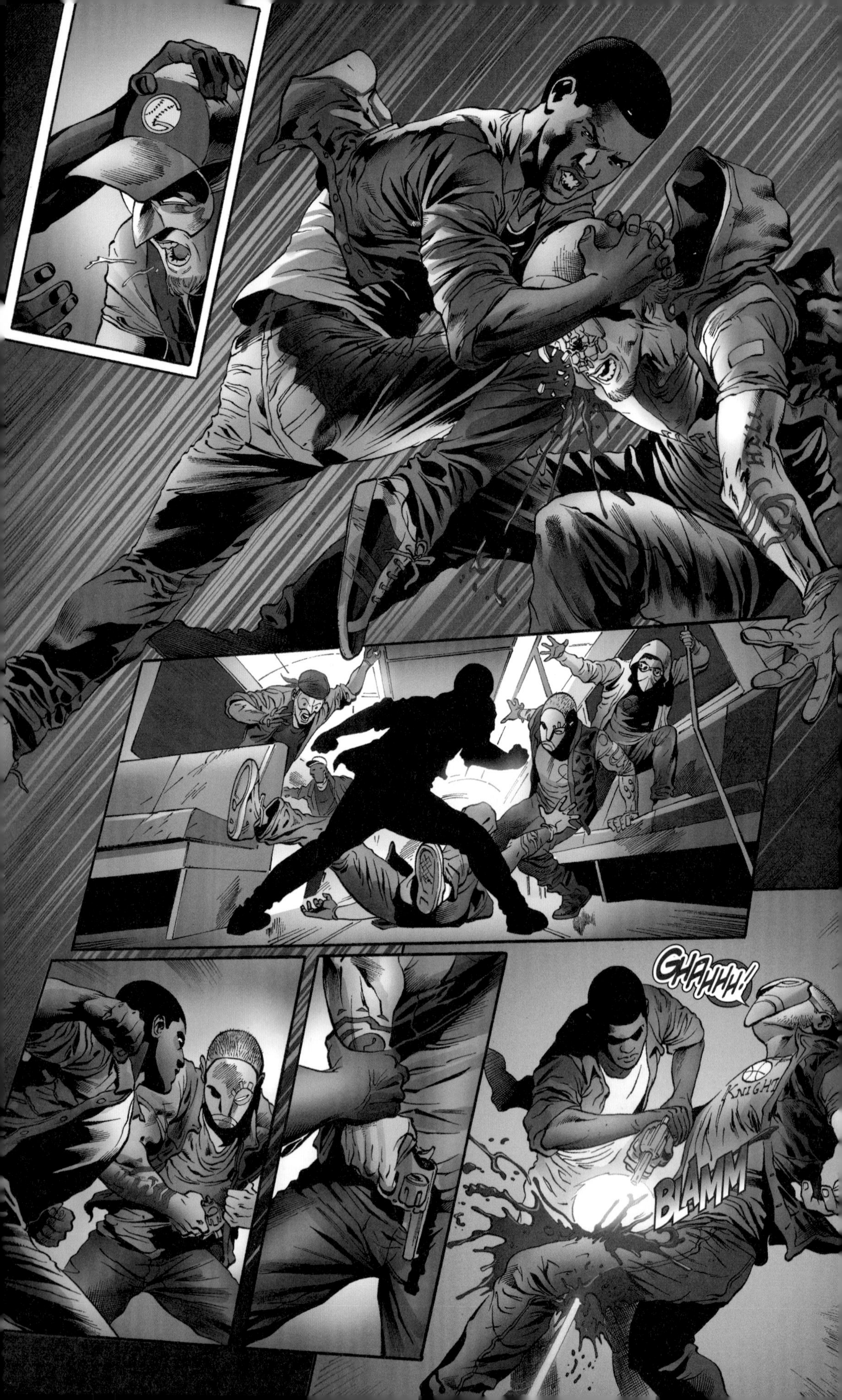
GHAHHH!
KNIGHT
BLAMM

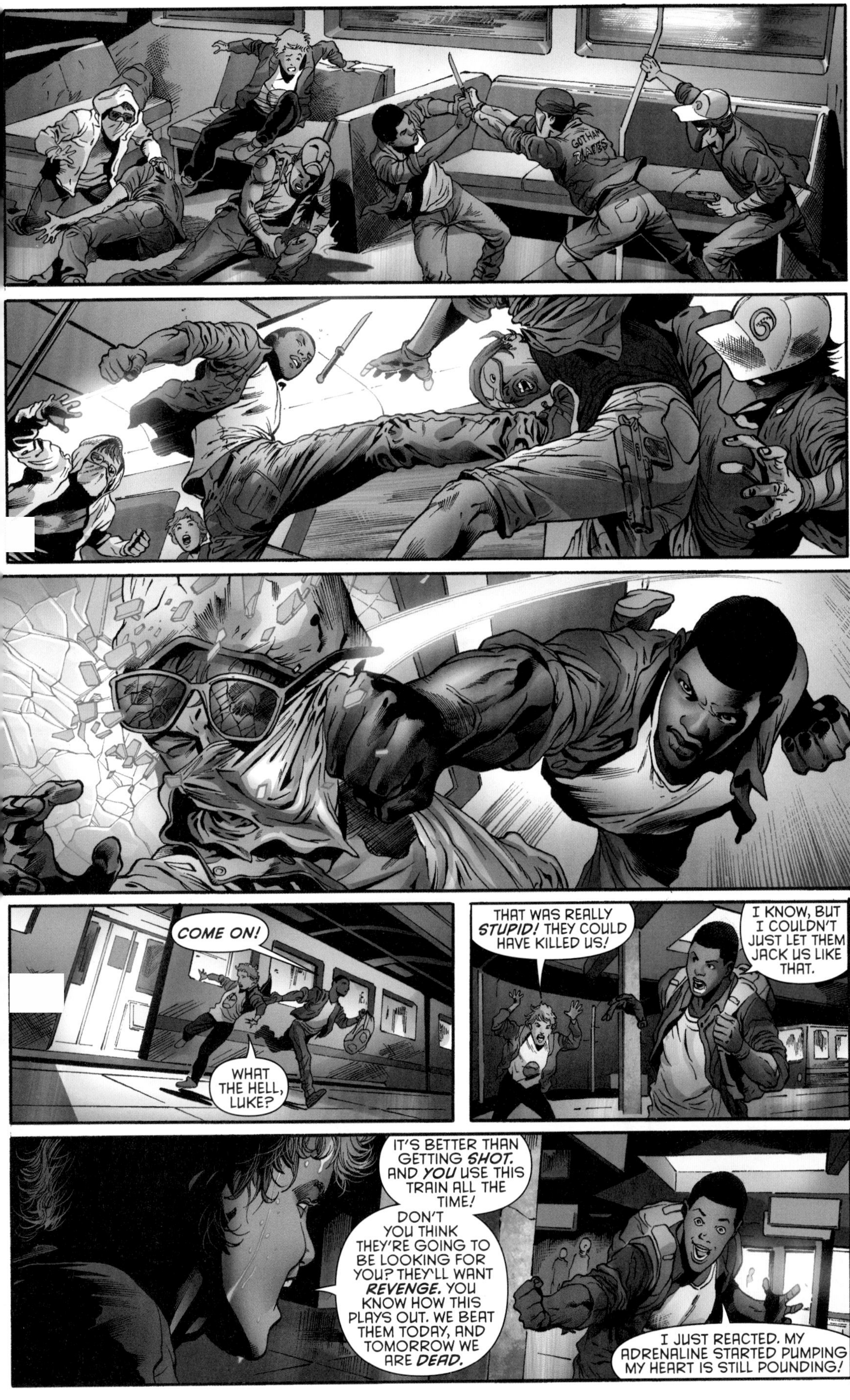
COME ON!
WHAT THE HELL, LUKE?
THAT WAS REALLY STUPID! THEY COULD HAVE KILLED US!
I KNOW, BUT I COULDN'T JUST LET THEM JACK US LIKE THAT.
IT'S BETTER THAN GETTING SHOT. AND YOU USE THIS TRAIN ALL THE TIME!
DON'T YOU THINK THEY'RE GOING TO BE LOOKING FOR YOU? THEY'LL WANT REVENGE. YOU KNOW HOW THIS PLAYS OUT. WE BEAT THEM TODAY, AND TOMORROW WE ARE DEAD.
I JUST REACTED. MY ADRENALINE STARTED PUMPING MY HEART IS STILL POUNDING!

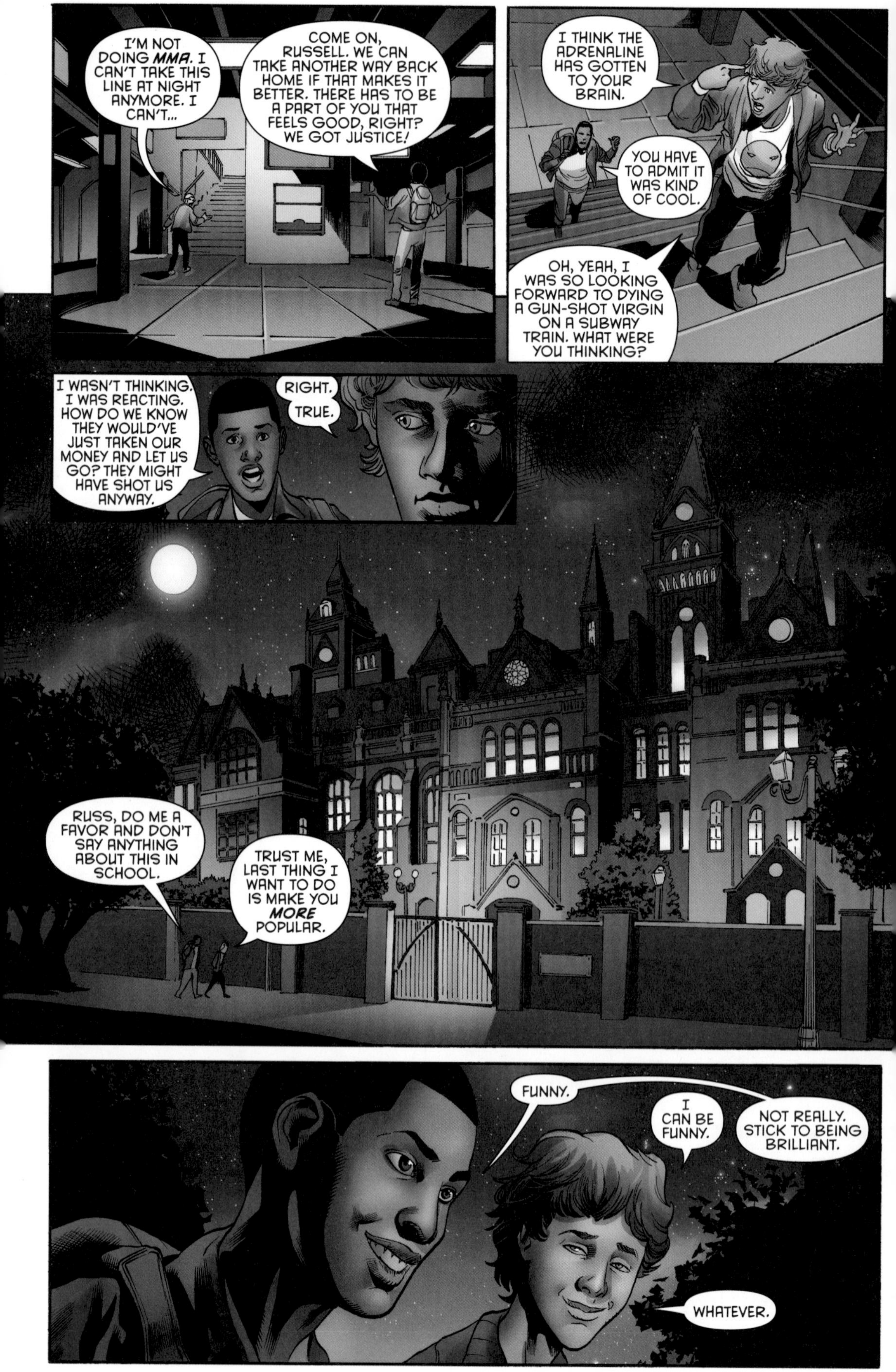
I'M NOT DOING MMA. I CAN'T TAKE THIS LINE AT NIGHT ANYMORE. I CAN'T...
COME ON, RUSSELL. WE CAN TAKE ANOTHER WAY BACK HOME IF THAT MAKES IT BETTER. THERE HAS TO BE A PART OF YOU THAT FEELS GOOD, RIGHT? WE GOT JUSTICE!
I THINK THE ADRENALINE HAS GOTTEN TO YOUR BRAIN.
YOU HAVE TO ADMIT IT WAS KIND OF COOL.
OH, YEAH, I WAS SO LOOKING FORWARD TO DYING A GUN-SHOT VIRGIN ON A SUBWAY TRAIN. WHAT WERE YOU THINKING?
I WASN'T THINKING. I WAS REACTING. HOW DO WE KNOW THEY WOULD'VE JUST TAKEN OUR MONEY AND LET US GO? THEY MIGHT HAVE SHOT US ANYWAY.
RIGHT.
TRUE.
RUSS, DO ME A FAVOR AND DON'T SAY ANYTHING ABOUT THIS IN SCHOOL.
TRUST ME, LAST THING I WANT TO DO IS MAKE YOU MORE POPULAR.
FUNNY.
I CAN BE FUNNY.
NOT REALLY. STICK TO BEING BRILLIANT.
WHATEVER.

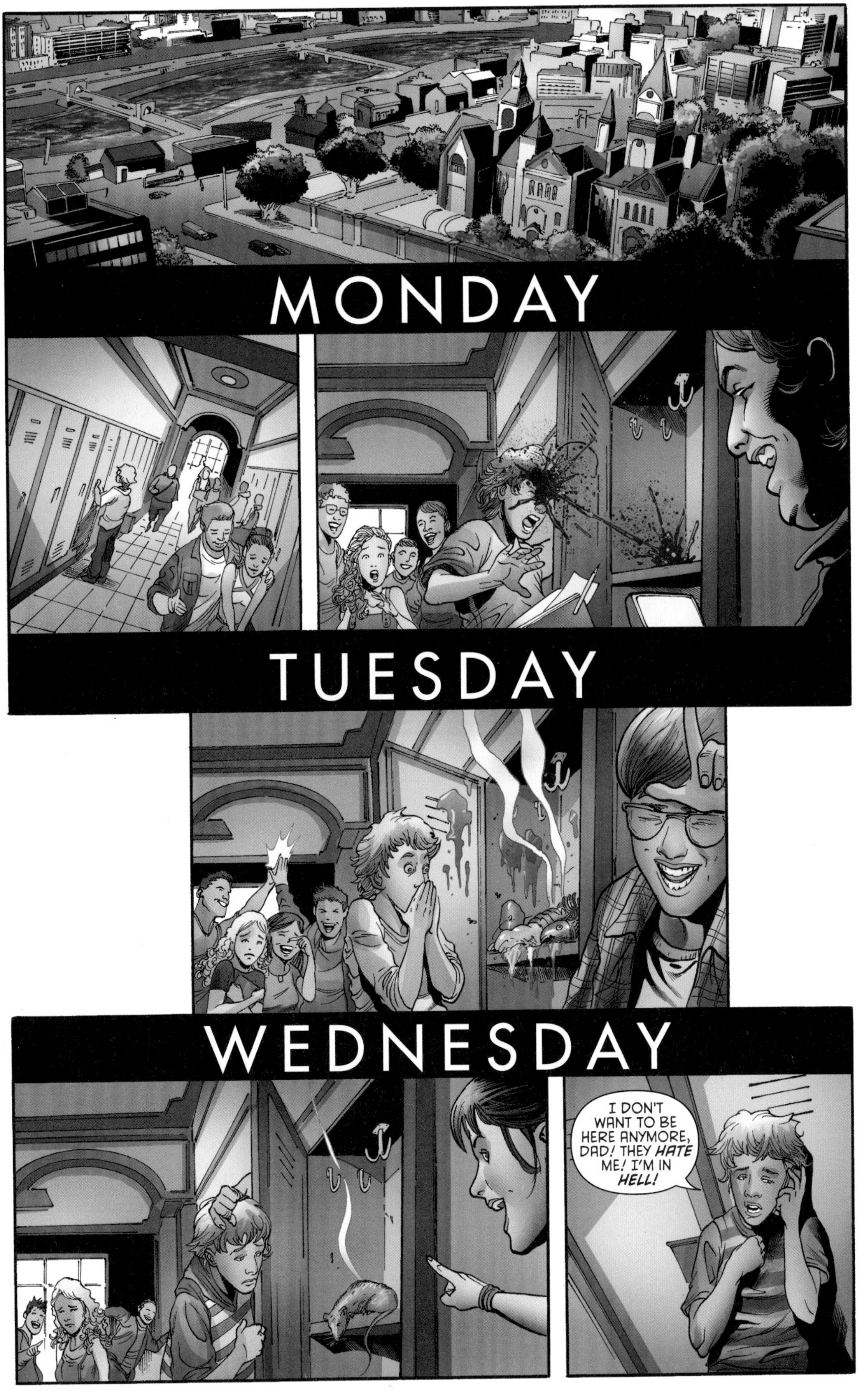
MONDAY
TUESDAY
WEDNESDAY
I DON'T WANT TO BE HERE ANYMORE, DAD! THEY HATE ME! I'M IN HELL!

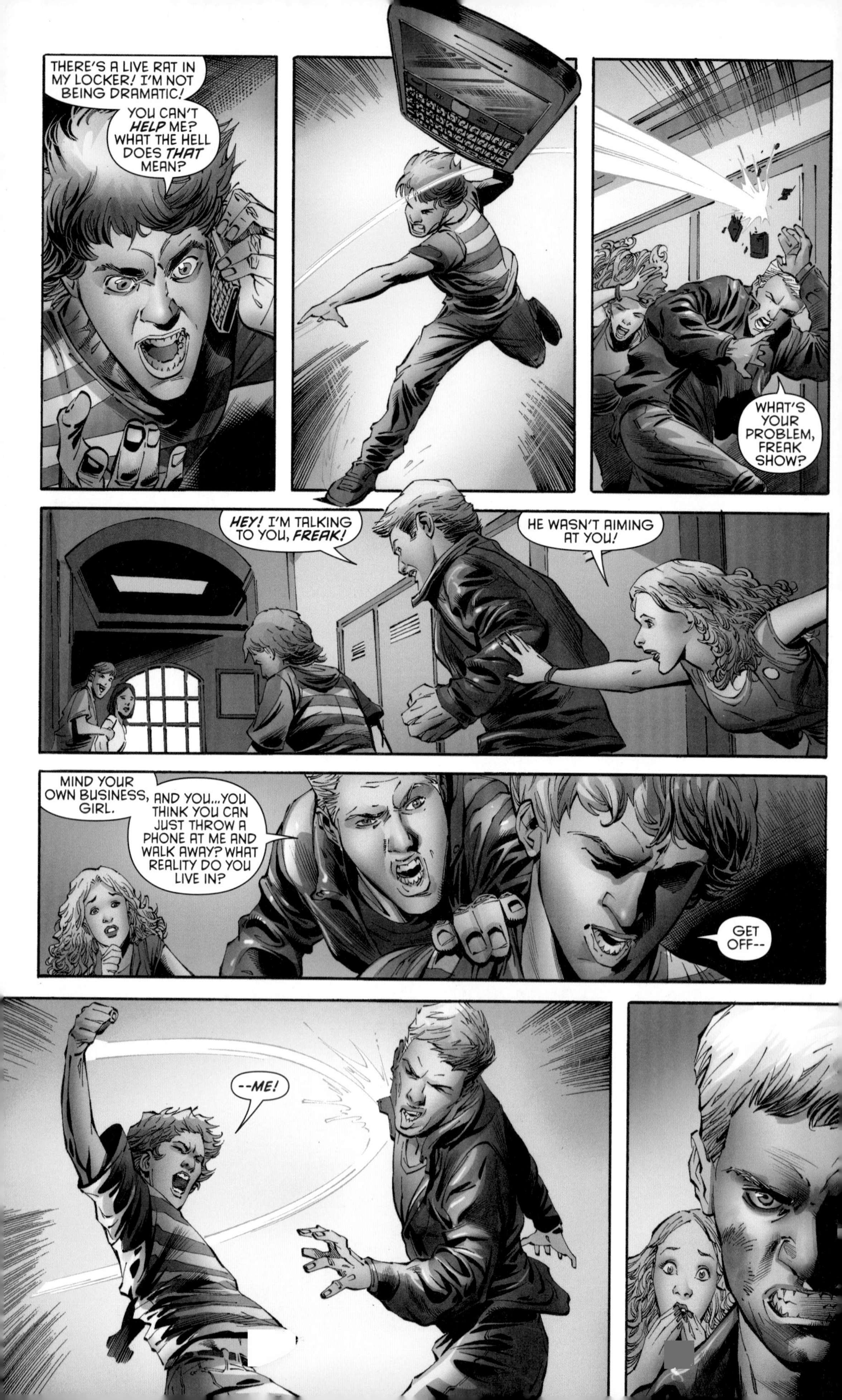

THERE'S A LIVE RAT IN MY LOCKER! I'M NOT BEING DRAMATIC!
YOU CAN'T HELP ME? WHAT THE HELL DOES THAT MEAN?
WHAT'S YOUR PROBLEM, FREAK SHOW?
HEY! I'M TALKING TO YOU, FREAK!
HE WASN'T AIMING AT YOU!
MIND YOUR OWN BUSINESS, GIRL.
AND YOU...YOU THINK YOU CAN JUST THROW A PHONE AT ME AND WALK AWAY? WHAT REALITY DO YOU LIVE IN?
GET OFF--
--ME!

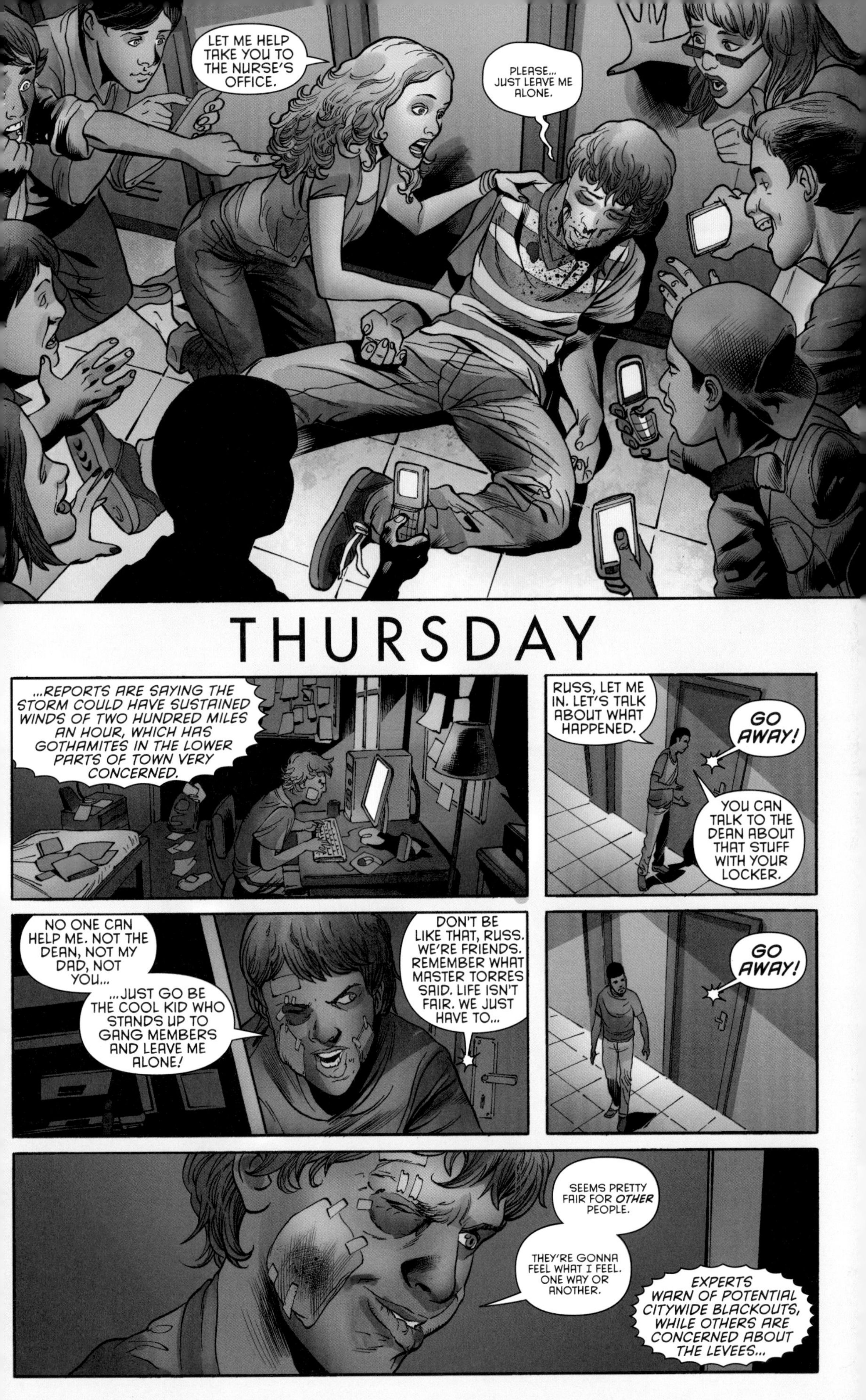
LET ME HELP TAKE YOU TO THE NURSE'S OFFICE.
PLEASE... JUST LEAVE ME ALONE.
THURSDAY
...REPORTS ARE SAYING THE STORM COULD HAVE SUSTAINED WINDS OF TWO HUNDRED MILES AN HOUR, WHICH HAS GOTHAMITES IN THE LOWER PARTS OF TOWN VERY CONCERNED.
RUSS, LET ME IN. LET'S TALK ABOUT WHAT HAPPENED.
GO AWAY!
YOU CAN TALK TO THE DEAN ABOUT THAT STUFF WITH YOUR LOCKER.
NO ONE CAN HELP ME. NOT THE DEAN, NOT MY DAD, NOT YOU...
...JUST GO BE THE COOL KID WHO STANDS UP TO GANG MEMBERS AND LEAVE ME ALONE!
DON'T BE LIKE THAT, RUSS. WE'RE FRIENDS. REMEMBER WHAT MASTER TORRES SAID. LIFE ISN'T FAIR. WE JUST HAVE TO...
GO AWAY!
SEEMS PRETTY FAIR FOR *OTHER* PEOPLE.
THEY'RE GONNA FEEL WHAT I FEEL. ONE WAY OR ANOTHER.
EXPERTS WARN OF POTENTIAL CITYWIDE BLACKOUTS, WHILE OTHERS ARE CONCERNED ABOUT THE LEVEES...

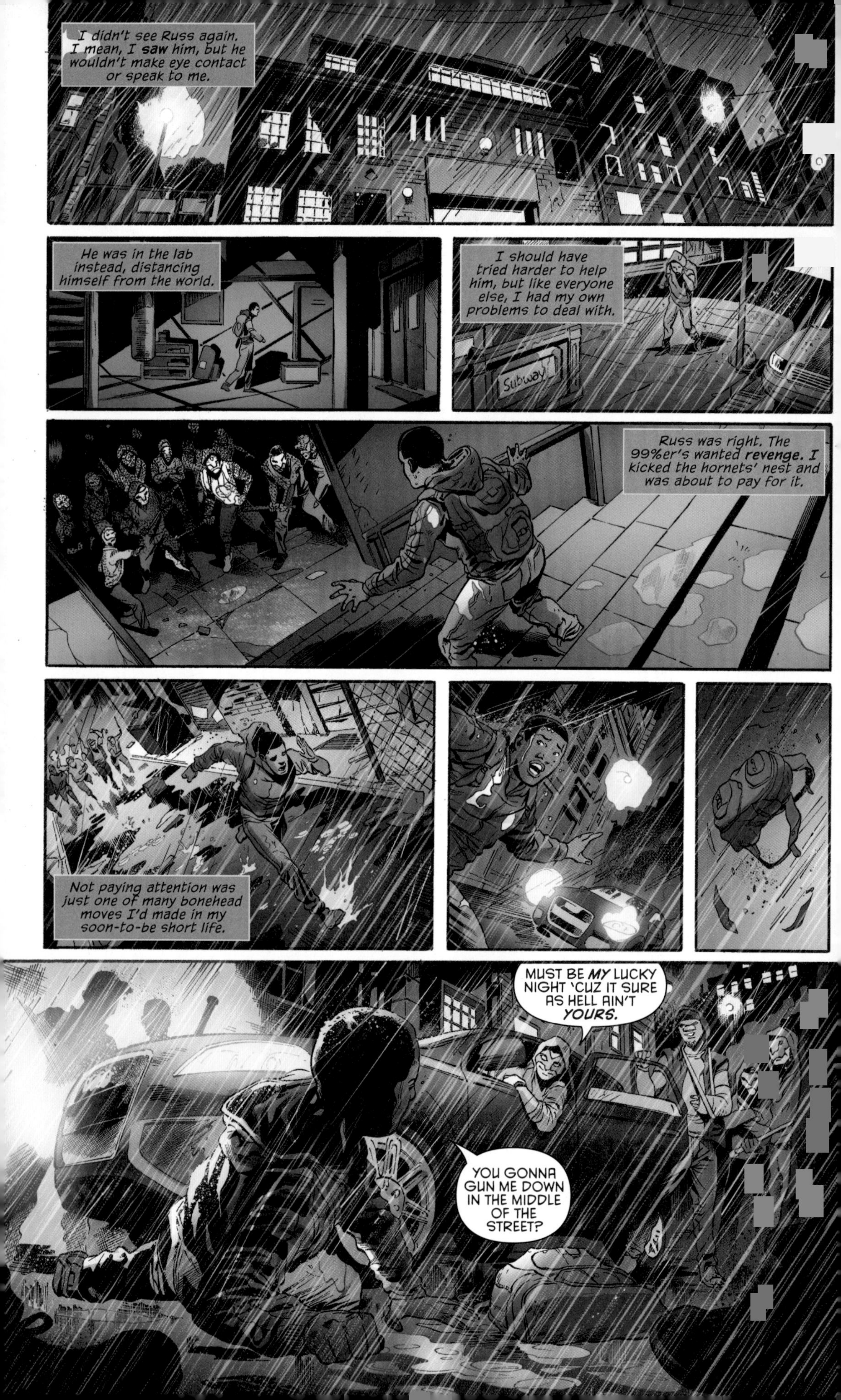
I didn't see Russ again. I mean, I saw him, but he wouldn't make eye contact or speak to me.
He was in the lab instead, distancing himself from the world.
I should have tried harder to help him, but like everyone else, I had my own problems to deal with.
Subway
Russ was right. The 99%er's wanted revenge. I kicked the hornets' nest and was about to pay for it.
Not paying attention was just one of many bonehead moves I'd made in my soon-to-be short life.
MUST BE MY LUCKY NIGHT 'CUZ IT SURE AS HELL AIN'T YOURS.
YOU GONNA GUN ME DOWN IN THE MIDDLE OF THE STREET?

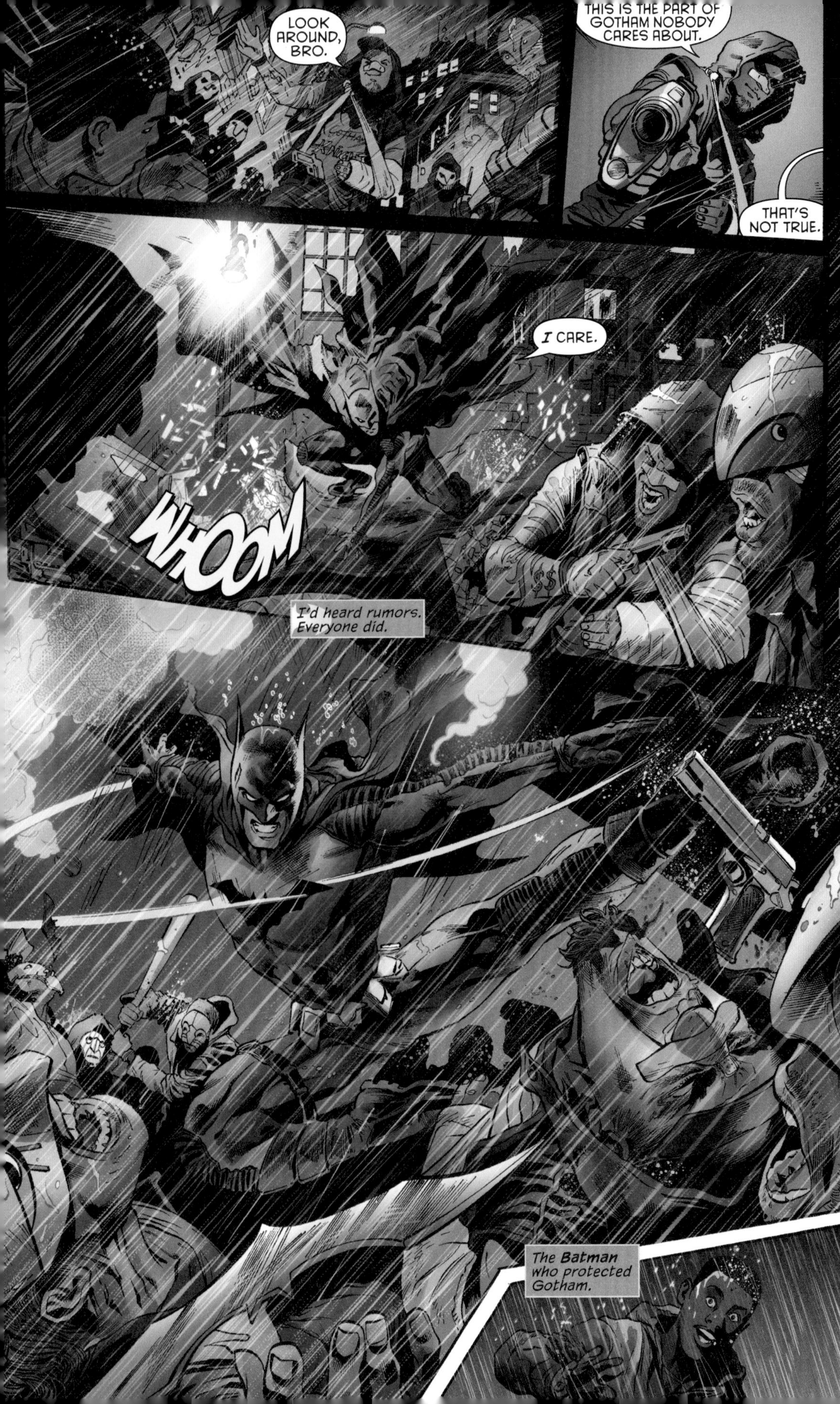

LOOK AROUND, BRO.
THIS IS THE PART OF GOTHAM NOBODY CARES ABOUT.
THAT'S NOT TRUE.
I CARE.
WHOOM
I'd heard rumors. Everyone did.
*The **Batman** who protected Gotham.*

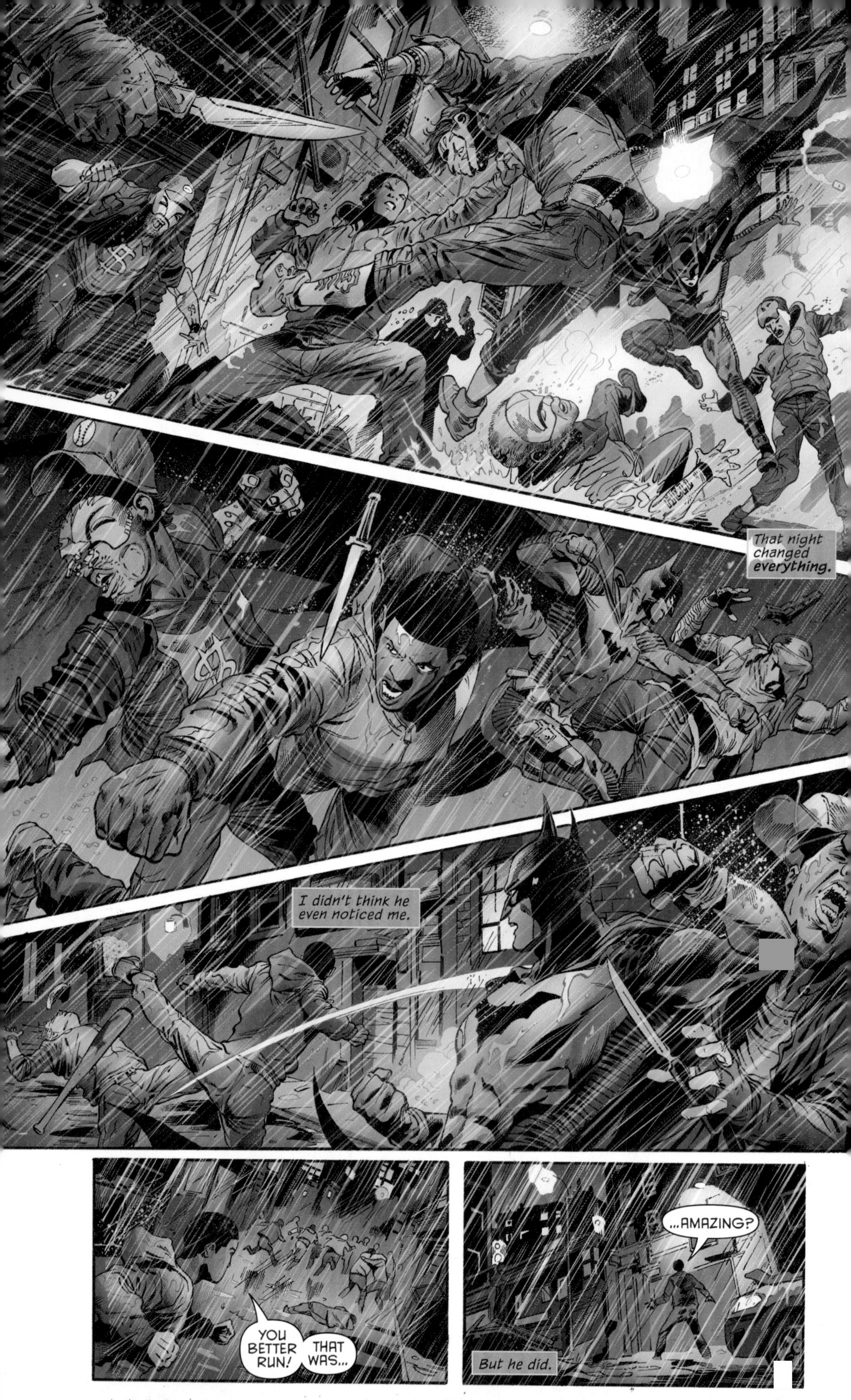
That night changed everything.
I didn't think he even noticed me.
YOU BETTER RUN!
THAT WAS...
...AMAZING?
But he did.

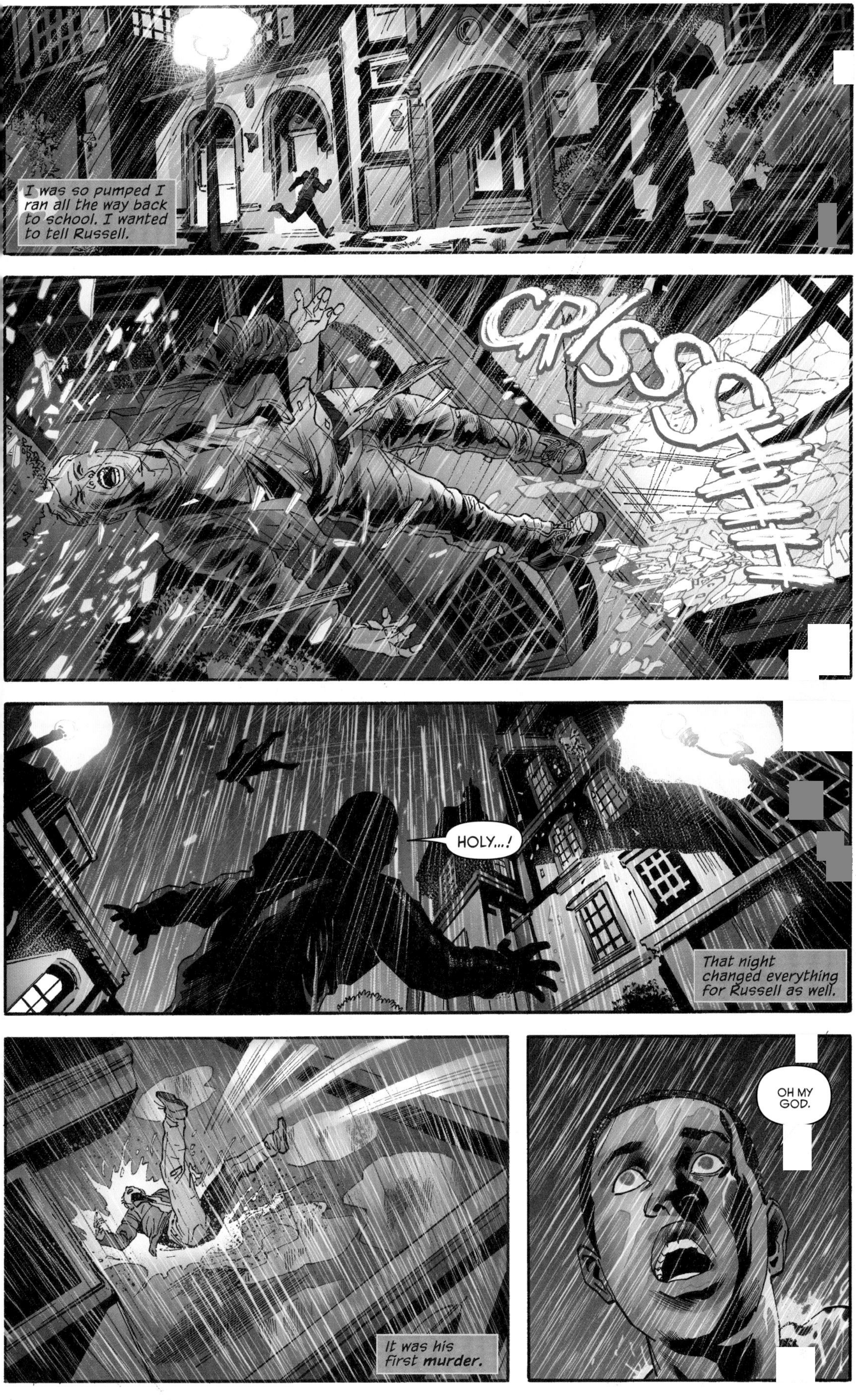
I was so pumped I ran all the way back to school. I wanted to tell Russell.
CRISSHHHH
HOLY...!
That night changed everything for Russell as well.
It was his first murder.
OH MY GOD.

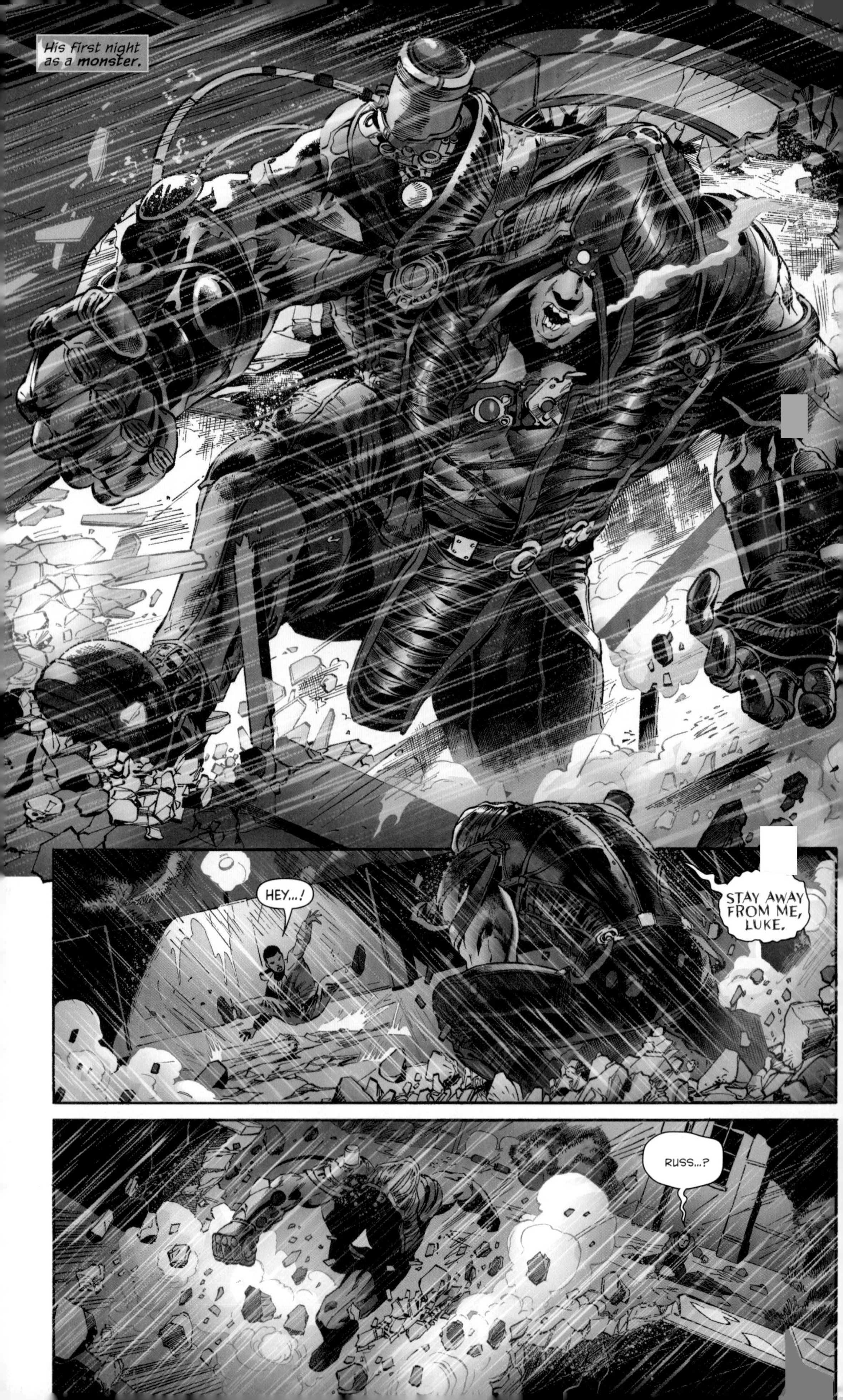
His first night as a monster.
HEY...!
STAY AWAY FROM ME, LUKE.
RUSS...?

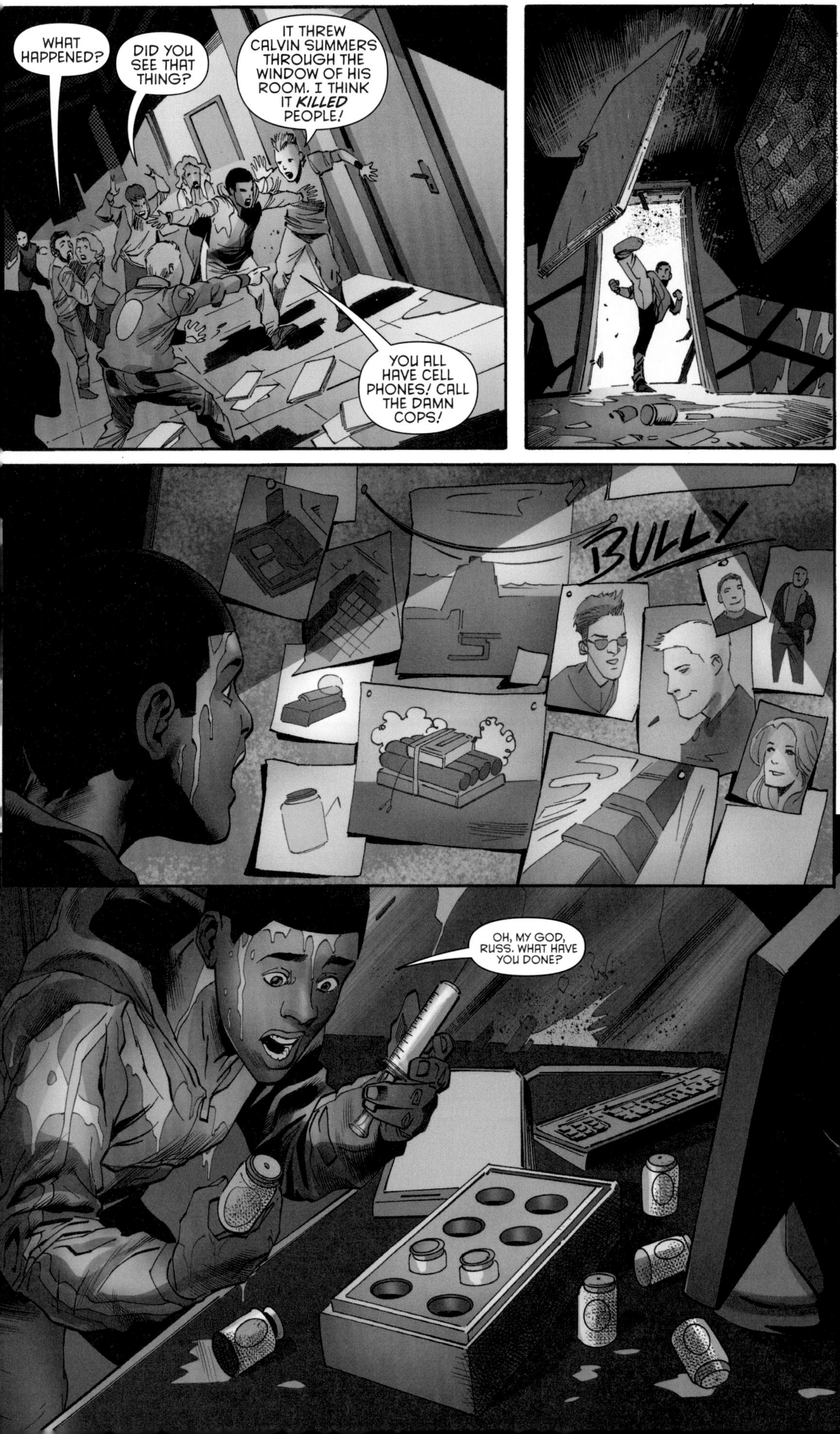
WHAT HAPPENED?
DID YOU SEE THAT THING?
IT THREW CALVIN SUMMERS THROUGH THE WINDOW OF HIS ROOM. I THINK IT KILLED PEOPLE!
YOU ALL HAVE CELL PHONES! CALL THE DAMN COPS!
BULLY
OH, MY GOD, RUSS. WHAT HAVE YOU DONE?

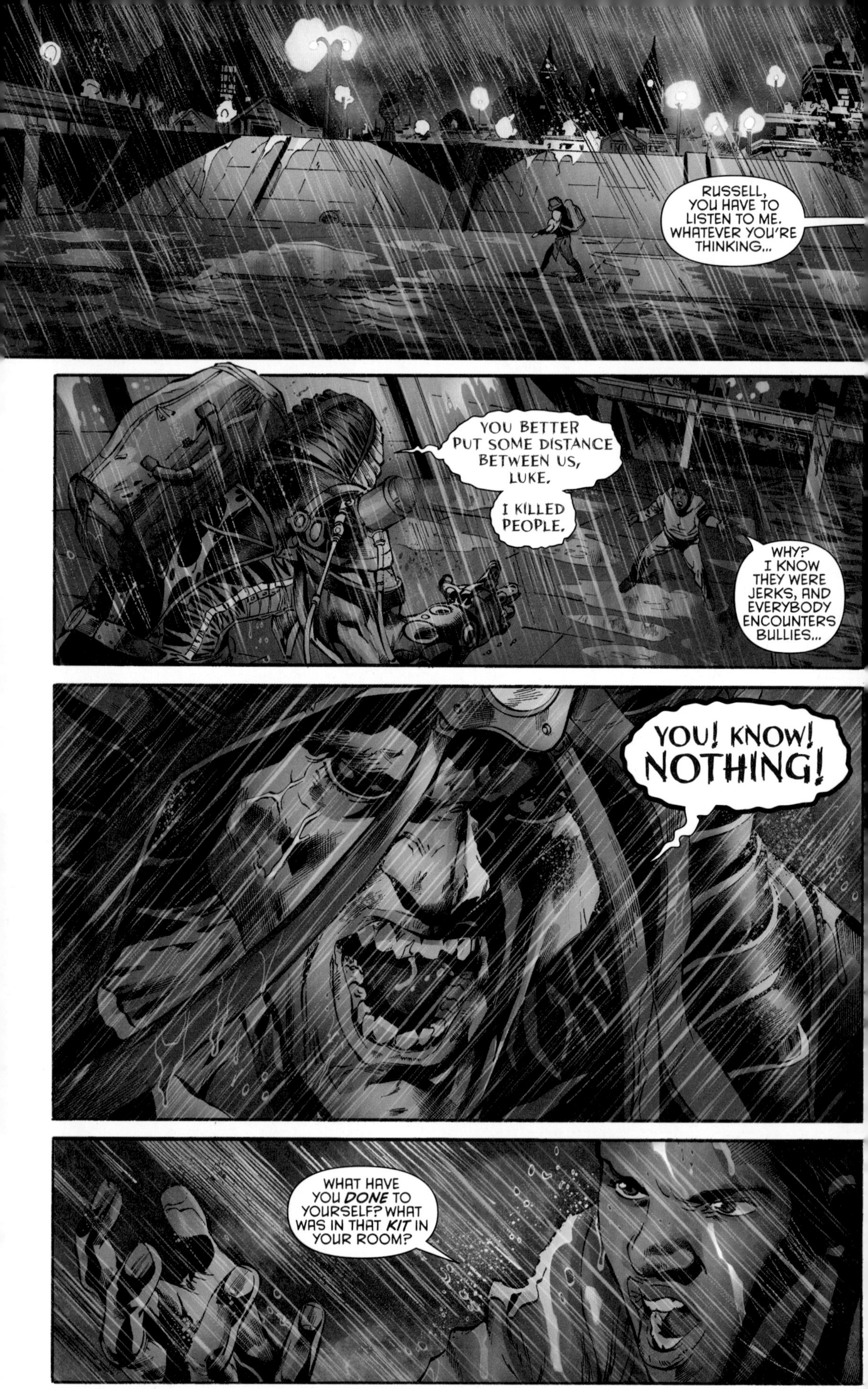
RUSSELL, YOU HAVE TO LISTEN TO ME. WHATEVER YOU'RE THINKING...
YOU BETTER PUT SOME DISTANCE BETWEEN US, LUKE.
I KILLED PEOPLE.
WHY? I KNOW THEY WERE JERKS, AND EVERYBODY ENCOUNTERS BULLIES...
YOU! KNOW! NOTHING!
WHAT HAVE YOU *DONE* TO YOURSELF? WHAT WAS IN THAT *KIT* IN YOUR ROOM?

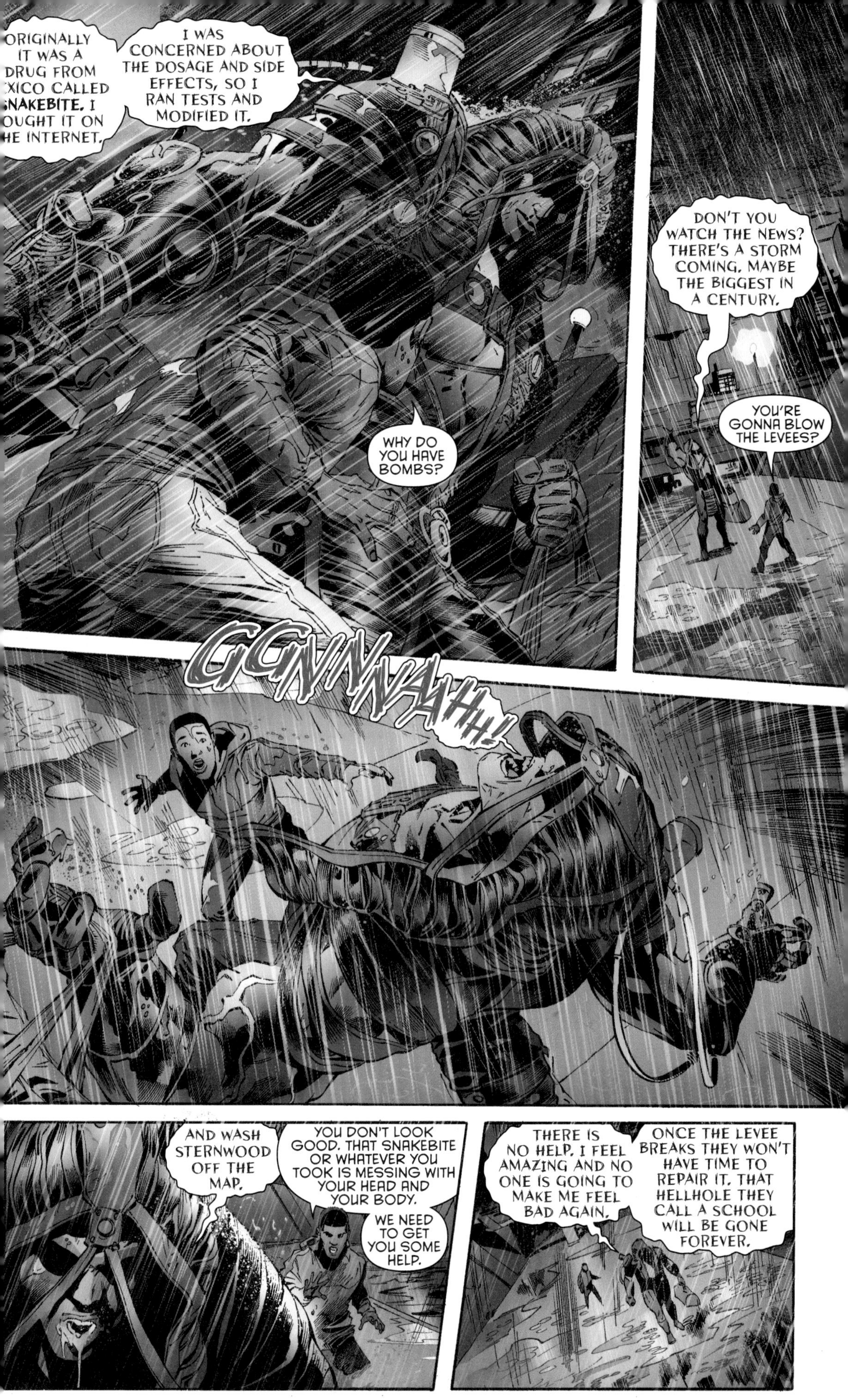
ORIGINALLY IT WAS A DRUG FROM XICO CALLED SNAKEBITE. I OUGHT IT ON HE INTERNET.
I WAS CONCERNED ABOUT THE DOSAGE AND SIDE EFFECTS, SO I RAN TESTS AND MODIFIED IT.
WHY DO YOU HAVE BOMBS?
DON'T YOU WATCH THE NEWS? THERE'S A STORM COMING. MAYBE THE BIGGEST IN A CENTURY.
YOU'RE GONNA BLOW THE LEVEES?
GGNNNAAHH!
AND WASH STERNWOOD OFF THE MAP.
YOU DON'T LOOK GOOD. THAT SNAKEBITE OR WHATEVER YOU TOOK IS MESSING WITH YOUR HEAD AND YOUR BODY.
WE NEED TO GET YOU SOME HELP.
THERE IS NO HELP. I FEEL AMAZING AND NO ONE IS GOING TO MAKE ME FEEL BAD AGAIN.
ONCE THE LEVEE BREAKS THEY WON'T HAVE TIME TO REPAIR IT. THAT HELLHOLE THEY CALL A SCHOOL WILL BE GONE FOREVER.

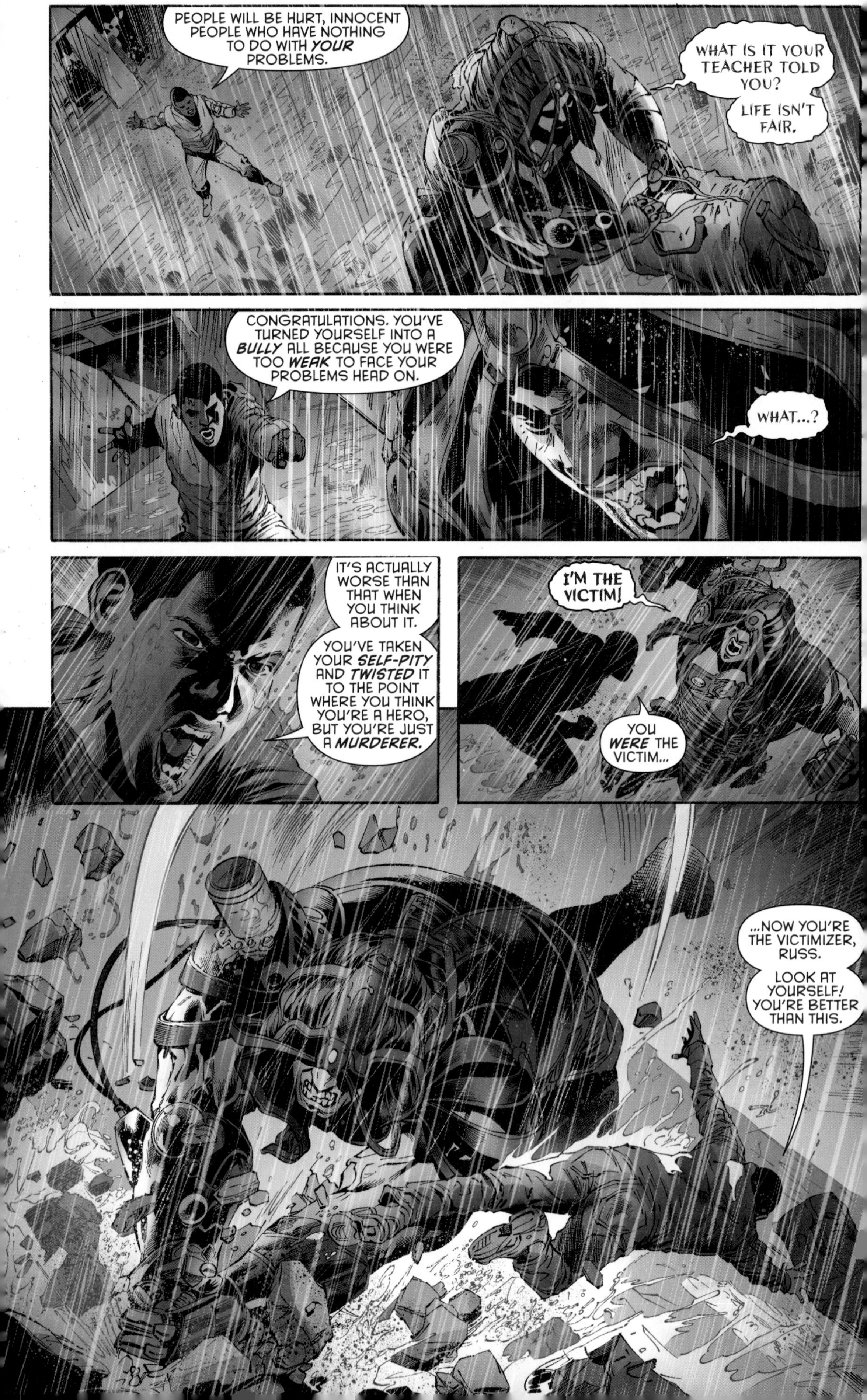
PEOPLE WILL BE HURT, INNOCENT PEOPLE WHO HAVE NOTHING TO DO WITH *YOUR* PROBLEMS.
WHAT IS IT YOUR TEACHER TOLD YOU?
LIFE ISN'T FAIR.
CONGRATULATIONS. YOU'VE TURNED YOURSELF INTO A *BULLY* ALL BECAUSE YOU WERE TOO *WEAK* TO FACE YOUR PROBLEMS HEAD ON.
WHAT...?
IT'S ACTUALLY WORSE THAN THAT WHEN YOU THINK ABOUT IT.
YOU'VE TAKEN YOUR *SELF-PITY* AND *TWISTED* IT TO THE POINT WHERE YOU THINK YOU'RE A HERO, BUT YOU'RE JUST A *MURDERER.*
I'M THE VICTIM!
YOU *WERE* THE VICTIM...
...NOW YOU'RE THE VICTIMIZER, RUSS.
LOOK AT YOURSELF! YOU'RE BETTER THAN THIS.

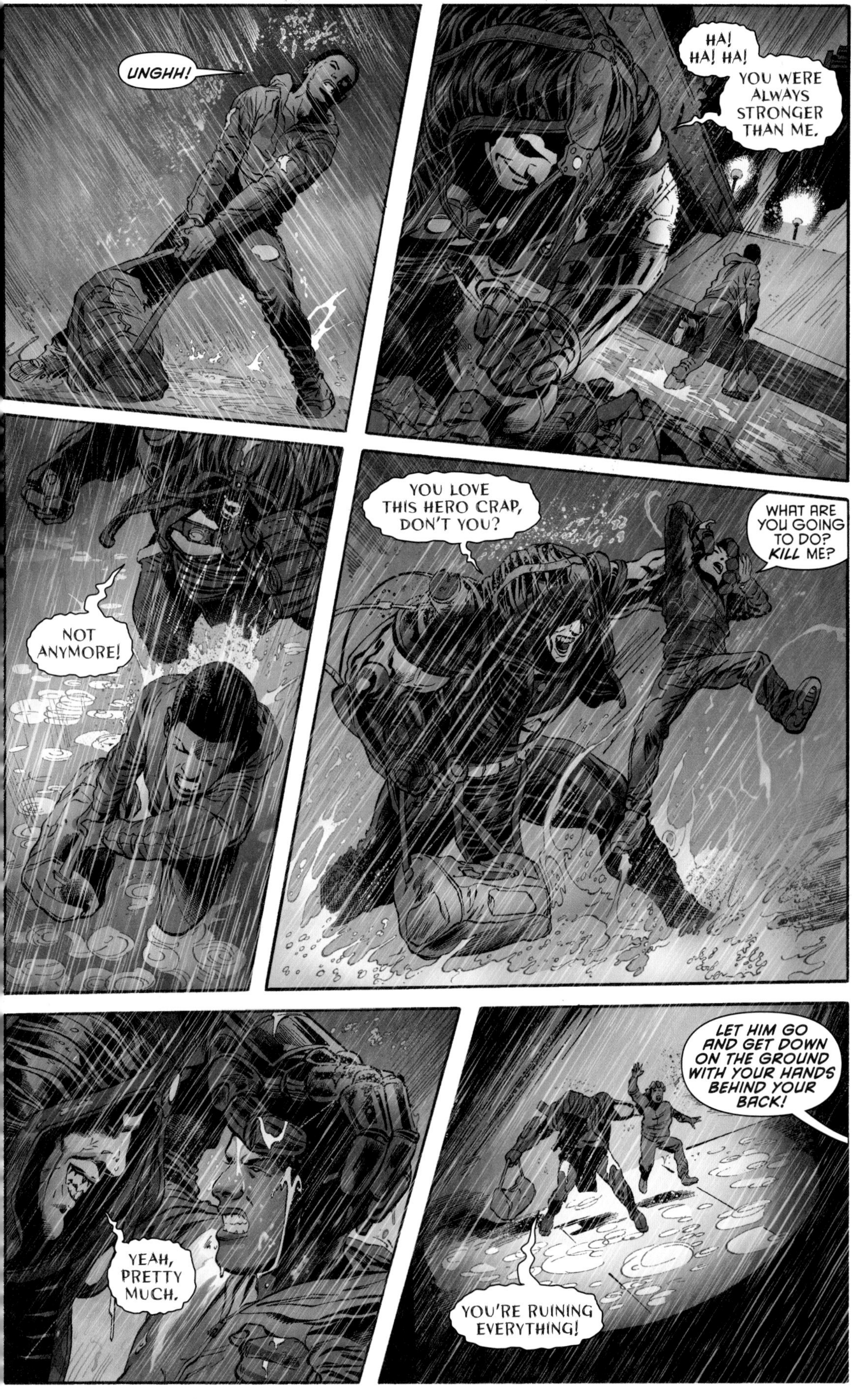
UNGHH!
HA! HA! HA!
YOU WERE ALWAYS STRONGER THAN ME.
NOT ANYMORE!
YOU LOVE THIS HERO CRAP, DON'T YOU?
WHAT ARE YOU GOING TO DO? KILL ME?
YEAH, PRETTY MUCH.
LET HIM GO AND GET DOWN ON THE GROUND WITH YOUR HANDS BEHIND YOUR BACK!
YOU'RE RUINING EVERYTHING!

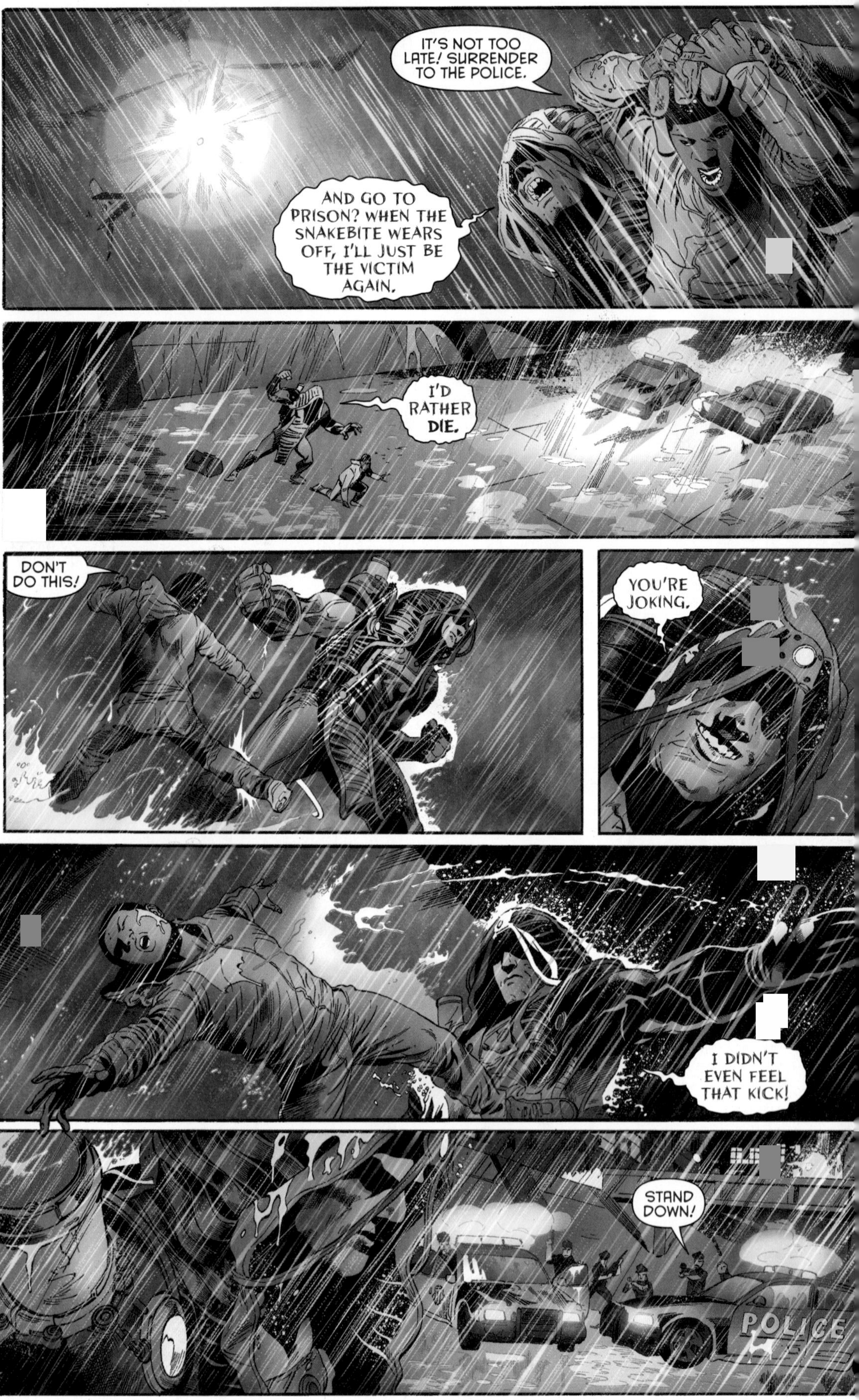
IT'S NOT TOO LATE! SURRENDER TO THE POLICE.
AND GO TO PRISON? WHEN THE SNAKEBITE WEARS OFF, I'LL JUST BE THE VICTIM AGAIN.
I'D RATHER DIE.
DON'T DO THIS!
YOU'RE JOKING.
I DIDN'T EVEN FEEL THAT KICK!
STAND DOWN!
POLICE

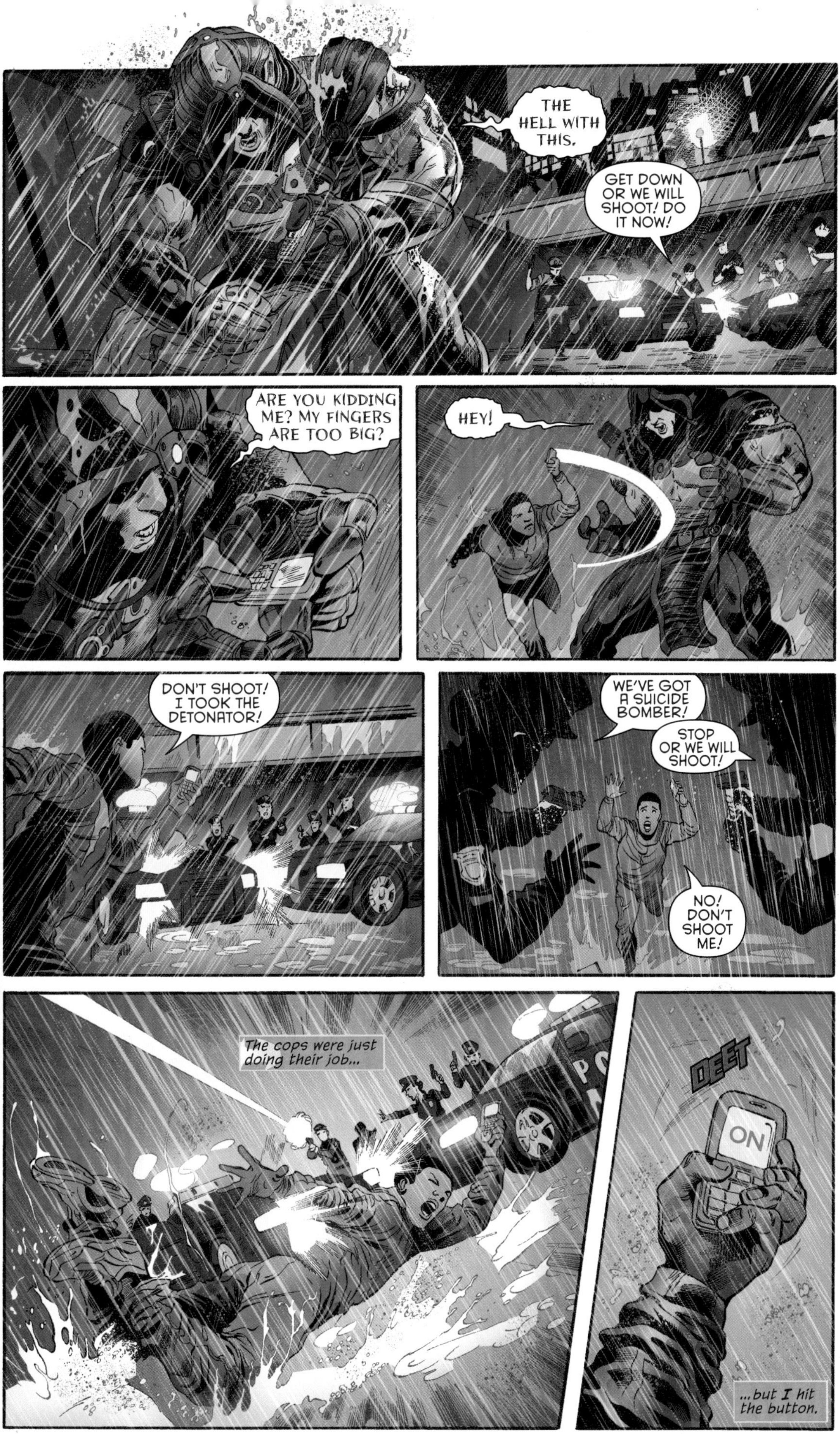
THE HELL WITH THIS.
GET DOWN OR WE WILL SHOOT! DO IT NOW!
ARE YOU KIDDING ME? MY FINGERS ARE TOO BIG?
HEY!
DON'T SHOOT! I TOOK THE DETONATOR!
WE'VE GOT A SUICIDE BOMBER!
STOP OR WE WILL SHOOT!
NO! DON'T SHOOT ME!
The cops were just doing their job...
DEET
ON
...but I hit the button.

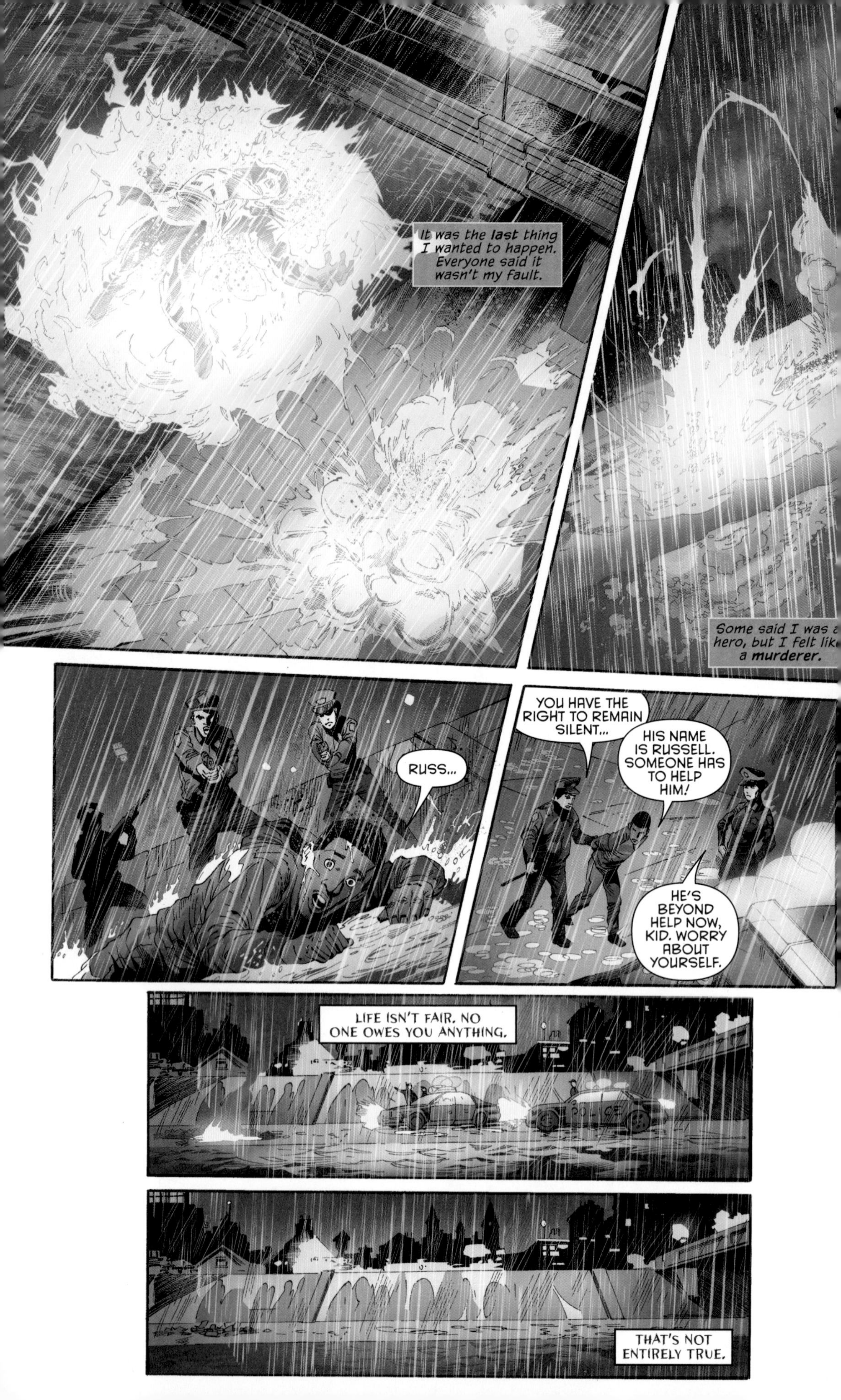
It was the last thing I wanted to happen. Everyone said it wasn't my fault.
Some said I was a hero, but I felt like a murderer.
RUSS...
YOU HAVE THE RIGHT TO REMAIN SILENT...
HIS NAME IS RUSSELL. SOMEONE HAS TO HELP HIM!
HE'S BEYOND HELP NOW, KID. WORRY ABOUT YOURSELF.
LIFE ISN'T FAIR. NO ONE OWES YOU ANYTHING.
THAT'S NOT ENTIRELY TRUE.

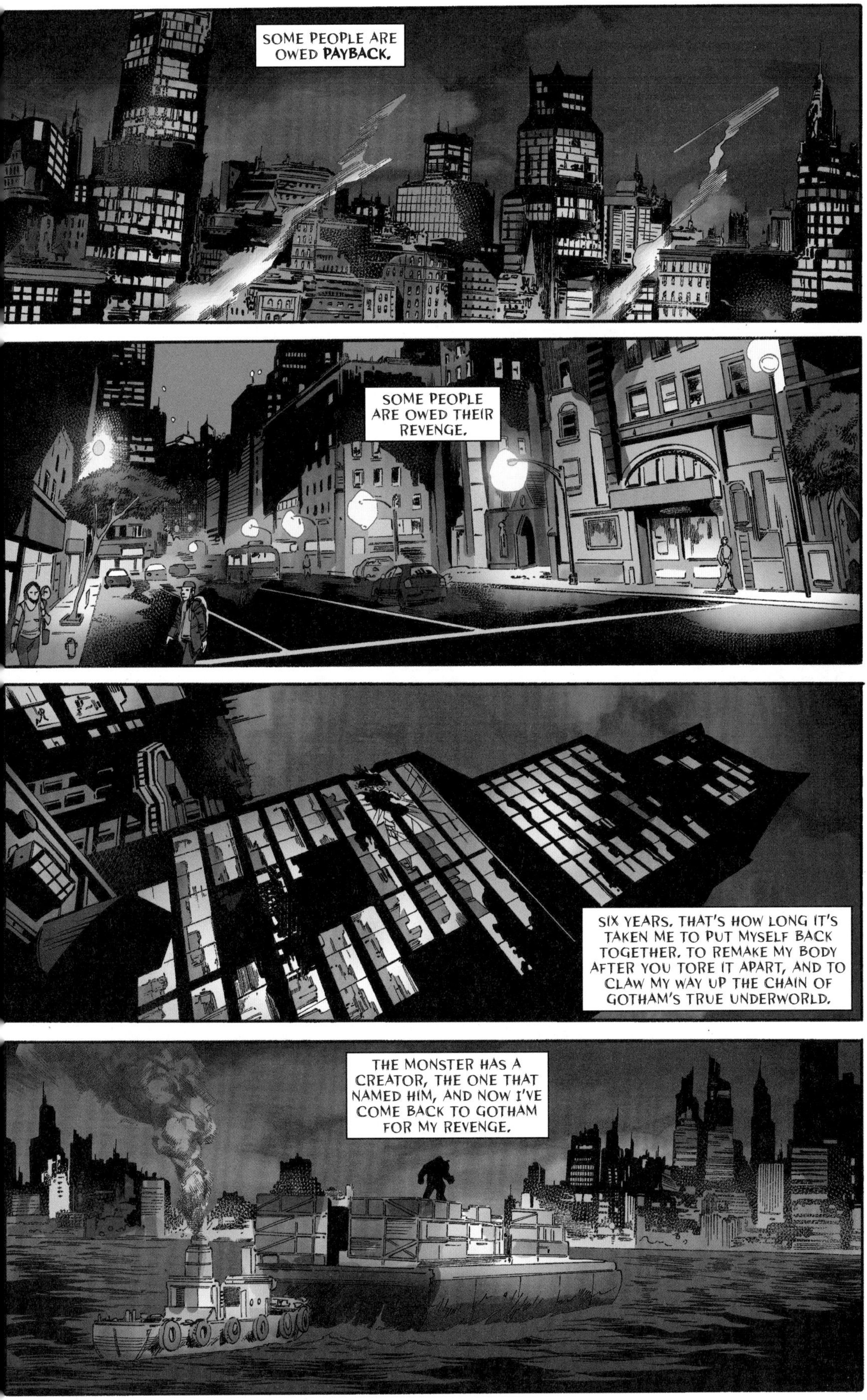
SOME PEOPLE ARE OWED **PAYBACK.**
SOME PEOPLE ARE OWED THEIR REVENGE.
SIX YEARS. THAT'S HOW LONG IT'S TAKEN ME TO PUT MYSELF BACK TOGETHER. TO REMAKE MY BODY AFTER YOU TORE IT APART, AND TO CLAW MY WAY UP THE CHAIN OF GOTHAM'S TRUE UNDERWORLD.
THE MONSTER HAS A CREATOR, THE ONE THAT NAMED HIM, AND NOW I'VE COME BACK TO GOTHAM FOR MY REVENGE.

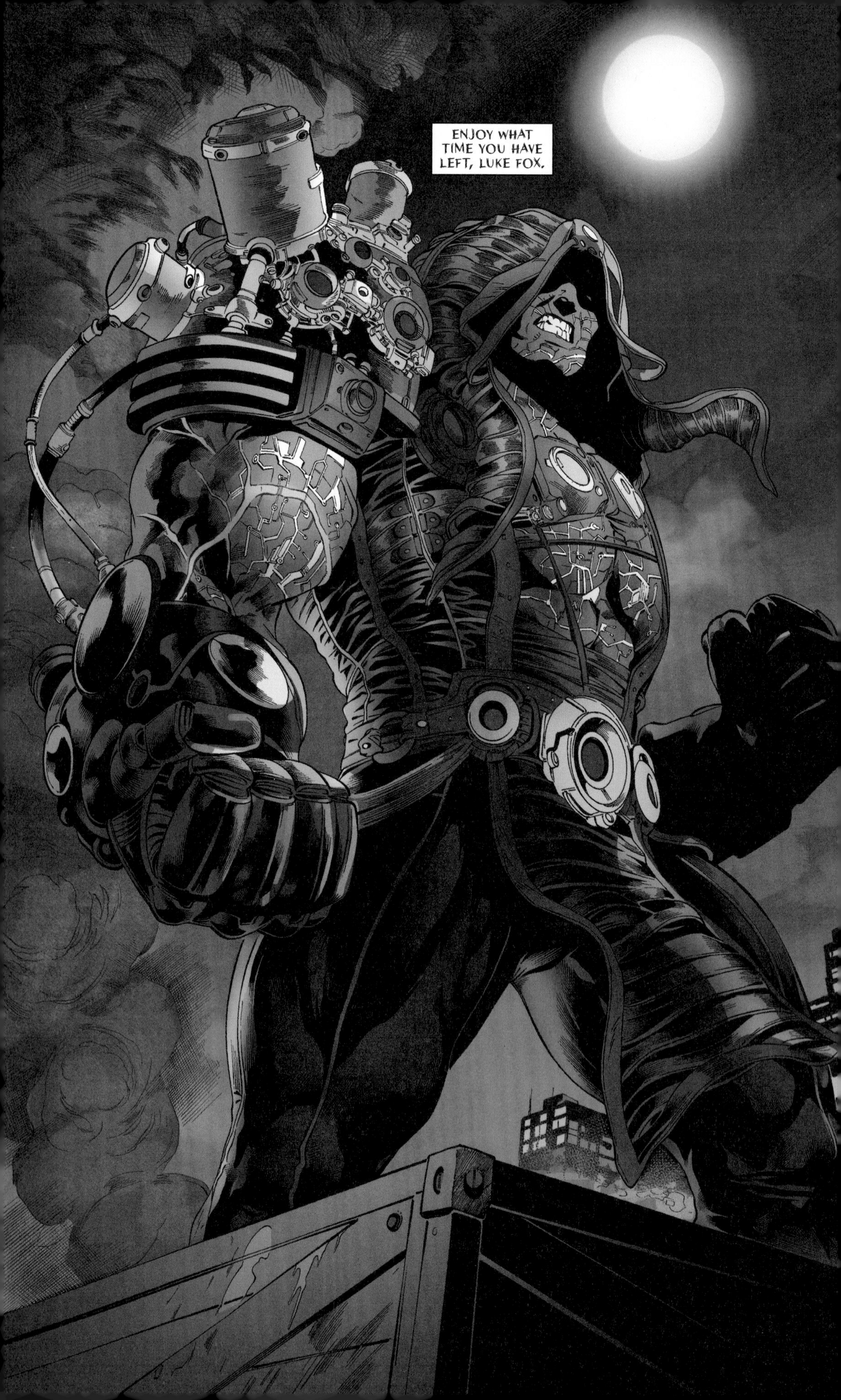
ENJOY WHAT TIME YOU HAVE LEFT, LUKE FOX.

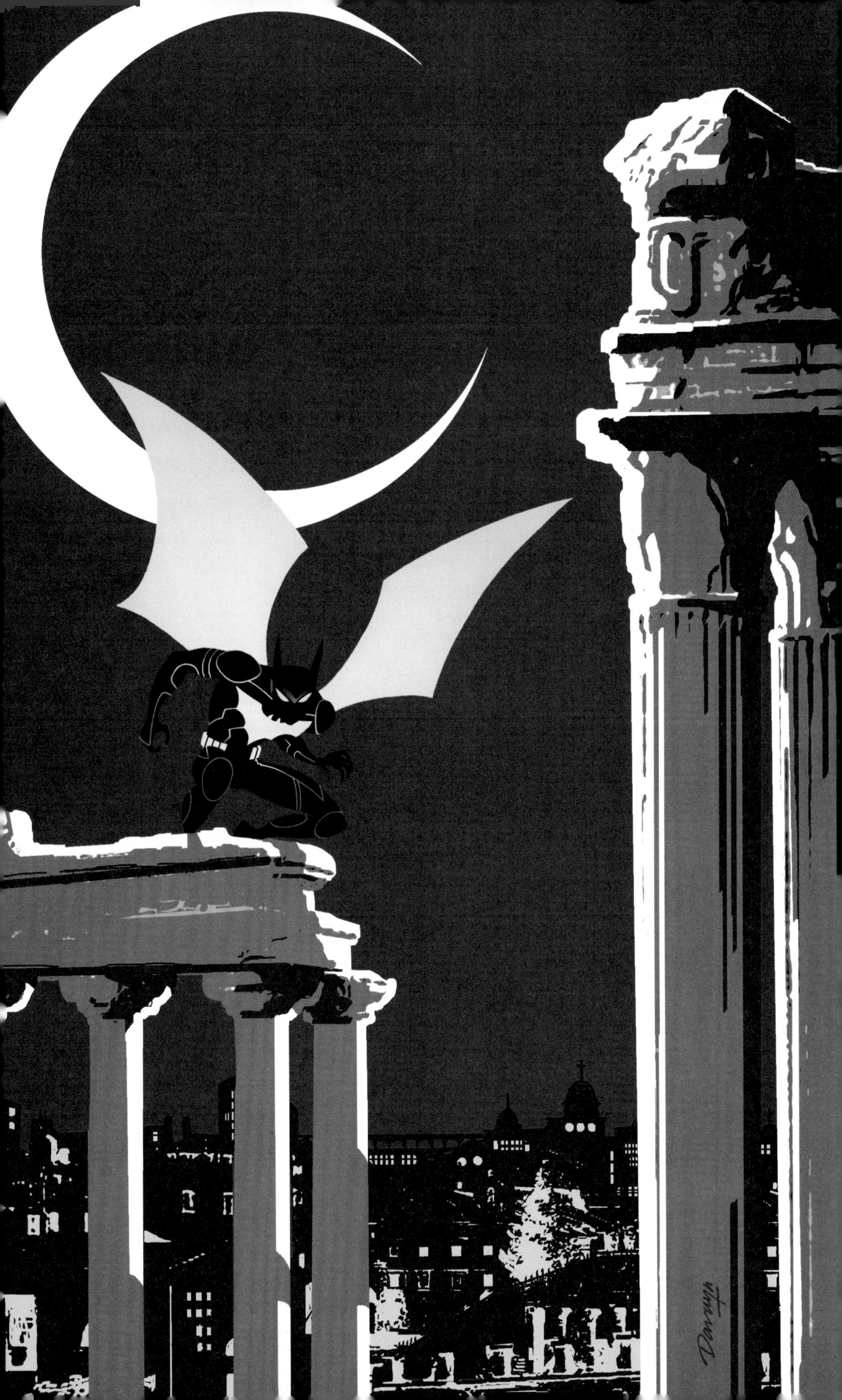

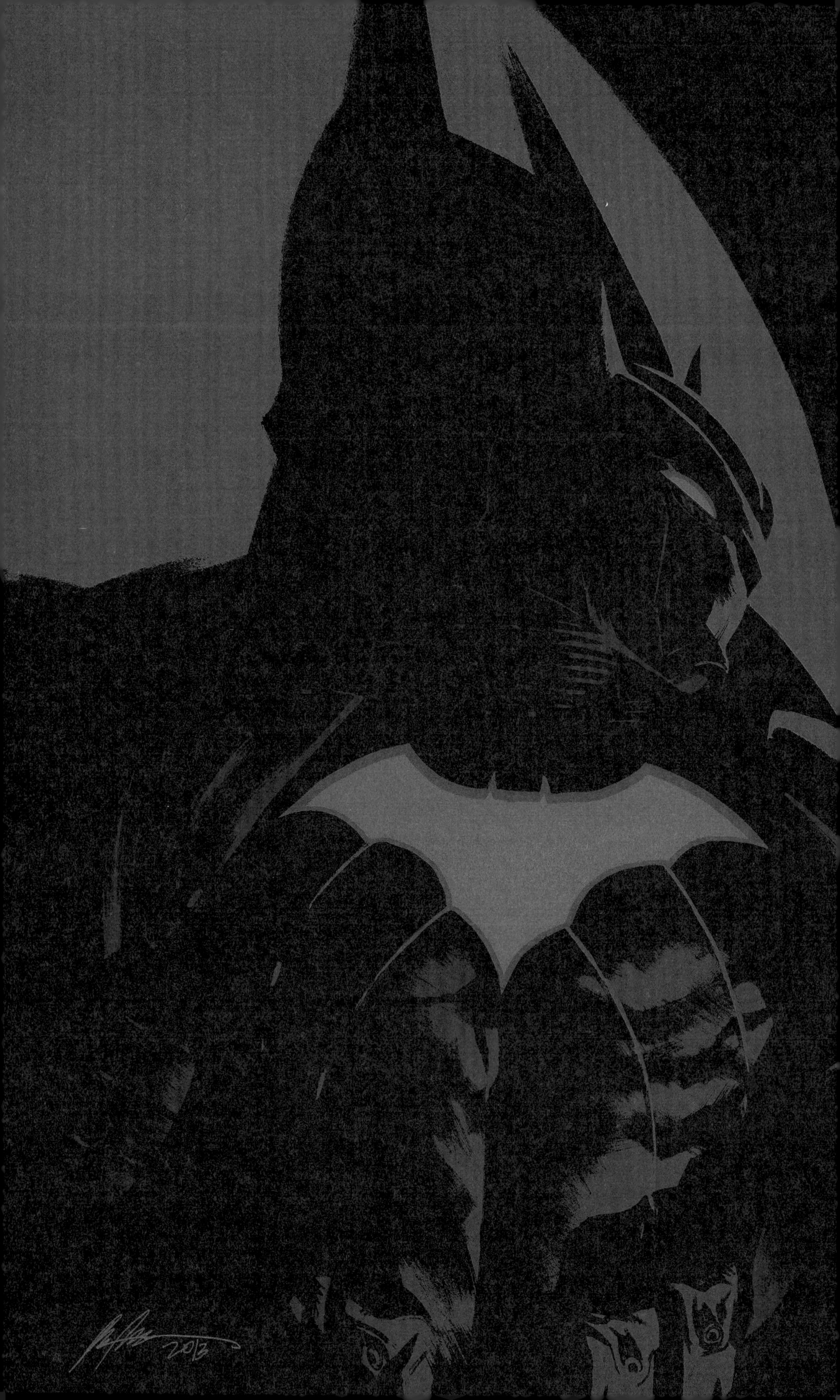

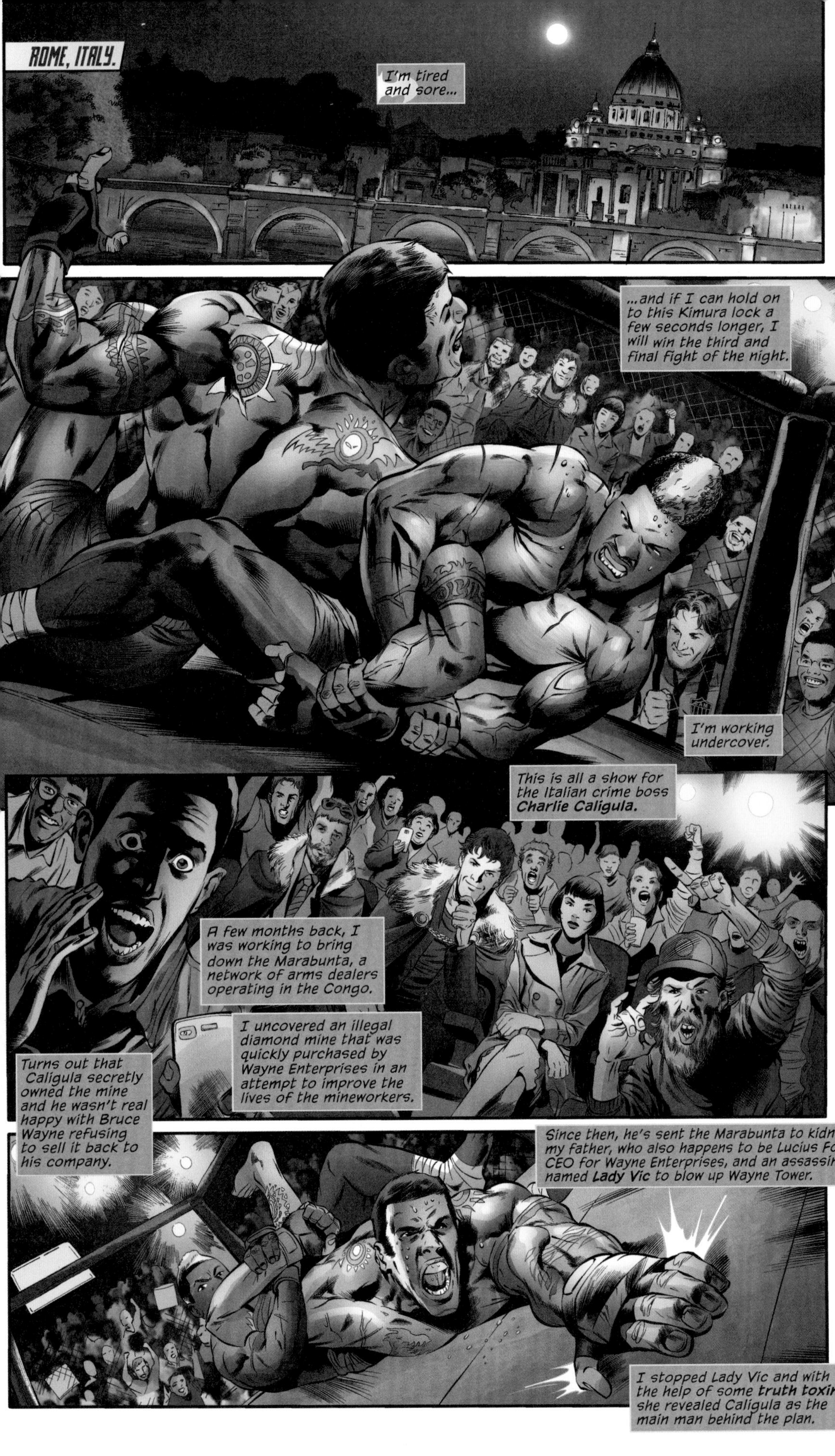
ROME, ITALY.
I'm tired and sore...
...and if I can hold on to this Kimura lock a few seconds longer, I will win the third and final fight of the night.
I'm working undercover.
This is all a show for the Italian crime boss Charlie Caligula.
A few months back, I was working to bring down the Marabunta, a network of arms dealers operating in the Congo.
I uncovered an illegal diamond mine that was quickly purchased by Wayne Enterprises in an attempt to improve the lives of the mineworkers.
Turns out that Caligula secretly owned the mine and he wasn't real happy with Bruce Wayne refusing to sell it back to his company.
Since then, he's sent the Marabunta to kidnap my father, who also happens to be Lucius Fox, CEO for Wayne Enterprises, and an assassin named Lady Vic to blow up Wayne Tower.
I stopped Lady Vic and with the help of some truth toxin, she revealed Caligula as the main man behind the plan.

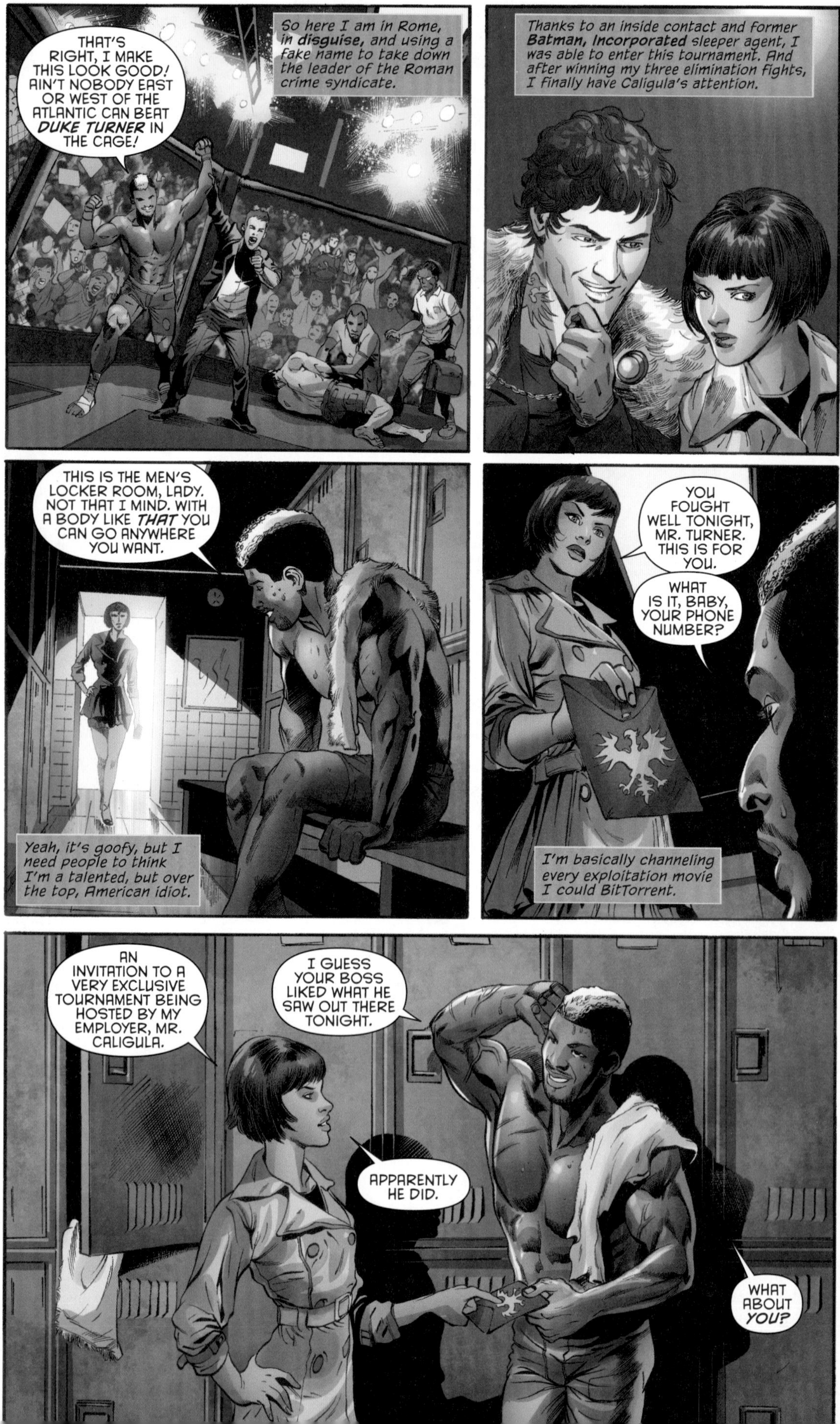
THAT'S RIGHT, I MAKE THIS LOOK GOOD! AIN'T NOBODY EAST OR WEST OF THE ATLANTIC CAN BEAT DUKE TURNER IN THE CAGE!
So here I am in Rome, in disguise, and using a fake name to take down the leader of the Roman crime syndicate.
Thanks to an inside contact and former Batman, Incorporated sleeper agent, I was able to enter this tournament. And after winning my three elimination fights, I finally have Caligula's attention.
THIS IS THE MEN'S LOCKER ROOM, LADY. NOT THAT I MIND. WITH A BODY LIKE THAT YOU CAN GO ANYWHERE YOU WANT.
Yeah, it's goofy, but I need people to think I'm a talented, but over the top, American idiot.
YOU FOUGHT WELL TONIGHT, MR. TURNER. THIS IS FOR YOU.
WHAT IS IT, BABY, YOUR PHONE NUMBER?
I'm basically channeling every exploitation movie I could BitTorrent.
AN INVITATION TO A VERY EXCLUSIVE TOURNAMENT BEING HOSTED BY MY EMPLOYER, MR. CALIGULA.
I GUESS YOUR BOSS LIKED WHAT HE SAW OUT THERE TONIGHT.
APPARENTLY HE DID.
WHAT ABOUT YOU?

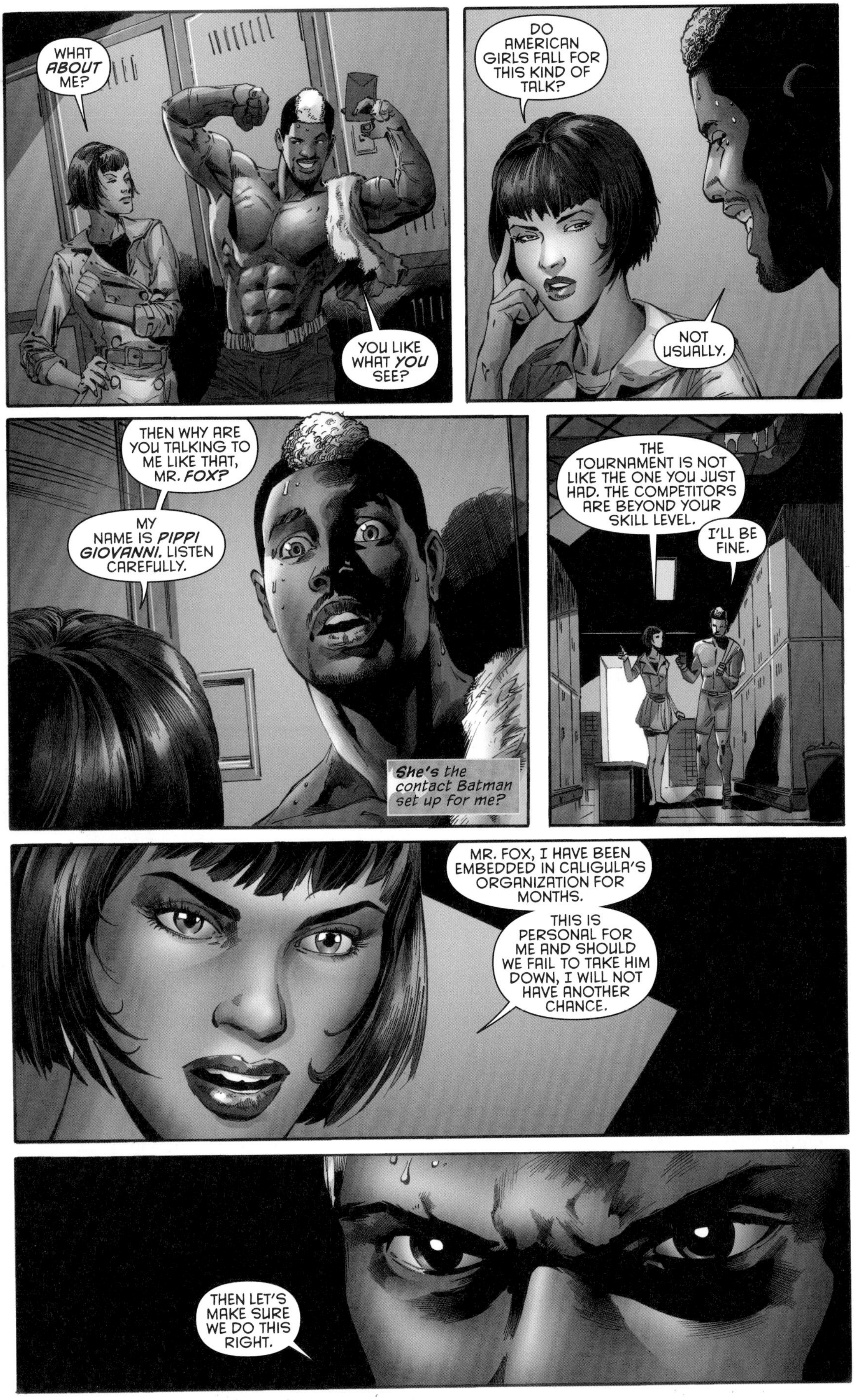
WHAT ABOUT ME?
YOU LIKE WHAT YOU SEE?
DO AMERICAN GIRLS FALL FOR THIS KIND OF TALK?
NOT USUALLY.
THEN WHY ARE YOU TALKING TO ME LIKE THAT, MR. FOX?
MY NAME IS PIPPI GIOVANNI. LISTEN CAREFULLY.
She's the contact Batman set up for me?
THE TOURNAMENT IS NOT LIKE THE ONE YOU JUST HAD. THE COMPETITORS ARE BEYOND YOUR SKILL LEVEL.
I'LL BE FINE.
MR. FOX, I HAVE BEEN EMBEDDED IN CALIGULA'S ORGANIZATION FOR MONTHS.
THIS IS PERSONAL FOR ME AND SHOULD WE FAIL TO TAKE HIM DOWN, I WILL NOT HAVE ANOTHER CHANCE.
THEN LET'S MAKE SURE WE DO THIS RIGHT.

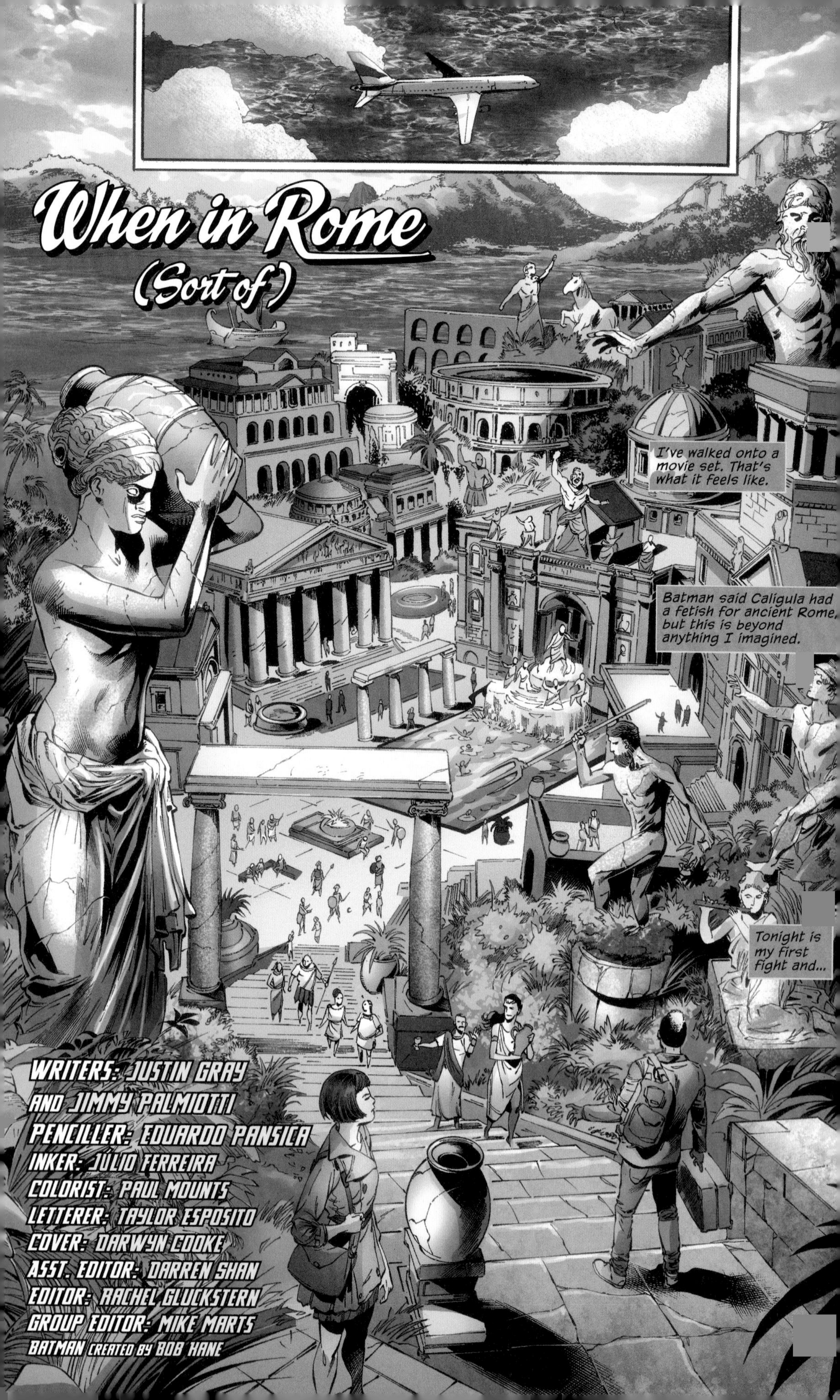
When in Rome
(Sort of)
I've walked onto a movie set. That's what it feels like.
Batman said Caligula had a fetish for ancient Rome, but this is beyond anything I imagined.
Tonight is my first fight and...
WRITERS: JUSTIN GRAY AND JIMMY PALMIOTTI
PENCILLER: EDUARDO PANSICA
INKER: JÚLIO FERREIRA
COLORIST: PAUL MOUNTS
LETTERER: TAYLOR ESPOSITO
COVER: DARWYN COOKE
ASST. EDITOR: DARREN SHAN
EDITOR: RACHEL GLUCKSTERN
GROUP EDITOR: MIKE MARTS
BATMAN CREATED BY BOB KANE

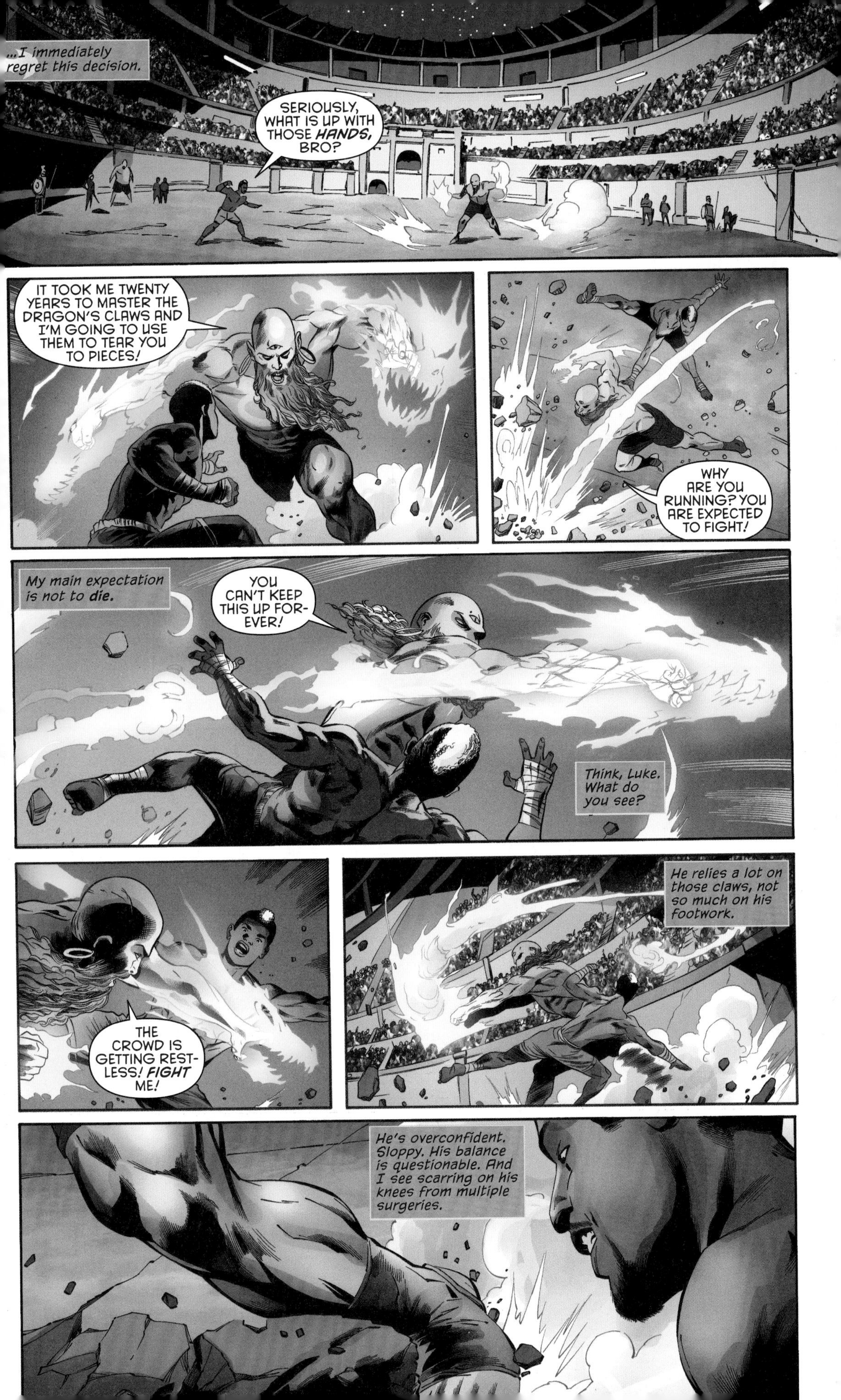

...I immediately regret this decision.
SERIOUSLY, WHAT IS UP WITH THOSE HANDS, BRO?
IT TOOK ME TWENTY YEARS TO MASTER THE DRAGON'S CLAWS AND I'M GOING TO USE THEM TO TEAR YOU TO PIECES!
WHY ARE YOU RUNNING? YOU ARE EXPECTED TO FIGHT!
My main expectation is not to die.
YOU CAN'T KEEP THIS UP FOR-EVER!
Think, Luke. What do you see?
THE CROWD IS GETTING REST-LESS! FIGHT ME!
He relies a lot on those claws, not so much on his footwork.
He's overconfident. Sloppy. His balance is questionable. And I see scarring on his knees from multiple surgeries.

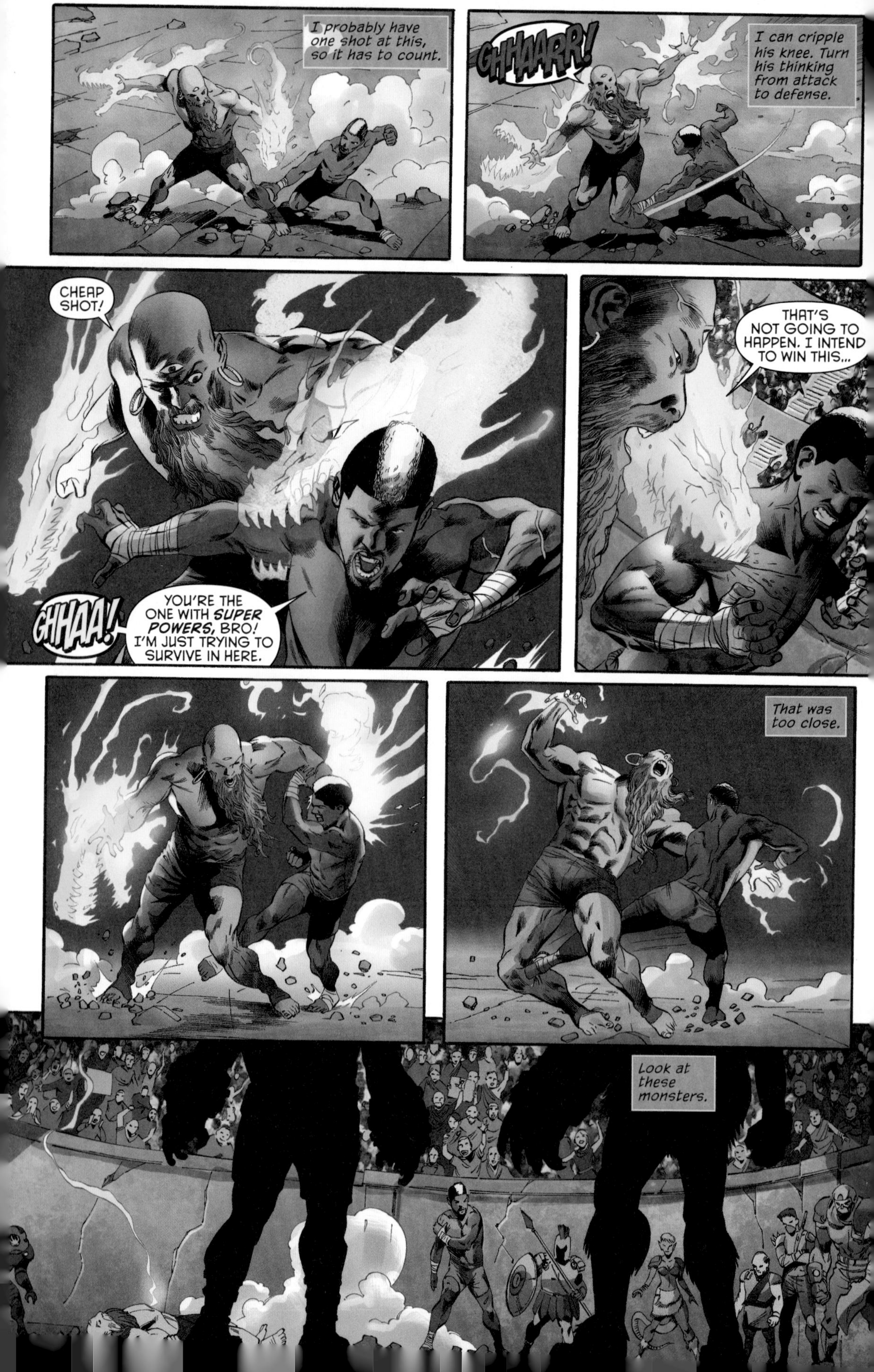
I probably have one shot at this, so it has to count.
GHHAARR!
I can cripple his knee. Turn his thinking from attack to defense.
CHEAP SHOT!
GHHAA!
YOU'RE THE ONE WITH SUPER POWERS, BRO! I'M JUST TRYING TO SURVIVE IN HERE.
THAT'S NOT GOING TO HAPPEN. I INTEND TO WIN THIS...
That was too close.
Look at these monsters.

I'm gonna get killed if I try to stay in the tourney.

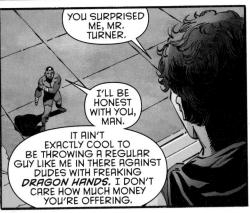

YOU SURPRISED ME, MR. TURNER.

I'LL BE HONEST WITH YOU, MAN.

IT AIN'T EXACTLY COOL TO BE THROWING A REGULAR GUY LIKE ME IN THERE AGAINST DUDES WITH FREAKING *DRAGON HANDS.* I DON'T CARE HOW MUCH MONEY YOU'RE OFFERING.

I AM YOUR *HOST,* MR. TURNER. YOU WILL ADDRESS ME AS *MR. CALIGULA,* OR I WILL HAVE YOU GUTTED AND THROWN IN THE OCEAN.

YOU WERE INVITED FOR ONE REASON AND ONE REASON ONLY. I NEEDED A LAMB FOR THE SLAUGHTER.

SORRY TO DISAPPOINT YOU.

I'M SURE YOU WON'T DISAPPOINT ME TOMORROW.

NEVER LET IT BE SAID I AM NOT A GENEROUS MAN. YOU MAY CHOOSE ANYONE SEATED WITH ME AS YOUR NIGHT'S ENTERTAINMENT.

YOU'RE SERIOUS? THEY'RE *PEOPLE.*

THEY'RE *MY* PEOPLE. THEY DO WHAT I SAY.

BOY OR GIRL, IT'S YOUR CHOICE, DUKE TURNER.

I WANT *HER.*

I'LL HAVE HER SENT TO YOUR ROOM.

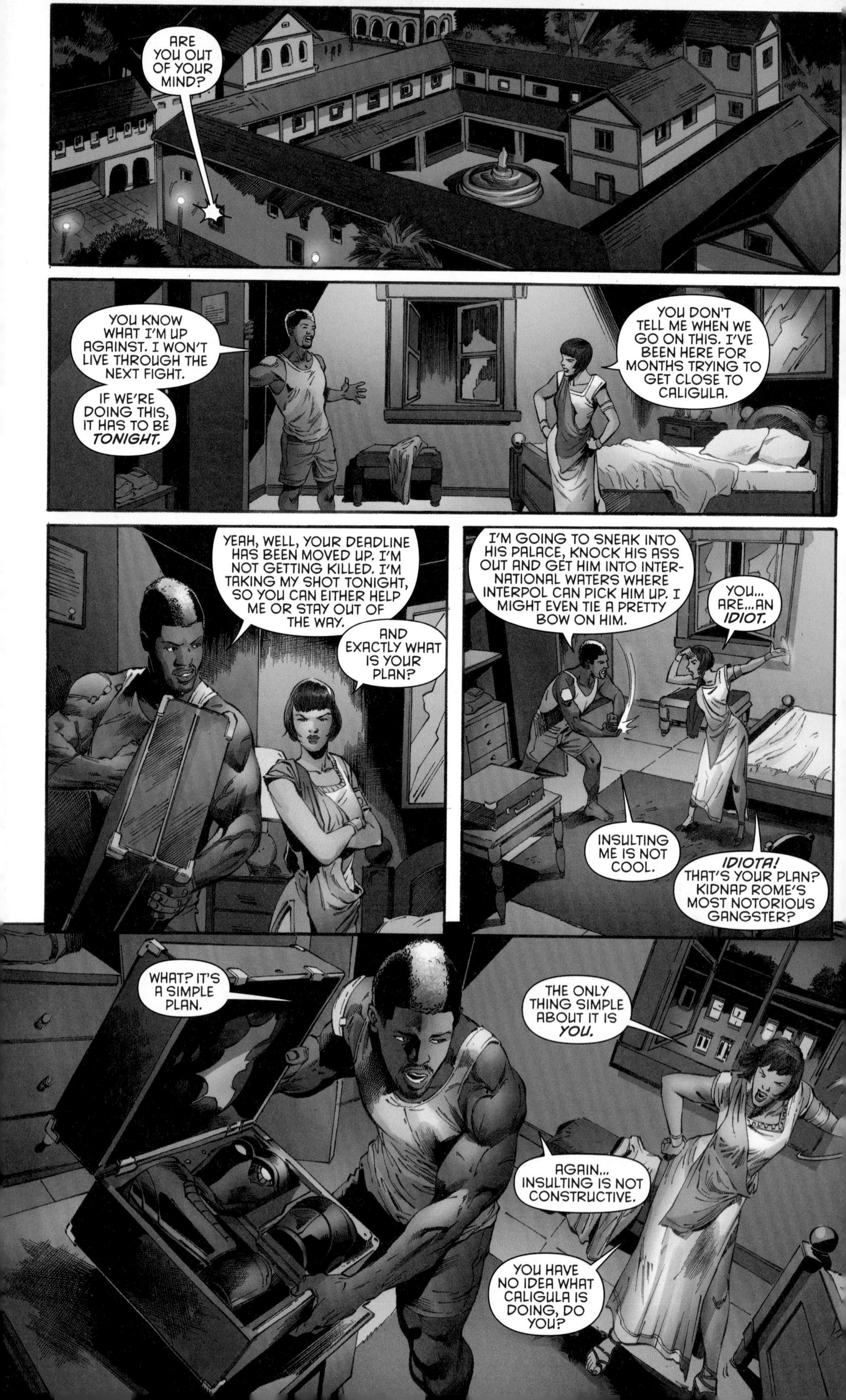

ARE YOU OUT OF YOUR MIND?
YOU KNOW WHAT I'M UP AGAINST. I WON'T LIVE THROUGH THE NEXT FIGHT.
IF WE'RE DOING THIS, IT HAS TO BE *TONIGHT.*
YOU DON'T TELL ME WHEN WE GO ON THIS. I'VE BEEN HERE FOR MONTHS TRYING TO GET CLOSE TO CALIGULA.
YEAH, WELL, YOUR DEADLINE HAS BEEN MOVED UP. I'M NOT GETTING KILLED. I'M TAKING MY SHOT TONIGHT, SO YOU CAN EITHER HELP ME OR STAY OUT OF THE WAY.
AND EXACTLY WHAT IS YOUR PLAN?
I'M GOING TO SNEAK INTO HIS PALACE, KNOCK HIS ASS OUT AND GET HIM INTO INTERNATIONAL WATERS WHERE INTERPOL CAN PICK HIM UP. I MIGHT EVEN TIE A PRETTY BOW ON HIM.
YOU... ARE...AN *IDIOT.*
INSULTING ME IS NOT COOL.
IDIOTA! THAT'S YOUR PLAN? KIDNAP ROME'S MOST NOTORIOUS GANGSTER?
WHAT? IT'S A SIMPLE PLAN.
THE ONLY THING SIMPLE ABOUT IT IS *YOU.*
AGAIN... INSULTING IS NOT CONSTRUCTIVE.
YOU HAVE NO IDEA WHAT CALIGULA IS DOING, DO YOU?

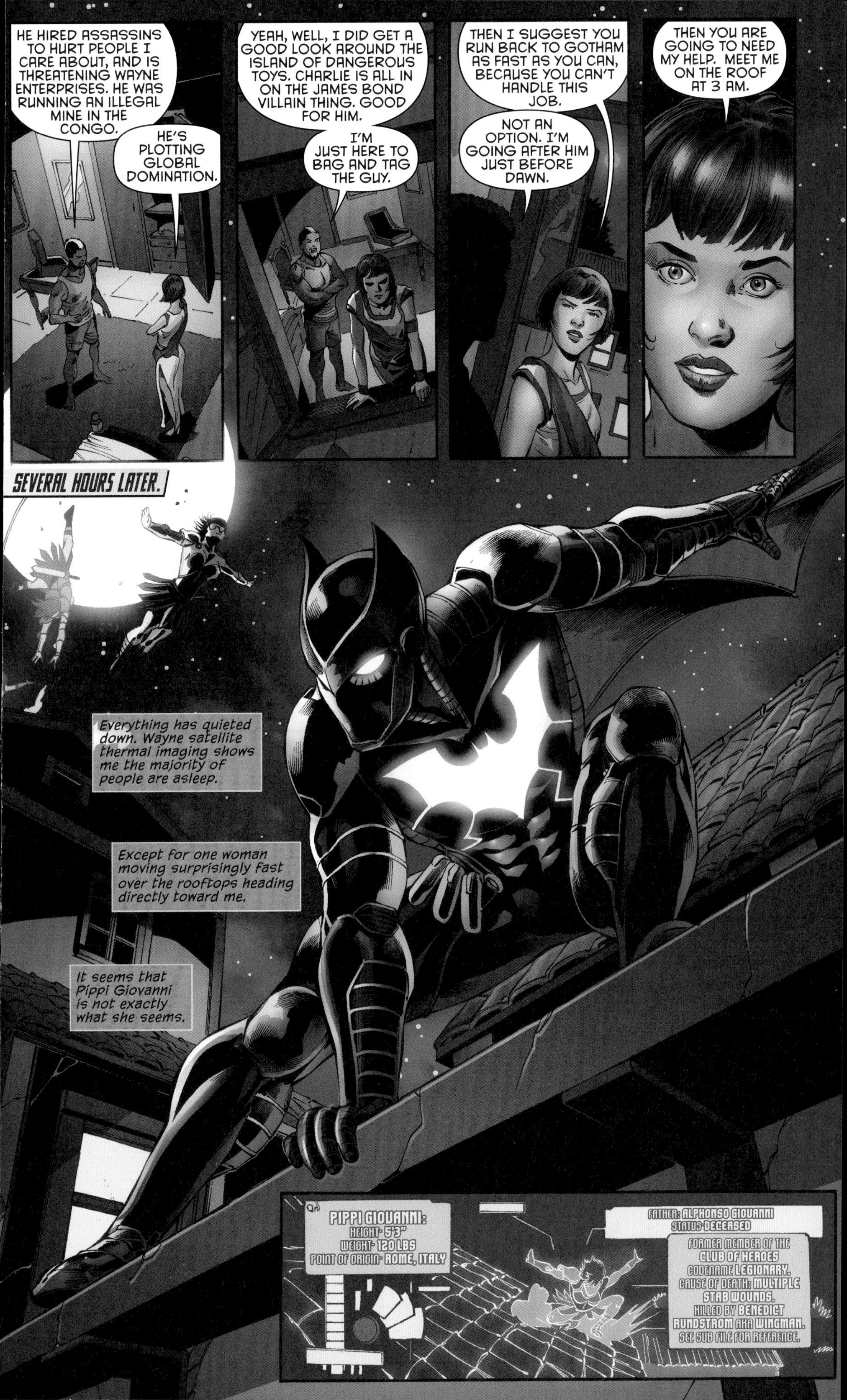
HE HIRED ASSASSINS TO HURT PEOPLE I CARE ABOUT, AND IS THREATENING WAYNE ENTERPRISES. HE WAS RUNNING AN ILLEGAL MINE IN THE CONGO.
HE'S PLOTTING GLOBAL DOMINATION.
YEAH, WELL, I DID GET A GOOD LOOK AROUND THE ISLAND OF DANGEROUS TOYS. CHARLIE IS ALL IN ON THE JAMES BOND VILLAIN THING. GOOD FOR HIM.
I'M JUST HERE TO BAG AND TAG THE GUY.
THEN I SUGGEST YOU RUN BACK TO GOTHAM AS FAST AS YOU CAN, BECAUSE YOU CAN'T HANDLE THIS JOB.
NOT AN OPTION. I'M GOING AFTER HIM JUST BEFORE DAWN.
THEN YOU ARE GOING TO NEED MY HELP. MEET ME ON THE ROOF AT 3 AM.
SEVERAL HOURS LATER.
Everything has quieted down. Wayne satellite thermal imaging shows me the majority of people are asleep.
Except for one woman moving surprisingly fast over the rooftops heading directly toward me.
It seems that Pippi Giovanni is not exactly what she seems.
PIPPI GIOVANNI:
HEIGHT- 5'3"
WEIGHT- 120 LBS
POINT OF ORIGIN- ROME, ITALY
FATHER: ALPHONSO GIOVANNI
STATUS-DECEASED
FORMER MEMBER OF THE CLUB OF HEROES CODENAME LEGIONARY. CAUSE OF DEATH: MULTIPLE STAB WOUNDS. KILLED BY BENEDICT RUNDSTROM AKA WINGMAN. SEE SUB FILE FOR REFERENCE.

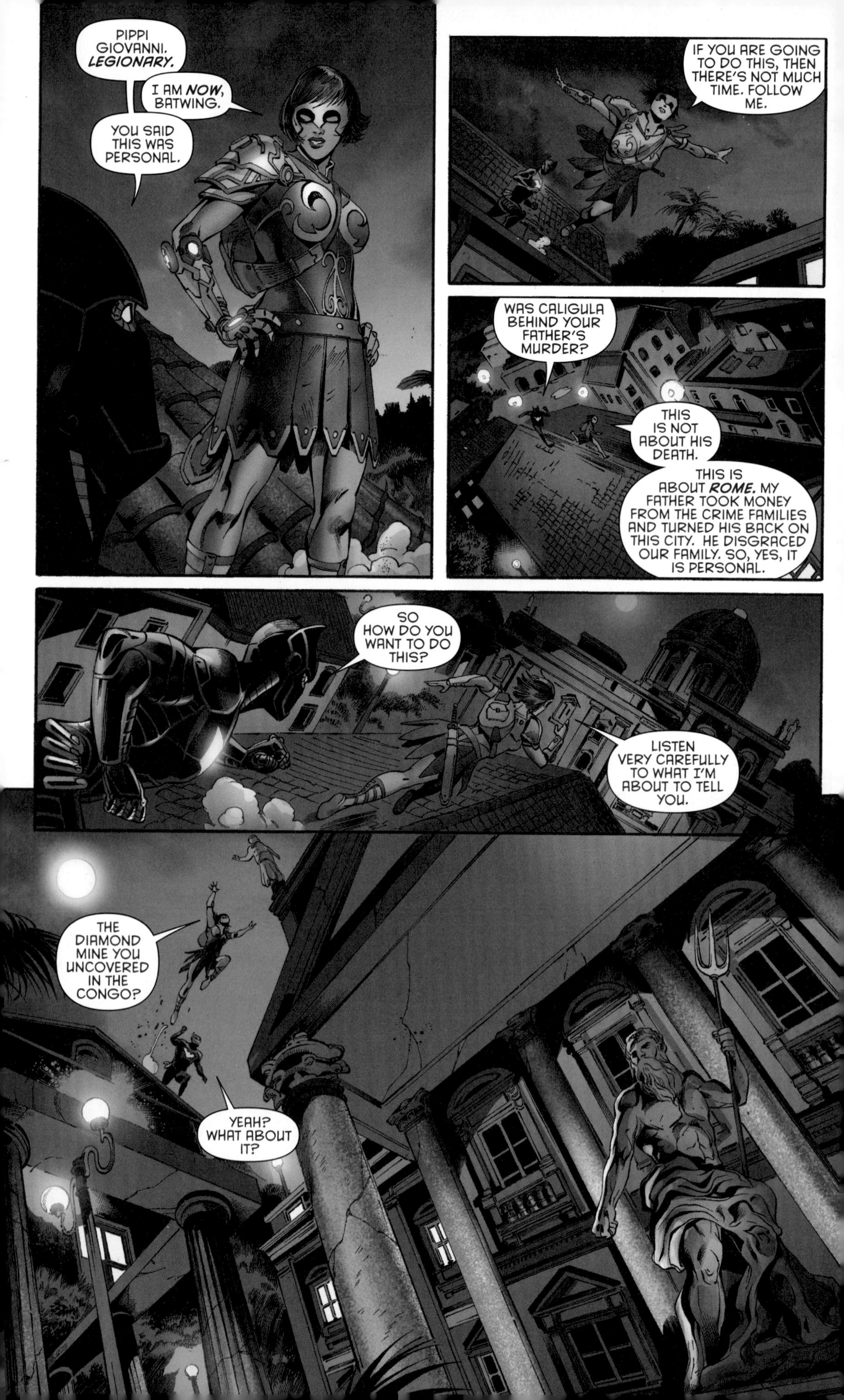
PIPPI GIOVANNI. LEGIONARY.
I AM NOW, BATWING.
YOU SAID THIS WAS PERSONAL.
IF YOU ARE GOING TO DO THIS, THEN THERE'S NOT MUCH TIME. FOLLOW ME.
WAS CALIGULA BEHIND YOUR FATHER'S MURDER?
THIS IS NOT ABOUT HIS DEATH.
THIS IS ABOUT ROME. MY FATHER TOOK MONEY FROM THE CRIME FAMILIES AND TURNED HIS BACK ON THIS CITY. HE DISGRACED OUR FAMILY. SO, YES, IT IS PERSONAL.
SO HOW DO YOU WANT TO DO THIS?
LISTEN VERY CAREFULLY TO WHAT I'M ABOUT TO TELL YOU.
THE DIAMOND MINE YOU UNCOVERED IN THE CONGO?
YEAH? WHAT ABOUT IT?

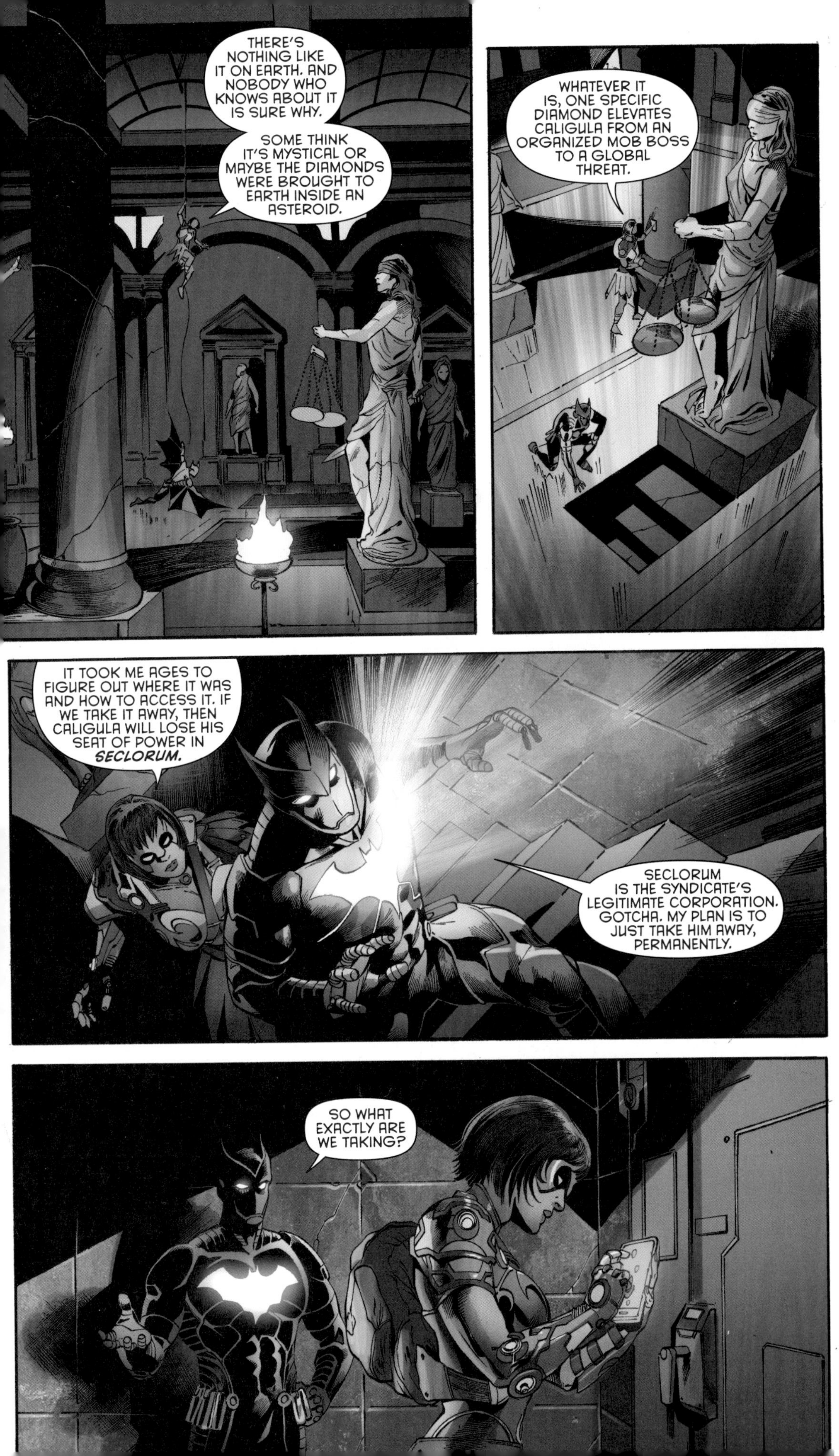
THERE'S NOTHING LIKE IT ON EARTH. AND NOBODY WHO KNOWS ABOUT IT IS SURE WHY.
SOME THINK IT'S MYSTICAL OR MAYBE THE DIAMONDS WERE BROUGHT TO EARTH INSIDE AN ASTEROID.
WHATEVER IT IS, ONE SPECIFIC DIAMOND ELEVATES CALIGULA FROM AN ORGANIZED MOB BOSS TO A GLOBAL THREAT.
IT TOOK ME AGES TO FIGURE OUT WHERE IT WAS AND HOW TO ACCESS IT. IF WE TAKE IT AWAY, THEN CALIGULA WILL LOSE HIS SEAT OF POWER IN SECLORUM.
SECLORUM IS THE SYNDICATE'S LEGITIMATE CORPORATION. GOTCHA. MY PLAN IS TO JUST TAKE HIM AWAY, PERMANENTLY.
SO WHAT EXACTLY ARE WE TAKING?

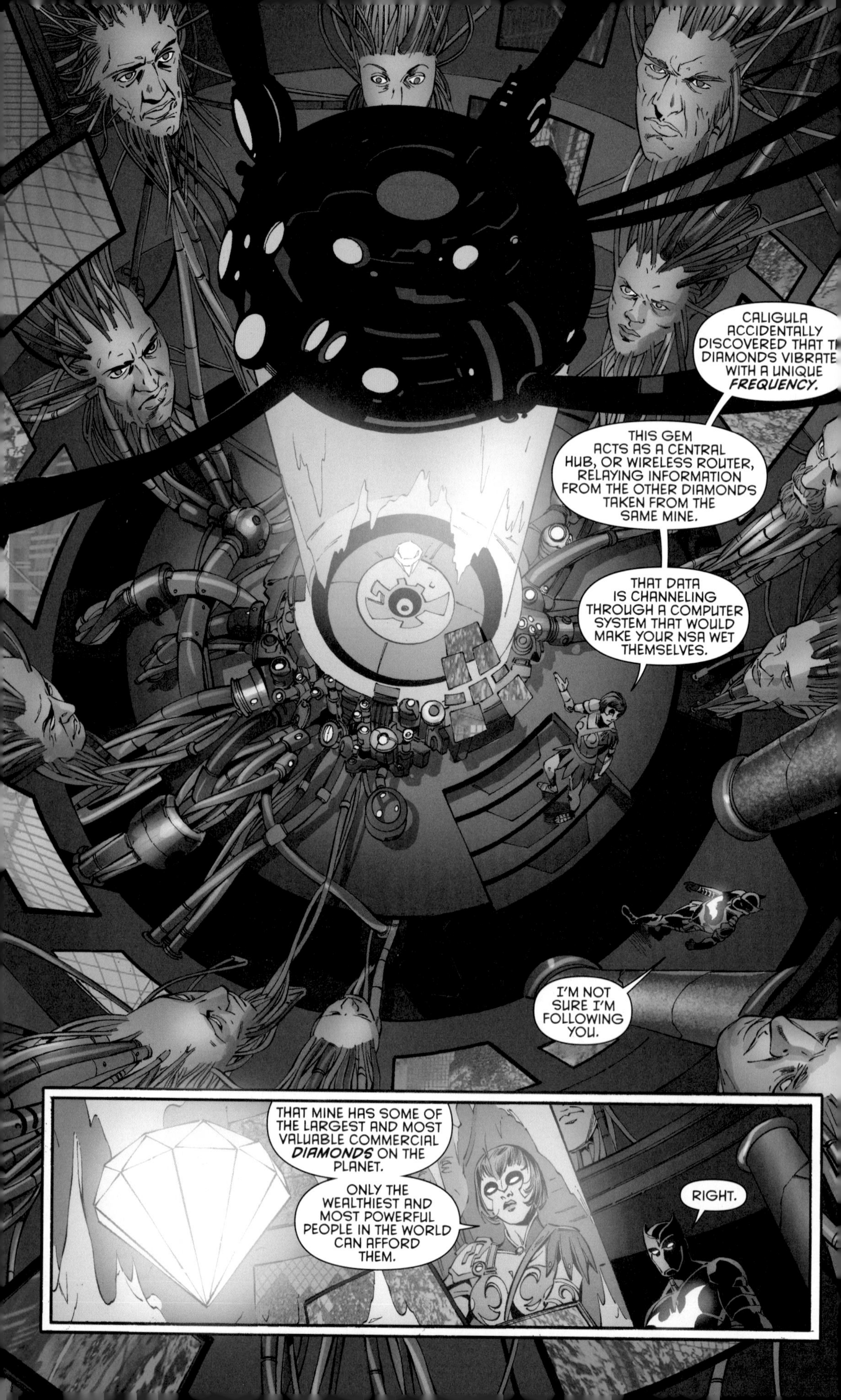

CALIGULA ACCIDENTALLY DISCOVERED THAT TH DIAMONDS VIBRATE WITH A UNIQUE *FREQUENCY.*
THIS GEM ACTS AS A CENTRAL HUB, OR WIRELESS ROUTER, RELAYING INFORMATION FROM THE OTHER DIAMONDS TAKEN FROM THE SAME MINE.
THAT DATA IS CHANNELING THROUGH A COMPUTER SYSTEM THAT WOULD MAKE YOUR NSA WET THEMSELVES.
I'M NOT SURE I'M FOLLOWING YOU.
THAT MINE HAS SOME OF THE LARGEST AND MOST VALUABLE COMMERCIAL *DIAMONDS* ON THE PLANET.
ONLY THE WEALTHIEST AND MOST POWERFUL PEOPLE IN THE WORLD CAN AFFORD THEM.
RIGHT.

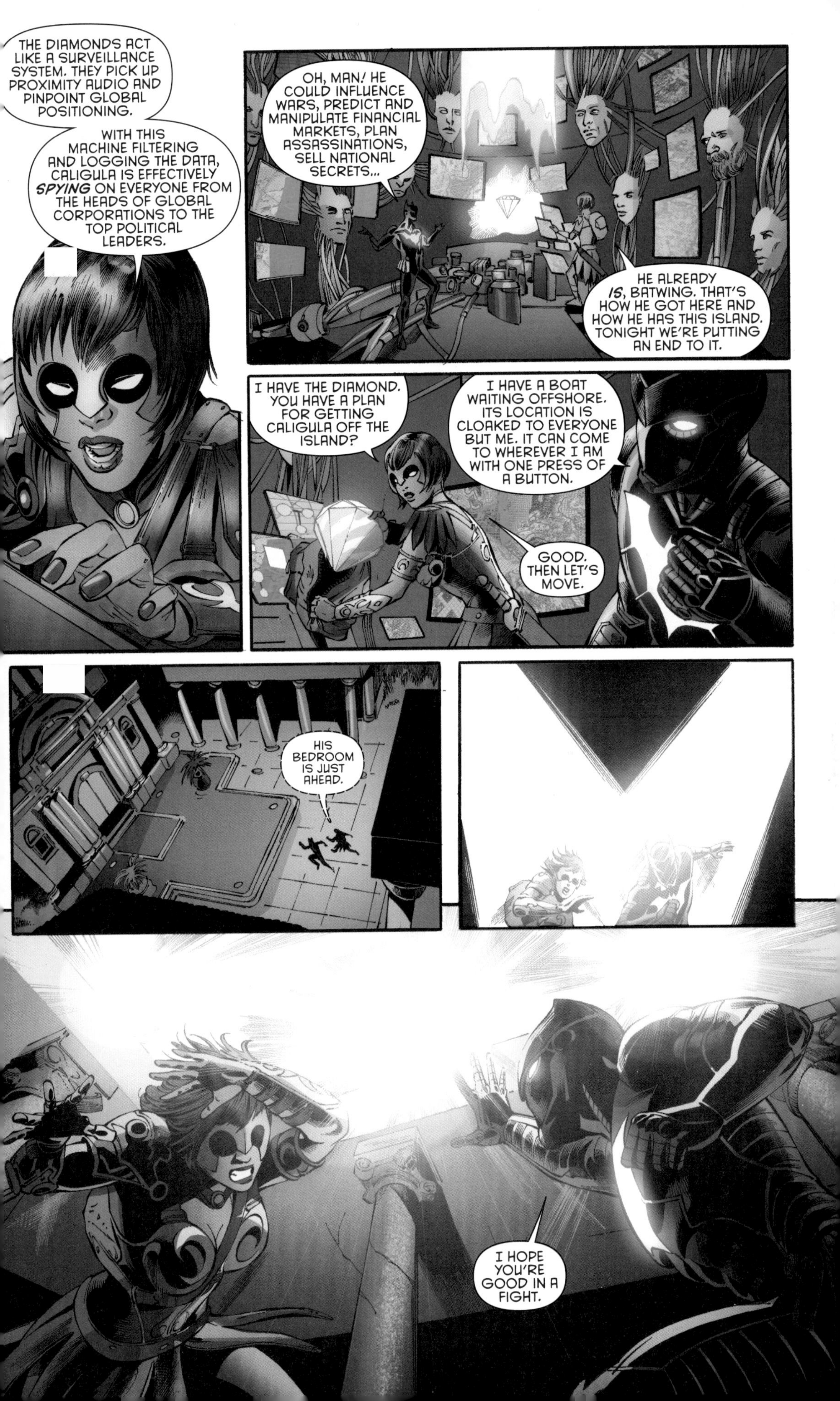
THE DIAMONDS ACT LIKE A SURVEILLANCE SYSTEM. THEY PICK UP PROXIMITY AUDIO AND PINPOINT GLOBAL POSITIONING.
WITH THIS MACHINE FILTERING AND LOGGING THE DATA, CALIGULA IS EFFECTIVELY SPYING ON EVERYONE FROM THE HEADS OF GLOBAL CORPORATIONS TO THE TOP POLITICAL LEADERS.
OH, MAN! HE COULD INFLUENCE WARS, PREDICT AND MANIPULATE FINANCIAL MARKETS, PLAN ASSASSINATIONS, SELL NATIONAL SECRETS...
HE ALREADY IS, BATWING. THAT'S HOW HE GOT HERE AND HOW HE HAS THIS ISLAND. TONIGHT WE'RE PUTTING AN END TO IT.
I HAVE THE DIAMOND. YOU HAVE A PLAN FOR GETTING CALIGULA OFF THE ISLAND?
I HAVE A BOAT WAITING OFFSHORE. ITS LOCATION IS CLOAKED TO EVERYONE BUT ME. IT CAN COME TO WHEREVER I AM WITH ONE PRESS OF A BUTTON.
GOOD. THEN LET'S MOVE.
HIS BEDROOM IS JUST AHEAD.
I HOPE YOU'RE GOOD IN A FIGHT.

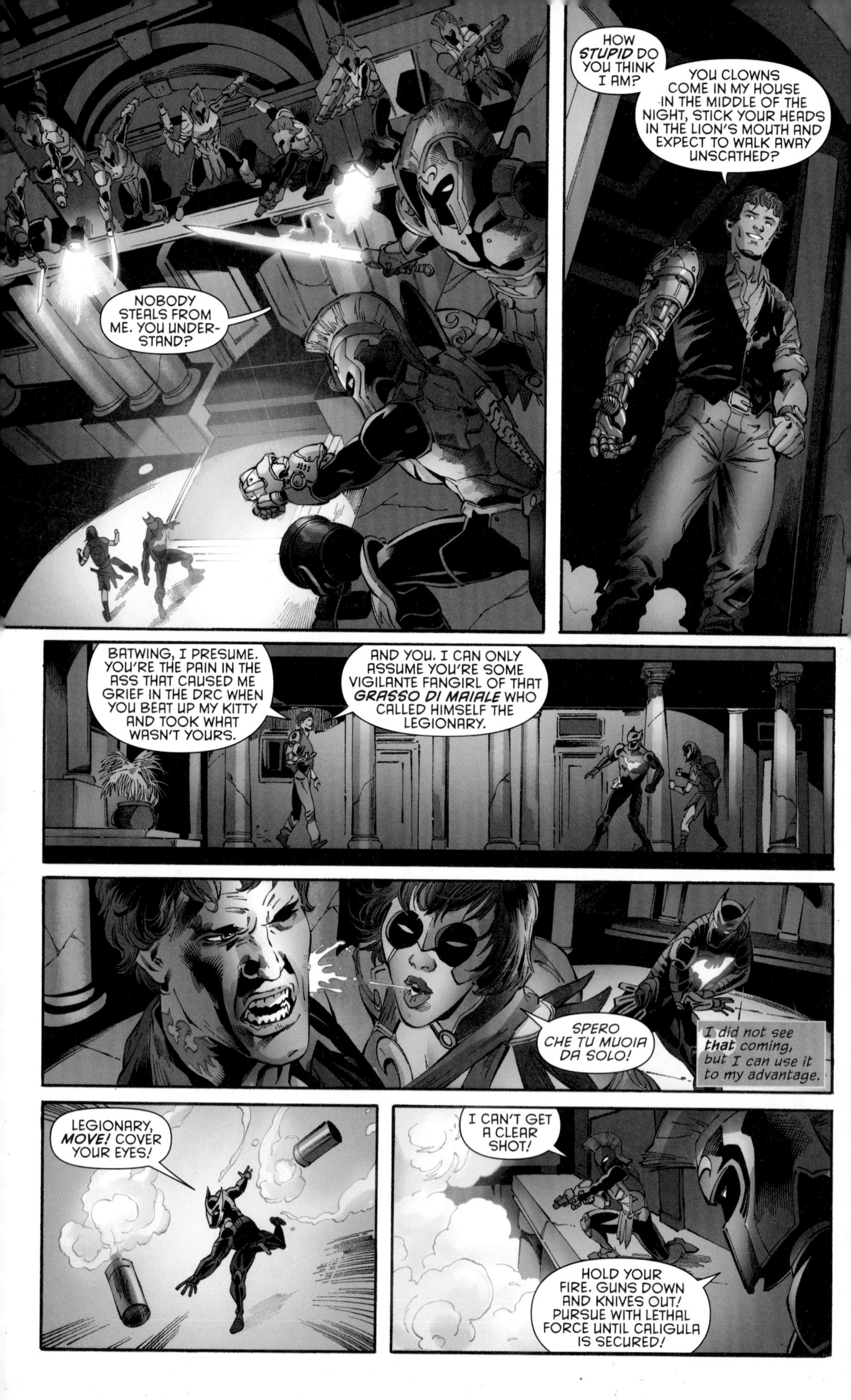
NOBODY STEALS FROM ME. YOU UNDER-STAND?
HOW STUPID DO YOU THINK I AM?
YOU CLOWNS COME IN MY HOUSE IN THE MIDDLE OF THE NIGHT, STICK YOUR HEADS IN THE LION'S MOUTH AND EXPECT TO WALK AWAY UNSCATHED?
BATWING, I PRESUME. YOU'RE THE PAIN IN THE ASS THAT CAUSED ME GRIEF IN THE DRC WHEN YOU BEAT UP MY KITTY AND TOOK WHAT WASN'T YOURS.
AND YOU. I CAN ONLY ASSUME YOU'RE SOME VIGILANTE FANGIRL OF THAT GRASSO DI MAIALE WHO CALLED HIMSELF THE LEGIONARY.
SPERO CHE TU MUOIA DA SOLO!
I did not see that coming, but I can use it to my advantage.
LEGIONARY, MOVE! COVER YOUR EYES!
I CAN'T GET A CLEAR SHOT!
HOLD YOUR FIRE. GUNS DOWN AND KNIVES OUT! PURSUE WITH LETHAL FORCE UNTIL CALIGULA IS SECURED!

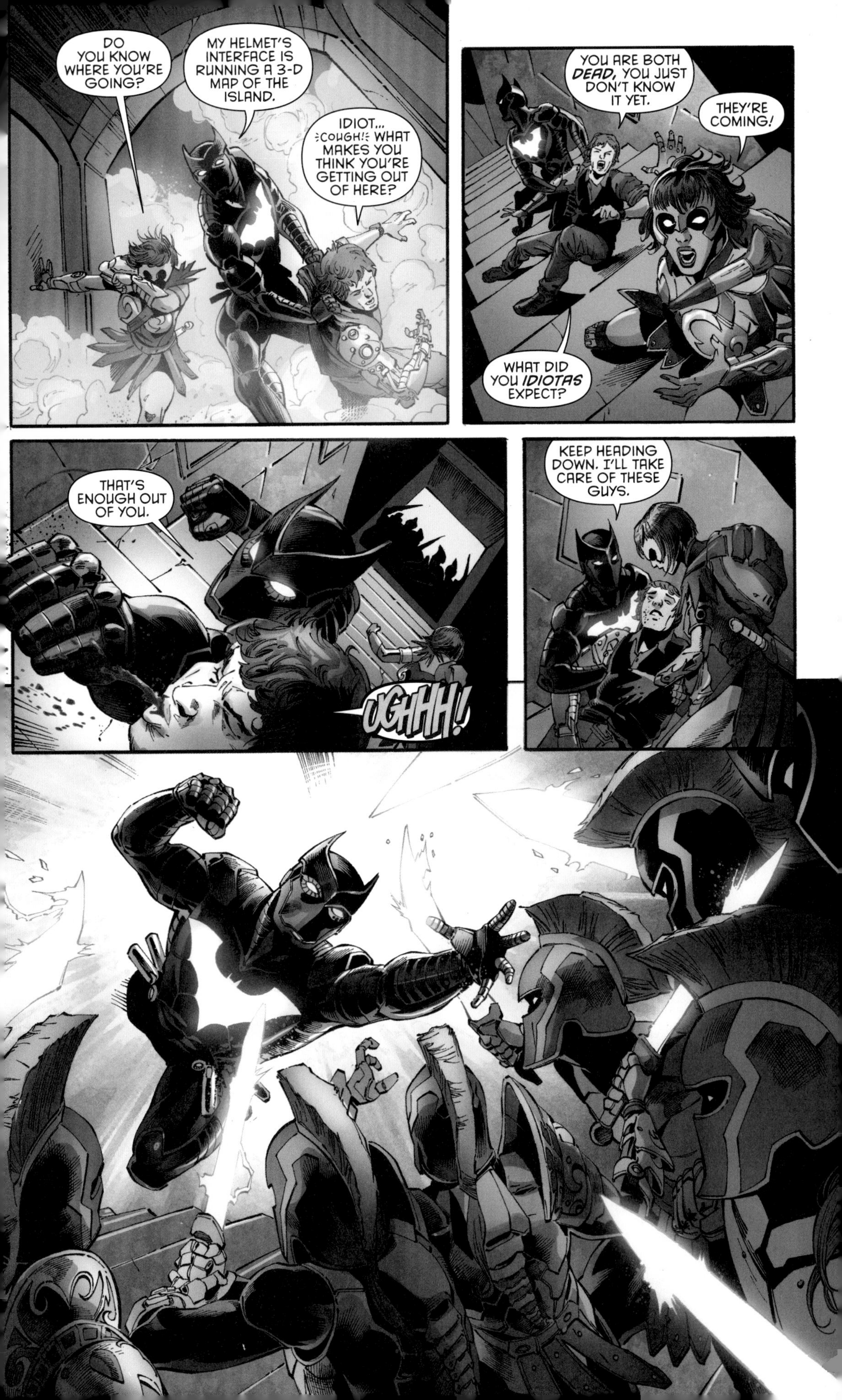
DO YOU KNOW WHERE YOU'RE GOING?
MY HELMET'S INTERFACE IS RUNNING A 3-D MAP OF THE ISLAND.
IDIOT... COUGH! WHAT MAKES YOU THINK YOU'RE GETTING OUT OF HERE?
YOU ARE BOTH DEAD, YOU JUST DON'T KNOW IT YET.
THEY'RE COMING!
WHAT DID YOU IDIOTAS EXPECT?
THAT'S ENOUGH OUT OF YOU.
UGHHH!
KEEP HEADING DOWN. I'LL TAKE CARE OF THESE GUYS.

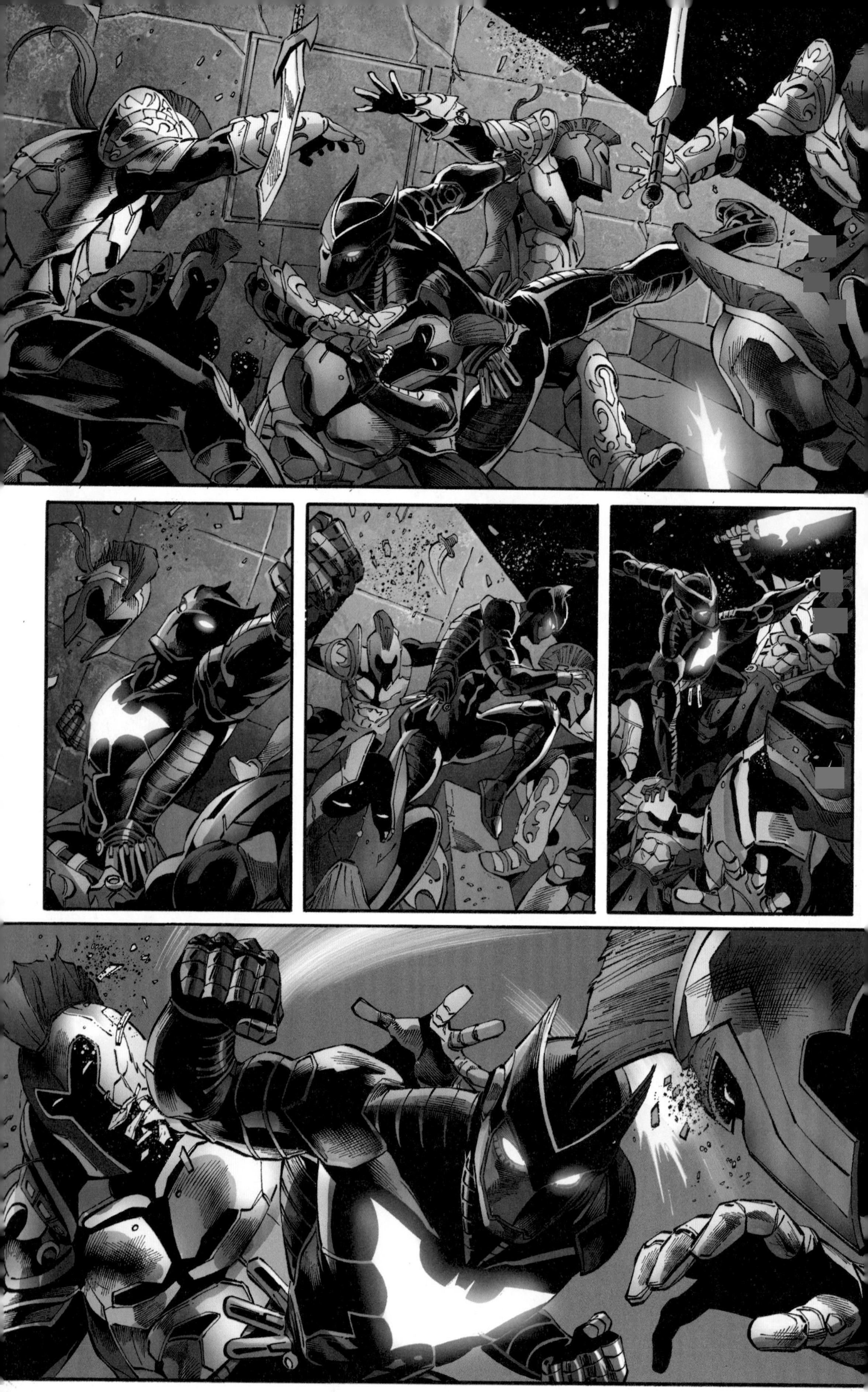

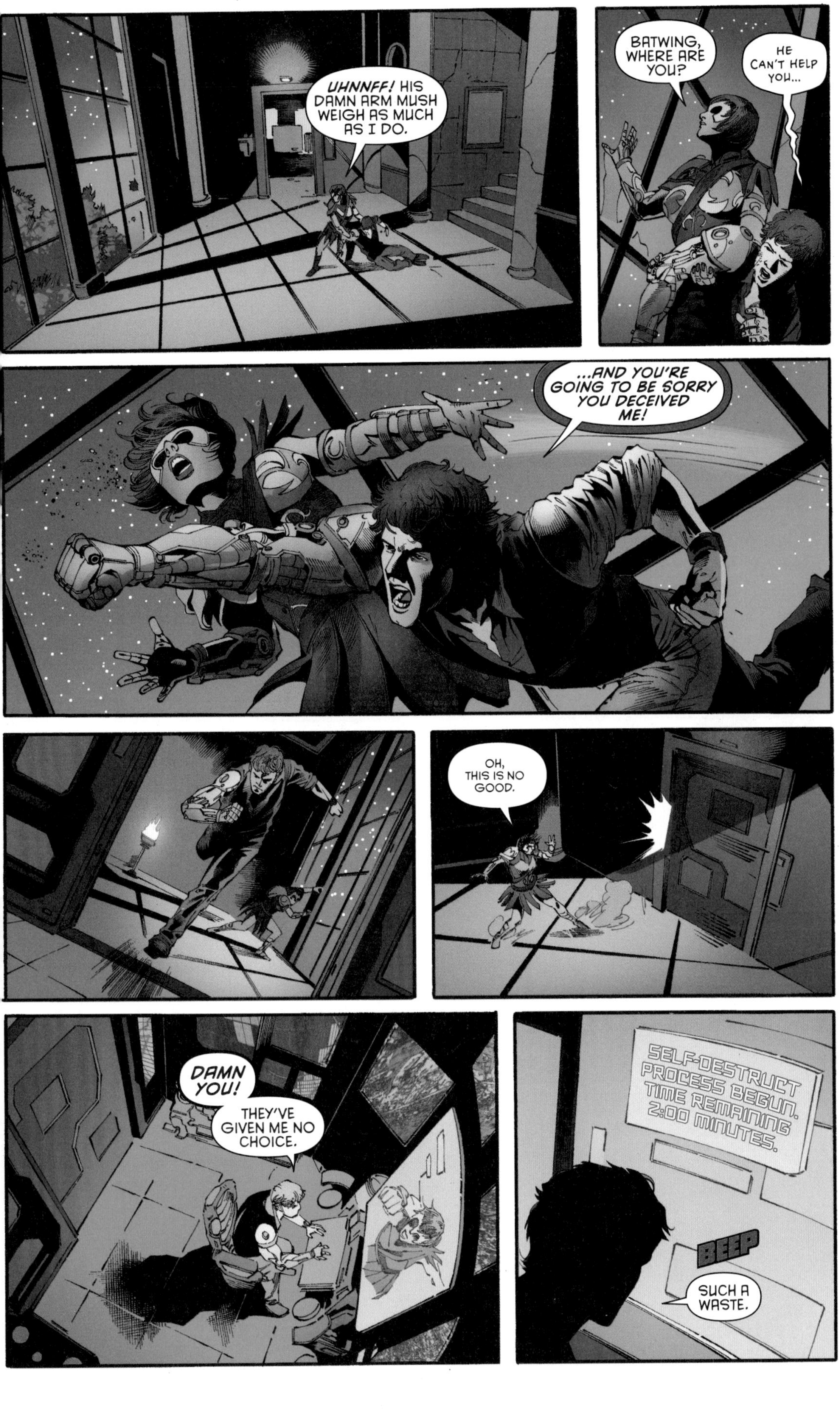
UHNNFF! HIS DAMN ARM MUSH WEIGH AS MUCH AS I DO.
BATWING, WHERE ARE YOU?
HE CAN'T HELP YOU...
...AND YOU'RE GOING TO BE SORRY YOU DECEIVED ME!
OH, THIS IS NO GOOD.
DAMN YOU!
THEY'VE GIVEN ME NO CHOICE.
SELF-DESTRUCT PROCESS BEGUN. TIME REMAINING 2:00 MINUTES.
BEEP
SUCH A WASTE.

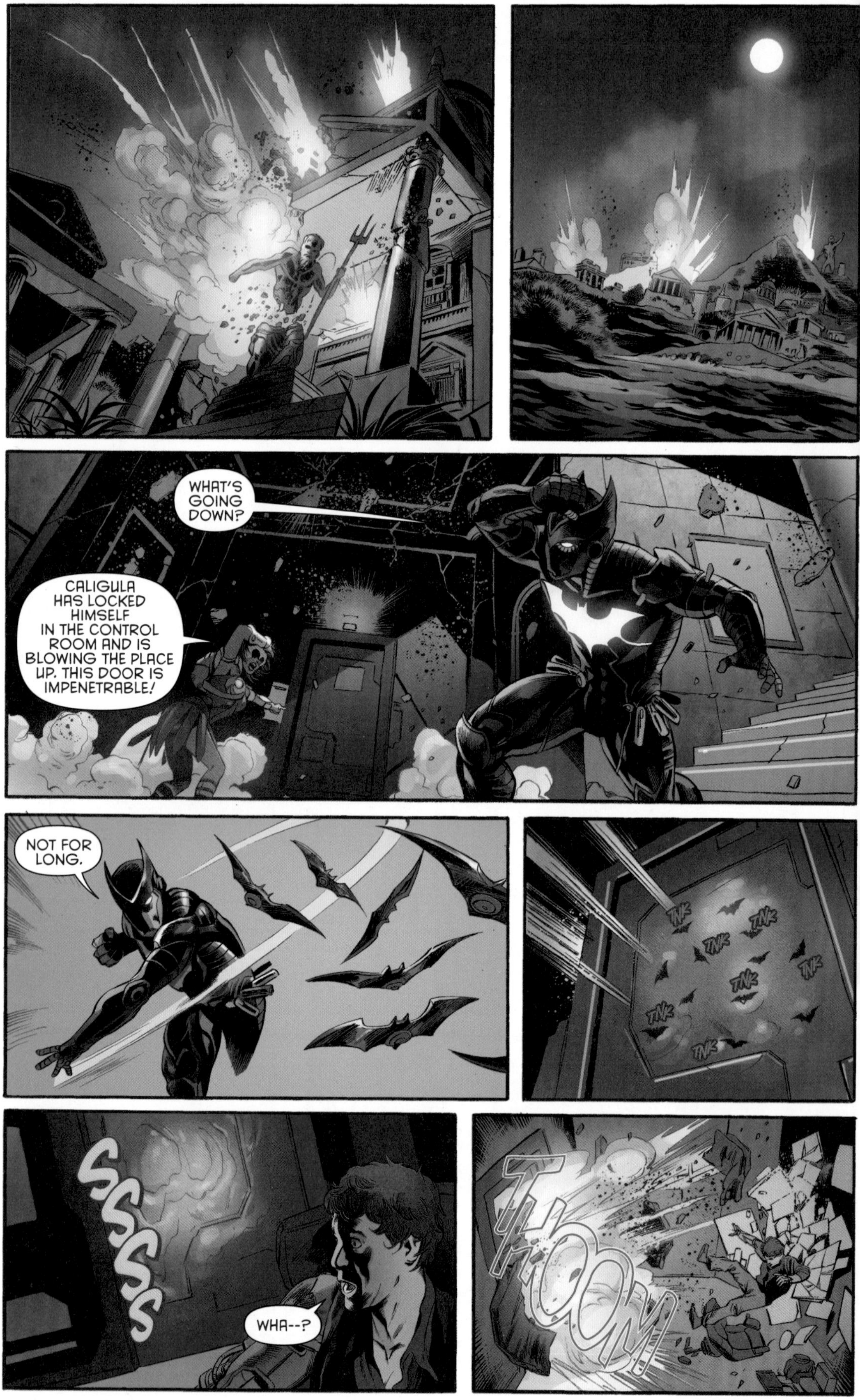
WHAT'S GOING DOWN?
CALIGULA HAS LOCKED HIMSELF IN THE CONTROL ROOM AND IS BLOWING THE PLACE UP. THIS DOOR IS IMPENETRABLE!
NOT FOR LONG.
TNK TNK TNK TNK TNK TNK TNK TNK
SSSSS
WHA--?
THOOOM

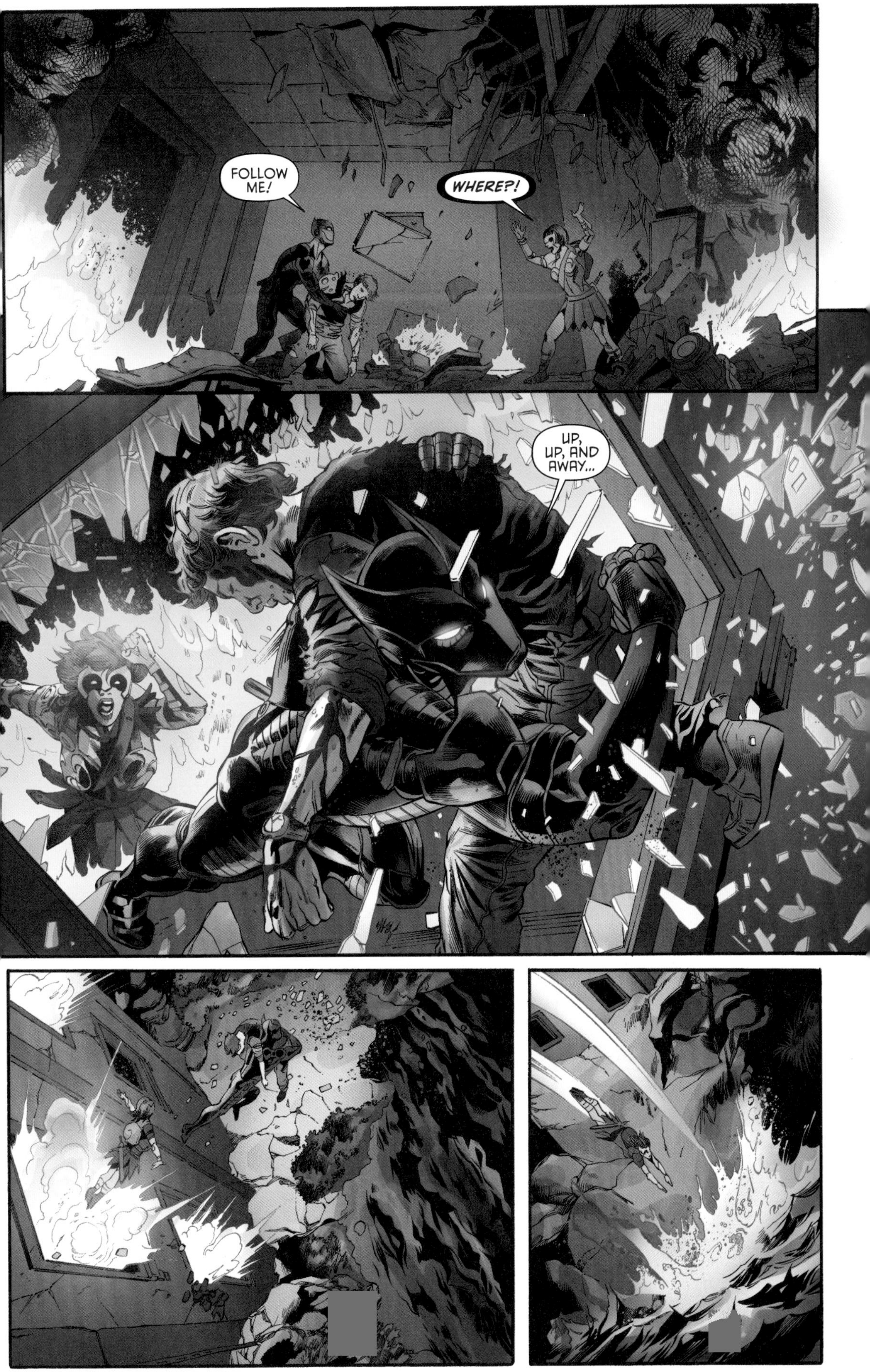
FOLLOW ME!
WHERE?!
UP, UP, AND AWAY...

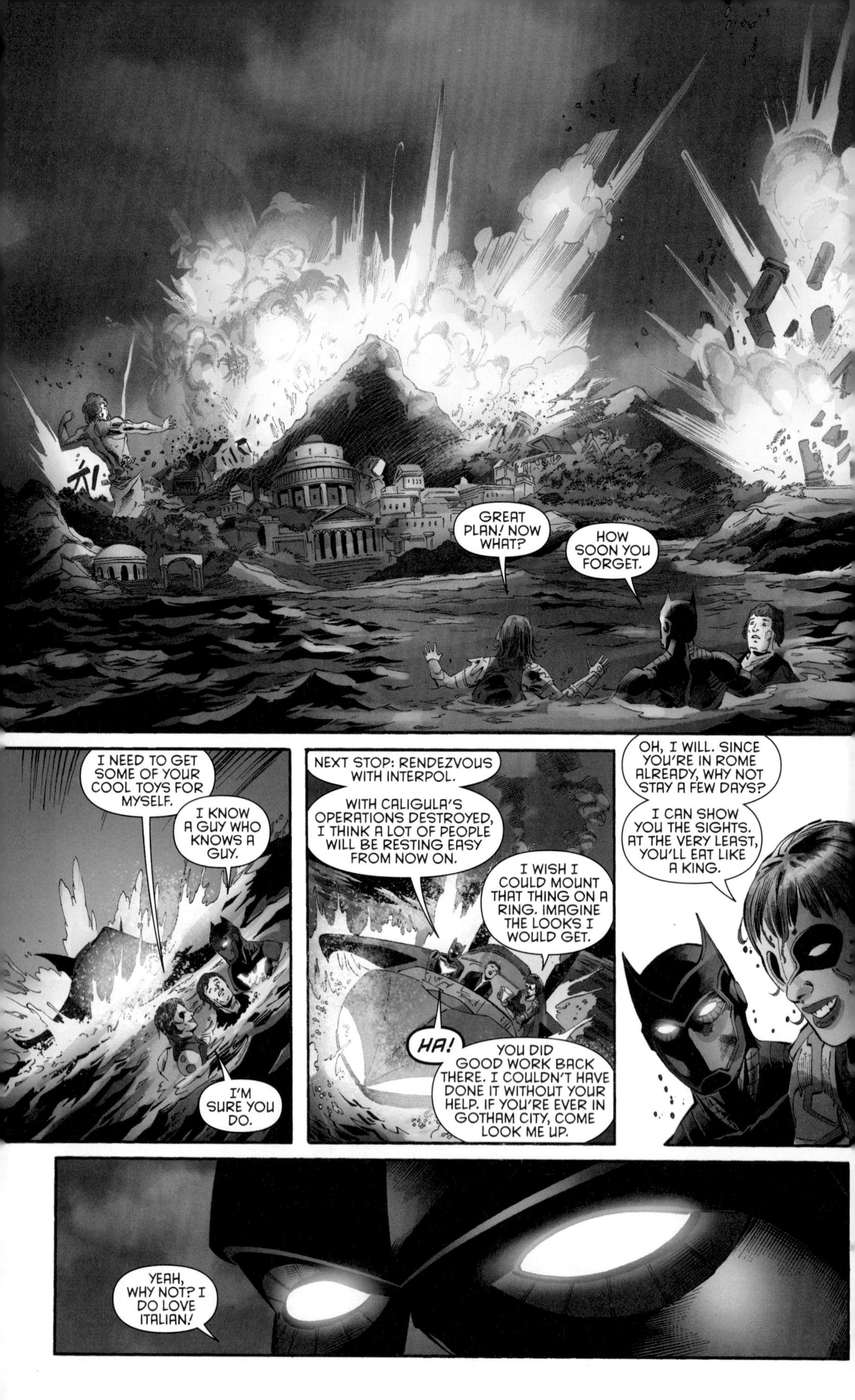

GREAT PLAN! NOW WHAT?
HOW SOON YOU FORGET.
I NEED TO GET SOME OF YOUR COOL TOYS FOR MYSELF.
I KNOW A GUY WHO KNOWS A GUY.
I'M SURE YOU DO.
NEXT STOP: RENDEZVOUS WITH INTERPOL.
WITH CALIGULA'S OPERATIONS DESTROYED, I THINK A LOT OF PEOPLE WILL BE RESTING EASY FROM NOW ON.
I WISH I COULD MOUNT THAT THING ON A RING. IMAGINE THE LOOKS I WOULD GET.
HA!
YOU DID GOOD WORK BACK THERE. I COULDN'T HAVE DONE IT WITHOUT YOUR HELP. IF YOU'RE EVER IN GOTHAM CITY, COME LOOK ME UP.
OH, I WILL. SINCE YOU'RE IN ROME ALREADY, WHY NOT STAY A FEW DAYS?
I CAN SHOW YOU THE SIGHTS. AT THE VERY LEAST, YOU'LL EAT LIKE A KING.
YEAH, WHY NOT? I DO LOVE ITALIAN!

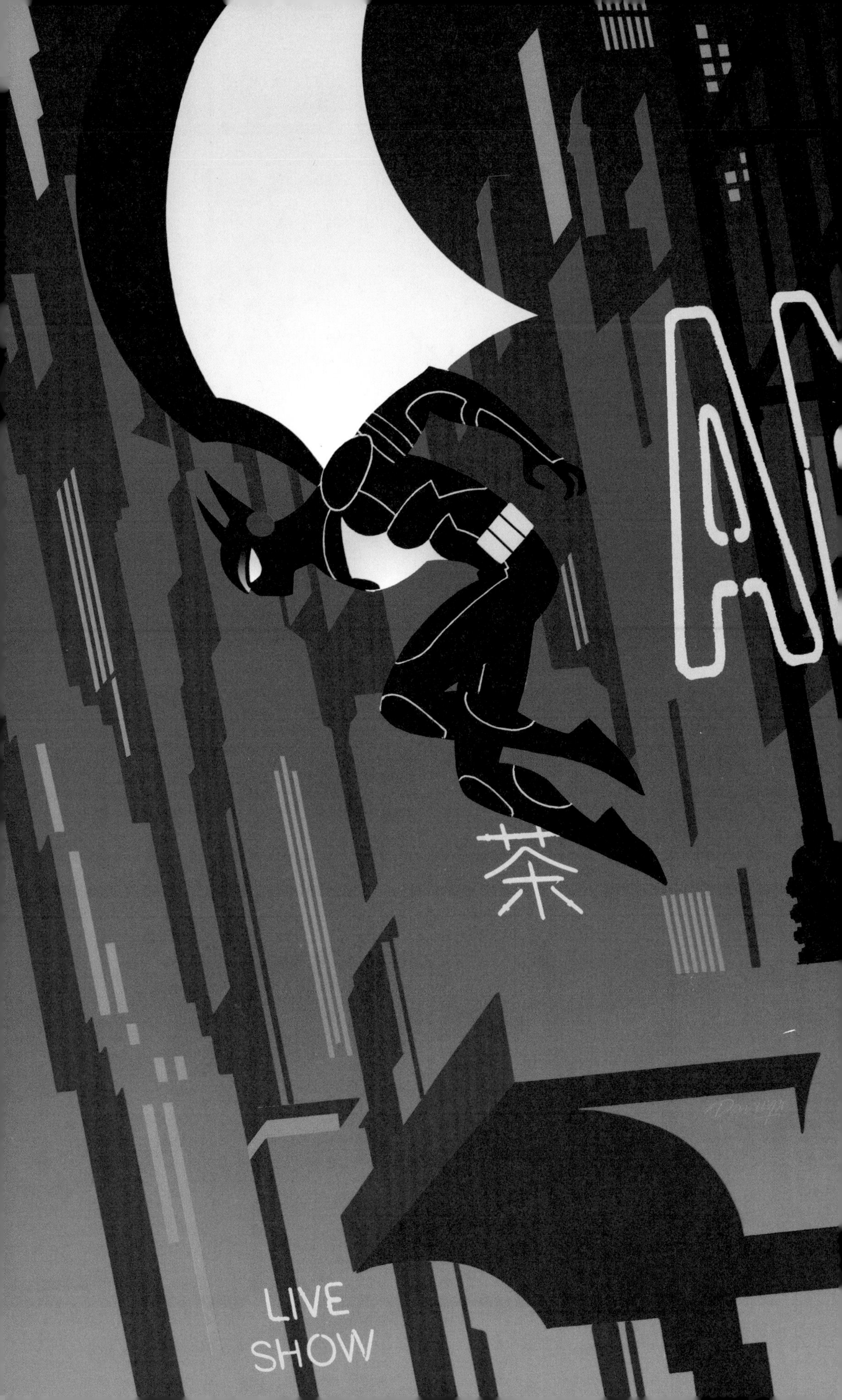
茶
LIVE
SHOW

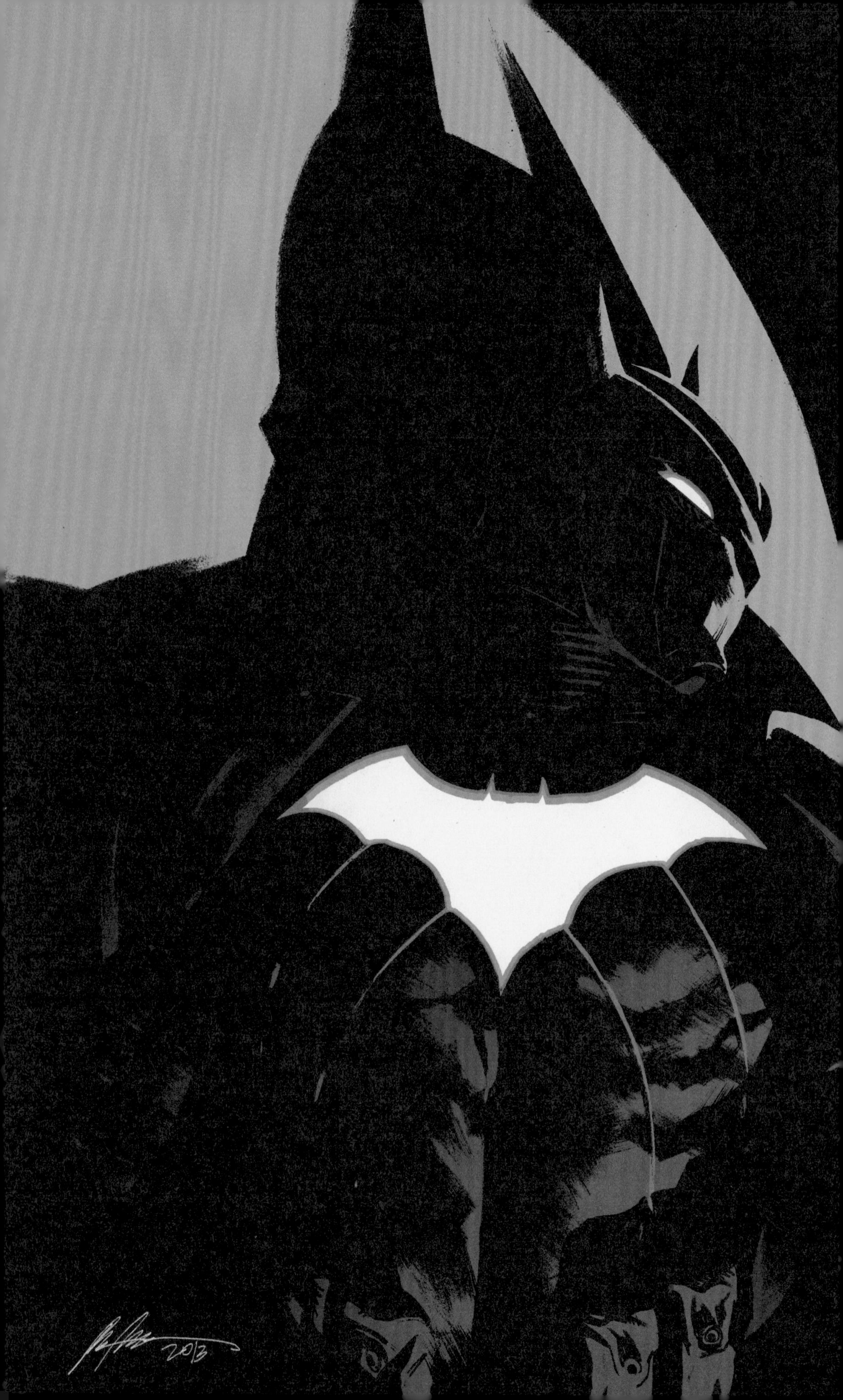
2013

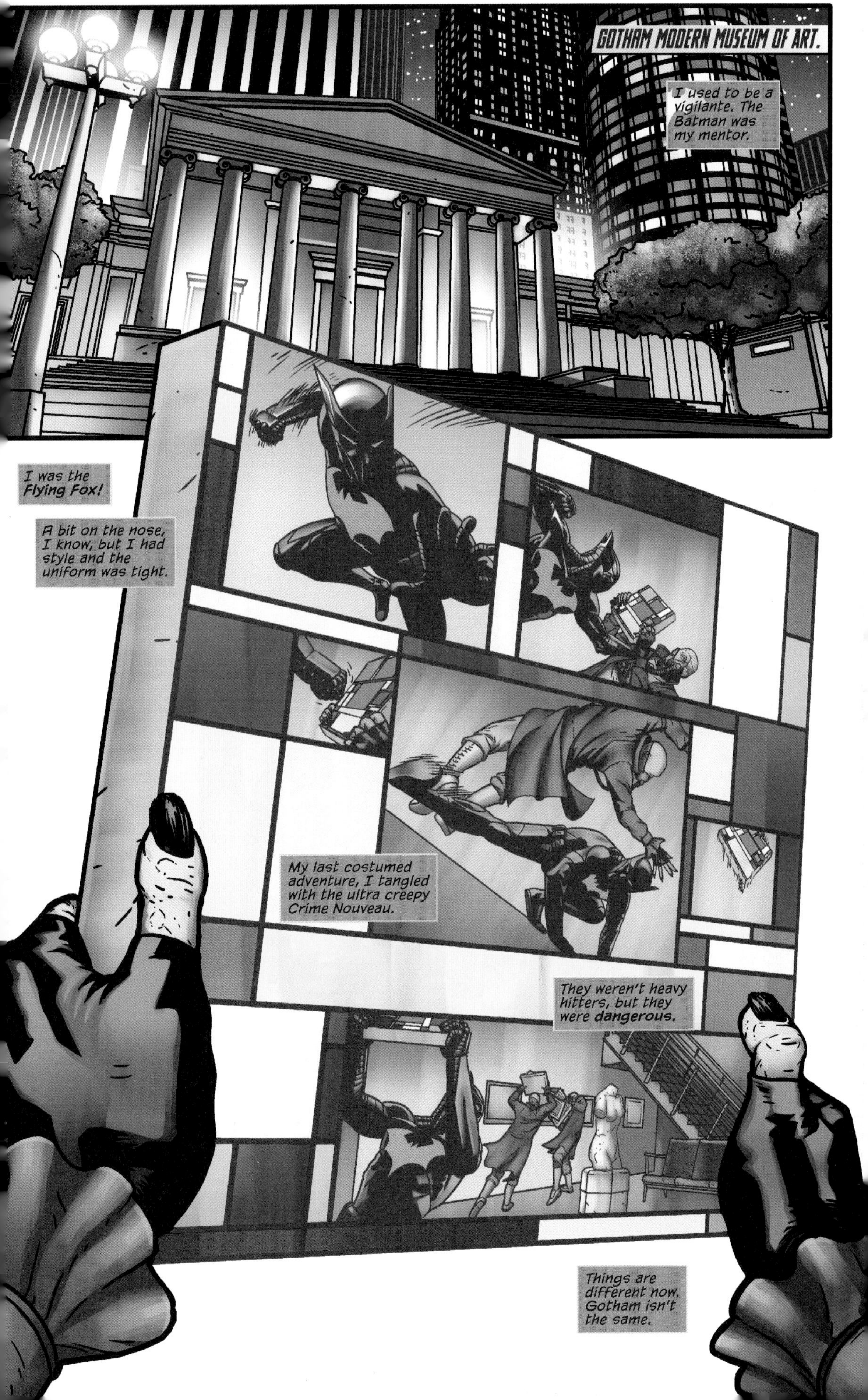

GOTHAM MODERN MUSEUM OF ART.
I used to be a vigilante. The Batman was my mentor.
I was the **Flying Fox!**
A bit on the nose, I know, but I had style and the uniform was tight.
My last costumed adventure, I tangled with the ultra creepy Crime Nouveau.
They weren't heavy hitters, but they were **dangerous.**
Things are different now. Gotham isn't the same.

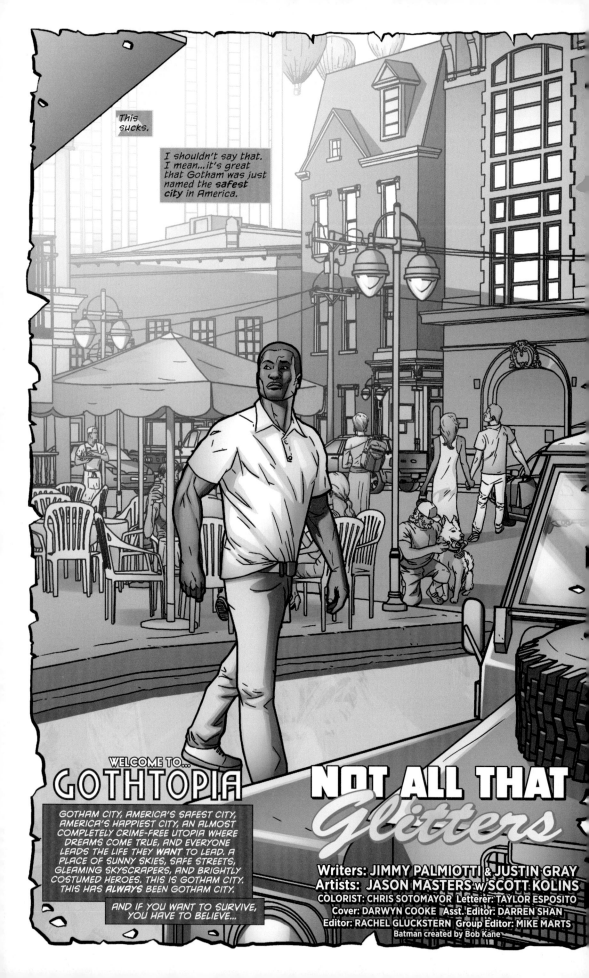

This sucks.

I shouldn't say that. I mean...it's great that Gotham was just named the **safest city** in America.

WELCOME TO...
GOTHTOPIA

GOTHAM CITY, AMERICA'S SAFEST CITY, AMERICA'S HAPPIEST CITY, AN ALMOST COMPLETELY CRIME-FREE UTOPIA WHERE DREAMS COME TRUE, AND EVERYONE LEADS THE LIFE THEY **WANT** TO LEAD. A PLACE OF SUNNY SKIES, SAFE STREETS, GLEAMING SKYSCRAPERS, AND BRIGHTLY COSTUMED HEROES. THIS IS GOTHAM CITY. THIS HAS **ALWAYS** BEEN GOTHAM CITY.

AND IF YOU WANT TO SURVIVE, YOU HAVE TO BELIEVE...

NOT ALL THAT *Glitters*

Writers: JIMMY PALMIOTTI & JUSTIN GRAY
Artists: JASON MASTERS w/SCOTT KOLINS
COLORIST: CHRIS SOTOMAYOR Letterer: TAYLOR ESPOSITO
Cover: DARWYN COOKE Asst. Editor: DARREN SHAN
Editor: RACHEL GLUCKSTERN Group Editor: MIKE MARTS
Batman created by Bob Kane

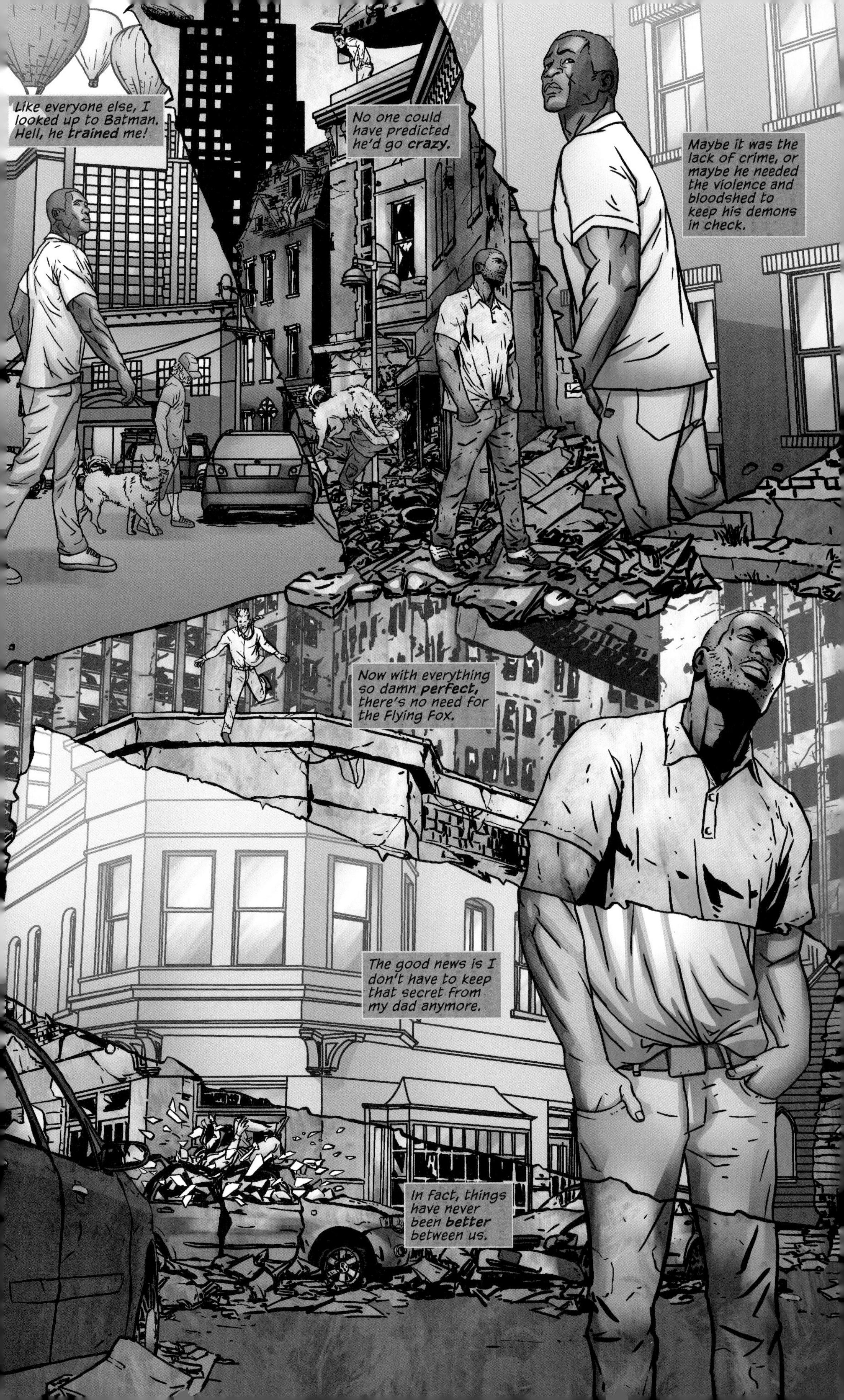

Like everyone else, I looked up to Batman. Hell, he trained me!
No one could have predicted he'd go crazy.
Maybe it was the lack of crime, or maybe he needed the violence and bloodshed to keep his demons in check.
Now with everything so damn perfect, there's no need for the Flying Fox.
The good news is I don't have to keep that secret from my dad anymore.
In fact, things have never been better between us.

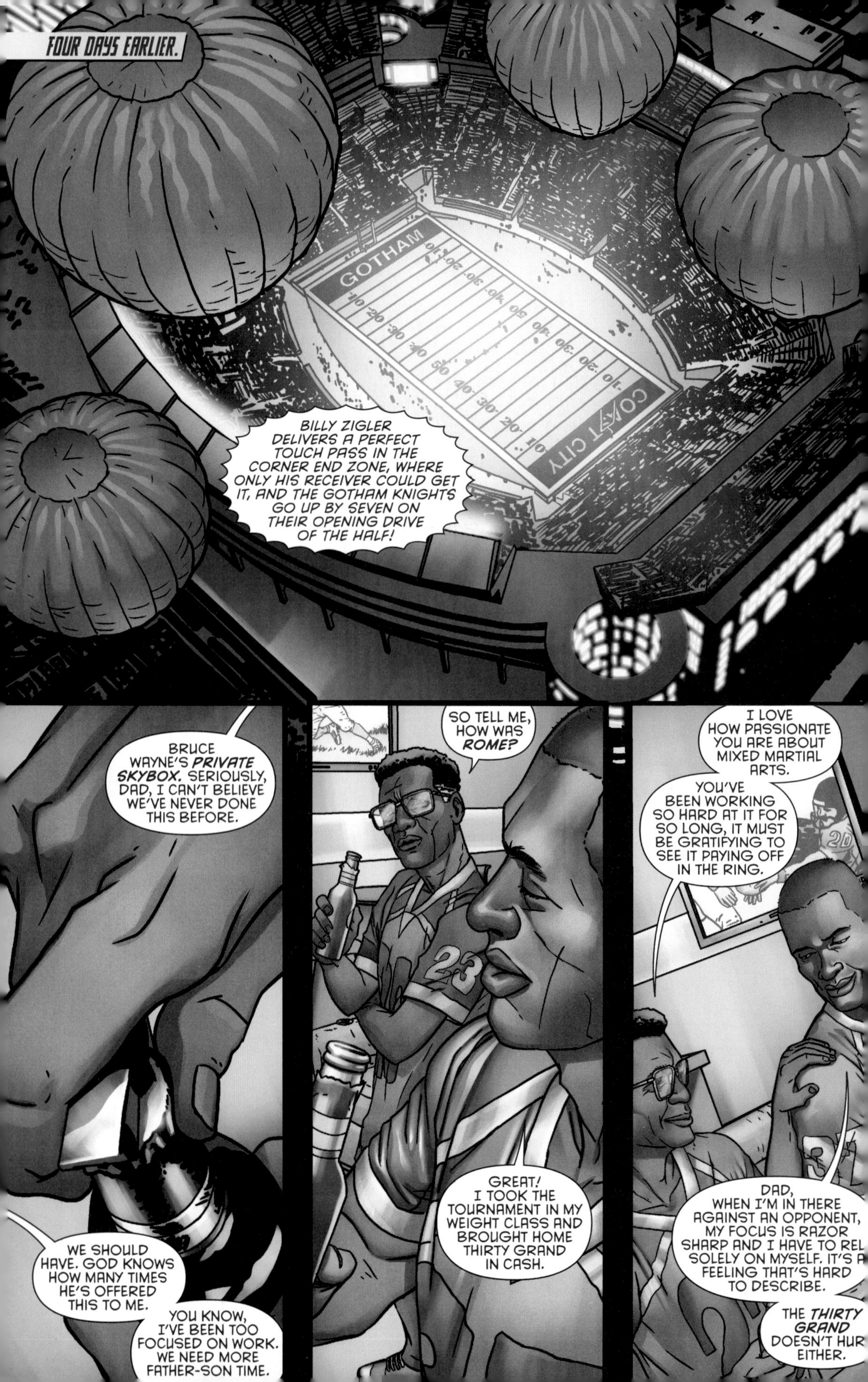
FOUR DAYS EARLIER.
GOTHAM
COAST CITY
BILLY ZIGLER DELIVERS A PERFECT TOUCH PASS IN THE CORNER END ZONE, WHERE ONLY HIS RECEIVER COULD GET IT, AND THE GOTHAM KNIGHTS GO UP BY SEVEN ON THEIR OPENING DRIVE OF THE HALF!
BRUCE WAYNE'S PRIVATE SKYBOX. SERIOUSLY, DAD, I CAN'T BELIEVE WE'VE NEVER DONE THIS BEFORE.
WE SHOULD HAVE. GOD KNOWS HOW MANY TIMES HE'S OFFERED THIS TO ME.
YOU KNOW, I'VE BEEN TOO FOCUSED ON WORK. WE NEED MORE FATHER-SON TIME.
SO TELL ME, HOW WAS ROME?
GREAT! I TOOK THE TOURNAMENT IN MY WEIGHT CLASS AND BROUGHT HOME THIRTY GRAND IN CASH.
I LOVE HOW PASSIONATE YOU ARE ABOUT MIXED MARTIAL ARTS.
YOU'VE BEEN WORKING SO HARD AT IT FOR SO LONG, IT MUST BE GRATIFYING TO SEE IT PAYING OFF IN THE RING.
DAD, WHEN I'M IN THERE AGAINST AN OPPONENT, MY FOCUS IS RAZOR SHARP AND I HAVE TO REL SOLELY ON MYSELF. IT'S A FEELING THAT'S HARD TO DESCRIBE.
THE THIRTY GRAND DOESN'T HUR EITHER.

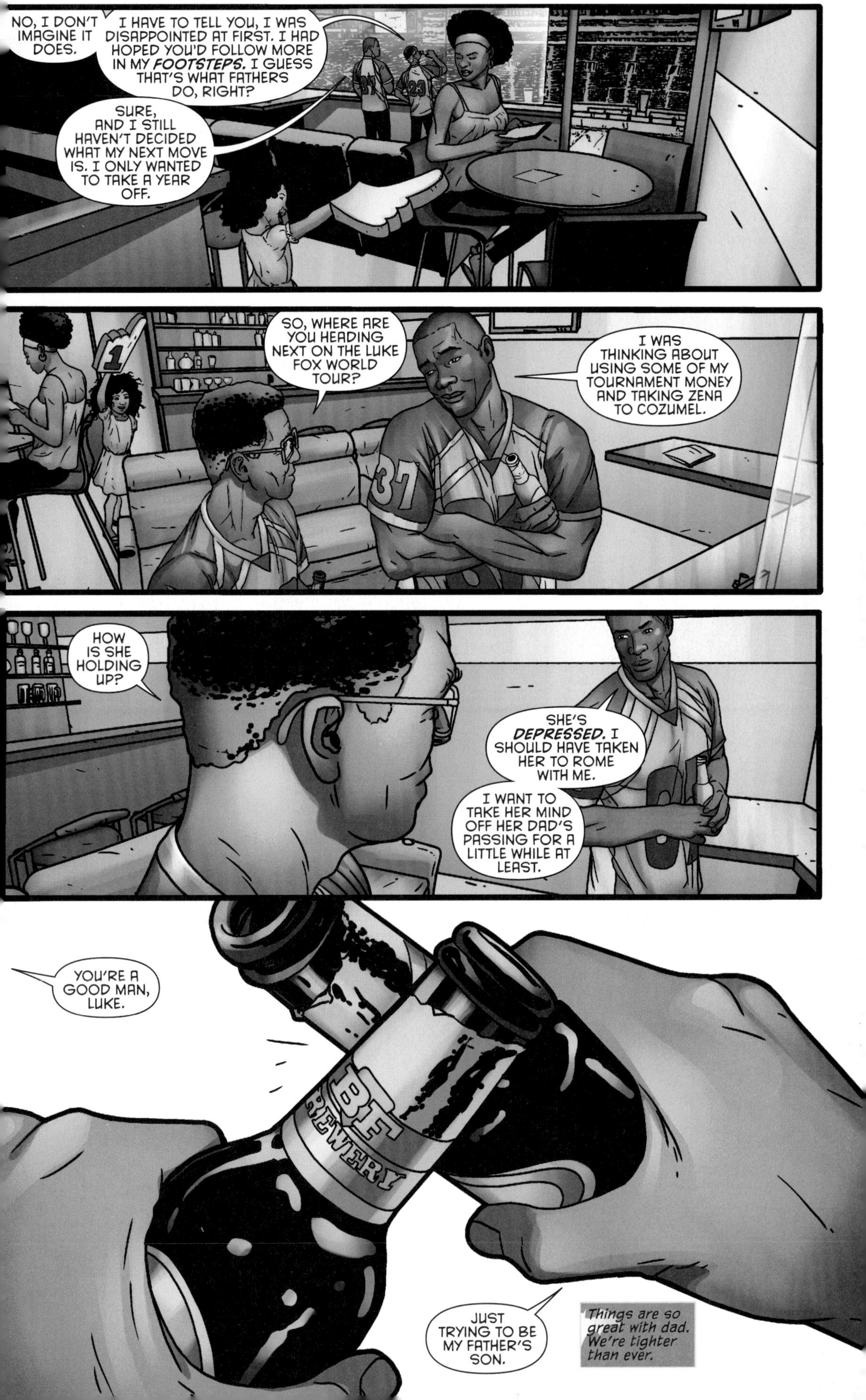
NO, I DON'T IMAGINE IT DOES.
I HAVE TO TELL YOU, I WAS DISAPPOINTED AT FIRST. I HAD HOPED YOU'D FOLLOW MORE IN MY *FOOTSTEPS.* I GUESS THAT'S WHAT FATHERS DO, RIGHT?
SURE, AND I STILL HAVEN'T DECIDED WHAT MY NEXT MOVE IS. I ONLY WANTED TO TAKE A YEAR OFF.
SO, WHERE ARE YOU HEADING NEXT ON THE LUKE FOX WORLD TOUR?
I WAS THINKING ABOUT USING SOME OF MY TOURNAMENT MONEY AND TAKING ZENA TO COZUMEL.
HOW IS SHE HOLDING UP?
SHE'S *DEPRESSED.* I SHOULD HAVE TAKEN HER TO ROME WITH ME.
I WANT TO TAKE HER MIND OFF HER DAD'S PASSING FOR A LITTLE WHILE AT LEAST.
YOU'RE A GOOD MAN, LUKE.
JUST TRYING TO BE MY FATHER'S SON.
Things are so great with dad. We're tighter than ever.

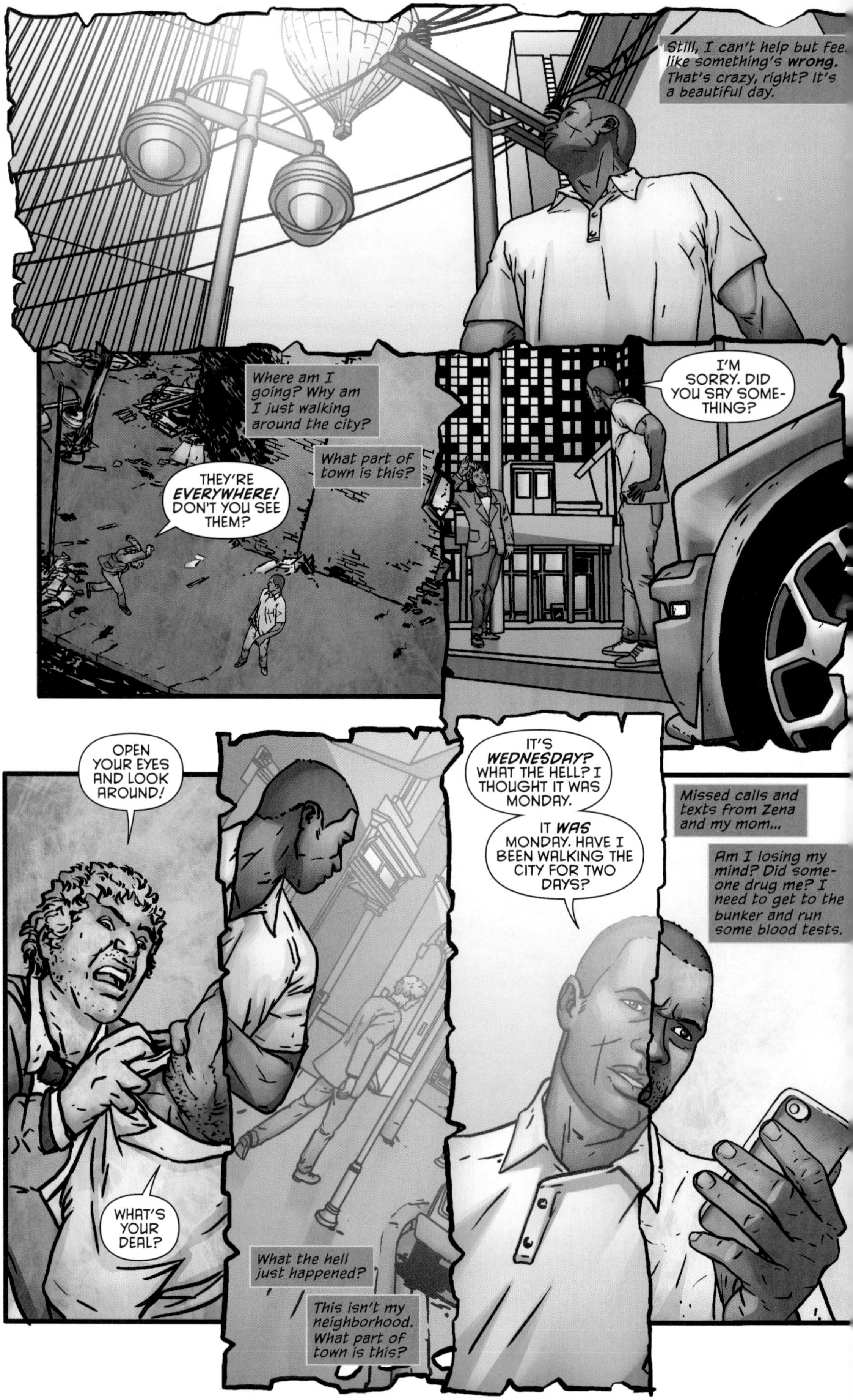

Still, I can't help but fee like something's wrong. That's crazy, right? It's a beautiful day.
Where am I going? Why am I just walking around the city?
What part of town is this?
THEY'RE EVERYWHERE! DON'T YOU SEE THEM?
I'M SORRY. DID YOU SAY SOME-THING?
OPEN YOUR EYES AND LOOK AROUND!
WHAT'S YOUR DEAL?
What the hell just happened?
This isn't my neighborhood. What part of town is this?
IT'S WEDNESDAY? WHAT THE HELL? I THOUGHT IT WAS MONDAY.
IT WAS MONDAY. HAVE I BEEN WALKING THE CITY FOR TWO DAYS?
Missed calls and texts from Zena and my mom...
Am I losing my mind? Did some-one drug me? I need to get to the bunker and run some blood tests.

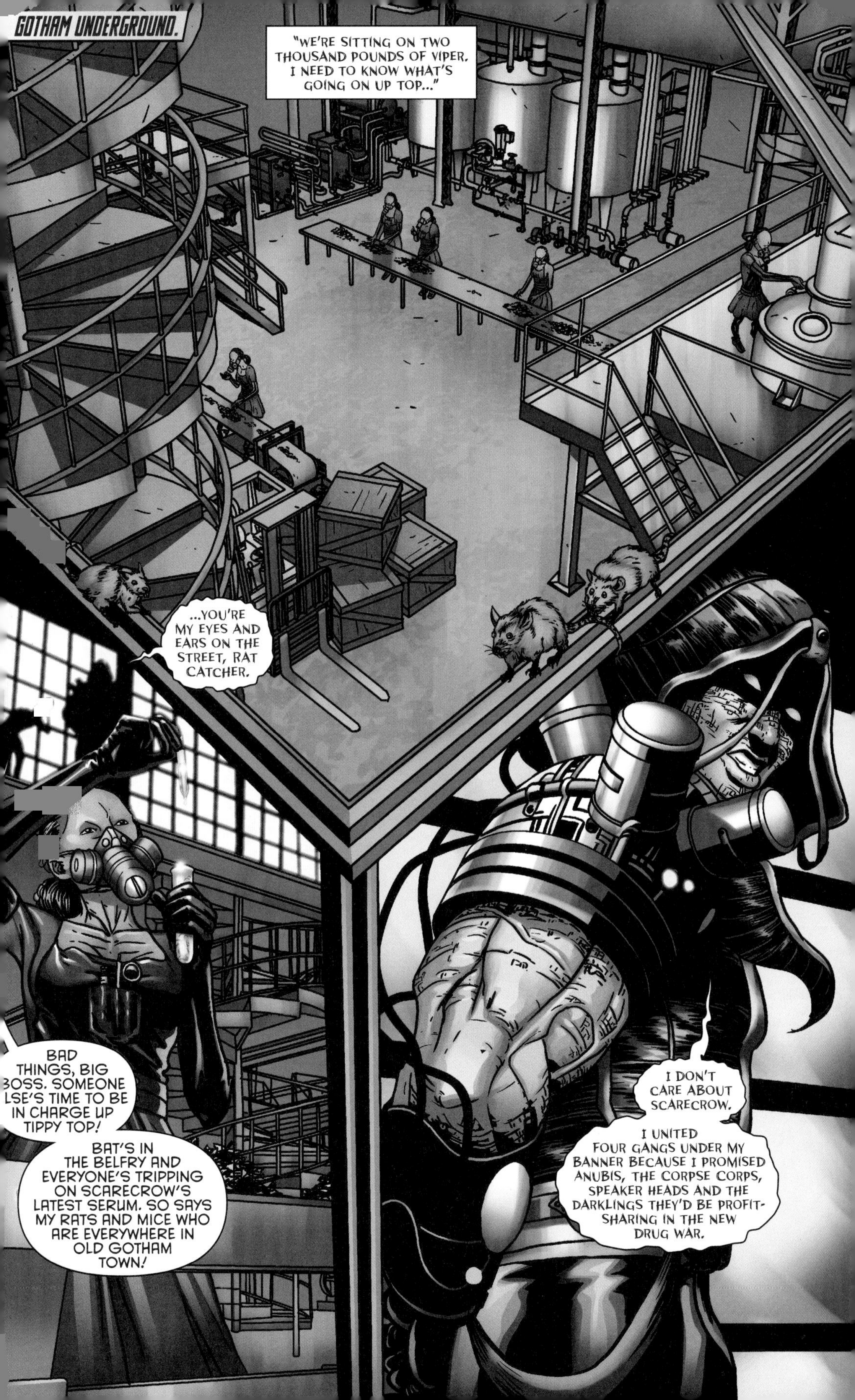

GOTHAM UNDERGROUND.
"WE'RE SITTING ON TWO THOUSAND POUNDS OF VIPER. I NEED TO KNOW WHAT'S GOING ON UP TOP..."
...YOU'RE MY EYES AND EARS ON THE STREET, RAT CATCHER.
BAD THINGS, BIG OSS. SOMEONE LSE'S TIME TO BE IN CHARGE UP TIPPY TOP!
BAT'S IN THE BELFRY AND EVERYONE'S TRIPPING ON SCARECROW'S LATEST SERUM. SO SAYS MY RATS AND MICE WHO ARE EVERYWHERE IN OLD GOTHAM TOWN!
I DON'T CARE ABOUT SCARECROW.
I UNITED FOUR GANGS UNDER MY BANNER BECAUSE I PROMISED ANUBIS, THE CORPSE CORPS, SPEAKER HEADS AND THE DARKLINGS THEY'D BE PROFIT-SHARING IN THE NEW DRUG WAR.

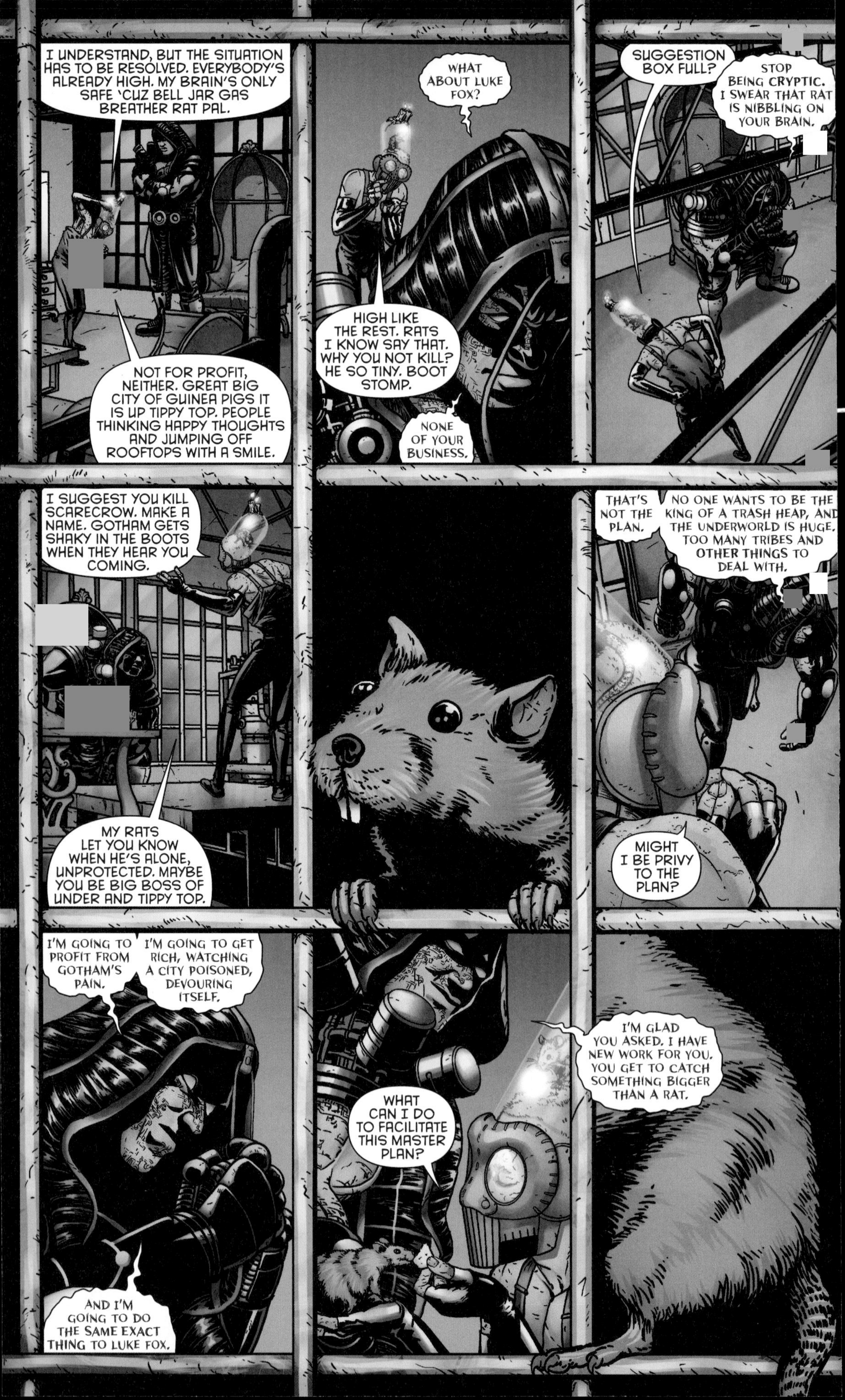
I UNDERSTAND, BUT THE SITUATION HAS TO BE RESOLVED. EVERYBODY'S ALREADY HIGH. MY BRAIN'S ONLY SAFE 'CUZ BELL JAR GAS BREATHER RAT PAL.
NOT FOR PROFIT, NEITHER. GREAT BIG CITY OF GUINEA PIGS IT IS UP TIPPY TOP. PEOPLE THINKING HAPPY THOUGHTS AND JUMPING OFF ROOFTOPS WITH A SMILE.
WHAT ABOUT LUKE FOX?
HIGH LIKE THE REST. RATS I KNOW SAY THAT. WHY YOU NOT KILL? HE SO TINY. BOOT STOMP.
NONE OF YOUR BUSINESS.
SUGGESTION BOX FULL?
STOP BEING CRYPTIC. I SWEAR THAT RAT IS NIBBLING ON YOUR BRAIN.
I SUGGEST YOU KILL SCARECROW. MAKE A NAME. GOTHAM GETS SHAKY IN THE BOOTS WHEN THEY HEAR YOU COMING.
MY RATS LET YOU KNOW WHEN HE'S ALONE, UNPROTECTED. MAYBE YOU BE BIG BOSS OF UNDER AND TIPPY TOP.
THAT'S NOT THE PLAN.
NO ONE WANTS TO BE THE KING OF A TRASH HEAP, AND THE UNDERWORLD IS HUGE. TOO MANY TRIBES AND OTHER THINGS TO DEAL WITH.
MIGHT I BE PRIVY TO THE PLAN?
I'M GOING TO PROFIT FROM GOTHAM'S PAIN.
I'M GOING TO GET RICH, WATCHING A CITY POISONED, DEVOURING ITSELF.
AND I'M GOING TO DO THE SAME EXACT THING TO LUKE FOX.
WHAT CAN I DO TO FACILITATE THIS MASTER PLAN?
I'M GLAD YOU ASKED. I HAVE NEW WORK FOR YOU. YOU GET TO CATCH SOMETHING BIGGER THAN A RAT.

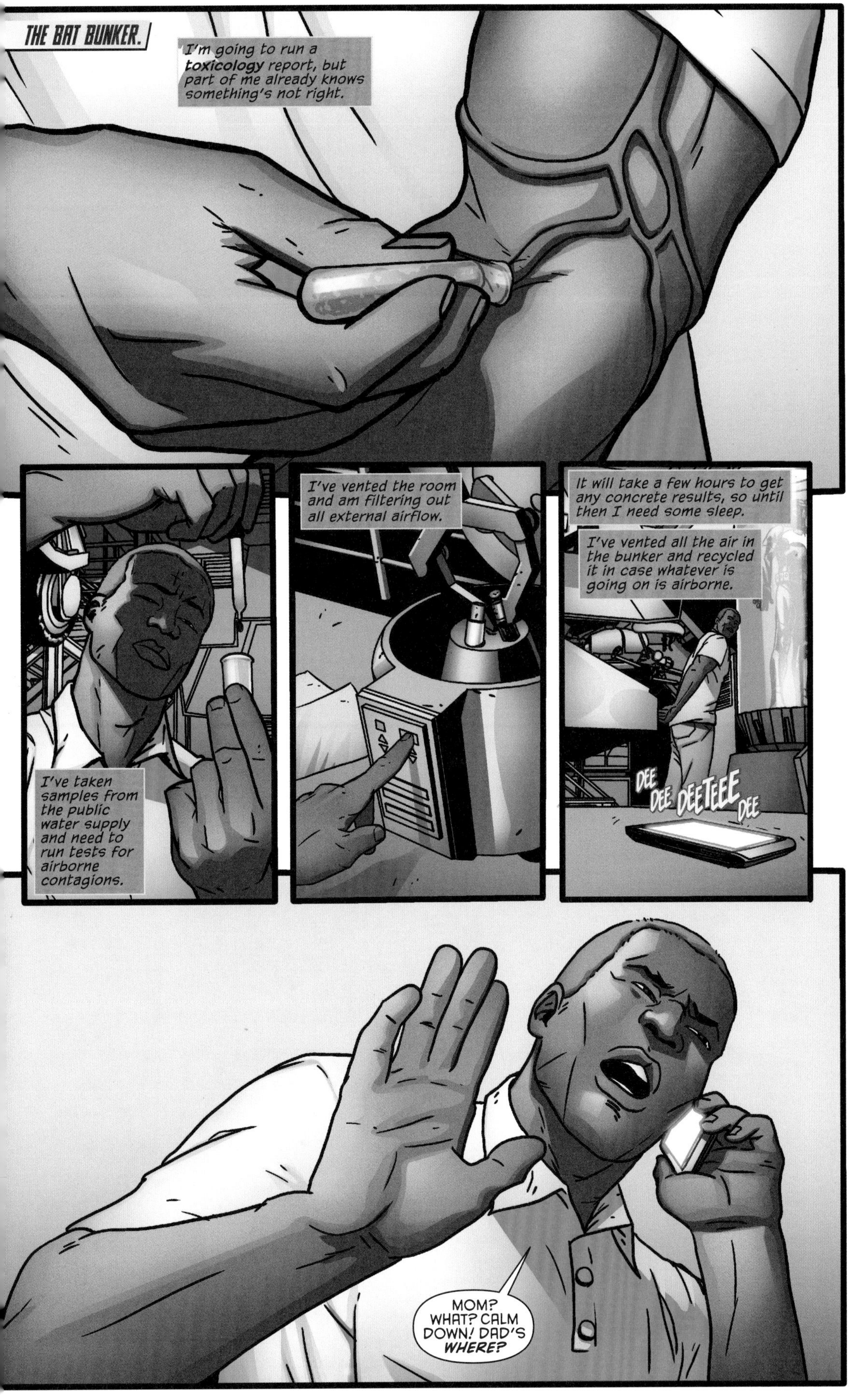

THE BAT BUNKER.
I'm going to run a **toxicology** report, but part of me already knows something's not right.
I've taken samples from the public water supply and need to run tests for airborne contagions.
I've vented the room and am filtering out all external airflow.
It will take a few hours to get any concrete results, so until then I need some sleep.
I've vented all the air in the bunker and recycled it in case whatever is going on is airborne.
DEE DEE DEETEEE DEE
MOM? WHAT? CALM DOWN! DAD'S *WHERE?*

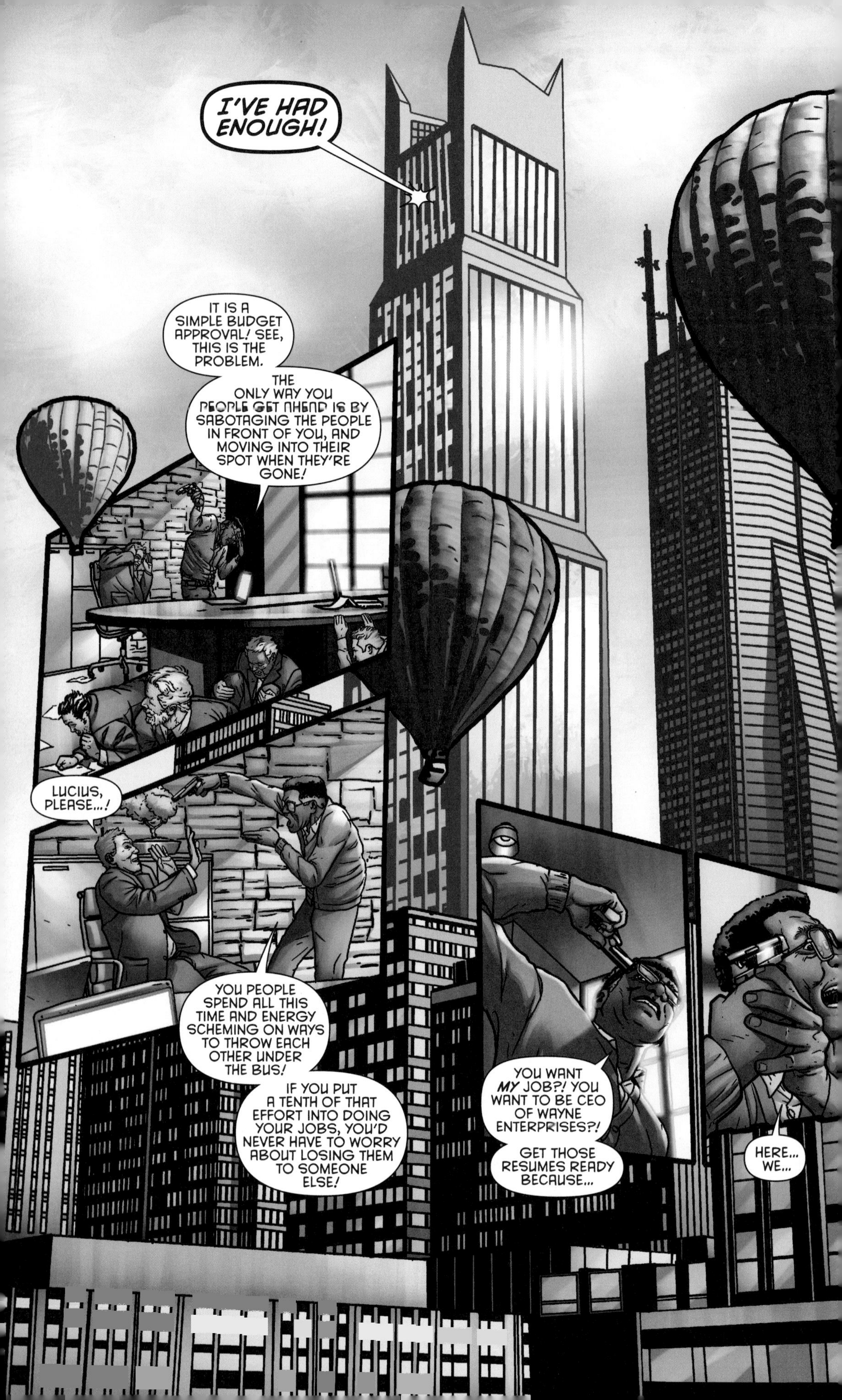
I'VE HAD ENOUGH!
IT IS A SIMPLE BUDGET APPROVAL! SEE, THIS IS THE PROBLEM.
THE ONLY WAY YOU PEOPLE GET AHEAD IS BY SABOTAGING THE PEOPLE IN FRONT OF YOU, AND MOVING INTO THEIR SPOT WHEN THEY'RE GONE!
LUCIUS, PLEASE...!
YOU PEOPLE SPEND ALL THIS TIME AND ENERGY SCHEMING ON WAYS TO THROW EACH OTHER UNDER THE BUS!
IF YOU PUT A TENTH OF THAT EFFORT INTO DOING YOUR JOBS, YOU'D NEVER HAVE TO WORRY ABOUT LOSING THEM TO SOMEONE ELSE!
YOU WANT MY JOB?! YOU WANT TO BE CEO OF WAYNE ENTERPRISES?!
GET THOSE RESUMES READY BECAUSE...
HERE... WE...

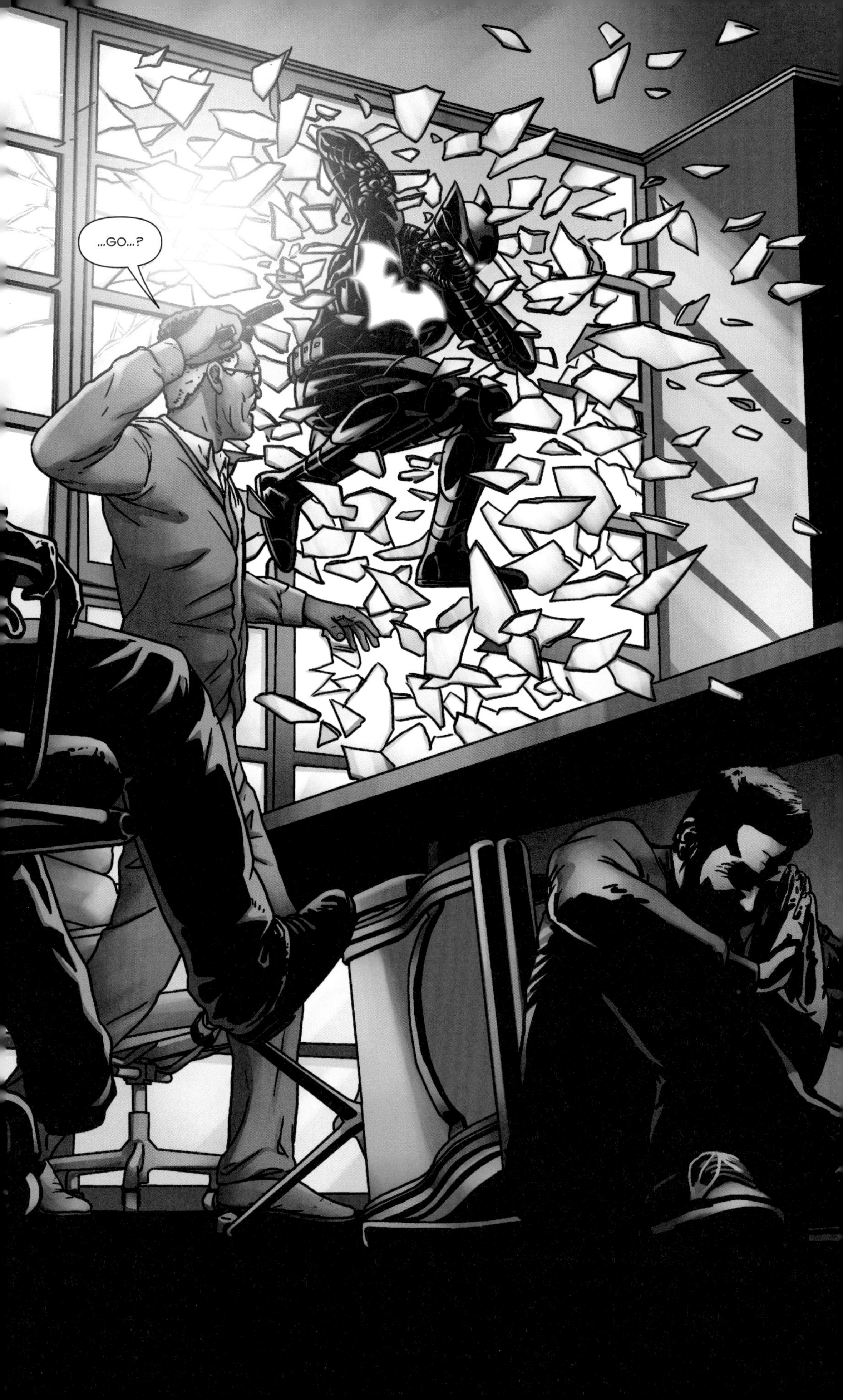
...GO...?

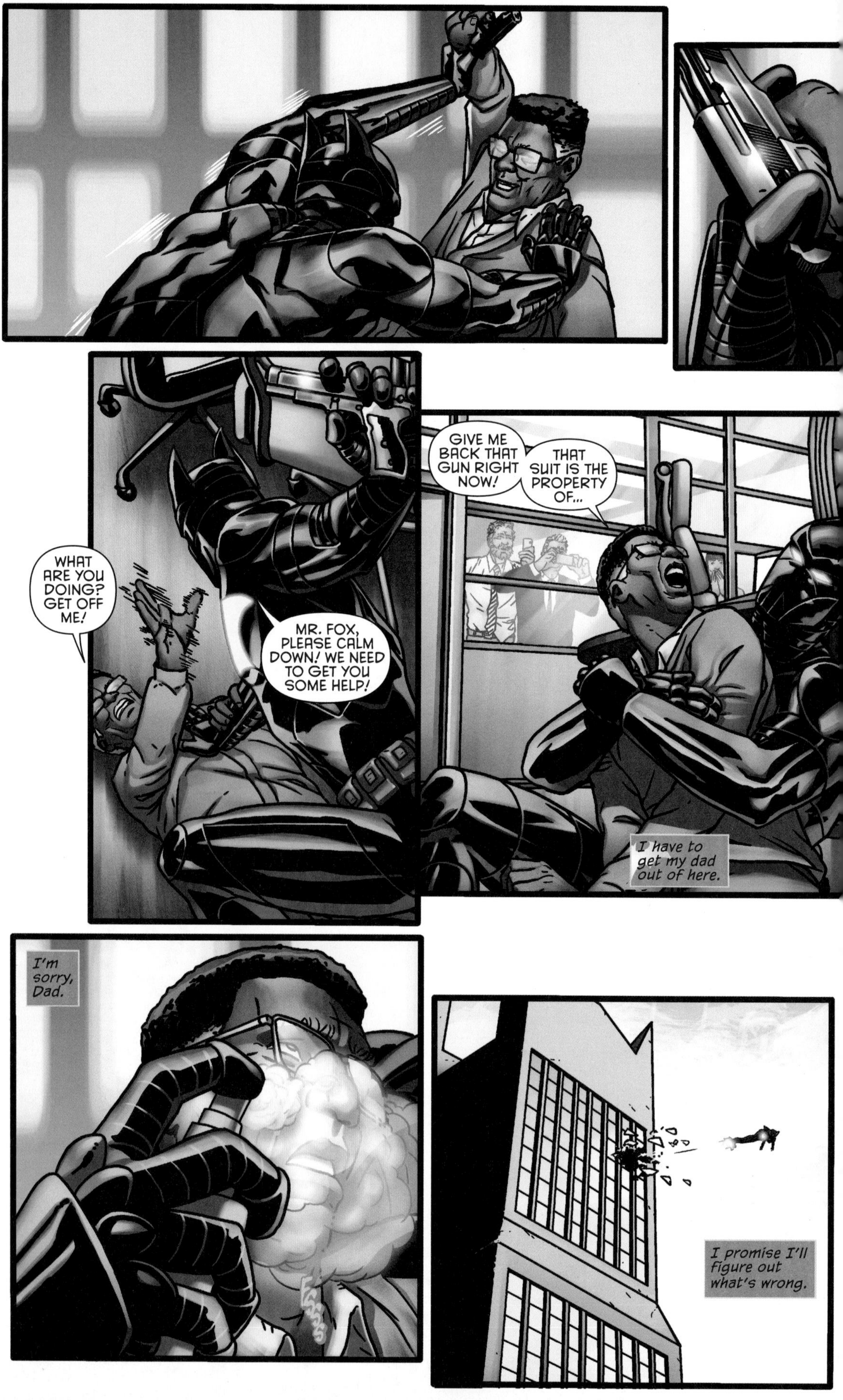
WHAT ARE YOU DOING? GET OFF ME!
MR. FOX, PLEASE CALM DOWN! WE NEED TO GET YOU SOME HELP!
GIVE ME BACK THAT GUN RIGHT NOW!
THAT SUIT IS THE PROPERTY OF...
I have to get my dad out of here.
I'm sorry, Dad.
I promise I'll figure out what's wrong.

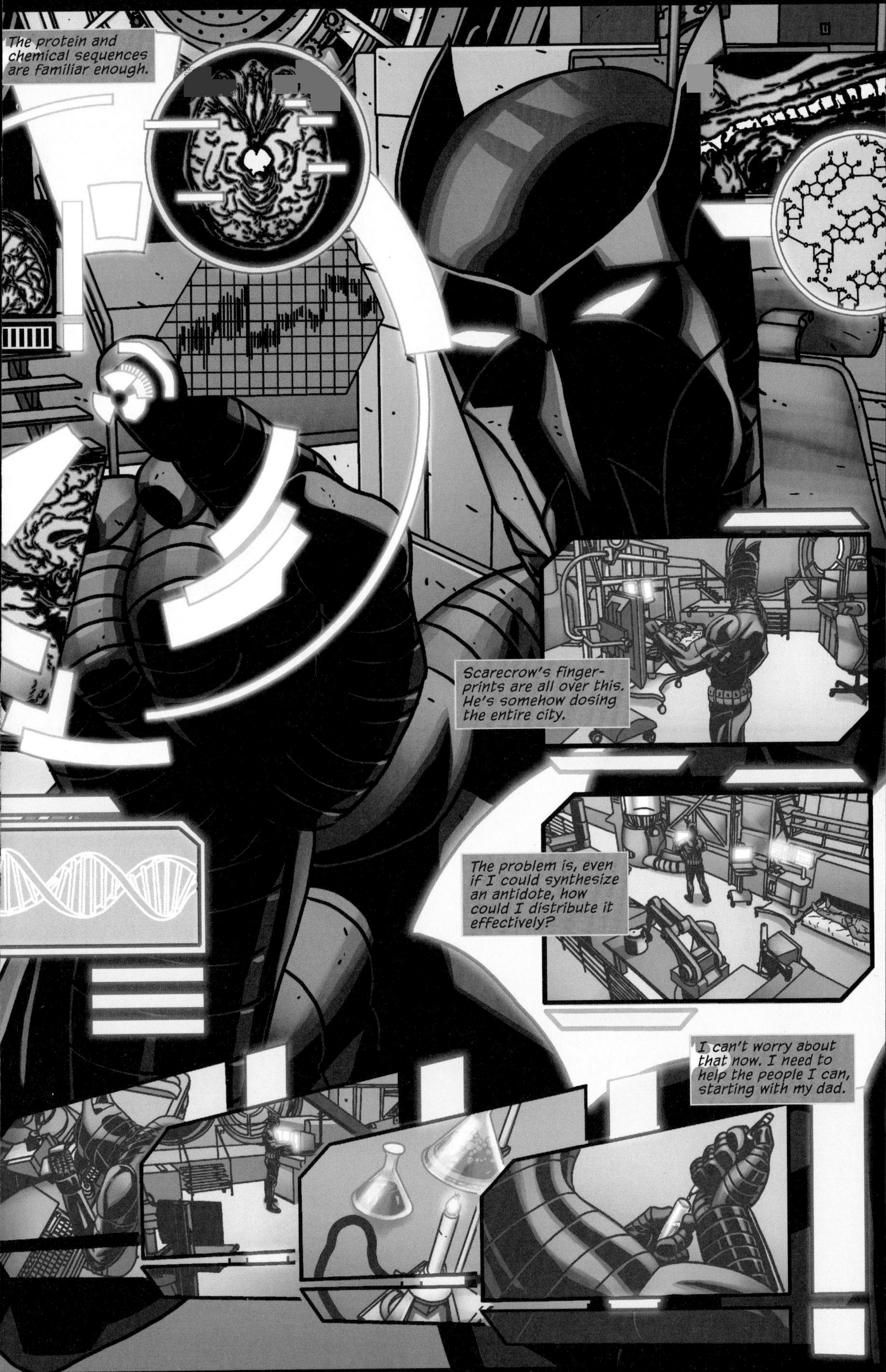
The protein and chemical sequences are familiar enough.
Scarecrow's finger-prints are all over this. He's somehow dosing the entire city.
The problem is, even if I could synthesize an antidote, how could I distribute it effectively?
I can't worry about that now. I need to help the people I can, starting with my dad.

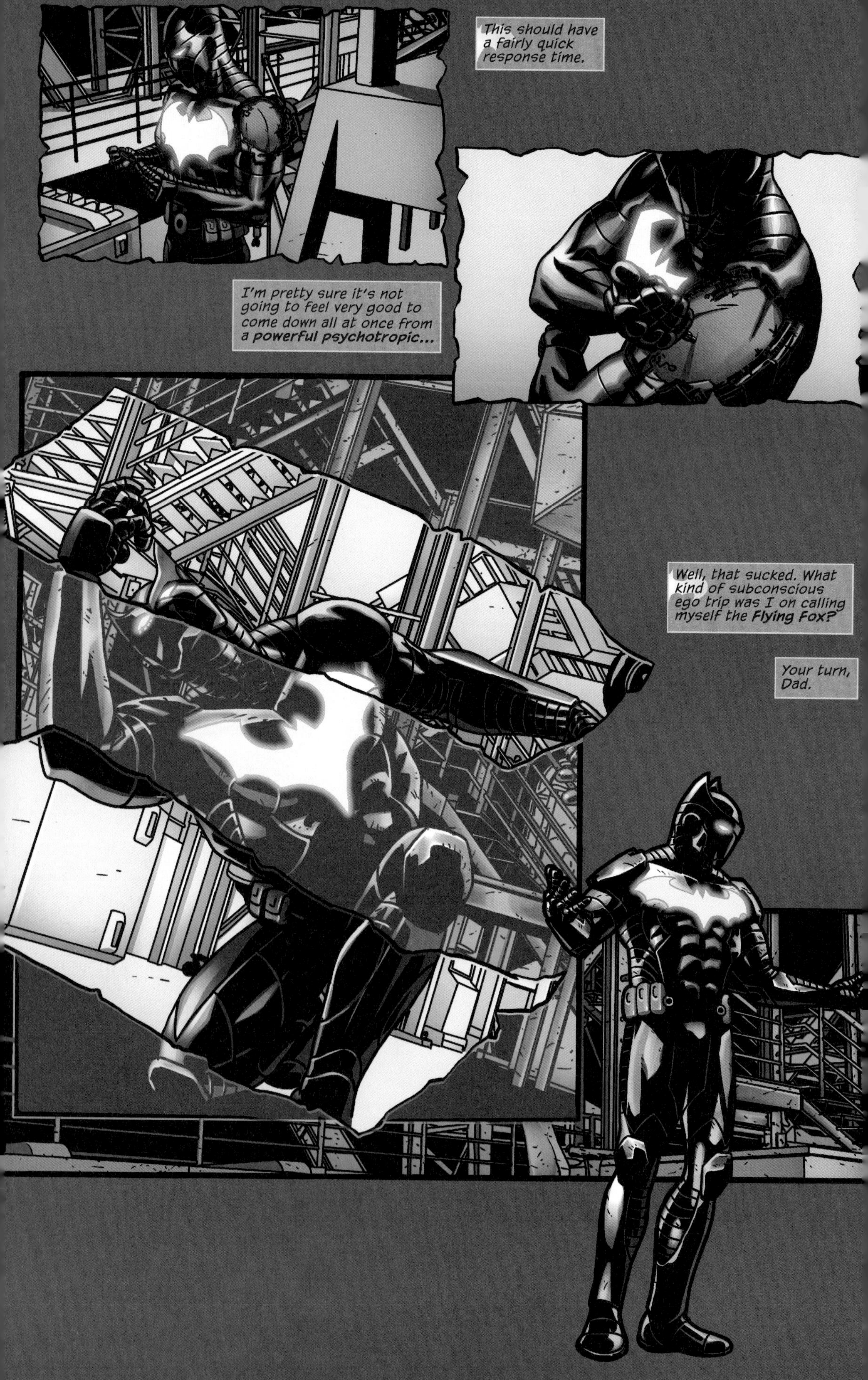
This should have a fairly quick response time.
I'm pretty sure it's not going to feel very good to come down all at once from a **powerful psychotropic...**
Well, that sucked. What kind of subconscious ego trip was I on calling myself the **Flying Fox?**
Your turn, Dad.

HOW ARE YOU FEELING, MR. FOX?

WHERE AM I?

YOU'RE SAFE. YOU WERE EXPOSED TO A KIND OF HALLUCINOGENIC DRUG, BUT I'VE DEVELOPED A NANO-ANTITOXIN THAT I BELIEVE WILL PROTECT YOU FROM FURTHER CONTAMINATION.

YOU'RE THAT NEW BATWING?

YES, SIR, I AM. I HAVE PRODUCED ENOUGH OF THE ANTITOXIN FOR YOU TO INOCULATE YOUR FAMILY.

THAT SHOULD KEEP THEM SAFE, BUT I WOULD RECOMMEND STAYING HOME UNTIL THE SITUATION HAS BEEN RESOLVED.

AND HOW EXACTLY IS THE SITUATION GOING TO BE RESOLVED?

I HAVE FAITH THAT WE CAN STOP THIS.

"WE"?

BATMAN AND OTHERS LIKE MYSELF.

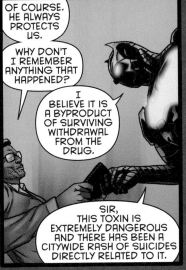

OF COURSE. HE ALWAYS PROTECTS US.

WHY DON'T I REMEMBER ANYTHING THAT HAPPENED?

I BELIEVE IT IS A BYPRODUCT OF SURVIVING WITHDRAWAL FROM THE DRUG.

SIR, THIS TOXIN IS EXTREMELY DANGEROUS AND THERE HAS BEEN A CITYWIDE RASH OF SUICIDES DIRECTLY RELATED TO IT.

I CAN'T MANUFACTURE ENOUGH TO CURE THE CITY, SO I HIGHLY RECOMMEND YOU INOCULATE YOUR LOVED ONES AS SOON AS POSSIBLE.

HOW DID YOU KNOW HOW MANY SHOTS I WOULD NEED?

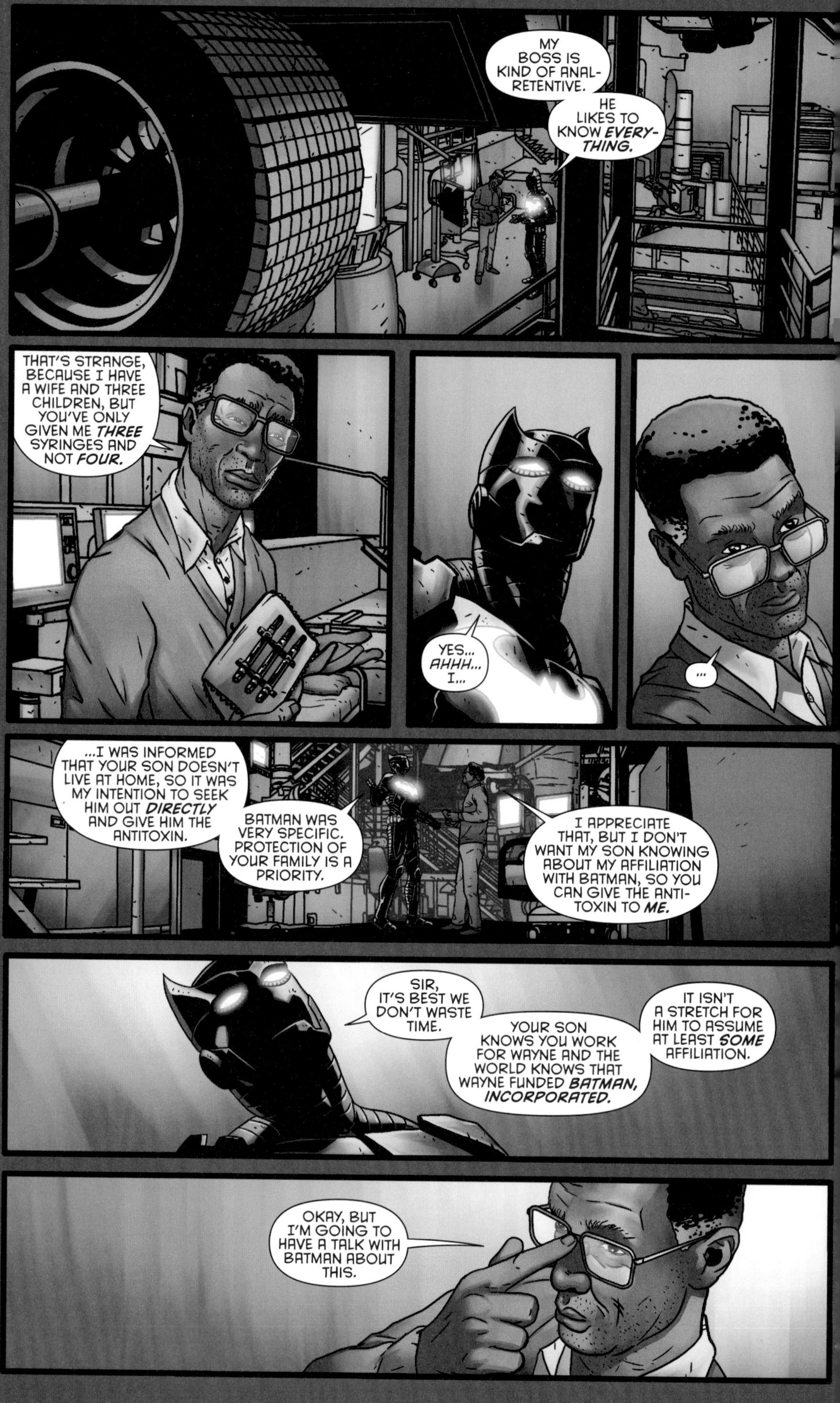

MY BOSS IS KIND OF ANAL-RETENTIVE.
HE LIKES TO KNOW EVERY-THING.
THAT'S STRANGE, BECAUSE I HAVE A WIFE AND THREE CHILDREN, BUT YOU'VE ONLY GIVEN ME THREE SYRINGES AND NOT FOUR.
YES... AHHH... I...
...
...I WAS INFORMED THAT YOUR SON DOESN'T LIVE AT HOME, SO IT WAS MY INTENTION TO SEEK HIM OUT DIRECTLY AND GIVE HIM THE ANTITOXIN.
BATMAN WAS VERY SPECIFIC. PROTECTION OF YOUR FAMILY IS A PRIORITY.
I APPRECIATE THAT, BUT I DON'T WANT MY SON KNOWING ABOUT MY AFFILIATION WITH BATMAN, SO YOU CAN GIVE THE ANTI-TOXIN TO ME.
SIR, IT'S BEST WE DON'T WASTE TIME.
YOUR SON KNOWS YOU WORK FOR WAYNE AND THE WORLD KNOWS THAT WAYNE FUNDED BATMAN, INCORPORATED.
IT ISN'T A STRETCH FOR HIM TO ASSUME AT LEAST SOME AFFILIATION.
OKAY, BUT I'M GOING TO HAVE A TALK WITH BATMAN ABOUT THIS.

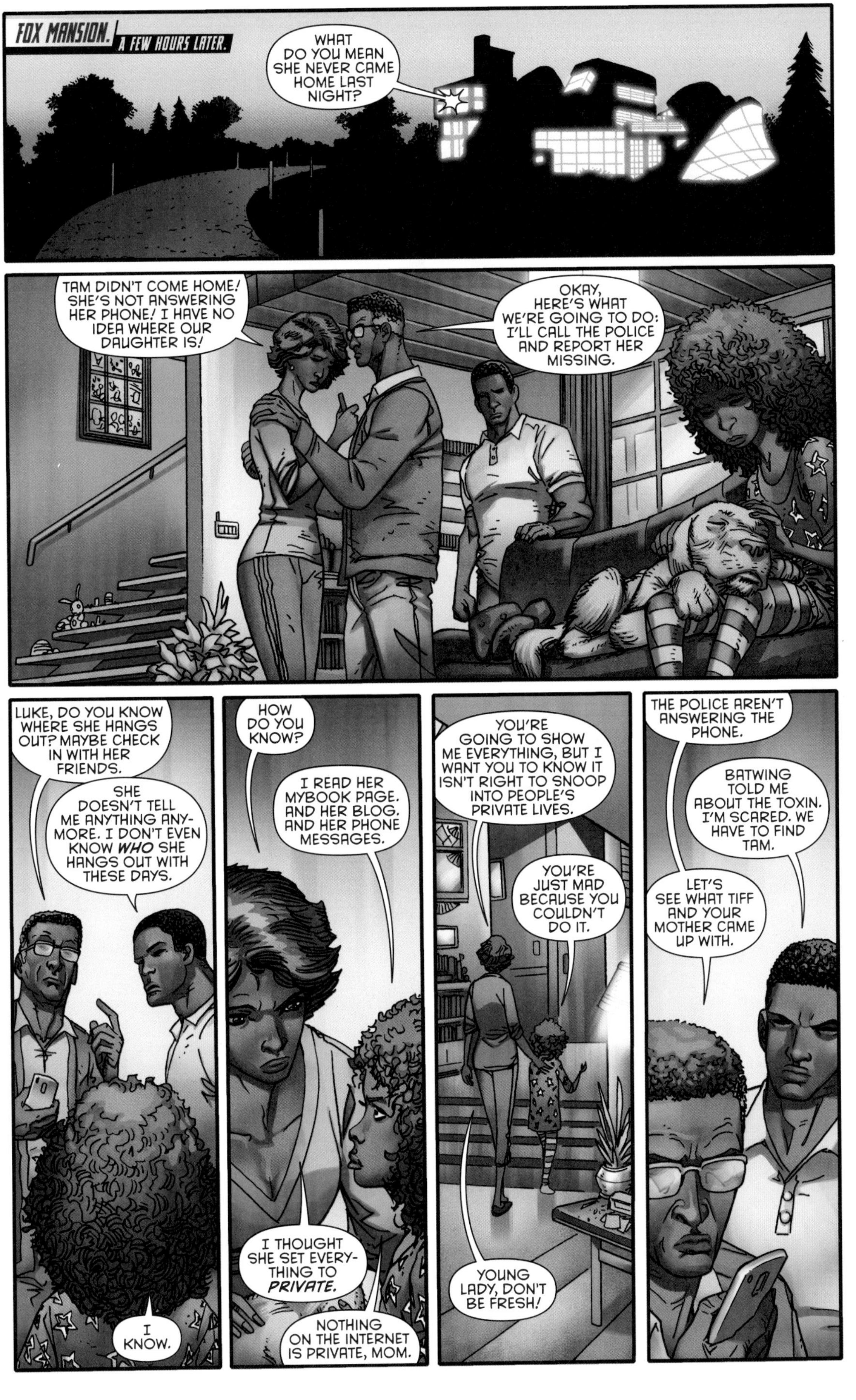
FOX MANSION.
A FEW HOURS LATER.
WHAT DO YOU MEAN SHE NEVER CAME HOME LAST NIGHT?
TAM DIDN'T COME HOME! SHE'S NOT ANSWERING HER PHONE! I HAVE NO IDEA WHERE OUR DAUGHTER IS!
OKAY, HERE'S WHAT WE'RE GOING TO DO: I'LL CALL THE POLICE AND REPORT HER MISSING.
LUKE, DO YOU KNOW WHERE SHE HANGS OUT? MAYBE CHECK IN WITH HER FRIENDS.
SHE DOESN'T TELL ME ANYTHING ANY-MORE. I DON'T EVEN KNOW *WHO* SHE HANGS OUT WITH THESE DAYS.
I KNOW.
HOW DO YOU KNOW?
I READ HER MYBOOK PAGE. AND HER BLOG. AND HER PHONE MESSAGES.
I THOUGHT SHE SET EVERY-THING TO *PRIVATE.*
NOTHING ON THE INTERNET IS PRIVATE, MOM.
YOU'RE GOING TO SHOW ME EVERYTHING, BUT I WANT YOU TO KNOW IT ISN'T RIGHT TO SNOOP INTO PEOPLE'S PRIVATE LIVES.
YOU'RE JUST MAD BECAUSE YOU COULDN'T DO IT.
YOUNG LADY, DON'T BE FRESH!
THE POLICE AREN'T ANSWERING THE PHONE.
BATWING TOLD ME ABOUT THE TOXIN. I'M SCARED. WE HAVE TO FIND TAM.
LET'S SEE WHAT TIFF AND YOUR MOTHER CAME UP WITH.

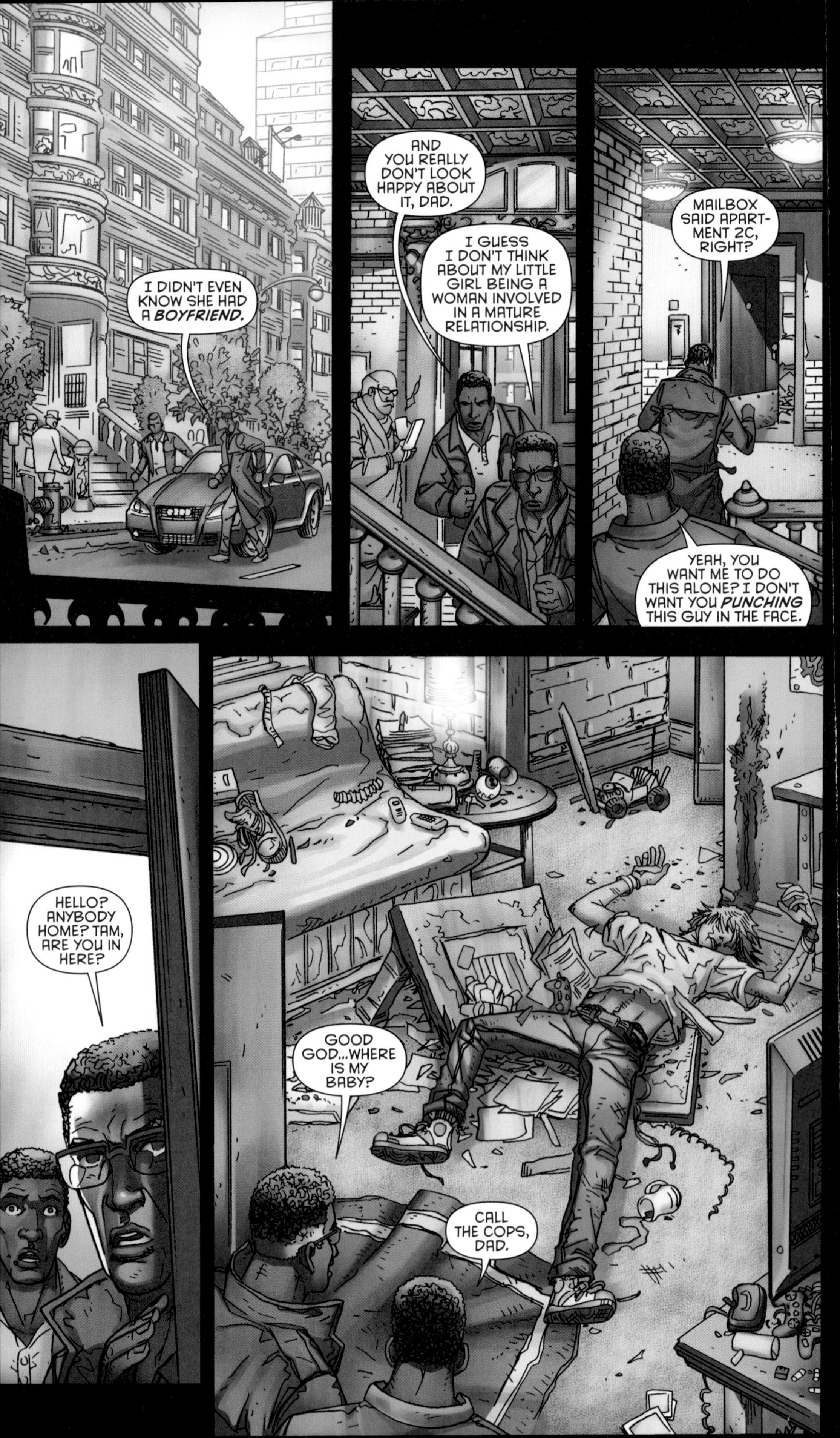
I DIDN'T EVEN KNOW SHE HAD A BOYFRIEND.
AND YOU REALLY DON'T LOOK HAPPY ABOUT IT, DAD.
I GUESS I DON'T THINK ABOUT MY LITTLE GIRL BEING A WOMAN INVOLVED IN A MATURE RELATIONSHIP.
MAILBOX SAID APARTMENT 2C, RIGHT?
YEAH, YOU WANT ME TO DO THIS ALONE? I DON'T WANT YOU PUNCHING THIS GUY IN THE FACE.
HELLO? ANYBODY HOME? TAM, ARE YOU IN HERE?
GOOD GOD...WHERE IS MY BABY?
CALL THE COPS, DAD.

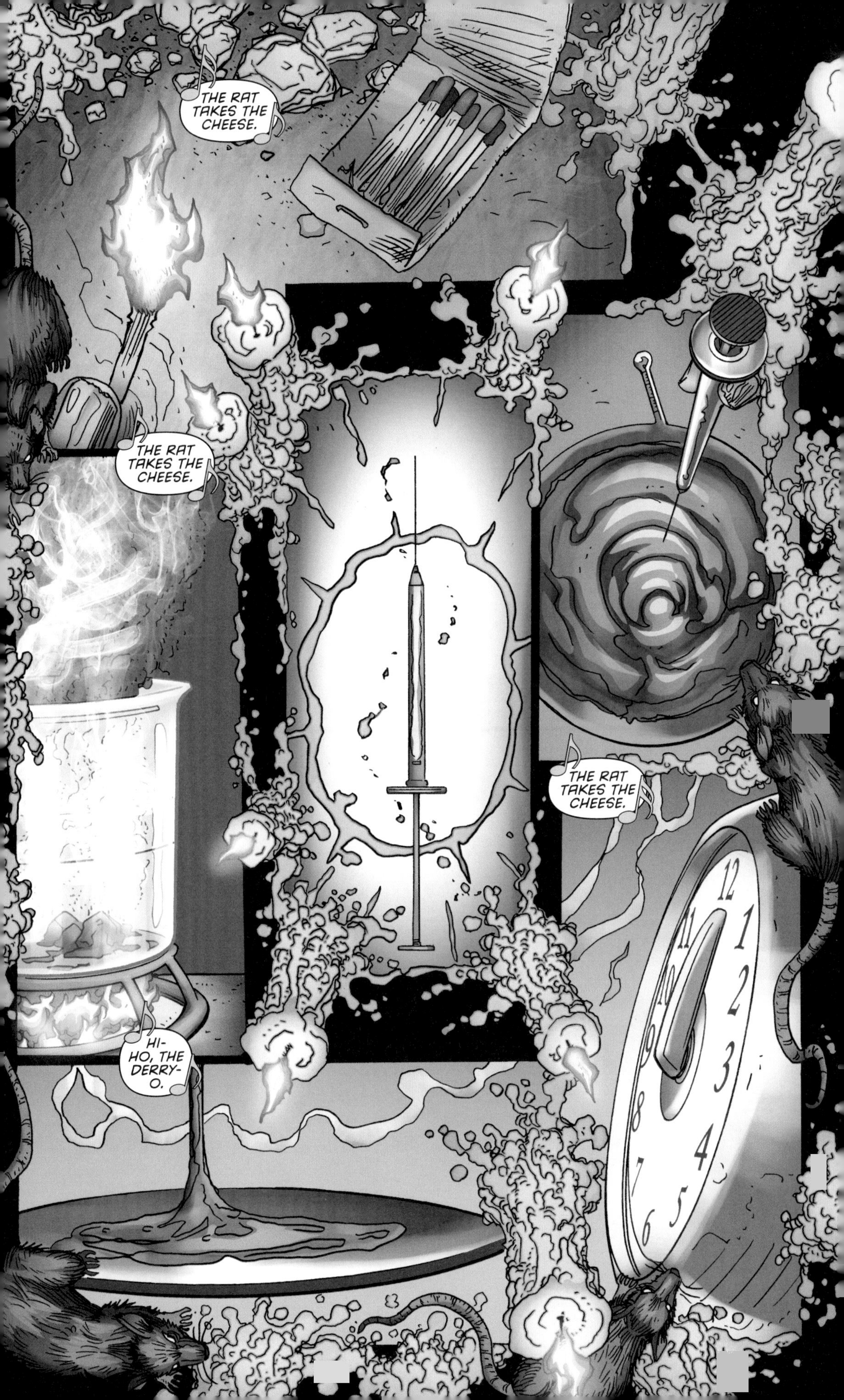
THE RAT TAKES THE CHEESE.
THE RAT TAKES THE CHEESE.
THE RAT TAKES THE CHEESE.
HI-HO, THE DERRY-O.

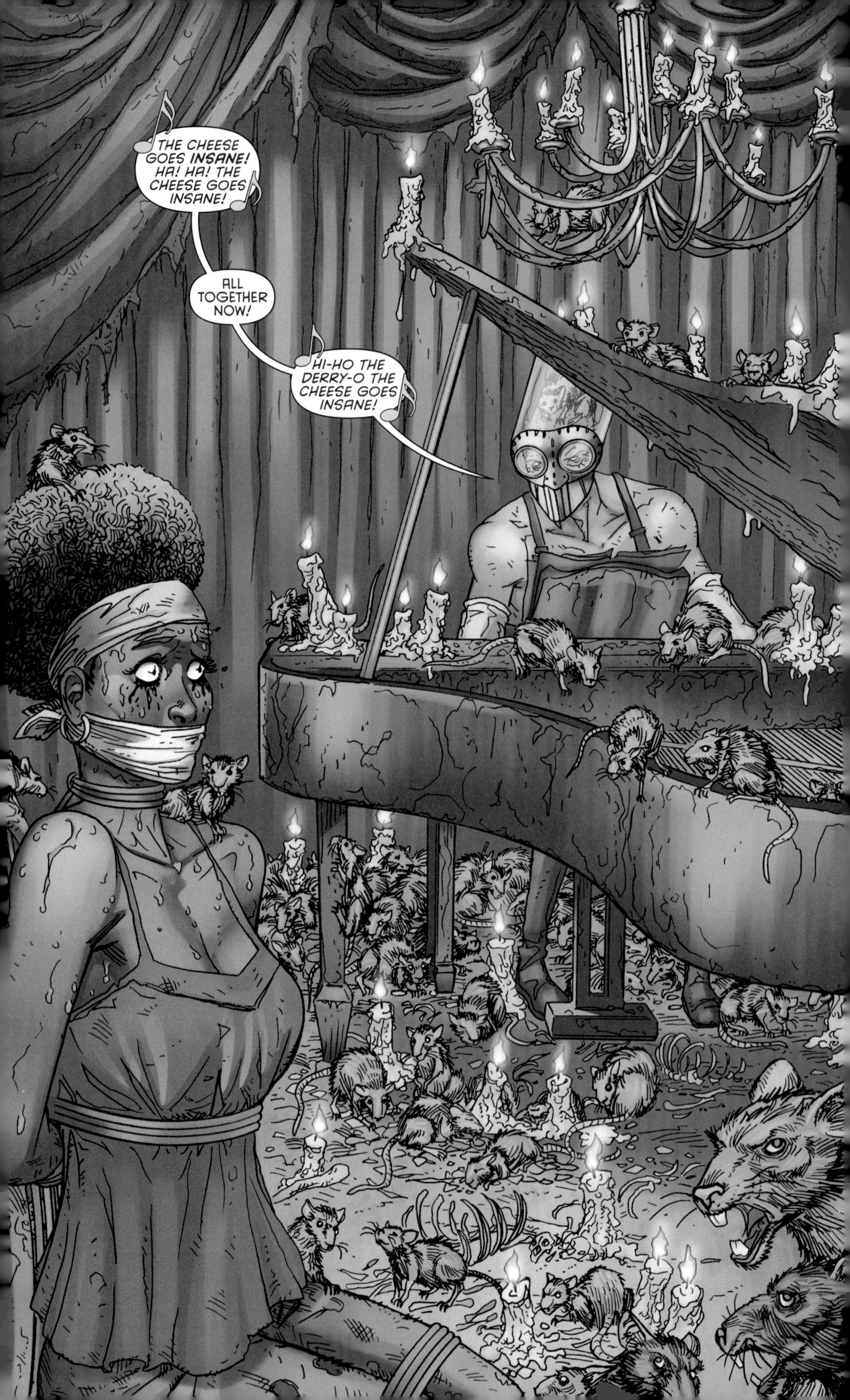
THE CHEESE GOES **INSANE!** HA! HA! THE CHEESE GOES INSANE!
ALL TOGETHER NOW!
HI-HO THE DERRY-O THE CHEESE GOES INSANE!

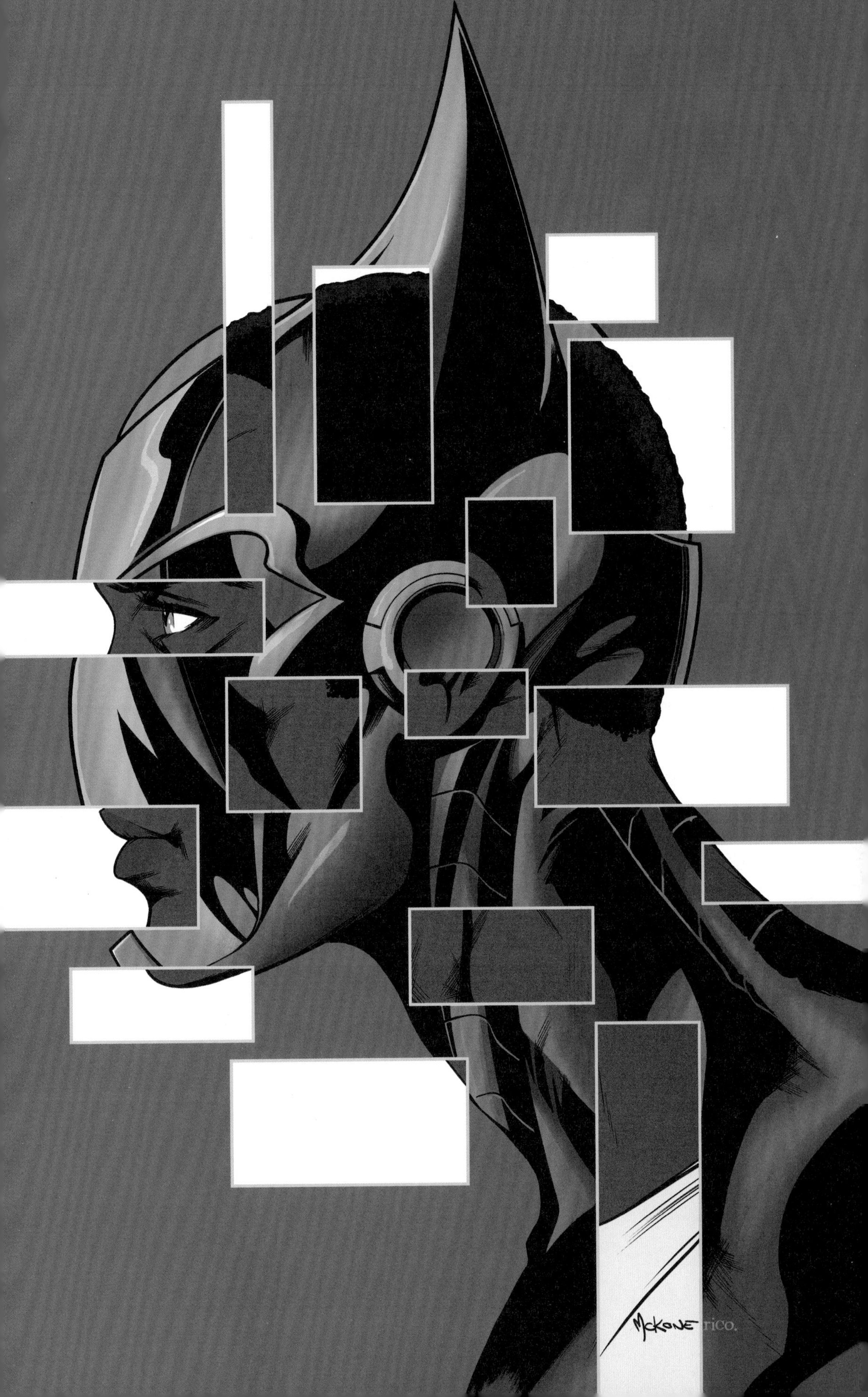
MCKONE rico.

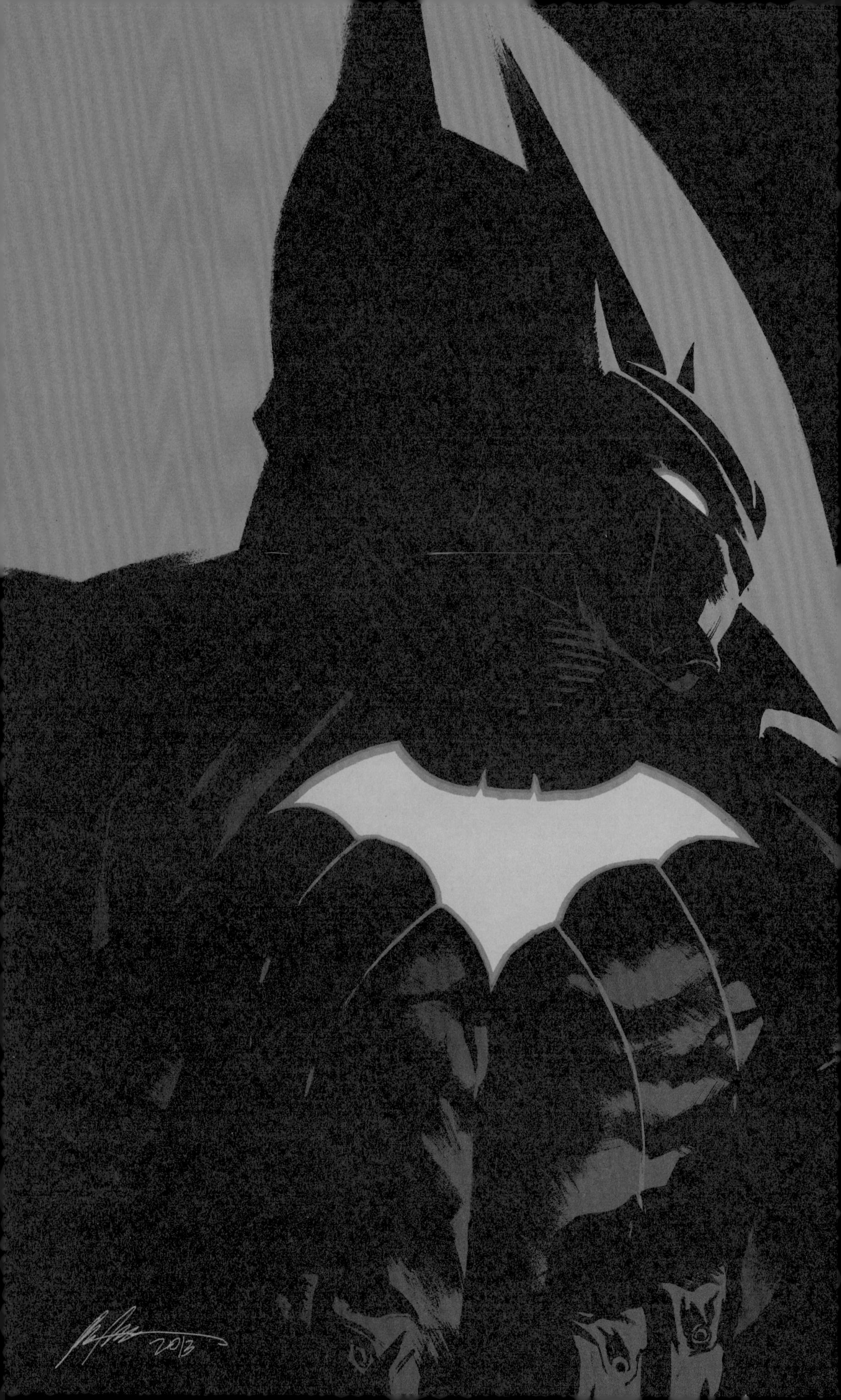

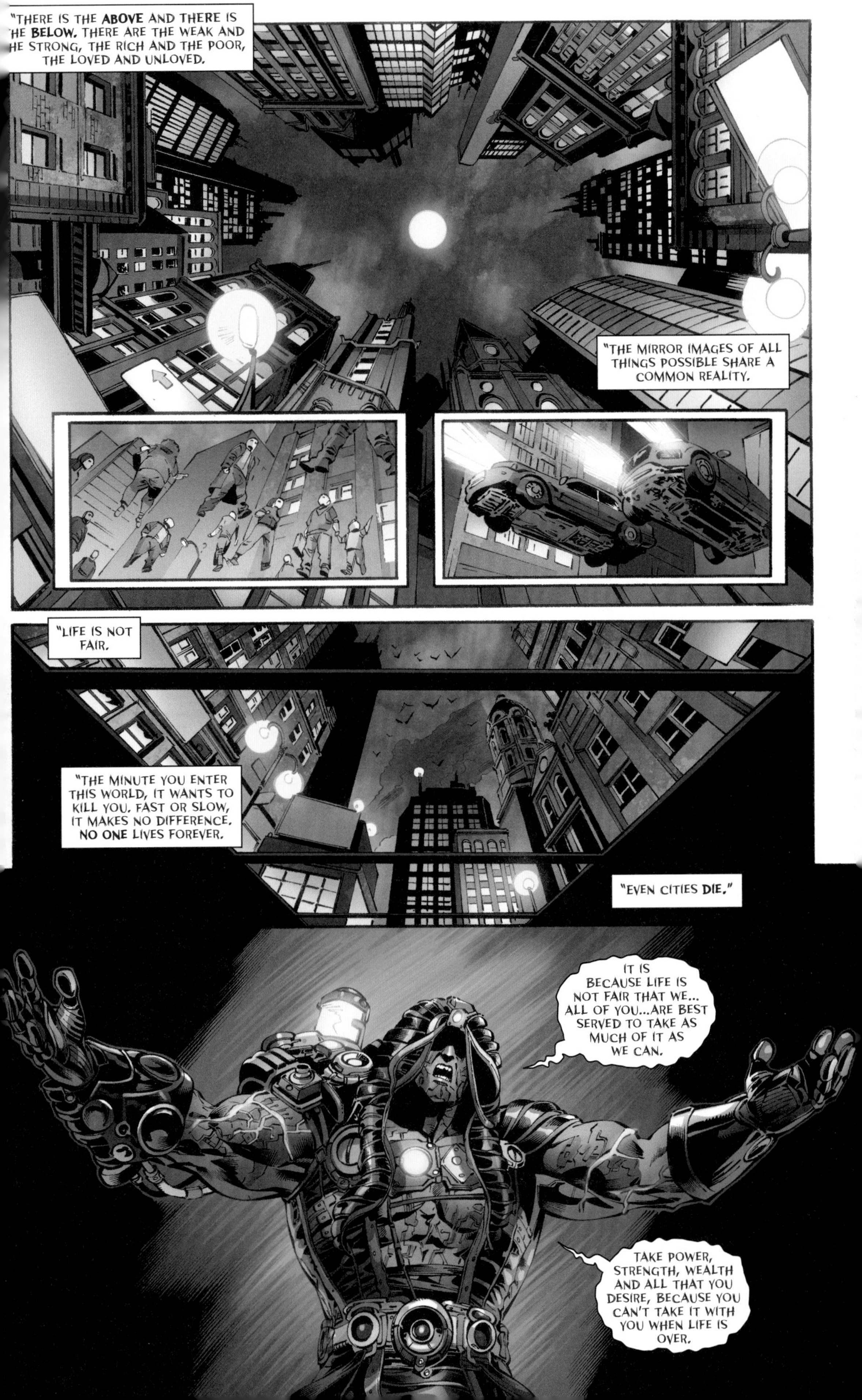
"THERE IS THE ABOVE AND THERE IS THE BELOW. THERE ARE THE WEAK AND THE STRONG, THE RICH AND THE POOR, THE LOVED AND UNLOVED.
"THE MIRROR IMAGES OF ALL THINGS POSSIBLE SHARE A COMMON REALITY.
"LIFE IS NOT FAIR.
"THE MINUTE YOU ENTER THIS WORLD, IT WANTS TO KILL YOU. FAST OR SLOW, IT MAKES NO DIFFERENCE. NO ONE LIVES FOREVER.
"EVEN CITIES DIE."
IT IS BECAUSE LIFE IS NOT FAIR THAT WE... ALL OF YOU...ARE BEST SERVED TO TAKE AS MUCH OF IT AS WE CAN.
TAKE POWER, STRENGTH, WEALTH AND ALL THAT YOU DESIRE, BECAUSE YOU CAN'T TAKE IT WITH YOU WHEN LIFE IS OVER.

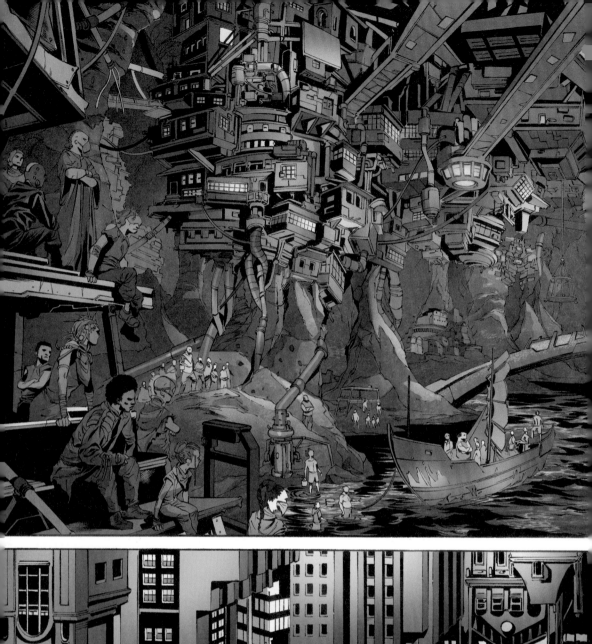

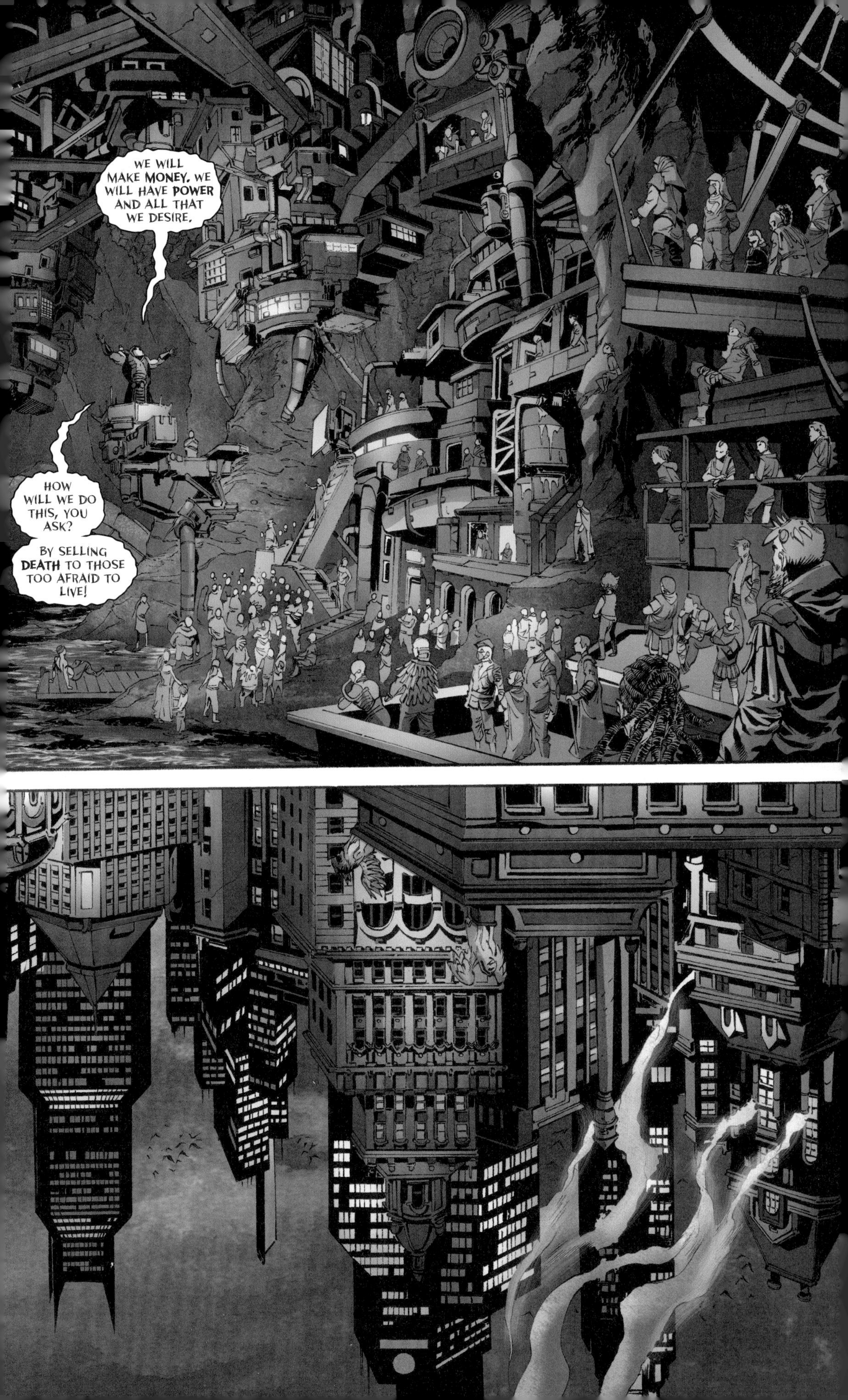
WE WILL MAKE **MONEY**. WE WILL HAVE **POWER** AND ALL THAT WE DESIRE.
HOW WILL WE DO THIS, YOU ASK?
BY SELLING **DEATH** TO THOSE TOO AFRAID TO LIVE!

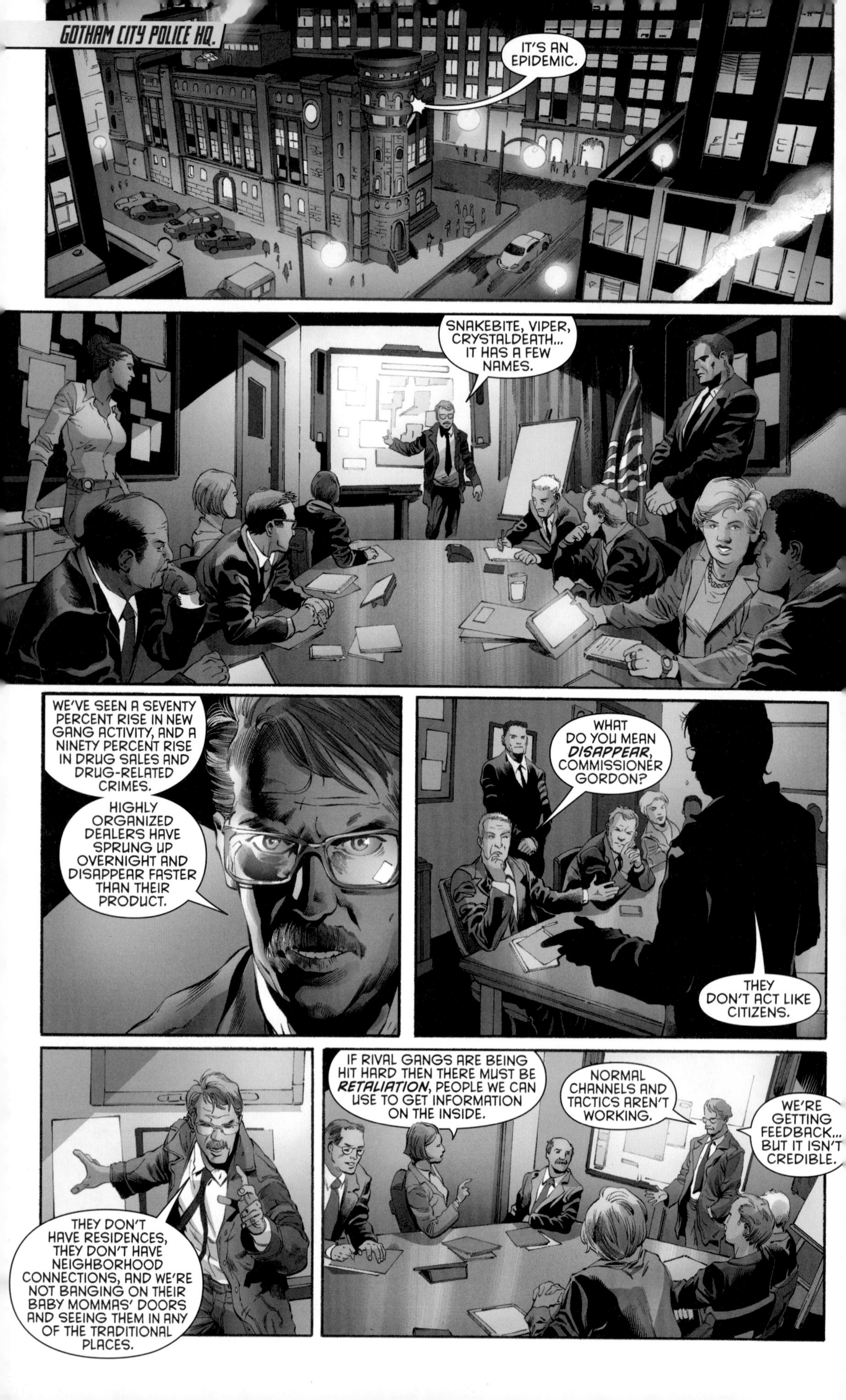
GOTHAM CITY POLICE HQ.
IT'S AN EPIDEMIC.
SNAKEBITE, VIPER, CRYSTALDEATH... IT HAS A FEW NAMES.
WE'VE SEEN A SEVENTY PERCENT RISE IN NEW GANG ACTIVITY, AND A NINETY PERCENT RISE IN DRUG SALES AND DRUG-RELATED CRIMES.
HIGHLY ORGANIZED DEALERS HAVE SPRUNG UP OVERNIGHT AND DISAPPEAR FASTER THAN THEIR PRODUCT.
WHAT DO YOU MEAN *DISAPPEAR,* COMMISSIONER GORDON?
THEY DON'T ACT LIKE CITIZENS.
THEY DON'T HAVE RESIDENCES, THEY DON'T HAVE NEIGHBORHOOD CONNECTIONS, AND WE'RE NOT BANGING ON THEIR BABY MOMMAS' DOORS AND SEEING THEM IN ANY OF THE TRADITIONAL PLACES.
IF RIVAL GANGS ARE BEING HIT HARD THEN THERE MUST BE *RETALIATION,* PEOPLE WE CAN USE TO GET INFORMATION ON THE INSIDE.
NORMAL CHANNELS AND TACTICS AREN'T WORKING.
WE'RE GETTING FEEDBACK... BUT IT ISN'T CREDIBLE.

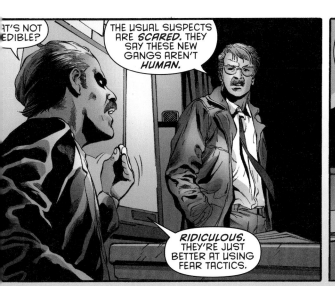

IT'S NOT EDIBLE?

THE USUAL SUSPECTS ARE *SCARED*. THEY SAY THESE NEW GANGS AREN'T *HUMAN*.

RIDICULOUS. THEY'RE JUST BETTER AT USING FEAR TACTICS.

COMMISSIONER, THE PUBLIC NEEDS TO BE AWARE THAT THE SIDE EFFECTS OF CRYSTALDEATH ARE DEVASTATING AND HAPPENING AT AN ALARMING RATE.

IN AS FEW AS THREE WEEKS, A HEAVY USER CAN BE REDUCED TO A VEGETATIVE STATE THAT REFLECTS YEARS OF HABITUAL ABUSE.

I HAVE THE REPORTS OF EVERYONE IN THIS ROOM, AND I'M TELLING YOU WE NEED A RADICALLY *DIFFERENT* APPROACH.

WE'RE FACING A NEW GENERATION OF CRIMINAL ENTERPRISES OPERATING WITH NEW CHANNELS OF DISTRIBUTION.

WHY CAN'T YOU PUT PEOPLE INTO DEEP COVER SCENARIOS?!

SO THERE HAVE BEEN *NO* ARRESTS AT ALL?

HAVE YOU NOT HEARD ANYTHING I'VE SAID?!

THEY ARE *IMPOSSIBLE* TO LOCATE OR TRACE AND HAVE NO RECORDS OF ANY KIND!

IT'S LIKE THEY'RE NOT EVEN LIVING IN GOTHAM CITY!

SOMETHING'S GOT TO BE DONE! THEY'RE STEPPING ALL OVER OUR TERRITORIES.

I SAY WE HANG BACK.

"HANG BACK"? ARE YOU OUT OF YOUR MIND?

LISTEN, THE FREAKS AR[E] STEPPING ON OUR TOE[S] AND IT SUCKS. BUT WE'[RE] *MINNOWS* AND THEY'R[E] EXPANDING THEIR OPERATIONS AT LIGHT SPEED, BRO.

BY NEXT MONTH, THEY'RE GONNA DR[AW] HEAVY HEAT FROM SHARKS IN THIS TANK. [I] SAY WE LET THEM SHAR[KS] DO WHAT SHARKS D[O] AND WE'LL GO BAC[K] TO B.U., BABY.

WHAT ARE YOU TALKING ABOUT "B.U."?

"BUSINESS AS USUAL", YO.

HELL NO! NO. NO. NOO!

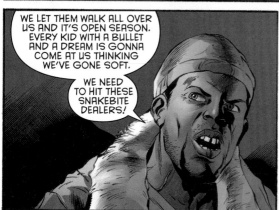

WE LET THEM WALK ALL OVER US AND IT'S OPEN SEASON. EVERY KID WITH A BULLET AND A DREAM IS GONNA COME AT US THINKING WE'VE GONE SOFT.

WE NEED TO HIT THESE SNAKEBITE DEALERS!

I AGREE. SORT OF.

OH CRAP, IT'S *BATMAN!*

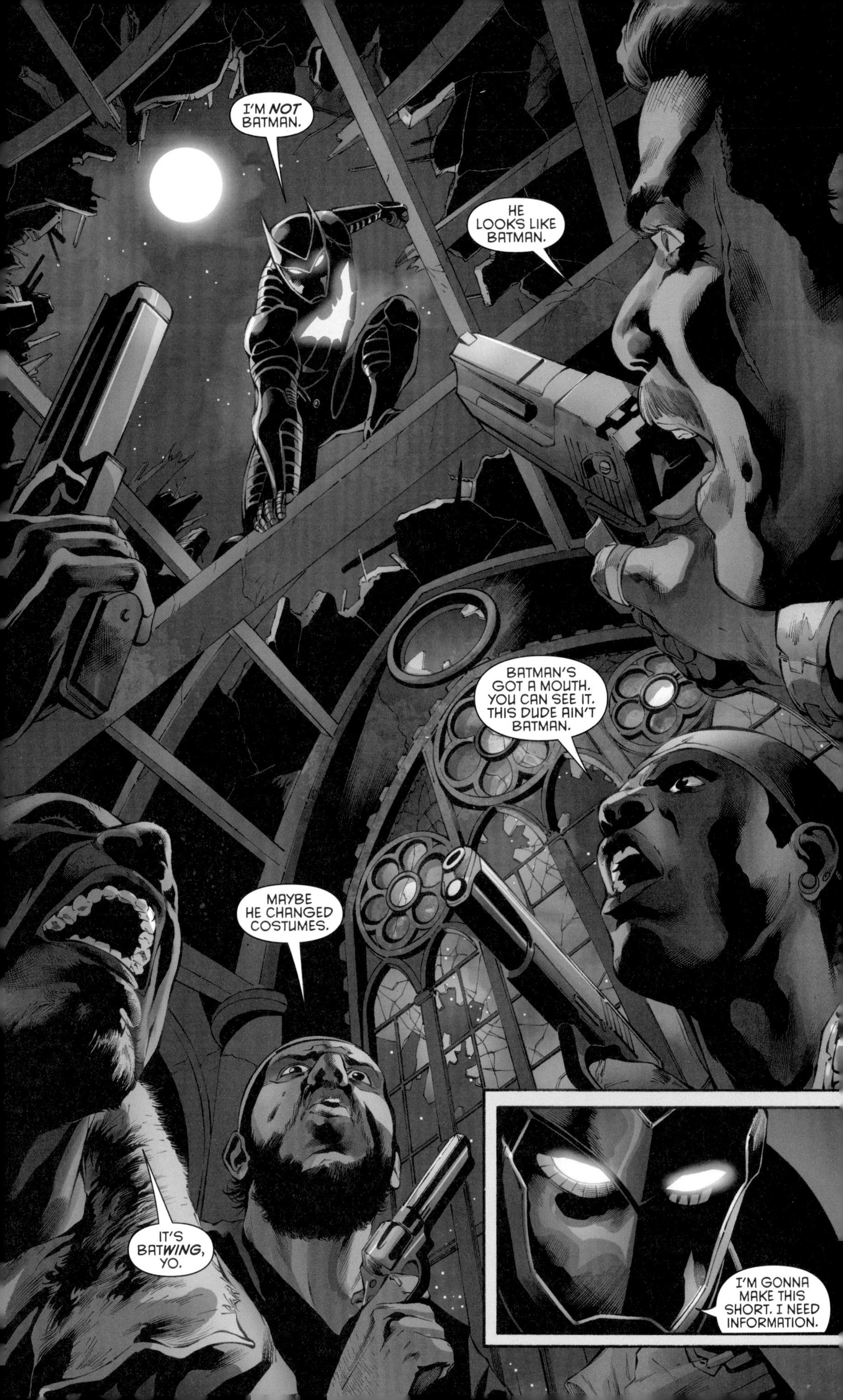
I'M *NOT* BATMAN.
HE LOOKS LIKE BATMAN.
BATMAN'S GOT A MOUTH. YOU CAN SEE IT. THIS DUDE AIN'T BATMAN.
MAYBE HE CHANGED COSTUMES.
IT'S BAT*WING*, YO.
I'M GONNA MAKE THIS SHORT. I NEED INFORMATION.

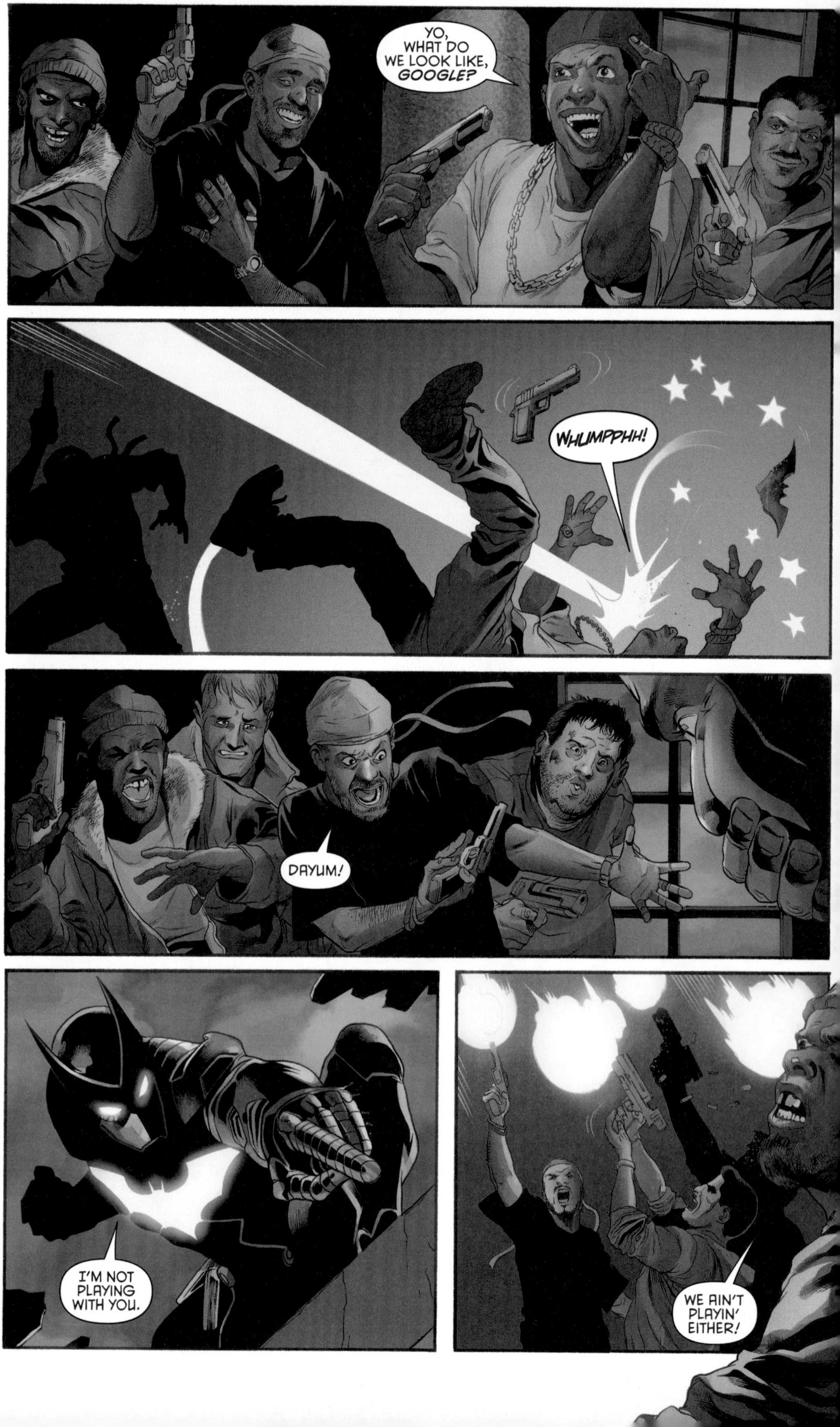
YO, WHAT DO WE LOOK LIKE, GOOGLE?
WHUMPPHH!
DAYUM!
I'M NOT PLAYING WITH YOU.
WE AIN'T PLAYIN' EITHER!

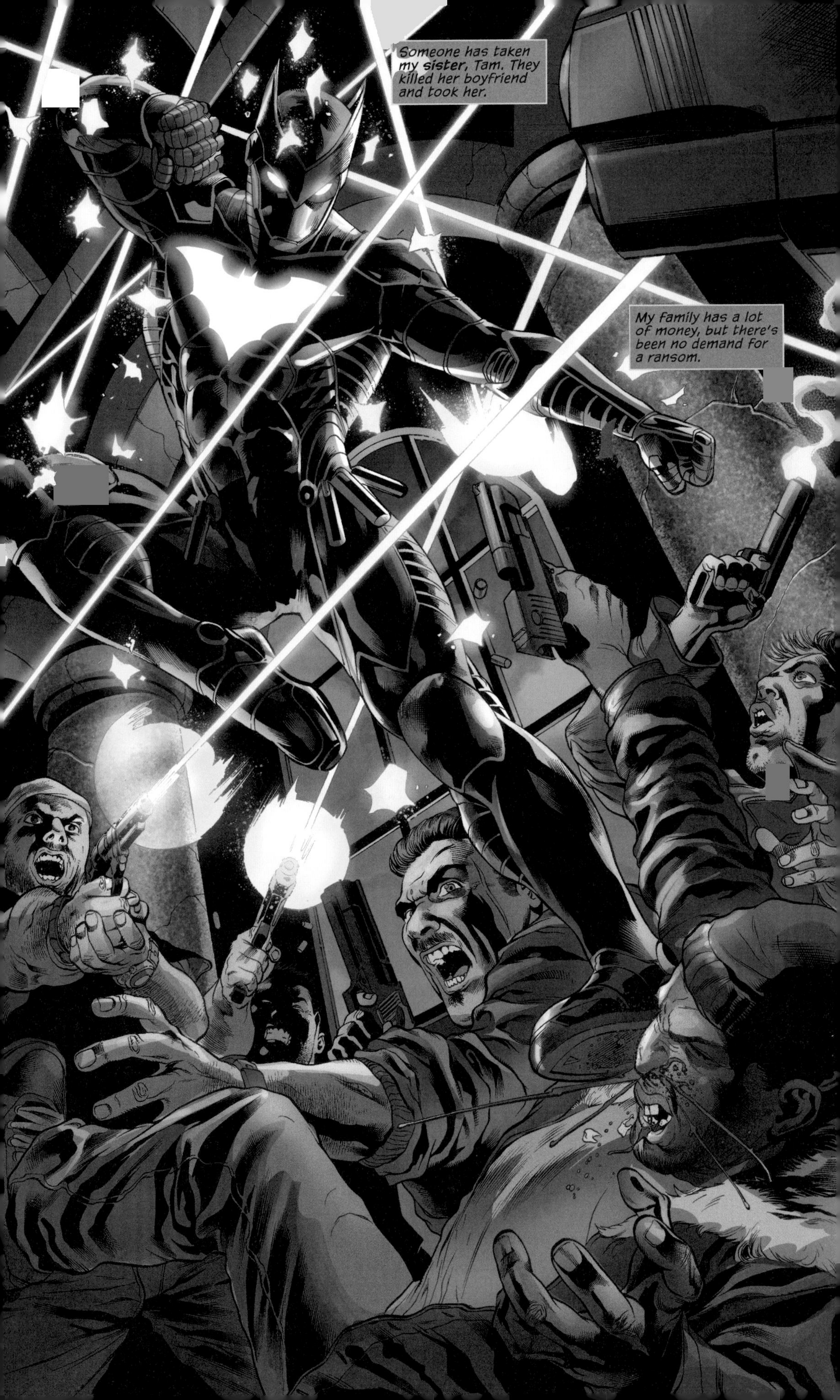
Someone has taken my sister, Tam. They killed her boyfriend and took her.
My family has a lot of money, but there's been no demand for a ransom.

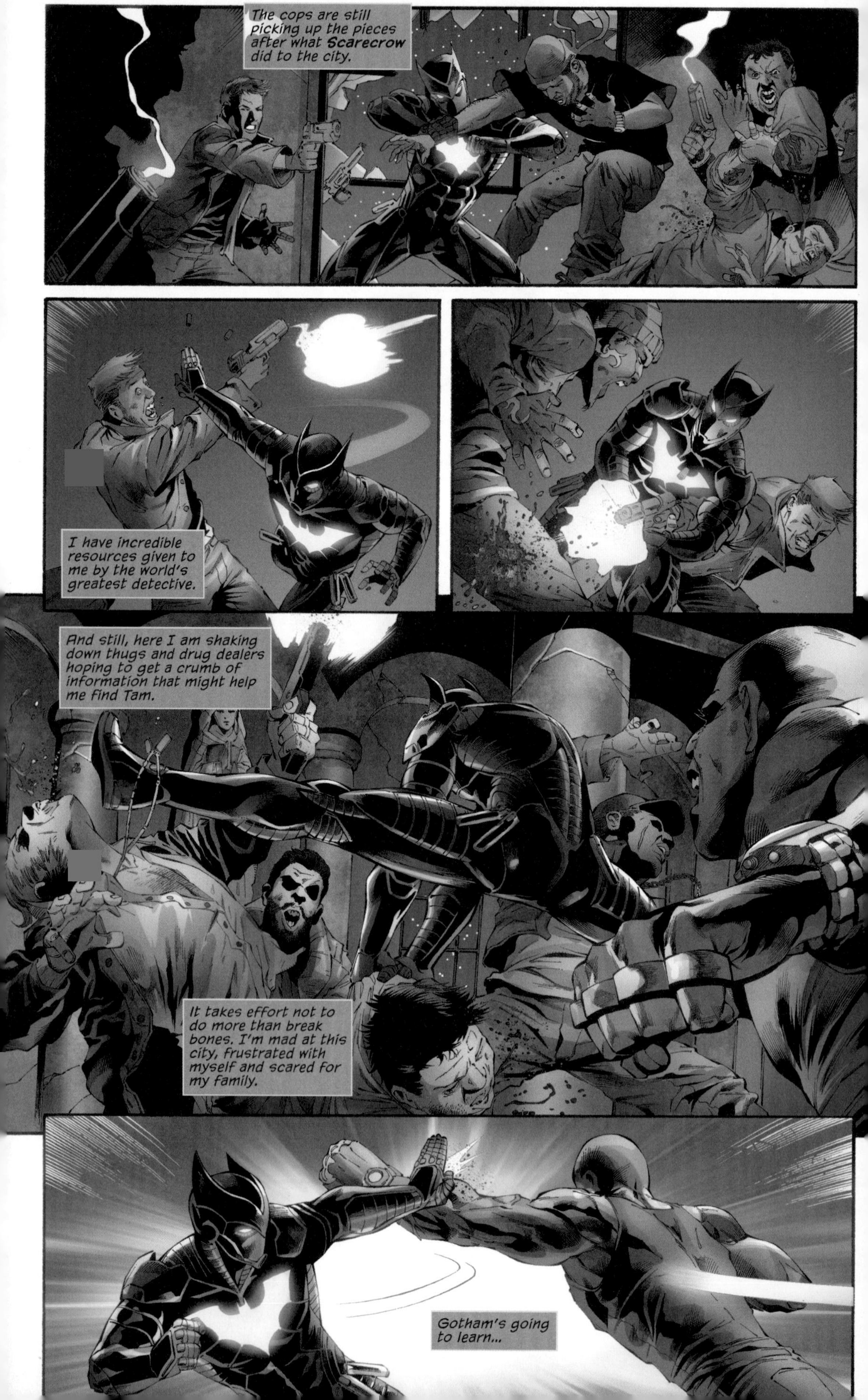
The cops are still picking up the pieces after what Scarecrow did to the city.
I have incredible resources given to me by the world's greatest detective.
And still, here I am shaking down thugs and drug dealers hoping to get a crumb of information that might help me find Tam.
It takes effort not to do more than break bones. I'm mad at this city, frustrated with myself and scared for my family.
Gotham's going to learn...

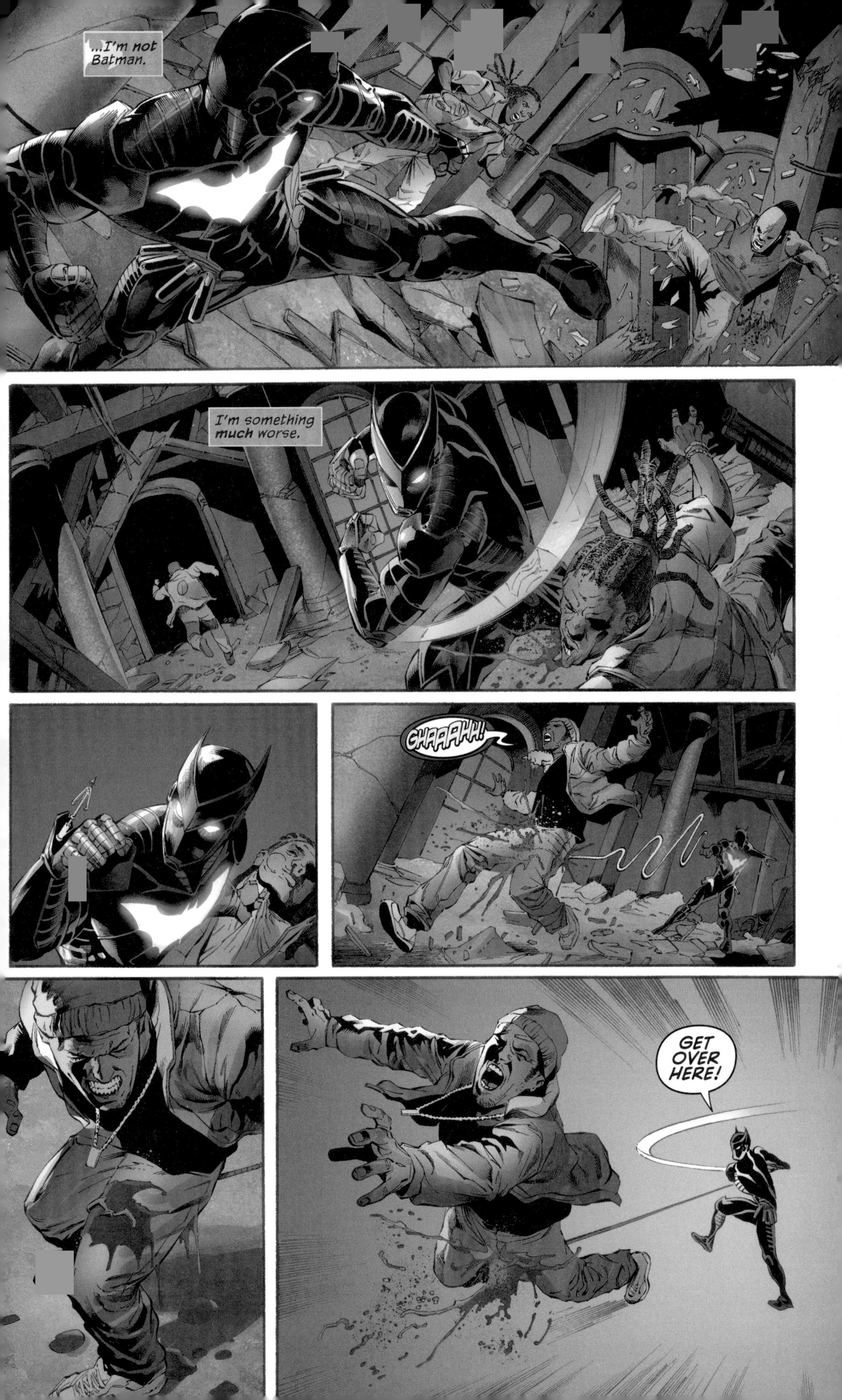
...I'm not Batman.
I'm something **much** worse.
GHAAAHH!
GET OVER HERE!

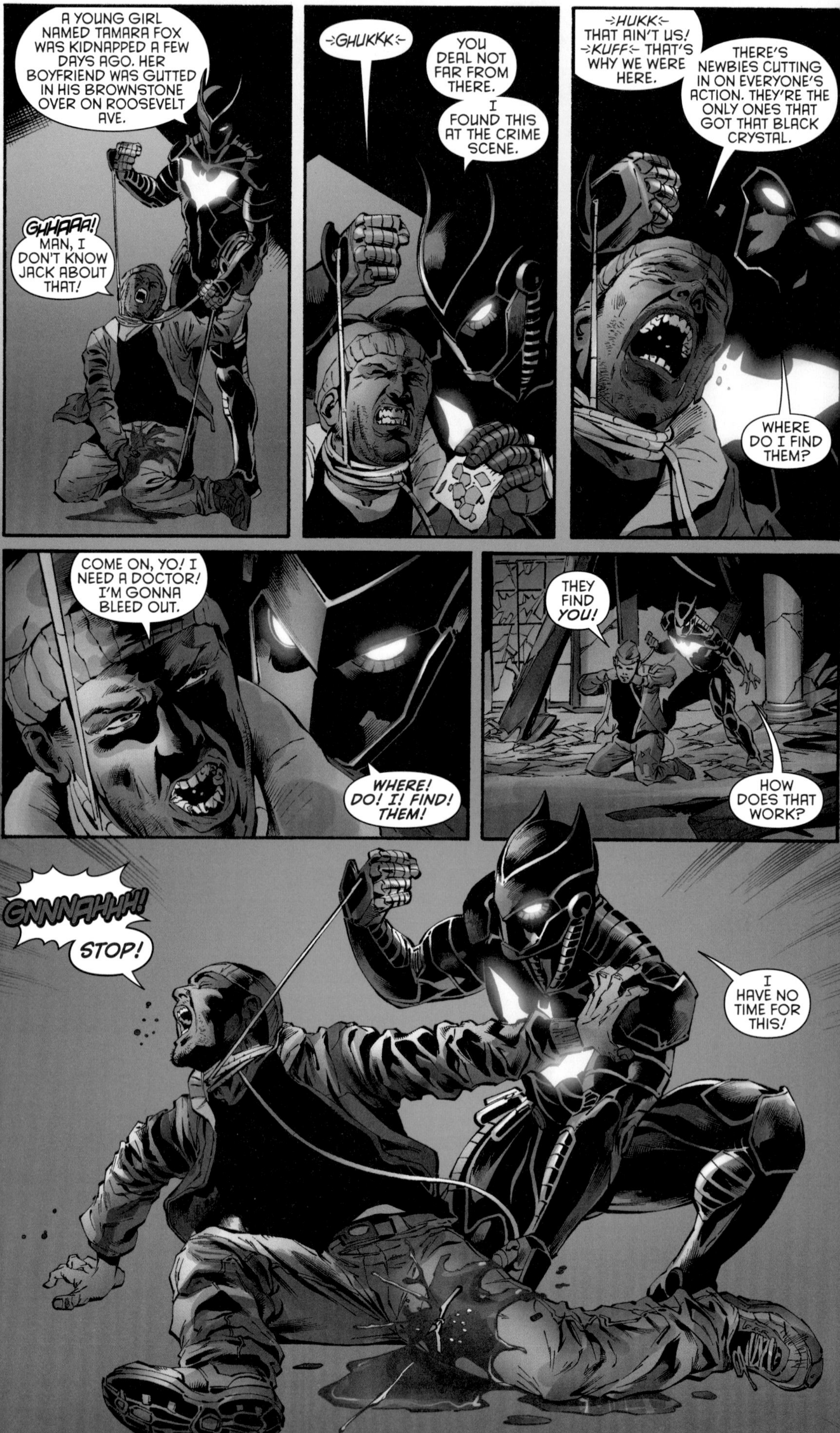
A YOUNG GIRL NAMED TAMARA FOX WAS KIDNAPPED A FEW DAYS AGO. HER BOYFRIEND WAS GUTTED IN HIS BROWNSTONE OVER ON ROOSEVELT AVE.
GHHAAA! MAN, I DON'T KNOW JACK ABOUT THAT!
-GHUKKK-
YOU DEAL NOT FAR FROM THERE.
I FOUND THIS AT THE CRIME SCENE.
-HUKK- THAT AIN'T US! -KUFF- THAT'S WHY WE WERE HERE.
THERE'S NEWBIES CUTTING IN ON EVERYONE'S ACTION. THEY'RE THE ONLY ONES THAT GOT THAT BLACK CRYSTAL.
WHERE DO I FIND THEM?
COME ON, YO! I NEED A DOCTOR! I'M GONNA BLEED OUT.
WHERE! DO! I! FIND! THEM!
THEY FIND YOU!
HOW DOES THAT WORK?
GNNAHHH!
STOP!
I HAVE NO TIME FOR THIS!

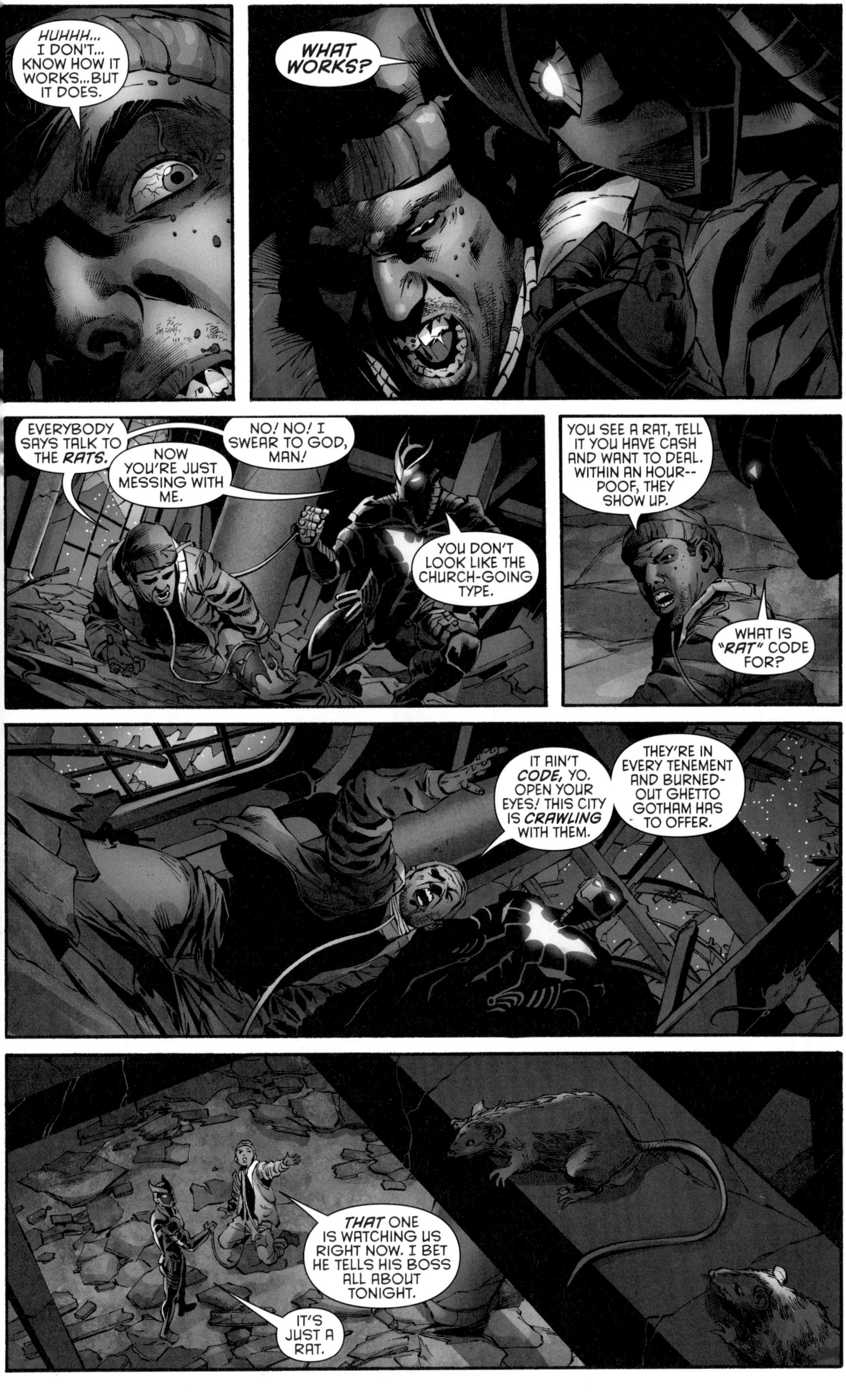
HUHHH... I DON'T... KNOW HOW IT WORKS...BUT IT DOES.
WHAT WORKS?
EVERYBODY SAYS TALK TO THE RATS.
NOW YOU'RE JUST MESSING WITH ME.
NO! NO! I SWEAR TO GOD, MAN!
YOU DON'T LOOK LIKE THE CHURCH-GOING TYPE.
YOU SEE A RAT, TELL IT YOU HAVE CASH AND WANT TO DEAL. WITHIN AN HOUR-- POOF, THEY SHOW UP.
WHAT IS "RAT" CODE FOR?
IT AIN'T CODE, YO. OPEN YOUR EYES! THIS CITY IS CRAWLING WITH THEM.
THEY'RE IN EVERY TENEMENT AND BURNED-OUT GHETTO GOTHAM HAS TO OFFER.
THAT ONE IS WATCHING US RIGHT NOW. I BET HE TELLS HIS BOSS ALL ABOUT TONIGHT.
IT'S JUST A RAT.

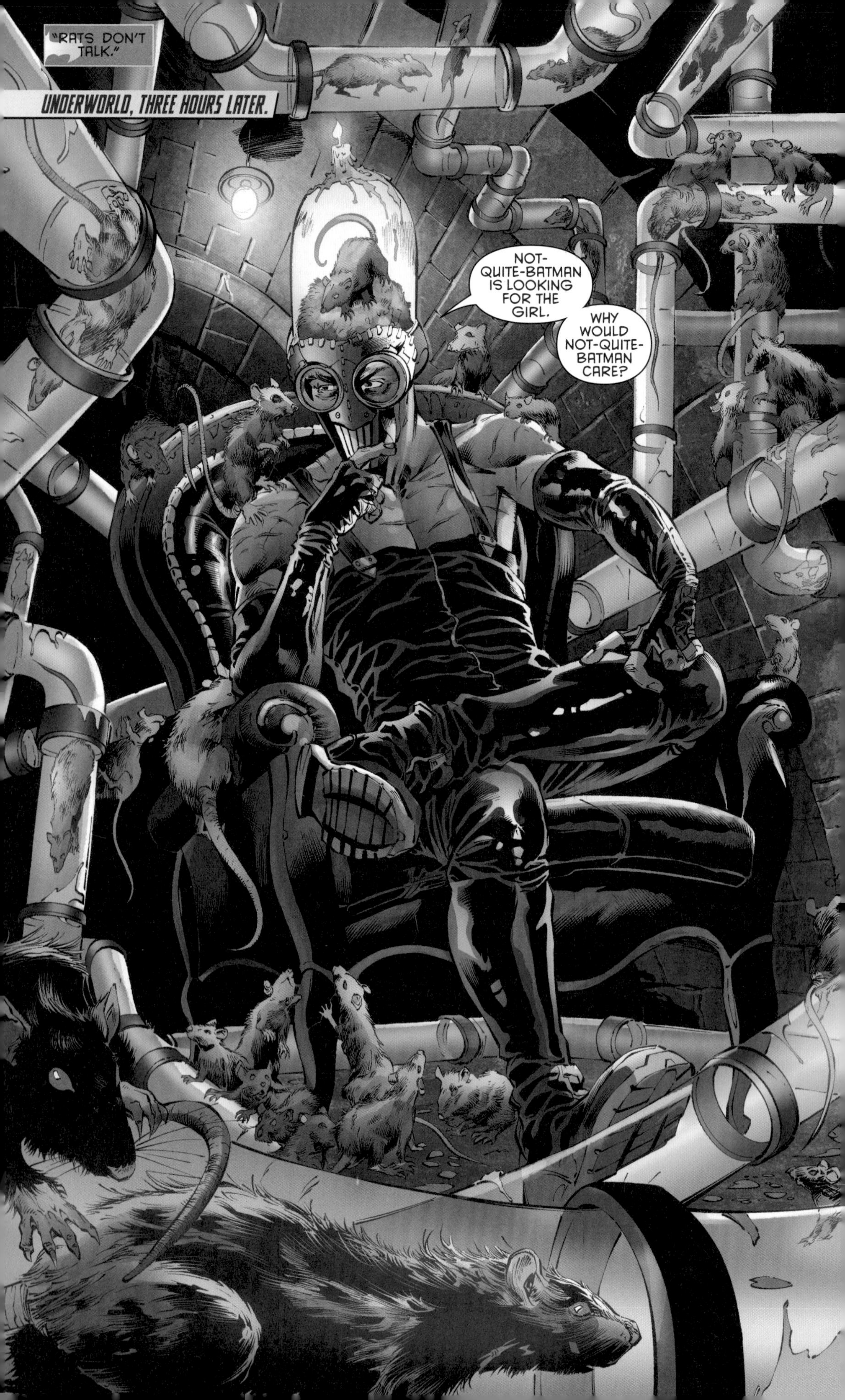
"RATS DON'T TALK."
UNDERWORLD, THREE HOURS LATER.
NOT-QUITE-BATMAN IS LOOKING FOR THE GIRL.
WHY WOULD NOT-QUITE-BATMAN CARE?

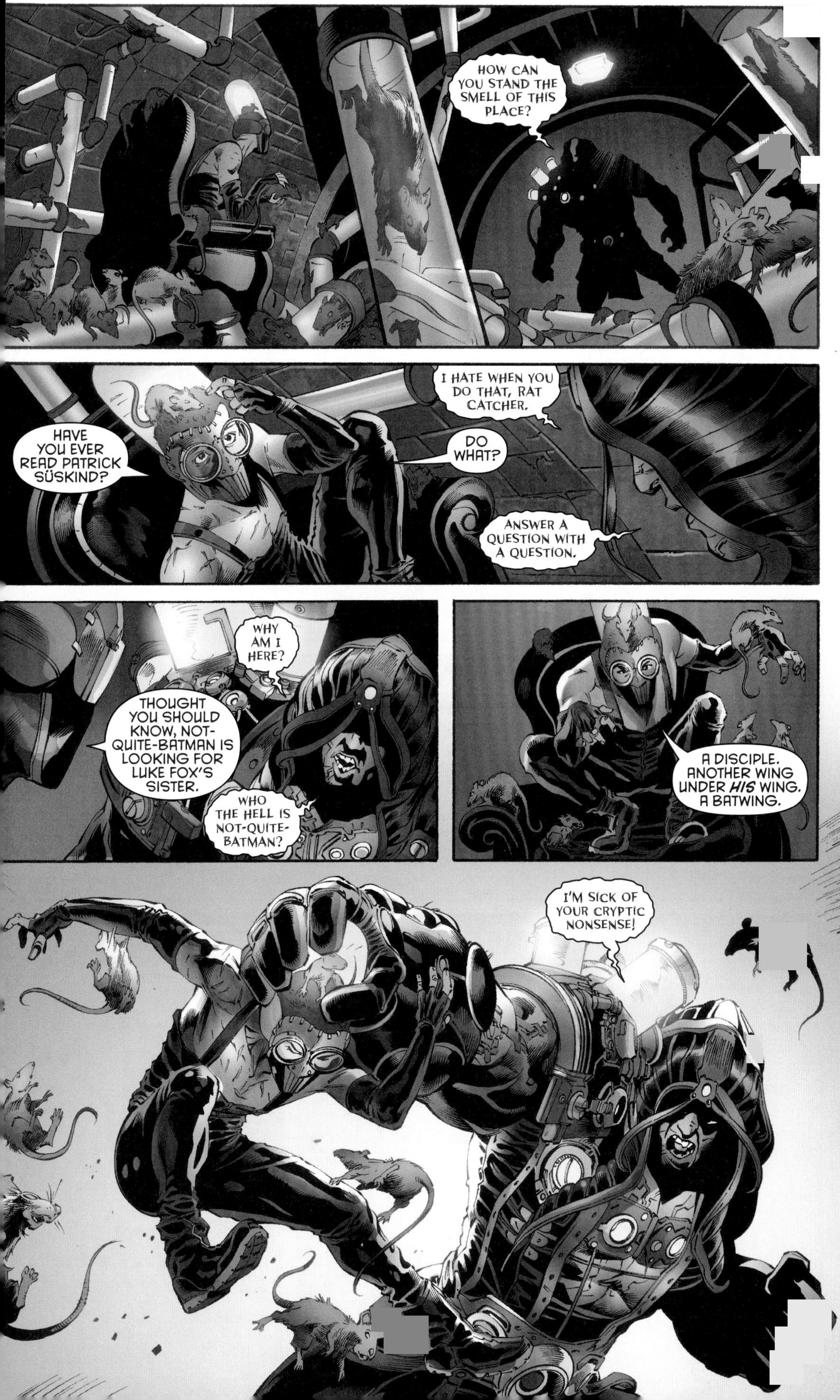
HOW CAN YOU STAND THE SMELL OF THIS PLACE?
HAVE YOU EVER READ PATRICK SÜSKIND?
I HATE WHEN YOU DO THAT, RAT CATCHER.
DO WHAT?
ANSWER A QUESTION WITH A QUESTION.
WHY AM I HERE?
THOUGHT YOU SHOULD KNOW, NOT-QUITE-BATMAN IS LOOKING FOR LUKE FOX'S SISTER.
WHO THE HELL IS NOT-QUITE-BATMAN?
A DISCIPLE. ANOTHER WING UNDER HIS WING. A BATWING.
I'M SICK OF YOUR CRYPTIC NONSENSE!

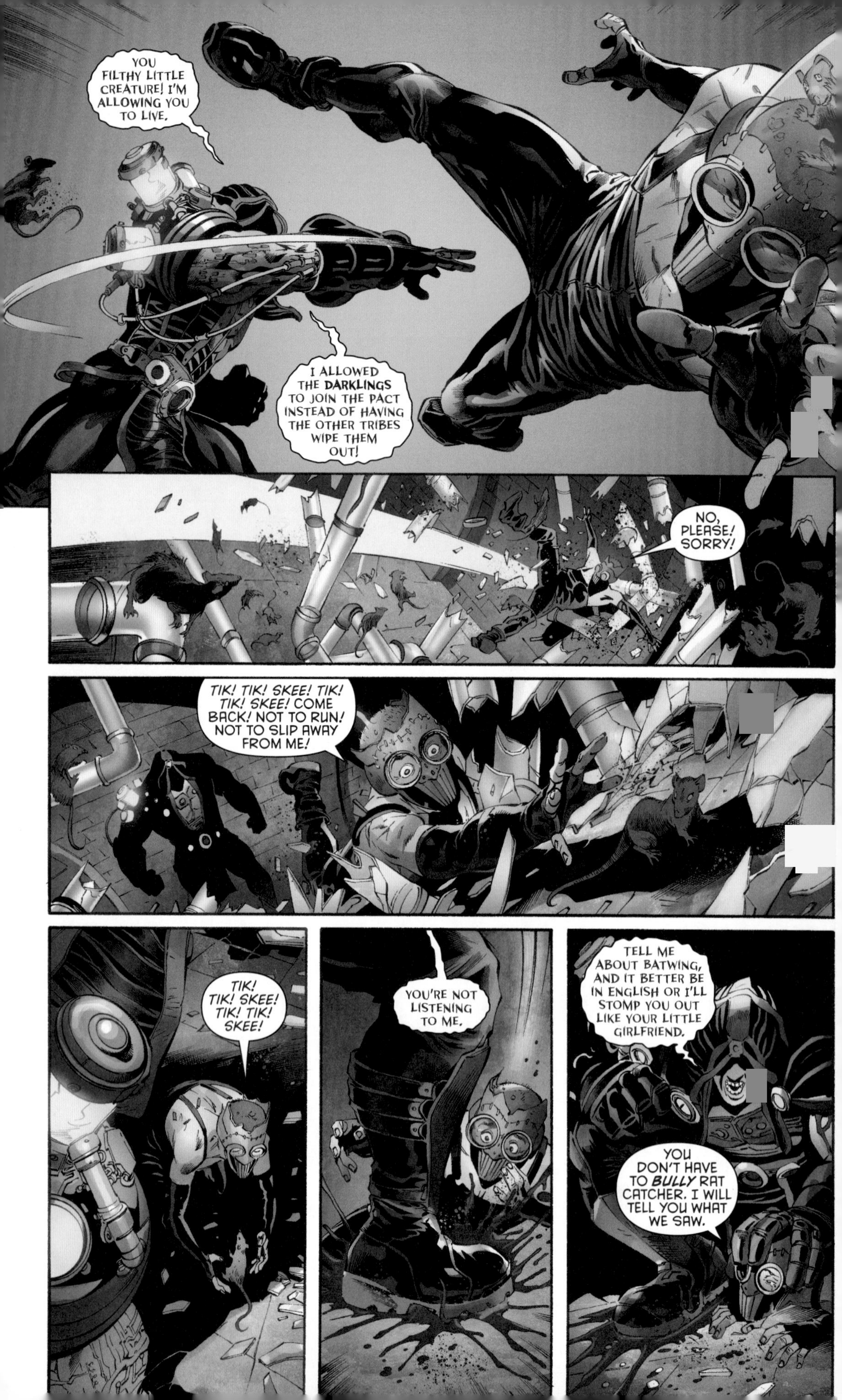

YOU FILTHY LITTLE CREATURE! I'M ALLOWING YOU TO LIVE.
I ALLOWED THE DARKLINGS TO JOIN THE PACT INSTEAD OF HAVING THE OTHER TRIBES WIPE THEM OUT!
NO, PLEASE! SORRY!
TIK! TIK! SKEE! TIK! TIK! SKEE! COME BACK! NOT TO RUN! NOT TO SLIP AWAY FROM ME!
TIK! TIK! SKEE! TIK! TIK! SKEE!
YOU'RE NOT LISTENING TO ME.
TELL ME ABOUT BATWING, AND IT BETTER BE IN ENGLISH OR I'LL STOMP YOU OUT LIKE YOUR LITTLE GIRLFRIEND.
YOU DON'T HAVE TO BULLY RAT CATCHER. I WILL TELL YOU WHAT WE SAW.

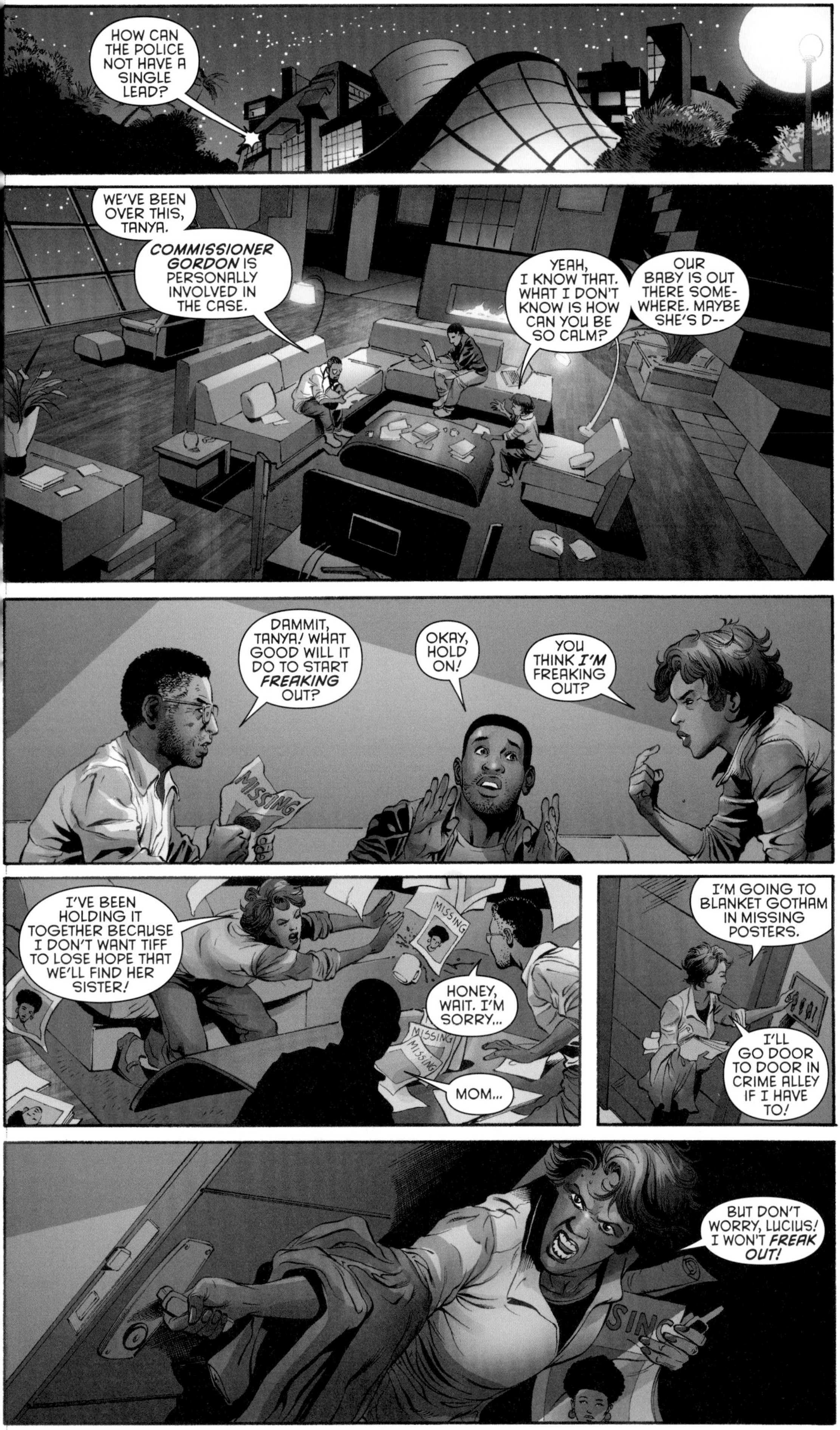
HOW CAN THE POLICE NOT HAVE A SINGLE LEAD?
WE'VE BEEN OVER THIS, TANYA.
COMMISSIONER GORDON IS PERSONALLY INVOLVED IN THE CASE.
YEAH, I KNOW THAT. WHAT I DON'T KNOW IS HOW CAN YOU BE SO CALM?
OUR BABY IS OUT THERE SOME-WHERE. MAYBE SHE'S D--
DAMMIT, TANYA! WHAT GOOD WILL IT DO TO START FREAKING OUT?
OKAY, HOLD ON!
YOU THINK I'M FREAKING OUT?
MISSING
I'VE BEEN HOLDING IT TOGETHER BECAUSE I DON'T WANT TIFF TO LOSE HOPE THAT WE'LL FIND HER SISTER!
HONEY, WAIT. I'M SORRY...
MOM...
I'M GOING TO BLANKET GOTHAM IN MISSING POSTERS.
I'LL GO DOOR TO DOOR IN CRIME ALLEY IF I HAVE TO!
BUT DON'T WORRY, LUCIUS! I WON'T FREAK OUT!

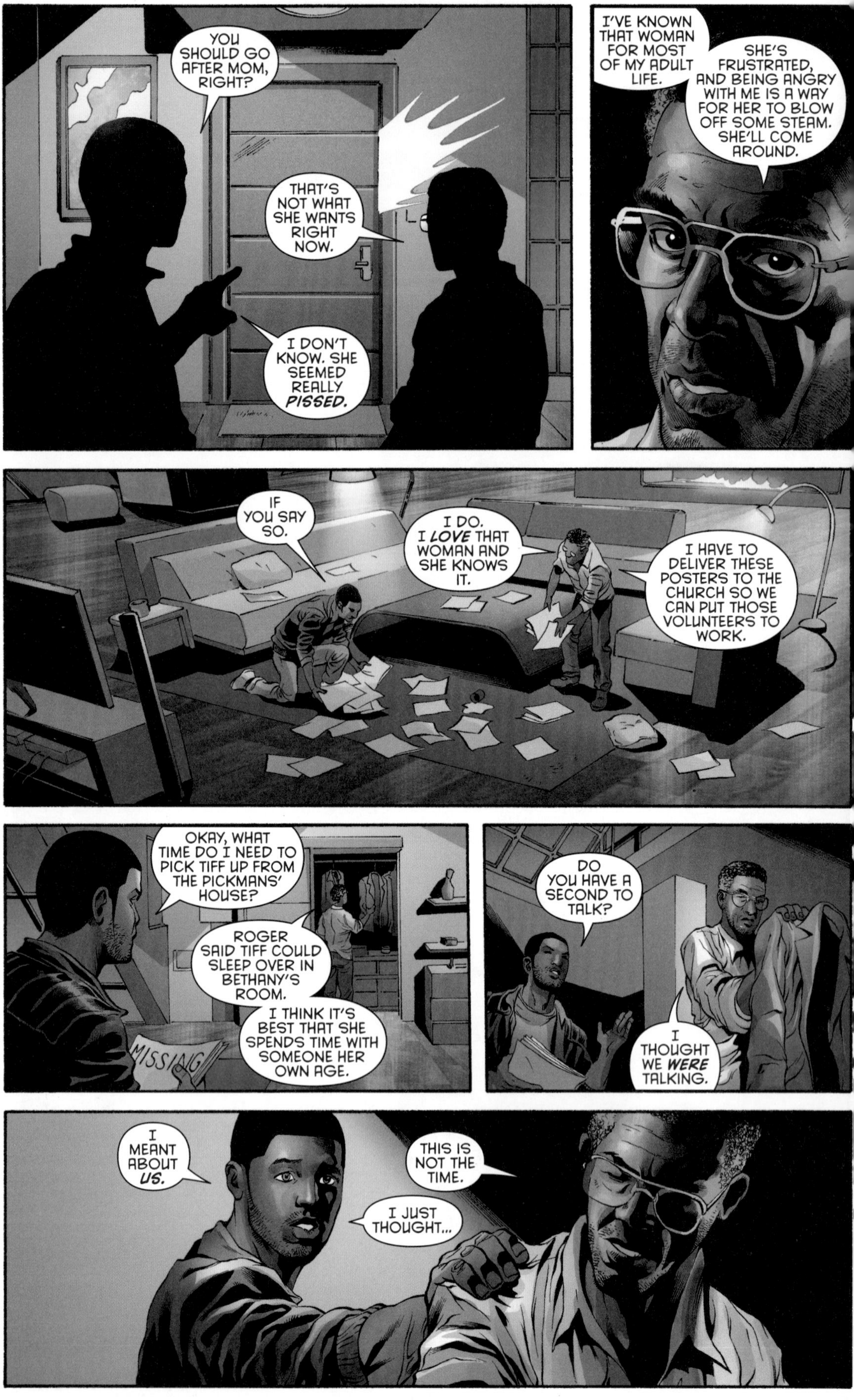

YOU SHOULD GO AFTER MOM, RIGHT?
THAT'S NOT WHAT SHE WANTS RIGHT NOW.
I DON'T KNOW. SHE SEEMED REALLY *PISSED.*
I'VE KNOWN THAT WOMAN FOR MOST OF MY ADULT LIFE.
SHE'S FRUSTRATED, AND BEING ANGRY WITH ME IS A WAY FOR HER TO BLOW OFF SOME STEAM. SHE'LL COME AROUND.
IF YOU SAY SO.
I DO. I *LOVE* THAT WOMAN AND SHE KNOWS IT.
I HAVE TO DELIVER THESE POSTERS TO THE CHURCH SO WE CAN PUT THOSE VOLUNTEERS TO WORK.
OKAY, WHAT TIME DO I NEED TO PICK TIFF UP FROM THE PICKMANS' HOUSE?
ROGER SAID TIFF COULD SLEEP OVER IN BETHANY'S ROOM.
I THINK IT'S BEST THAT SHE SPENDS TIME WITH SOMEONE HER OWN AGE.
MISSING
DO YOU HAVE A SECOND TO TALK?
I THOUGHT WE *WERE* TALKING.
I MEANT ABOUT *US.*
THIS IS NOT THE TIME.
I JUST THOUGHT...

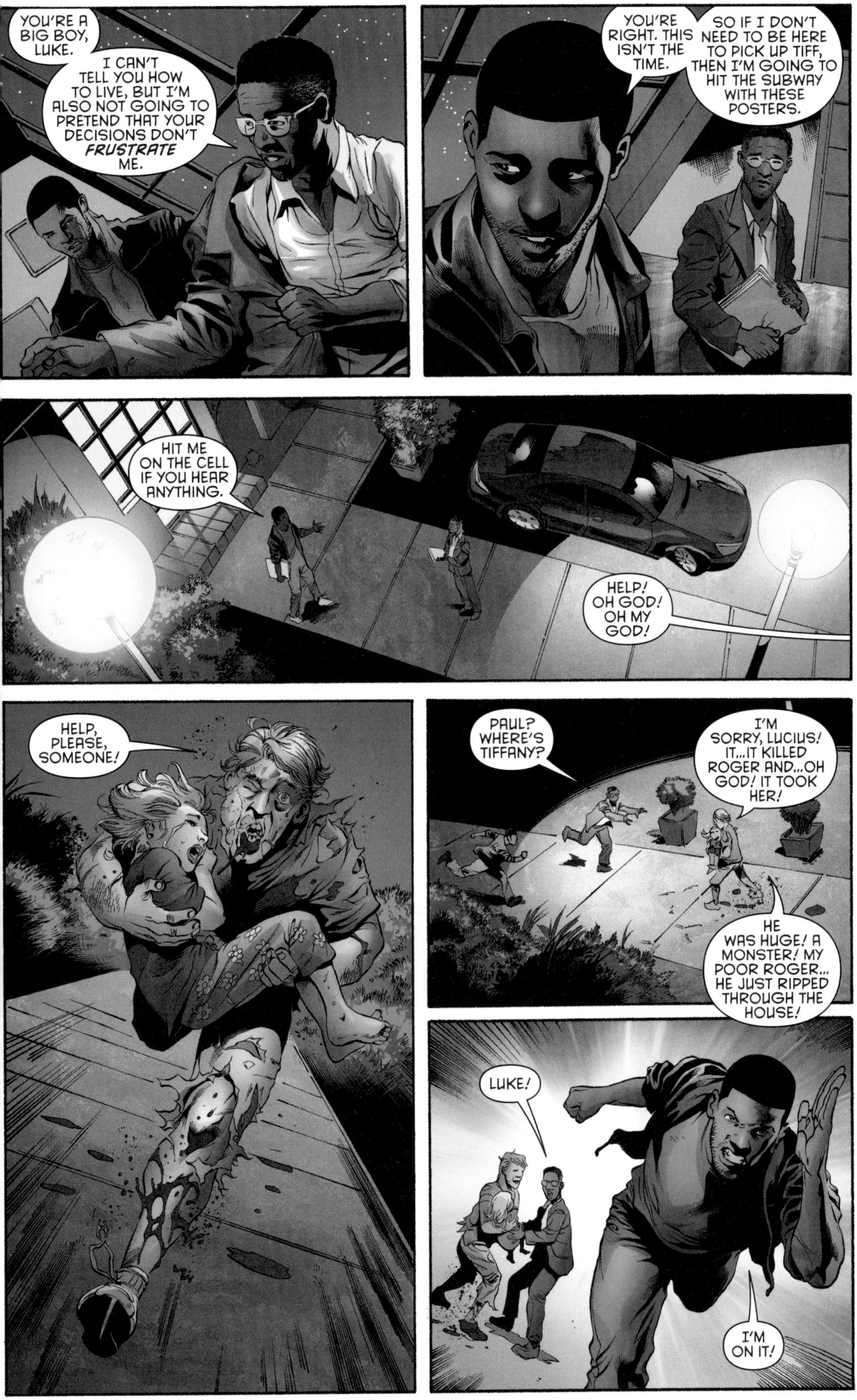
YOU'RE A BIG BOY, LUKE.
I CAN'T TELL YOU HOW TO LIVE, BUT I'M ALSO NOT GOING TO PRETEND THAT YOUR DECISIONS DON'T *FRUSTRATE* ME.
YOU'RE RIGHT. THIS ISN'T THE TIME.
SO IF I DON'T NEED TO BE HERE TO PICK UP TIFF, THEN I'M GOING TO HIT THE SUBWAY WITH THESE POSTERS.
HIT ME ON THE CELL IF YOU HEAR ANYTHING.
HELP! OH GOD! OH MY GOD!
HELP, PLEASE, SOMEONE!
PAUL? WHERE'S TIFFANY?
I'M SORRY, LUCIUS! IT...IT KILLED ROGER AND...OH GOD! IT TOOK HER!
HE WAS HUGE! A MONSTER! MY POOR ROGER... HE JUST RIPPED THROUGH THE HOUSE!
LUKE!
I'M ON IT!

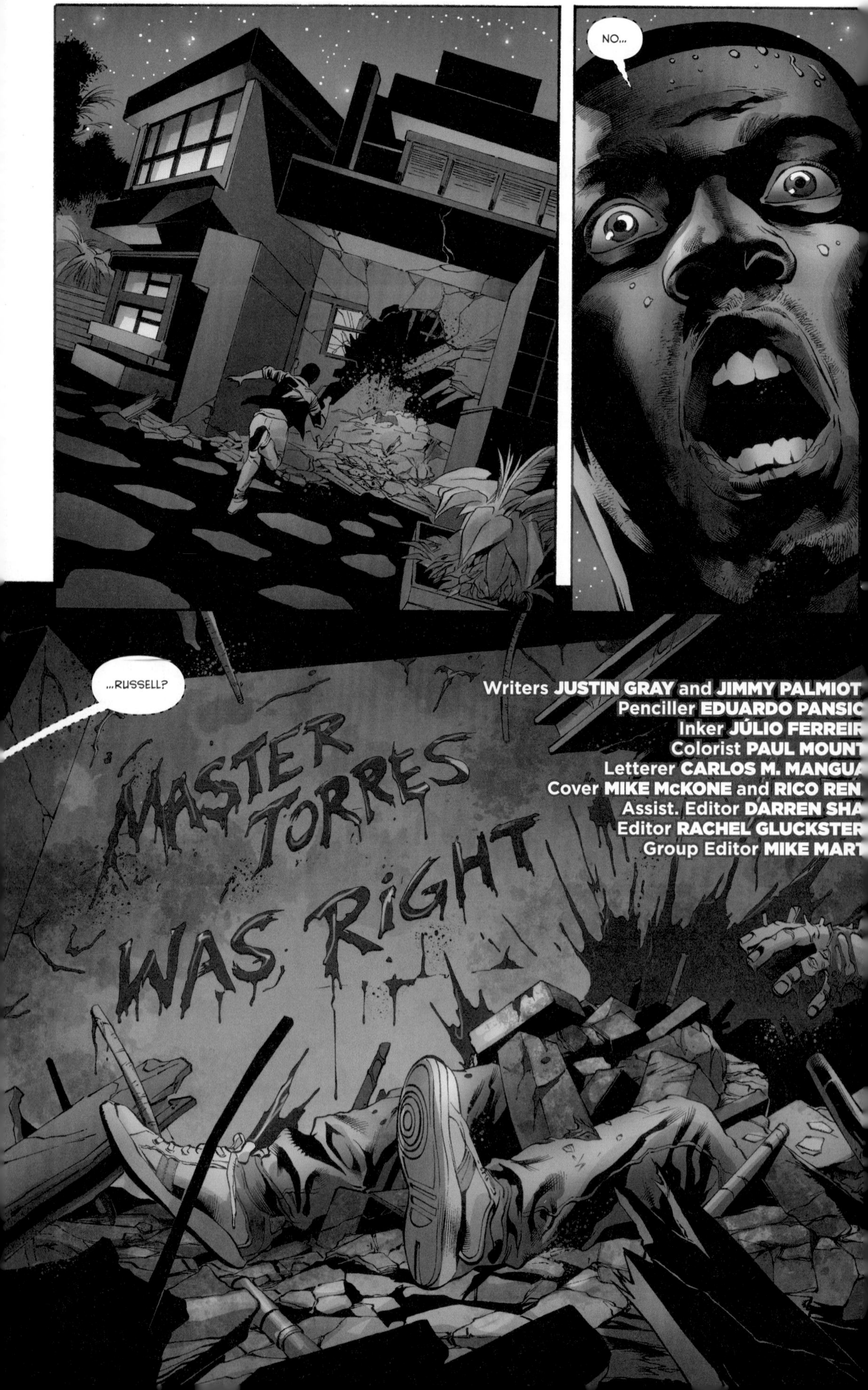
NO...
...RUSSELL?
MASTER TORRES WAS RIGHT
Writers JUSTIN GRAY and JIMMY PALMIOT
Penciller EDUARDO PANSIC
Inker JÚLIO FERREIR
Colorist PAUL MOUNT
Letterer CARLOS M. MANGU
Cover MIKE McKONE and RICO REN
Assist. Editor DARREN SHA
Editor RACHEL GLUCKSTER
Group Editor MIKE MART

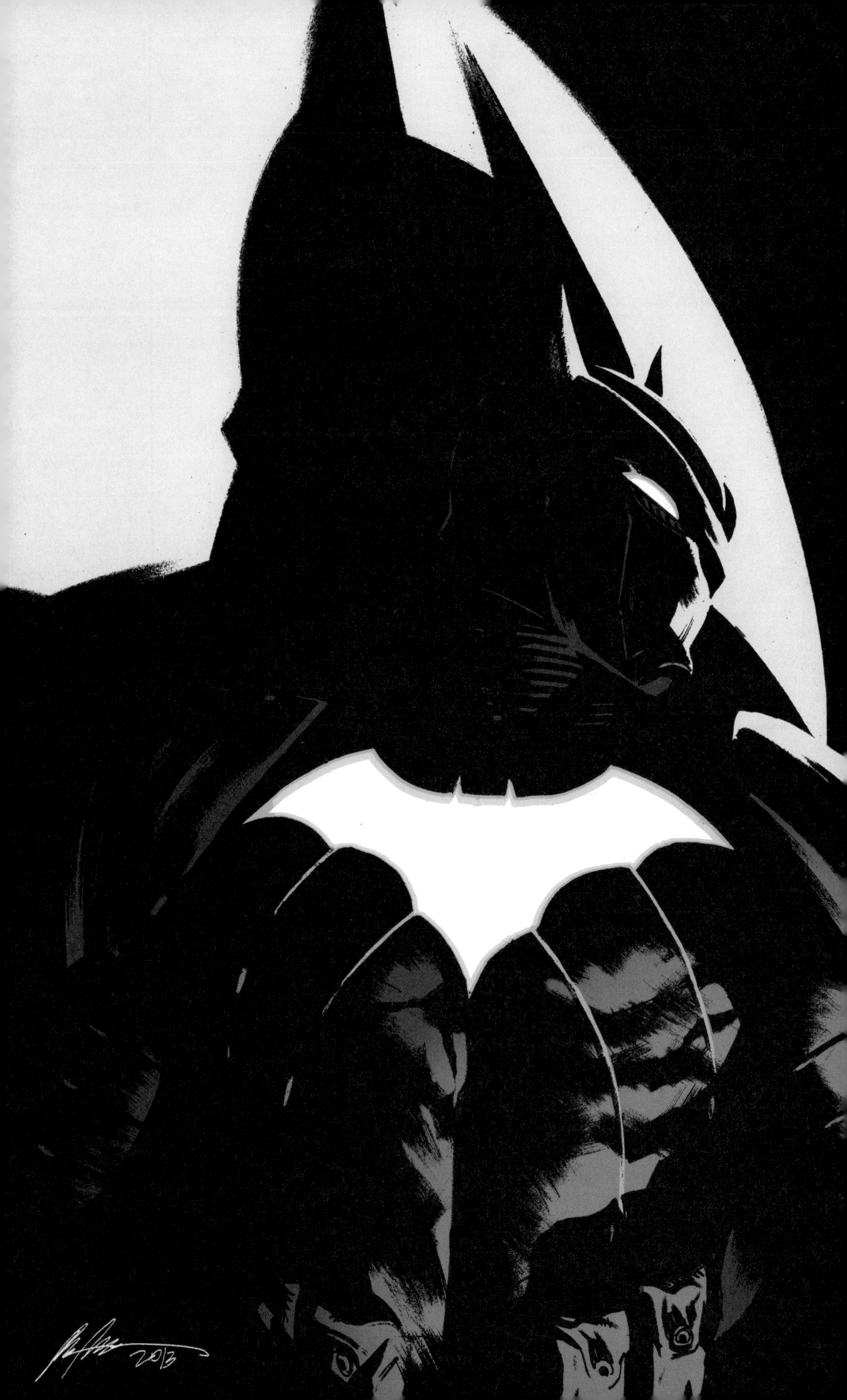
2013

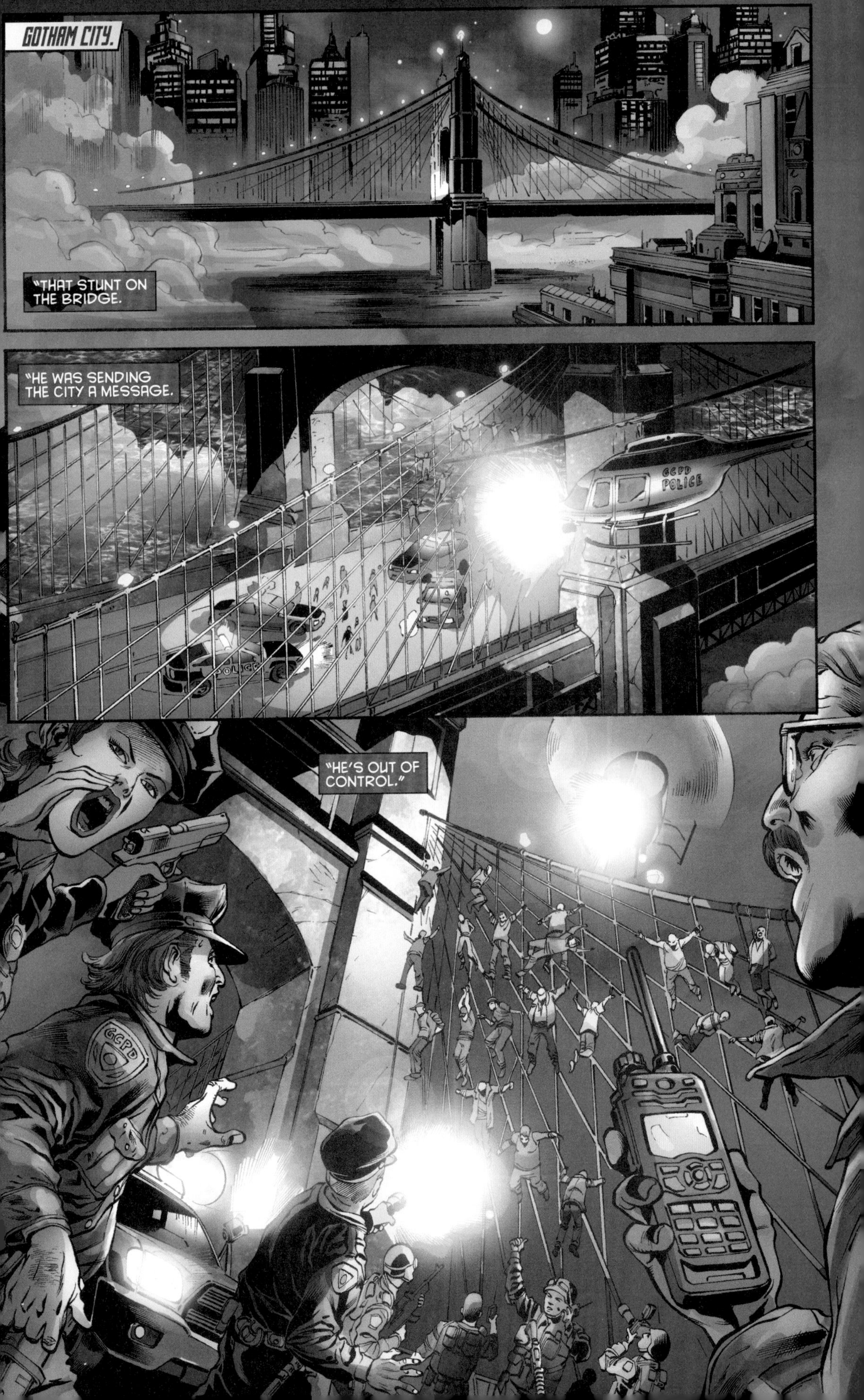
GOTHAM CITY.
"THAT STUNT ON THE BRIDGE.
"HE WAS SENDING THE CITY A MESSAGE.
"HE'S OUT OF CONTROL."

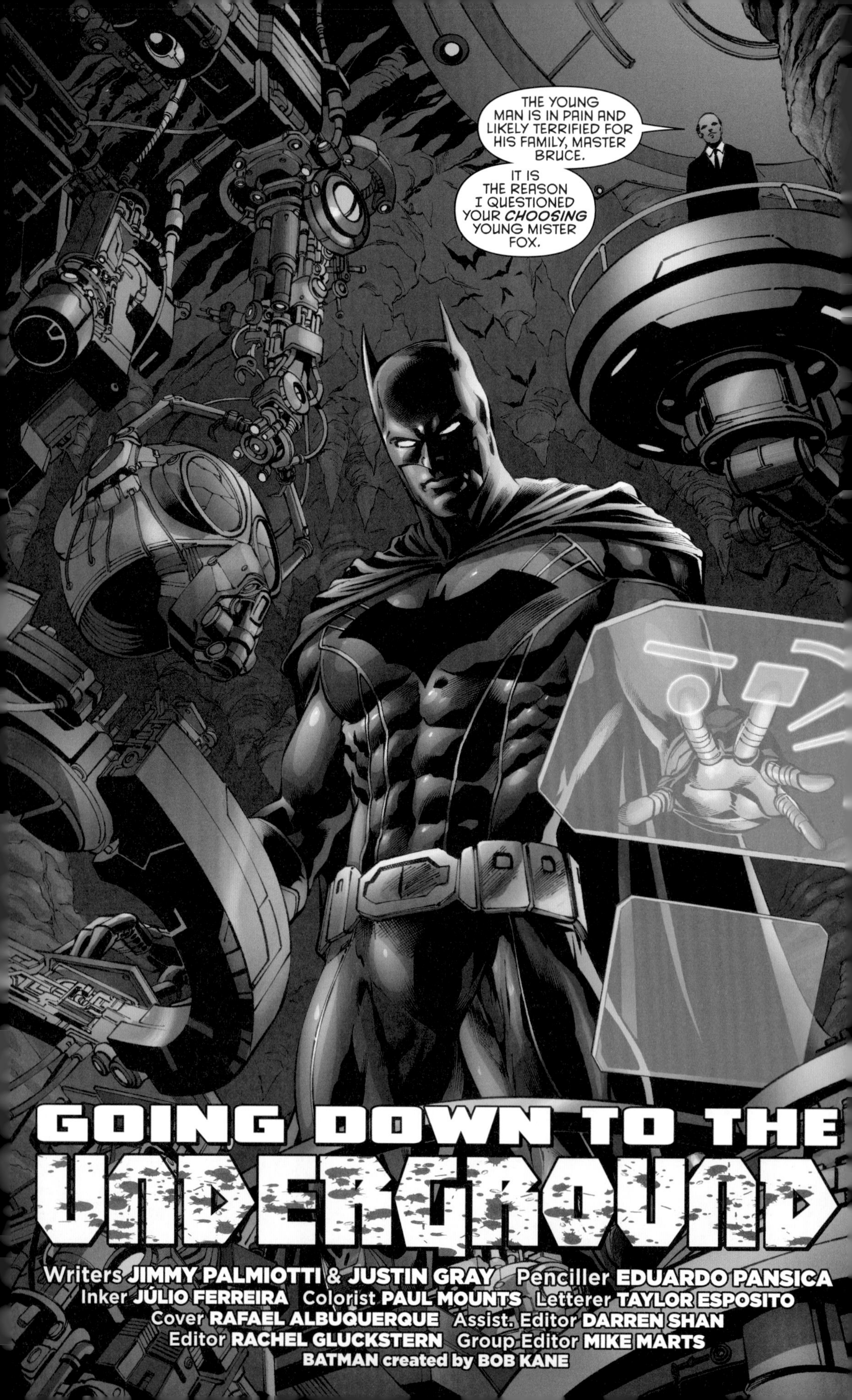
THE YOUNG MAN IS IN PAIN AND LIKELY TERRIFIED FOR HIS FAMILY, MASTER BRUCE.
IT IS THE REASON I QUESTIONED YOUR *CHOOSING* YOUNG MISTER FOX.
GOING DOWN TO THE
UNDERGROUND
Writers **JIMMY PALMIOTTI & JUSTIN GRAY** Penciller **EDUARDO PANSICA**
Inker **JÚLIO FERREIRA** Colorist **PAUL MOUNTS** Letterer **TAYLOR ESPOSITO**
Cover **RAFAEL ALBUQUERQUE** Assist. Editor **DARREN SHAN**
Editor **RACHEL GLUCKSTERN** Group Editor **MIKE MARTS**
BATMAN created by **BOB KANE**

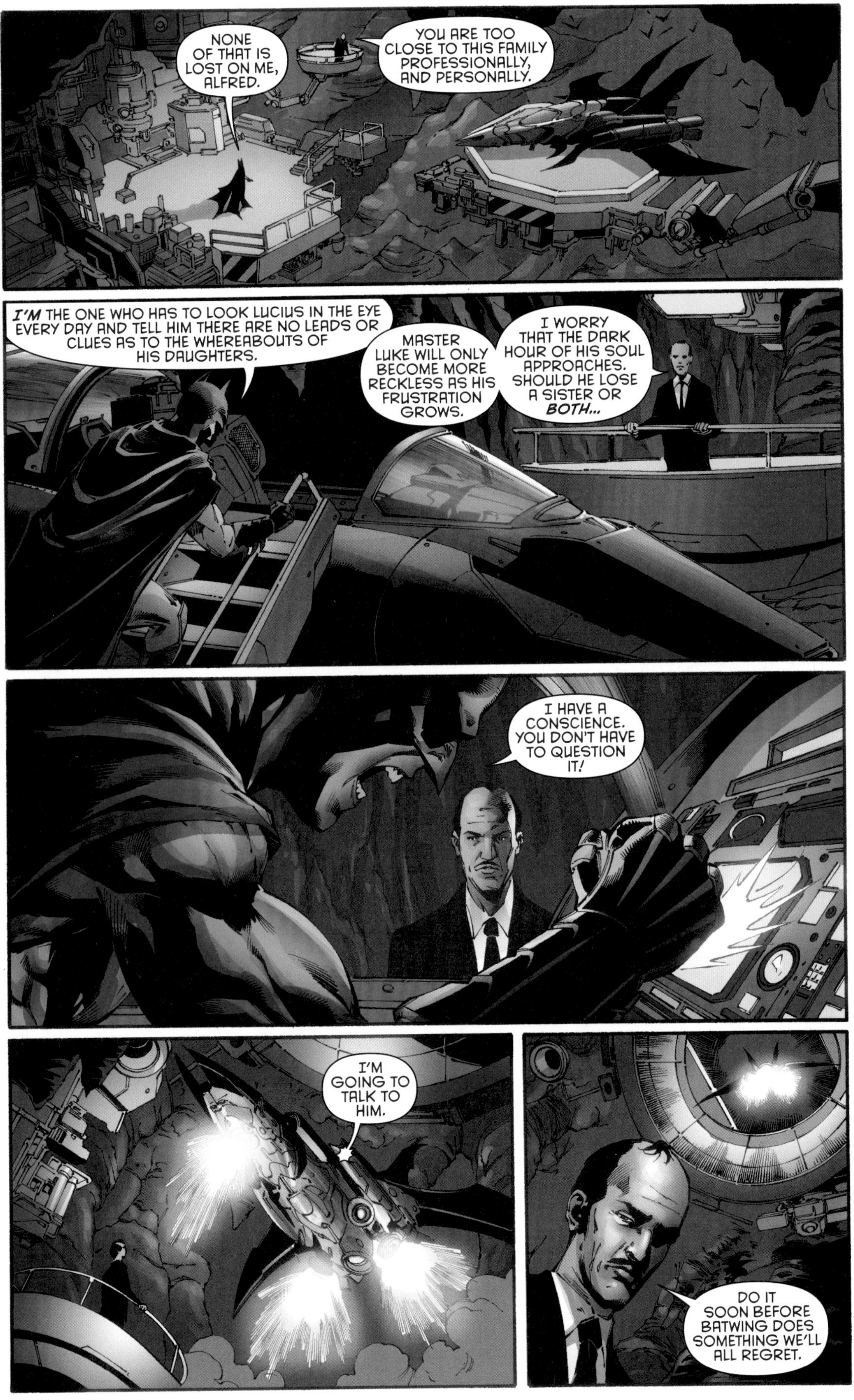
NONE OF THAT IS LOST ON ME, ALFRED.
YOU ARE TOO CLOSE TO THIS FAMILY PROFESSIONALLY, AND PERSONALLY.
I'M THE ONE WHO HAS TO LOOK LUCIUS IN THE EYE EVERY DAY AND TELL HIM THERE ARE NO LEADS OR CLUES AS TO THE WHEREABOUTS OF HIS DAUGHTERS.
MASTER LUKE WILL ONLY BECOME MORE RECKLESS AS HIS FRUSTRATION GROWS.
I WORRY THAT THE DARK HOUR OF HIS SOUL APPROACHES. SHOULD HE LOSE A SISTER OR BOTH...
I HAVE A CONSCIENCE. YOU DON'T HAVE TO QUESTION IT!
I'M GOING TO TALK TO HIM.
DO IT SOON BEFORE BATWING DOES SOMETHING WE'LL ALL REGRET.

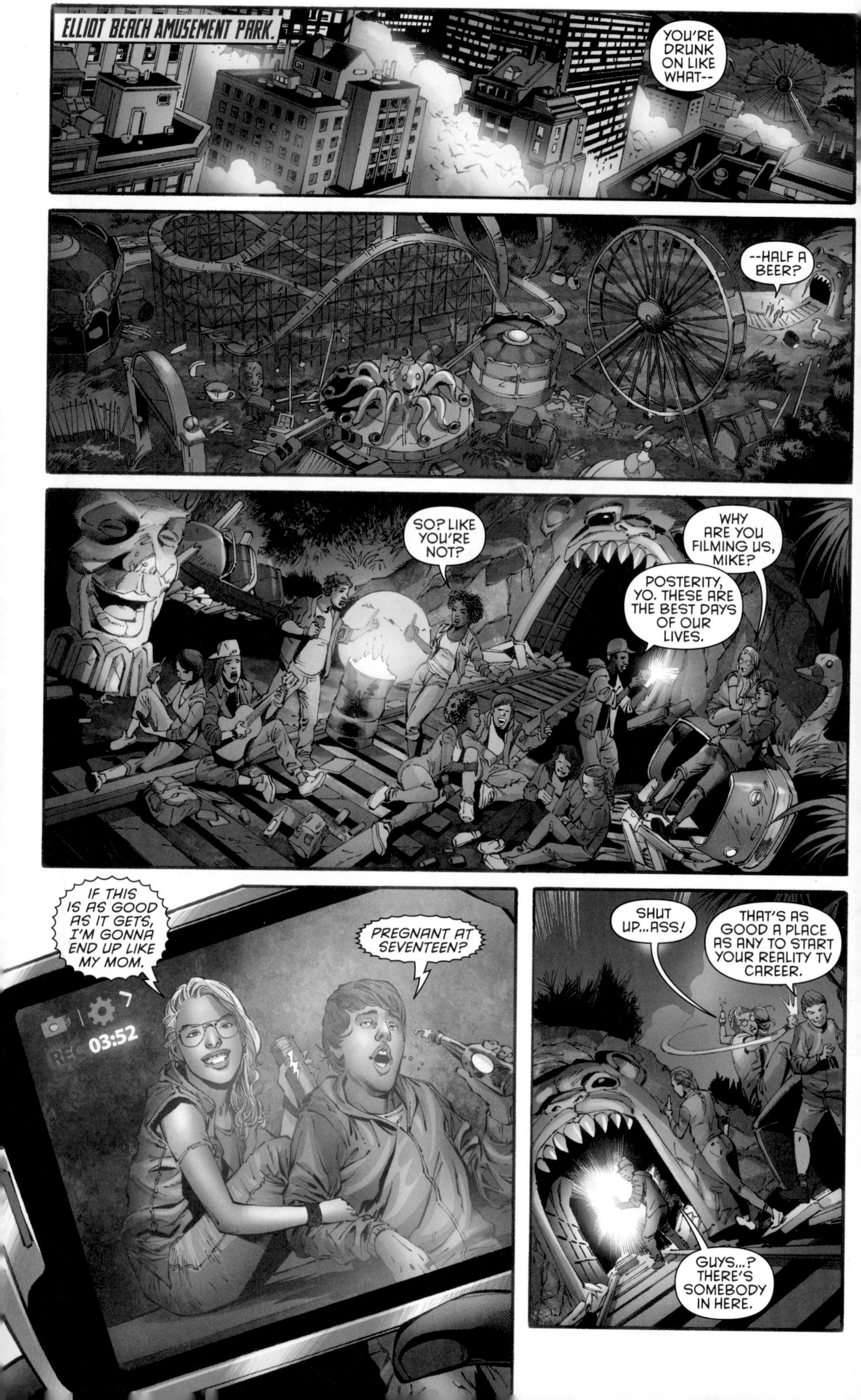
ELLIOT BEACH AMUSEMENT PARK.
YOU'RE DRUNK ON LIKE WHAT--
--HALF A BEER?
SO? LIKE YOU'RE NOT?
WHY ARE YOU FILMING US, MIKE?
POSTERITY, YO. THESE ARE THE BEST DAYS OF OUR LIVES.
IF THIS IS AS GOOD AS IT GETS, I'M GONNA END UP LIKE MY MOM.
PREGNANT AT SEVENTEEN?
03:52
REC
SHUT UP...ASS!
THAT'S AS GOOD A PLACE AS ANY TO START YOUR REALITY TV CAREER.
GUYS...? THERE'S SOMEBODY IN HERE.

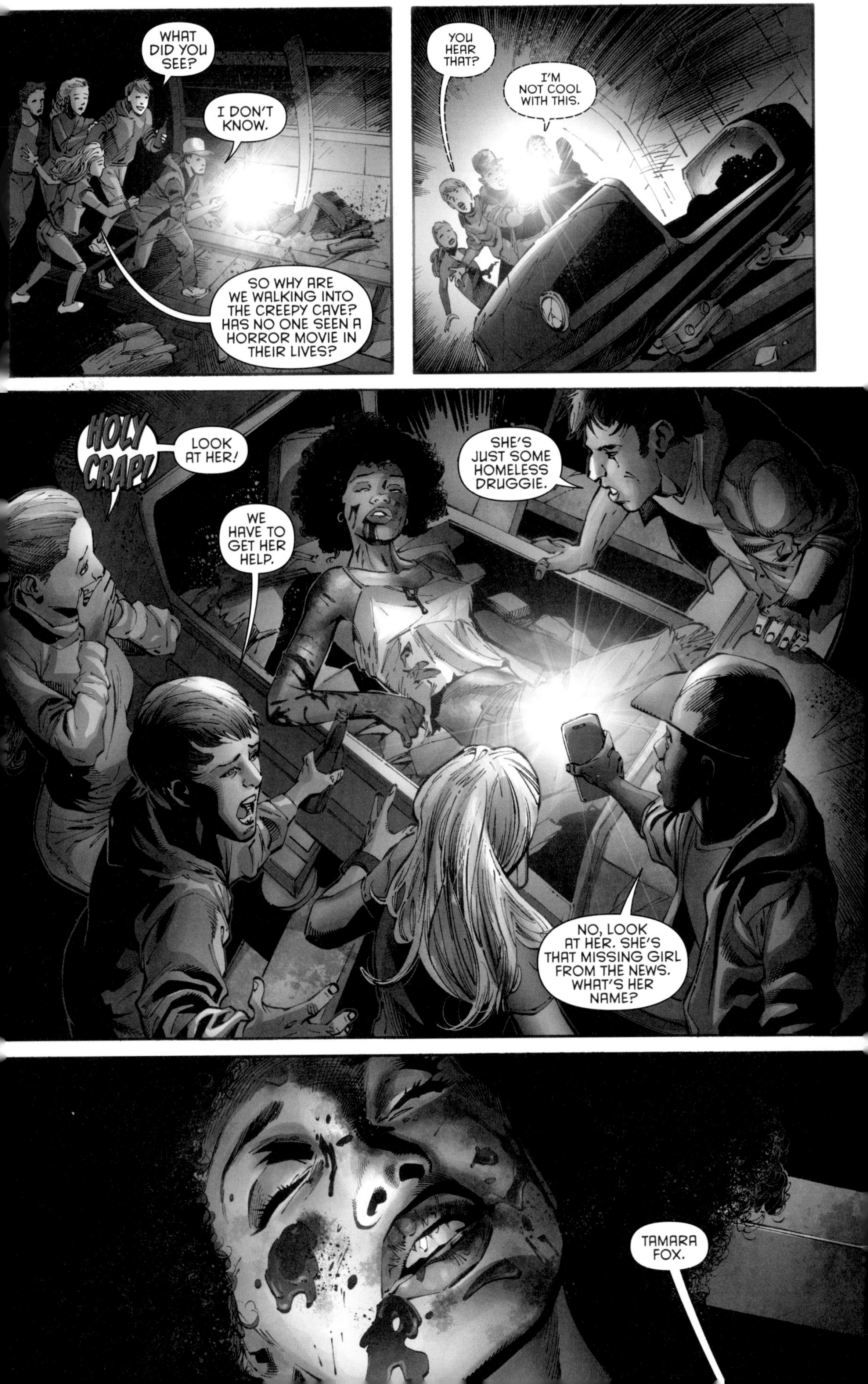
WHAT DID YOU SEE?
I DON'T KNOW.
SO WHY ARE WE WALKING INTO THE CREEPY CAVE? HAS NO ONE SEEN A HORROR MOVIE IN THEIR LIVES?
YOU HEAR THAT?
I'M NOT COOL WITH THIS.
HOLY CRAP!
LOOK AT HER!
WE HAVE TO GET HER HELP.
SHE'S JUST SOME HOMELESS DRUGGIE.
NO, LOOK AT HER. SHE'S THAT MISSING GIRL FROM THE NEWS. WHAT'S HER NAME?
TAMARA FOX.

I KNOW THIS IS HARD TO HEAR...

GOTHAM MEMORIAL

...SO I'LL JUST COME OUT AND SAY IT.

YOUR DAUGHTER IS DEHYDRATED AND MALNOURISHED. WE'VE RUN A BATTERY OF TESTS. NOT ALL OF THE RESULTS ARE IN, BUT I CAN TELL YOU SHE WAS NOT SEXUALLY ASSAULTED.

HOW LONG HAS YOUR DAUGHTER BEEN INVOLVED WITH HEAVY *DRUG USE?*

OUR DAUGHTER HAS *NEVER* USED DRUGS.

SOMETIMES PARENTS MISS THE SIGNS.

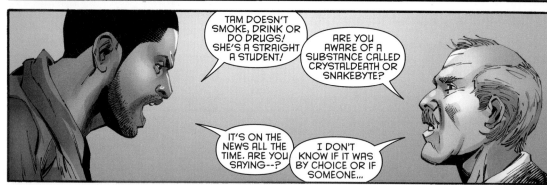

TAM DOESN'T SMOKE, DRINK OR DO DRUGS! SHE'S A STRAIGHT A STUDENT!

ARE YOU AWARE OF A SUBSTANCE CALLED CRYSTALDEATH OR SNAKEBYTE?

IT'S ON THE NEWS ALL THE TIME. ARE YOU SAYING--?

I DON'T KNOW IF IT WAS BY CHOICE OR IF SOMEONE...

I'M SORRY. TAMARA HAS EXTENSIVE BRAIN DAMAGE FROM REPEATED AND DELIBERATE EXPOSURE TO CRYSTALDEATH.

SHE'S GOING TO REQUIRE LIFELONG CARE.

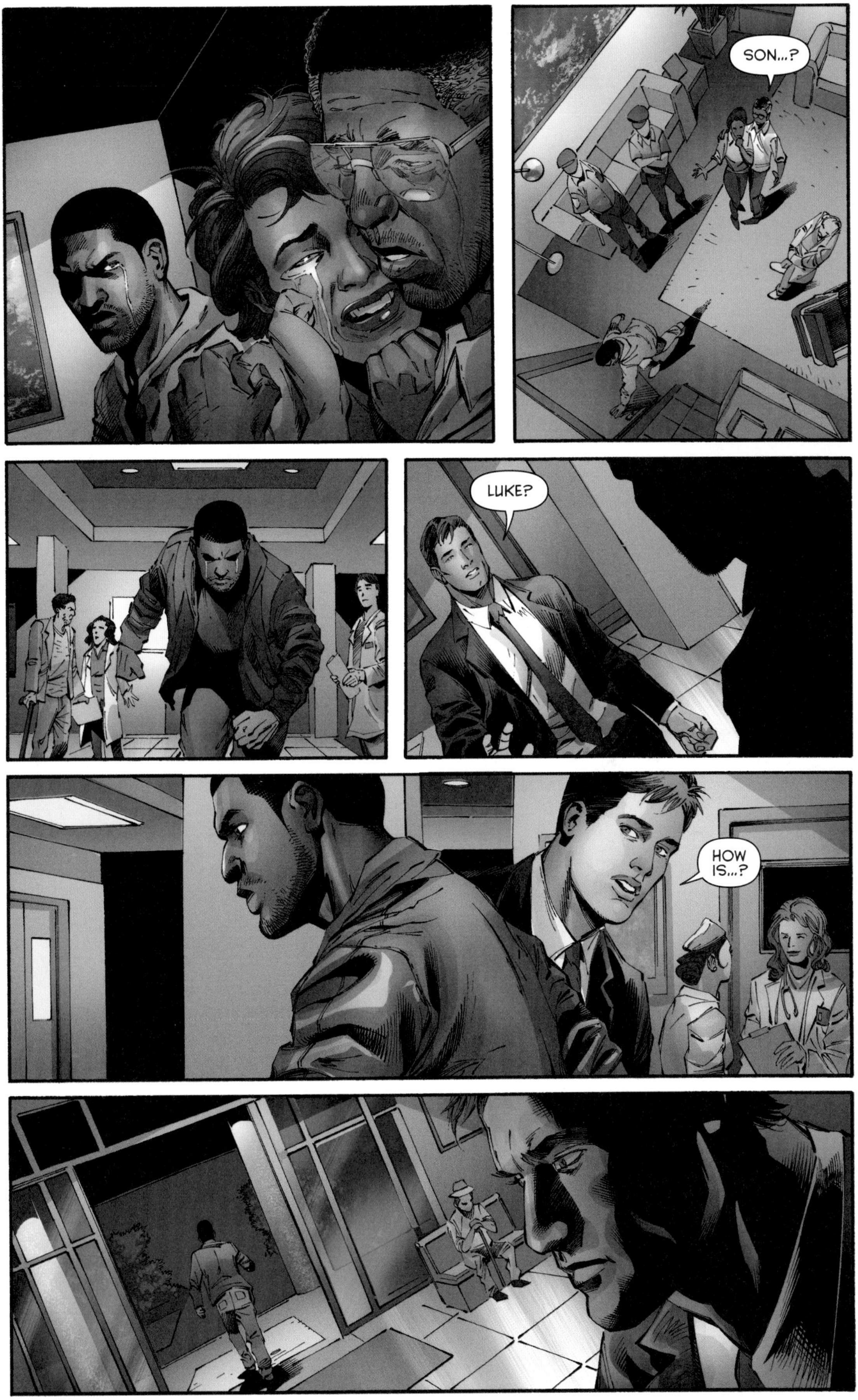
SON...?
LUKE?
HOW IS...?

I'm so angry. I have to act. Just can't sit still.

The police won't find anything useful. They don't have the right equipment.

But me, I can go to the dark places.

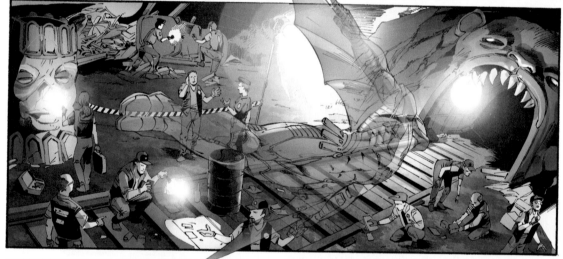

Down the hatch.

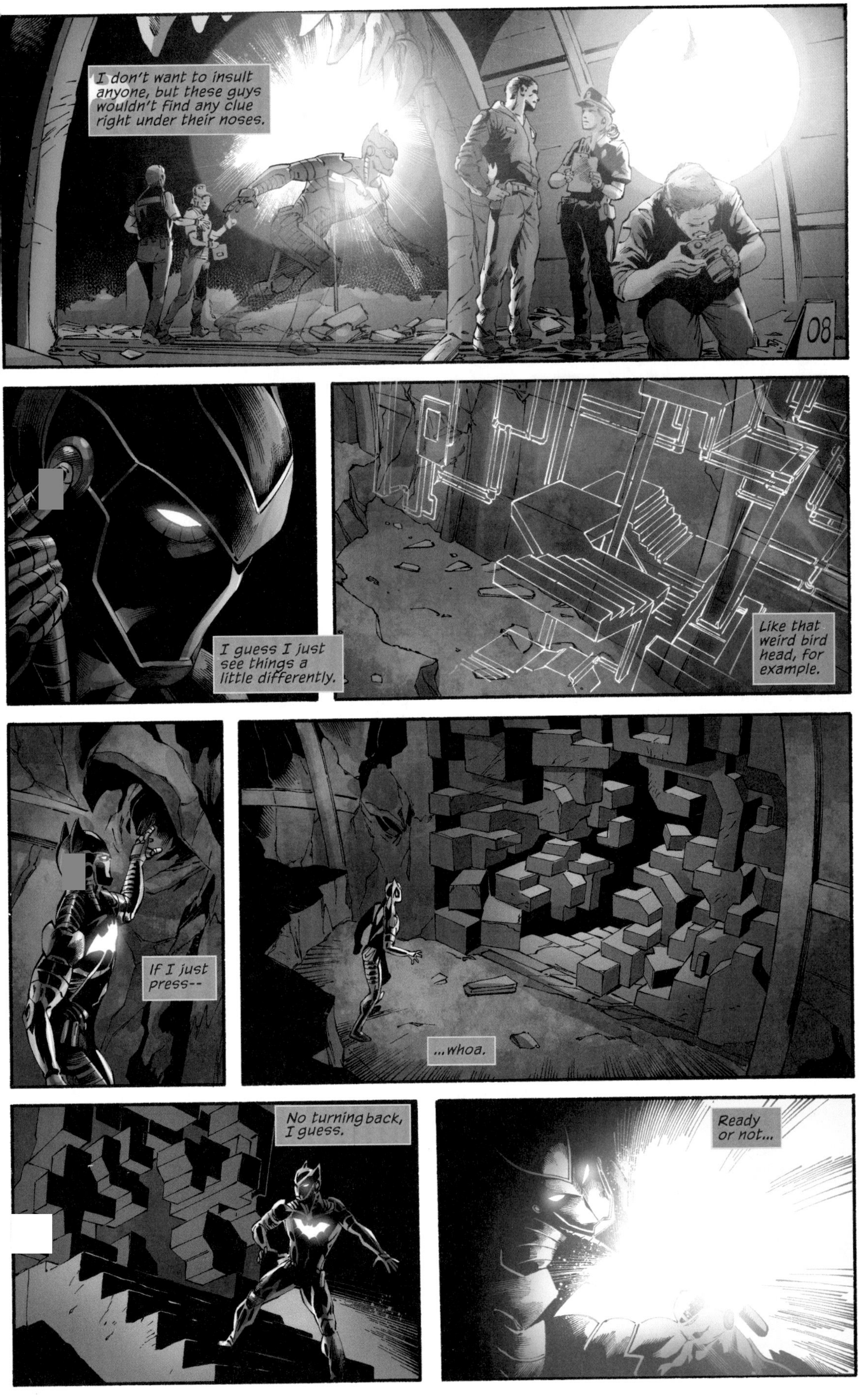
I don't want to insult anyone, but these guys wouldn't find any clue right under their noses.
08
I guess I just see things a little differently.
Like that weird bird head, for example.
If I just press--
...whoa.
No turning back, I guess.
Ready or not...

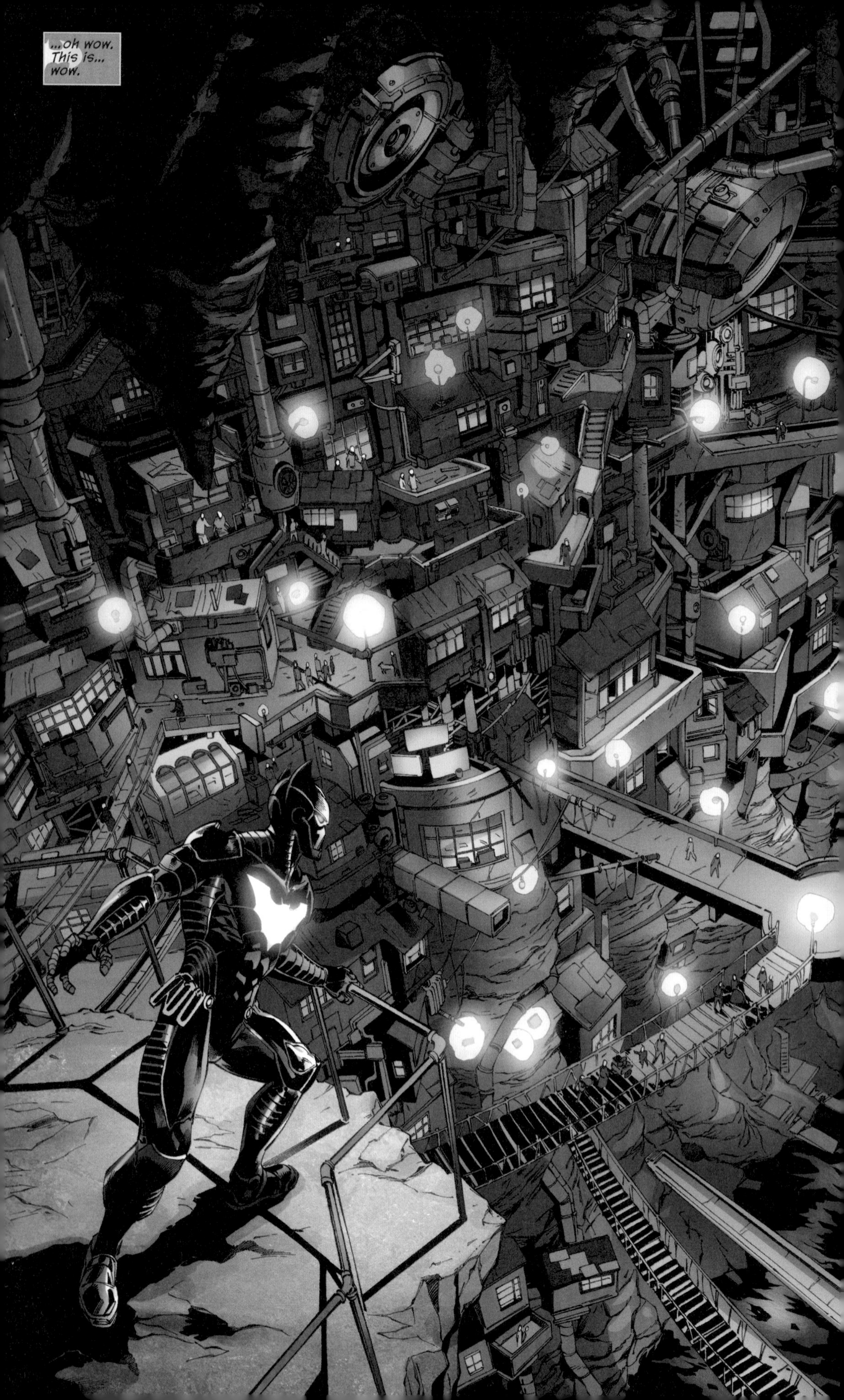
...oh wow. This is... wow.

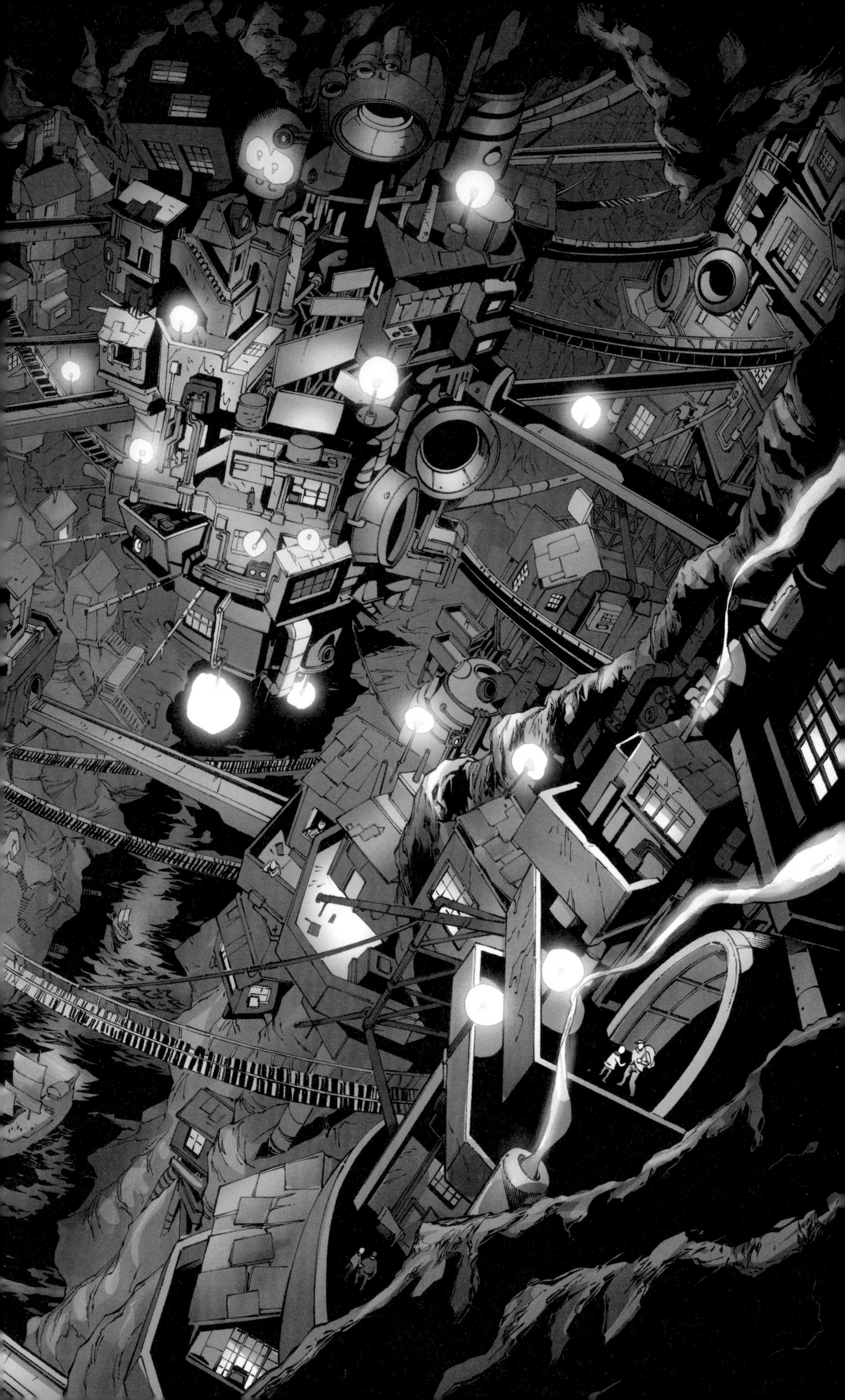

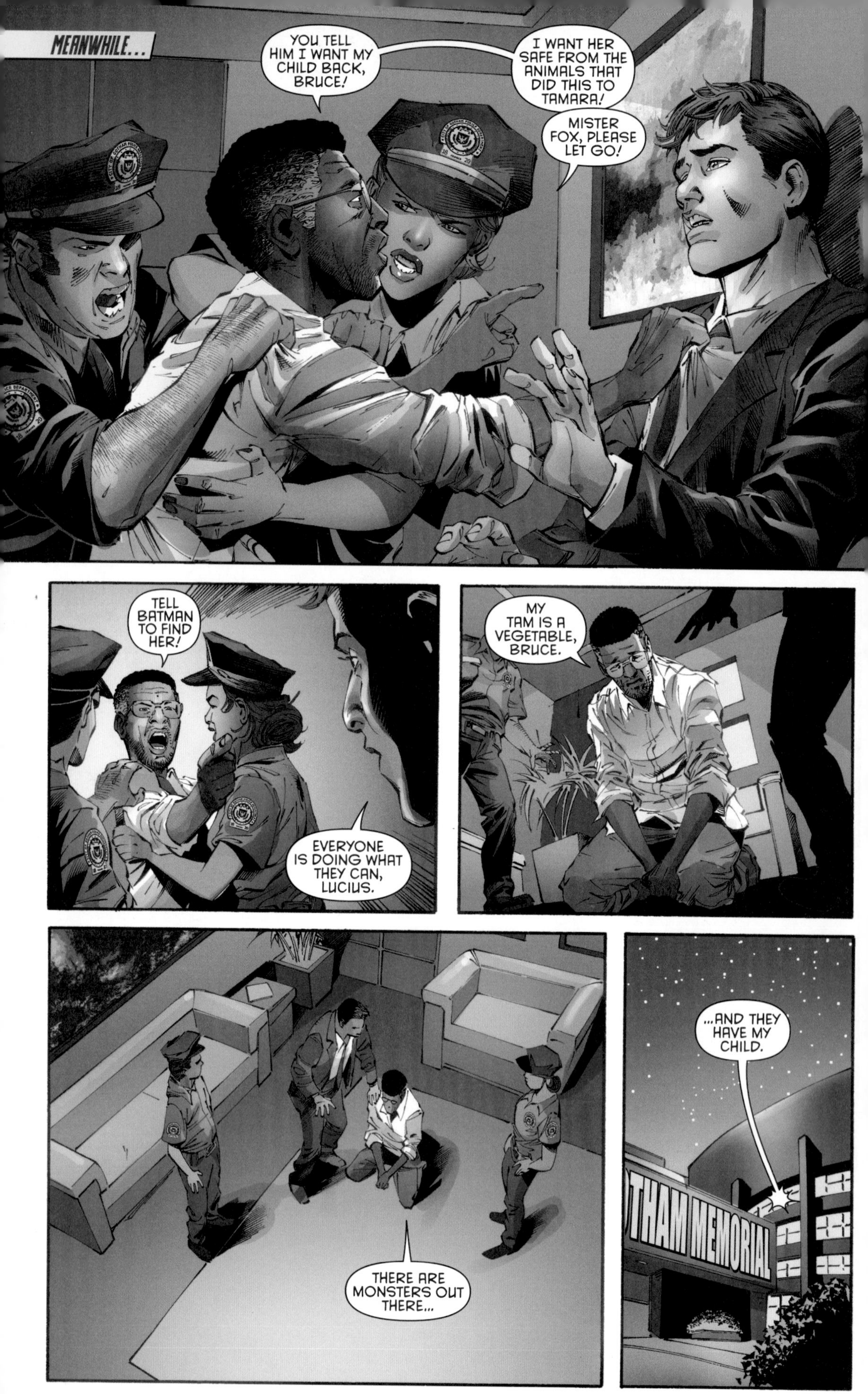
MEANWHILE...
YOU TELL HIM I WANT MY CHILD BACK, BRUCE!
I WANT HER SAFE FROM THE ANIMALS THAT DID THIS TO TAMARA!
MISTER FOX, PLEASE LET GO!
TELL BATMAN TO FIND HER!
EVERYONE IS DOING WHAT THEY CAN, LUCIUS.
MY TAM IS A VEGETABLE, BRUCE.
THERE ARE MONSTERS OUT THERE...
...AND THEY HAVE MY CHILD.
THAM MEMORIAL

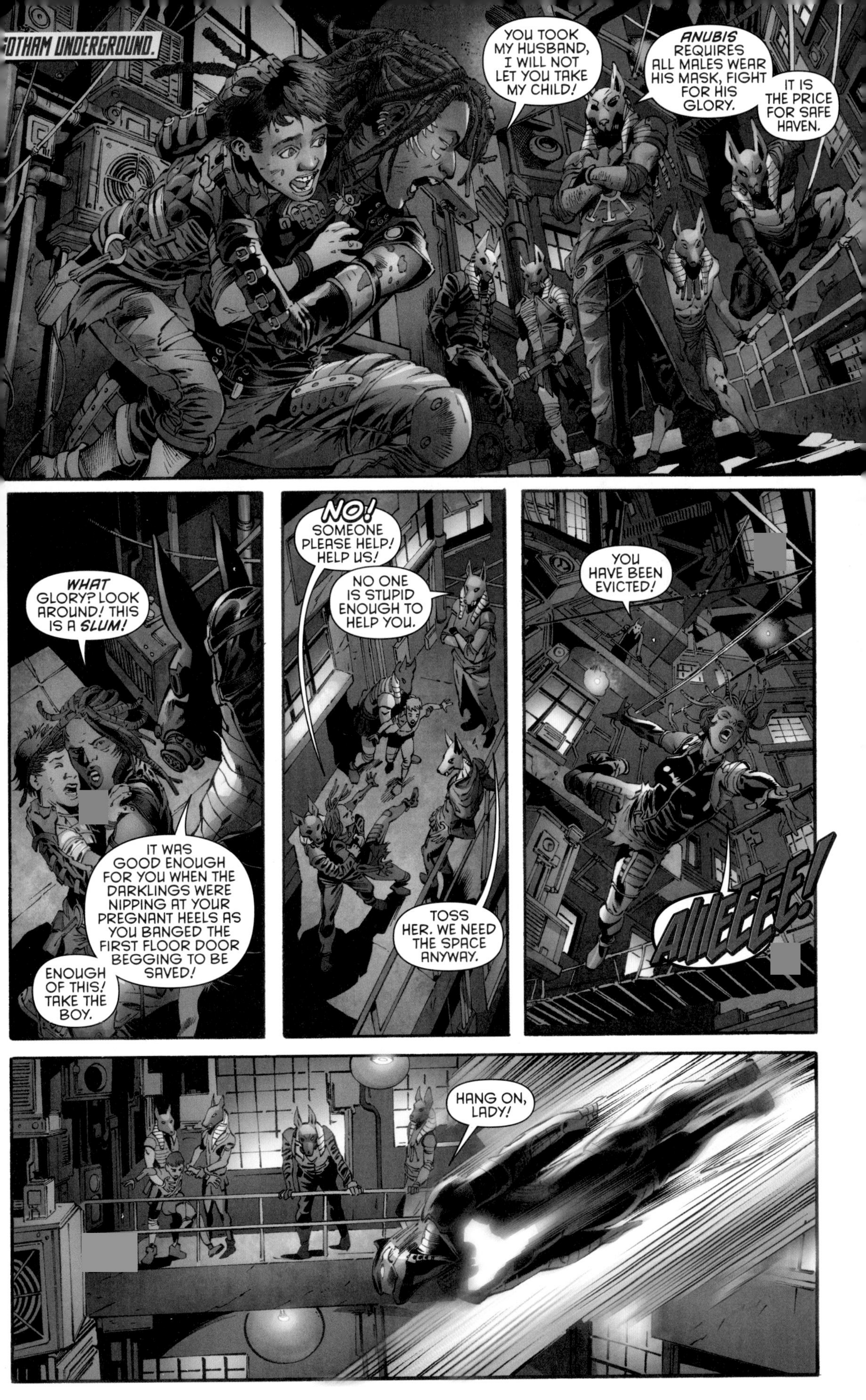
GOTHAM UNDERGROUND.
YOU TOOK MY HUSBAND, I WILL NOT LET YOU TAKE MY CHILD!
ANUBIS REQUIRES ALL MALES WEAR HIS MASK, FIGHT FOR HIS GLORY.
IT IS THE PRICE FOR SAFE HAVEN.
WHAT GLORY? LOOK AROUND! THIS IS A SLUM!
IT WAS GOOD ENOUGH FOR YOU WHEN THE DARKLINGS WERE NIPPING AT YOUR PREGNANT HEELS AS YOU BANGED THE FIRST FLOOR DOOR BEGGING TO BE SAVED!
ENOUGH OF THIS! TAKE THE BOY.
NO! SOMEONE PLEASE HELP! HELP US!
NO ONE IS STUPID ENOUGH TO HELP YOU.
TOSS HER. WE NEED THE SPACE ANYWAY.
YOU HAVE BEEN EVICTED!
AIIEEEE!
HANG ON, LADY!

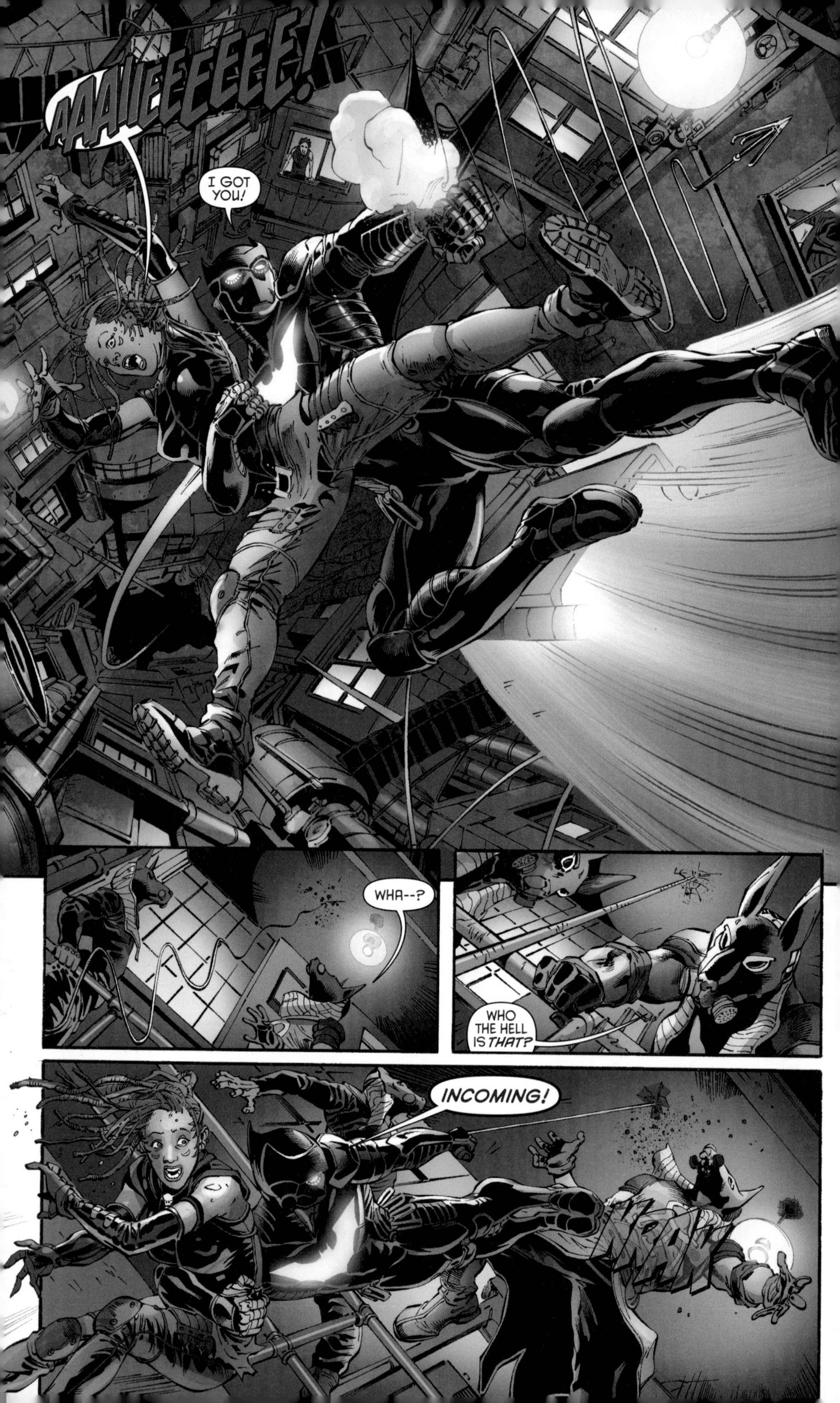
AAAIIEEEEEE!
I GOT YOU!
WHA--?
WHO THE HELL IS *THAT?*
INCOMING!

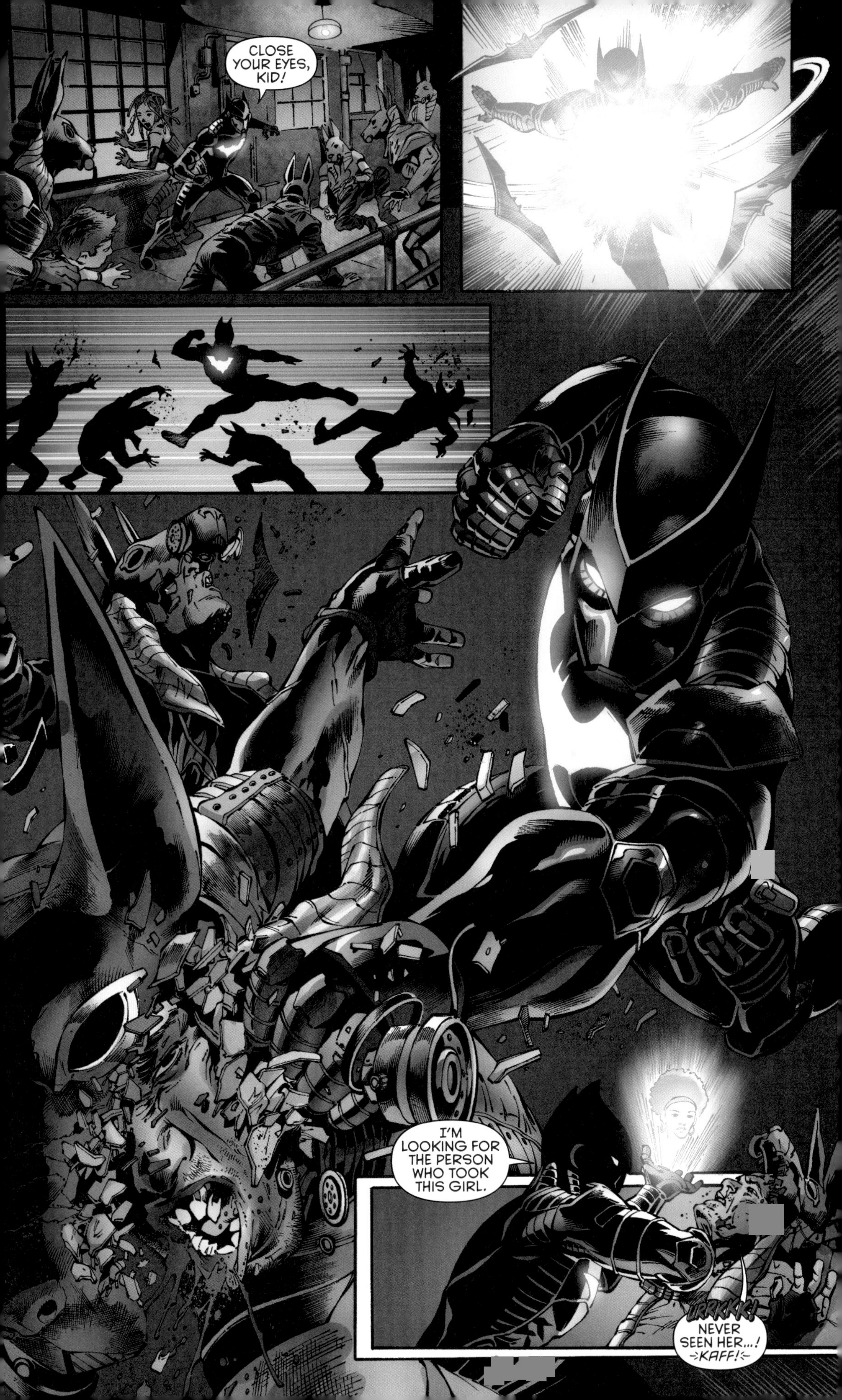

CLOSE YOUR EYES, KID!
I'M LOOKING FOR THE PERSON WHO TOOK THIS GIRL.
URRKKK!
NEVER SEEN HER...! -KAFF!-

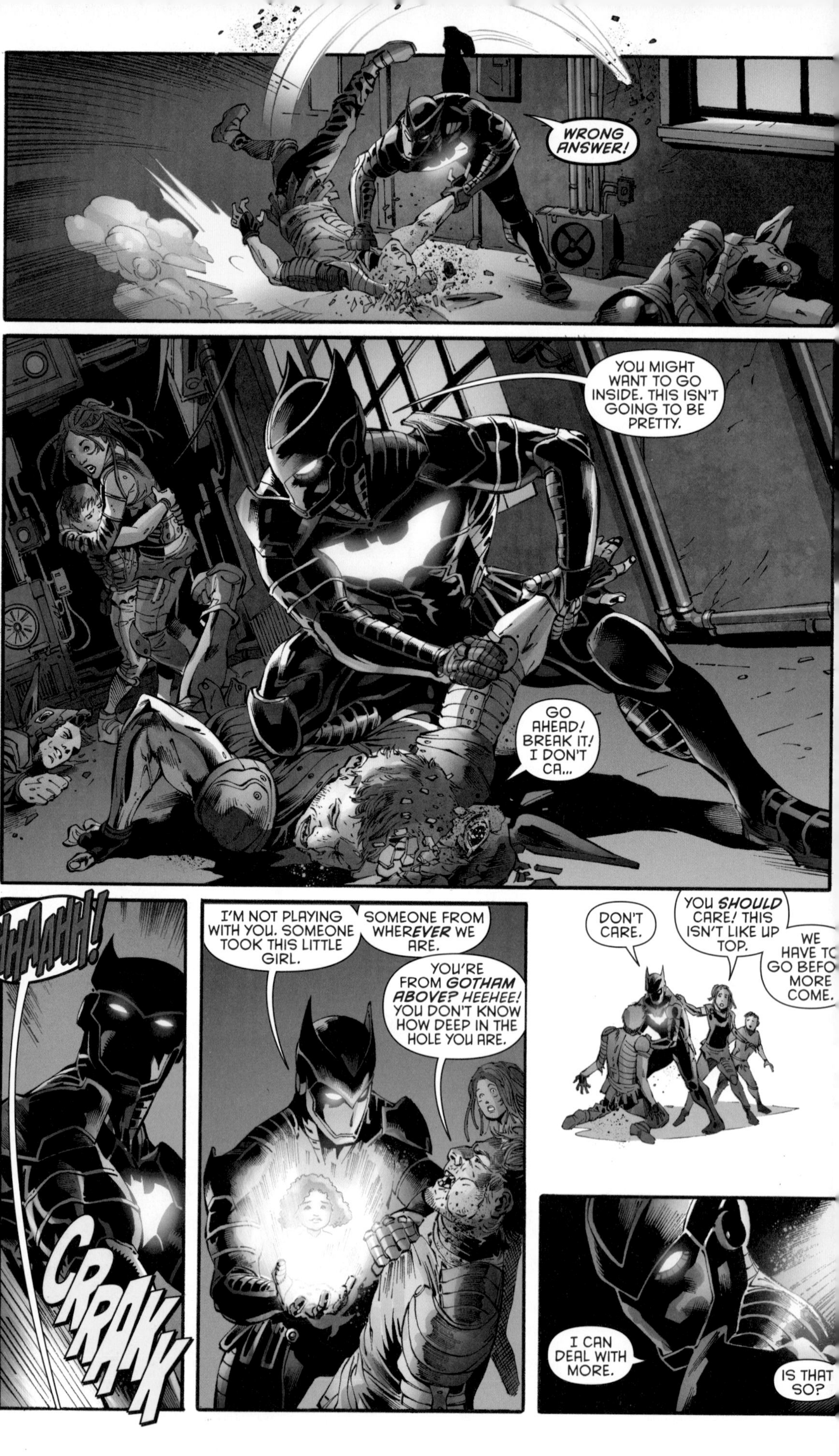

WRONG ANSWER!
YOU MIGHT WANT TO GO INSIDE. THIS ISN'T GOING TO BE PRETTY.
GO AHEAD! BREAK IT! I DON'T CA...
GHHAAHH!
CRRAKK
I'M NOT PLAYING WITH YOU. SOMEONE TOOK THIS LITTLE GIRL.
SOMEONE FROM WHEREVER WE ARE.
YOU'RE FROM GOTHAM ABOVE? HEEHEE! YOU DON'T KNOW HOW DEEP IN THE HOLE YOU ARE.
DON'T CARE.
YOU SHOULD CARE! THIS ISN'T LIKE UP TOP.
WE HAVE TO GO BEFO MORE COME.
I CAN DEAL WITH MORE.
IS THAT SO?

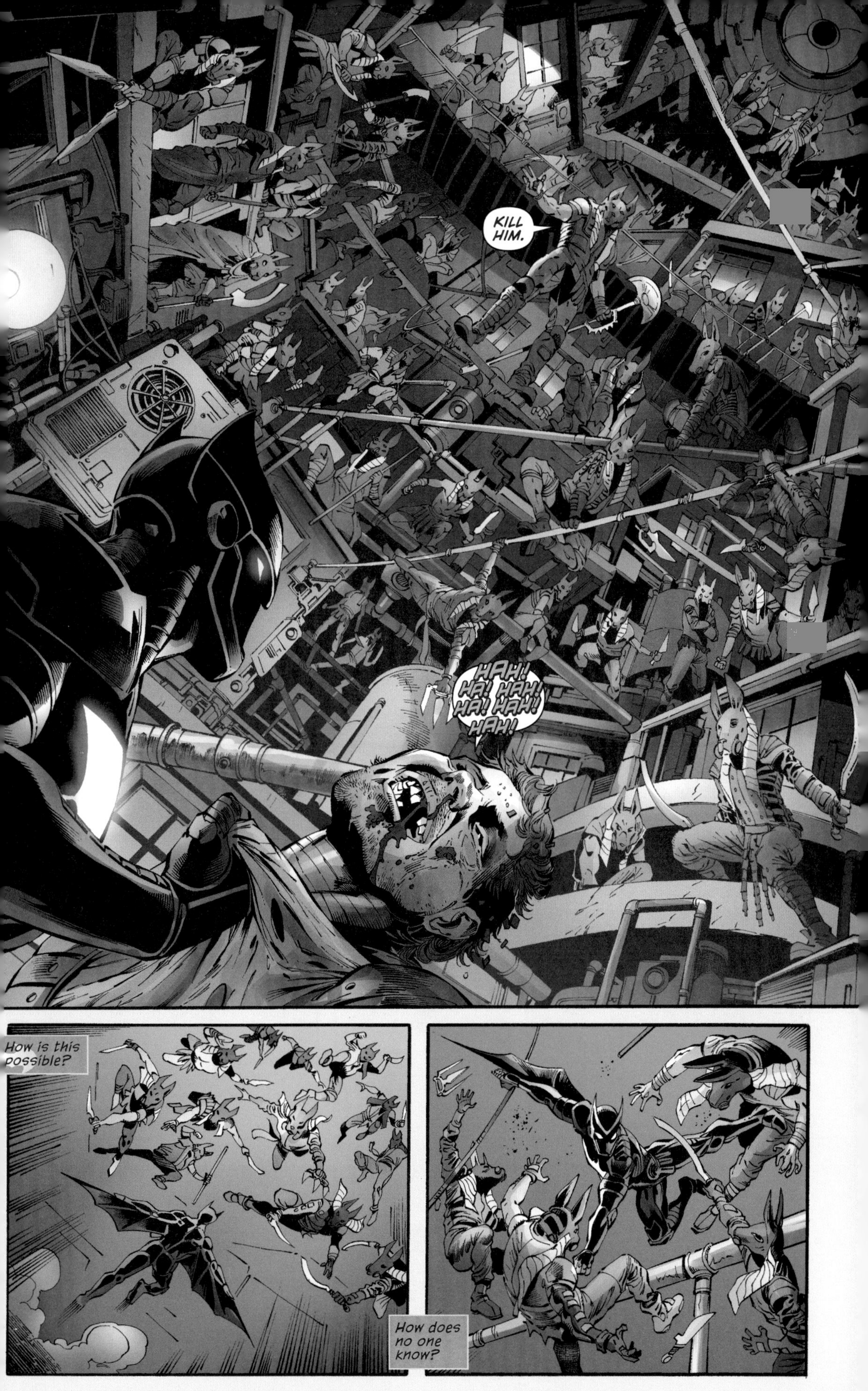
KILL HIM.
HAH! HA! HAH! HA! HAH! HAH!
How is this possible?
How does no one know?

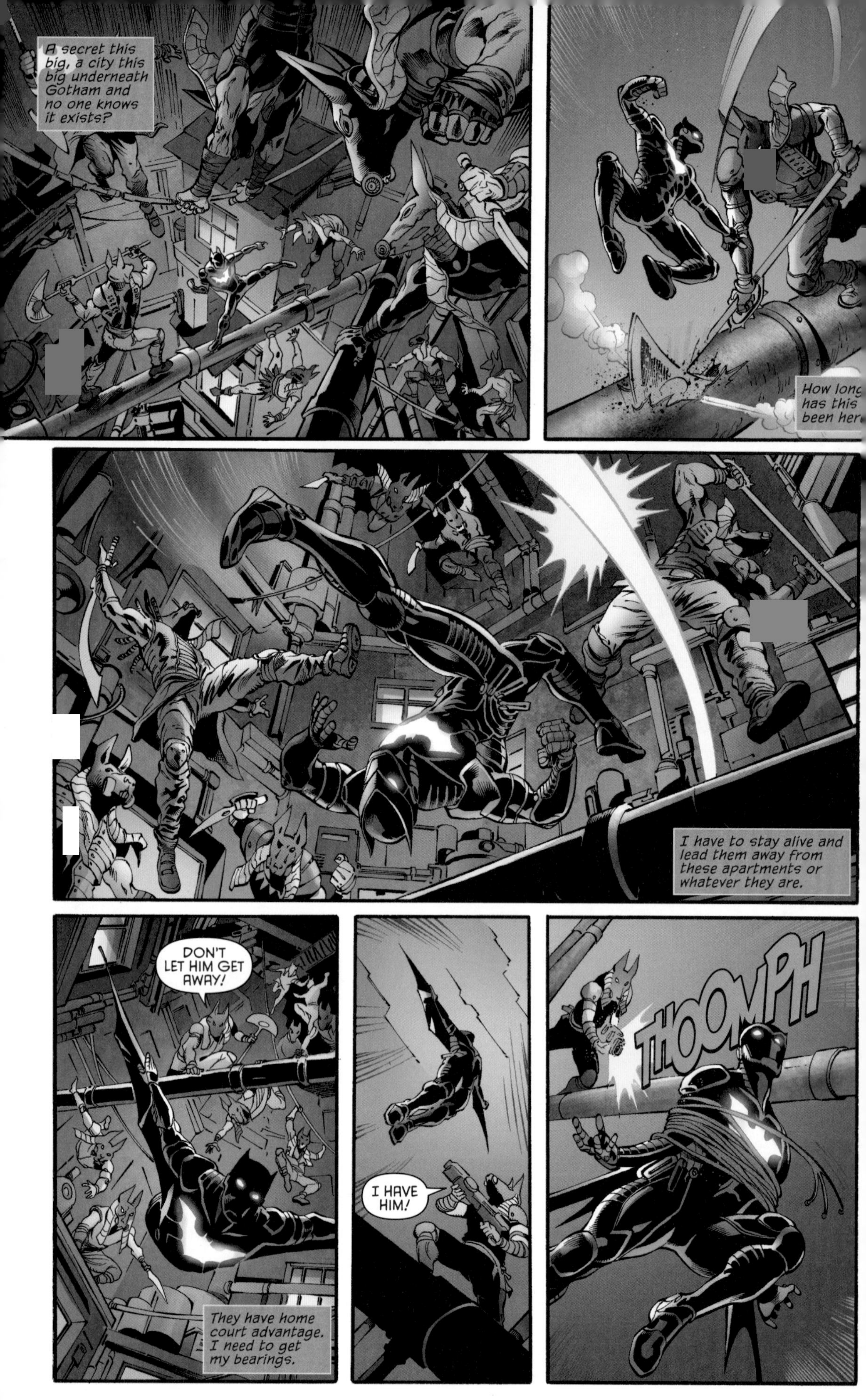
A secret this big, a city this big underneath Gotham and no one knows it exists?
How long has this been her
I have to stay alive and lead them away from these apartments or whatever they are.
DON'T LET HIM GET AWAY!
They have home court advantage. I need to get my bearings.
I HAVE HIM!
THOOMPH

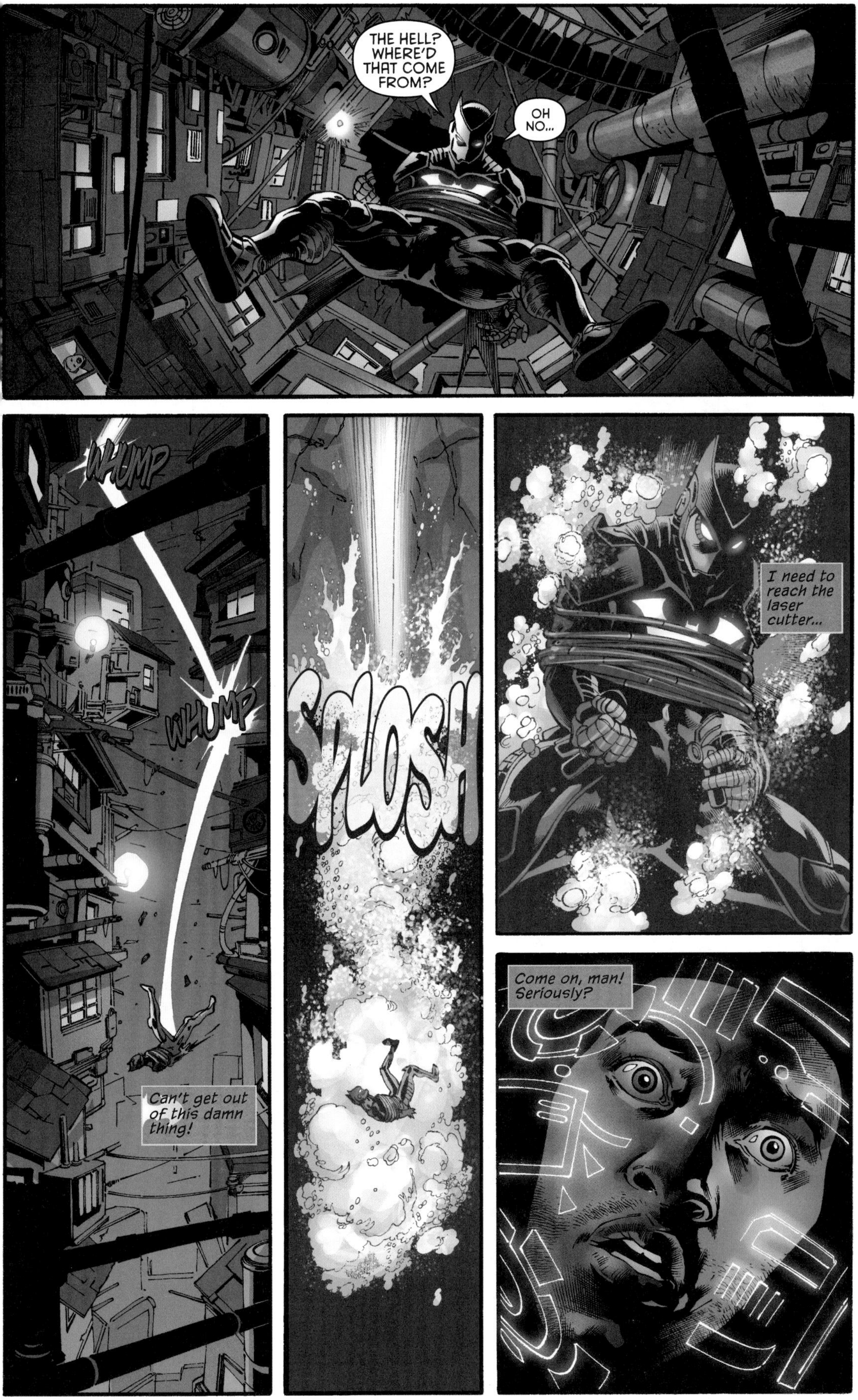
THE HELL? WHERE'D THAT COME FROM?
OH NO...
WHUMP
WHUMP
Can't get out of this damn thing!
SPLOSH
I need to reach the laser cutter...
Come on, man! Seriously?

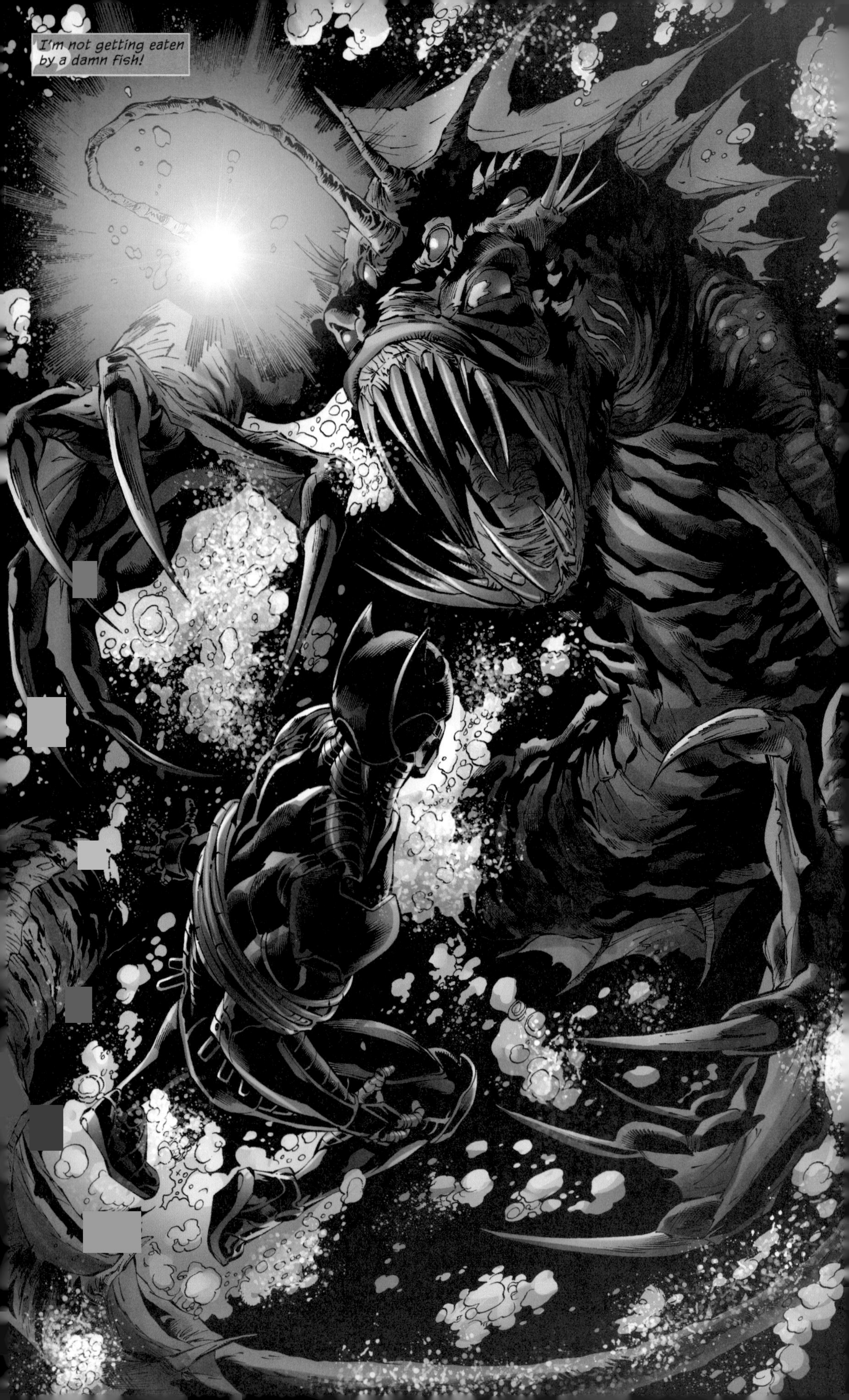
I'm not getting eaten by a damn fish!

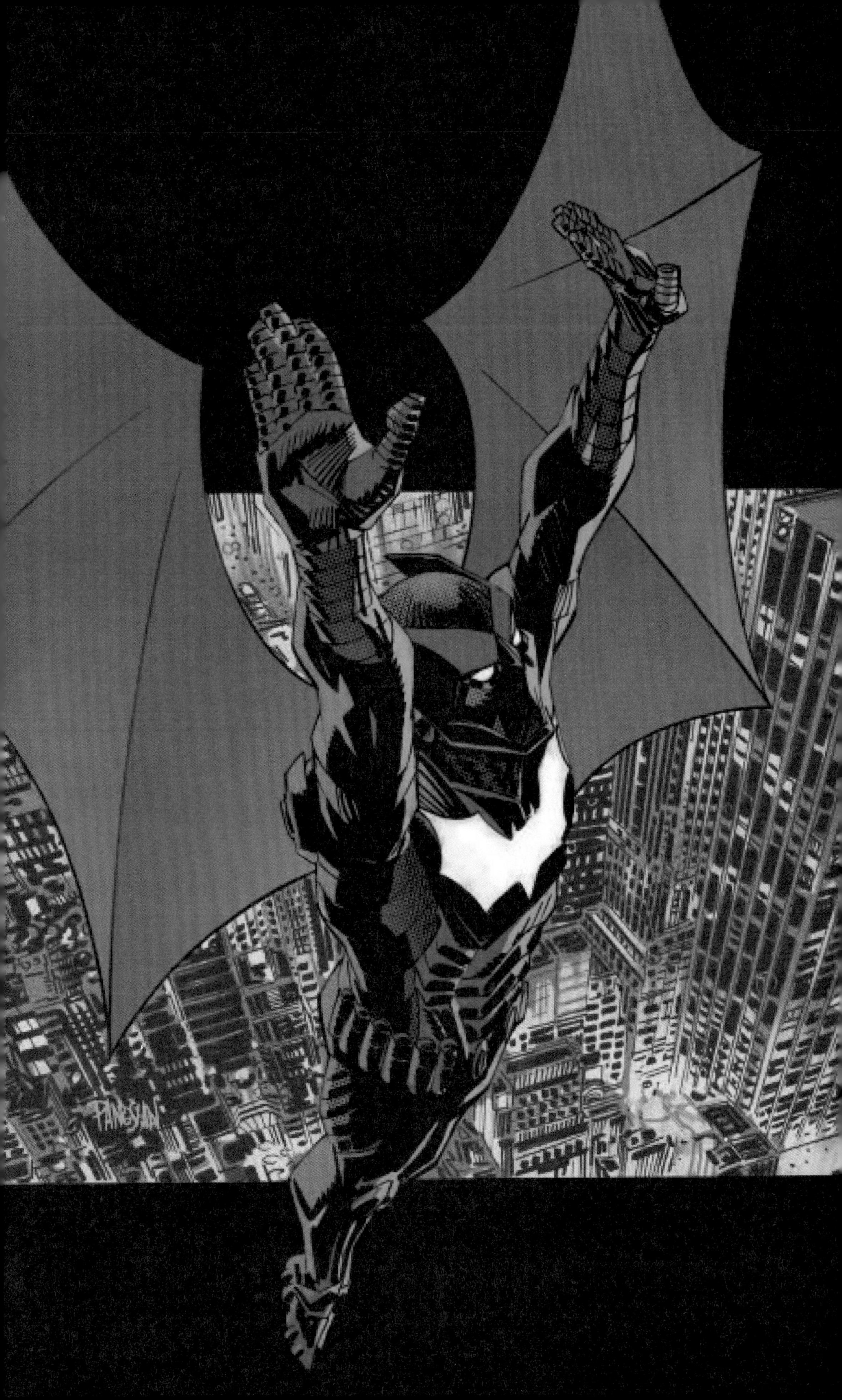

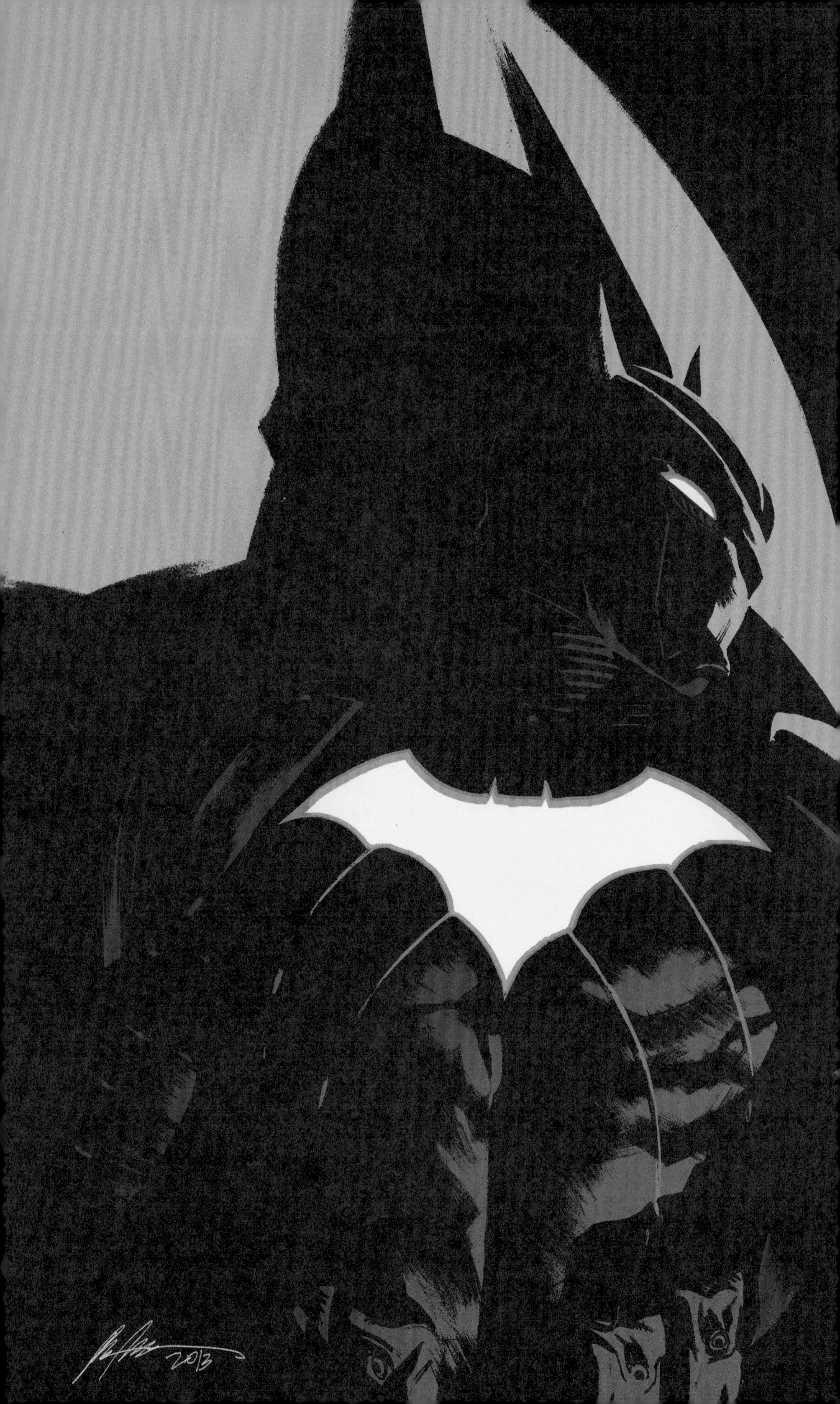

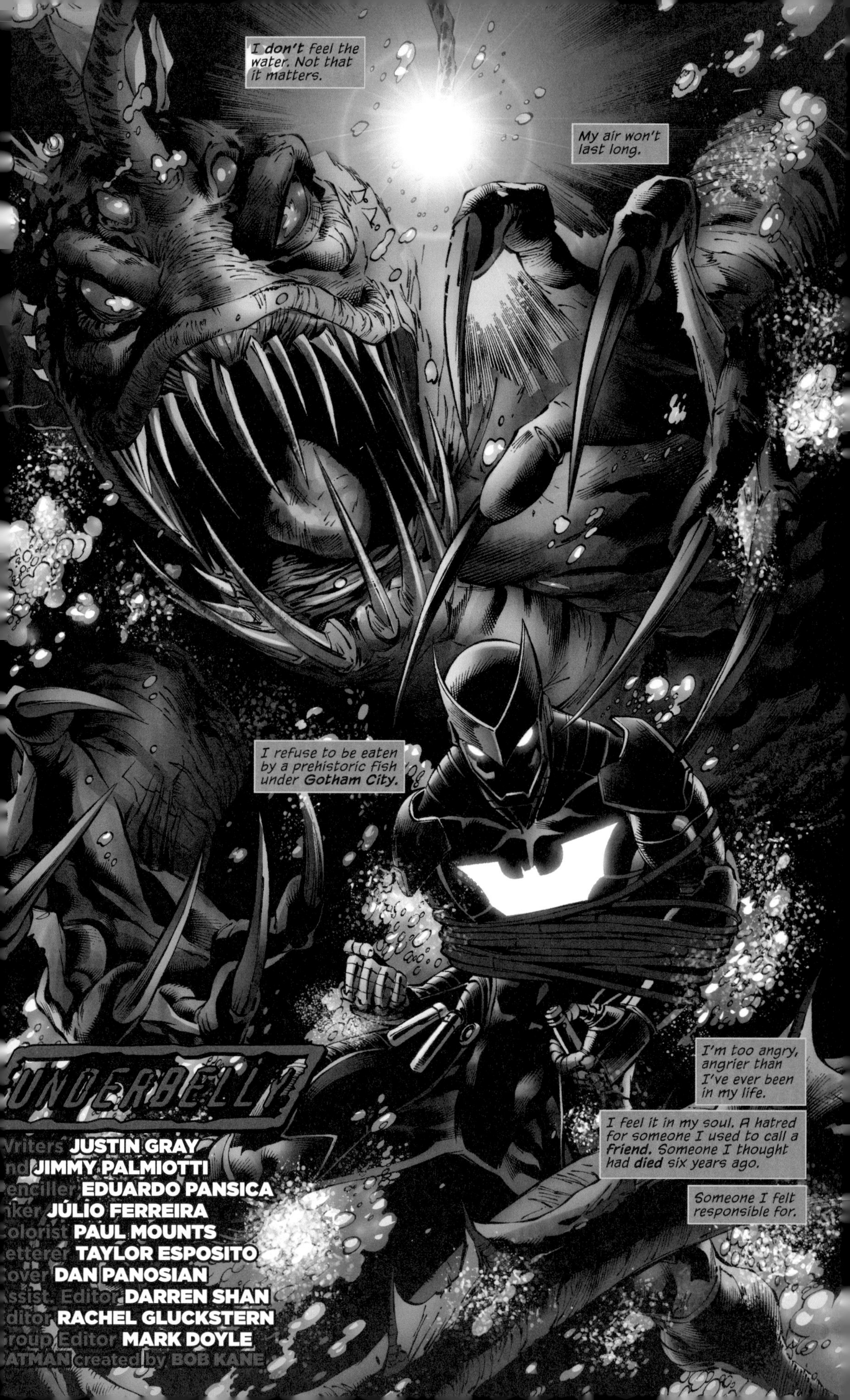
I don't feel the water. Not that it matters.
My air won't last long.
I refuse to be eaten by a prehistoric fish under Gotham City.
I'm too angry, angrier than I've ever been in my life.
I feel it in my soul. A hatred for someone I used to call a friend. Someone I thought had died six years ago.
Someone I felt responsible for.
UNDERBELLY
Vriters JUSTIN GRAY
nd JIMMY PALMIOTTI
enciller EDUARDO PANSICA
nker JÚLIO FERREIRA
olorist PAUL MOUNTS
etterer TAYLOR ESPOSITO
over DAN PANOSIAN
ssist. Editor DARREN SHAN
ditor RACHEL GLUCKSTERN
roup Editor MARK DOYLE
ATMAN created by BOB KANE

That someone is *Russell Tavaroff.* He hurt my sister in a way I can't wrap my head around.

My heart is broken my stomach is sick and my heart is pumping acid.

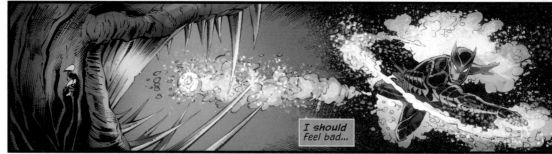

The fish is just being a fish. All it does is swim and eat. Today it picked the wrong meal.

I should feel bad...

But I don't.

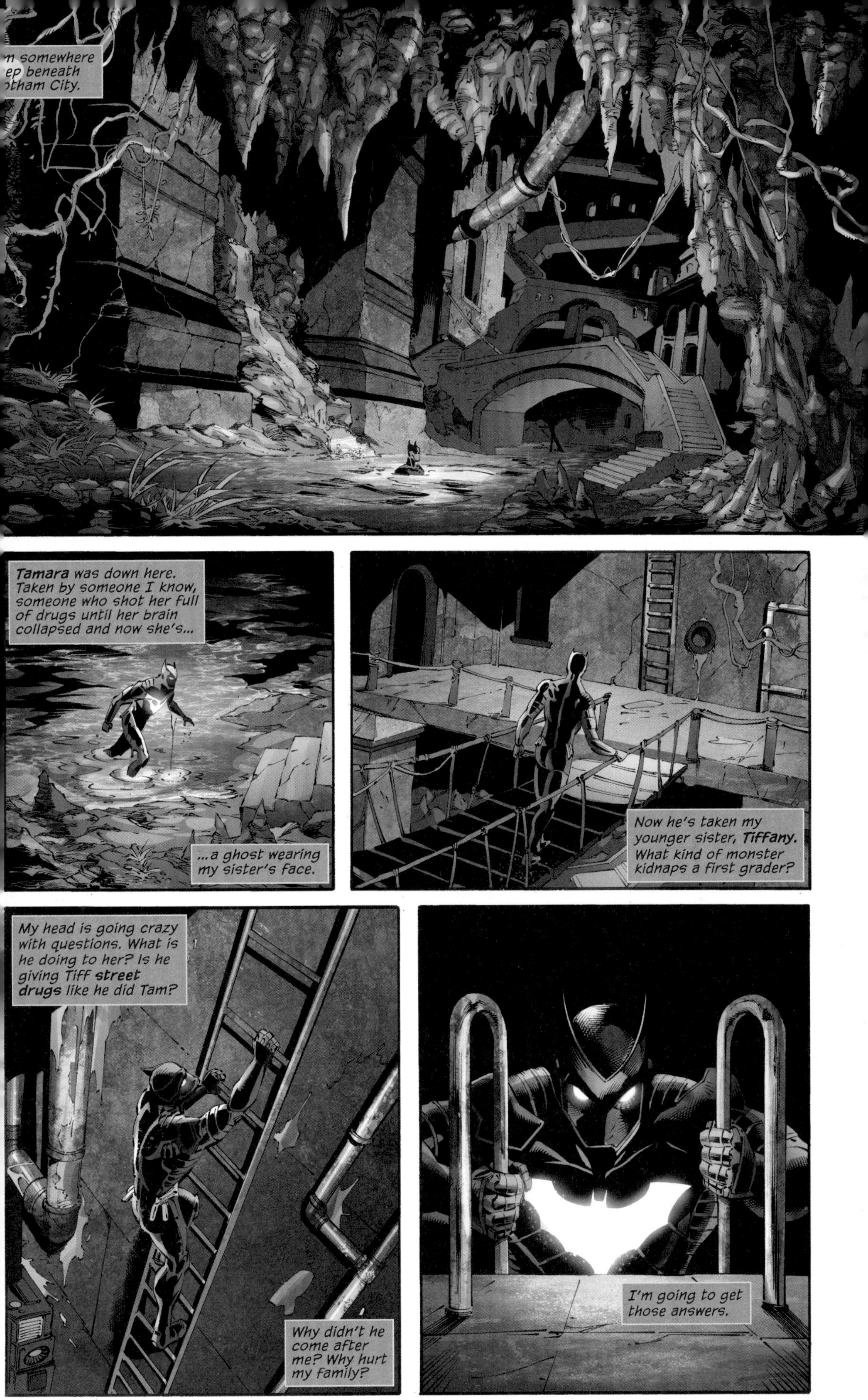
m somewhere
ep beneath
otham City.
Tamara was down here. Taken by someone I know, someone who shot her full of drugs until her brain collapsed and now she's...
...a ghost wearing my sister's face.
Now he's taken my younger sister, Tiffany. What kind of monster kidnaps a first grader?
My head is going crazy with questions. What is he doing to her? Is he giving Tiff street drugs like he did Tam?
Why didn't he come after me? Why hurt my family?
I'm going to get those answers.

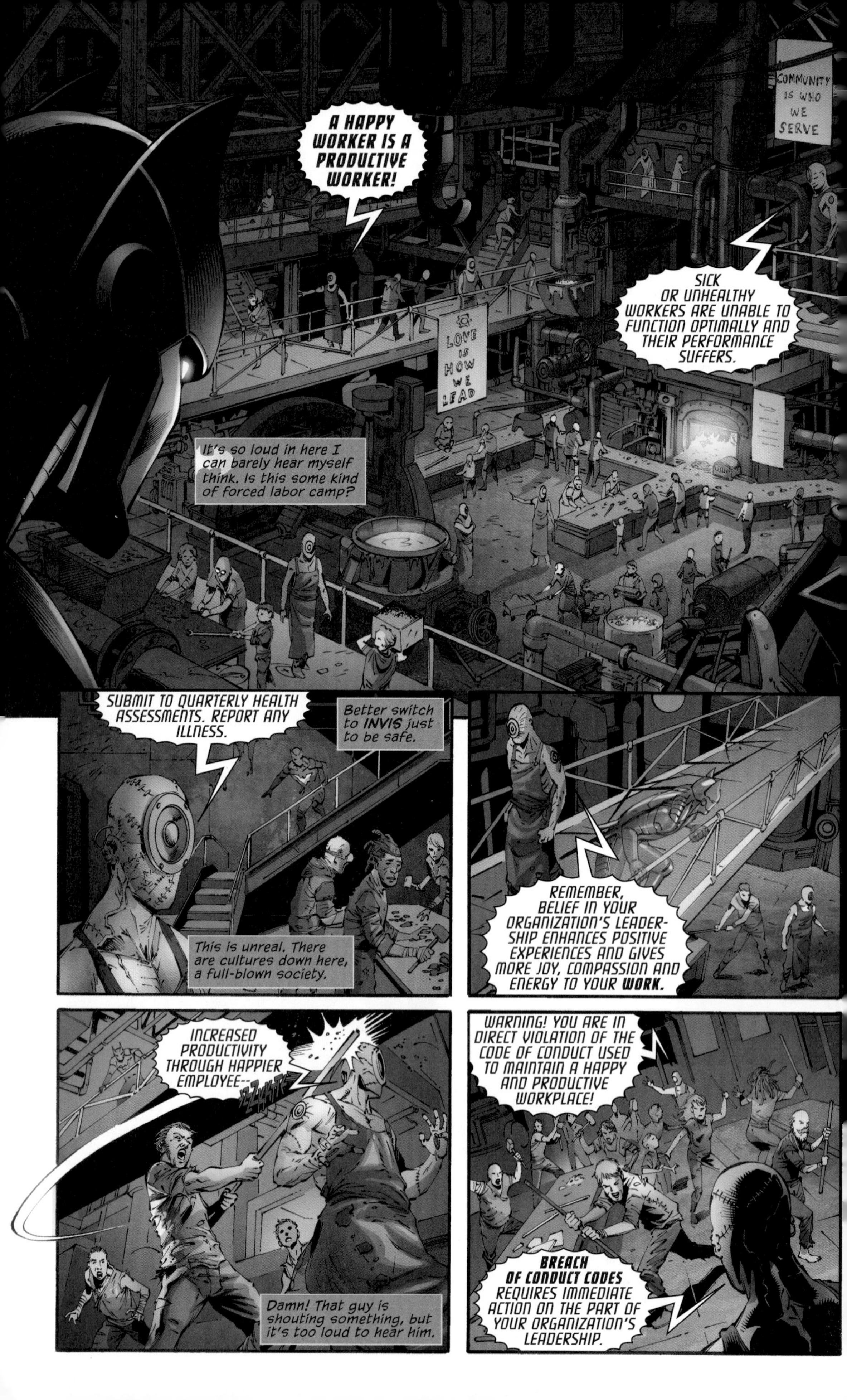

A HAPPY WORKER IS A PRODUCTIVE WORKER!
COMMUNITY IS WHO WE SERVE
LOVE IS HOW WE LEAD
SICK OR UNHEALTHY WORKERS ARE UNABLE TO FUNCTION OPTIMALLY AND THEIR PERFORMANCE SUFFERS.
It's so loud in here I can barely hear myself think. Is this some kind of forced labor camp?
SUBMIT TO QUARTERLY HEALTH ASSESSMENTS. REPORT ANY ILLNESS.
Better switch to INVIS just to be safe.
This is unreal. There are cultures down here, a full-blown society.
REMEMBER, BELIEF IN YOUR ORGANIZATION'S LEADERSHIP ENHANCES POSITIVE EXPERIENCES AND GIVES MORE JOY, COMPASSION AND ENERGY TO YOUR WORK.
INCREASED PRODUCTIVITY THROUGH HAPPIER EMPLOYEE--
ZZZHHT
Damn! That guy is shouting something, but it's too loud to hear him.
WARNING! YOU ARE IN DIRECT VIOLATION OF THE CODE OF CONDUCT USED TO MAINTAIN A HAPPY AND PRODUCTIVE WORKPLACE!
BREACH OF CONDUCT CODES REQUIRES IMMEDIATE ACTION ON THE PART OF YOUR ORGANIZATION'S LEADERSHIP.

They're killing them with sound!

The suit's audio dampeners are working well enough.

Still, there's no reason to risk a direct *sonic blast* from these freaks.

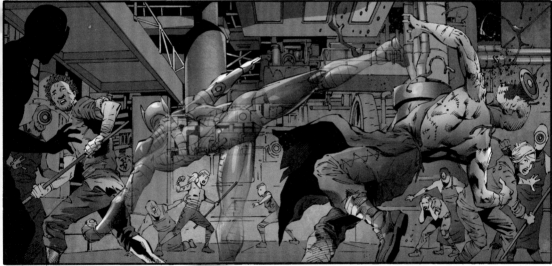

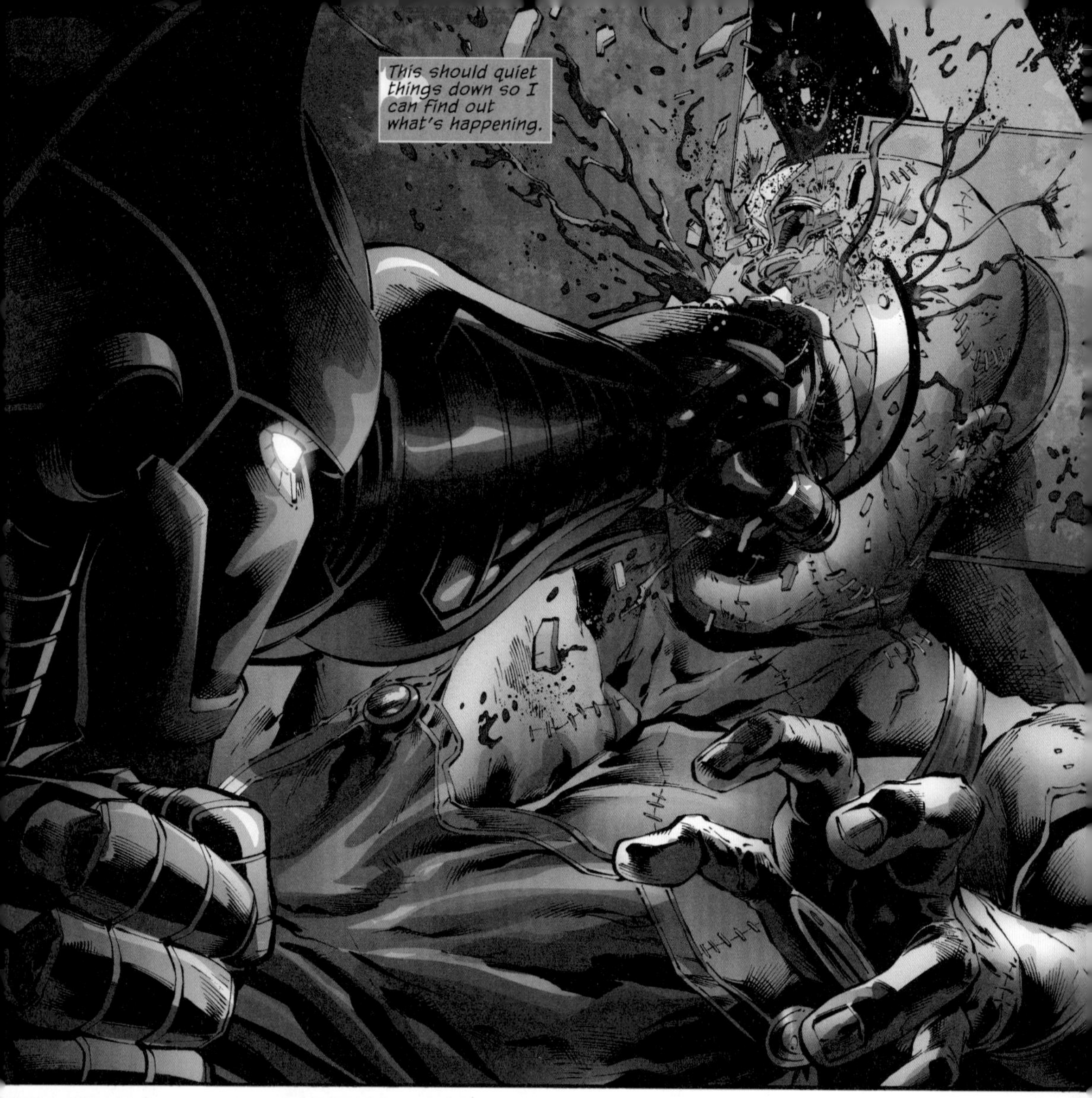
This should quiet things down so I can find out what's happening.

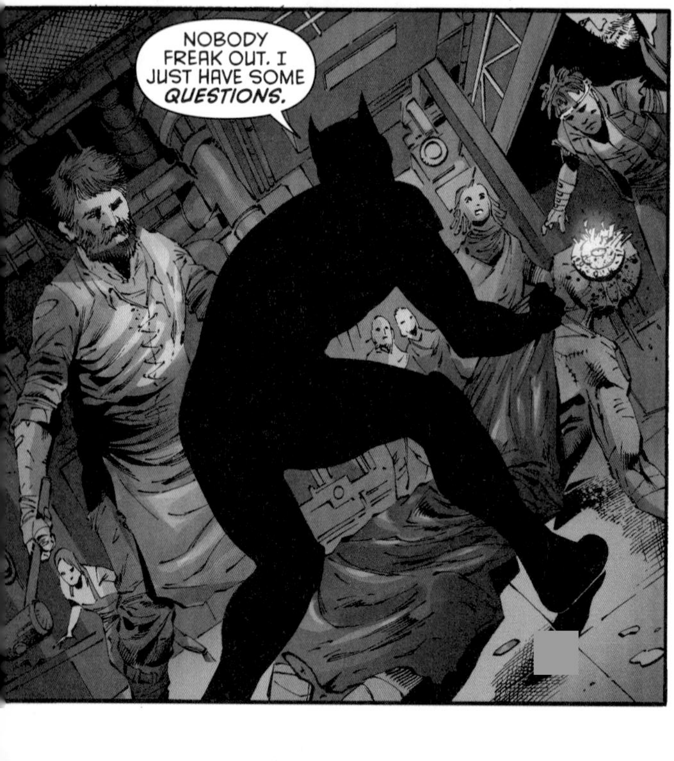
NOBODY FREAK OUT. I JUST HAVE SOME *QUESTIONS.*

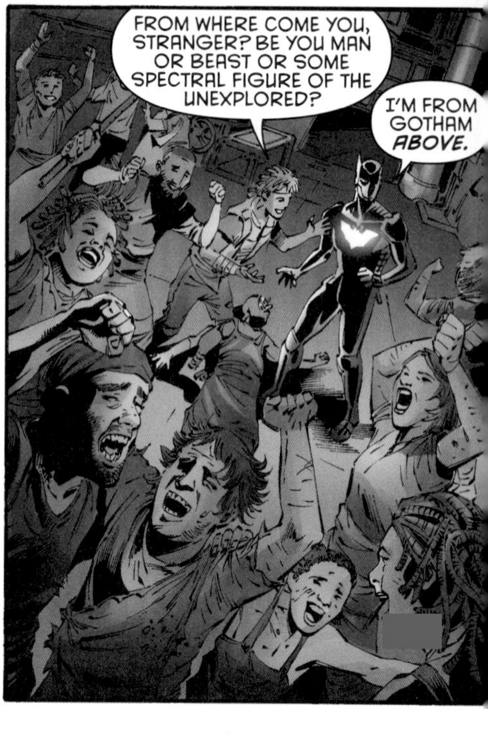
FROM WHERE COME YOU, STRANGER? BE YOU MAN OR BEAST OR SOME SPECTRAL FIGURE OF THE UNEXPLORED?
I'M FROM GOTHAM *ABOVE.*

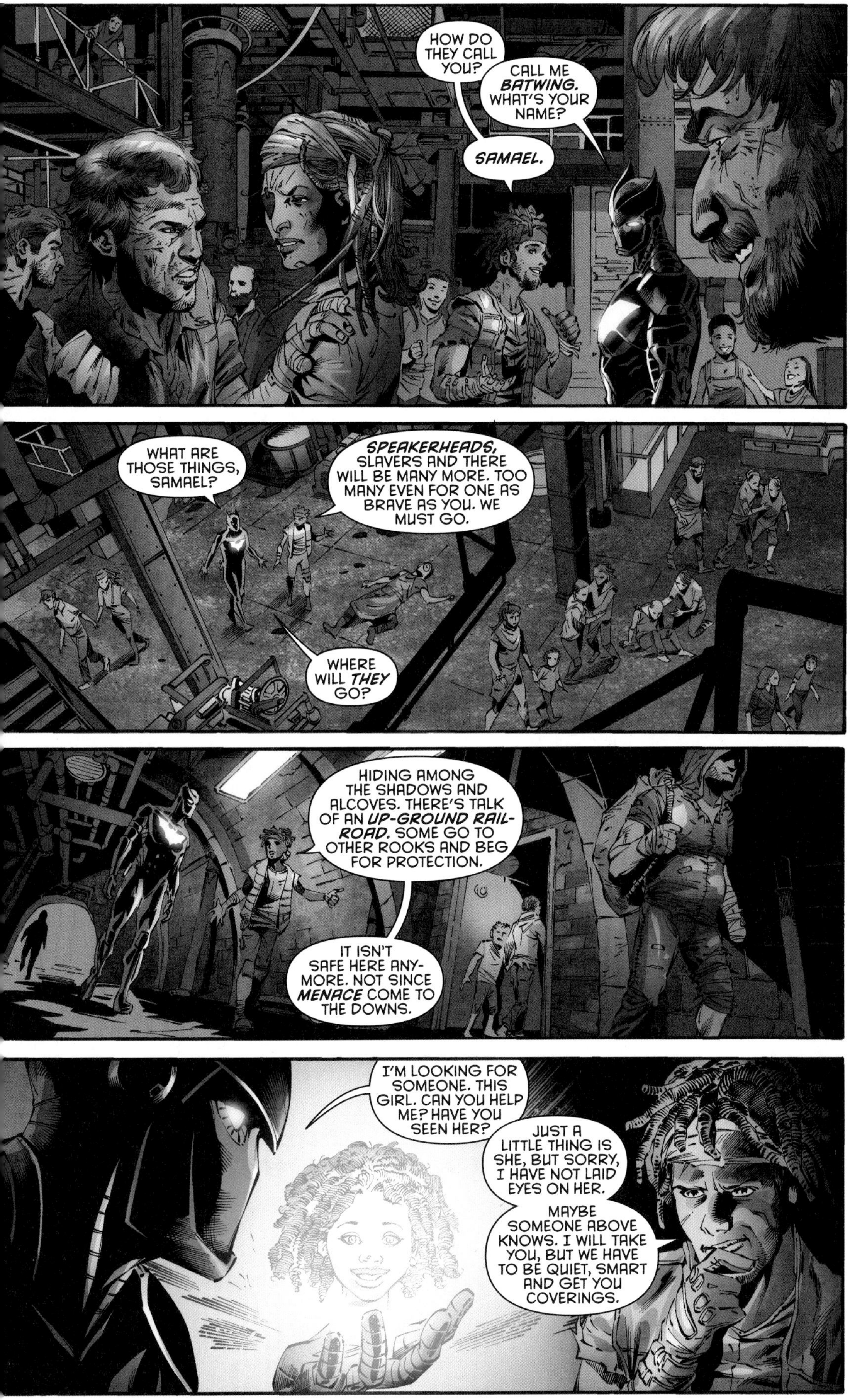
HOW DO THEY CALL YOU?
CALL ME BATWING. WHAT'S YOUR NAME?
SAMAEL.
WHAT ARE THOSE THINGS, SAMAEL?
SPEAKERHEADS, SLAVERS AND THERE WILL BE MANY MORE. TOO MANY EVEN FOR ONE AS BRAVE AS YOU. WE MUST GO.
WHERE WILL THEY GO?
HIDING AMONG THE SHADOWS AND ALCOVES. THERE'S TALK OF AN UP-GROUND RAIL-ROAD. SOME GO TO OTHER ROOKS AND BEG FOR PROTECTION.
IT ISN'T SAFE HERE ANY-MORE. NOT SINCE MENACE COME TO THE DOWNS.
I'M LOOKING FOR SOMEONE. THIS GIRL. CAN YOU HELP ME? HAVE YOU SEEN HER?
JUST A LITTLE THING IS SHE, BUT SORRY, I HAVE NOT LAID EYES ON HER.
MAYBE SOMEONE ABOVE KNOWS. I WILL TAKE YOU, BUT WE HAVE TO BE QUIET, SMART AND GET YOU COVERINGS.

I'M BEGGING YOU FOR HELP.

I'M DOING WHAT I CAN, *LUCIUS.*

YOU CAN'T BE! NOT WITH THE TECHNOLOGY WE HAVE, NOT WITH YOUR SKILL AND UNDERSTANDING OF THIS CITY!

I HAVE A DAUGHTER... SOMEONE SHOT MY TEENAGE DAUGHTER TAMARA FULL OF DRUGS AND NOW...SHE... OH GOD...!

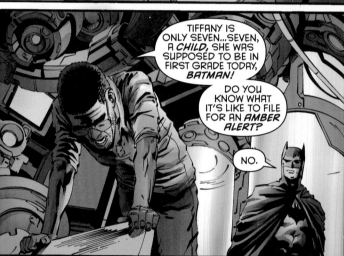

TIFFANY IS ONLY SEVEN...SEVEN, A *CHILD,* SHE WAS SUPPOSED TO BE IN FIRST GRADE TODAY, *BATMAN!*

DO YOU KNOW WHAT IT'S LIKE TO FILE FOR AN *AMBER ALERT?*

NO.

AND NOW MY BOY, *LUKE,* HAS VANISHED, PROBABLY GOD KNOWS WHERE LOOKING FOR HER, AND HE'S DANGEROUS ENOUGH TO GET HIMSELF KILLED!

MY FAMILY IS COMING APART!

EVERY COP IN GOTHAM IS WORKING ON THE CASE. I'M TAPPING EVERY RESOURCE AND STREET CONNECTION I HAVE.

IT ISN'T GOOD ENOUGH.

WE'LL FIND LUKE AND TIFFANY AND THE PEOPLE RESPONSIBLE, LUCIUS.

WHERE ARE YOU, *BATWING?*

WHY ISN'T THE LOCATION SOFTWARE IN THE SUIT FUNCTIONING?

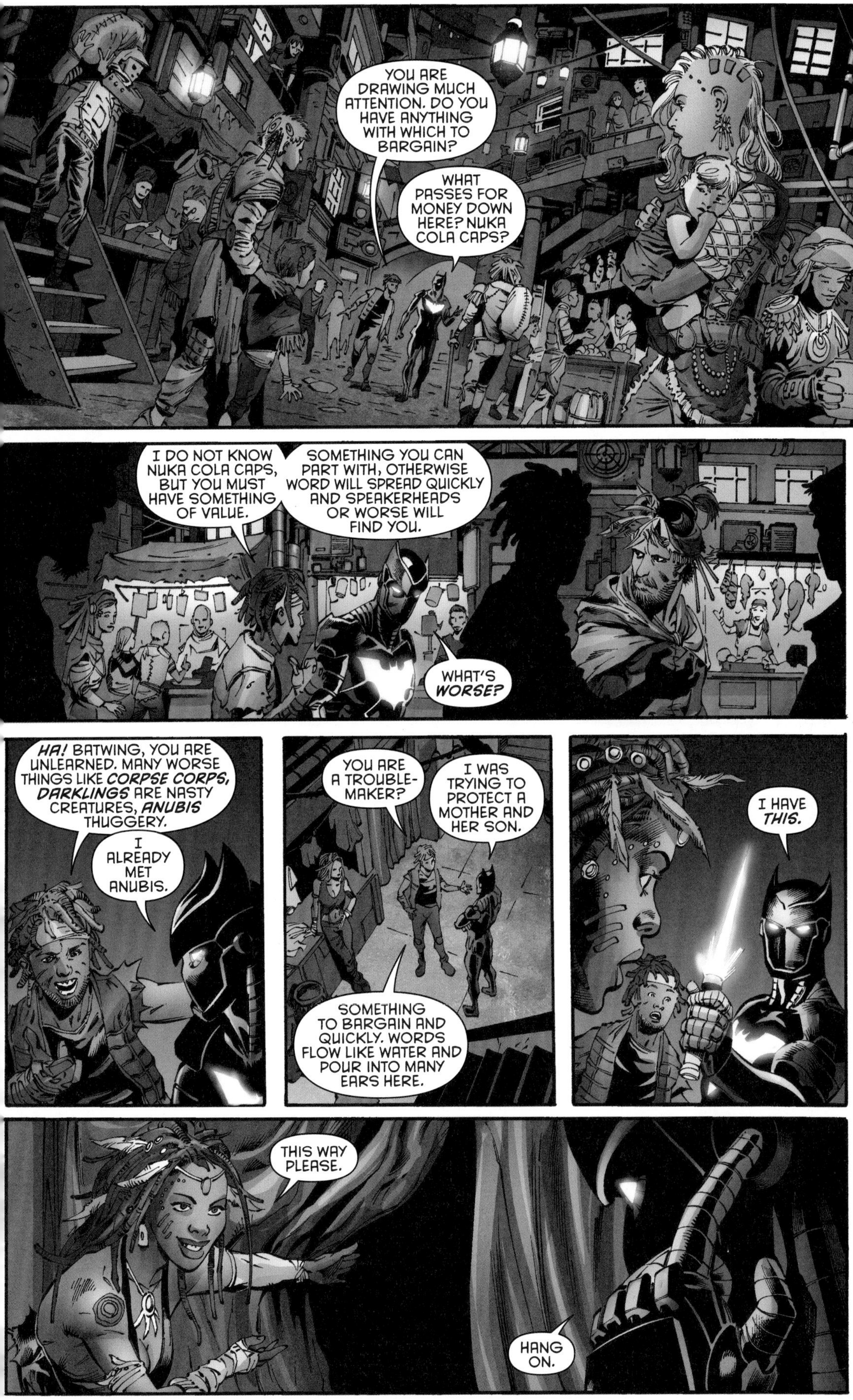
YOU ARE DRAWING MUCH ATTENTION. DO YOU HAVE ANYTHING WITH WHICH TO BARGAIN?
WHAT PASSES FOR MONEY DOWN HERE? NUKA COLA CAPS?
I DO NOT KNOW NUKA COLA CAPS, BUT YOU MUST HAVE SOMETHING OF VALUE.
SOMETHING YOU CAN PART WITH, OTHERWISE WORD WILL SPREAD QUICKLY AND SPEAKERHEADS OR WORSE WILL FIND YOU.
WHAT'S *WORSE?*
HA! BATWING, YOU ARE UNLEARNED. MANY WORSE THINGS LIKE *CORPSE CORPS, DARKLINGS* ARE NASTY CREATURES, *ANUBIS* THUGGERY.
I ALREADY MET ANUBIS.
YOU ARE A TROUBLE-MAKER?
I WAS TRYING TO PROTECT A MOTHER AND HER SON.
SOMETHING TO BARGAIN AND QUICKLY. WORDS FLOW LIKE WATER AND POUR INTO MANY EARS HERE.
I HAVE *THIS.*
THIS WAY PLEASE.
HANG ON.

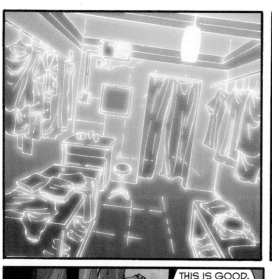

WHAT CAN I GET FOR THE LASER KNIFE?

A WHOLE LOT. EVEN ME.

I...uhhh, JUST CLOTHES SHOULD DO IT.

THIS IS GOOD, NEUTRAL, NO GANG COLORS, BUT CLOSE ENOUGH TO DARKLING THAT MOST PEOPLE WILL LEAVE YOU BE.

LIKE A MASK. GO IN THE BACK AND CHANGE. WE DECIDE IF YOU LOOK PRESENTABLE.

I GOT A *BETTER* IDEA.

WE MUST MOVE.

I HAVE AN IDEA WHO MAY KNOW WHERE THE GIRL YOU SEEK IS OR WHO SHE IS WITH.

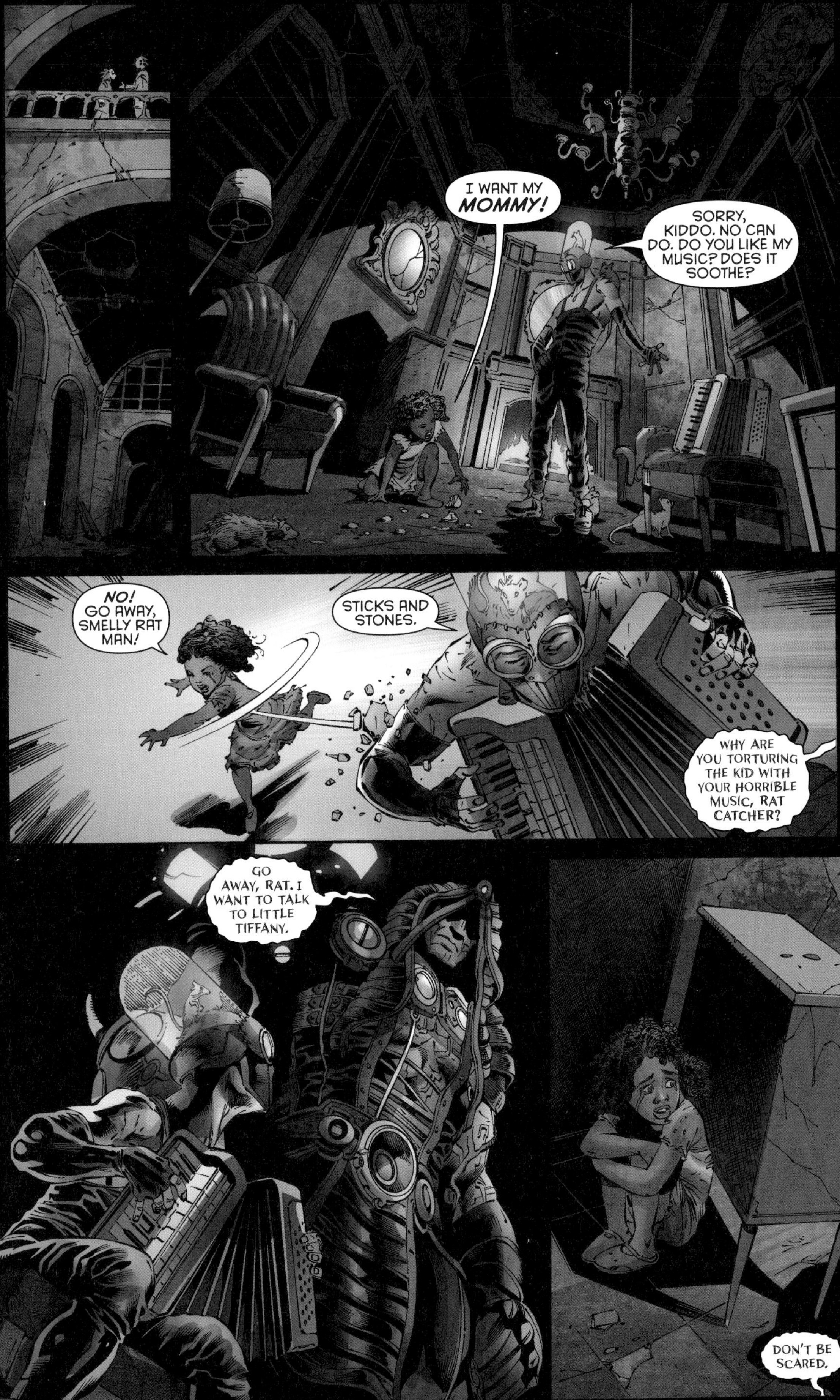
I WANT MY MOMMY!
SORRY, KIDDO. NO CAN DO. DO YOU LIKE MY MUSIC? DOES IT SOOTHE?
NO! GO AWAY, SMELLY RAT MAN!
STICKS AND STONES.
WHY ARE YOU TORTURING THE KID WITH YOUR HORRIBLE MUSIC, RAT CATCHER?
GO AWAY, RAT. I WANT TO TALK TO LITTLE TIFFANY.
DON'T BE SCARED.

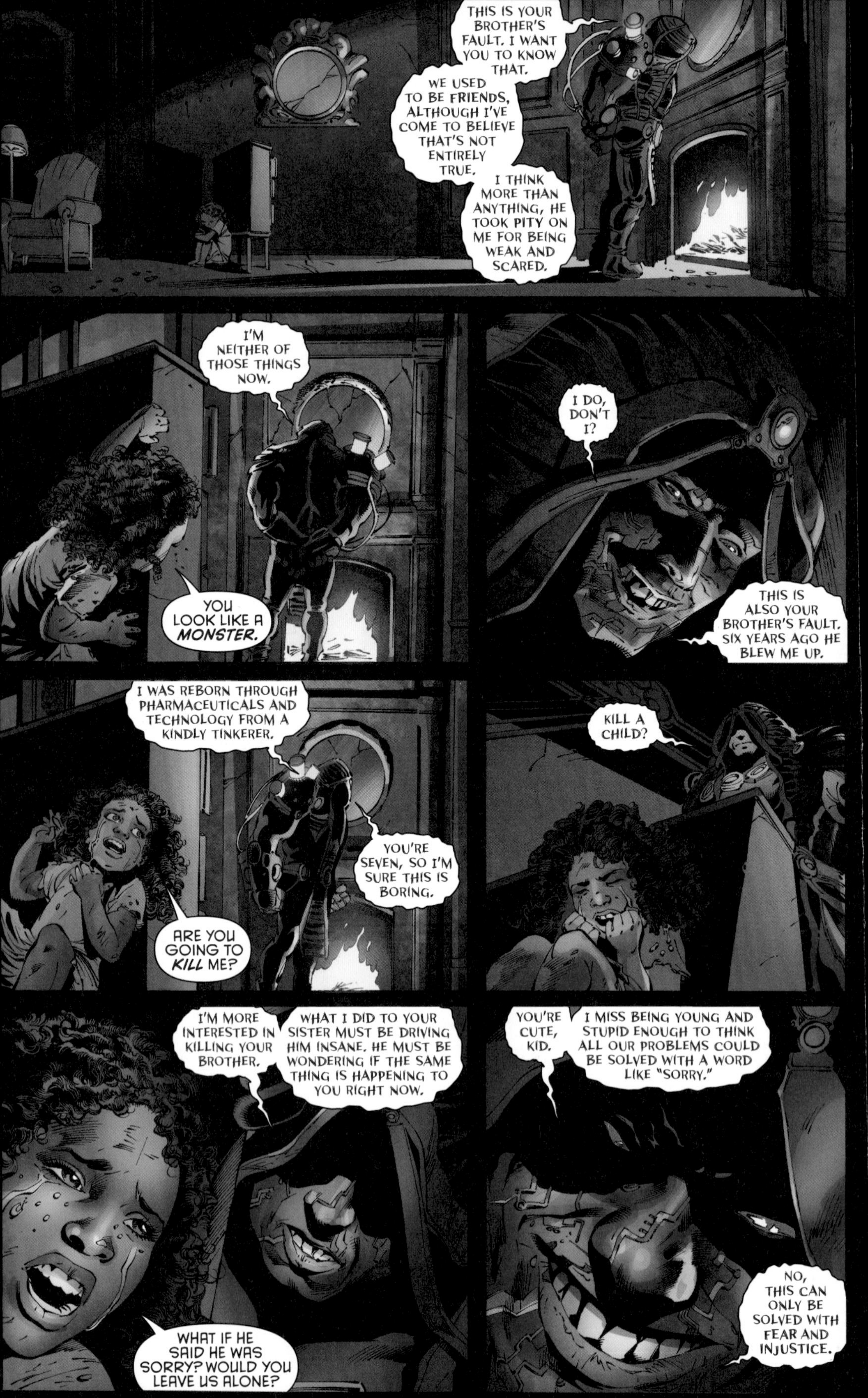
THIS IS YOUR BROTHER'S FAULT. I WANT YOU TO KNOW THAT.
WE USED TO BE FRIENDS, ALTHOUGH I'VE COME TO BELIEVE THAT'S NOT ENTIRELY TRUE.
I THINK MORE THAN ANYTHING, HE TOOK PITY ON ME FOR BEING WEAK AND SCARED.
I'M NEITHER OF THOSE THINGS NOW.
YOU LOOK LIKE A MONSTER.
I DO, DON'T I?
THIS IS ALSO YOUR BROTHER'S FAULT. SIX YEARS AGO HE BLEW ME UP.
I WAS REBORN THROUGH PHARMACEUTICALS AND TECHNOLOGY FROM A KINDLY TINKERER.
YOU'RE SEVEN, SO I'M SURE THIS IS BORING.
ARE YOU GOING TO KILL ME?
KILL A CHILD?
I'M MORE INTERESTED IN KILLING YOUR BROTHER.
WHAT I DID TO YOUR SISTER MUST BE DRIVING HIM INSANE. HE MUST BE WONDERING IF THE SAME THING IS HAPPENING TO YOU RIGHT NOW.
WHAT IF HE SAID HE WAS SORRY? WOULD YOU LEAVE US ALONE?
YOU'RE CUTE, KID.
I MISS BEING YOUNG AND STUPID ENOUGH TO THINK ALL OUR PROBLEMS COULD BE SOLVED WITH A WORD LIKE "SORRY."
NO, THIS CAN ONLY BE SOLVED WITH FEAR AND INJUSTICE.

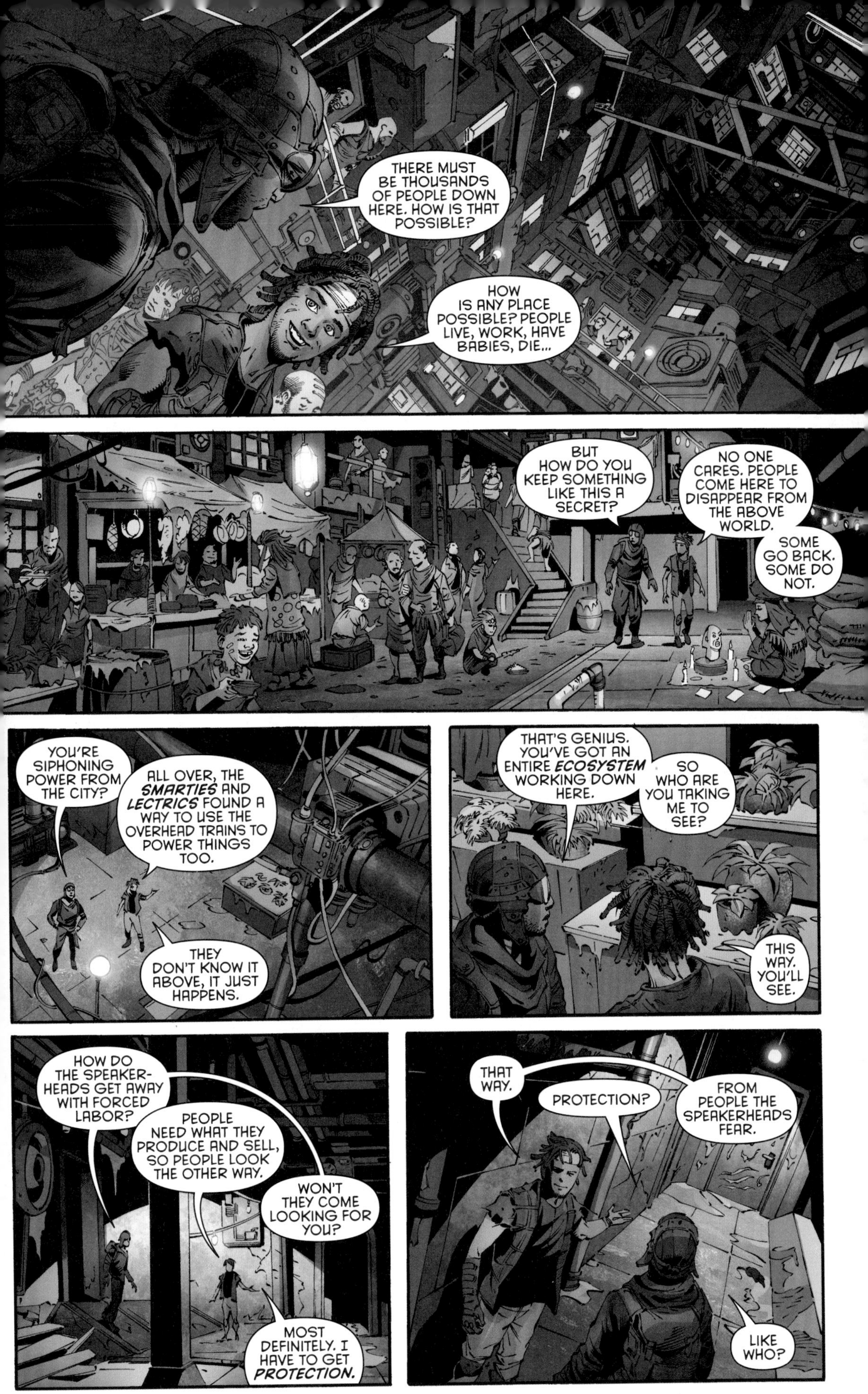

THERE MUST BE THOUSANDS OF PEOPLE DOWN HERE. HOW IS THAT POSSIBLE?
HOW IS ANY PLACE POSSIBLE? PEOPLE LIVE, WORK, HAVE BABIES, DIE...
BUT HOW DO YOU KEEP SOMETHING LIKE THIS A SECRET?
NO ONE CARES. PEOPLE COME HERE TO DISAPPEAR FROM THE ABOVE WORLD.
SOME GO BACK. SOME DO NOT.
YOU'RE SIPHONING POWER FROM THE CITY?
ALL OVER, THE SMARTIES AND LECTRICS FOUND A WAY TO USE THE OVERHEAD TRAINS TO POWER THINGS TOO.
THEY DON'T KNOW IT ABOVE, IT JUST HAPPENS.
THAT'S GENIUS. YOU'VE GOT AN ENTIRE ECOSYSTEM WORKING DOWN HERE.
SO WHO ARE YOU TAKING ME TO SEE?
THIS WAY. YOU'LL SEE.
HOW DO THE SPEAKER-HEADS GET AWAY WITH FORCED LABOR?
PEOPLE NEED WHAT THEY PRODUCE AND SELL, SO PEOPLE LOOK THE OTHER WAY.
WON'T THEY COME LOOKING FOR YOU?
MOST DEFINITELY. I HAVE TO GET PROTECTION.
THAT WAY.
PROTECTION?
FROM PEOPLE THE SPEAKERHEADS FEAR.
LIKE WHO?

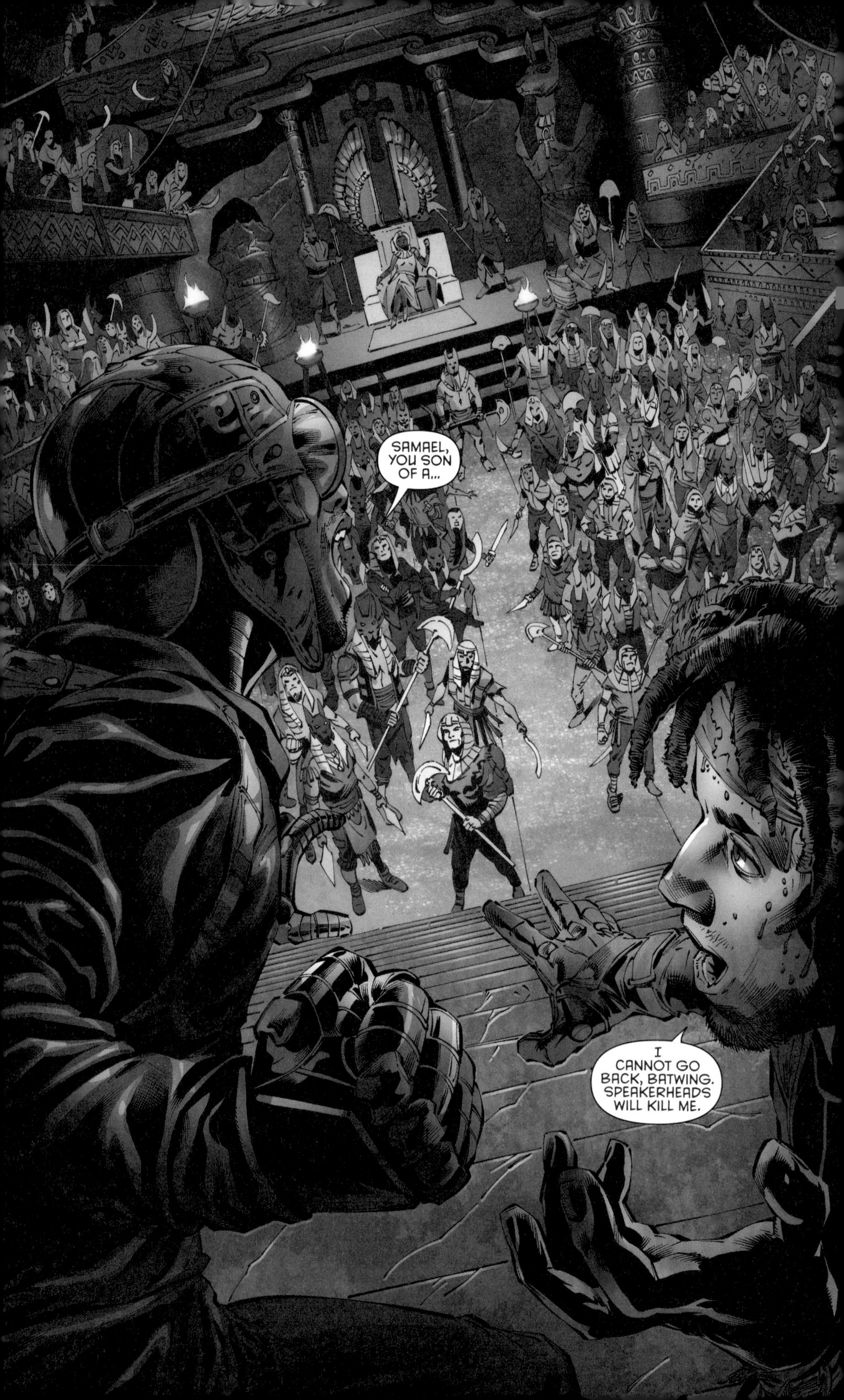
SAMAEL, YOU SON OF A...
I CANNOT GO BACK, BATWING. SPEAKERHEADS WILL KILL ME.

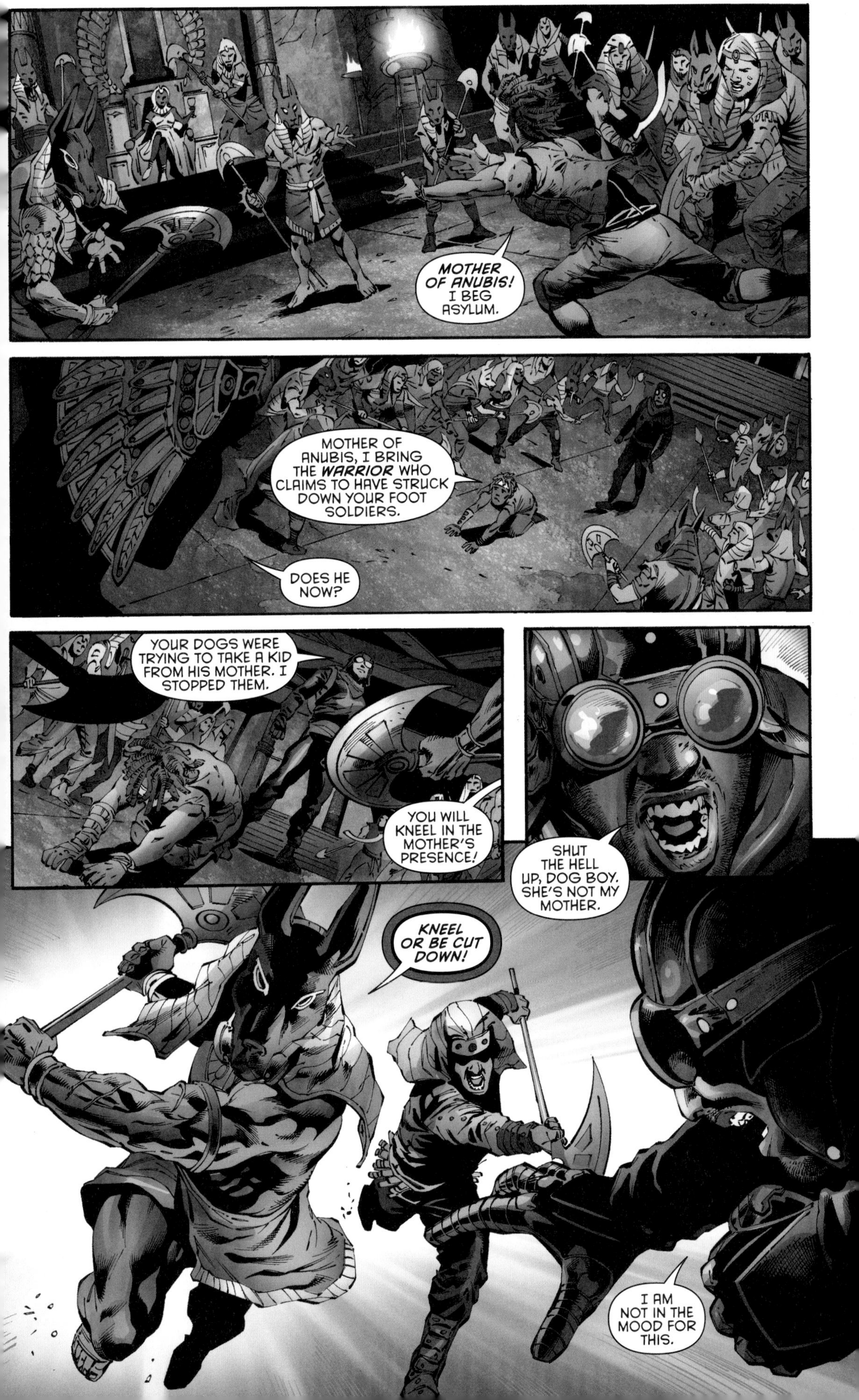

MOTHER OF ANUBIS! I BEG ASYLUM.
MOTHER OF ANUBIS, I BRING THE WARRIOR WHO CLAIMS TO HAVE STRUCK DOWN YOUR FOOT SOLDIERS.
DOES HE NOW?
YOUR DOGS WERE TRYING TO TAKE A KID FROM HIS MOTHER. I STOPPED THEM.
YOU WILL KNEEL IN THE MOTHER'S PRESENCE!
SHUT THE HELL UP, DOG BOY. SHE'S NOT MY MOTHER.
KNEEL OR BE CUT DOWN!
I AM NOT IN THE MOOD FOR THIS.

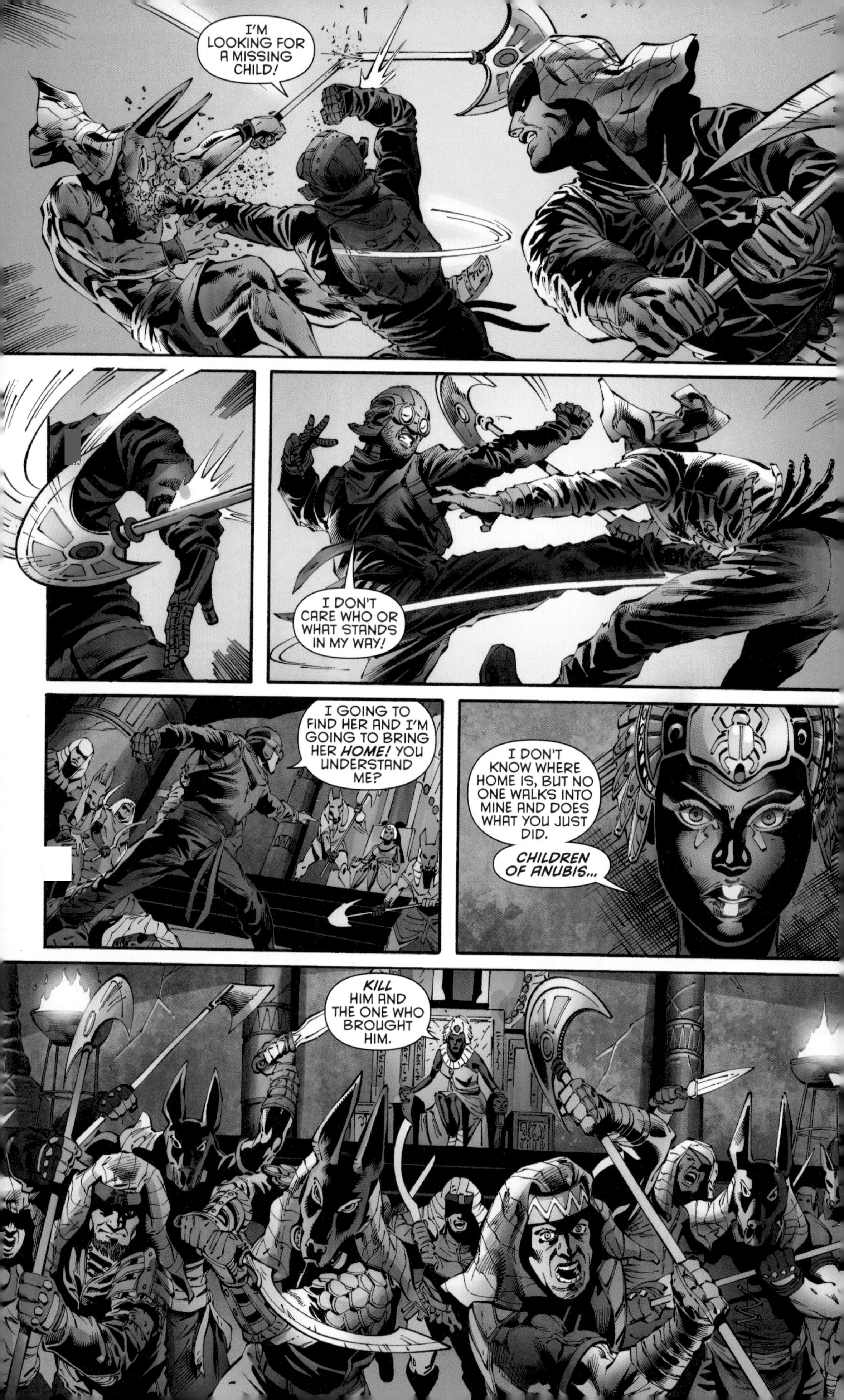
I'M LOOKING FOR A MISSING CHILD!
I DON'T CARE WHO OR WHAT STANDS IN MY WAY!
I GOING TO FIND HER AND I'M GOING TO BRING HER *HOME!* YOU UNDERSTAND ME?
I DON'T KNOW WHERE HOME IS, BUT NO ONE WALKS INTO MINE AND DOES WHAT YOU JUST DID.
CHILDREN OF ANUBIS...
KILL HIM AND THE ONE WHO BROUGHT HIM.

I'm trying not to get sucked into that dark place, but I welcome the rage in me. I embrace it.

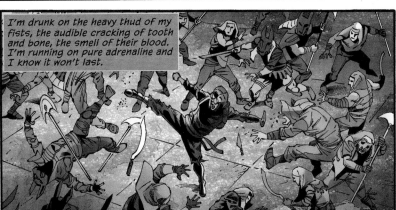

I'm drunk on the heavy thud of my fists, the audible cracking of tooth and bone, the smell of their blood. I'm running on pure adrenaline and I know it won't last.

How does Batman do it? Does he cut off his emotions? Does he have no one he cares about?

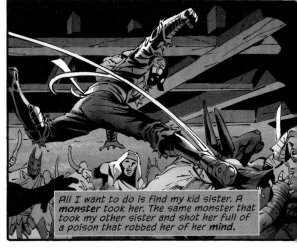

All I want to do is find my kid sister. A monster took her. The same monster that took my other sister and shot her full of a poison that robbed her of her mind.

I'm going to get tired soon. I might be used to five-minute rounds, but they come with breaks and water and smelling salts.

Fighting these Anubis idiots is a waste of time and energy.

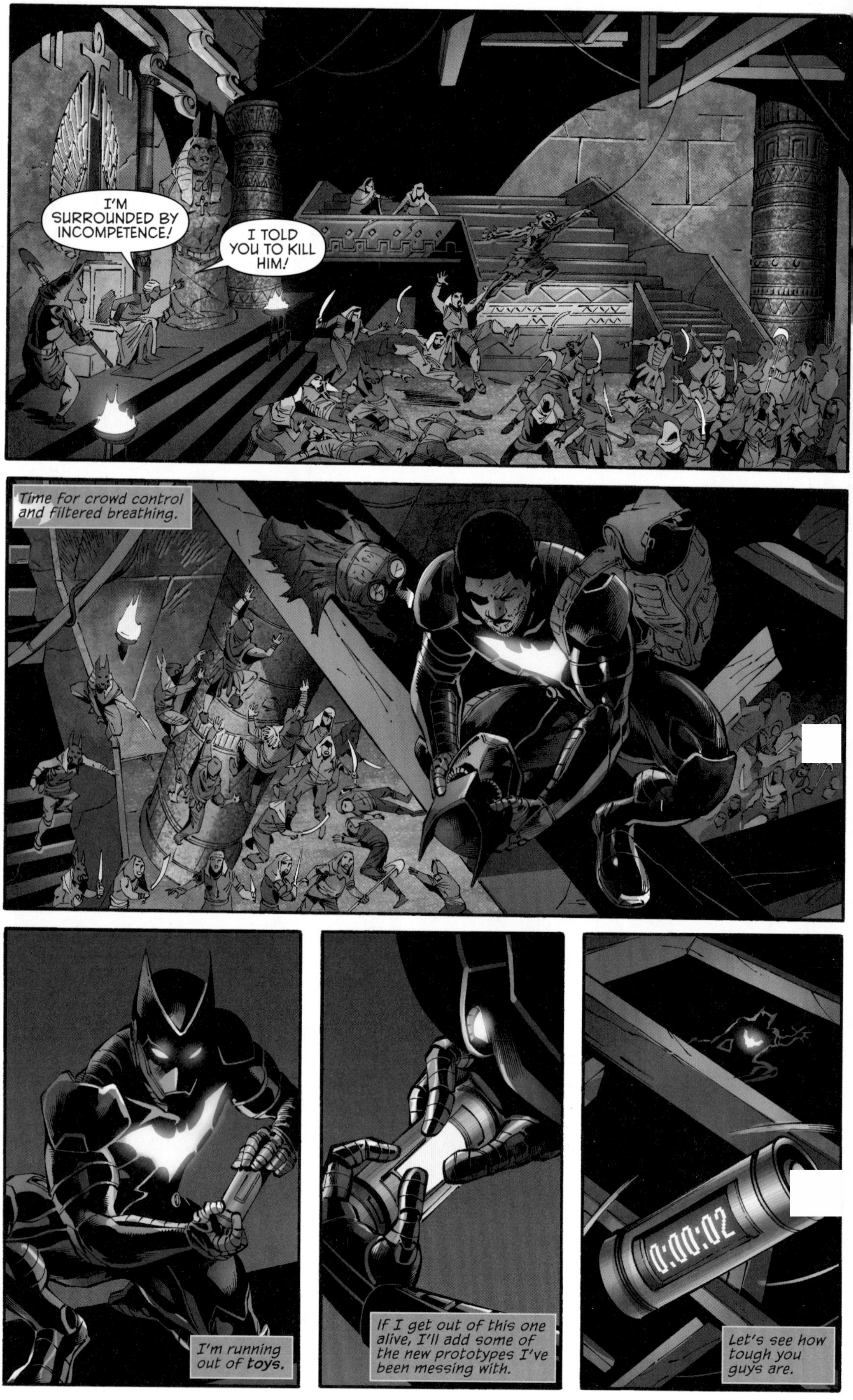
I'M SURROUNDED BY INCOMPETENCE!
I TOLD YOU TO KILL HIM!
Time for crowd control and filtered breathing.
I'm running out of toys.
If I get out of this one alive, I'll add some of the new prototypes I've been messing with.
0:00:02
Let's see how tough you guys are.

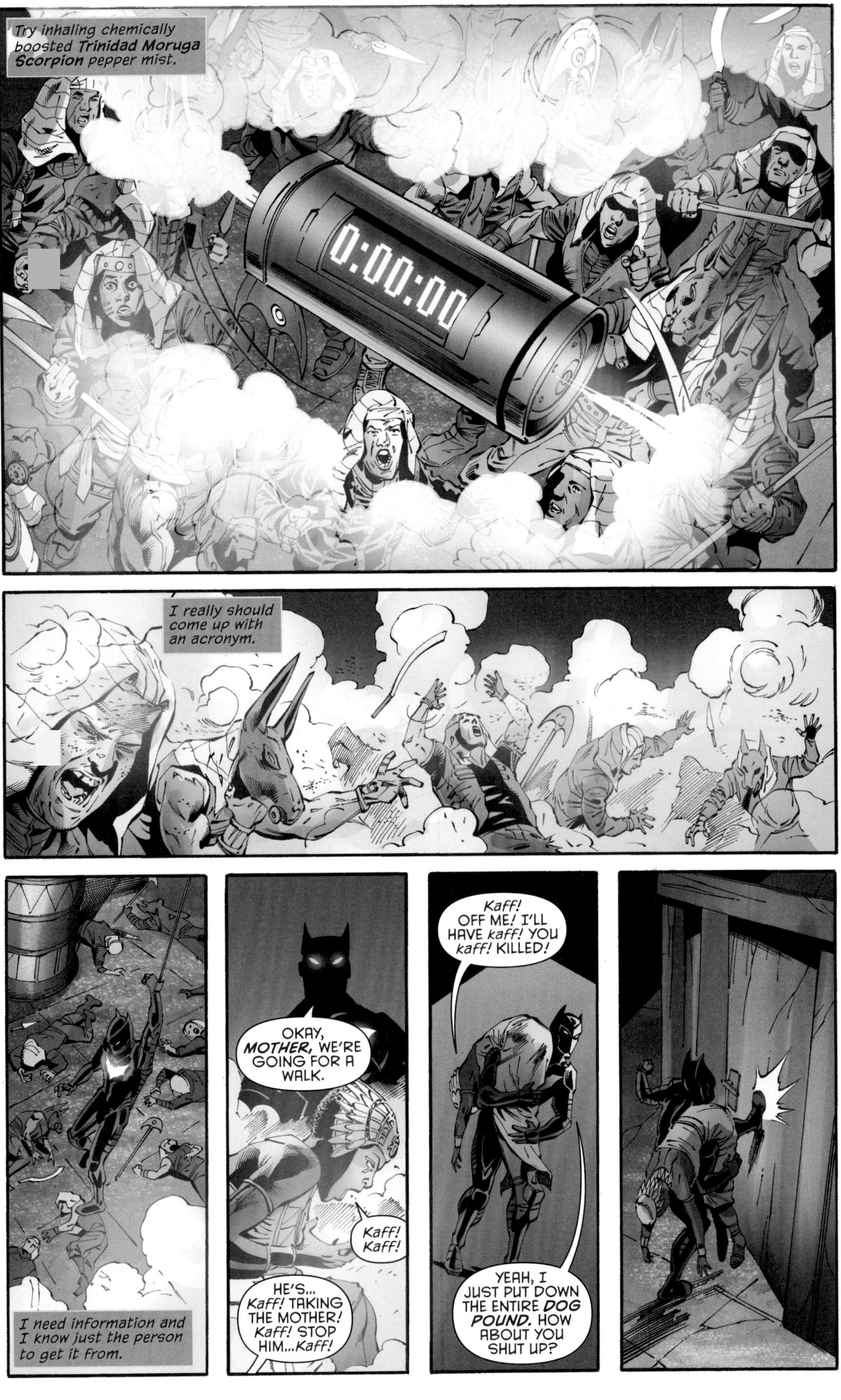
Try inhaling chemically boosted Trinidad Moruga Scorpion pepper mist.
0:00:00
I really should come up with an acronym.
I need information and I know just the person to get it from.
OKAY, MOTHER, WE'RE GOING FOR A WALK.
Kaff! Kaff!
HE'S... Kaff! TAKING THE MOTHER! Kaff! STOP HIM...Kaff!
Kaff! OFF ME! I'LL HAVE kaff! YOU kaff! KILLED!
YEAH, I JUST PUT DOWN THE ENTIRE DOG POUND. HOW ABOUT YOU SHUT UP?

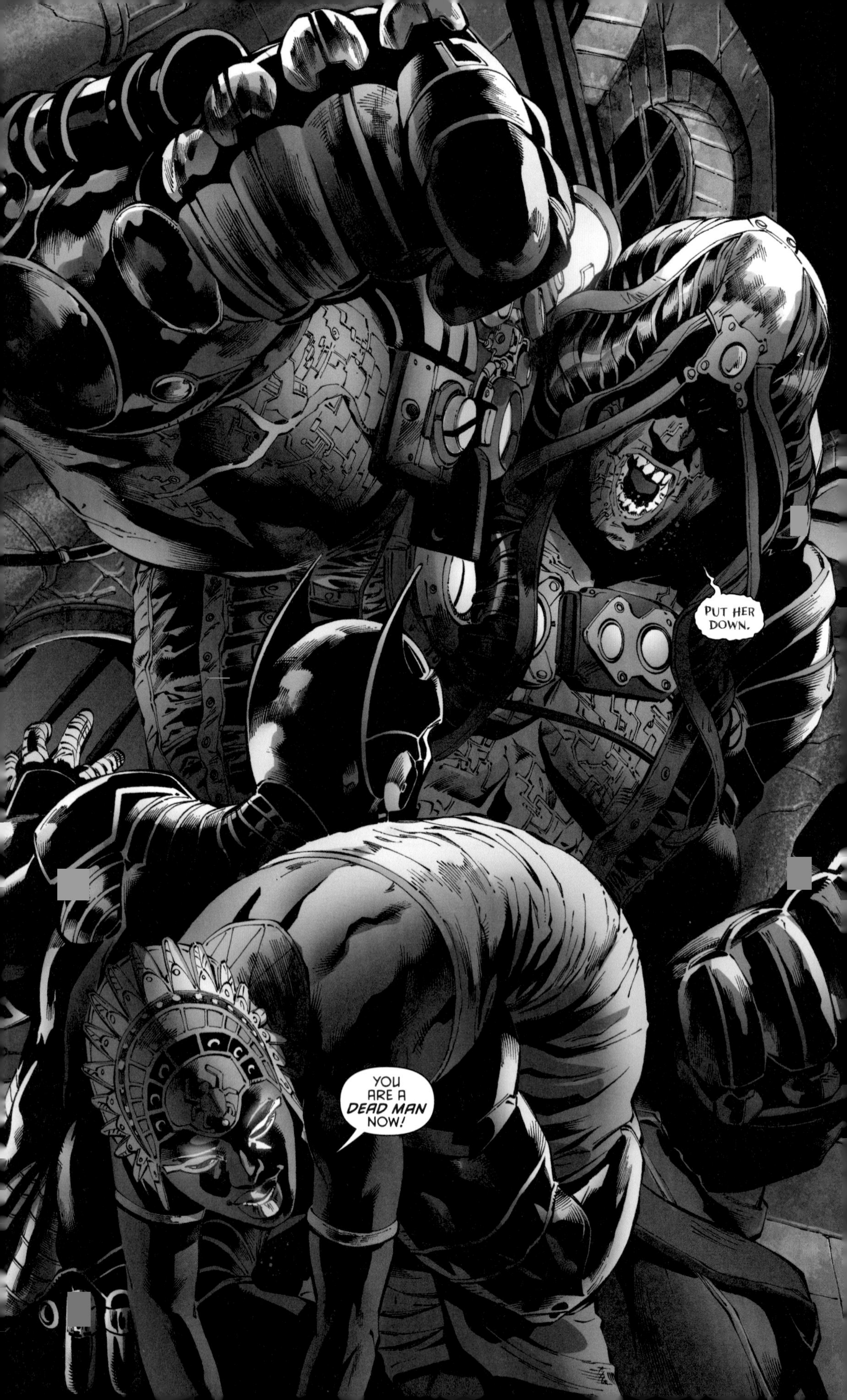
PUT HER DOWN.
YOU ARE A DEAD MAN NOW!

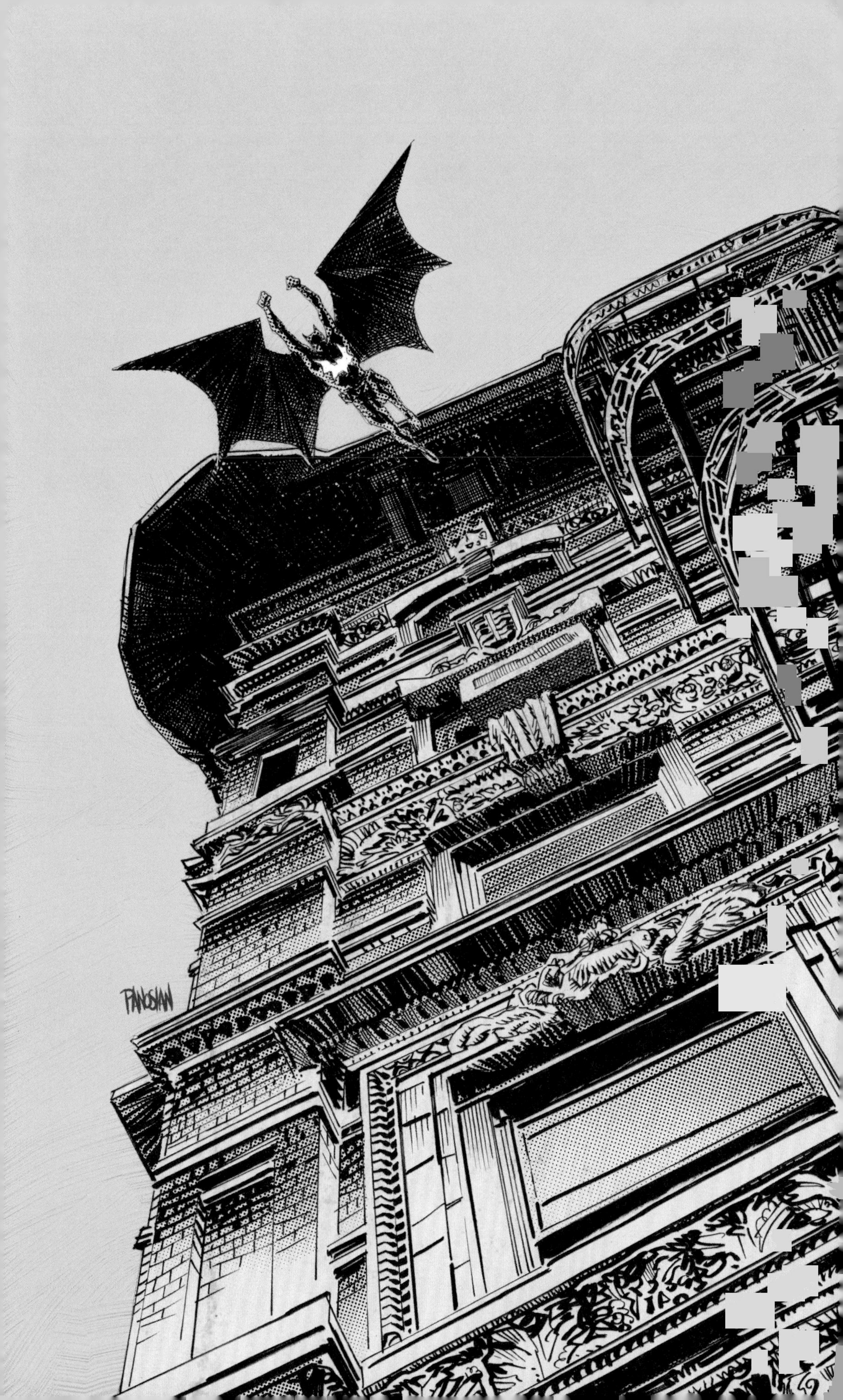
PANOSIAN

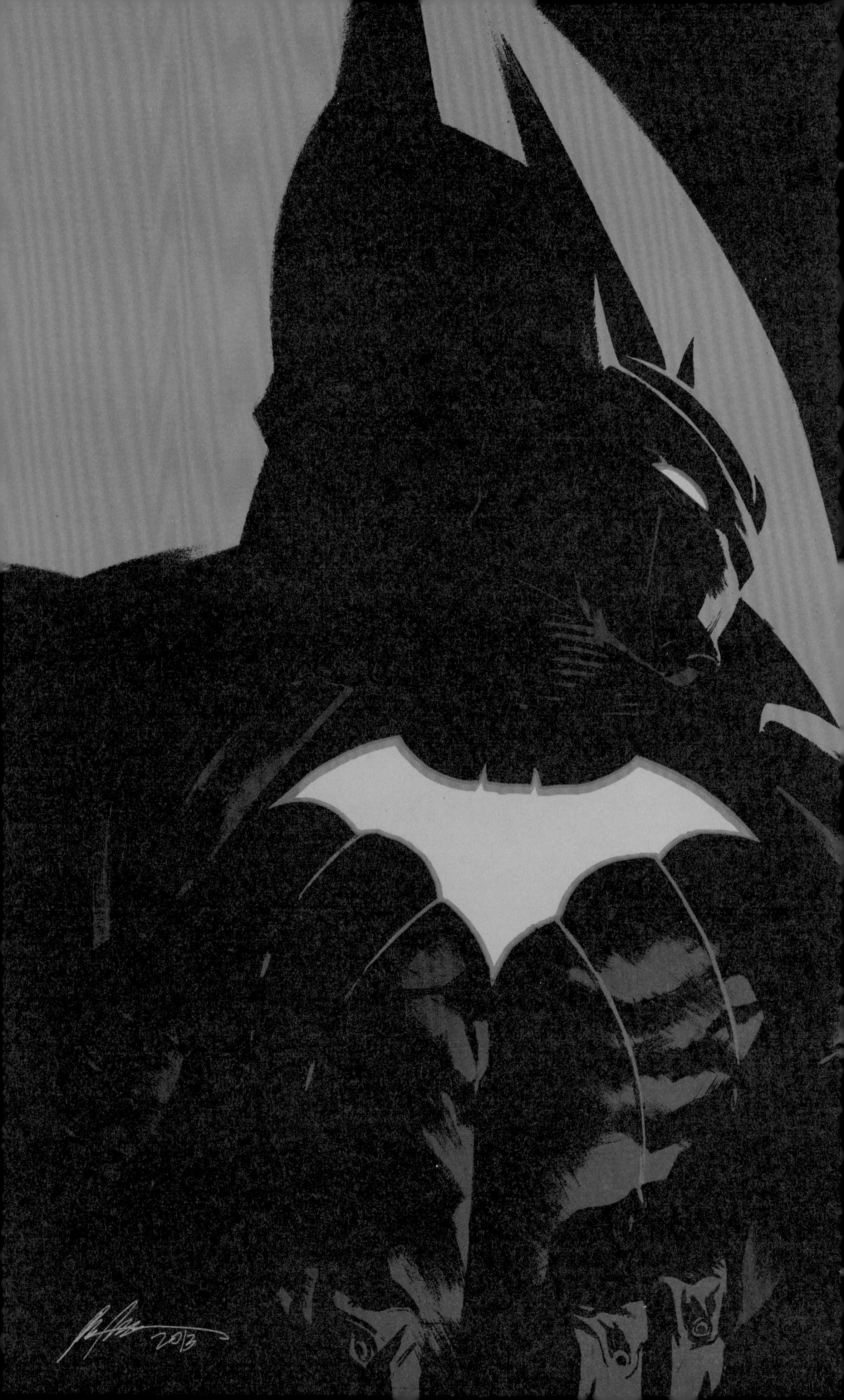

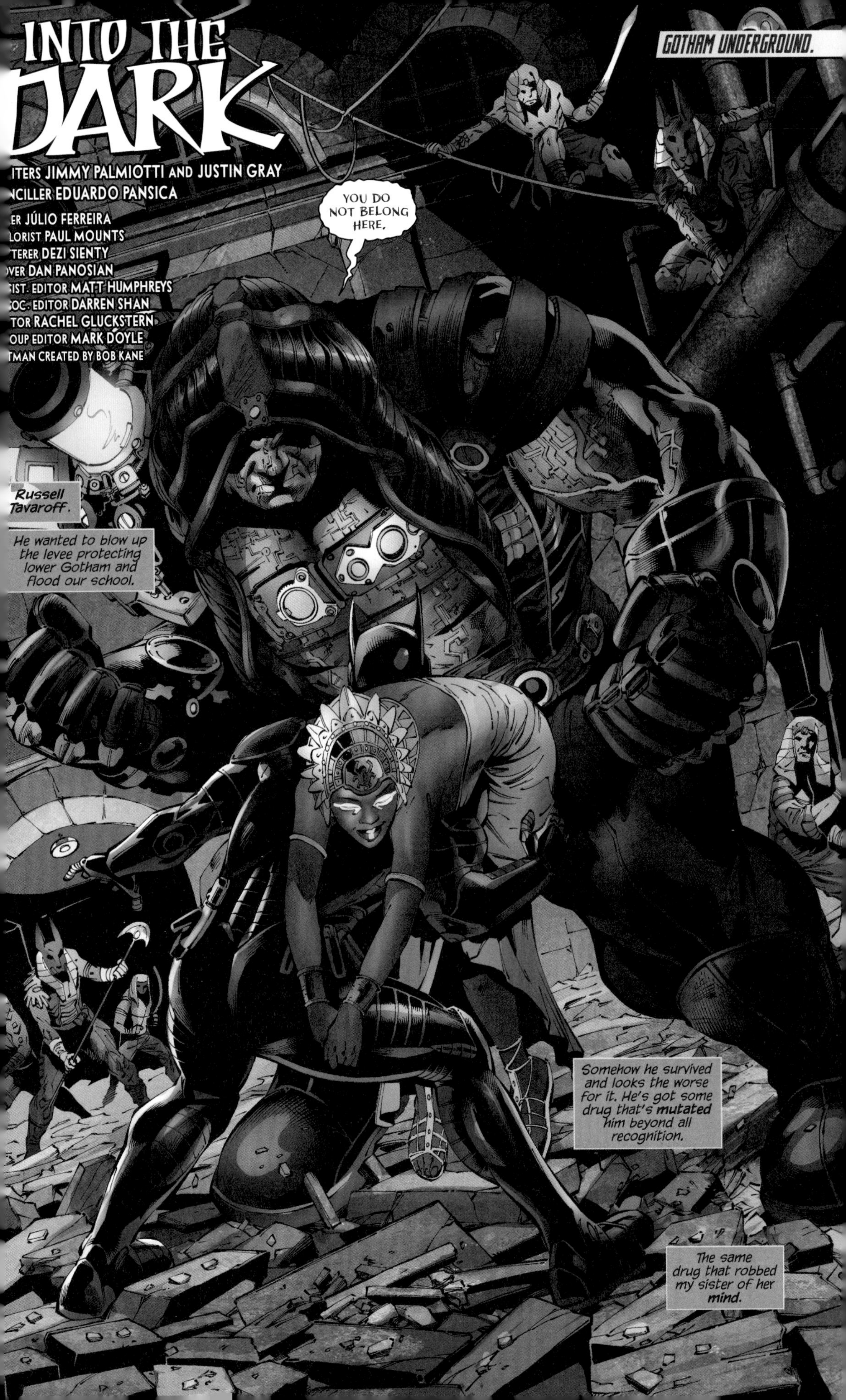
INTO THE DARK
ITERS JIMMY PALMIOTTI AND JUSTIN GRAY
NCILLER EDUARDO PANSICA
ER JÚLIO FERREIRA
LORIST PAUL MOUNTS
TERER DEZI SIENTY
VER DAN PANOSIAN
SIST. EDITOR MATT HUMPHREYS
SOC. EDITOR DARREN SHAN
TOR RACHEL GLUCKSTERN
OUP EDITOR MARK DOYLE
TMAN CREATED BY BOB KANE
GOTHAM UNDERGROUND.
YOU DO NOT BELONG HERE.
Russell Tavaroff.
He wanted to blow up the levee protecting lower Gotham and flood our school.
Somehow he survived and looks the worse for it. He's got some drug that's **mutated** him beyond all recognition.
The same drug that robbed my sister of her **mind**.

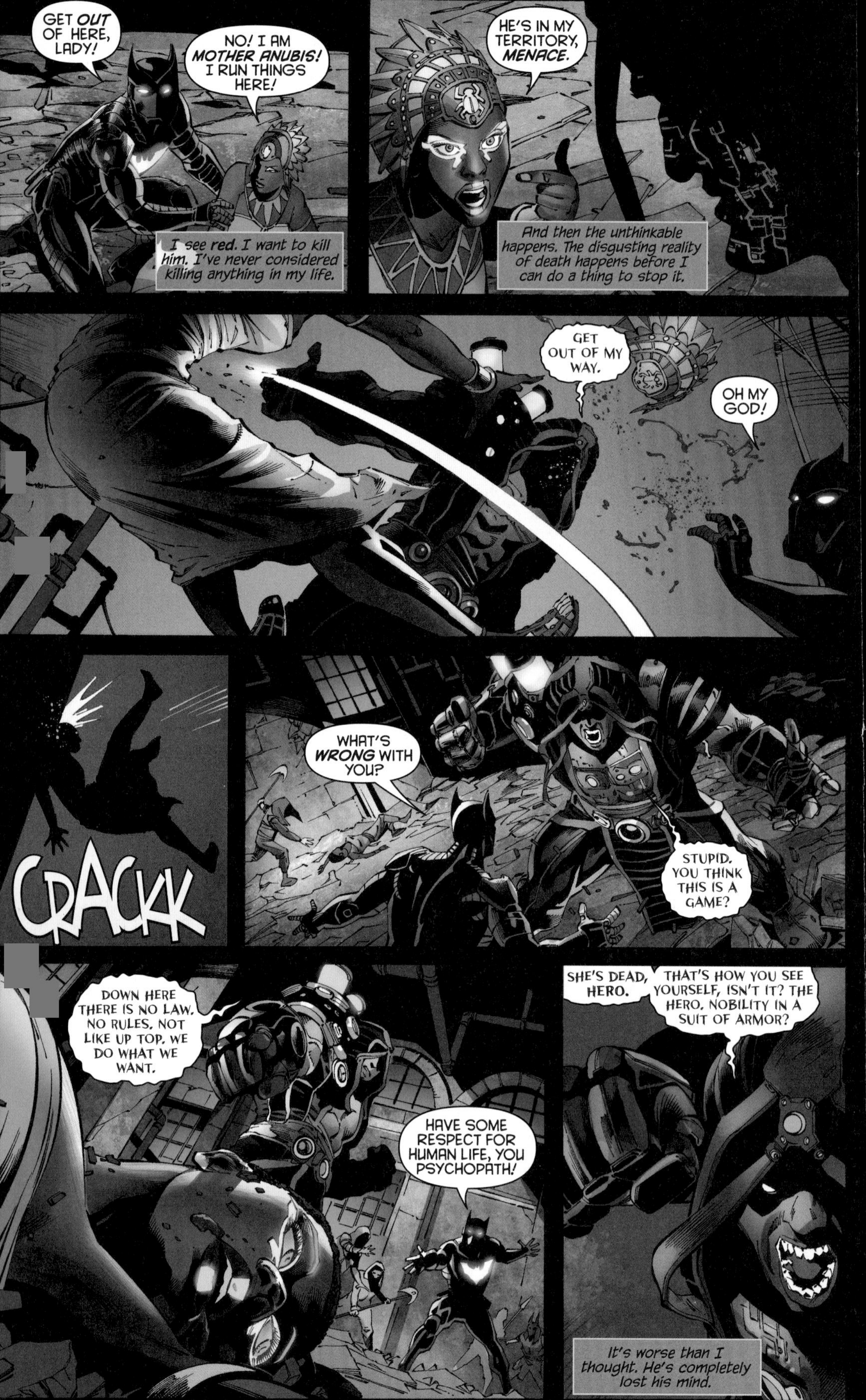
GET OUT OF HERE, LADY!
NO! I AM MOTHER ANUBIS! I RUN THINGS HERE!
I see red. I want to kill him. I've never considered killing anything in my life.
HE'S IN MY TERRITORY, MENACE.
And then the unthinkable happens. The disgusting reality of death happens before I can do a thing to stop it.
GET OUT OF MY WAY.
OH MY GOD!
CRACKK
WHAT'S WRONG WITH YOU?
STUPID. YOU THINK THIS IS A GAME?
DOWN HERE THERE IS NO LAW. NO RULES. NOT LIKE UP TOP. WE DO WHAT WE WANT.
HAVE SOME RESPECT FOR HUMAN LIFE, YOU PSYCHOPATH!
SHE'S DEAD, HERO.
THAT'S HOW YOU SEE YOURSELF, ISN'T IT? THE HERO. NOBILITY IN A SUIT OF ARMOR?
It's worse than I thought. He's completely lost his mind.

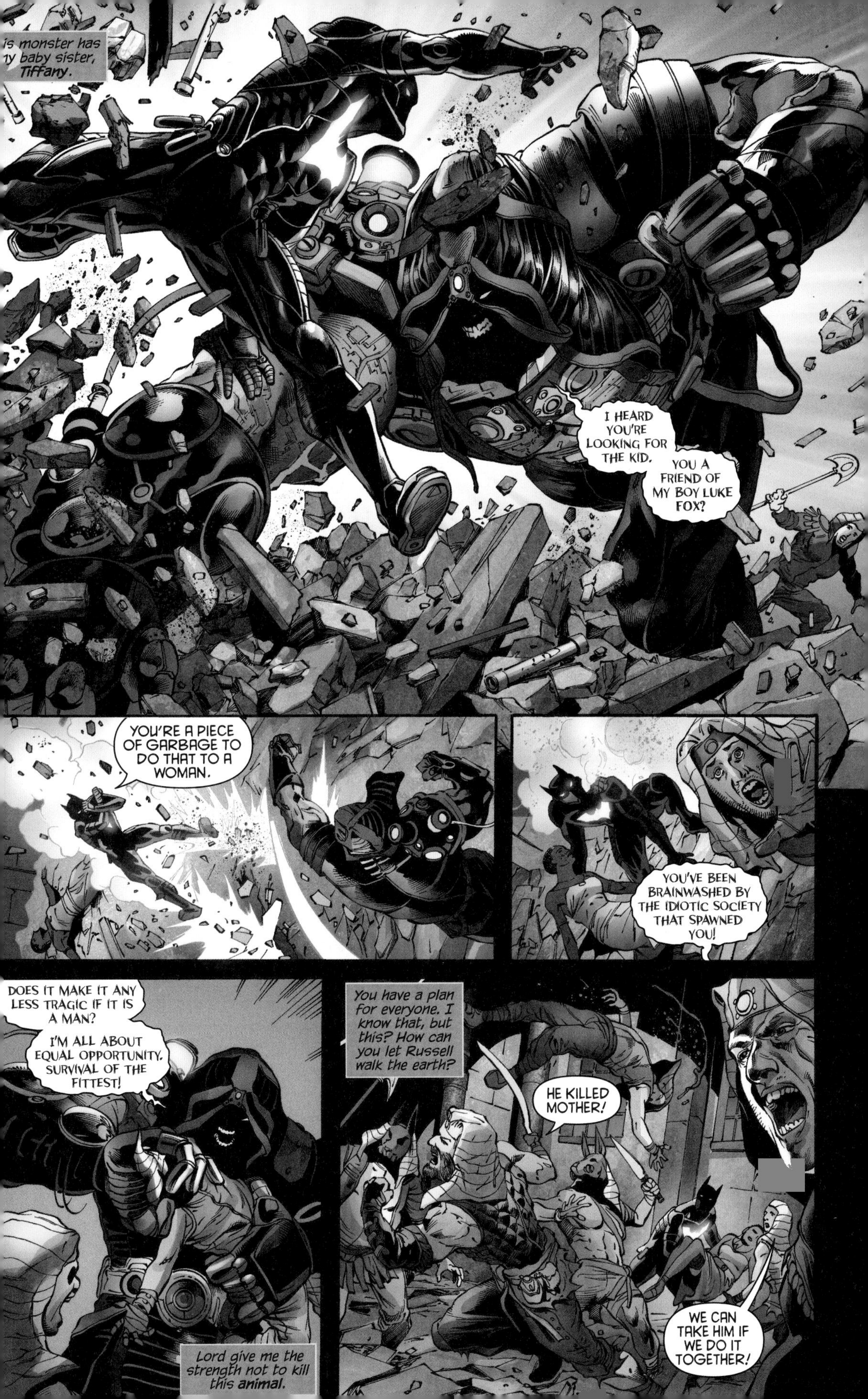
is monster has
ny baby sister,
Tiffany.
I HEARD YOU'RE LOOKING FOR THE KID.
YOU A FRIEND OF MY BOY LUKE FOX?
YOU'RE A PIECE OF GARBAGE TO DO THAT TO A WOMAN.
YOU'VE BEEN BRAINWASHED BY THE IDIOTIC SOCIETY THAT SPAWNED YOU!
DOES IT MAKE IT ANY LESS TRAGIC IF IT IS A MAN?
I'M ALL ABOUT EQUAL OPPORTUNITY. SURVIVAL OF THE FITTEST!
Lord give me the strength not to kill this **animal**.
You have a plan for everyone. I know that, but this? How can you let Russell walk the earth?
HE KILLED MOTHER!
WE CAN TAKE HIM IF WE DO IT TOGETHER!

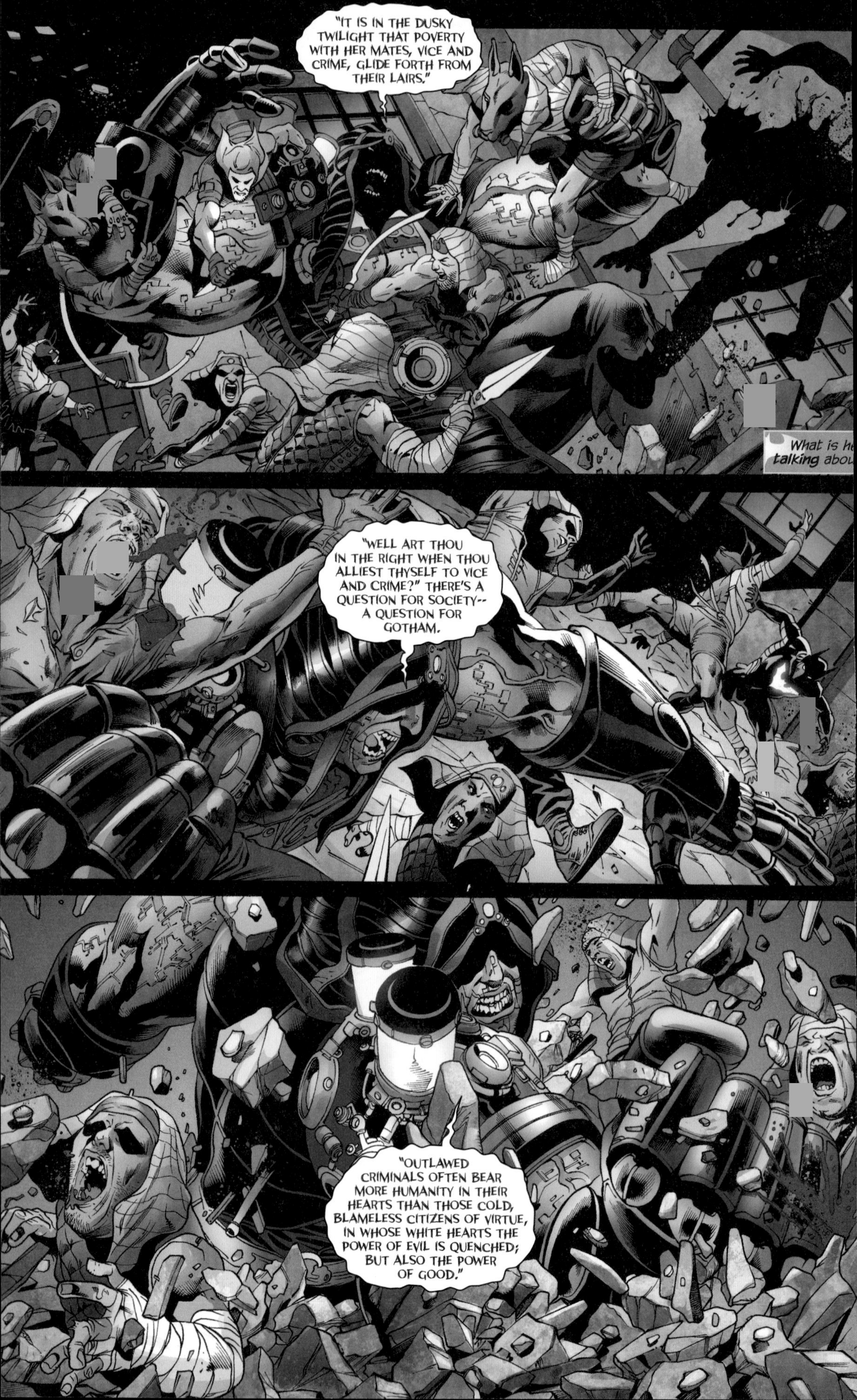
"IT IS IN THE DUSKY TWILIGHT THAT POVERTY WITH HER MATES, VICE AND CRIME, GLIDE FORTH FROM THEIR LAIRS."
What is he talking about
"WELL ART THOU IN THE RIGHT WHEN THOU ALLIEST THYSELF TO VICE AND CRIME?" THERE'S A QUESTION FOR SOCIETY-- A QUESTION FOR GOTHAM.
"OUTLAWED CRIMINALS OFTEN BEAR MORE HUMANITY IN THEIR HEARTS THAN THOSE COLD, BLAMELESS CITIZENS OF VIRTUE, IN WHOSE WHITE HEARTS THE POWER OF EVIL IS QUENCHED; BUT ALSO THE POWER OF GOOD."

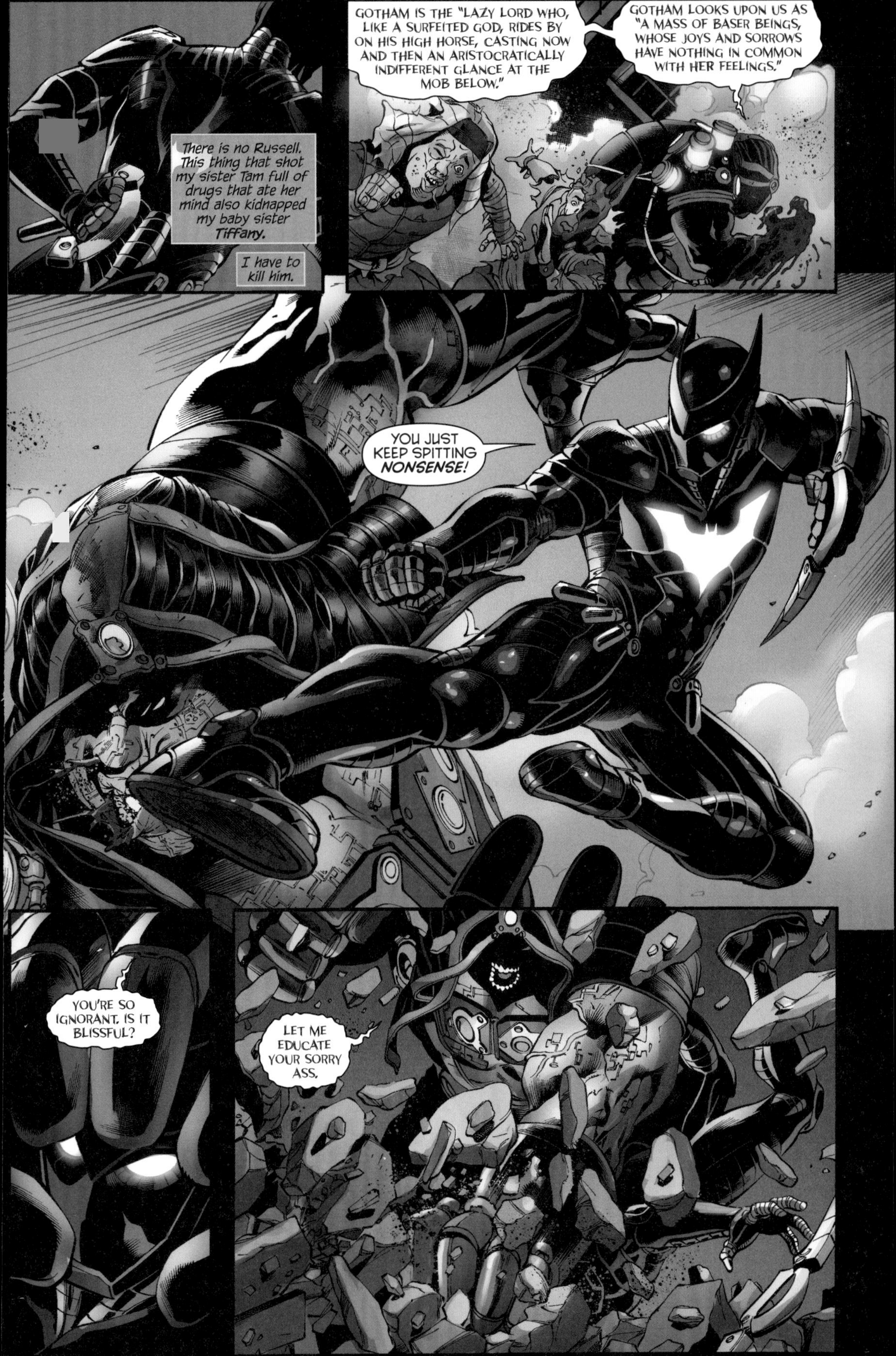
There is no Russell. This thing that shot my sister Tam full of drugs that ate her mind also kidnapped my baby sister Tiffany.
I have to kill him.
GOTHAM IS THE "LAZY LORD WHO, LIKE A SURFEITED GOD, RIDES BY ON HIS HIGH HORSE, CASTING NOW AND THEN AN ARISTOCRATICALLY INDIFFERENT GLANCE AT THE MOB BELOW."
GOTHAM LOOKS UPON US AS "A MASS OF BASER BEINGS, WHOSE JOYS AND SORROWS HAVE NOTHING IN COMMON WITH HER FEELINGS."
YOU JUST KEEP SPITTING NONSENSE!
YOU'RE SO IGNORANT. IS IT BLISSFUL?
LET ME EDUCATE YOUR SORRY ASS.

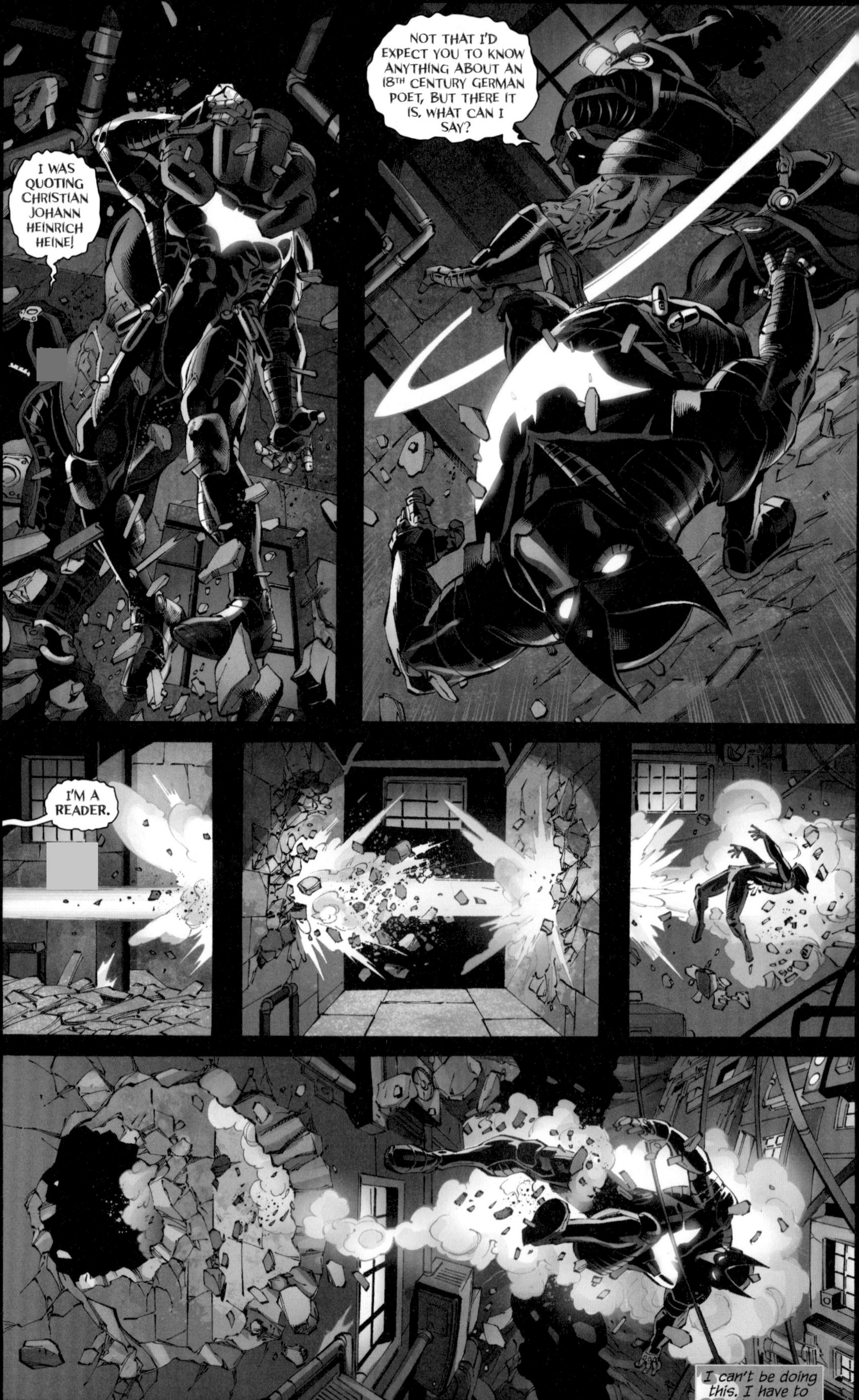
I WAS QUOTING CHRISTIAN JOHANN HEINRICH HEINE!
NOT THAT I'D EXPECT YOU TO KNOW ANYTHING ABOUT AN 18TH CENTURY GERMAN POET, BUT THERE IT IS. WHAT CAN I SAY?
I'M A READER.
I can't be doing this. I have to find Tiffany.

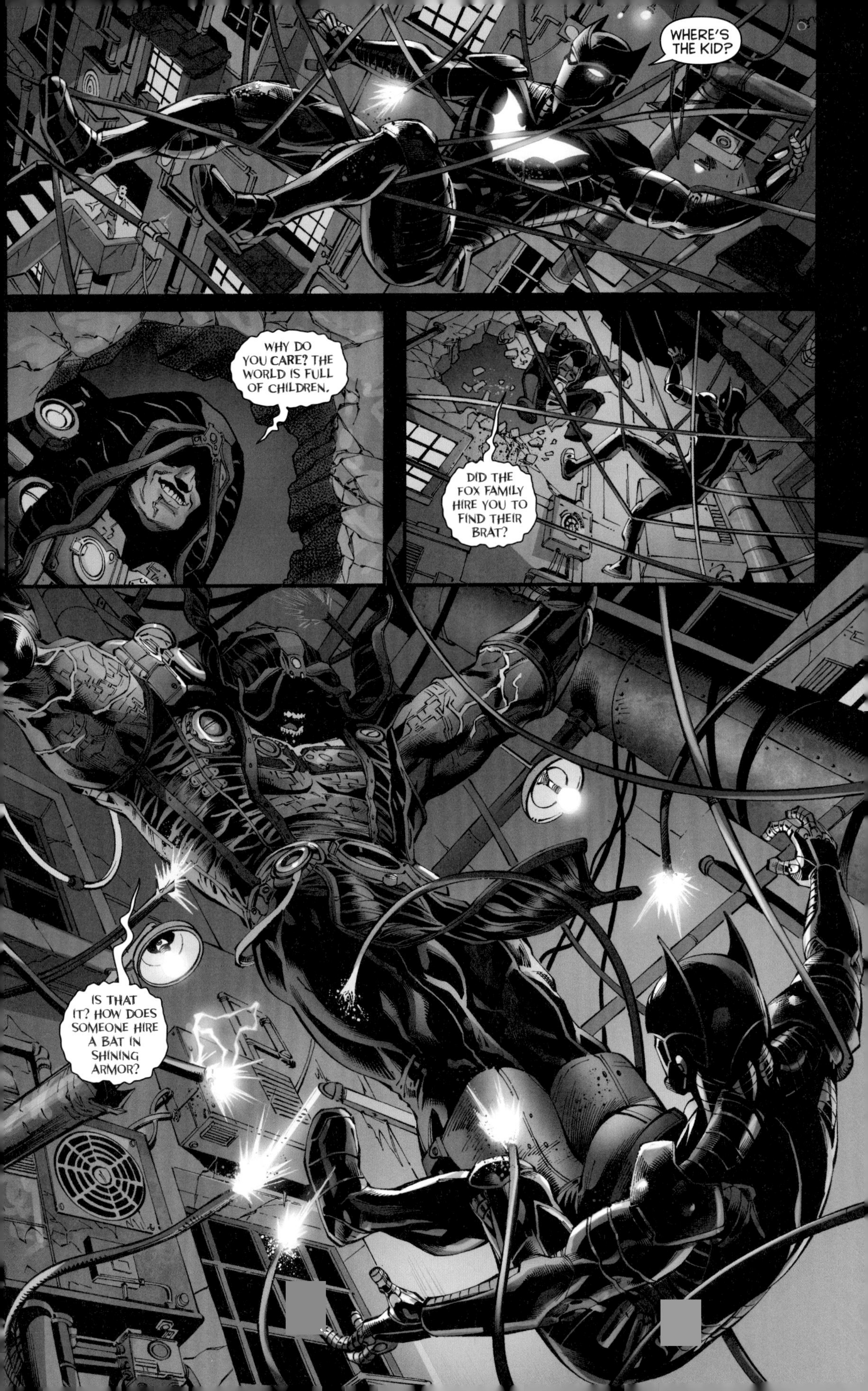
WHERE'S THE KID?
WHY DO YOU CARE? THE WORLD IS FULL OF CHILDREN.
DID THE FOX FAMILY HIRE YOU TO FIND THEIR BRAT?
IS THAT IT? HOW DOES SOMEONE HIRE A BAT IN SHINING ARMOR?

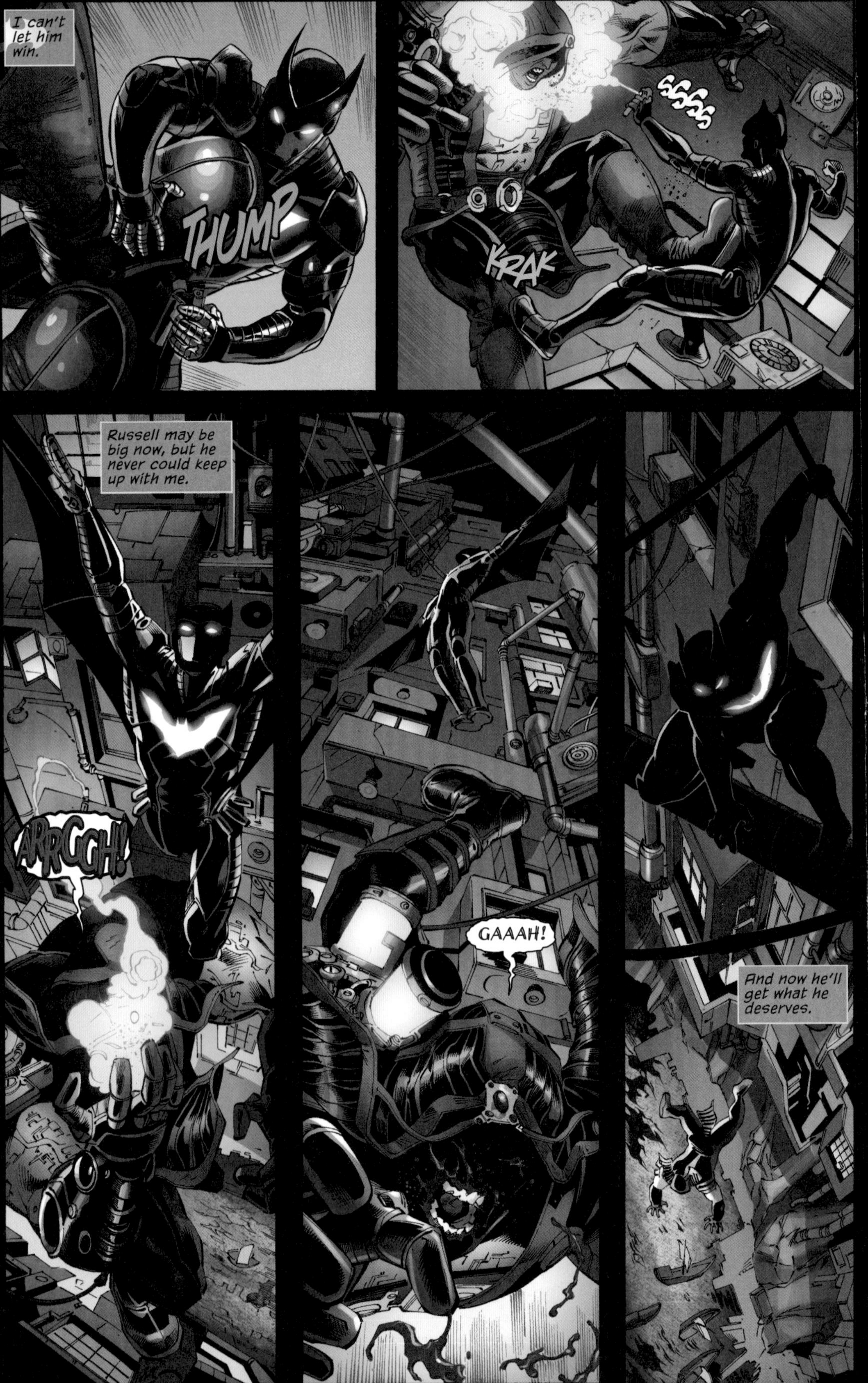

I can't let him win.
THUMP
SSSS
KRAK
Russell may be big now, but he never could keep up with me.
ARRGGH!
GAAAH!
And now he'll get what he deserves.

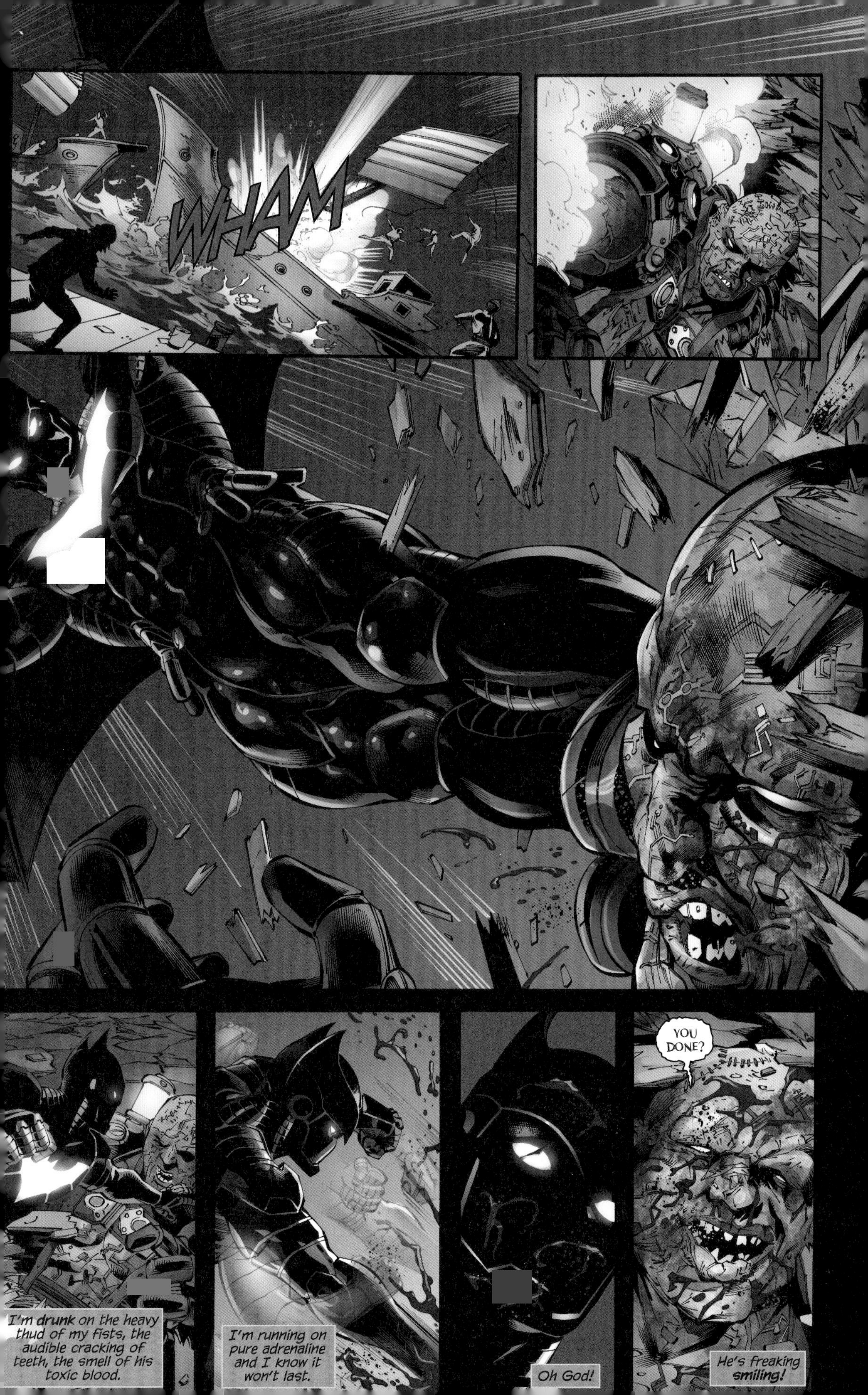
WHAM
I'm drunk on the heavy thud of my fists, the audible cracking of teeth, the smell of his toxic blood.
I'm running on pure adrenaline and I know it won't last.
Oh God!
YOU DONE?
He's freaking smiling!

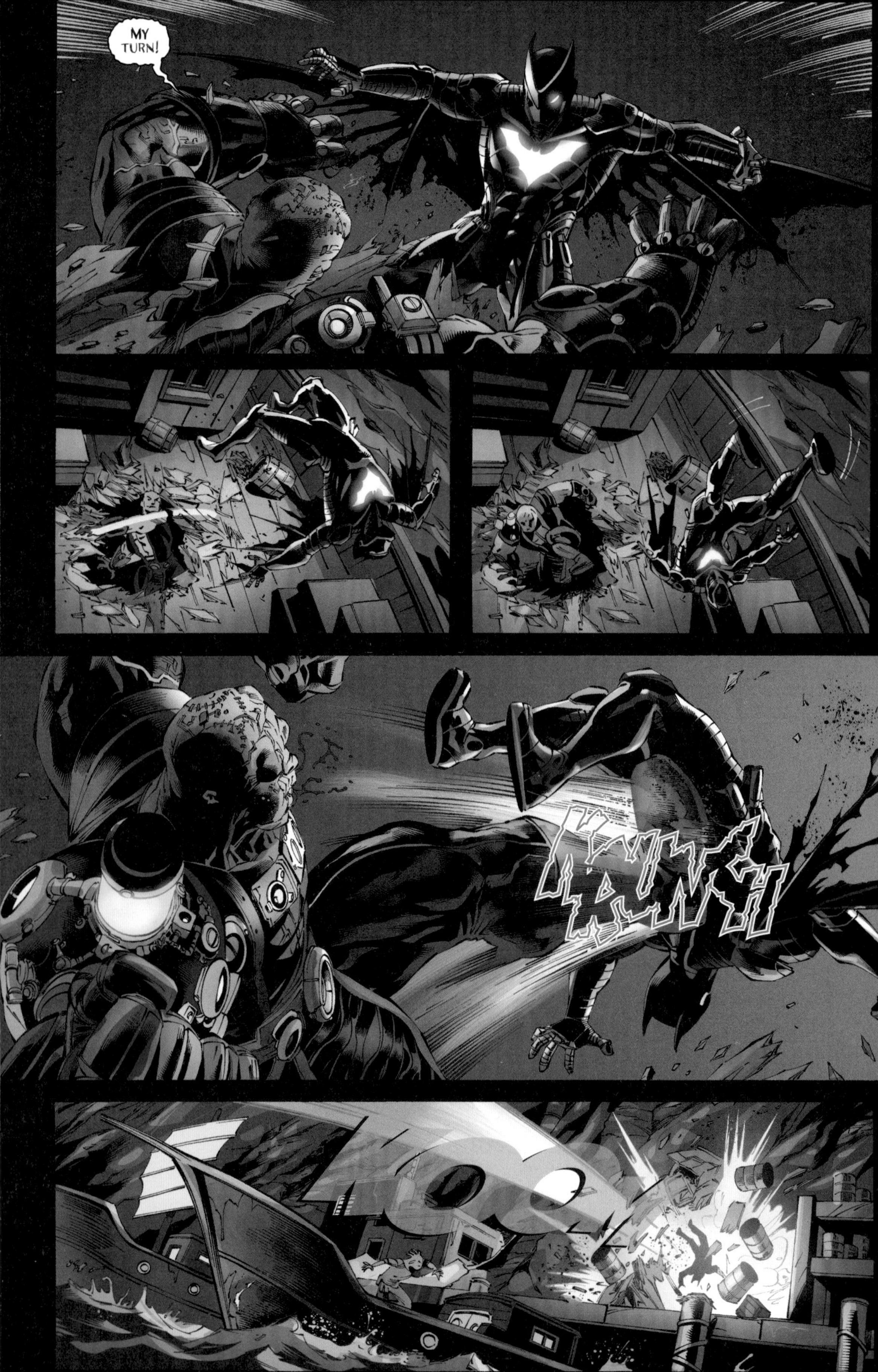
MY TURN!
KRUNCH

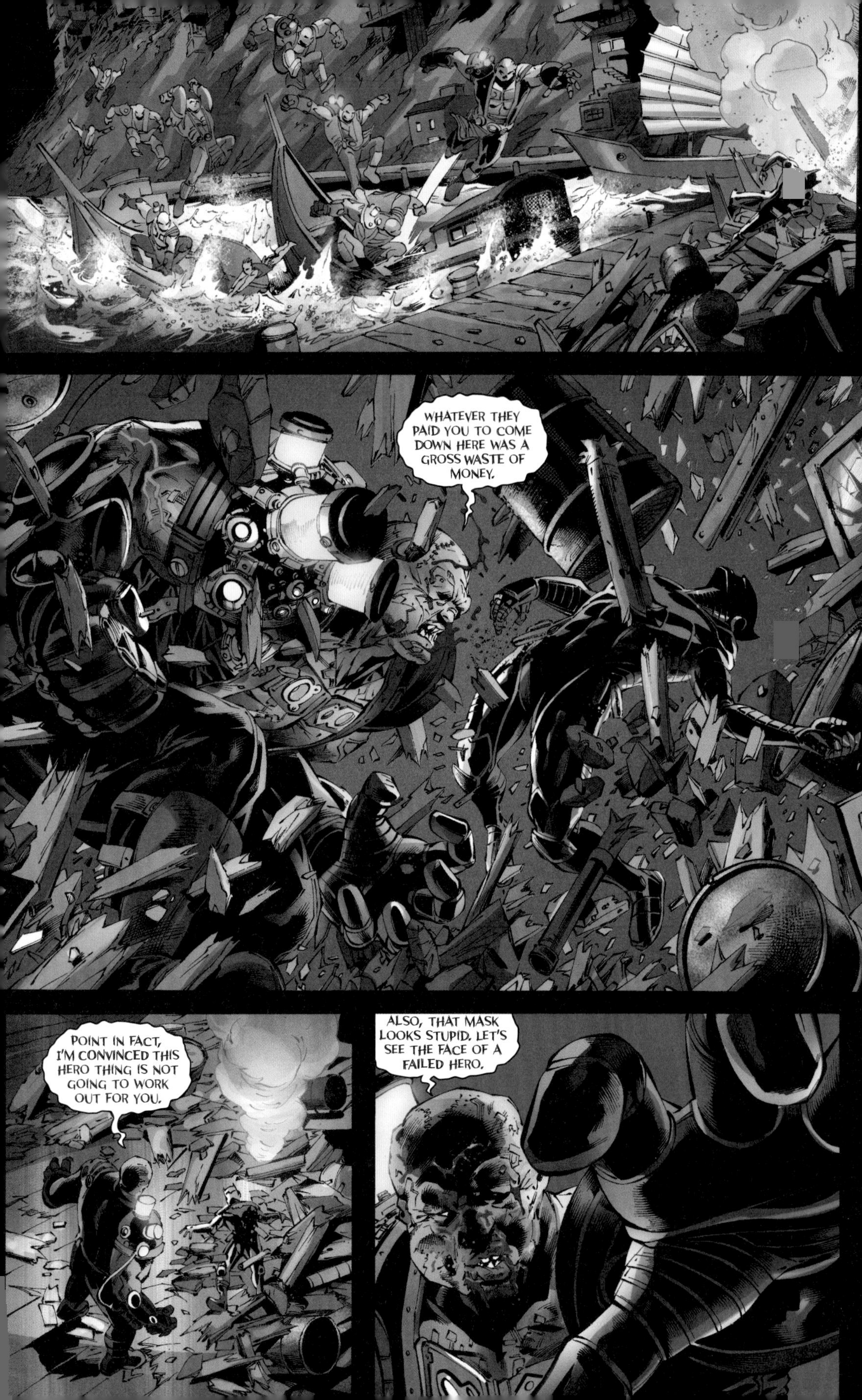
WHATEVER THEY PAID YOU TO COME DOWN HERE WAS A GROSS WASTE OF MONEY.
POINT IN FACT, I'M CONVINCED THIS HERO THING IS NOT GOING TO WORK OUT FOR YOU.
ALSO, THAT MASK LOOKS STUPID. LET'S SEE THE FACE OF A FAILED HERO.

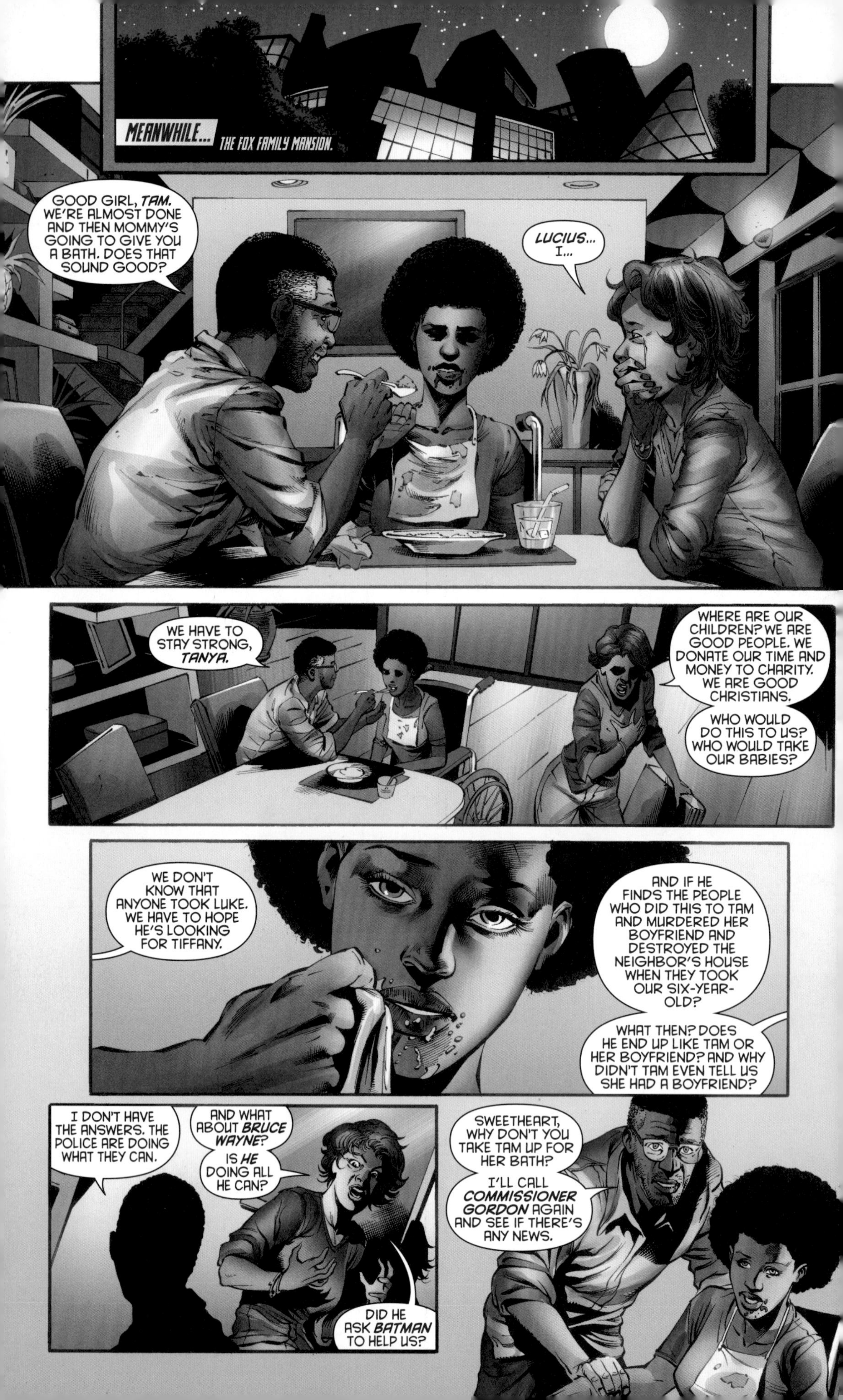

MEANWHILE... THE FOX FAMILY MANSION.
GOOD GIRL, TAM. WE'RE ALMOST DONE AND THEN MOMMY'S GOING TO GIVE YOU A BATH. DOES THAT SOUND GOOD?
LUCIUS... I...
WE HAVE TO STAY STRONG, TANYA.
WHERE ARE OUR CHILDREN? WE ARE GOOD PEOPLE. WE DONATE OUR TIME AND MONEY TO CHARITY. WE ARE GOOD CHRISTIANS.
WHO WOULD DO THIS TO US? WHO WOULD TAKE OUR BABIES?
WE DON'T KNOW THAT ANYONE TOOK LUKE. WE HAVE TO HOPE HE'S LOOKING FOR TIFFANY.
AND IF HE FINDS THE PEOPLE WHO DID THIS TO TAM AND MURDERED HER BOYFRIEND AND DESTROYED THE NEIGHBOR'S HOUSE WHEN THEY TOOK OUR SIX-YEAR-OLD?
WHAT THEN? DOES HE END UP LIKE TAM OR HER BOYFRIEND? AND WHY DIDN'T TAM EVEN TELL US SHE HAD A BOYFRIEND?
I DON'T HAVE THE ANSWERS. THE POLICE ARE DOING WHAT THEY CAN.
AND WHAT ABOUT BRUCE WAYNE?
IS HE DOING ALL HE CAN?
DID HE ASK BATMAN TO HELP US?
SWEETHEART, WHY DON'T YOU TAKE TAM UP FOR HER BATH?
I'LL CALL COMMISSIONER GORDON AGAIN AND SEE IF THERE'S ANY NEWS.

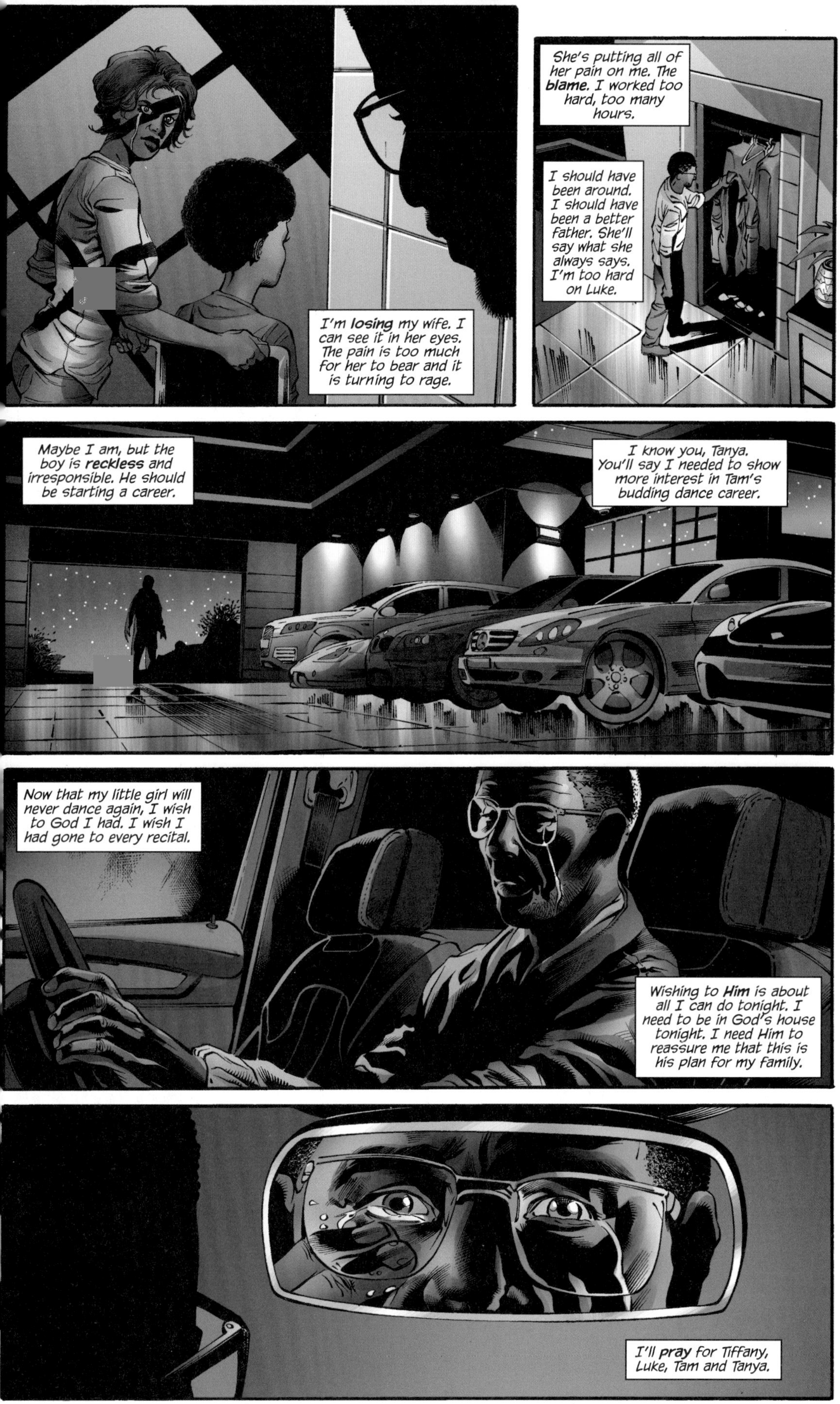
I'm **losing** my wife. I can see it in her eyes. The pain is too much for her to bear and it is turning to rage.
She's putting all of her pain on me. The **blame.** I worked too hard, too many hours.
I should have been around. I should have been a better father. She'll say what she always says. I'm too hard on Luke.
Maybe I am, but the boy is **reckless** and irresponsible. He should be starting a career.
I know you, Tanya. You'll say I needed to show more interest in Tam's budding dance career.
Now that my little girl will never dance again, I wish to God I had. I wish I had gone to every recital.
Wishing to **Him** is about all I can do tonight. I need to be in God's house tonight. I need Him to reassure me that this is his plan for my family.
I'll **pray** for Tiffany, Luke, Tam and Tanya.

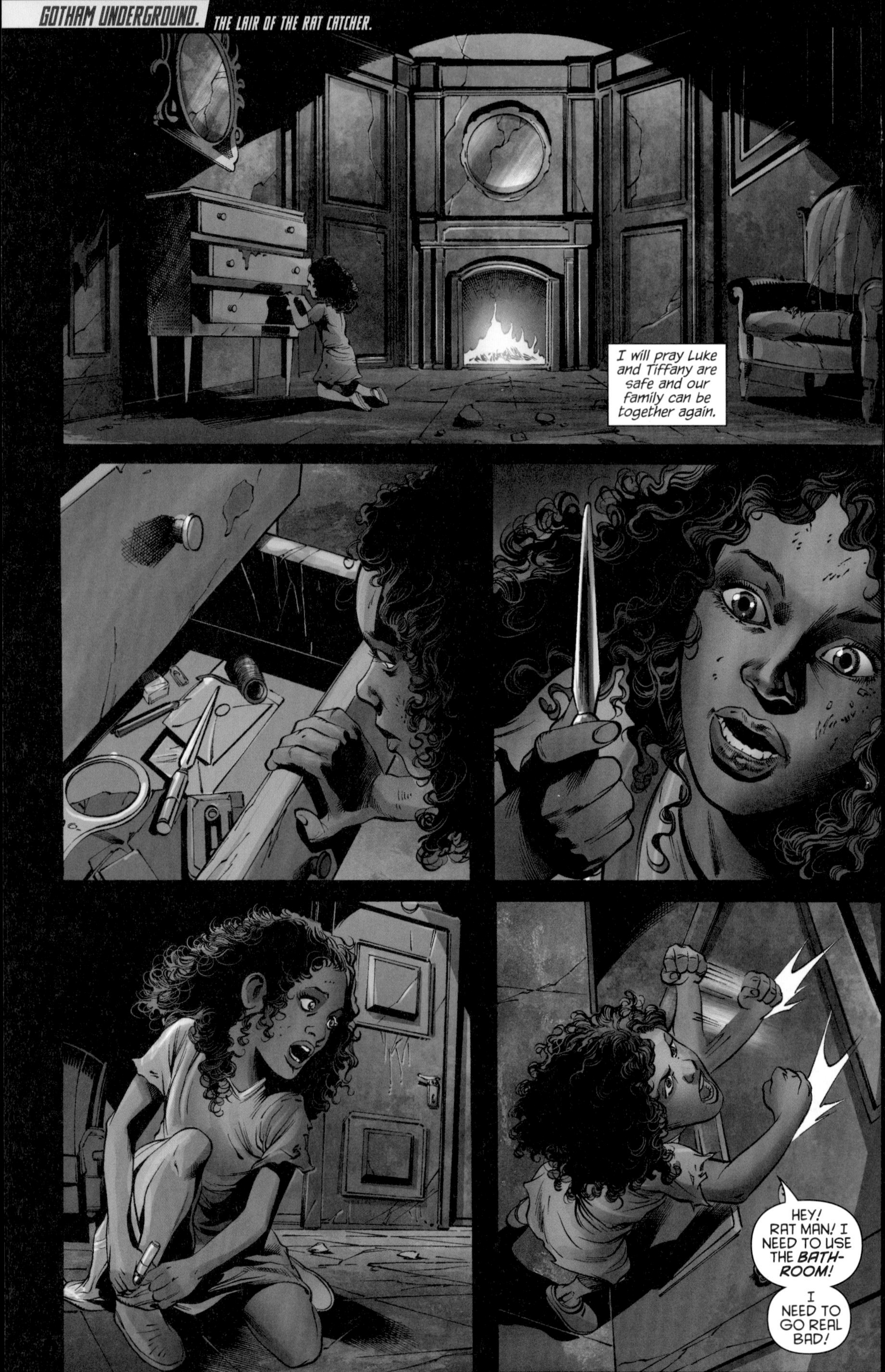
GOTHAM UNDERGROUND.
THE LAIR OF THE RAT CATCHER.
I will pray Luke and Tiffany are safe and our family can be together again.
HEY! RAT MAN! I NEED TO USE THE BATH-ROOM!
I NEED TO GO REAL BAD!

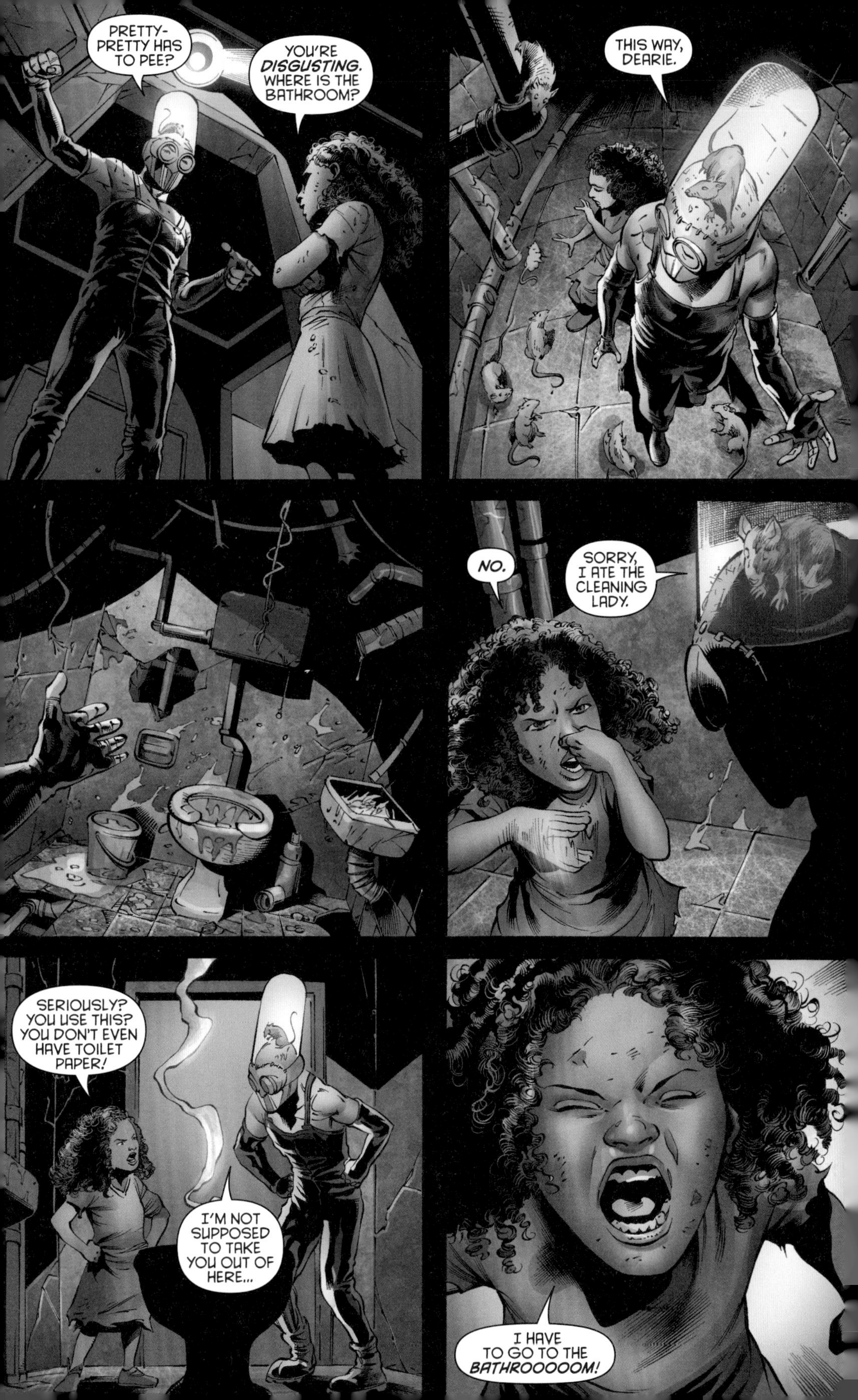
PRETTY-PRETTY HAS TO PEE?
YOU'RE DISGUSTING. WHERE IS THE BATHROOM?
THIS WAY, DEARIE.
NO.
SORRY, I ATE THE CLEANING LADY.
SERIOUSLY? YOU USE THIS? YOU DON'T EVEN HAVE TOILET PAPER!
I'M NOT SUPPOSED TO TAKE YOU OUT OF HERE...
I HAVE TO GO TO THE BATHROOOOOM!

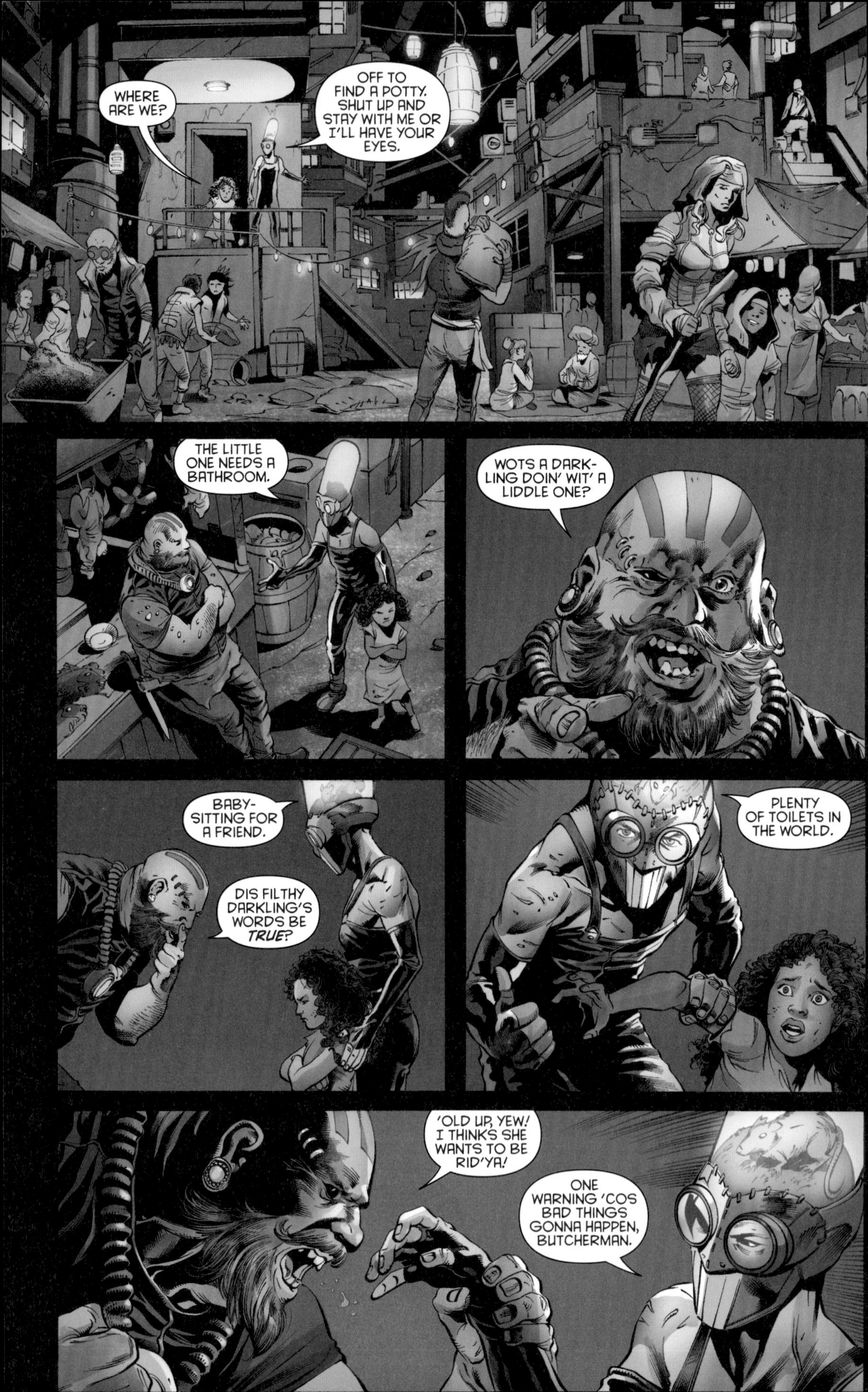
WHERE ARE WE?
OFF TO FIND A POTTY. SHUT UP AND STAY WITH ME OR I'LL HAVE YOUR EYES.
THE LITTLE ONE NEEDS A BATHROOM.
WOTS A DARK-LING DOIN' WIT' A LIDDLE ONE?
BABY-SITTING FOR A FRIEND.
DIS FILTHY DARKLING'S WORDS BE *TRUE*?
PLENTY OF TOILETS IN THE WORLD.
'OLD UP, YEW! I THINKS SHE WANTS TO BE RID'YA!
ONE WARNING 'COS BAD THINGS GONNA HAPPEN, BUTCHERMAN.

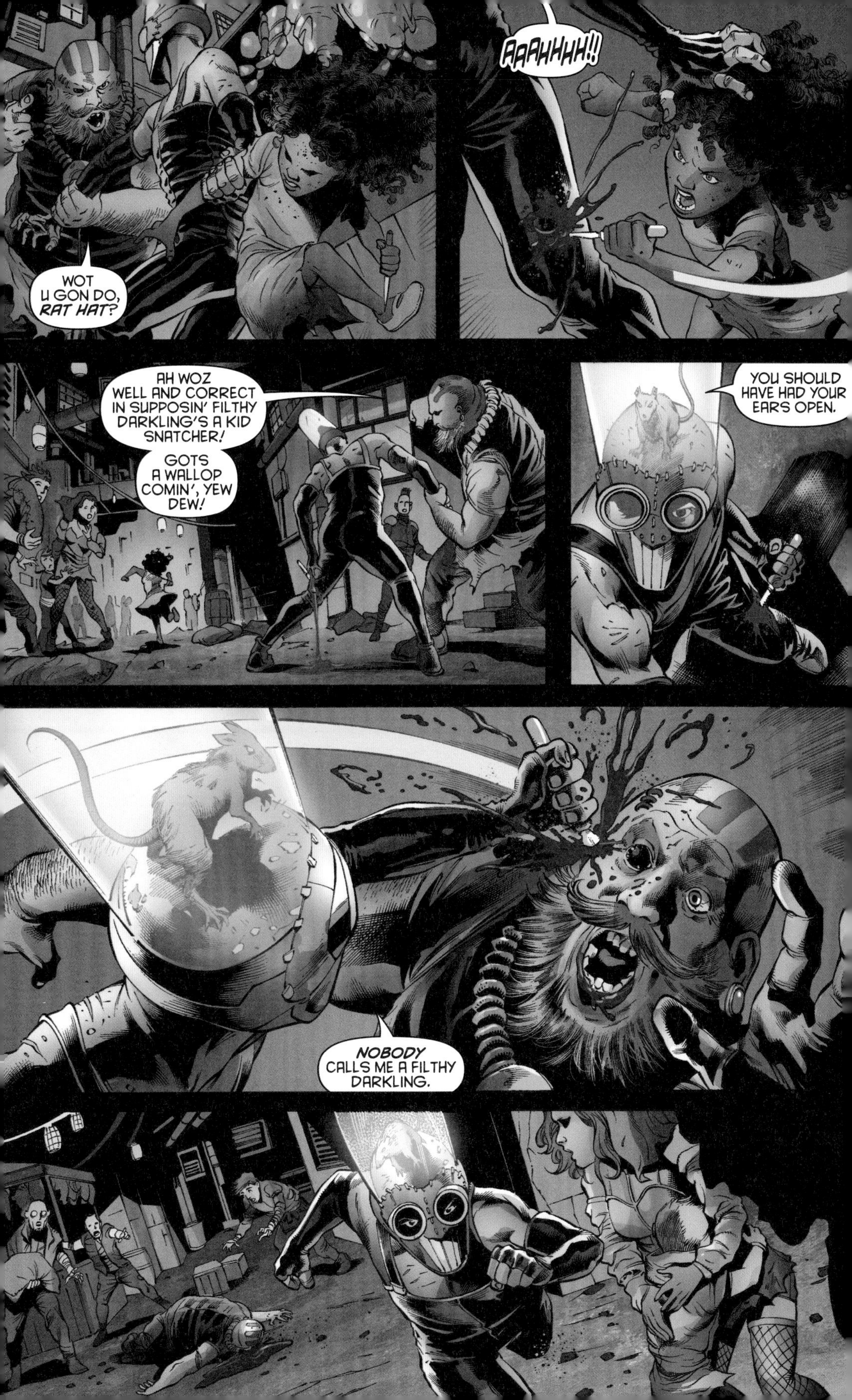
WOT U GON DO, *RAT HAT?*
AAAHHHH!!
AH WOZ WELL AND CORRECT IN SUPPOSIN' FILTHY DARKLING'S A KID SNATCHER!
GOTS A WALLOP COMIN', YEW DEW!
YOU SHOULD HAVE HAD YOUR EARS OPEN.
NOBODY CALLS ME A FILTHY DARKLING.

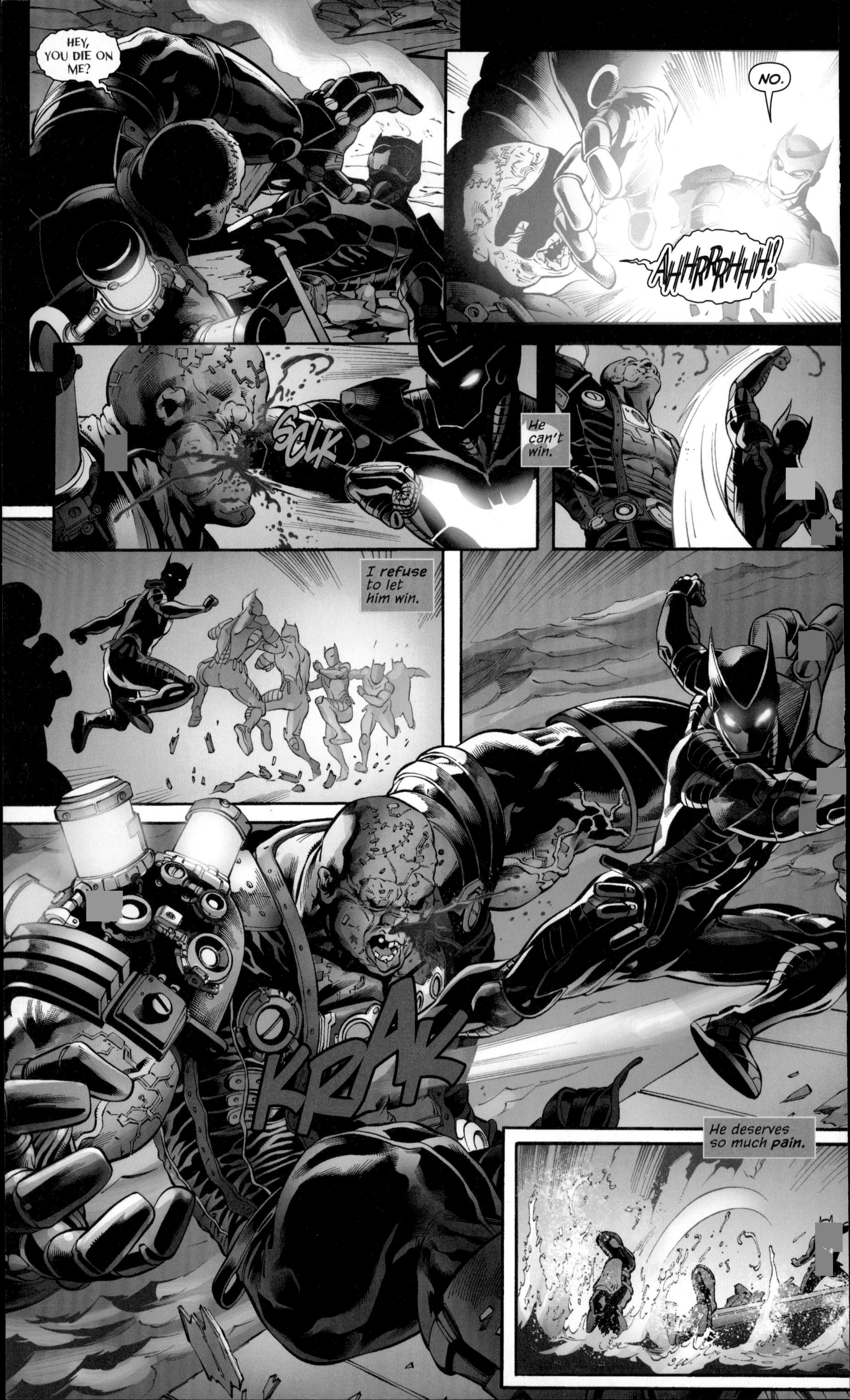

HEY, YOU DIE ON ME?
NO.
AHHRRRHHH!
SCLK
He can't win.
I refuse to let him win.
KRAK
He deserves so much pain.

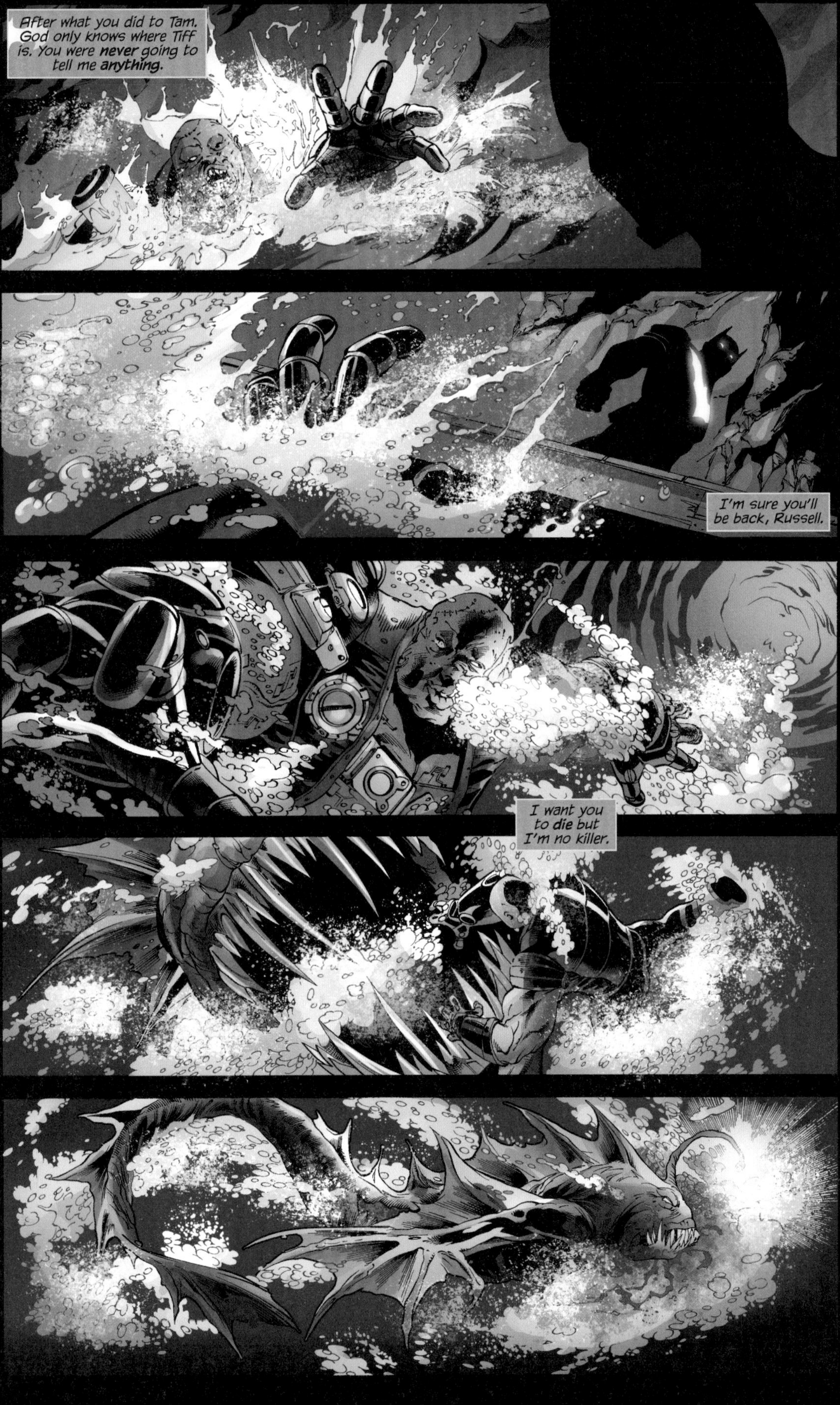
After what you did to Tam. God only knows where Tiff is. You were **never** going to tell me **anything**.
I'm sure you'll be back, Russell.
I want you to **die** but I'm no killer.

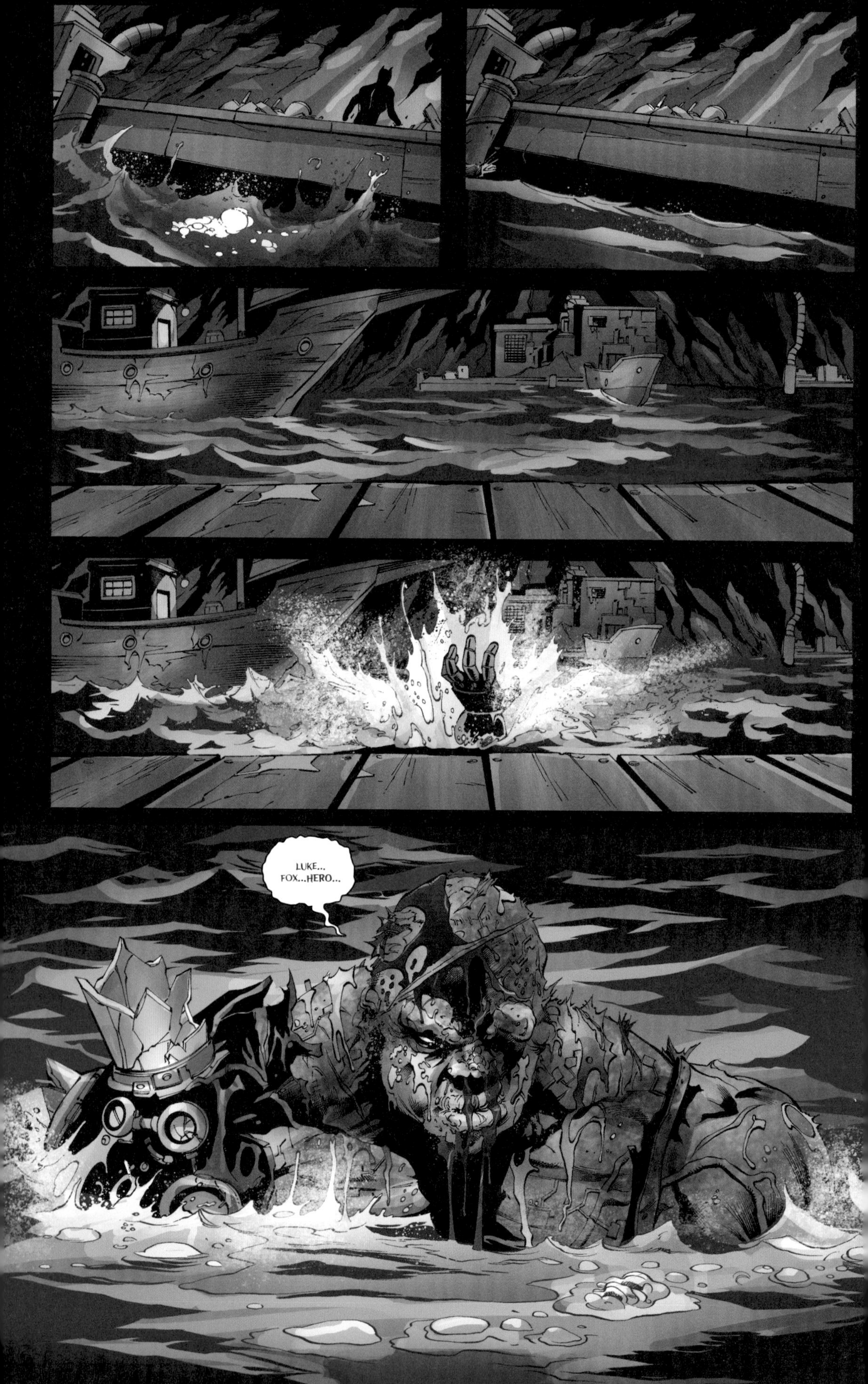
LUKE...
FOX...HERO...

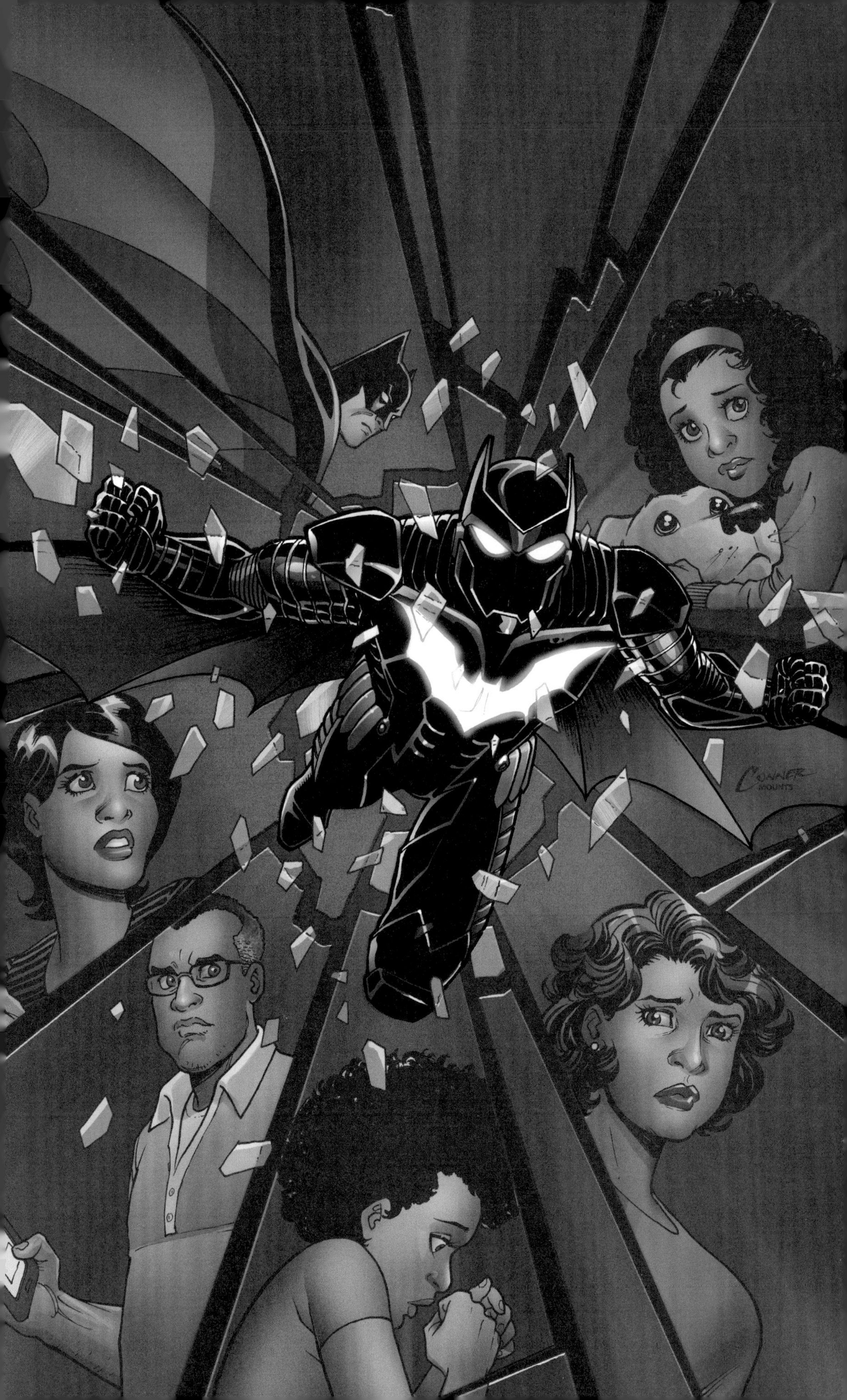
CONNER
MOUNTS

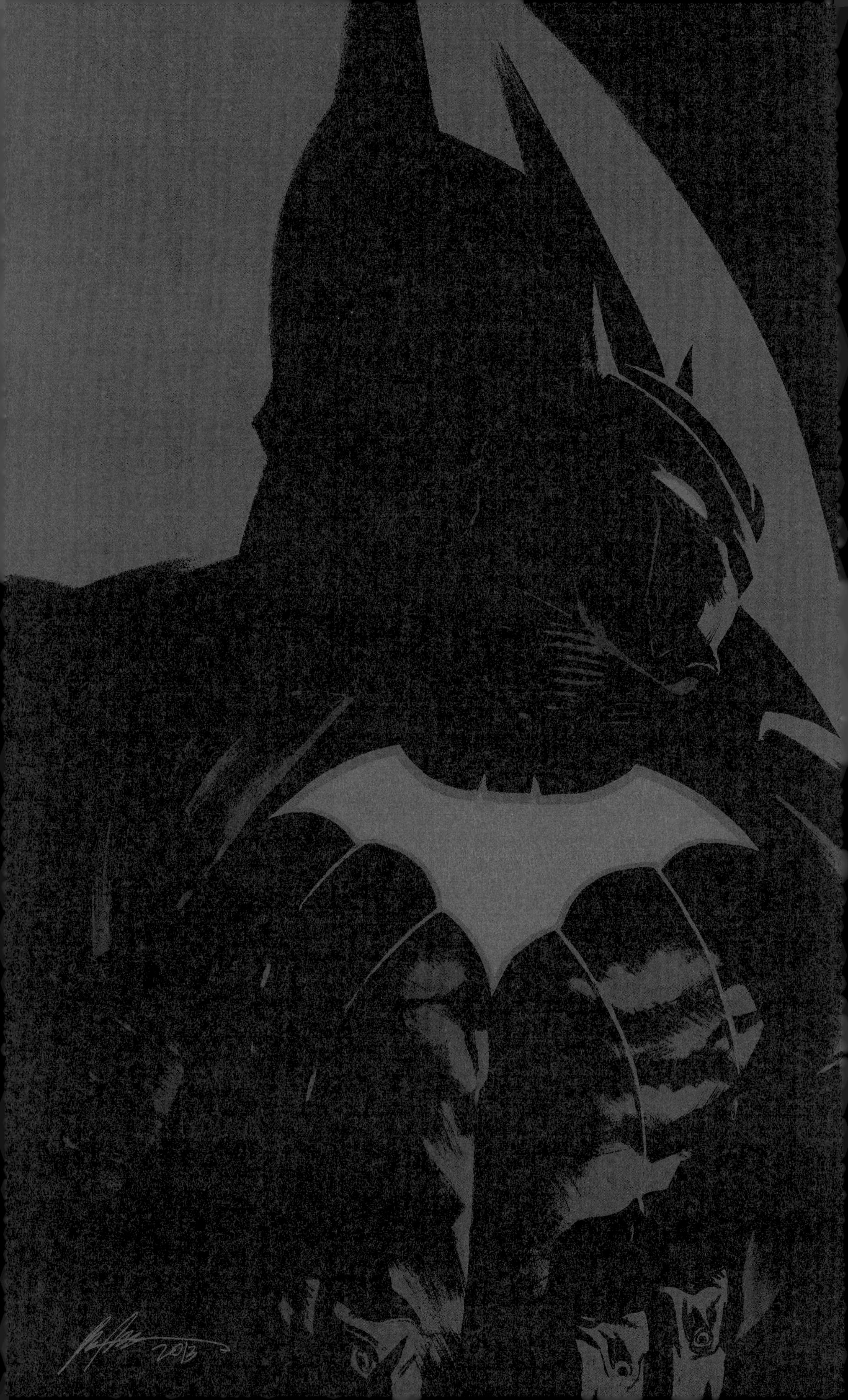
2013

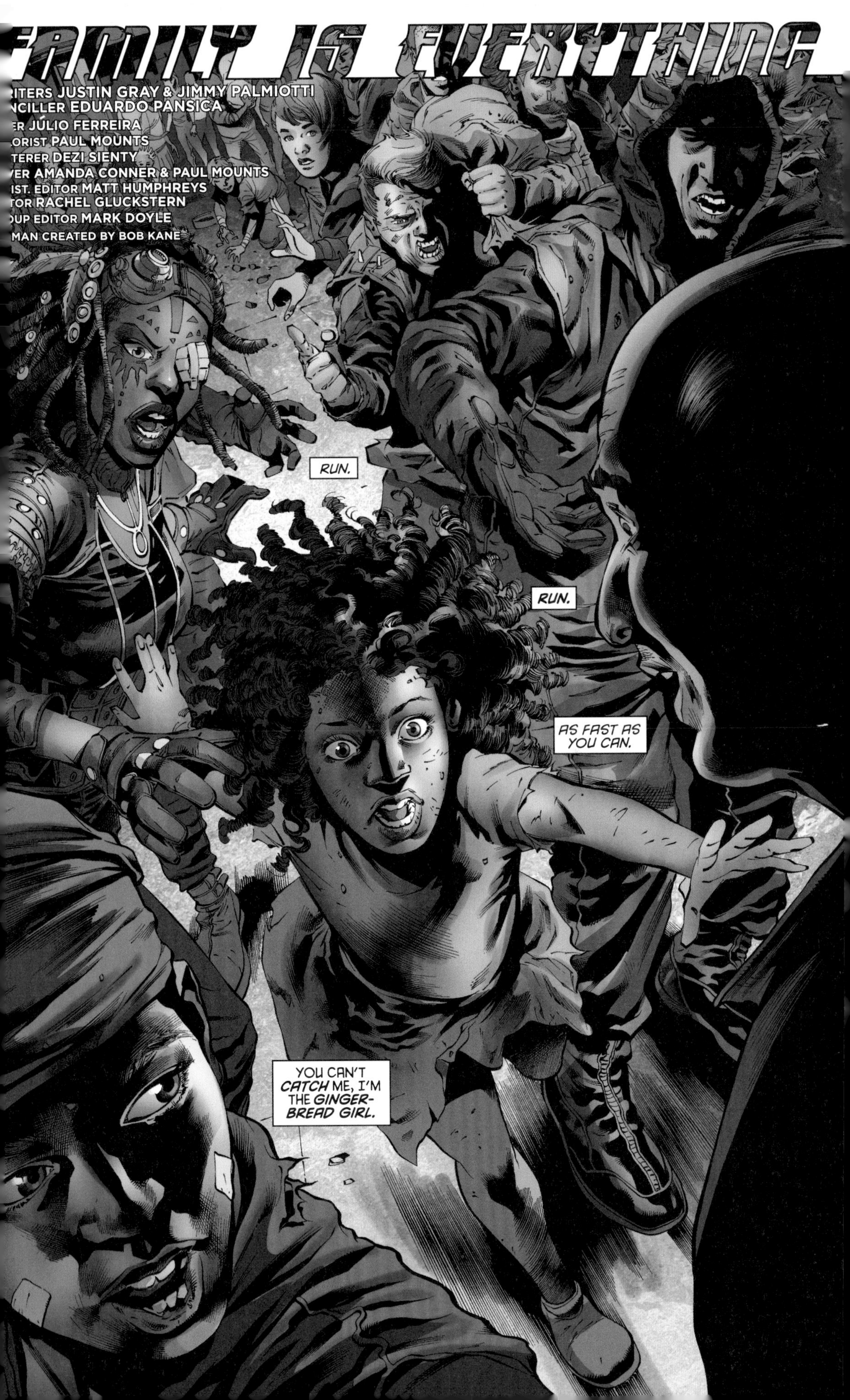
FAMILY IS EVERYTHING
RITERS JUSTIN GRAY & JIMMY PALMIOTTI
NCILLER EDUARDO PANSICA
ER JÚLIO FERREIRA
ORIST PAUL MOUNTS
TERER DEZI SIENTY
VER AMANDA CONNER & PAUL MOUNTS
IST. EDITOR MATT HUMPHREYS
TOR RACHEL GLUCKSTERN
OUP EDITOR MARK DOYLE
MAN CREATED BY BOB KANE
RUN.
RUN.
AS FAST AS YOU CAN.
YOU CAN'T CATCH ME, I'M THE GINGER-BREAD GIRL.

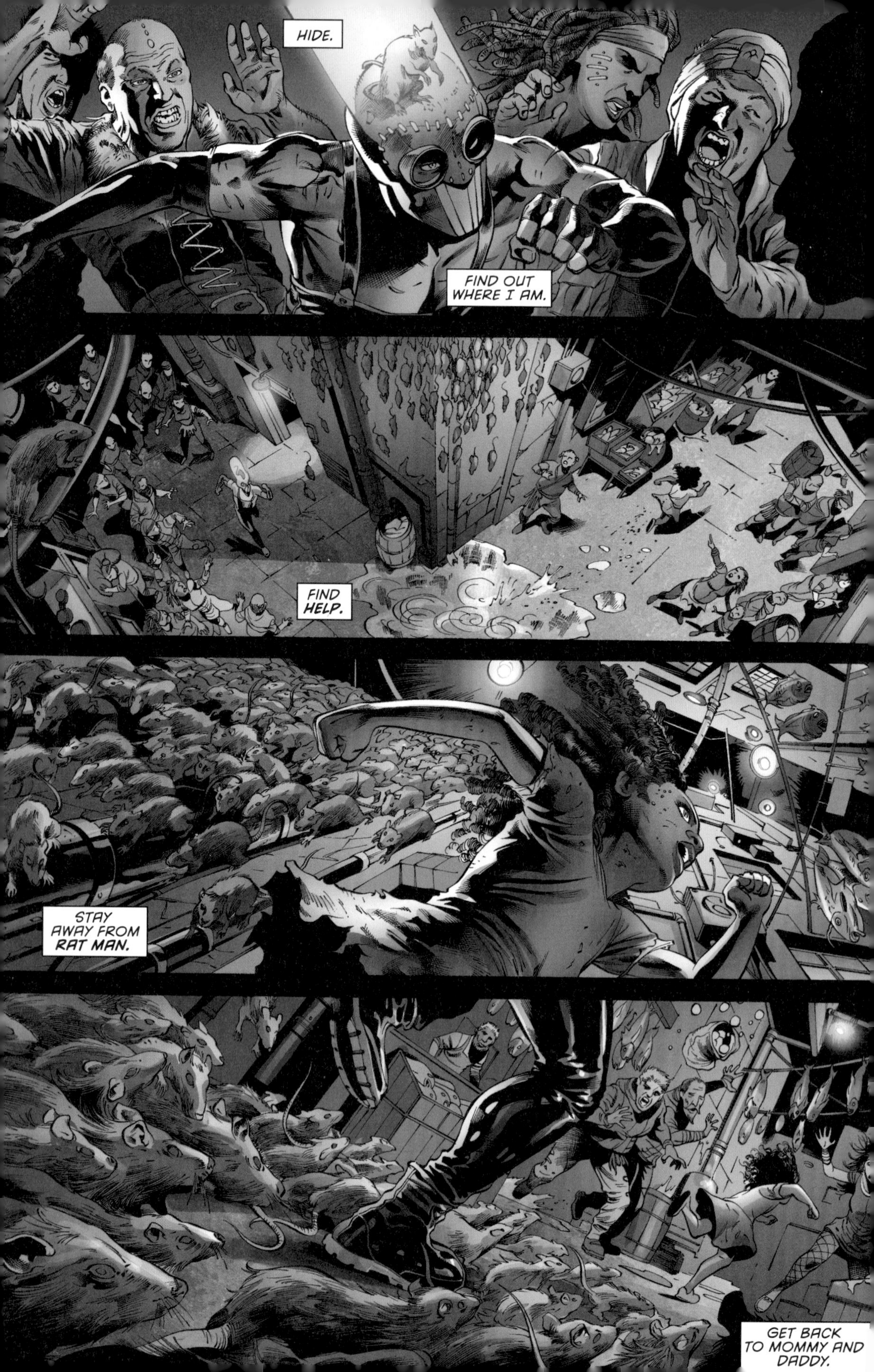
HIDE.
FIND OUT WHERE I AM.
FIND HELP.
STAY AWAY FROM RAT MAN.
GET BACK TO MOMMY AND DADDY.

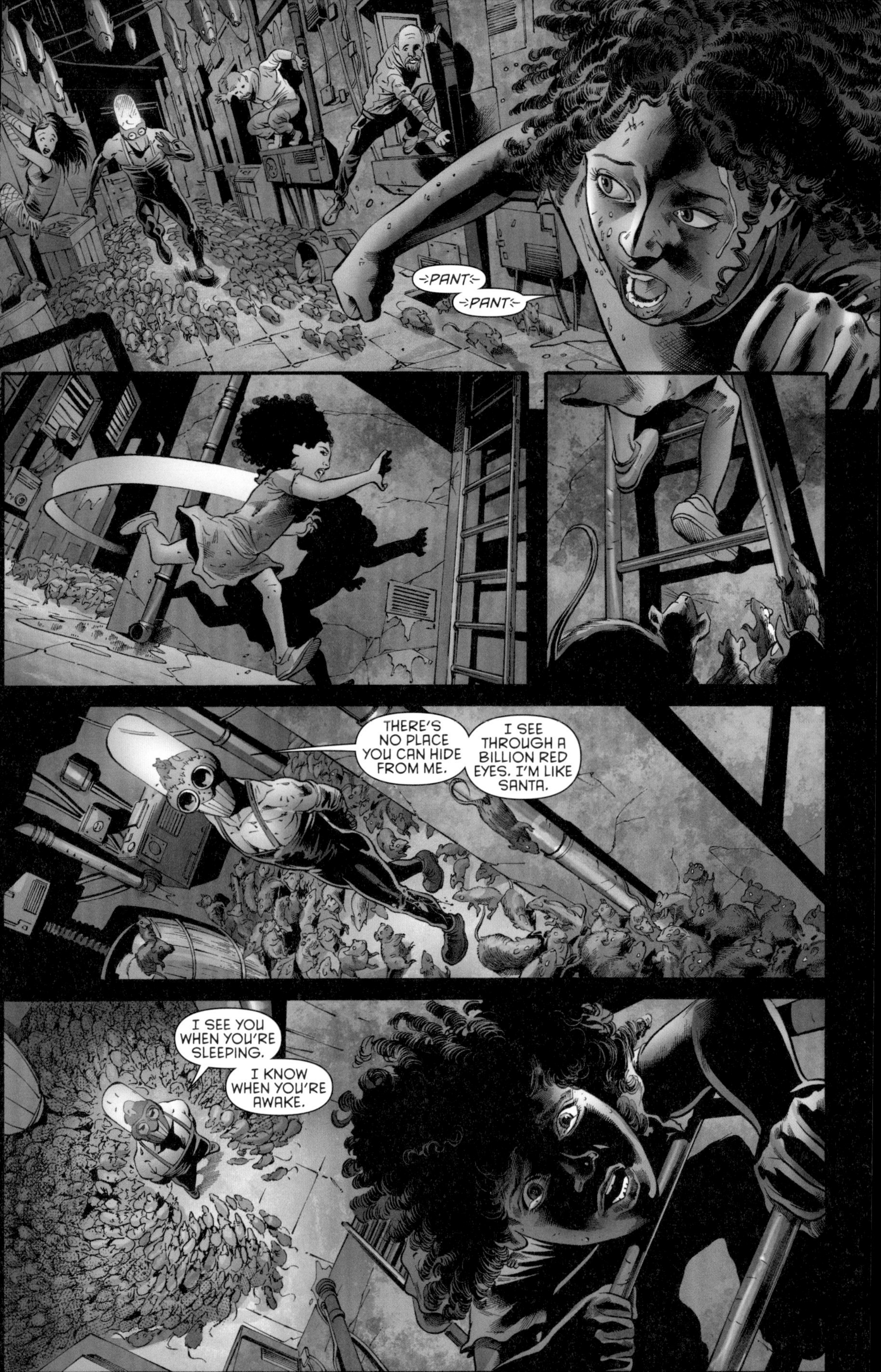
PANT
PANT
THERE'S NO PLACE YOU CAN HIDE FROM ME.
I SEE THROUGH A BILLION RED EYES. I'M LIKE SANTA.
I SEE YOU WHEN YOU'RE SLEEPING.
I KNOW WHEN YOU'RE AWAKE.

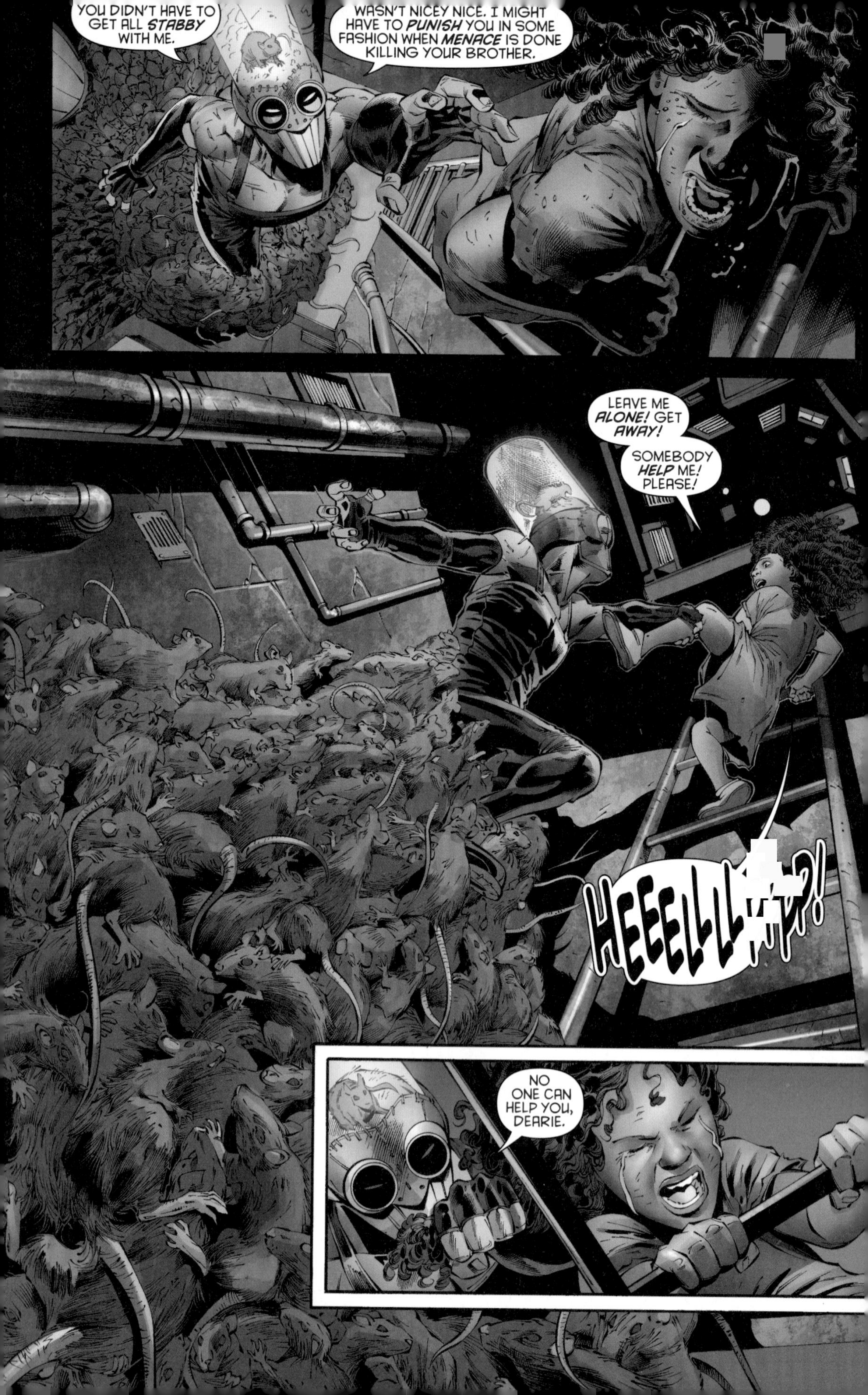
YOU DIDN'T HAVE TO GET ALL STABBY WITH ME.
WASN'T NICEY NICE. I MIGHT HAVE TO PUNISH YOU IN SOME FASHION WHEN MENACE IS DONE KILLING YOUR BROTHER.
LEAVE ME ALONE! GET AWAY!
SOMEBODY HELP ME! PLEASE!
HEEELLL P!
NO ONE CAN HELP YOU, DEARIE.

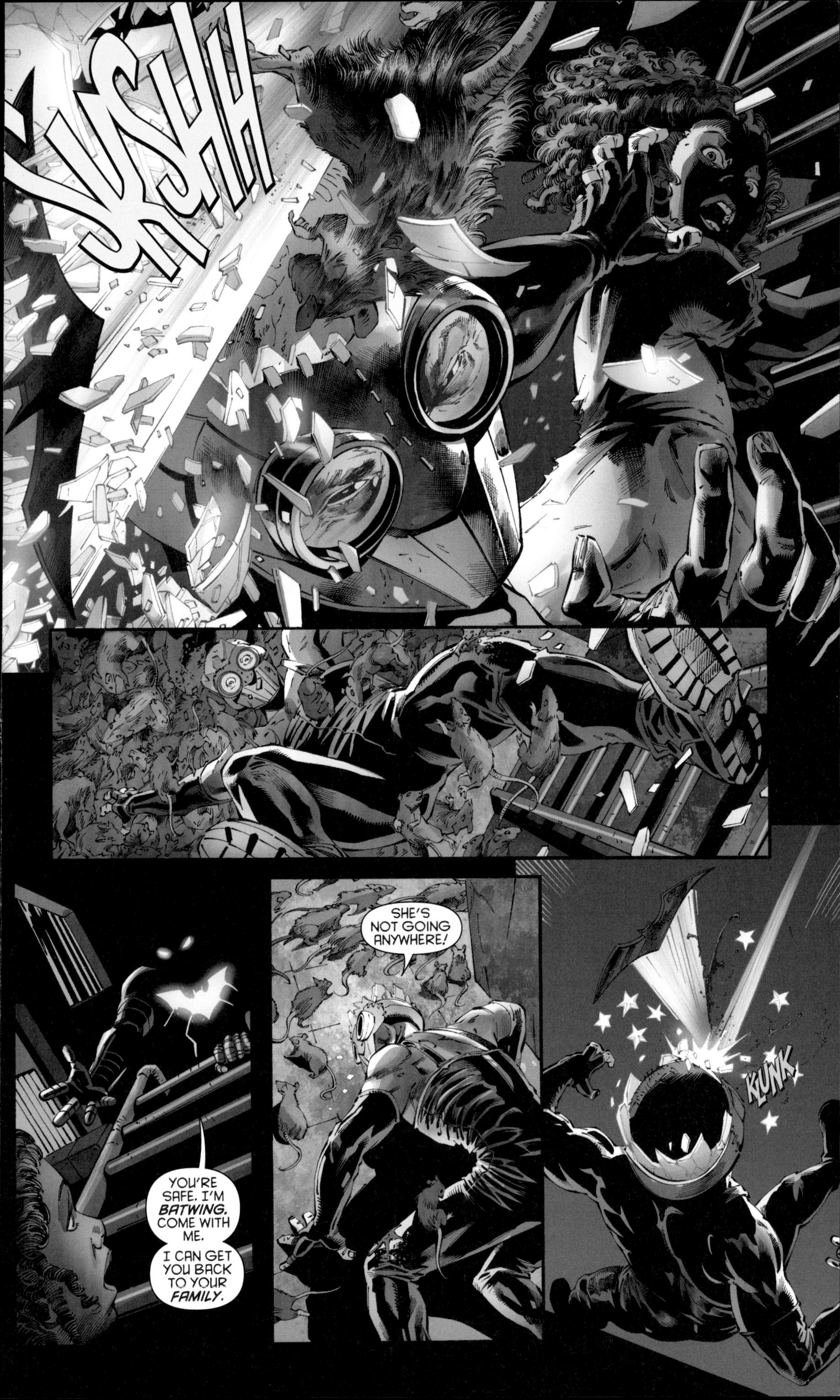
SKSHH
YOU'RE SAFE. I'M BATWING. COME WITH ME.
I CAN GET YOU BACK TO YOUR FAMILY.
SHE'S NOT GOING ANYWHERE!
KLUNK

MEANWHILE...
WAYNE TOWER.

THE SEARCH IS STILL ON FOR SIX-YEAR-OLD *TIFFANY FOX,* DAUGHTER OF WAYNE ENTERPRISES CEO *LUCIUS FOX.*

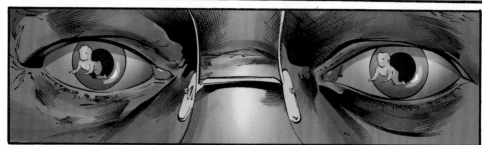

YOU GOT IT, TIFFANY! THAT'S IT... YOU'RE *WALKING...* THAT'S MY BIG GIRL...

DADDY PICKED THE *RIGHT* DAY TO WORK FROM HOME, DIDN'T HE?

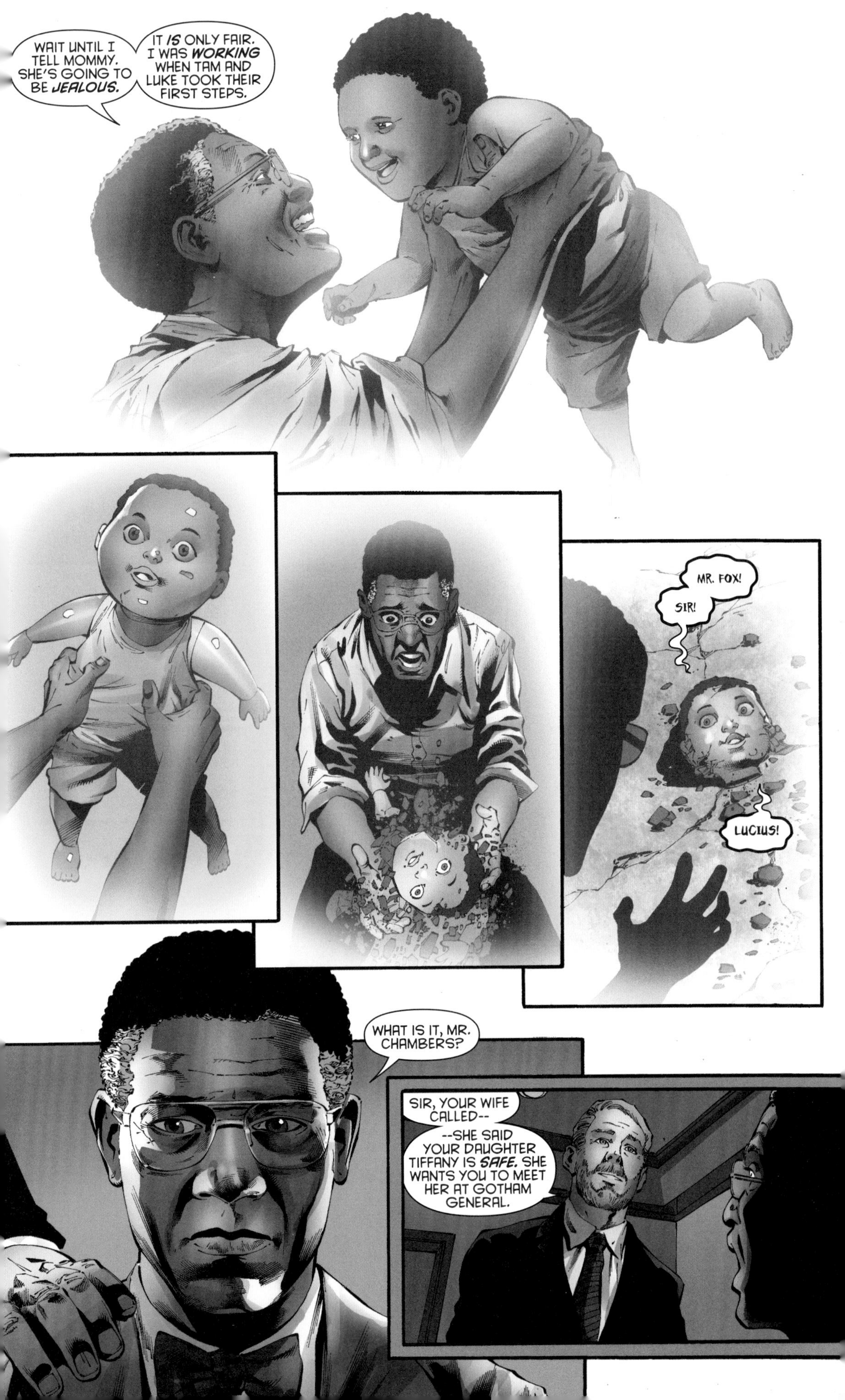
WAIT UNTIL I TELL MOMMY. SHE'S GOING TO BE *JEALOUS.*
IT *IS* ONLY FAIR. I WAS *WORKING* WHEN TAM AND LUKE TOOK THEIR FIRST STEPS.
MR. FOX!
SIR!
LUCIUS!
WHAT IS IT, MR. CHAMBERS?
SIR, YOUR WIFE CALLED--
--SHE SAID YOUR DAUGHTER TIFFANY IS *SAFE.* SHE WANTS YOU TO MEET HER AT GOTHAM GENERAL.

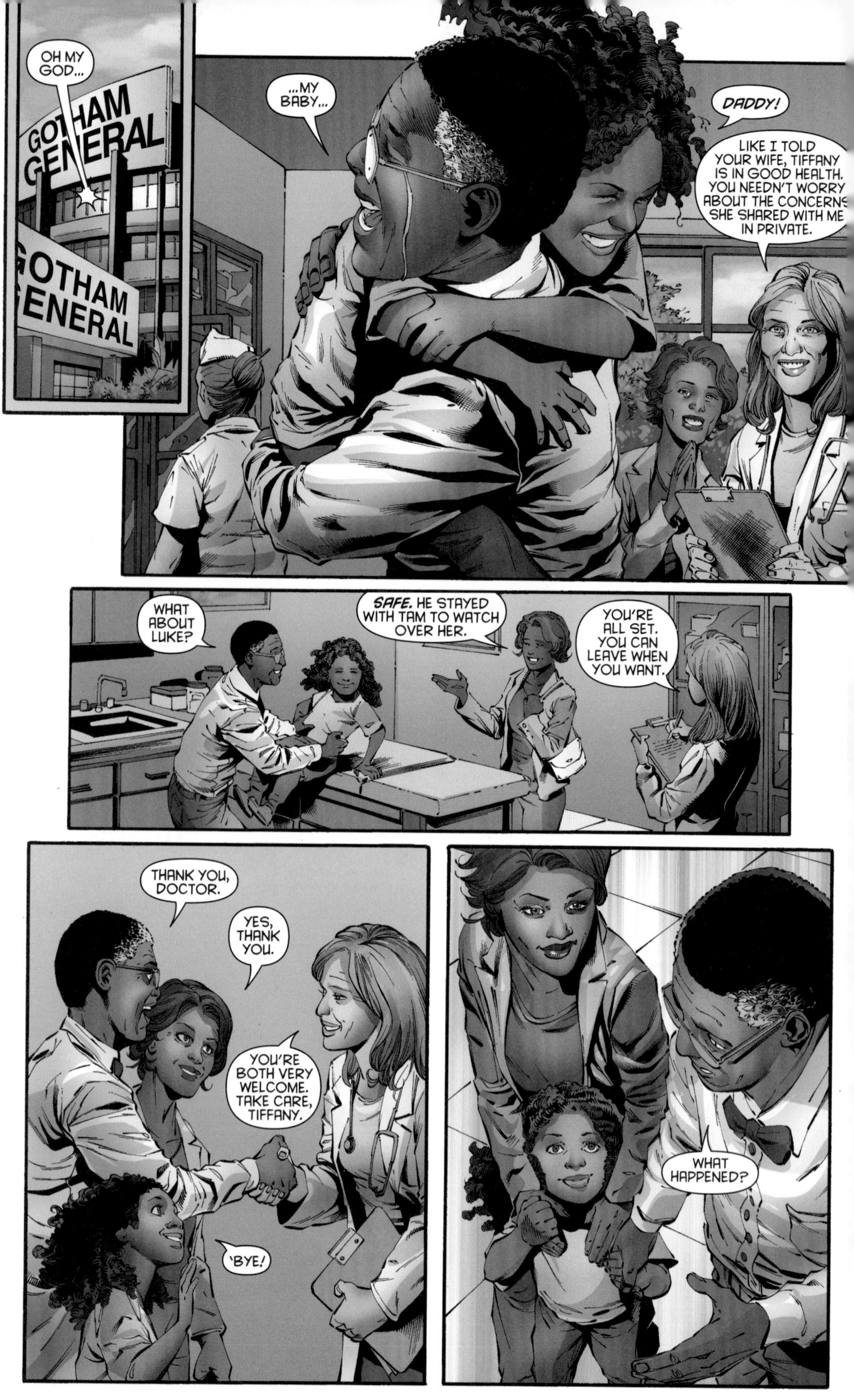
OH MY GOD...
GOTHAM GENERAL
GOTHAM GENERAL
...MY BABY...
DADDY!
LIKE I TOLD YOUR WIFE, TIFFANY IS IN GOOD HEALTH. YOU NEEDN'T WORRY ABOUT THE CONCERNS SHE SHARED WITH ME IN PRIVATE.
WHAT ABOUT LUKE?
SAFE. HE STAYED WITH TAM TO WATCH OVER HER.
YOU'RE ALL SET. YOU CAN LEAVE WHEN YOU WANT.
THANK YOU, DOCTOR.
YES, THANK YOU.
YOU'RE BOTH VERY WELCOME. TAKE CARE, TIFFANY.
'BYE!
WHAT HAPPENED?

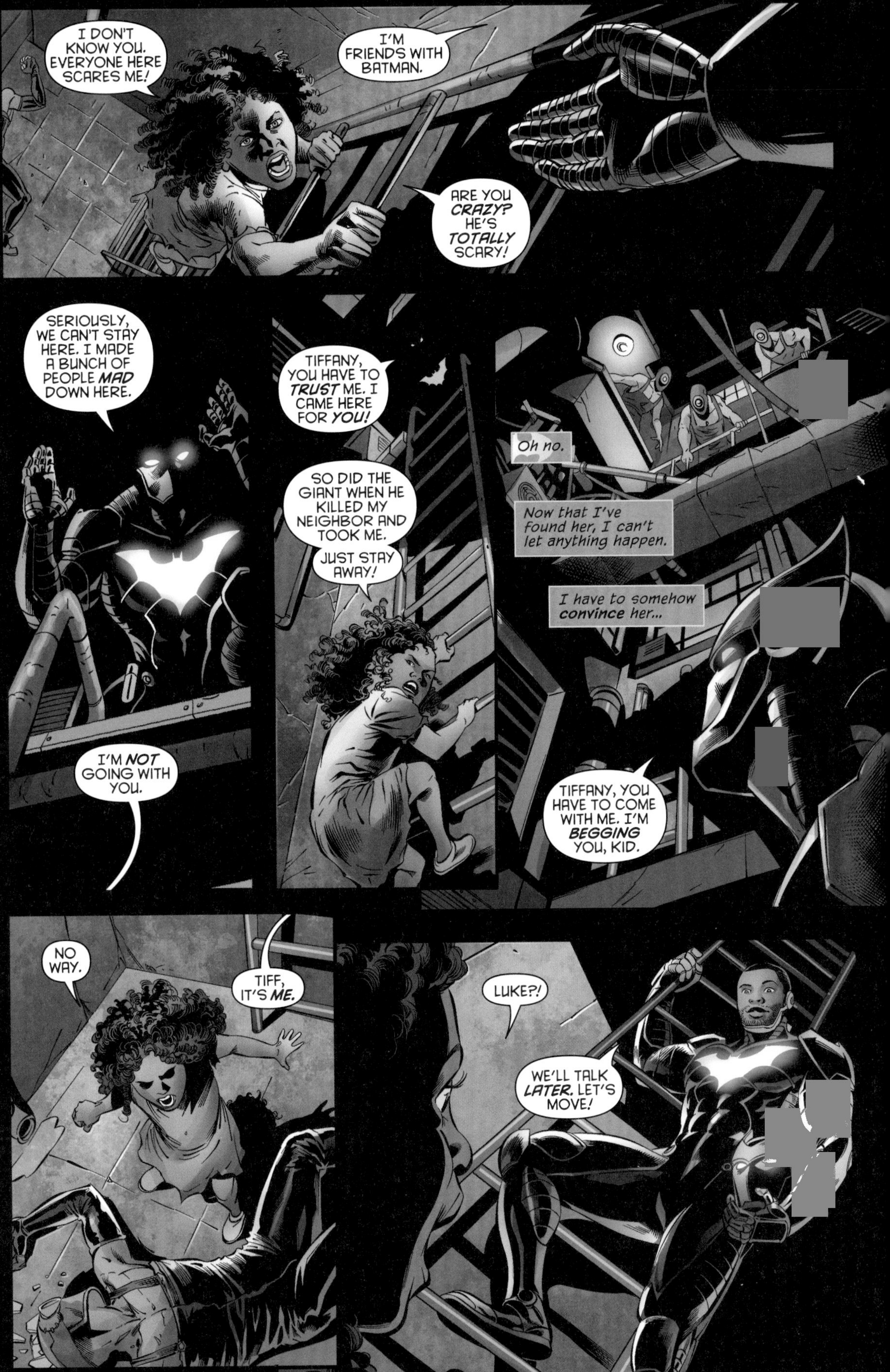
I DON'T KNOW YOU. EVERYONE HERE SCARES ME!
I'M FRIENDS WITH BATMAN.
ARE YOU CRAZY? HE'S TOTALLY SCARY!
SERIOUSLY, WE CAN'T STAY HERE. I MADE A BUNCH OF PEOPLE MAD DOWN HERE.
I'M NOT GOING WITH YOU.
TIFFANY, YOU HAVE TO TRUST ME. I CAME HERE FOR YOU!
SO DID THE GIANT WHEN HE KILLED MY NEIGHBOR AND TOOK ME.
JUST STAY AWAY!
Oh no.
Now that I've found her, I can't let anything happen.
I have to somehow convince her...
TIFFANY, YOU HAVE TO COME WITH ME. I'M BEGGING YOU, KID.
NO WAY.
TIFF, IT'S ME.
LUKE?!
WE'LL TALK LATER. LET'S MOVE!

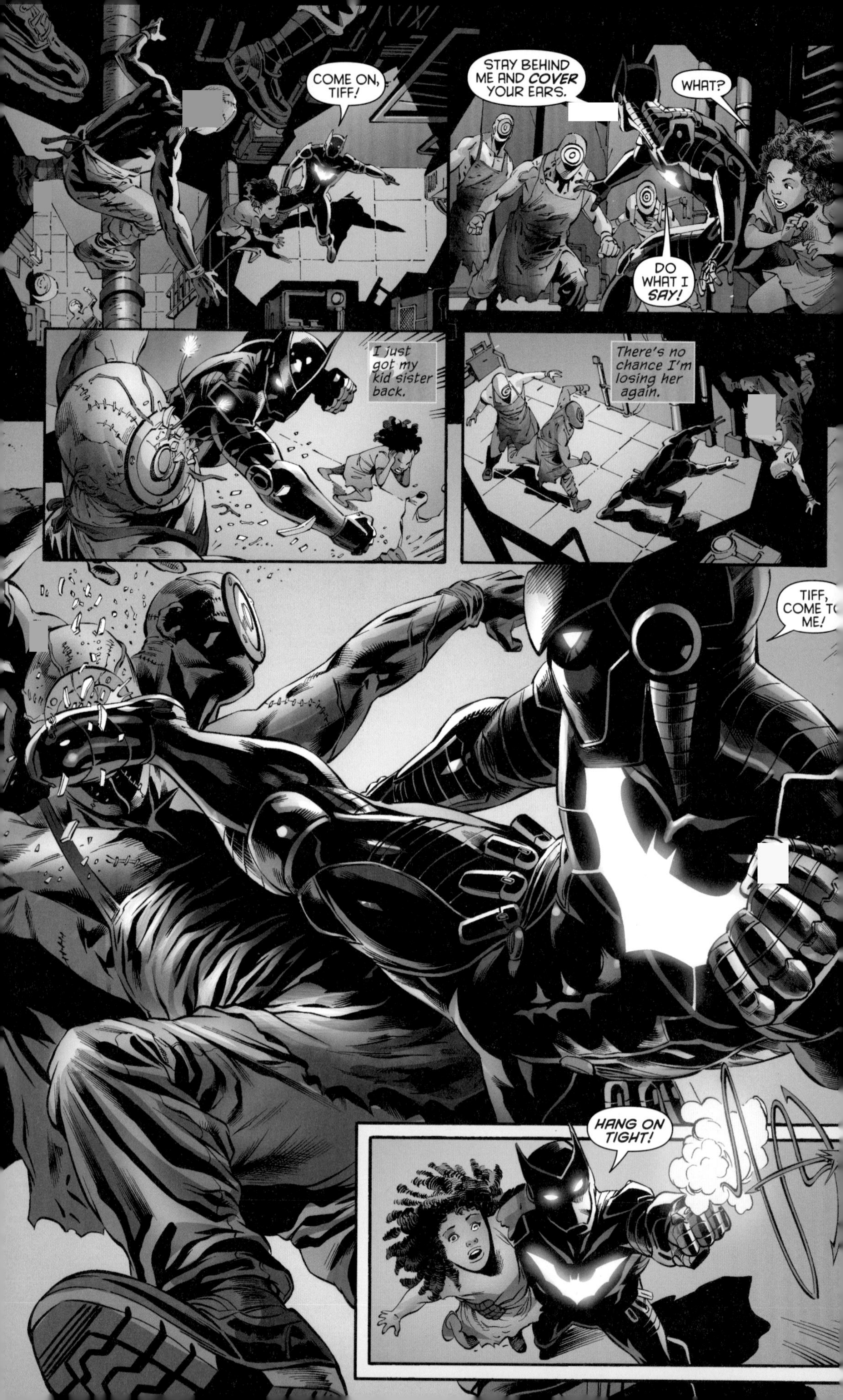
COME ON, TIFF!
STAY BEHIND ME AND COVER YOUR EARS.
WHAT?
DO WHAT I SAY!
I just got my kid sister back.
There's no chance I'm losing her again.
TIFF, COME TO ME!
HANG ON TIGHT!

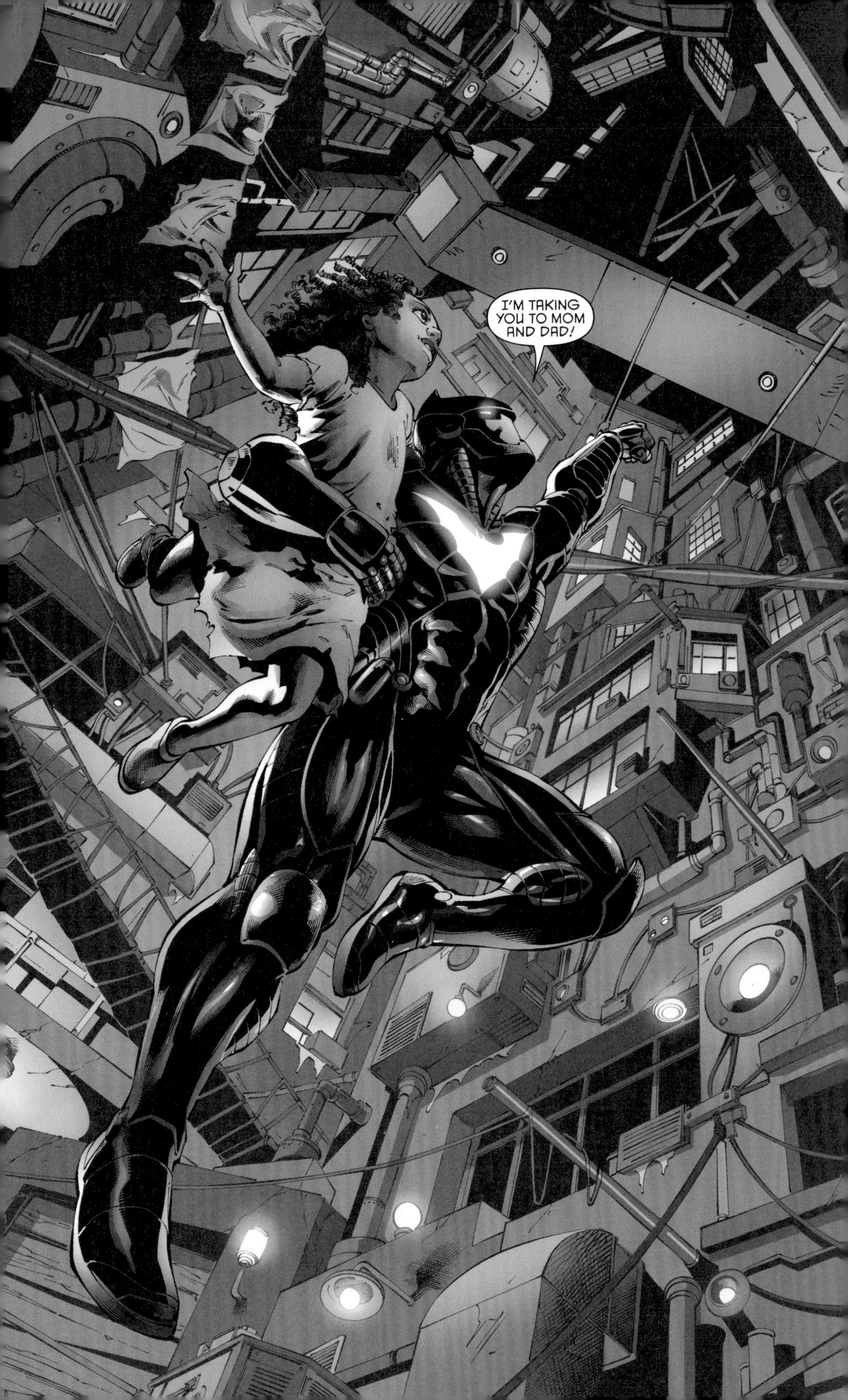
I'M TAKING YOU TO MOM AND DAD!

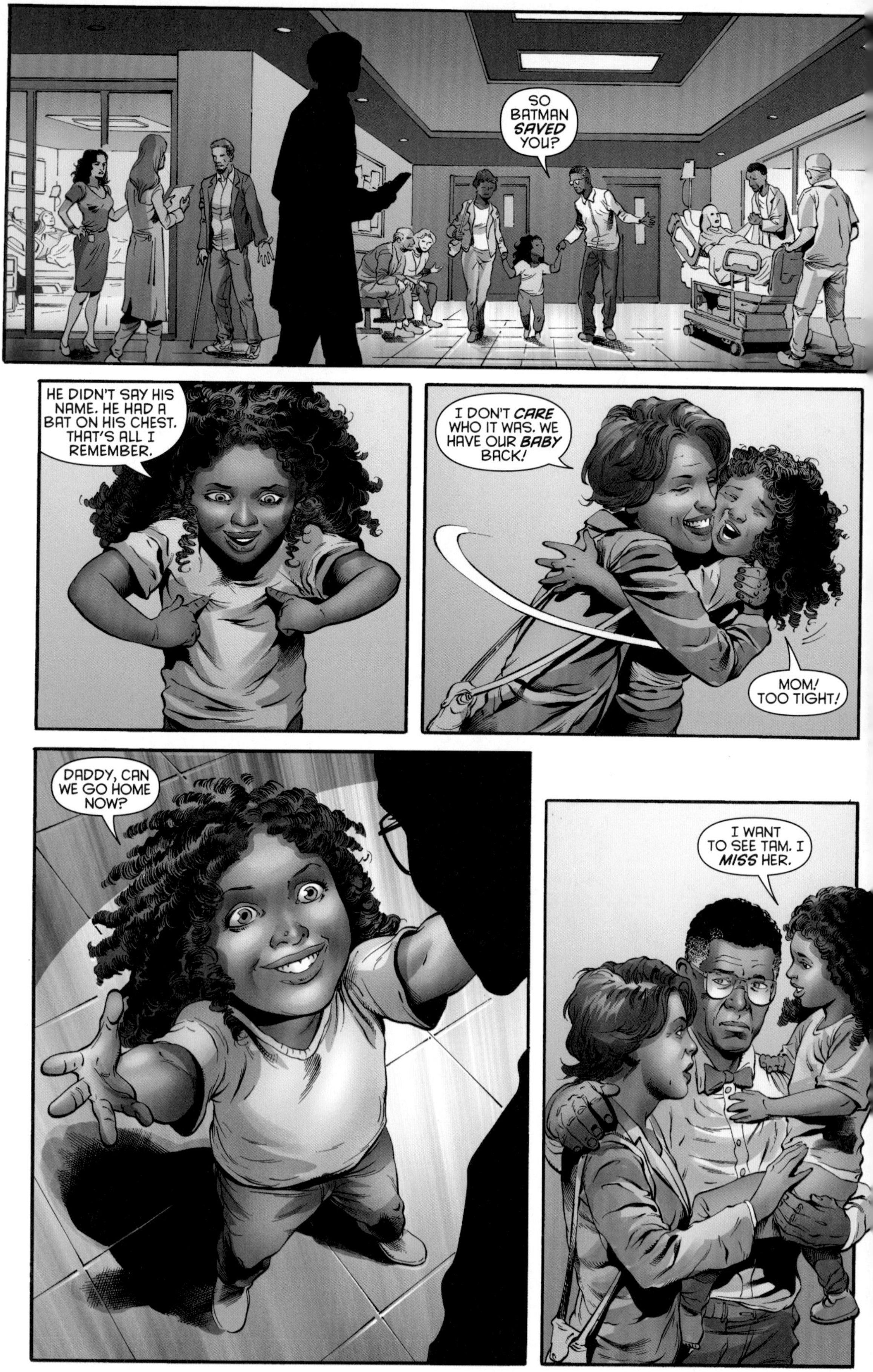
SO BATMAN SAVED YOU?
HE DIDN'T SAY HIS NAME. HE HAD A BAT ON HIS CHEST. THAT'S ALL I REMEMBER.
I DON'T CARE WHO IT WAS. WE HAVE OUR BABY BACK!
MOM! TOO TIGHT!
DADDY, CAN WE GO HOME NOW?
I WANT TO SEE TAM. I MISS HER.

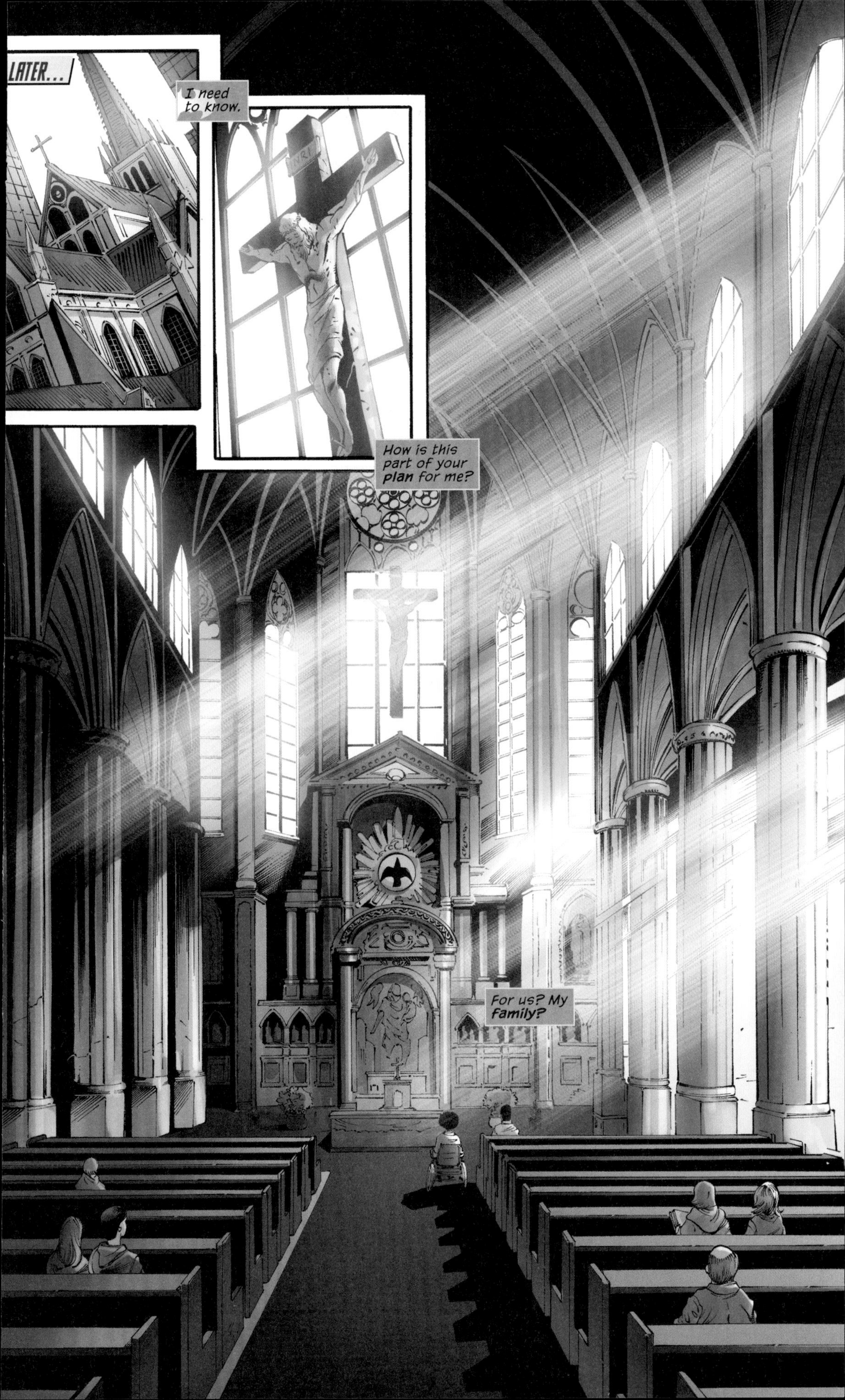
LATER...
I need to know.
How is this part of your plan for me?
For us? My family?

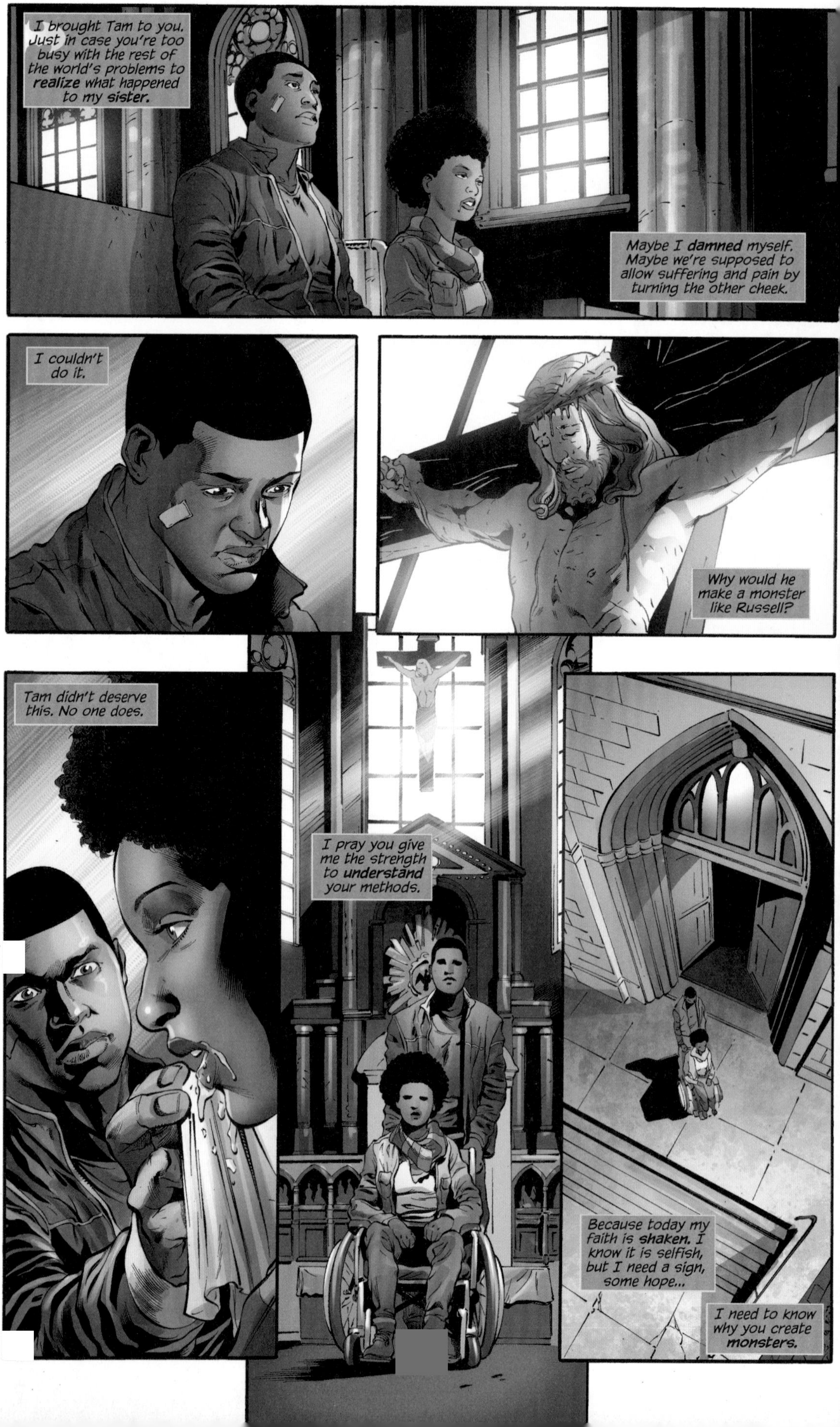
I brought Tam to you. Just in case you're too busy with the rest of the world's problems to **realize** what happened to my **sister.**
Maybe I **damned** myself. Maybe we're supposed to allow suffering and pain by turning the other cheek.
I couldn't do it.
Why would he make a monster like Russell?
Tam didn't deserve this. No one does.
I pray you give me the strength to **understand** your methods.
Because today my faith is **shaken.** I know it is selfish, but I need a sign, some hope...
I need to know why you create **monsters.**

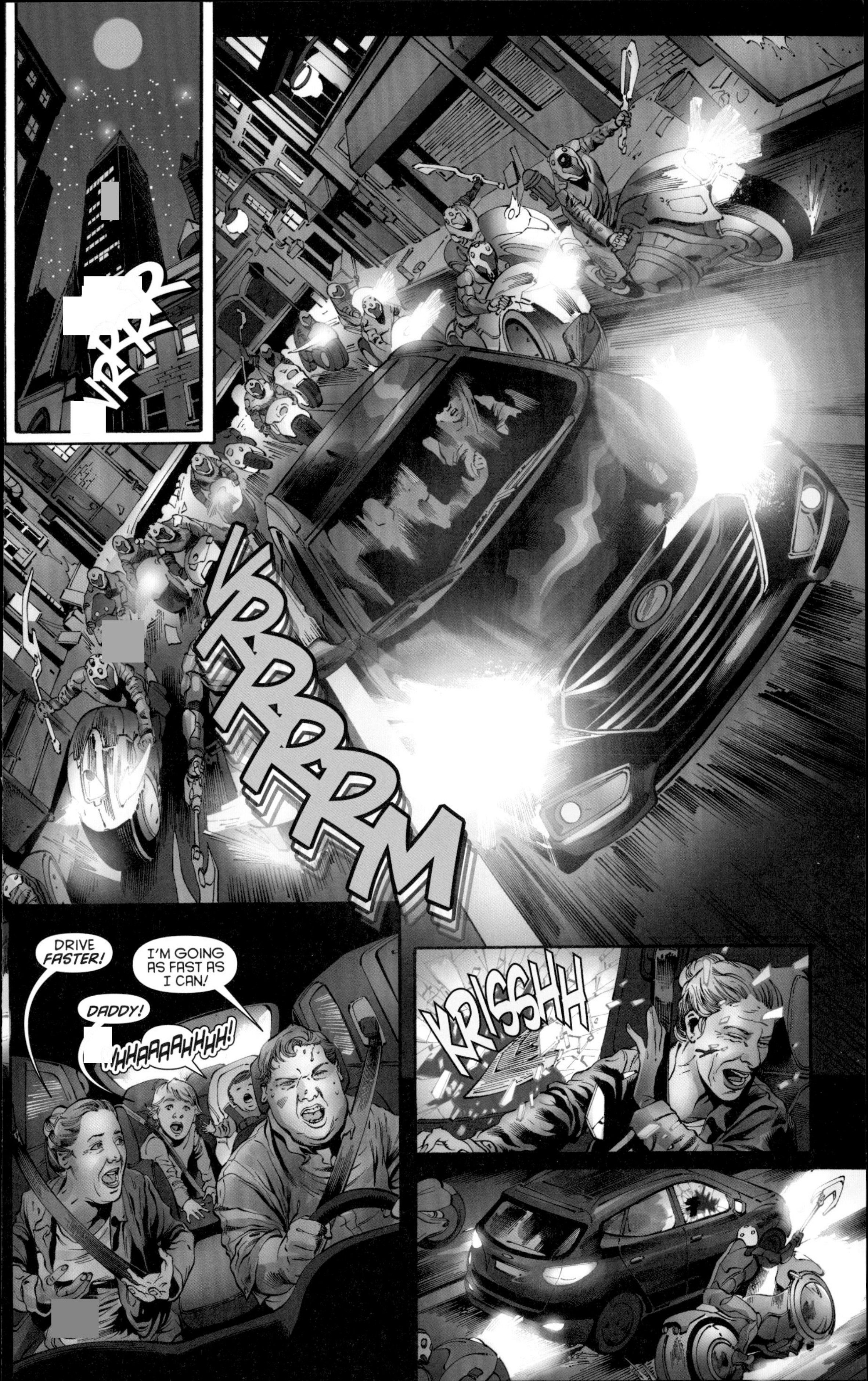
VRRRRM
DRIVE FASTER!
I'M GOING AS FAST AS I CAN!
DADDY!
KRISSHH

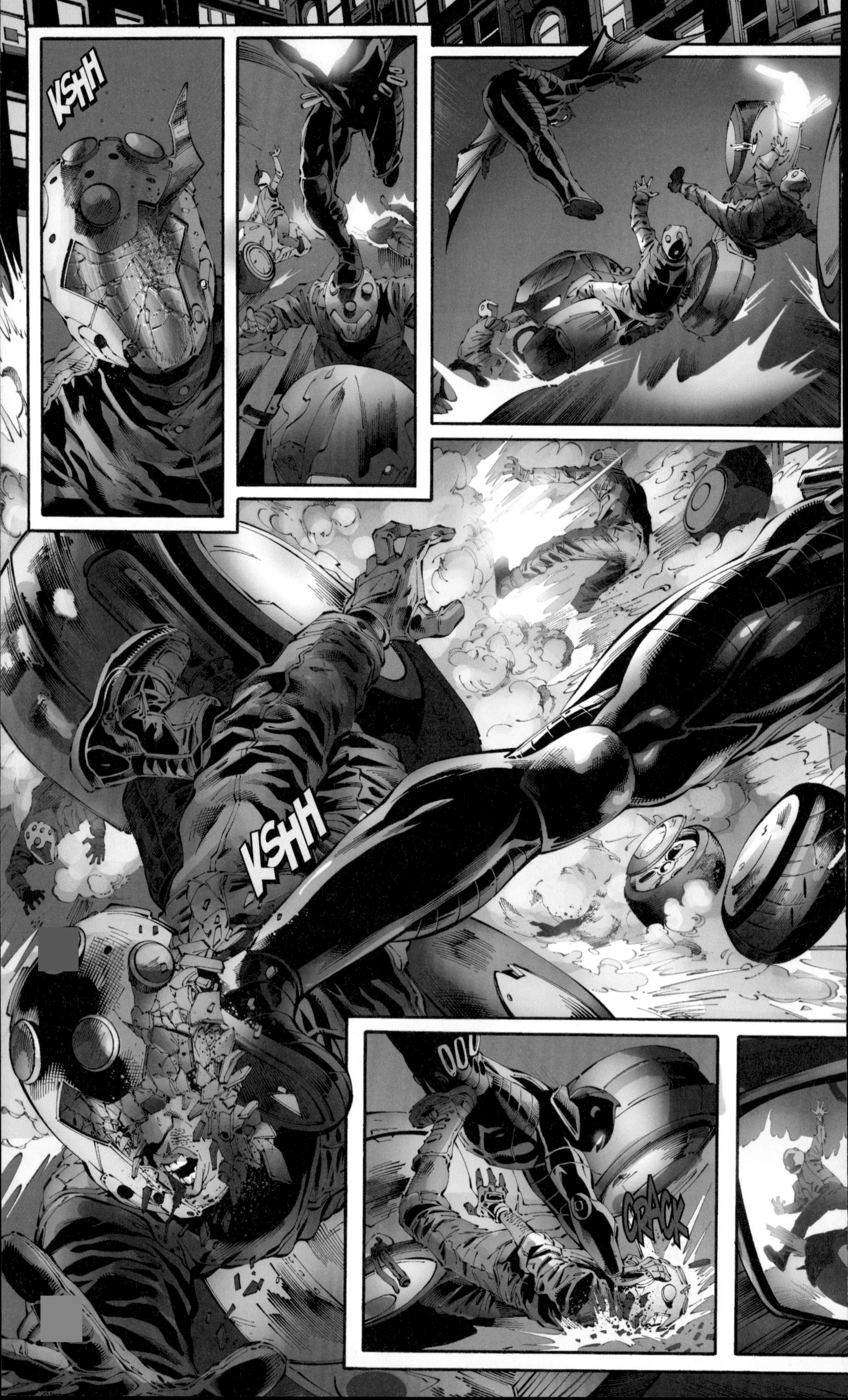
KSHH
KSHH
CRACK

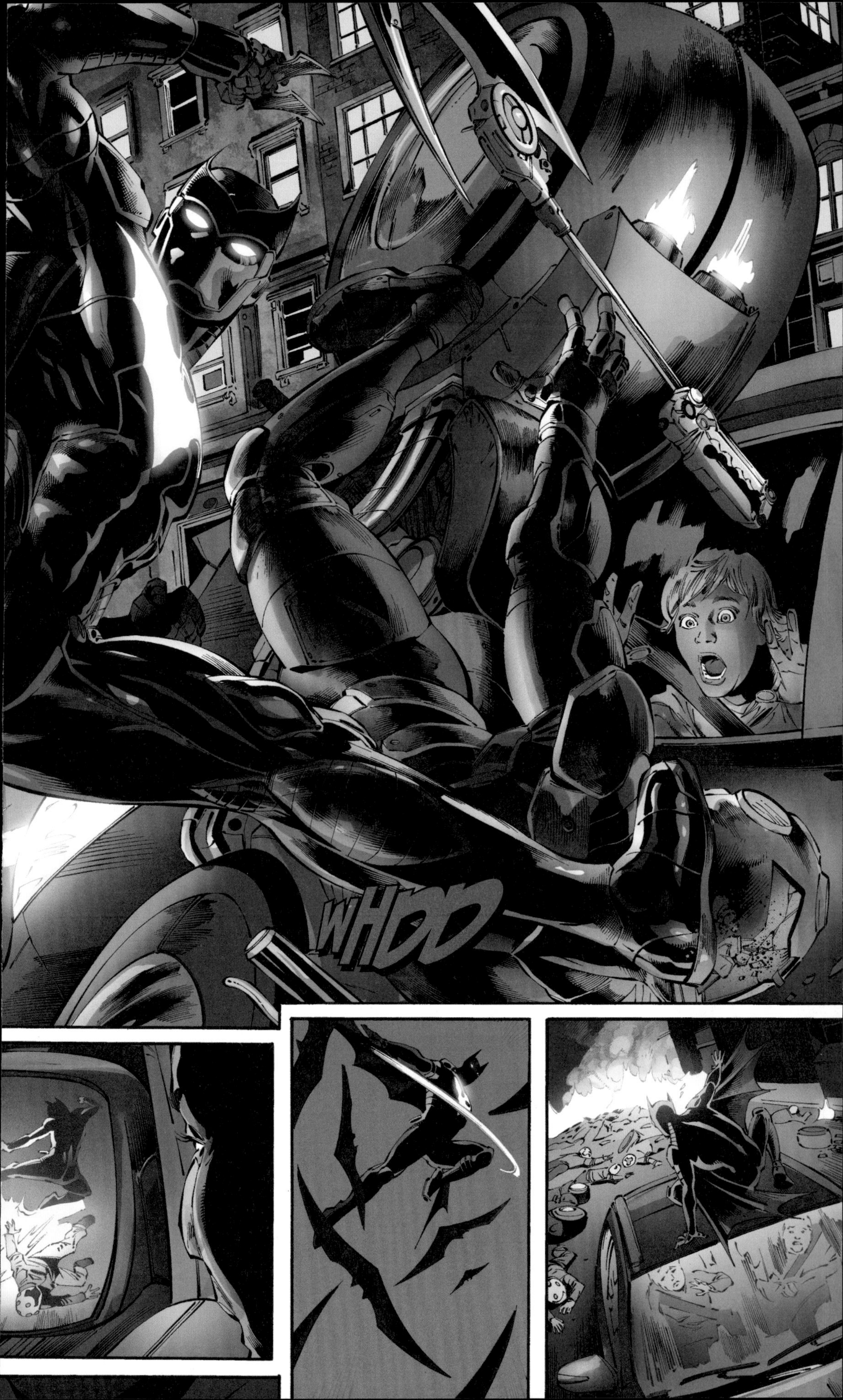
WHDD

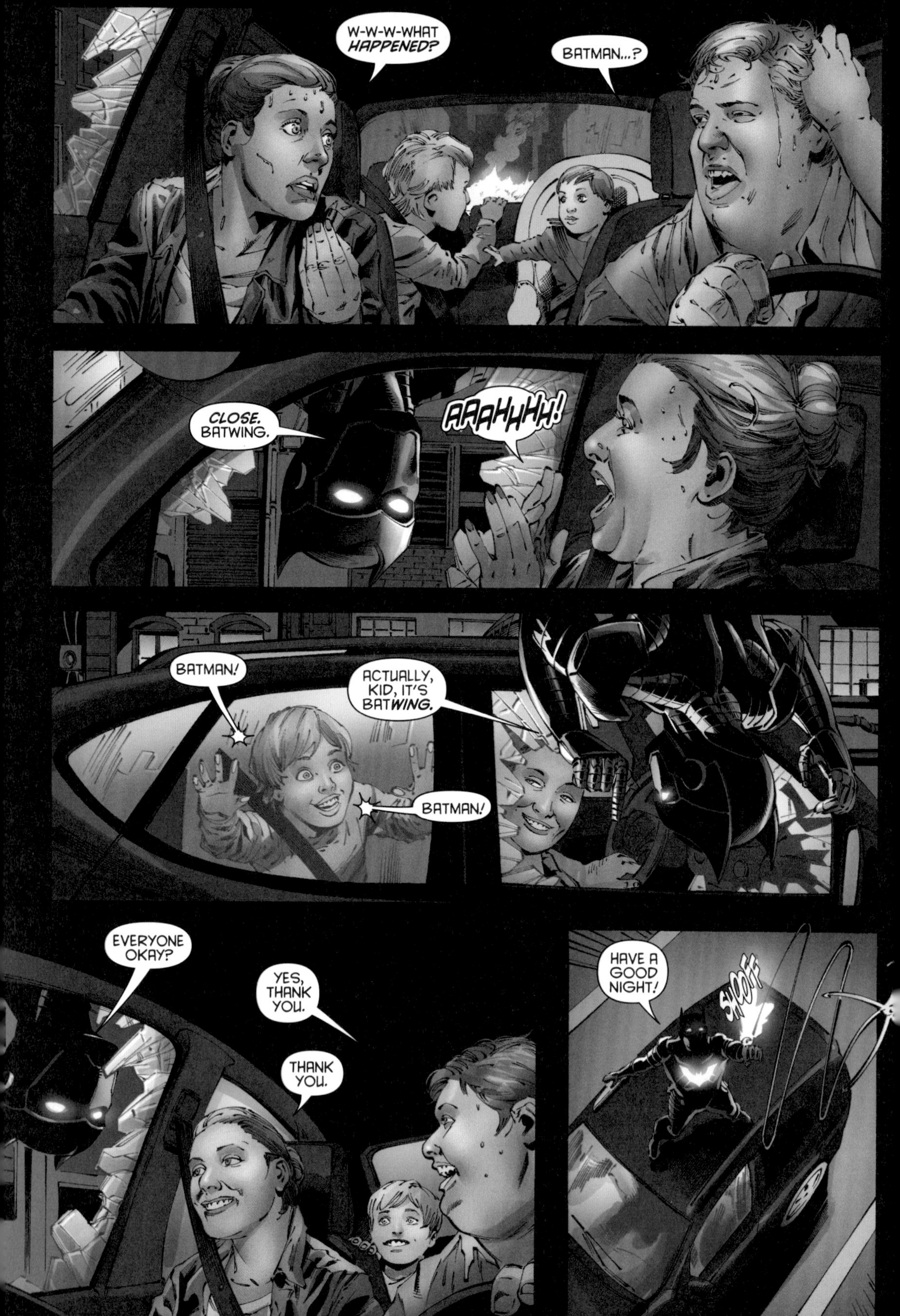
W-W-W-WHAT *HAPPENED?*
BATMAN...?
CLOSE. BATWING.
AAAHHHH!
BATMAN!
ACTUALLY, KID, IT'S BAT*WING.*
BATMAN!
EVERYONE OKAY?
YES, THANK YOU.
THANK YOU.
HAVE A GOOD NIGHT!
SHOOFF

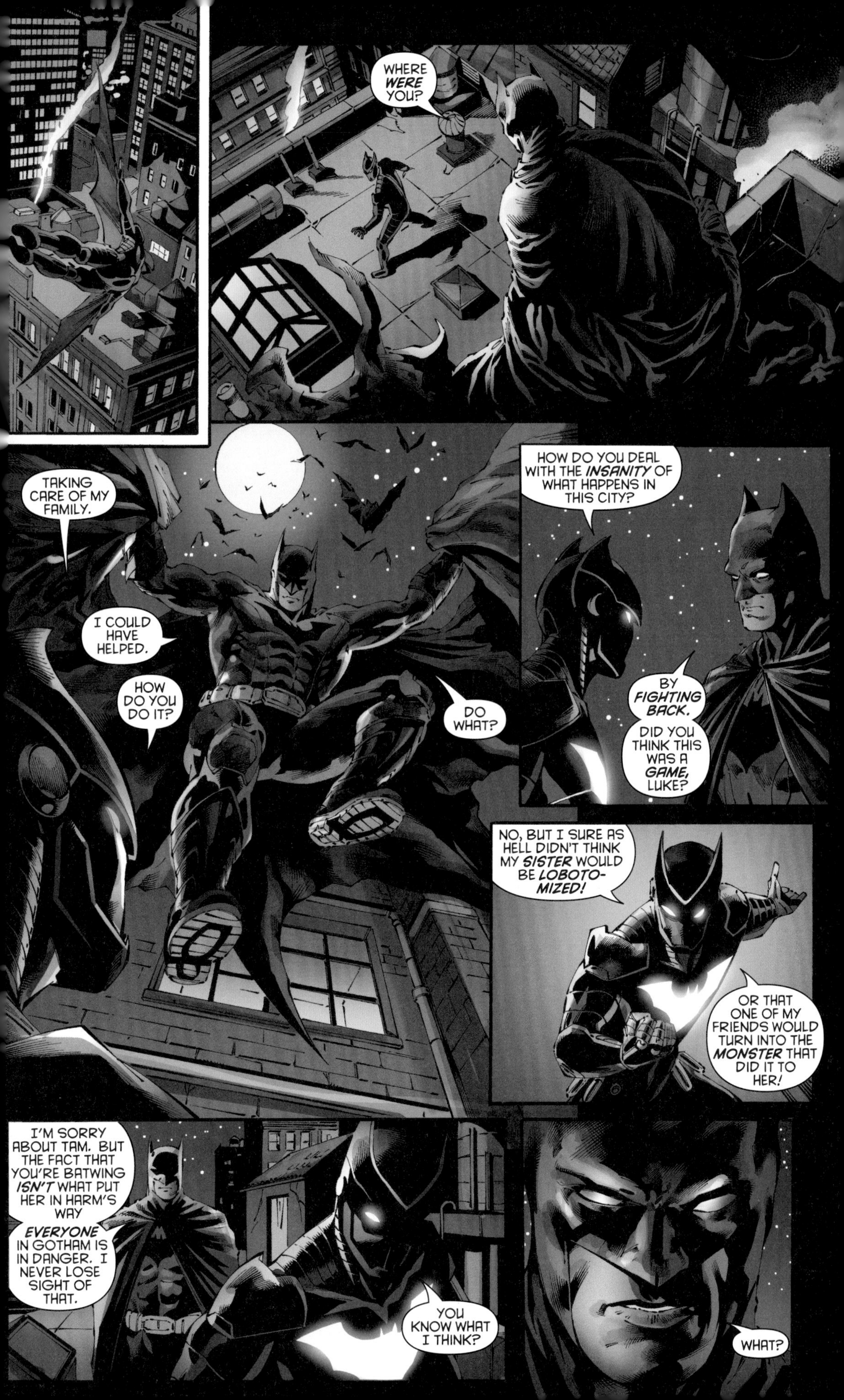
WHERE WERE YOU?
TAKING CARE OF MY FAMILY.
I COULD HAVE HELPED.
HOW DO YOU DO IT?
DO WHAT?
HOW DO YOU DEAL WITH THE INSANITY OF WHAT HAPPENS IN THIS CITY?
BY FIGHTING BACK.
DID YOU THINK THIS WAS A GAME, LUKE?
NO, BUT I SURE AS HELL DIDN'T THINK MY SISTER WOULD BE LOBOTO-MIZED!
OR THAT ONE OF MY FRIENDS WOULD TURN INTO THE MONSTER THAT DID IT TO HER!
I'M SORRY ABOUT TAM. BUT THE FACT THAT YOU'RE BATWING ISN'T WHAT PUT HER IN HARM'S WAY
EVERYONE IN GOTHAM IS IN DANGER. I NEVER LOSE SIGHT OF THAT.
YOU KNOW WHAT I THINK?
WHAT?

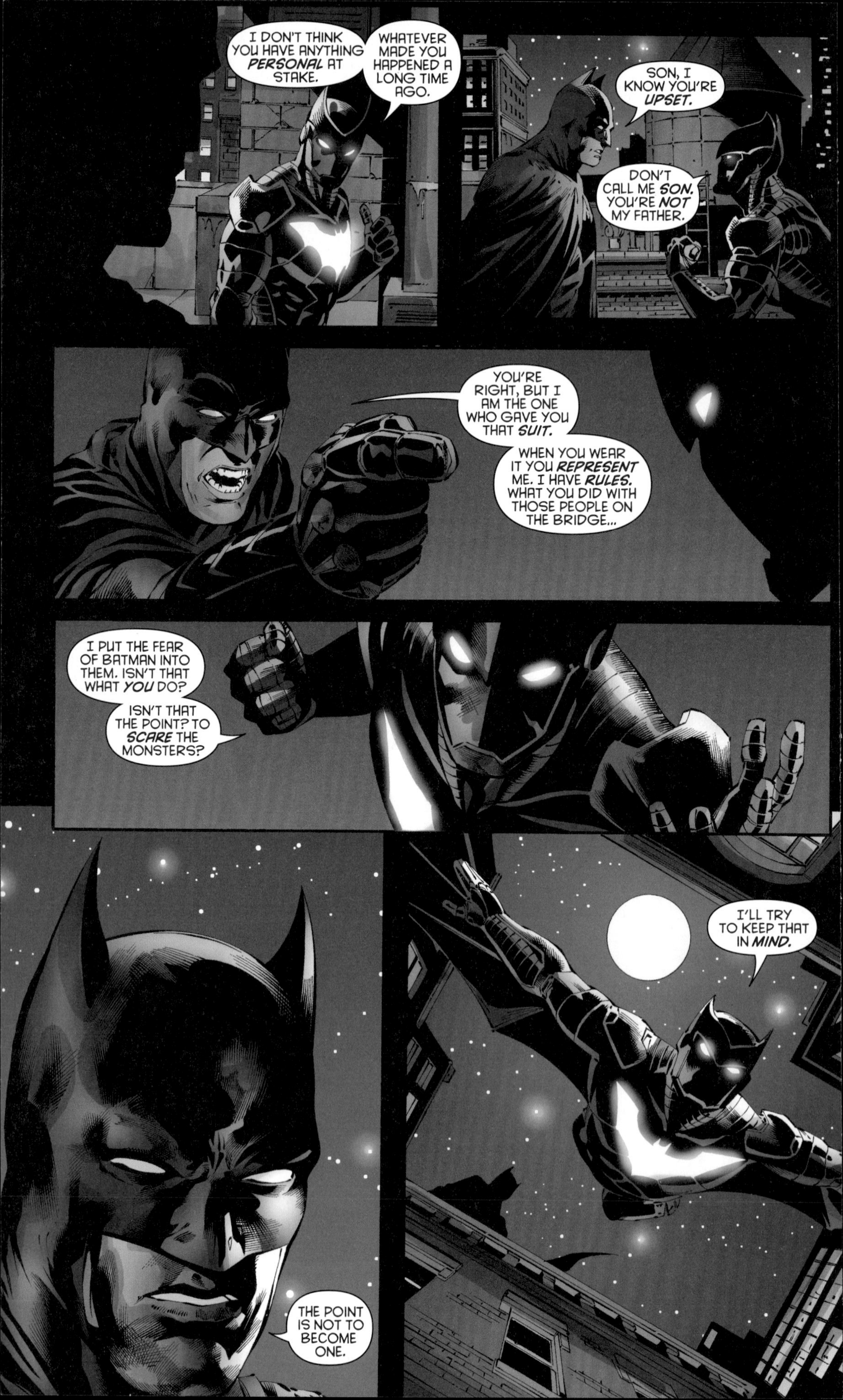
I DON'T THINK YOU HAVE ANYTHING *PERSONAL* AT STAKE.
WHATEVER MADE YOU HAPPENED A LONG TIME AGO.
SON, I KNOW YOU'RE *UPSET.*
DON'T CALL ME *SON.* YOU'RE *NOT* MY FATHER.
YOU'RE RIGHT, BUT I AM THE ONE WHO GAVE YOU THAT *SUIT.*
WHEN YOU WEAR IT YOU *REPRESENT* ME. I HAVE *RULES.* WHAT YOU DID WITH THOSE PEOPLE ON THE BRIDGE...
I PUT THE FEAR OF BATMAN INTO THEM. ISN'T THAT WHAT *YOU* DO?
ISN'T THAT THE POINT? TO *SCARE* THE MONSTERS?
THE POINT IS NOT TO BECOME ONE.
I'LL TRY TO KEEP THAT IN *MIND.*

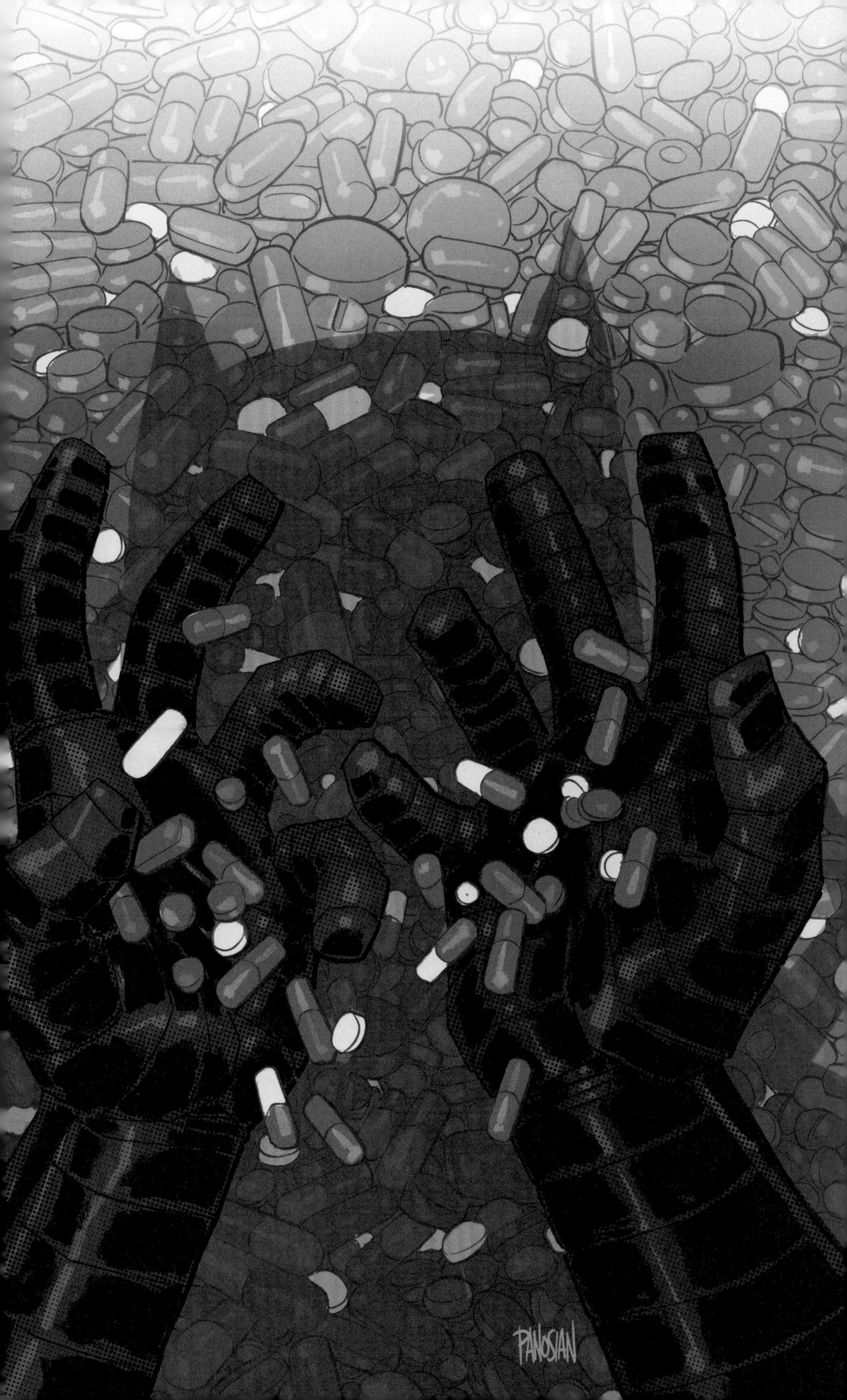
PANOSIAN

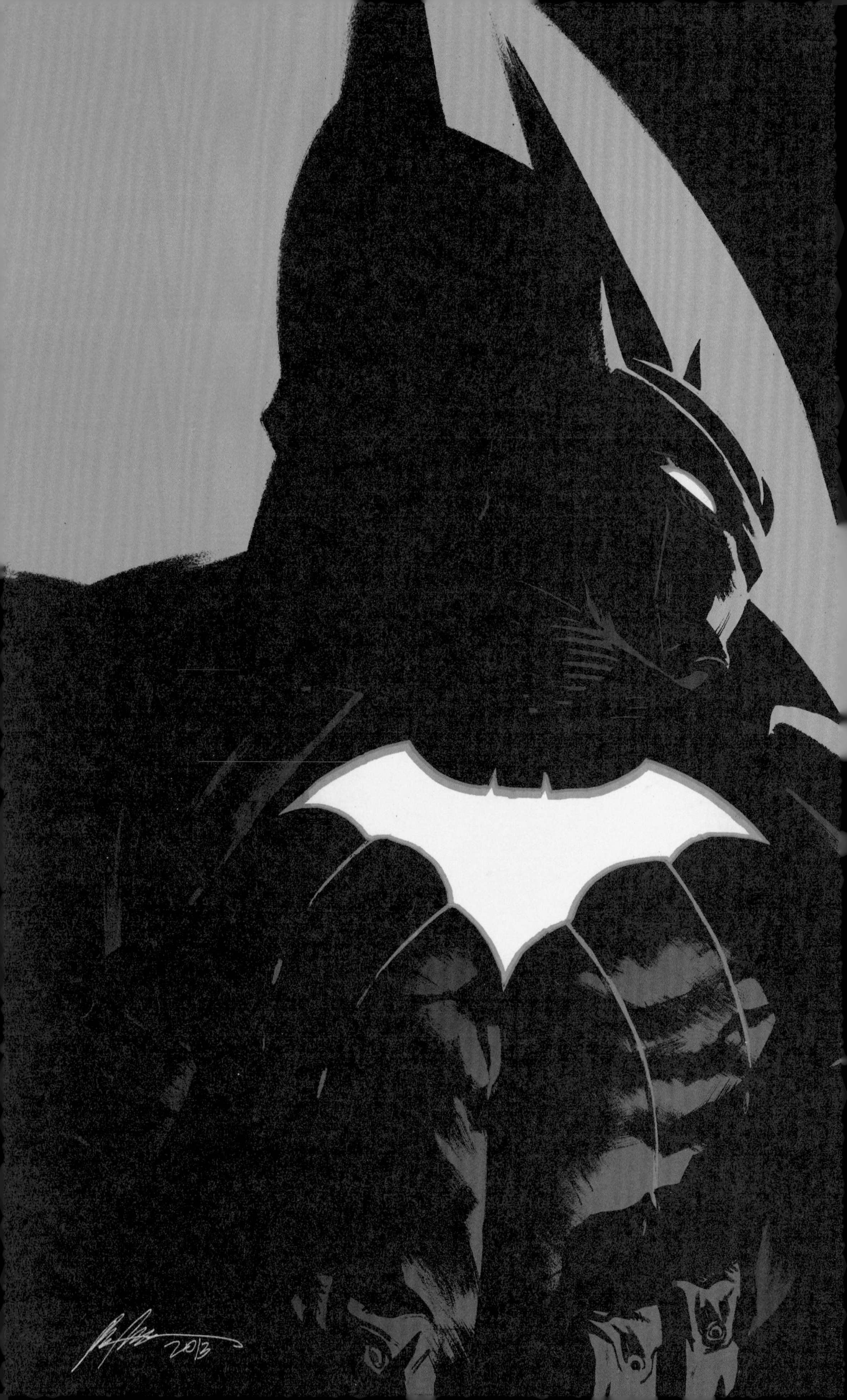

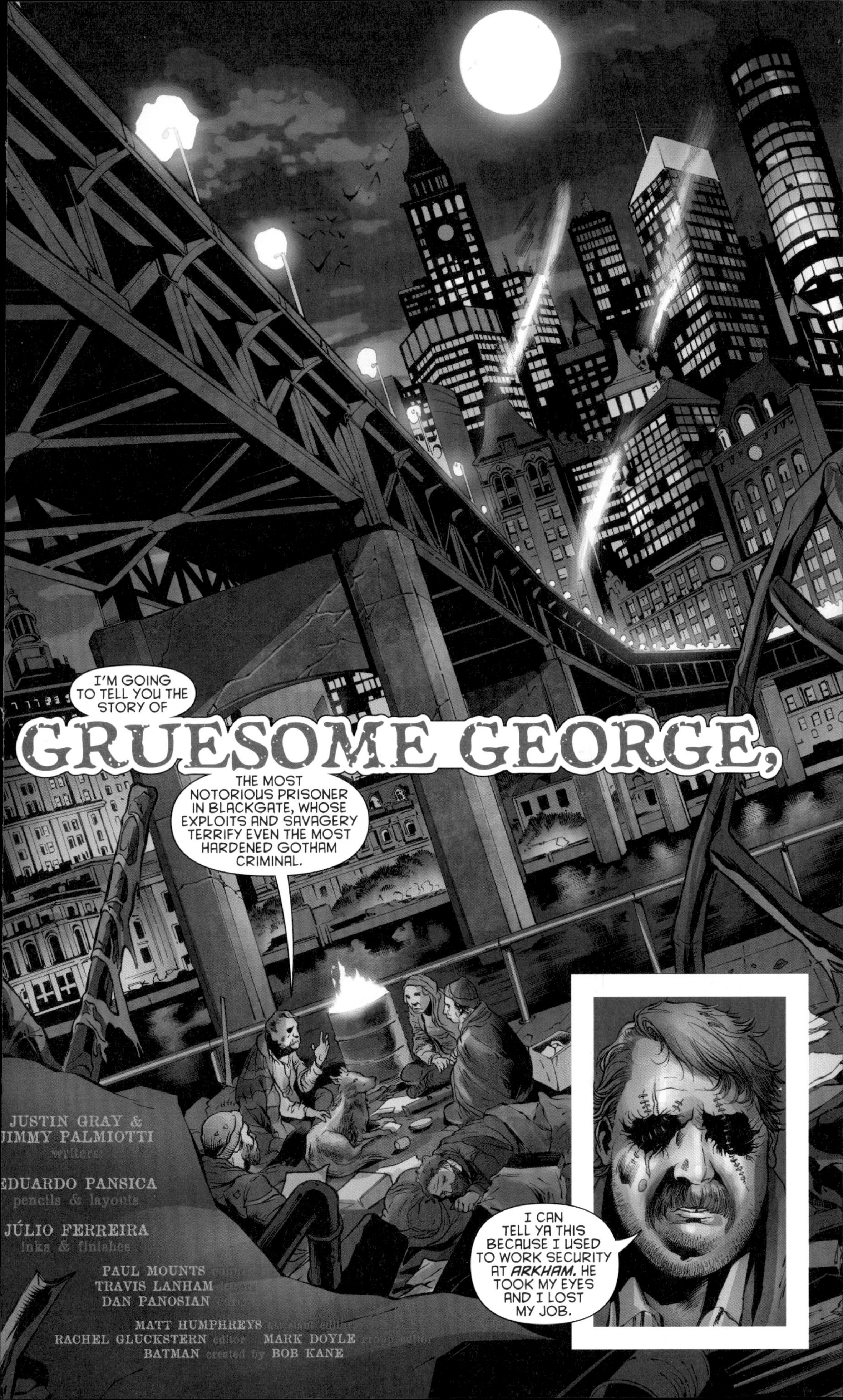
I'M GOING TO TELL YOU THE STORY OF
GRUESOME GEORGE,
THE MOST NOTORIOUS PRISONER IN BLACKGATE, WHOSE EXPLOITS AND SAVAGERY TERRIFY EVEN THE MOST HARDENED GOTHAM CRIMINAL.
I CAN TELL YA THIS BECAUSE I USED TO WORK SECURITY AT ARKHAM. HE TOOK MY EYES AND I LOST MY JOB.
JUSTIN GRAY & JIMMY PALMIOTTI writers
EDUARDO PANSICA pencils & layouts
JÚLIO FERREIRA inks & finishes
PAUL MOUNTS
TRAVIS LANHAM
DAN PANOSIAN
MATT HUMPHREYS
RACHEL GLUCKSTERN editor
MARK DOYLE
BATMAN created by BOB KANE

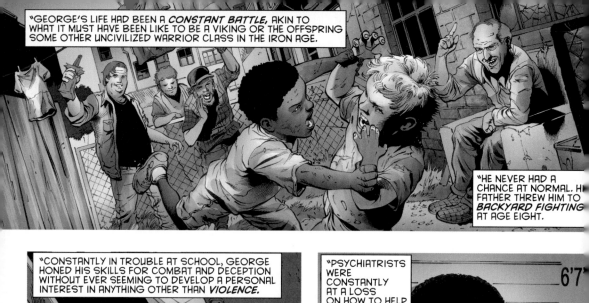

"GEORGE'S LIFE HAD BEEN A *CONSTANT BATTLE*, AKIN TO WHAT IT MUST HAVE BEEN LIKE TO BE A VIKING OR THE OFFSPRING SOME OTHER UNCIVILIZED WARRIOR CLASS IN THE IRON AGE.

"HE NEVER HAD A CHANCE AT NORMAL. H FATHER THREW HIM TO *BACKYARD FIGHTING* AT AGE EIGHT.

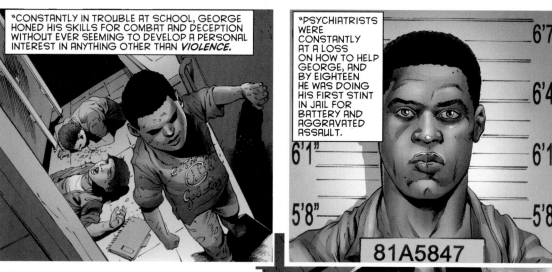

"CONSTANTLY IN TROUBLE AT SCHOOL, GEORGE HONED HIS SKILLS FOR COMBAT AND DECEPTION WITHOUT EVER SEEMING TO DEVELOP A PERSONAL INTEREST IN ANYTHING OTHER THAN *VIOLENCE.*

"PSYCHIATRISTS WERE CONSTANTLY AT A LOSS ON HOW TO HELP GEORGE, AND BY EIGHTEEN HE WAS DOING HIS FIRST STINT IN JAIL FOR BATTERY AND AGGRAVATED ASSAULT.

6'7"
6'4"
6'1"
6'1"
5'8"
5'8"

81A5847

"ONCE INSIDE, HIS REACTION TO PRISON WAS THE COMPLETE OPPOSITE OF ITS INTENDED EFFECT--HE *LOVED* IT.

"HE HAD ACCESS TO CONSTANT CONFLICT AND VIOLENCE.

"IT DIDN'T *MATTER* IF HE WON OR LOST FIGHT--THE ACT WAS ALL THAT MATTERED. TRADING BLOWS, BLOOD, THE SMELL (SWEAT AND FEAR--IT WAS HIS *ART FORM*

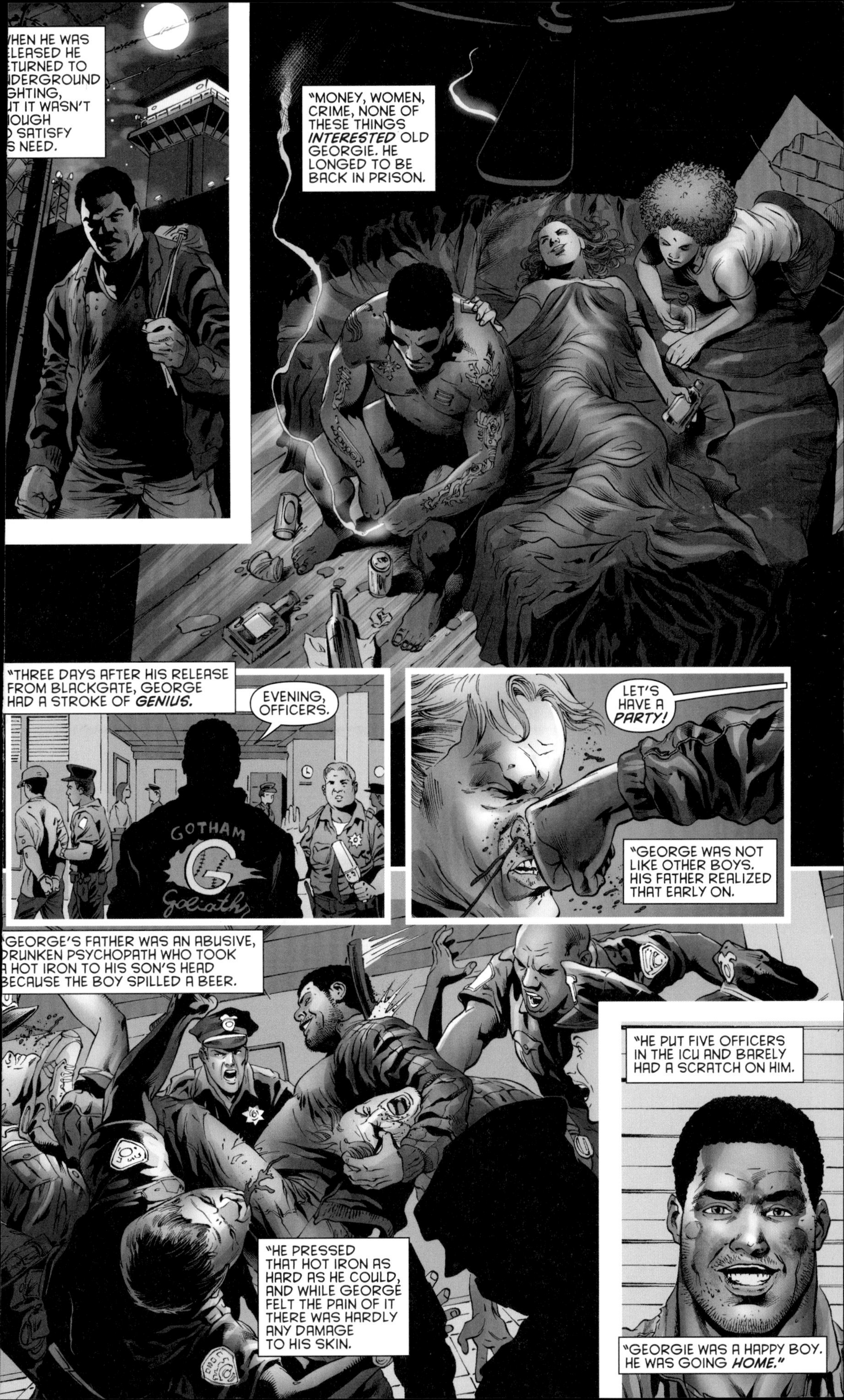

HEN HE WAS
ELEASED HE
ETURNED TO
NDERGROUND
GHTING,
UT IT WASN'T
NOUGH
O SATISFY
S NEED.
"MONEY, WOMEN, CRIME, NONE OF THESE THINGS INTERESTED OLD GEORGIE. HE LONGED TO BE BACK IN PRISON.
"THREE DAYS AFTER HIS RELEASE FROM BLACKGATE, GEORGE HAD A STROKE OF GENIUS.
EVENING, OFFICERS.
GOTHAM
Goliaths
LET'S HAVE A PARTY!
"GEORGE WAS NOT LIKE OTHER BOYS. HIS FATHER REALIZED THAT EARLY ON.
"GEORGE'S FATHER WAS AN ABUSIVE, DRUNKEN PSYCHOPATH WHO TOOK A HOT IRON TO HIS SON'S HEAD BECAUSE THE BOY SPILLED A BEER.
"HE PUT FIVE OFFICERS IN THE ICU AND BARELY HAD A SCRATCH ON HIM.
"HE PRESSED THAT HOT IRON AS HARD AS HE COULD, AND WHILE GEORGE FELT THE PAIN OF IT THERE WAS HARDLY ANY DAMAGE TO HIS SKIN.
"GEORGIE WAS A HAPPY BOY. HE WAS GOING HOME."

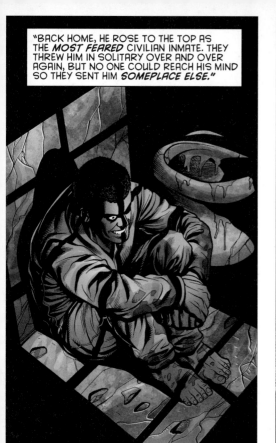

"BACK HOME, HE ROSE TO THE TOP AS THE *MOST FEARED* CIVILIAN INMATE. THEY THREW HIM IN SOLITARY OVER AND OVER AGAIN, BUT NO ONE COULD REACH HIS MIND SO THEY SENT HIM *SOMEPLACE ELSE.*"

I WANT TO GO *HOME!*

THIS IS NOT FOR ME!

"GEORGIE DIDN'T LIKE ARKHAM ASYLUM ONE BIT. HE COULDN'T TASTE ANYTHING. HE WAS ALWAYS SLEEPY.

"WORST OF ALL, HE COULDN'T *PUNCH* ANYONE.

"HE WAS STILL CAPABLE OF SEEING THROUGH THE HAZE OF HIS MEDICATION CLEARLY ENOUGH TO REALIZE HE NEEDED A PURPOSE.

"SOMETHING TO LIVE FOR."

SEVERAL OF THE MEN TAKEN INTO CUSTODY SAID THEY WERE *ATTACKED* BY A MAN WEARING A BATSUIT.

THIS BATMAN SUBDUED MORE THAN A *DOZEN* GANG MEMBERS SINGLE-HANDEDLY.

"THEN ONE NIGHT HE GETS A *SIGN.* HE GETS THE HOPE FOR A BETTER DAY.

"PROBLEM IS, POOR GEORGIE'S STILL IN THE LOONY BIN.

"THEN, FIVE YEARS LATER, A MIRACLE OF MIRACLES WHEN ONE NIGHT THE WHOLE WORLD GOES TOPSY-TURVY, THE LUNATICS AND SUPER-WACKOS BUST OUT OF THE CUCKOO'S NEST."

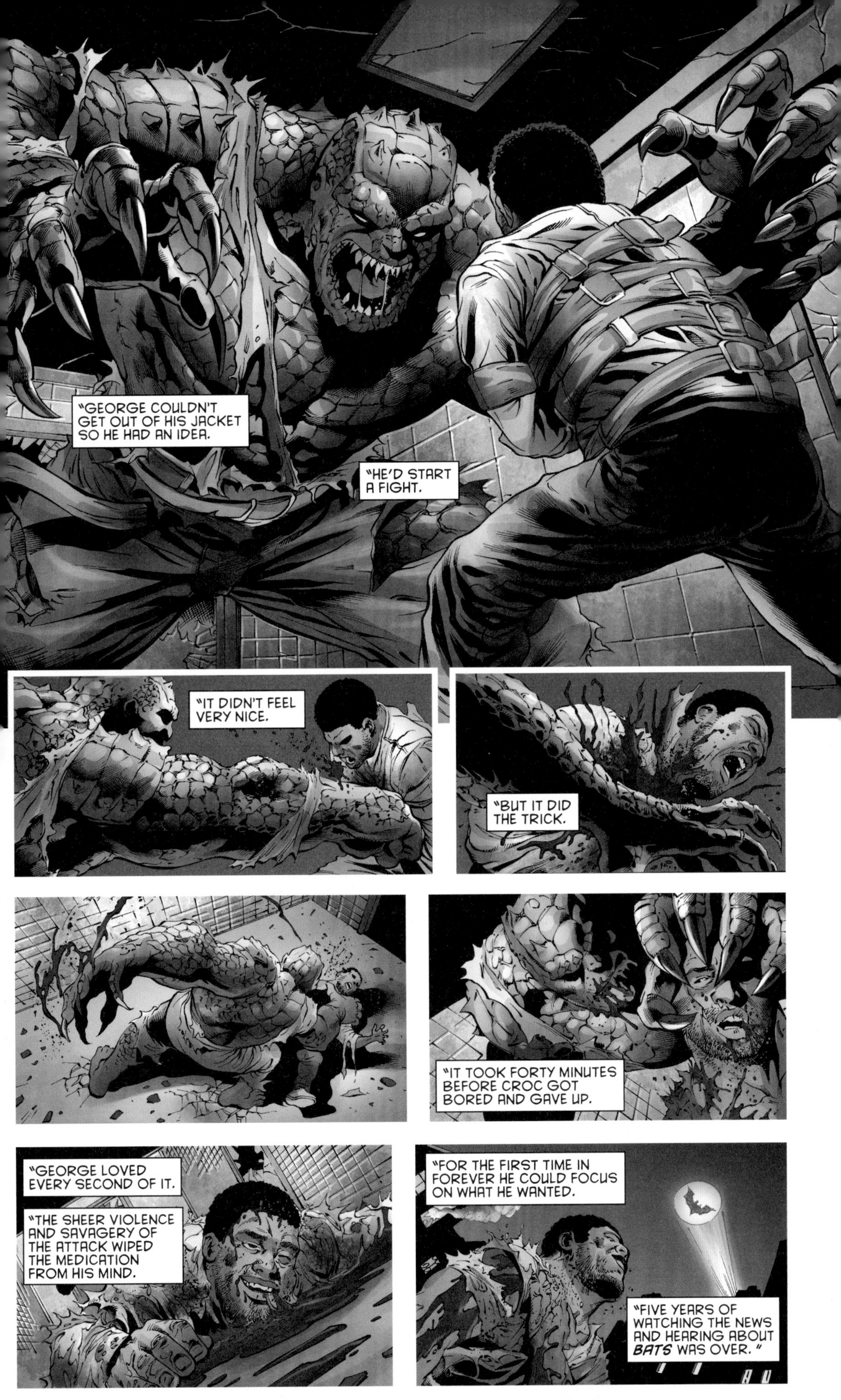
"GEORGE COULDN'T GET OUT OF HIS JACKET SO HE HAD AN IDEA.
"HE'D START A FIGHT.
"IT DIDN'T FEEL VERY NICE.
"BUT IT DID THE TRICK.
"IT TOOK FORTY MINUTES BEFORE CROC GOT BORED AND GAVE UP.
"GEORGE LOVED EVERY SECOND OF IT.
"THE SHEER VIOLENCE AND SAVAGERY OF THE ATTACK WIPED THE MEDICATION FROM HIS MIND.
"FOR THE FIRST TIME IN FOREVER HE COULD FOCUS ON WHAT HE WANTED.
"FIVE YEARS OF WATCHING THE NEWS AND HEARING ABOUT *BATS* WAS OVER."

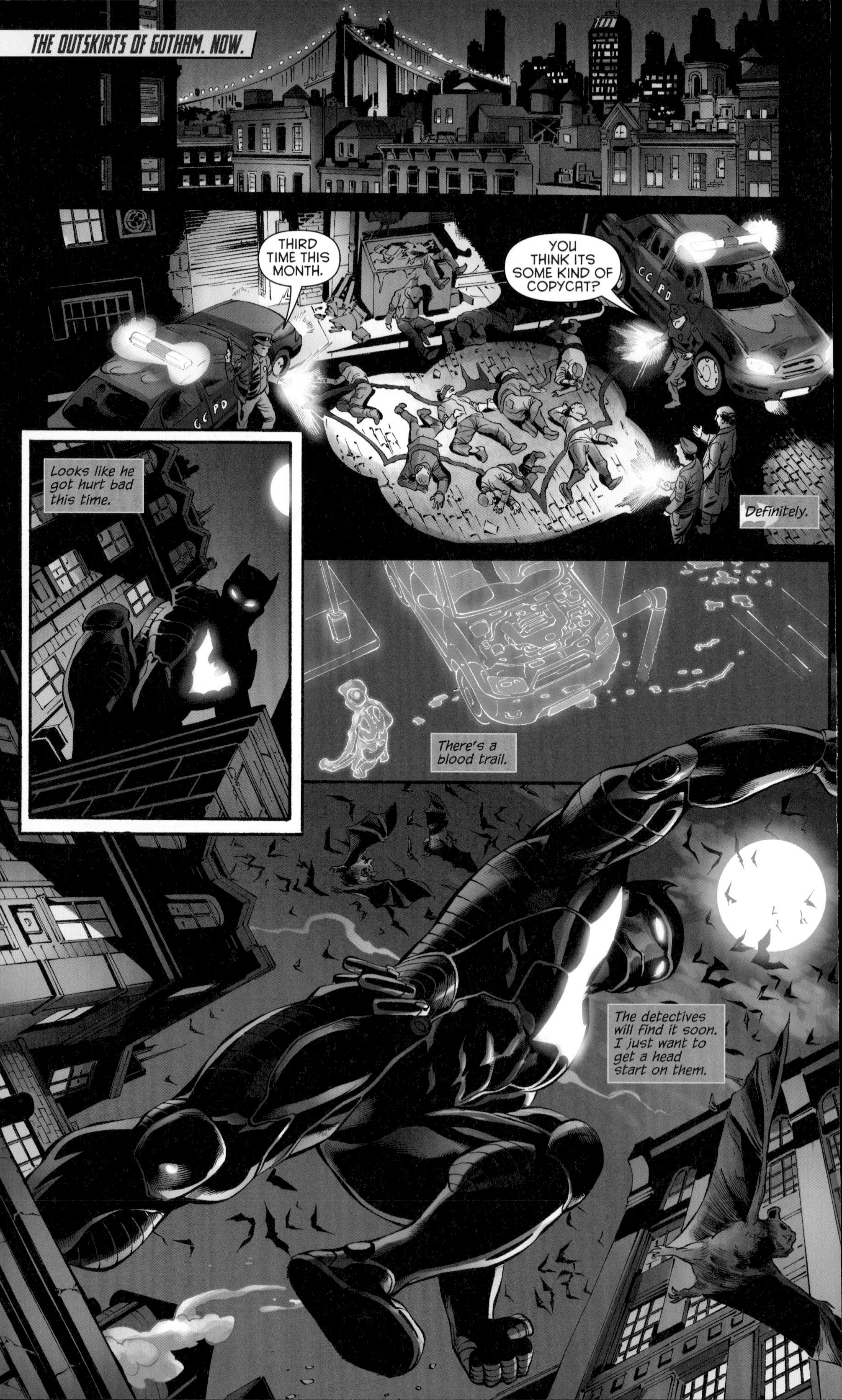
THE OUTSKIRTS OF GOTHAM. NOW.
THIRD TIME THIS MONTH.
YOU THINK ITS SOME KIND OF COPYCAT?
Definitely.
Looks like he got hurt bad this time.
There's a blood trail.
The detectives will find it soon. I just want to get a head start on them.

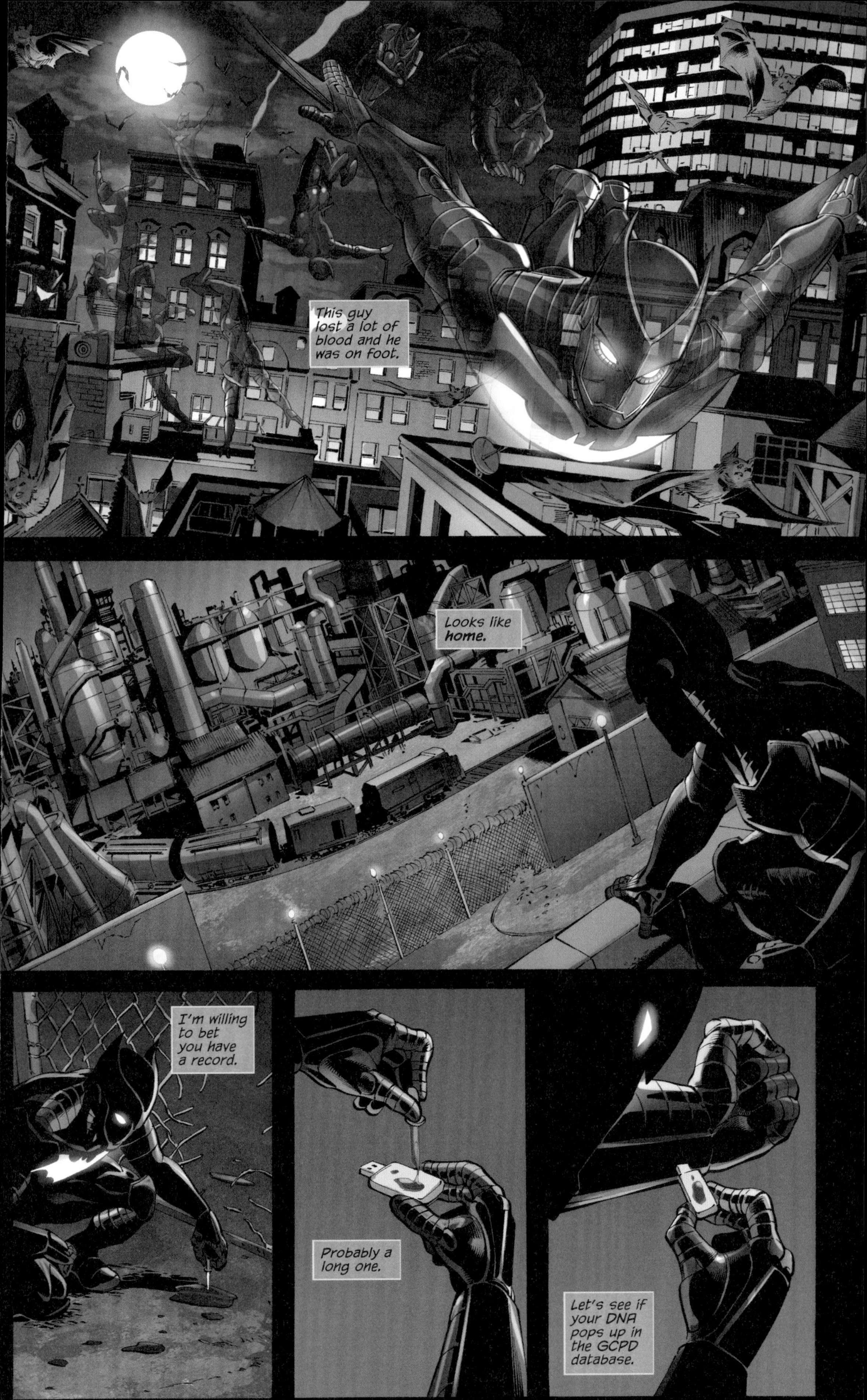
This guy lost a lot of blood and he was on foot.
Looks like **home.**
I'm willing to bet you have a record.
Probably a long one.
Let's see if your DNA pops up in the GCPD database.

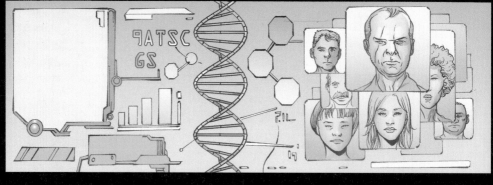

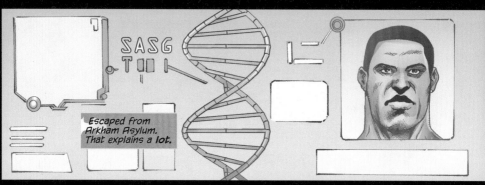

Escaped from Arkham Asylum. That explains a *lot.*

He's wounded and down a few quarts. Shouldn't be too much trouble once I find a way inside.

INCOMING CALL FROM ENCRYPTED PERSONAL CELL PHONE.

CALLER ID?

MOM.

RESTRICT EXTERNAL AUDIO. BROADCAST INSIDE THE HELMET AND ANSWER.

HEY, MOM. WHAT'S UP? WHY ARE YOU CALLING ME IN THE MIDDLE OF THE NIGHT?

HI, BABY. I COULDN'T SLEEP.

I WANTED TO ASK IF YOU'D PICK UP TAM'S *BIRTHDAY CAKE* FROM THE BAKERY.

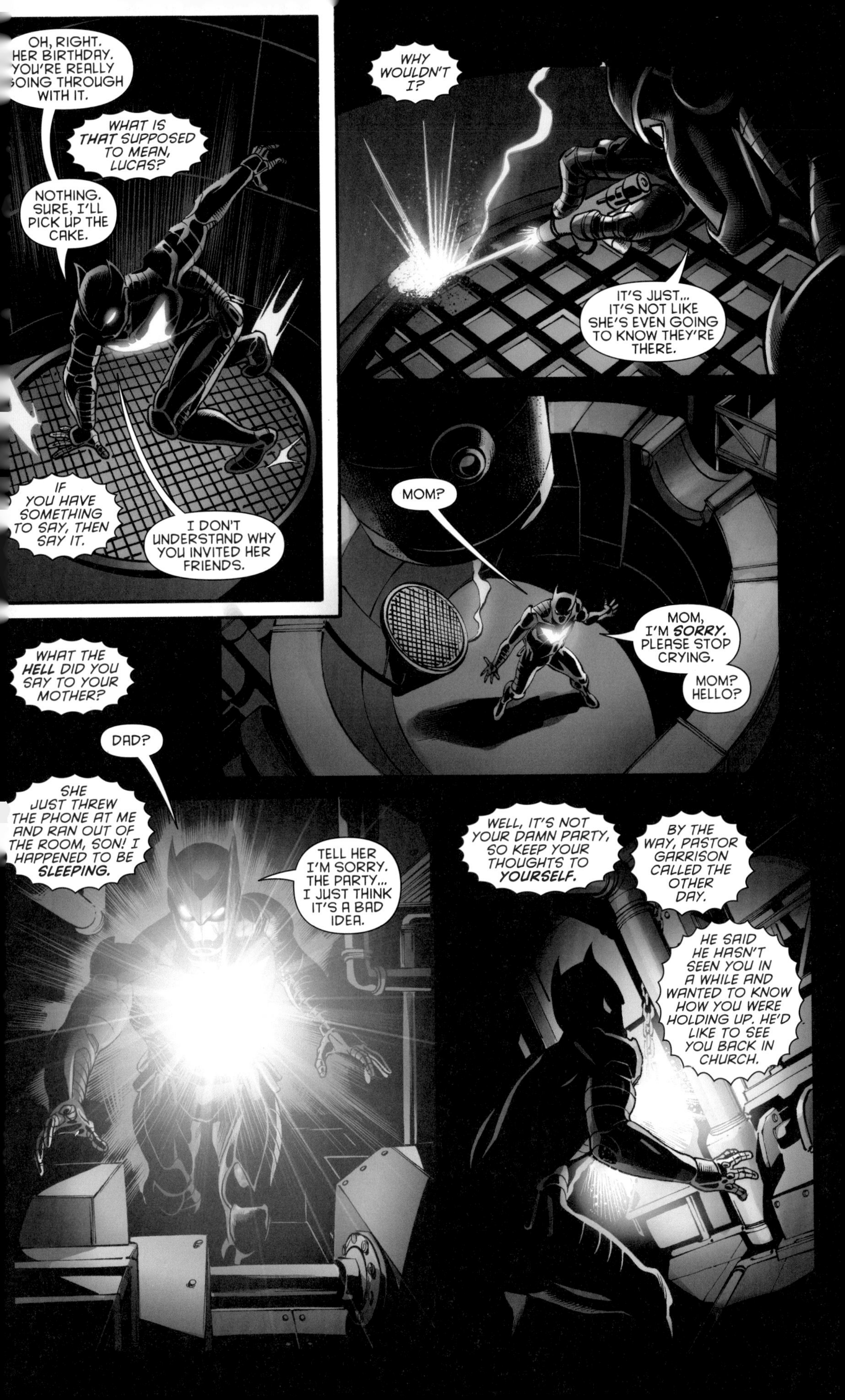
OH, RIGHT. HER BIRTHDAY. YOU'RE REALLY GOING THROUGH WITH IT.
WHAT IS THAT SUPPOSED TO MEAN, LUCAS?
NOTHING. SURE, I'LL PICK UP THE CAKE.
WHY WOULDN'T I?
IT'S JUST... IT'S NOT LIKE SHE'S EVEN GOING TO KNOW THEY'RE THERE.
IF YOU HAVE SOMETHING TO SAY, THEN SAY IT.
I DON'T UNDERSTAND WHY YOU INVITED HER FRIENDS.
MOM?
MOM, I'M SORRY. PLEASE STOP CRYING.
MOM? HELLO?
WHAT THE HELL DID YOU SAY TO YOUR MOTHER?
DAD?
SHE JUST THREW THE PHONE AT ME AND RAN OUT OF THE ROOM, SON! I HAPPENED TO BE SLEEPING.
TELL HER I'M SORRY. THE PARTY... I JUST THINK IT'S A BAD IDEA.
WELL, IT'S NOT YOUR DAMN PARTY, SO KEEP YOUR THOUGHTS TO YOURSELF.
BY THE WAY, PASTOR GARRISON CALLED THE OTHER DAY.
HE SAID HE HASN'T SEEN YOU IN A WHILE AND WANTED TO KNOW HOW YOU WERE HOLDING UP. HE'D LIKE TO SEE YOU BACK IN CHURCH.

I'VE BEEN BUSY.
DOING WHAT? AS FAR AS I KNOW YOU DON'T HAVE A JOB, AND YOU STILL HAVEN'T ENROLLED IN A COLLEGE.
GREAT, IS THIS A PREVIEW OF TOMORROW NIGHT? YOU'RE GOING TO GET ON ME AT THE PARTY?
I'M DONE BOTHERING YOU ABOUT YOUR FUTURE.
IT WOULDN'T HURT TO CALL TIFFANY ONCE IN A WHILE. SHE'S ALWAYS ASKING ABOUT YOU, AND I'M TIRED OF MAKING EXCUSES.
TELL HER I'LL BE THERE TOMORROW NIGHT AND APOLOGIZE TO MOM FOR ME.
TELL HER YOURSELF.
CLICK
GREAT. HANG UP ON ME. THANKS, DAD.

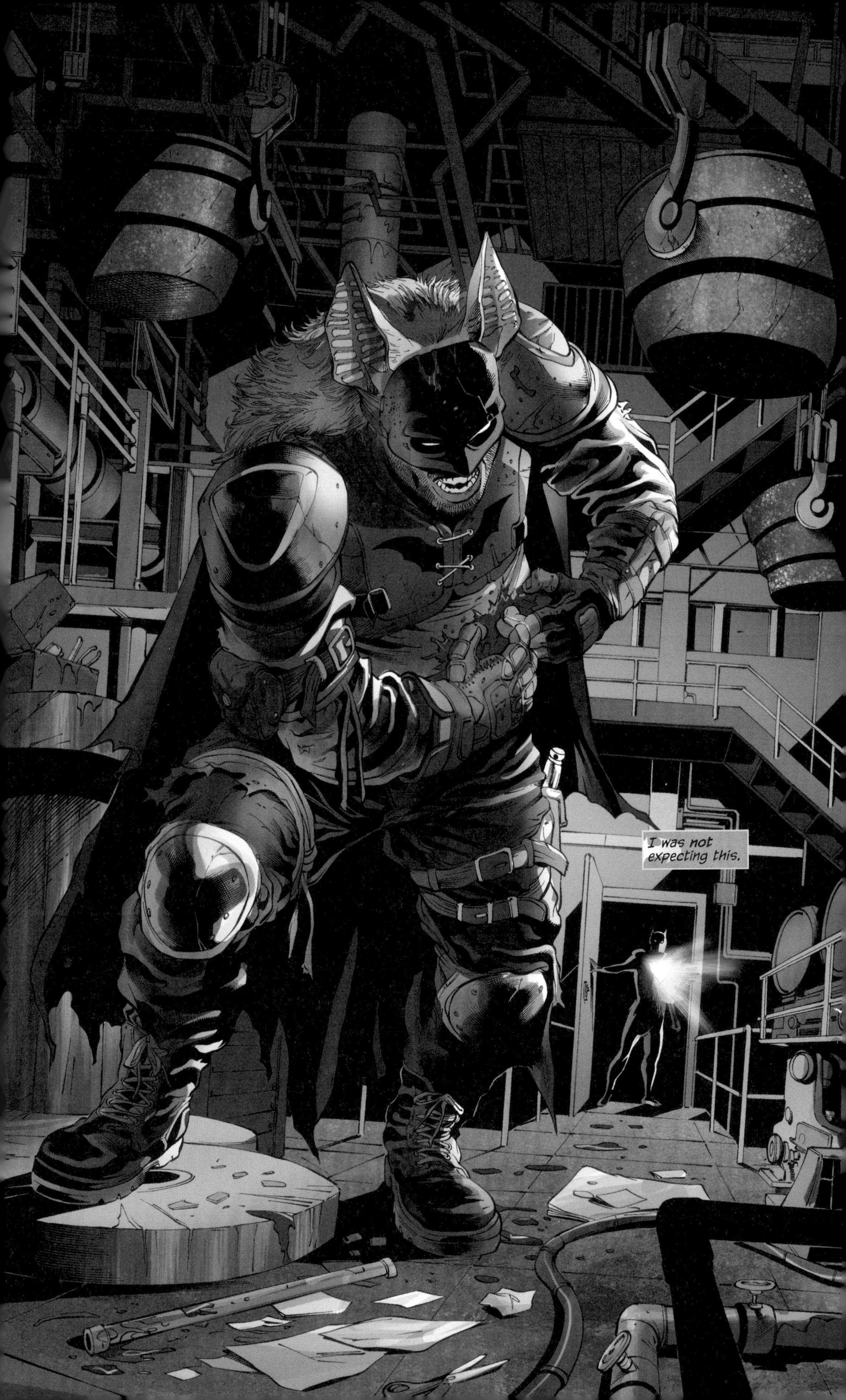
I was not expecting this.

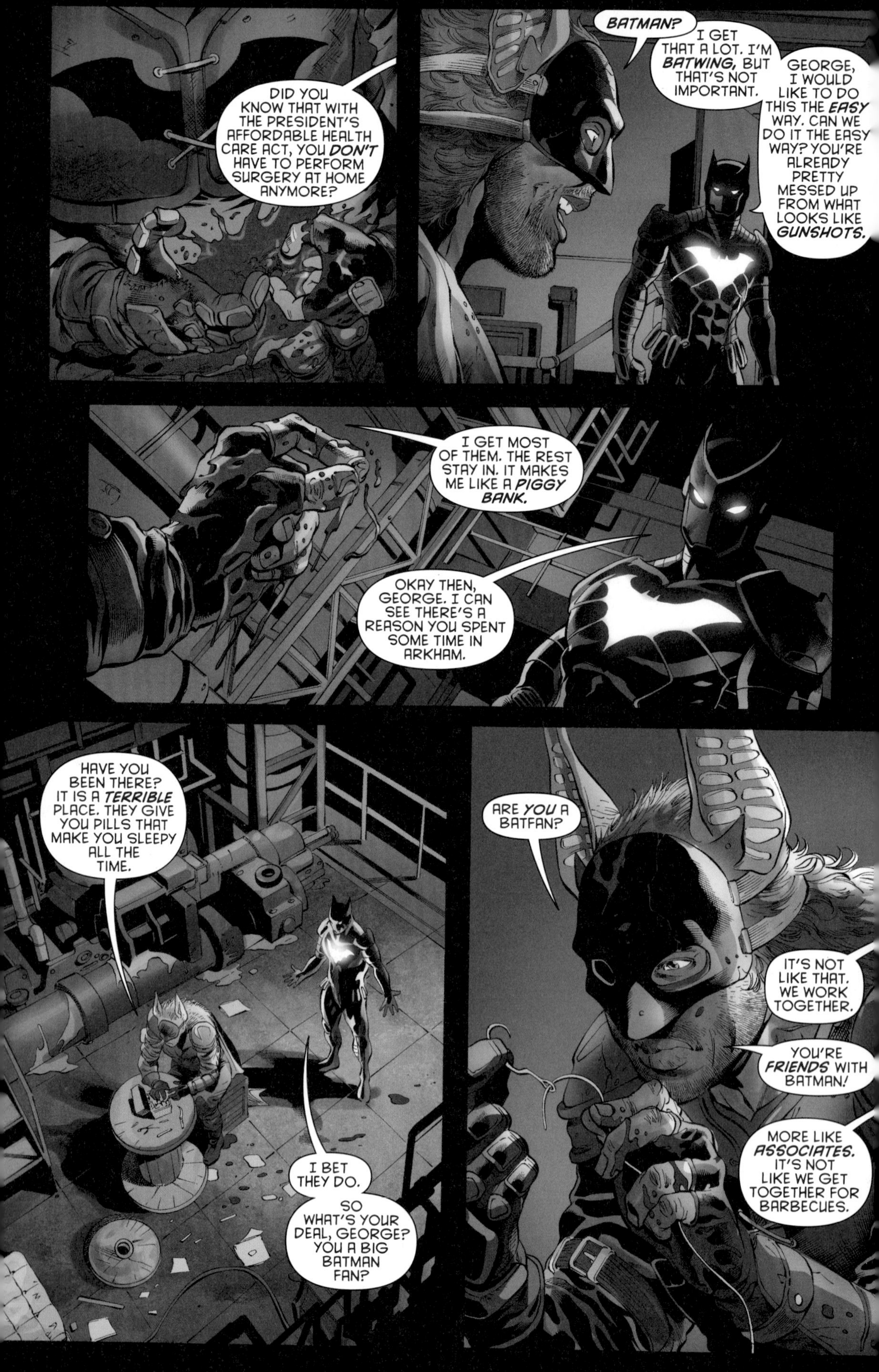

DID YOU KNOW THAT WITH THE PRESIDENT'S AFFORDABLE HEALTH CARE ACT, YOU DON'T HAVE TO PERFORM SURGERY AT HOME ANYMORE?
BATMAN?
I GET THAT A LOT. I'M BATWING, BUT THAT'S NOT IMPORTANT.
GEORGE, I WOULD LIKE TO DO THIS THE EASY WAY. CAN WE DO IT THE EASY WAY? YOU'RE ALREADY PRETTY MESSED UP FROM WHAT LOOKS LIKE GUNSHOTS.
I GET MOST OF THEM. THE REST STAY IN. IT MAKES ME LIKE A PIGGY BANK.
OKAY THEN, GEORGE. I CAN SEE THERE'S A REASON YOU SPENT SOME TIME IN ARKHAM.
HAVE YOU BEEN THERE? IT IS A TERRIBLE PLACE. THEY GIVE YOU PILLS THAT MAKE YOU SLEEPY ALL THE TIME.
I BET THEY DO.
SO WHAT'S YOUR DEAL, GEORGE? YOU A BIG BATMAN FAN?
ARE YOU A BATFAN?
IT'S NOT LIKE THAT. WE WORK TOGETHER.
YOU'RE FRIENDS WITH BATMAN!
MORE LIKE ASSOCIATES. IT'S NOT LIKE WE GET TOGETHER FOR BARBECUES.

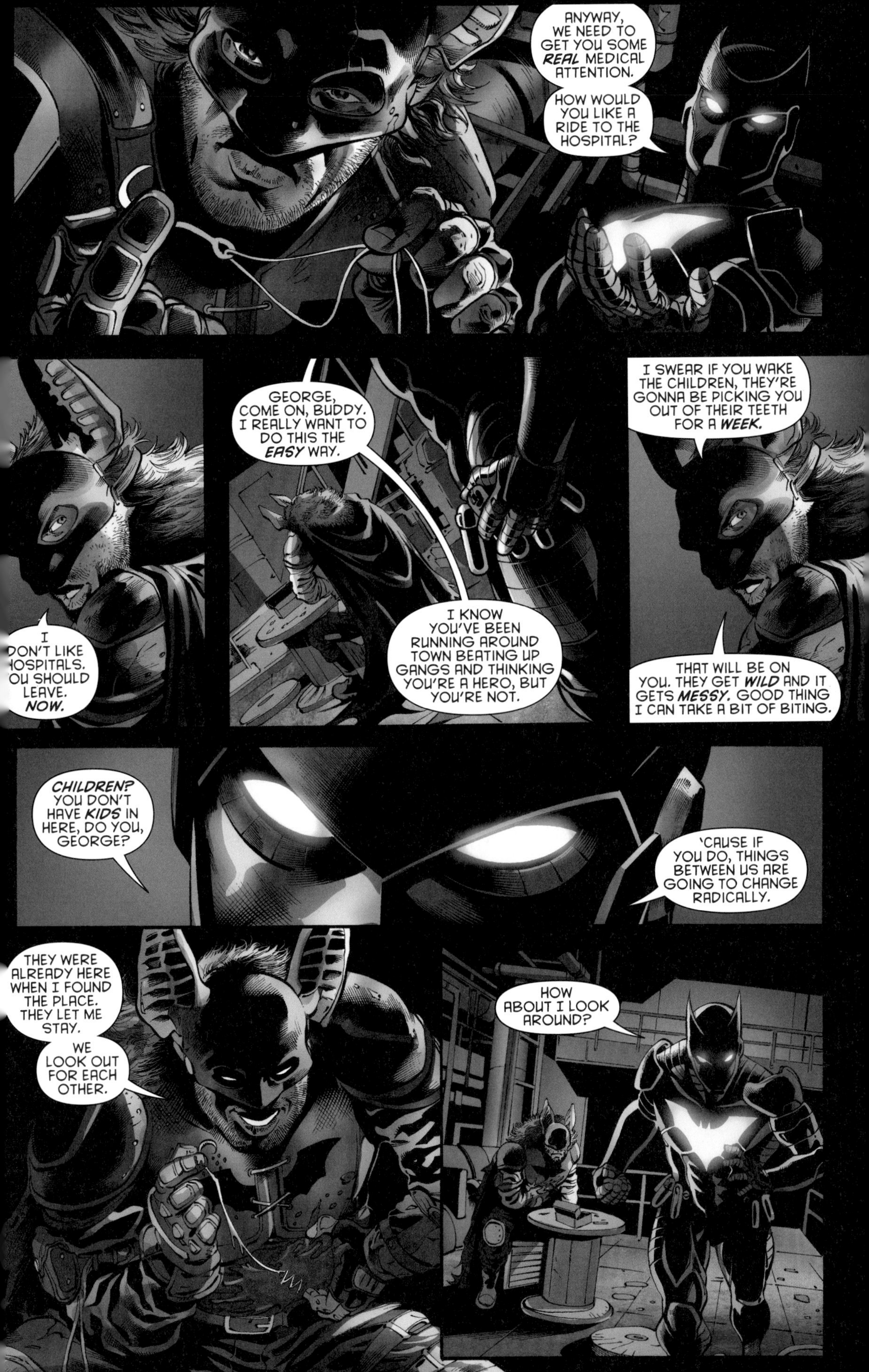

ANYWAY, WE NEED TO GET YOU SOME **REAL** MEDICAL ATTENTION.
HOW WOULD YOU LIKE A RIDE TO THE HOSPITAL?
I DON'T LIKE HOSPITALS. YOU SHOULD LEAVE. **NOW.**
GEORGE, COME ON, BUDDY. I REALLY WANT TO DO THIS THE **EASY** WAY.
I KNOW YOU'VE BEEN RUNNING AROUND TOWN BEATING UP GANGS AND THINKING YOU'RE A HERO, BUT YOU'RE NOT.
I SWEAR IF YOU WAKE THE CHILDREN, THEY'RE GONNA BE PICKING YOU OUT OF THEIR TEETH FOR A **WEEK.**
THAT WILL BE ON YOU. THEY GET **WILD** AND IT GETS **MESSY.** GOOD THING I CAN TAKE A BIT OF BITING.
CHILDREN? YOU DON'T HAVE **KIDS** IN HERE, DO YOU, GEORGE?
'CAUSE IF YOU DO, THINGS BETWEEN US ARE GOING TO CHANGE RADICALLY.
THEY WERE ALREADY HERE WHEN I FOUND THE PLACE. THEY LET ME STAY.
WE LOOK OUT FOR EACH OTHER.
HOW ABOUT I LOOK AROUND?

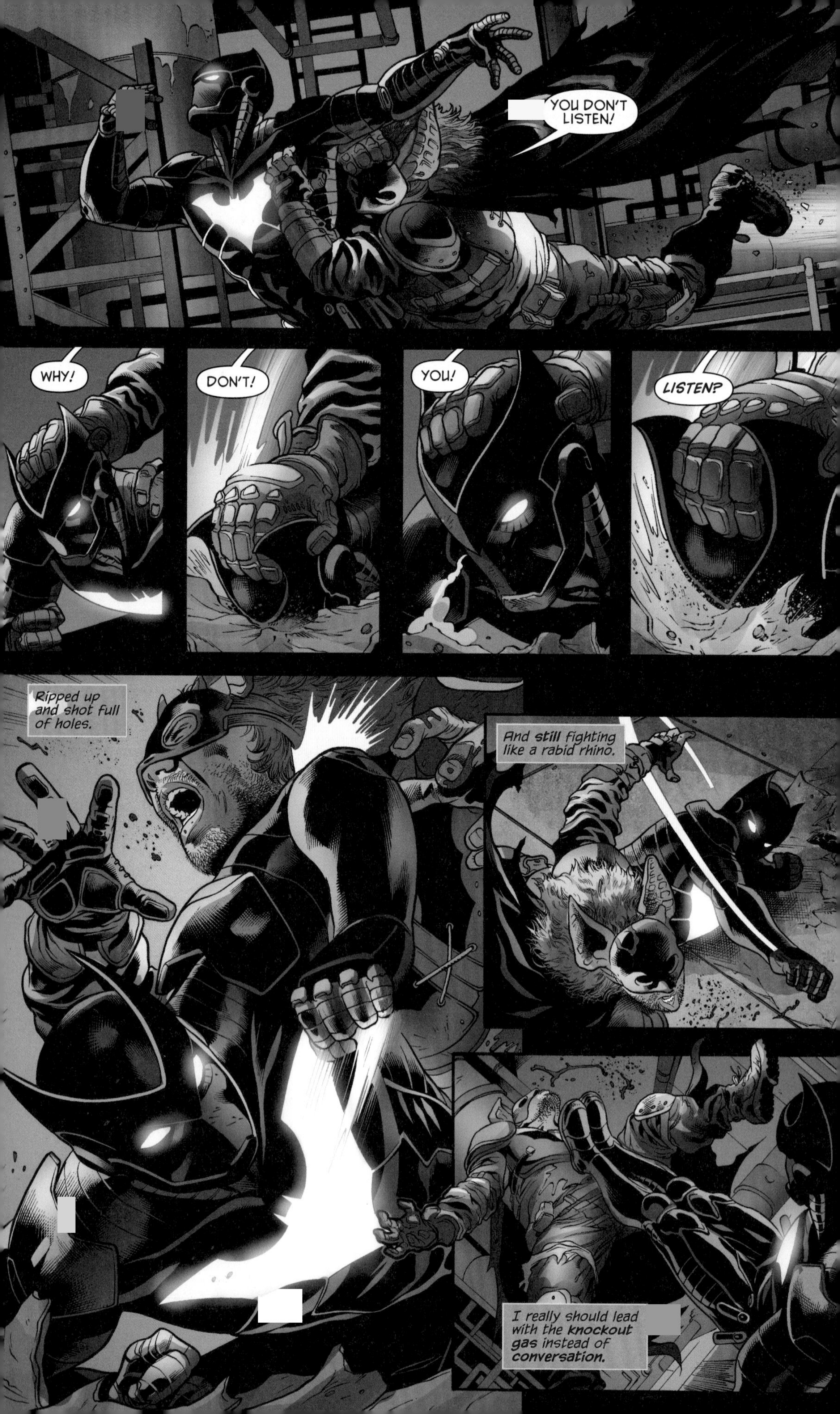
YOU DON'T LISTEN!
WHY!
DON'T!
YOU!
LISTEN?
Ripped up and shot full of holes.
And still fighting like a rabid rhino.
I really should lead with the knockout gas instead of conversation.

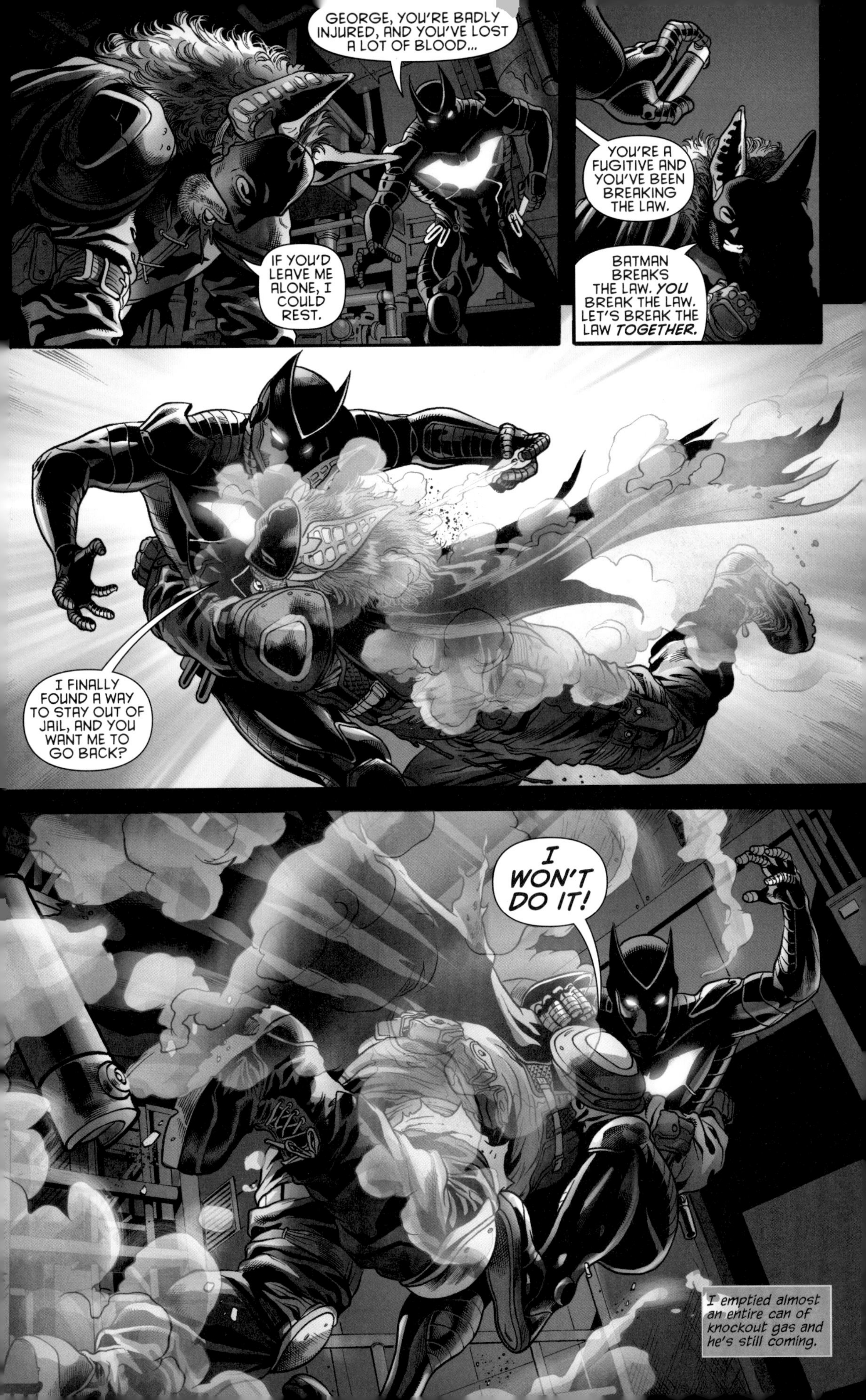
GEORGE, YOU'RE BADLY INJURED, AND YOU'VE LOST A LOT OF BLOOD...
IF YOU'D LEAVE ME ALONE, I COULD REST.
YOU'RE A FUGITIVE AND YOU'VE BEEN BREAKING THE LAW.
BATMAN BREAKS THE LAW. *YOU* BREAK THE LAW. LET'S BREAK THE LAW *TOGETHER.*
I FINALLY FOUND A WAY TO STAY OUT OF JAIL, AND YOU WANT ME TO GO BACK?
I WON'T DO IT!
I emptied almost an entire can of knockout gas and he's still coming.

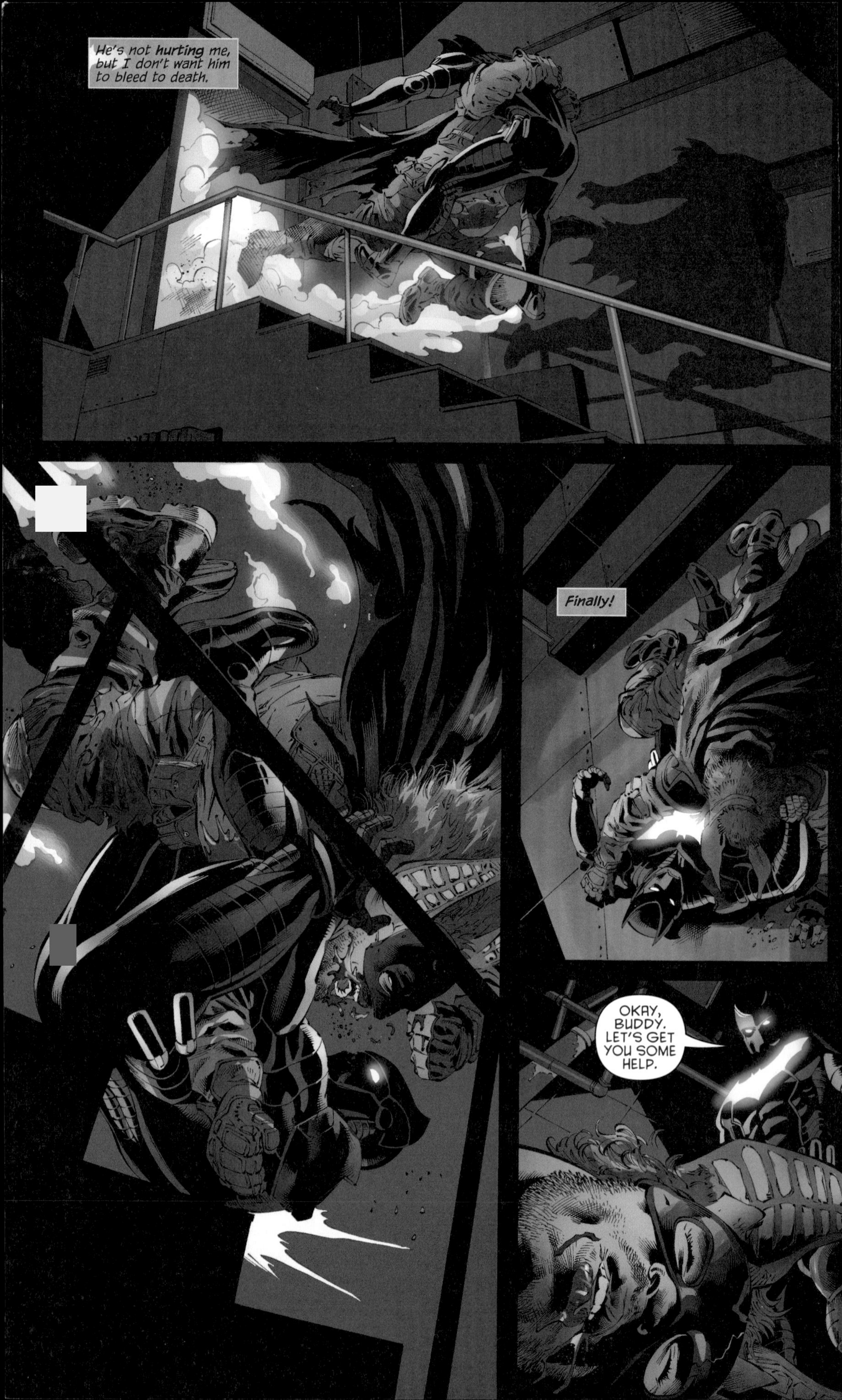
He's not hurting me, but I don't want him to bleed to death.
Finally!
OKAY, BUDDY. LET'S GET YOU SOME HELP.

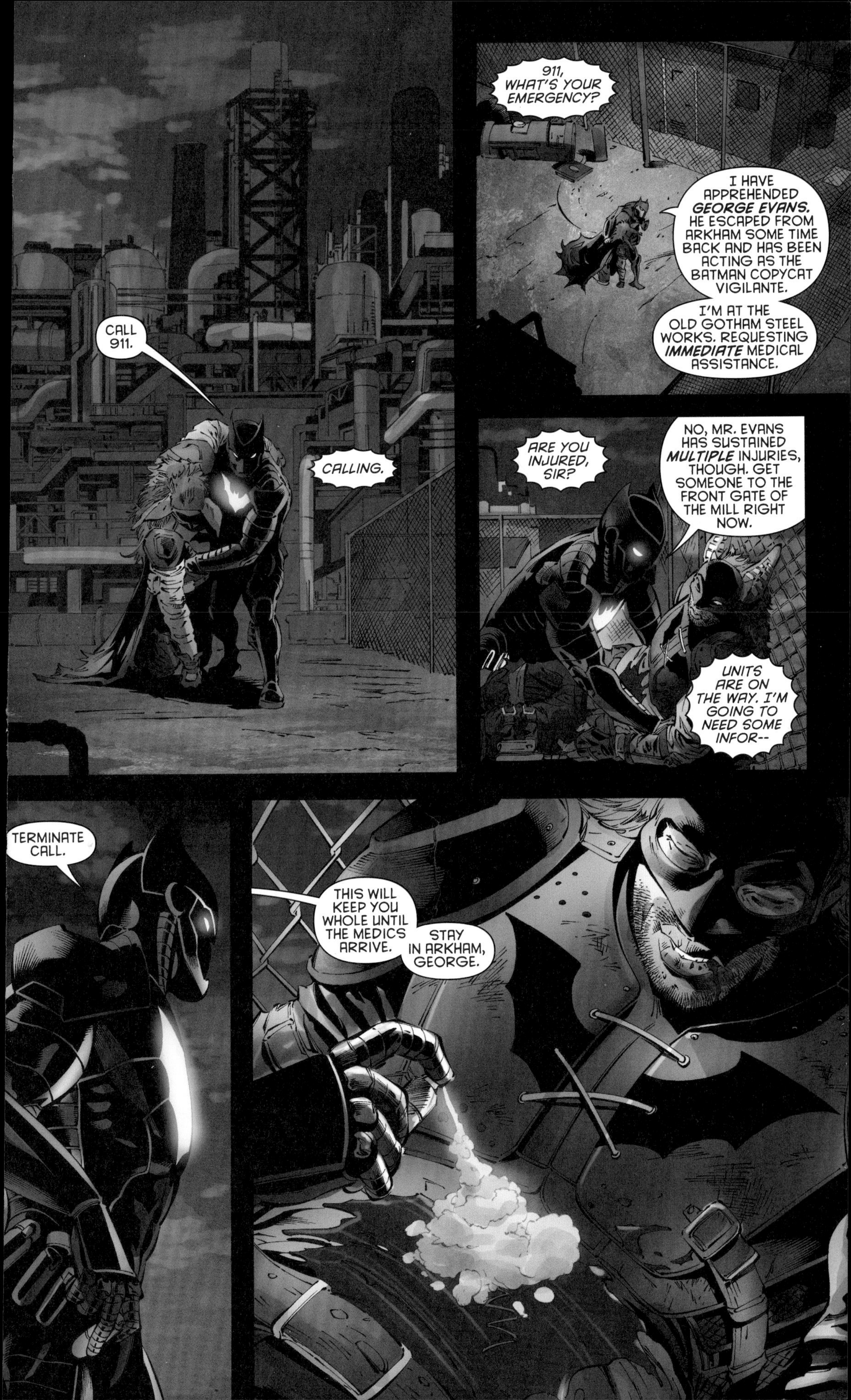
CALL 911.
CALLING.
911, WHAT'S YOUR EMERGENCY?
I HAVE APPREHENDED *GEORGE EVANS.* HE ESCAPED FROM ARKHAM SOME TIME BACK AND HAS BEEN ACTING AS THE BATMAN COPYCAT VIGILANTE.
I'M AT THE OLD GOTHAM STEEL WORKS. REQUESTING *IMMEDIATE* MEDICAL ASSISTANCE.
ARE YOU INJURED, SIR?
NO, MR. EVANS HAS SUSTAINED *MULTIPLE* INJURIES, THOUGH. GET SOMEONE TO THE FRONT GATE OF THE MILL RIGHT NOW.
UNITS ARE ON THE WAY. I'M GOING TO NEED SOME INFOR--
TERMINATE CALL.
THIS WILL KEEP YOU WHOLE UNTIL THE MEDICS ARRIVE.
STAY IN ARKHAM, GEORGE.

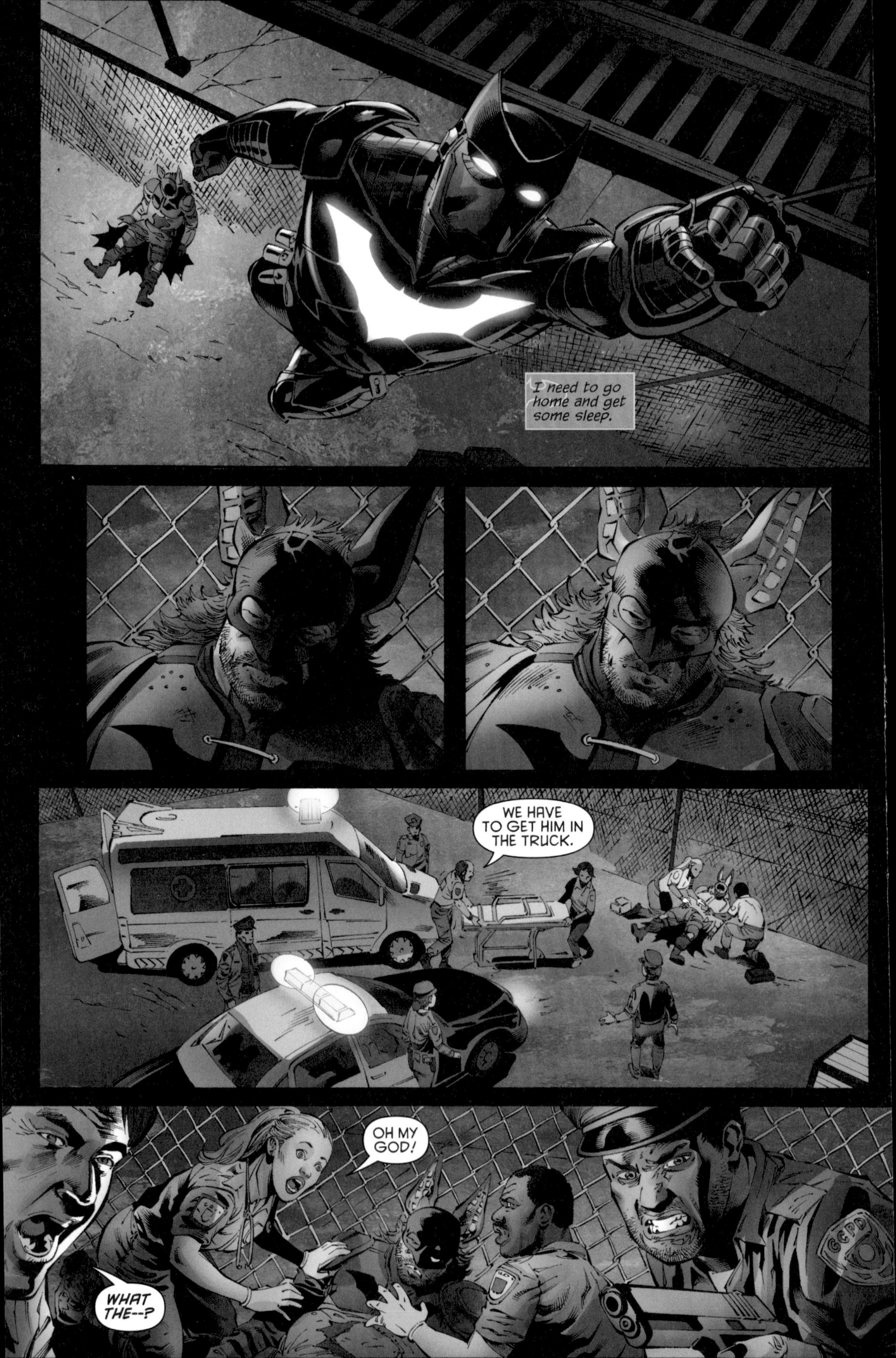
I need to go home and get some sleep.
WE HAVE TO GET HIM IN THE TRUCK.
OH MY GOD!
WHAT THE--?

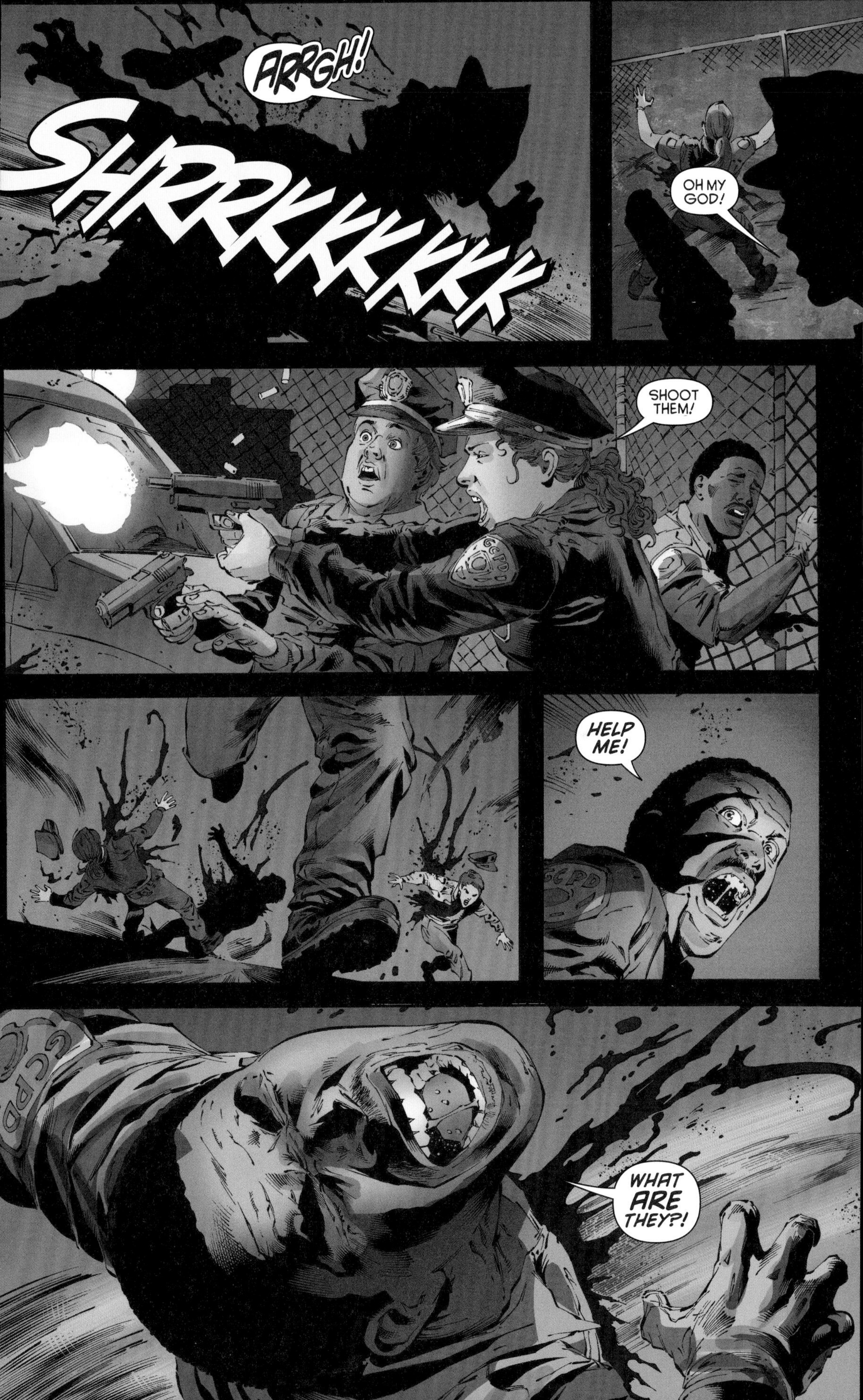
ARRGH!
SHRRKKKKKK
OH MY GOD!
SHOOT THEM!
HELP ME!
WHAT ARE THEY?!

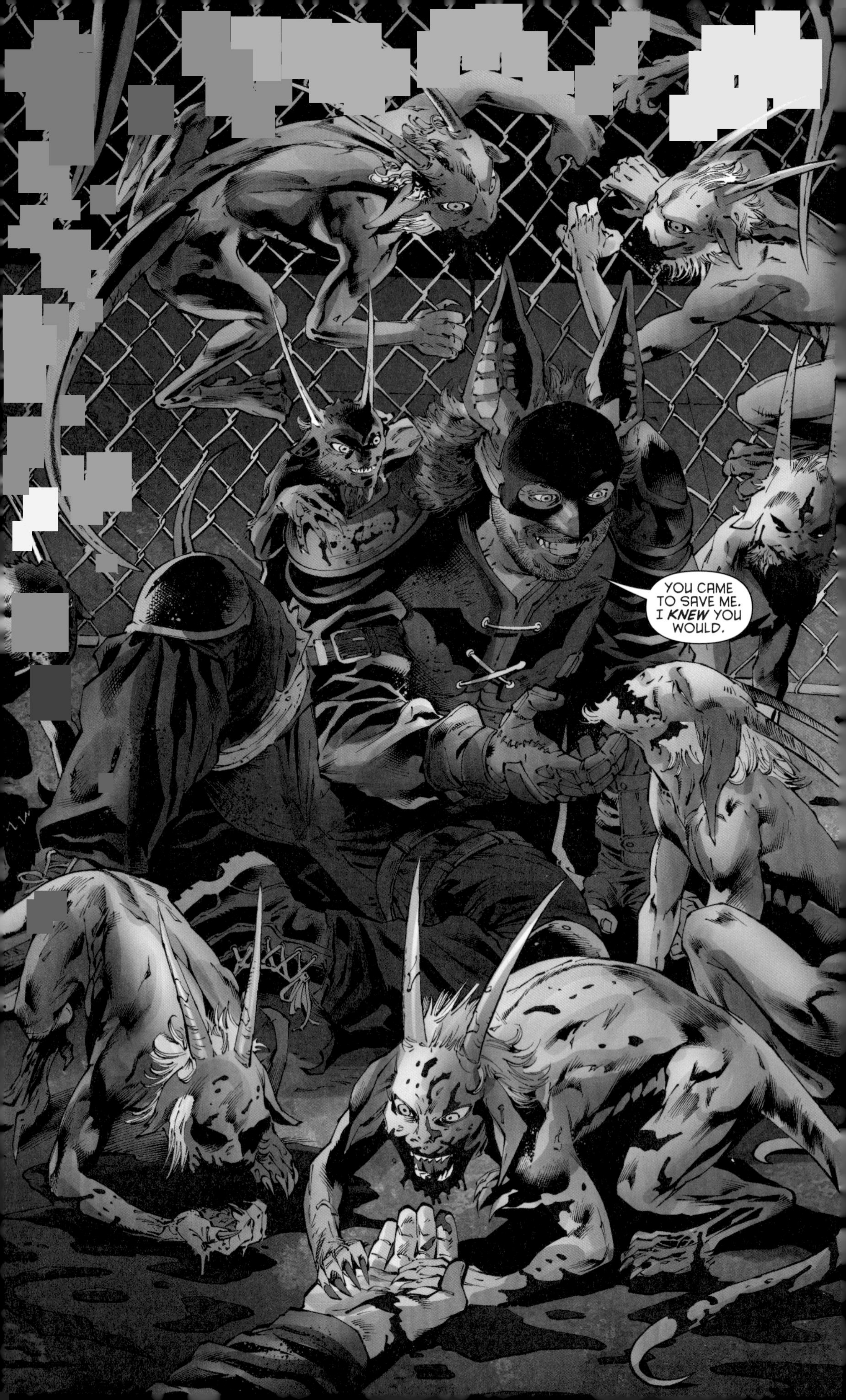
YOU CAME TO SAVE ME. I KNEW YOU WOULD.

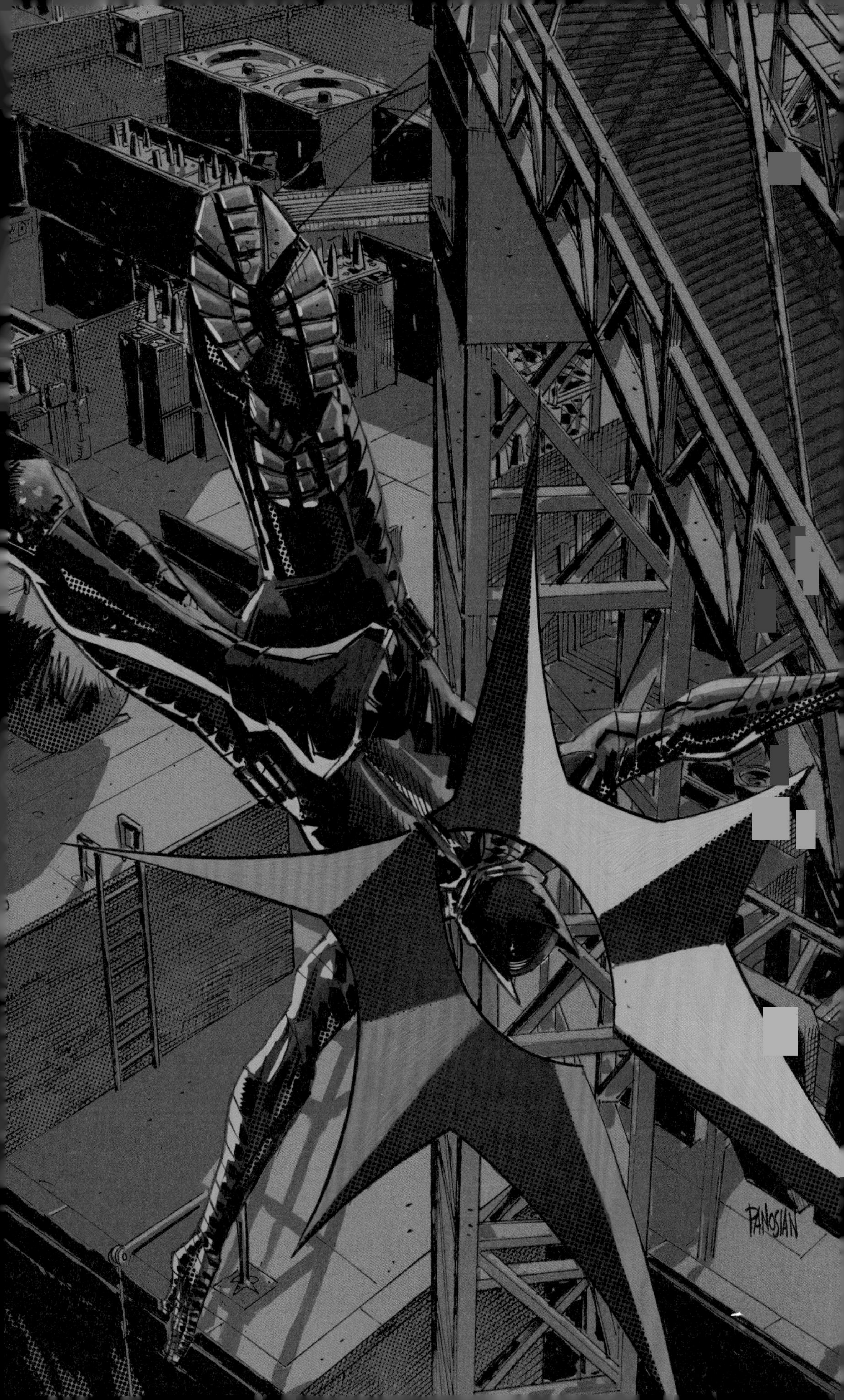
PANOSIAN

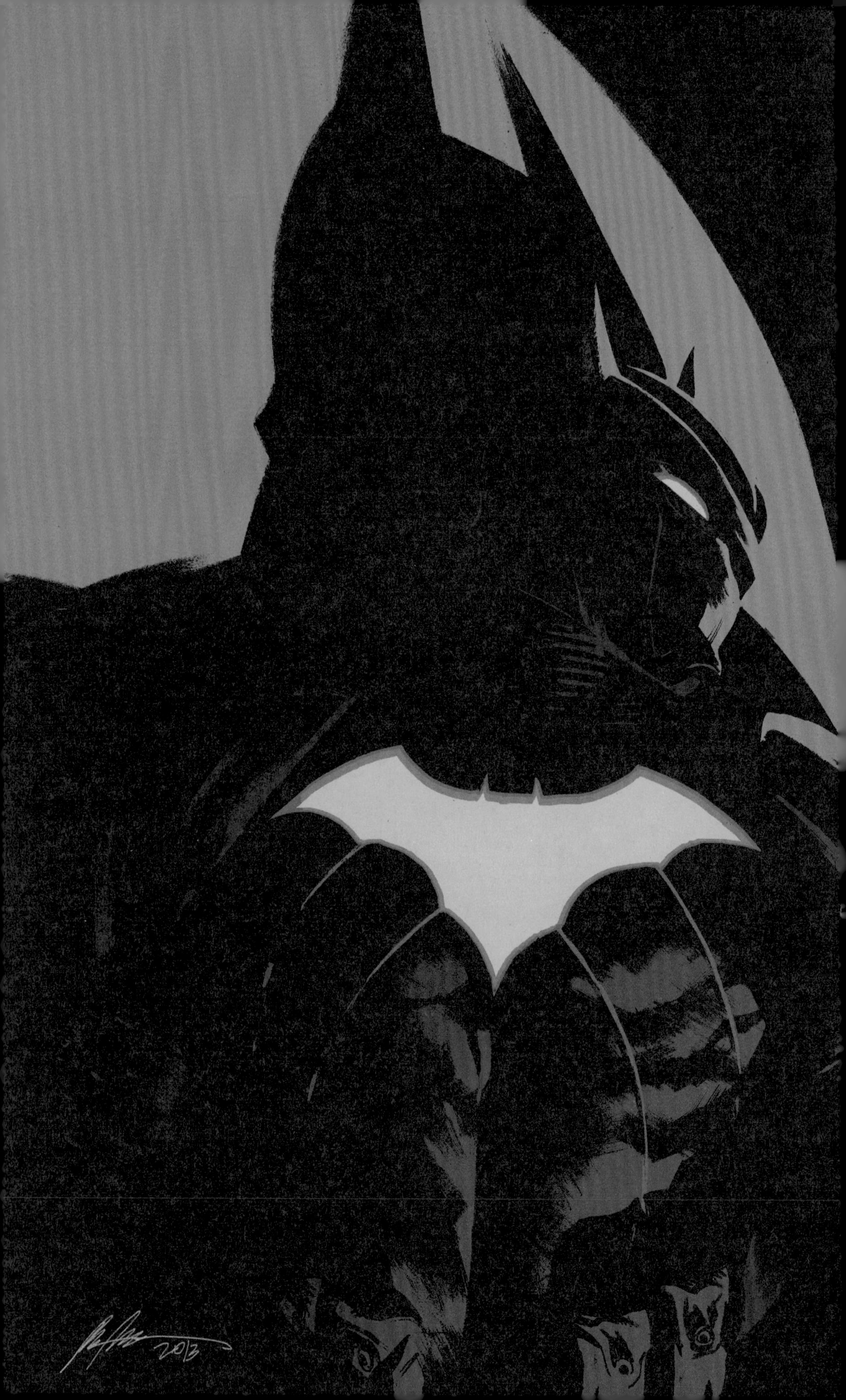
2013

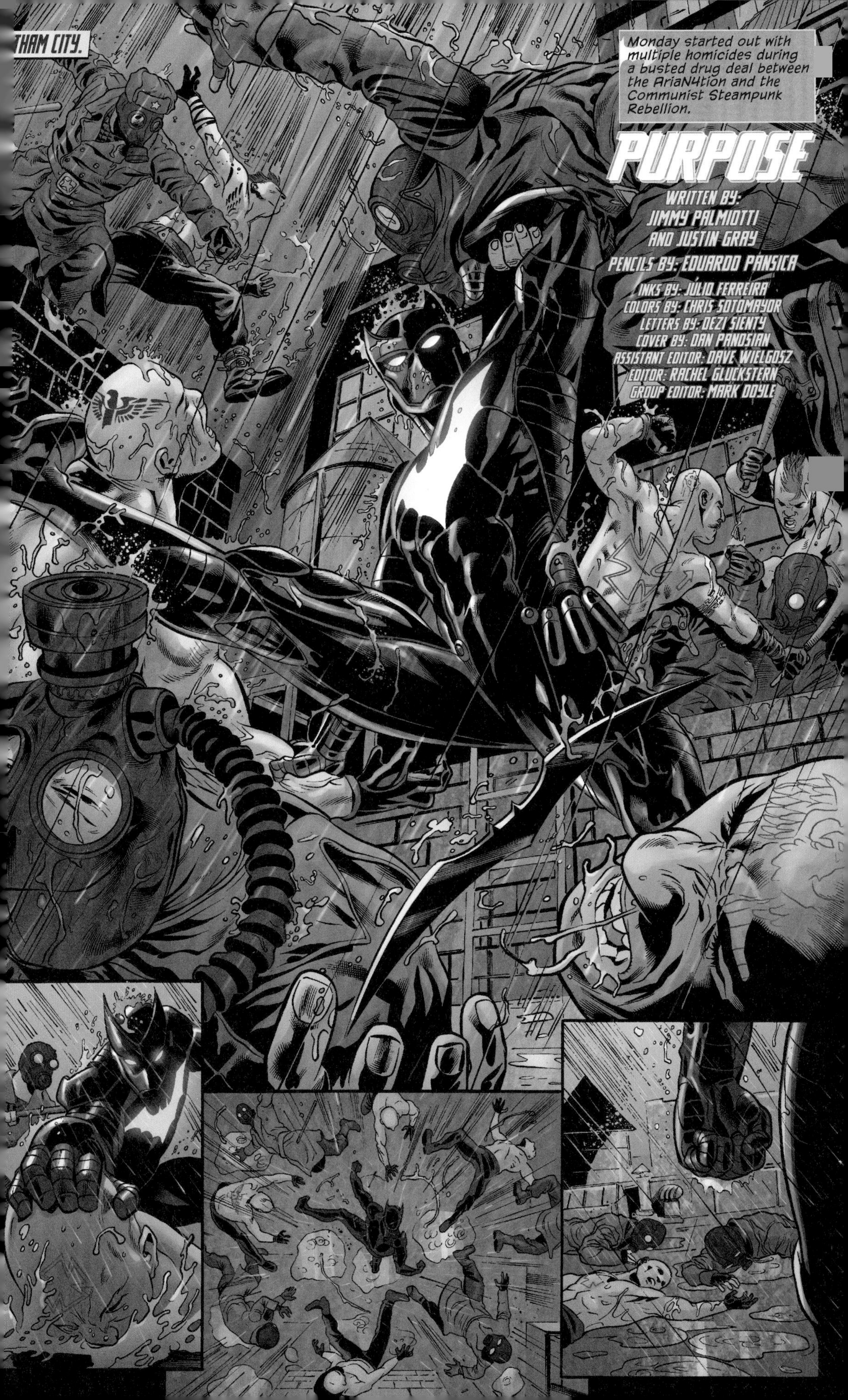
THAM CITY.
Monday started out with multiple homicides during a busted drug deal between the AriaN4tion and the Communist Steampunk Rebellion.
PURPOSE
WRITTEN BY: JIMMY PALMIOTTI AND JUSTIN GRAY
PENCILS BY: EDUARDO PANSICA
INKS BY: JÚLIO FERREIRA
COLORS BY: CHRIS SOTOMAYOR
LETTERS BY: DEZI SIENTY
COVER BY: DAN PANOSIAN
ASSISTANT EDITOR: DAVE WIELGOSZ
EDITOR: RACHEL GLUCKSTERN
GROUP EDITOR: MARK DOYLE

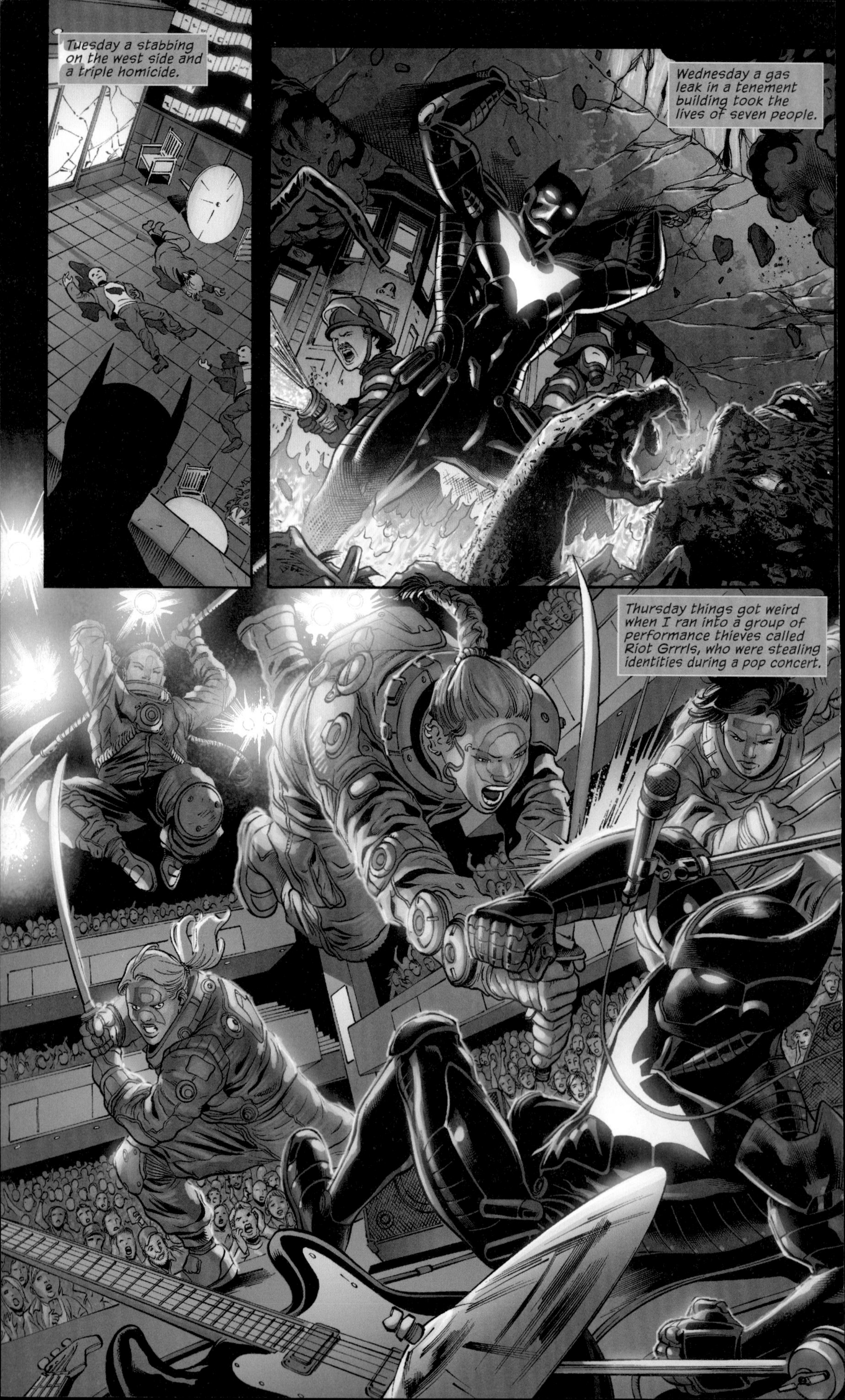
Tuesday a stabbing on the west side and a triple homicide.
Wednesday a gas leak in a tenement building took the lives of seven people.
Thursday things got weird when I ran into a group of performance thieves called Riot Grrrls, who were stealing identities during a pop concert.

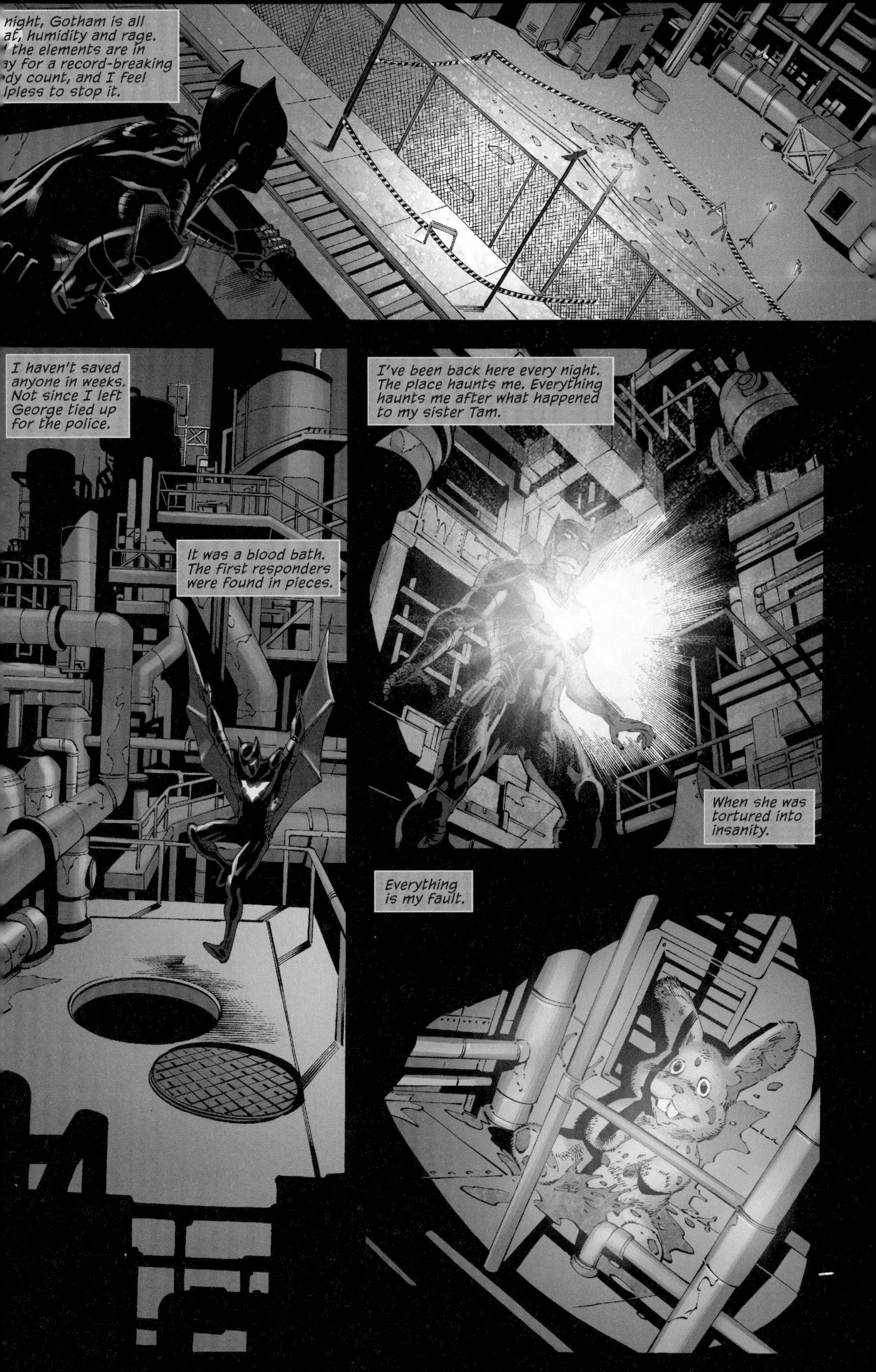

night, Gotham is all
at, humidity and rage.
the elements are in
ay for a record-breaking
dy count, and I feel
lpless to stop it.
I haven't saved anyone in weeks. Not since I left George tied up for the police.
It was a blood bath. The first responders were found in pieces.
I've been back here every night. The place haunts me. Everything haunts me after what happened to my sister Tam.
When she was tortured into insanity.
Everything is my fault.

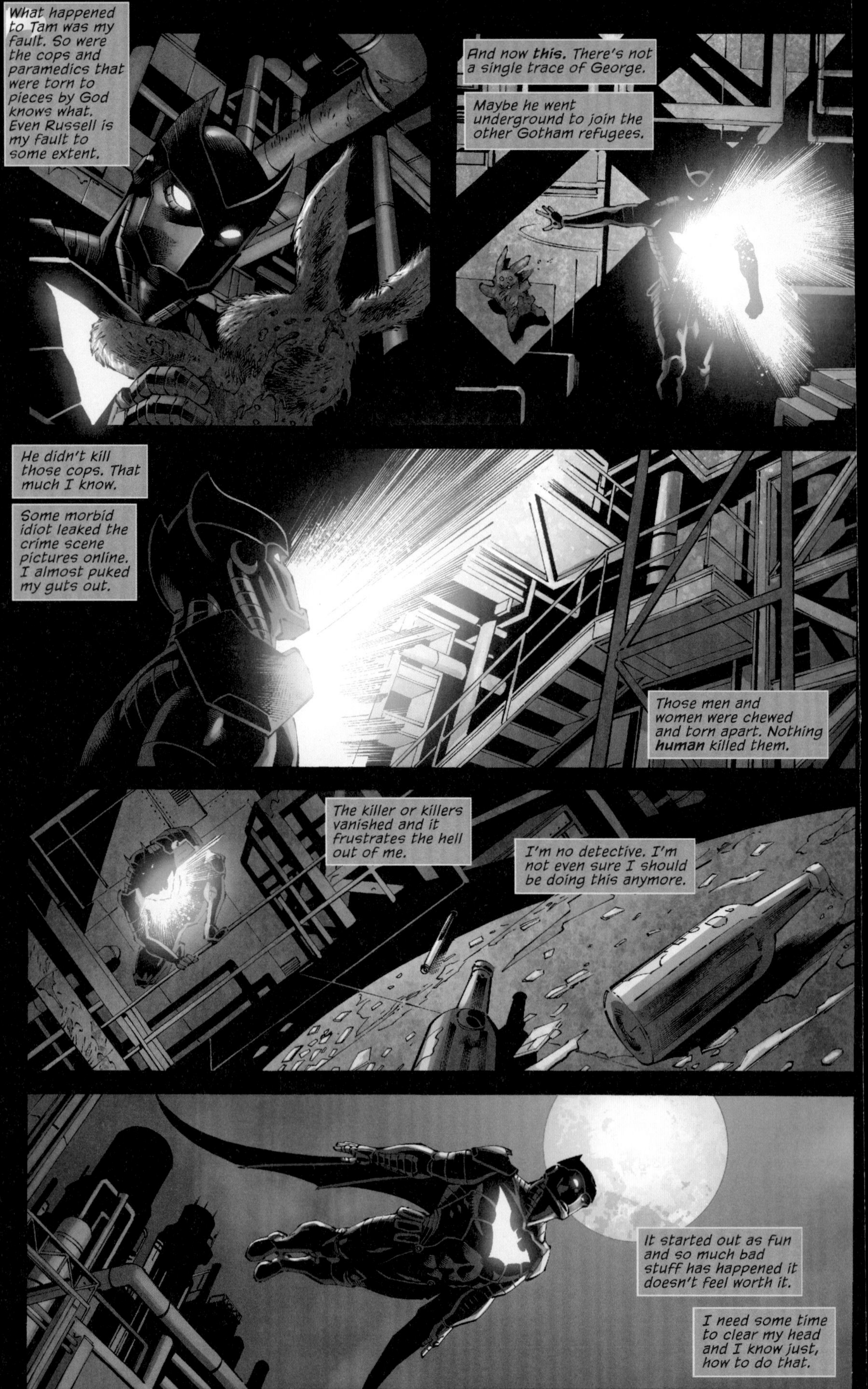

What happened to Tam was my fault. So were the cops and paramedics that were torn to pieces by God knows what. Even Russell is my fault to some extent.
And now this. There's not a single trace of George.
Maybe he went underground to join the other Gotham refugees.
He didn't kill those cops. That much I know.
Some morbid idiot leaked the crime scene pictures online. I almost puked my guts out.
Those men and women were chewed and torn apart. Nothing human killed them.
The killer or killers vanished and it frustrates the hell out of me.
I'm no detective. I'm not even sure I should be doing this anymore.
It started out as fun and so much bad stuff has happened it doesn't feel worth it.
I need some time to clear my head and I know just how to do that.

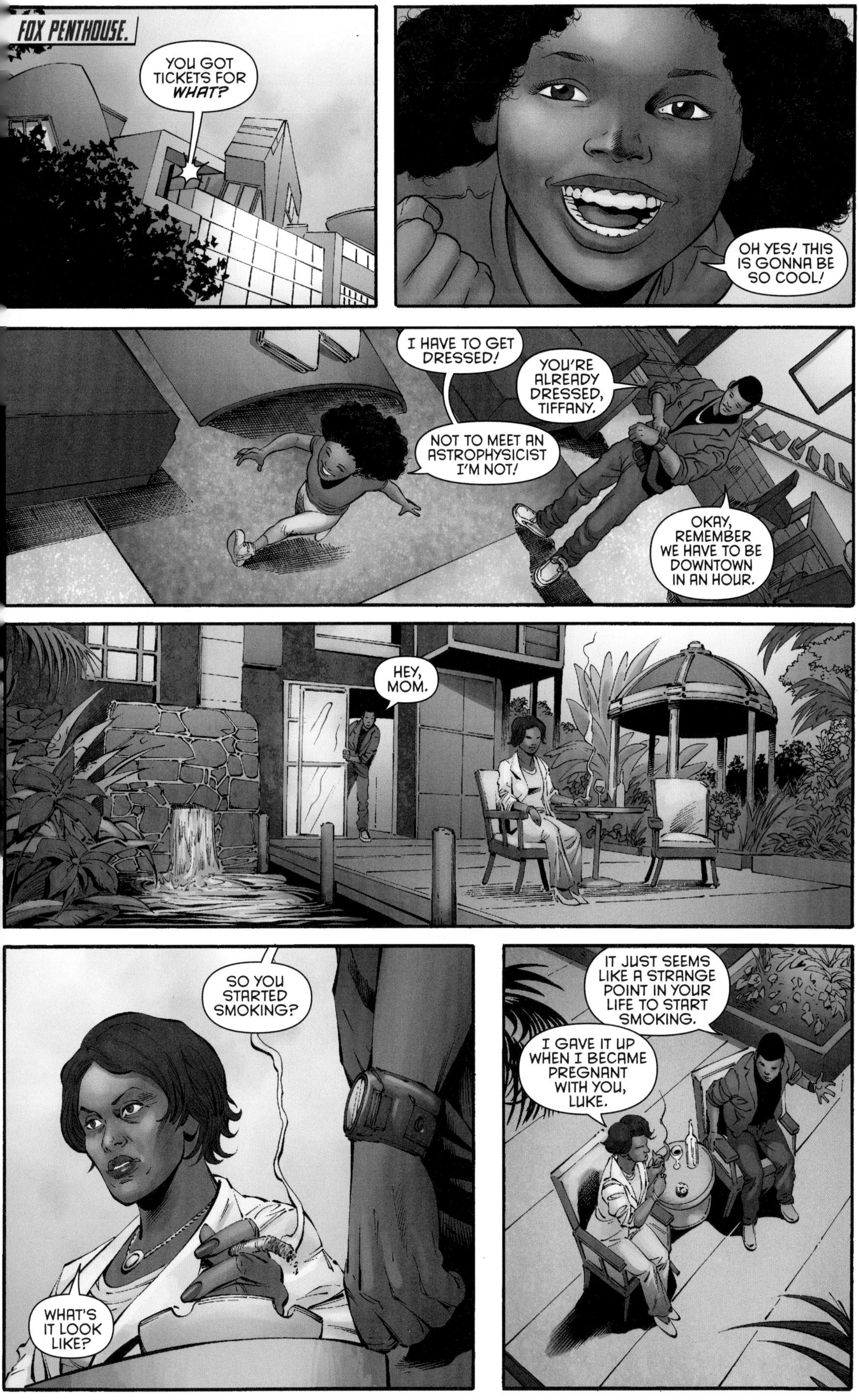
FOX PENTHOUSE.
YOU GOT TICKETS FOR WHAT?
OH YES! THIS IS GONNA BE SO COOL!
I HAVE TO GET DRESSED!
YOU'RE ALREADY DRESSED, TIFFANY.
NOT TO MEET AN ASTROPHYSICIST I'M NOT!
OKAY, REMEMBER WE HAVE TO BE DOWNTOWN IN AN HOUR.
HEY, MOM.
SO YOU STARTED SMOKING?
WHAT'S IT LOOK LIKE?
IT JUST SEEMS LIKE A STRANGE POINT IN YOUR LIFE TO START SMOKING.
I GAVE IT UP WHEN I BECAME PREGNANT WITH YOU, LUKE.

DO YOU THINK KILLING YOURSELF IS GOING TO MAKE YOU FEEL BETTER?

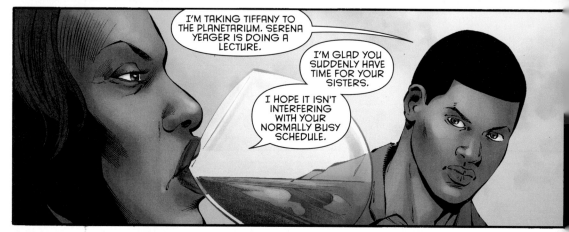

I'M TAKING TIFFANY TO THE PLANETARIUM. SERENA YEAGER IS DOING A LECTURE.

I'M GLAD YOU SUDDENLY HAVE TIME FOR YOUR SISTERS.

I HOPE IT ISN'T INTERFERING WITH YOUR NORMALLY BUSY SCHEDULE.

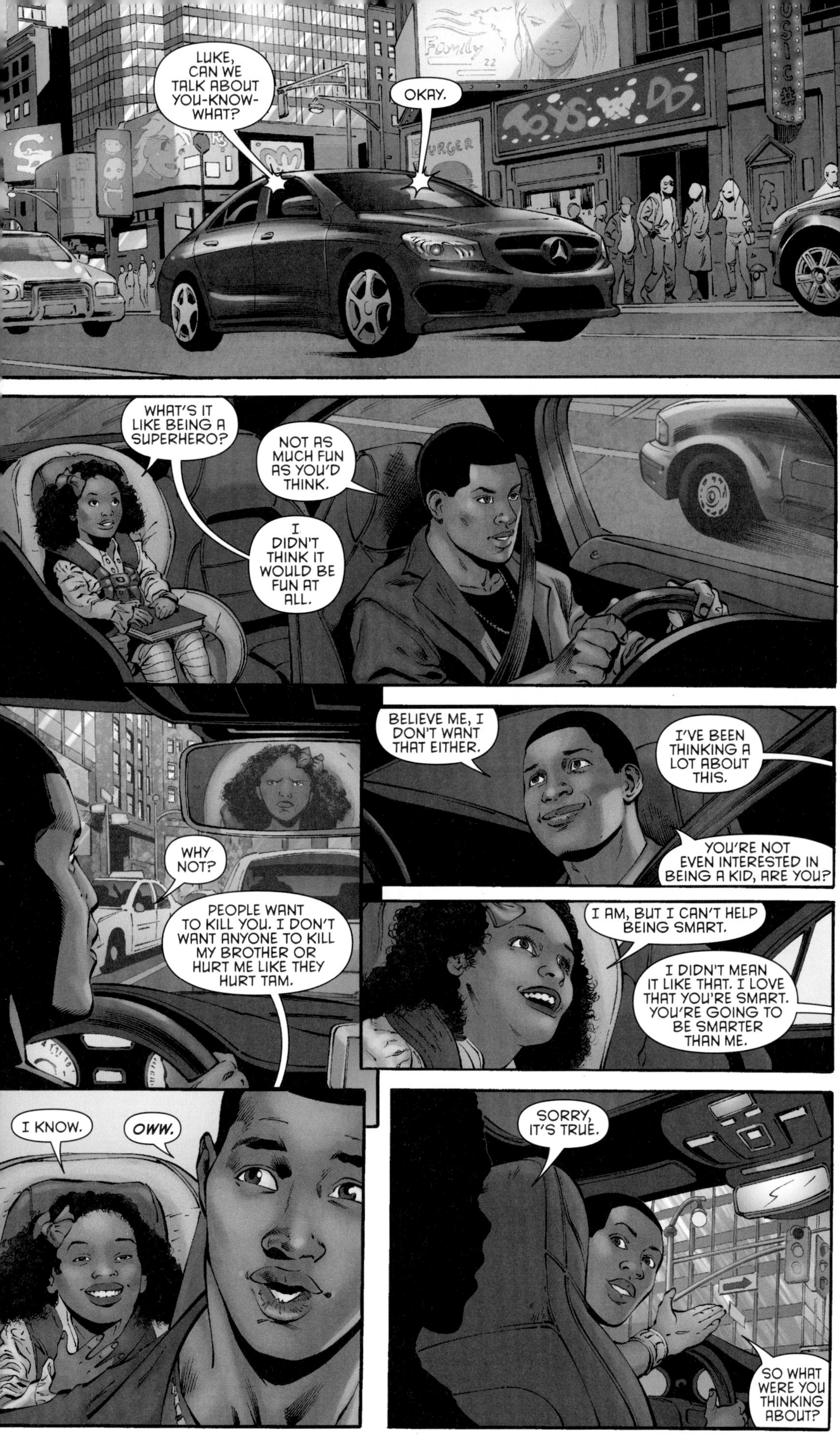
LUKE, CAN WE TALK ABOUT YOU-KNOW-WHAT?
OKAY.
WHAT'S IT LIKE BEING A SUPERHERO?
NOT AS MUCH FUN AS YOU'D THINK.
I DIDN'T THINK IT WOULD BE FUN AT ALL.
WHY NOT?
PEOPLE WANT TO KILL YOU. I DON'T WANT ANYONE TO KILL MY BROTHER OR HURT ME LIKE THEY HURT TAM.
BELIEVE ME, I DON'T WANT THAT EITHER.
I'VE BEEN THINKING A LOT ABOUT THIS.
YOU'RE NOT EVEN INTERESTED IN BEING A KID, ARE YOU?
I AM, BUT I CAN'T HELP BEING SMART.
I DIDN'T MEAN IT LIKE THAT. I LOVE THAT YOU'RE SMART. YOU'RE GOING TO BE SMARTER THAN ME.
I KNOW.
OWW.
SORRY, IT'S TRUE.
SO WHAT WERE YOU THINKING ABOUT?

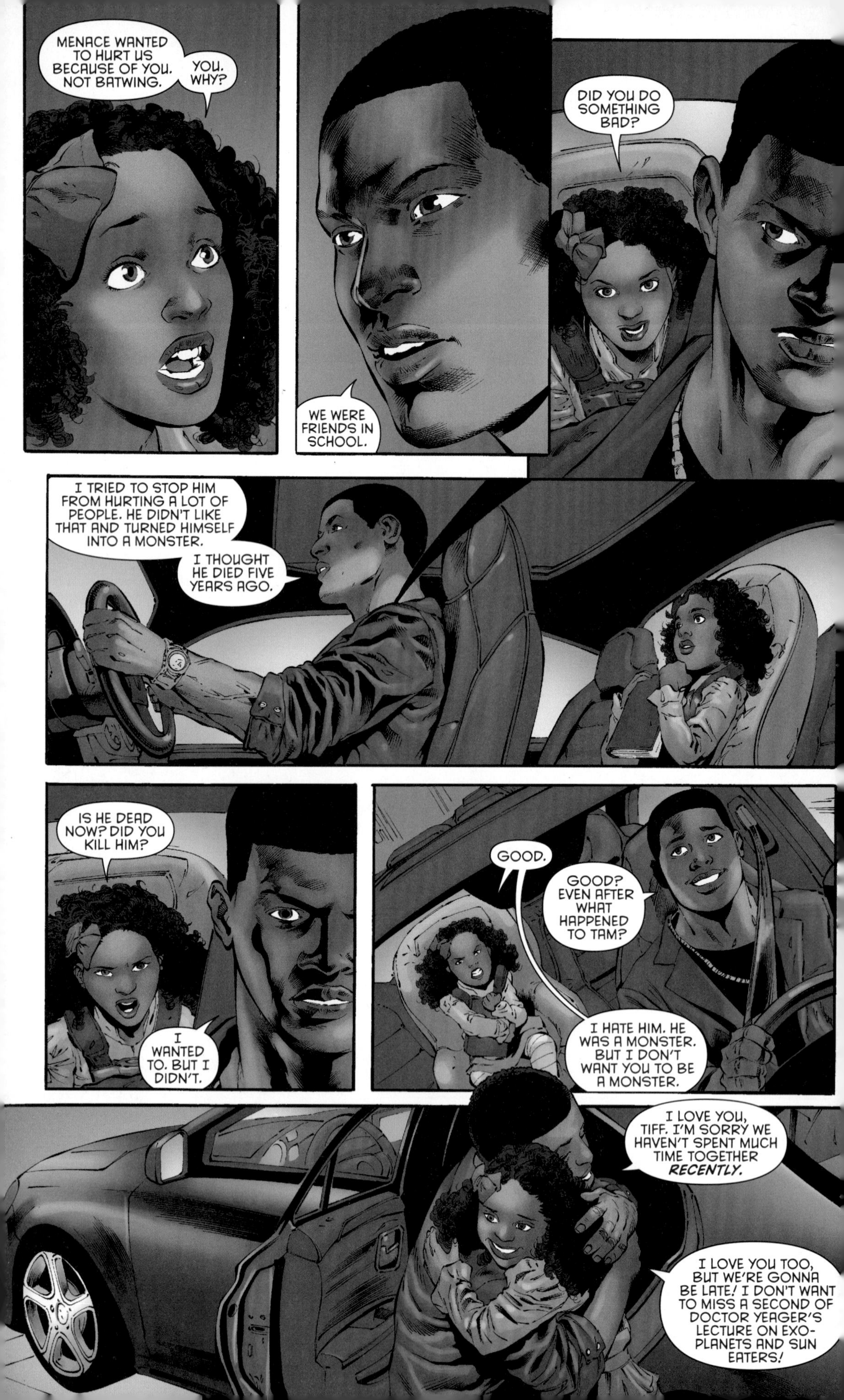
MENACE WANTED TO HURT US BECAUSE OF YOU. NOT BATWING.
YOU. WHY?
WE WERE FRIENDS IN SCHOOL.
DID YOU DO SOMETHING BAD?
I TRIED TO STOP HIM FROM HURTING A LOT OF PEOPLE. HE DIDN'T LIKE THAT AND TURNED HIMSELF INTO A MONSTER.
I THOUGHT HE DIED FIVE YEARS AGO.
IS HE DEAD NOW? DID YOU KILL HIM?
I WANTED TO. BUT I DIDN'T.
GOOD.
GOOD? EVEN AFTER WHAT HAPPENED TO TAM?
I HATE HIM. HE WAS A MONSTER. BUT I DON'T WANT YOU TO BE A MONSTER.
I LOVE YOU, TIFF. I'M SORRY WE HAVEN'T SPENT MUCH TIME TOGETHER ***RECENTLY.***
I LOVE YOU TOO, BUT WE'RE GONNA BE LATE! I DON'T WANT TO MISS A SECOND OF DOCTOR YEAGER'S LECTURE ON EXO-PLANETS AND SUN EATERS!

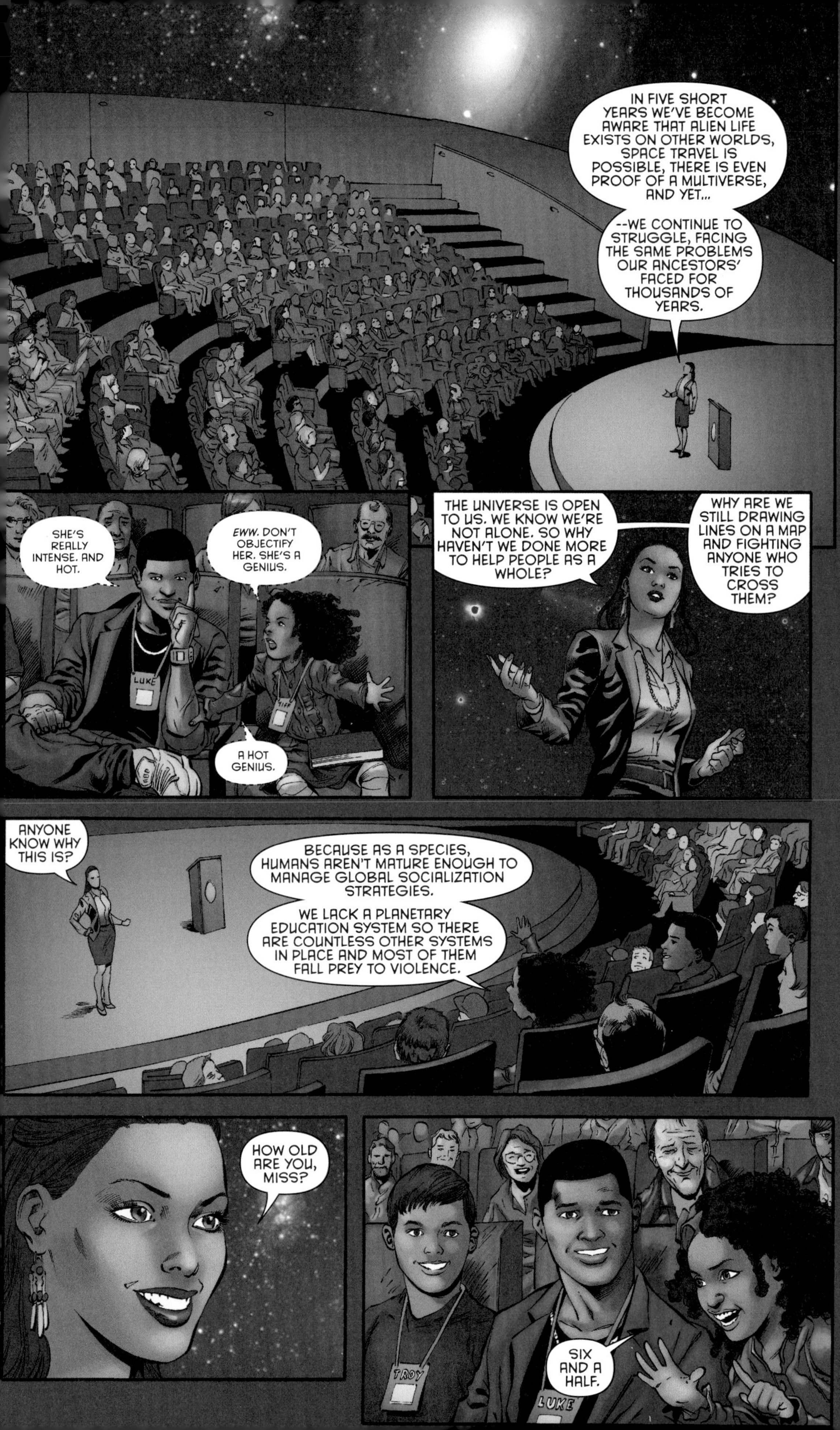
IN FIVE SHORT YEARS WE'VE BECOME AWARE THAT ALIEN LIFE EXISTS ON OTHER WORLDS, SPACE TRAVEL IS POSSIBLE, THERE IS EVEN PROOF OF A MULTIVERSE, AND YET...
--WE CONTINUE TO STRUGGLE, FACING THE SAME PROBLEMS OUR ANCESTORS' FACED FOR THOUSANDS OF YEARS.
SHE'S REALLY INTENSE. AND HOT.
EWW. DON'T OBJECTIFY HER. SHE'S A GENIUS.
A HOT GENIUS.
LUKE
TIFF
THE UNIVERSE IS OPEN TO US. WE KNOW WE'RE NOT ALONE. SO WHY HAVEN'T WE DONE MORE TO HELP PEOPLE AS A WHOLE?
WHY ARE WE STILL DRAWING LINES ON A MAP AND FIGHTING ANYONE WHO TRIES TO CROSS THEM?
ANYONE KNOW WHY THIS IS?
BECAUSE AS A SPECIES, HUMANS AREN'T MATURE ENOUGH TO MANAGE GLOBAL SOCIALIZATION STRATEGIES.
WE LACK A PLANETARY EDUCATION SYSTEM SO THERE ARE COUNTLESS OTHER SYSTEMS IN PLACE AND MOST OF THEM FALL PREY TO VIOLENCE.
HOW OLD ARE YOU, MISS?
SIX AND A HALF.
TROY
LUKE

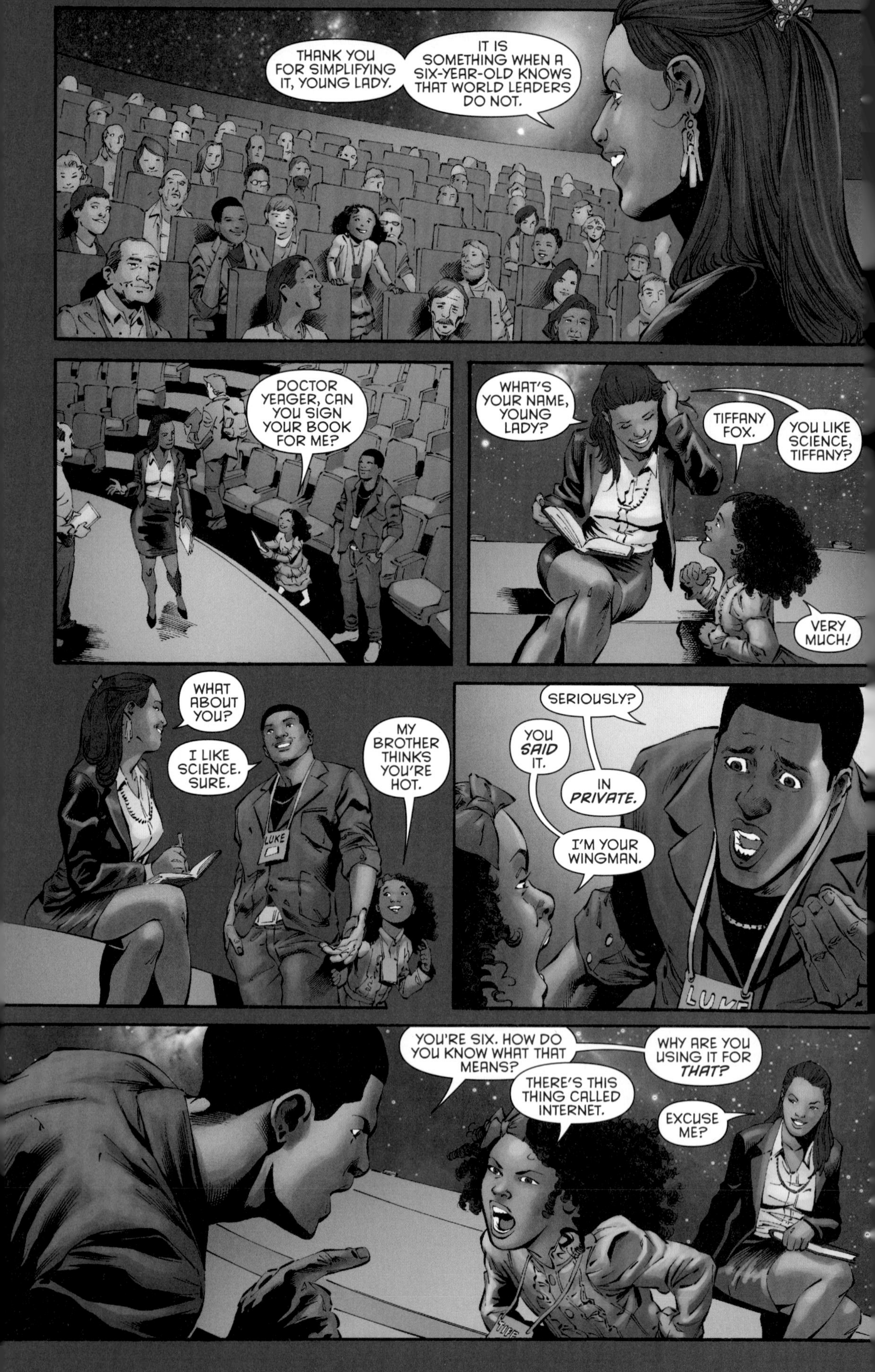
THANK YOU FOR SIMPLIFYING IT, YOUNG LADY.
IT IS SOMETHING WHEN A SIX-YEAR-OLD KNOWS THAT WORLD LEADERS DO NOT.
DOCTOR YEAGER, CAN YOU SIGN YOUR BOOK FOR ME?
WHAT'S YOUR NAME, YOUNG LADY?
TIFFANY FOX.
YOU LIKE SCIENCE, TIFFANY?
VERY MUCH!
WHAT ABOUT YOU?
I LIKE SCIENCE. SURE.
MY BROTHER THINKS YOU'RE HOT.
LUKE
SERIOUSLY?
YOU *SAID* IT.
IN *PRIVATE.*
I'M YOUR WINGMAN.
YOU'RE SIX. HOW DO YOU KNOW WHAT THAT MEANS?
THERE'S THIS THING CALLED INTERNET.
WHY ARE YOU USING IT FOR *THAT?*
EXCUSE ME?

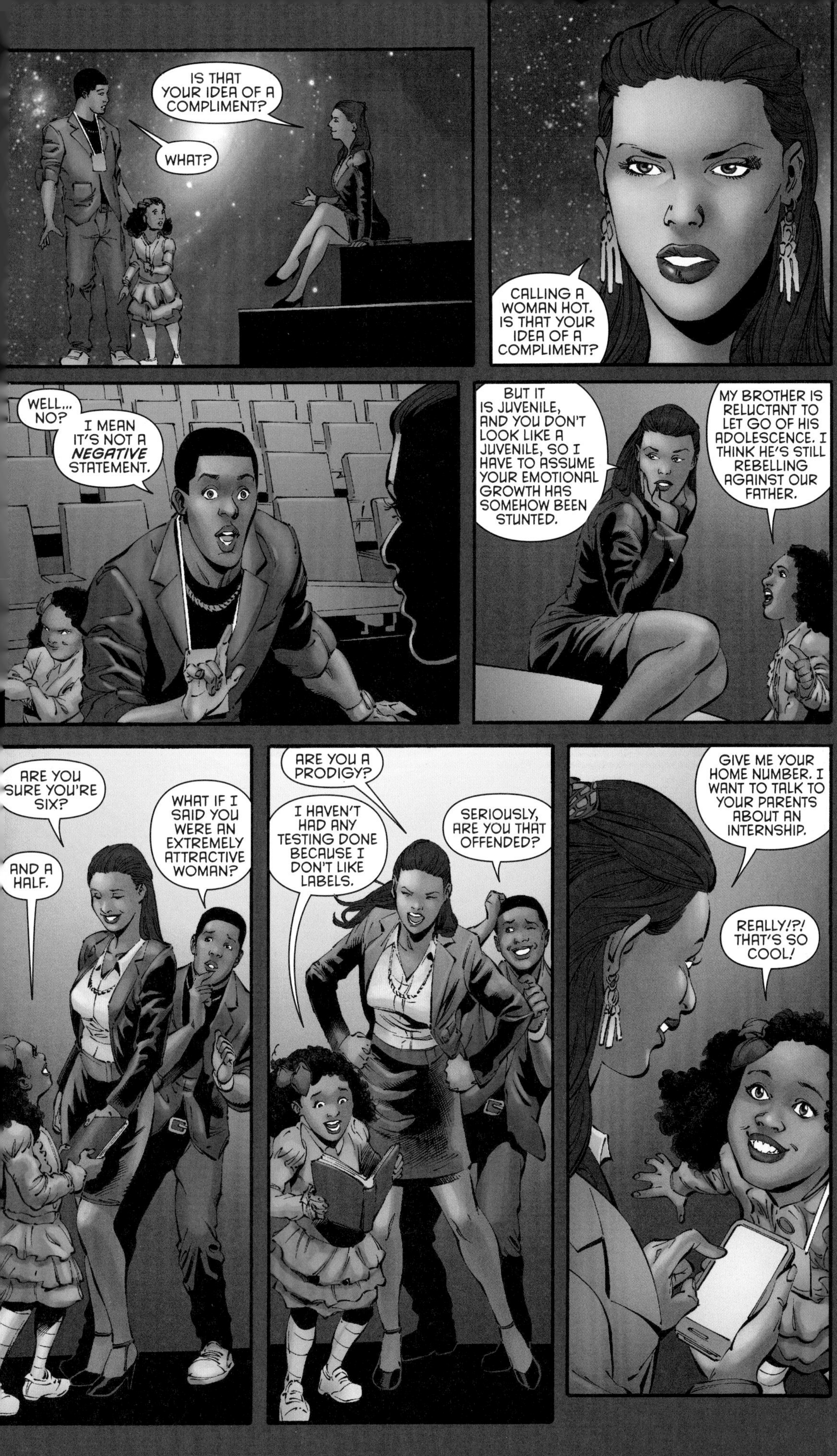
IS THAT YOUR IDEA OF A COMPLIMENT?
WHAT?
CALLING A WOMAN HOT. IS THAT YOUR IDEA OF A COMPLIMENT?
WELL... NO?
I MEAN IT'S NOT A NEGATIVE STATEMENT.
BUT IT IS JUVENILE, AND YOU DON'T LOOK LIKE A JUVENILE, SO I HAVE TO ASSUME YOUR EMOTIONAL GROWTH HAS SOMEHOW BEEN STUNTED.
MY BROTHER IS RELUCTANT TO LET GO OF HIS ADOLESCENCE. I THINK HE'S STILL REBELLING AGAINST OUR FATHER.
ARE YOU SURE YOU'RE SIX?
AND A HALF.
WHAT IF I SAID YOU WERE AN EXTREMELY ATTRACTIVE WOMAN?
ARE YOU A PRODIGY?
I HAVEN'T HAD ANY TESTING DONE BECAUSE I DON'T LIKE LABELS.
SERIOUSLY, ARE YOU THAT OFFENDED?
GIVE ME YOUR HOME NUMBER. I WANT TO TALK TO YOUR PARENTS ABOUT AN INTERNSHIP.
REALLY!?! THAT'S SO COOL!

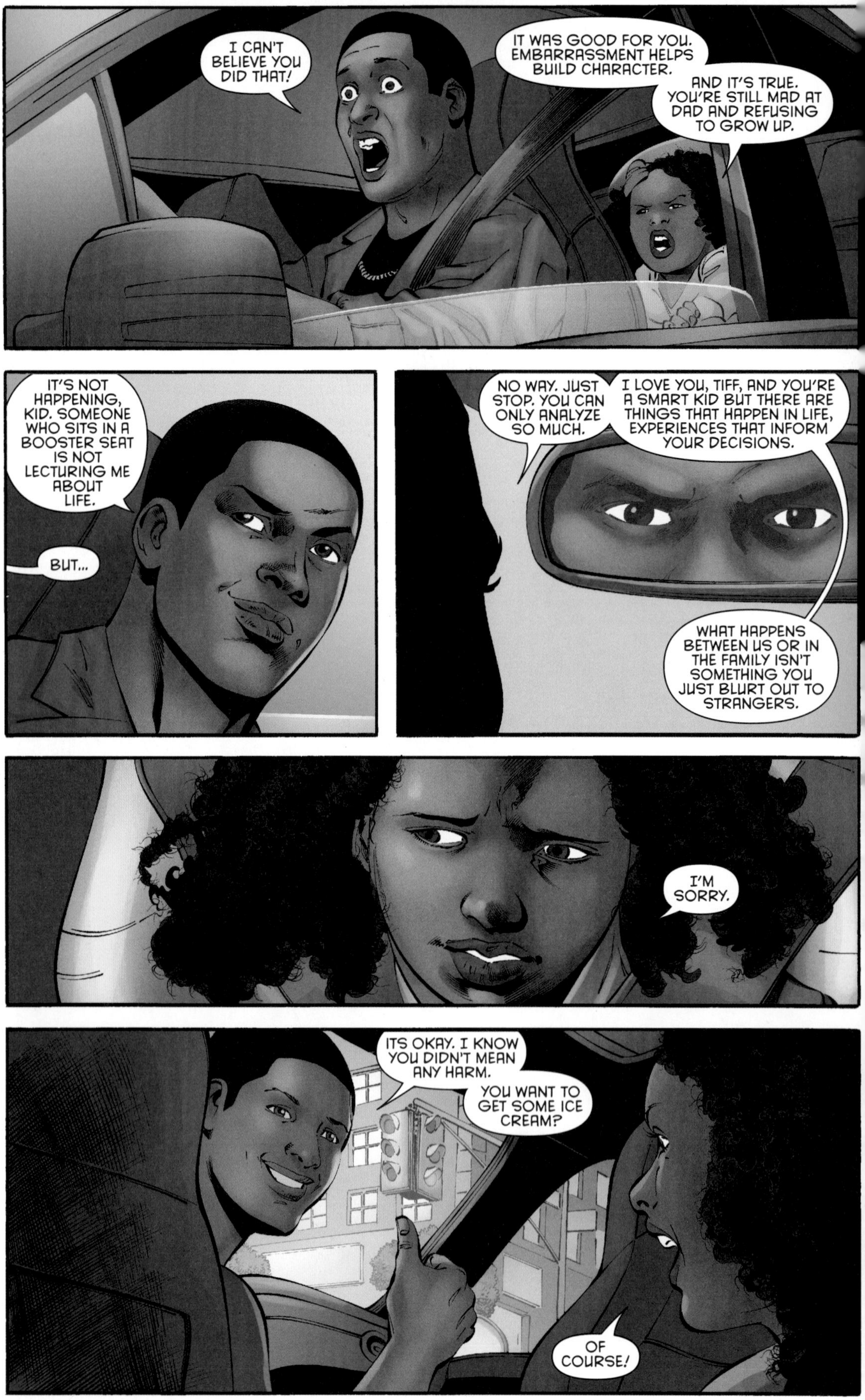
I CAN'T BELIEVE YOU DID THAT!
IT WAS GOOD FOR YOU. EMBARRASSMENT HELPS BUILD CHARACTER.
AND IT'S TRUE. YOU'RE STILL MAD AT DAD AND REFUSING TO GROW UP.
IT'S NOT HAPPENING, KID. SOMEONE WHO SITS IN A BOOSTER SEAT IS NOT LECTURING ME ABOUT LIFE.
BUT...
NO WAY. JUST STOP. YOU CAN ONLY ANALYZE SO MUCH.
I LOVE YOU, TIFF, AND YOU'RE A SMART KID BUT THERE ARE THINGS THAT HAPPEN IN LIFE, EXPERIENCES THAT INFORM YOUR DECISIONS.
WHAT HAPPENS BETWEEN US OR IN THE FAMILY ISN'T SOMETHING YOU JUST BLURT OUT TO STRANGERS.
I'M SORRY.
ITS OKAY. I KNOW YOU DIDN'T MEAN ANY HARM.
YOU WANT TO GET SOME ICE CREAM?
OF COURSE!

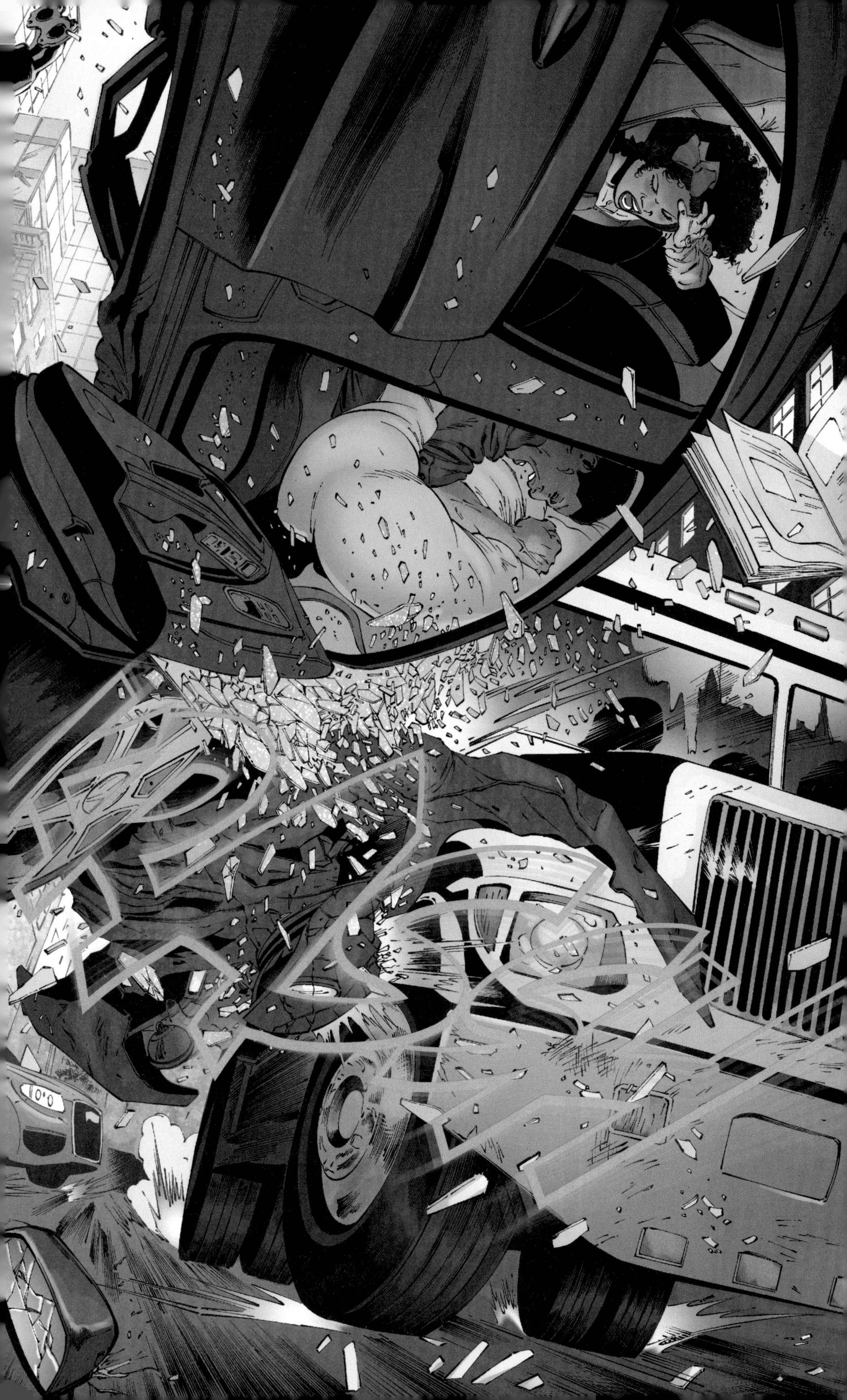

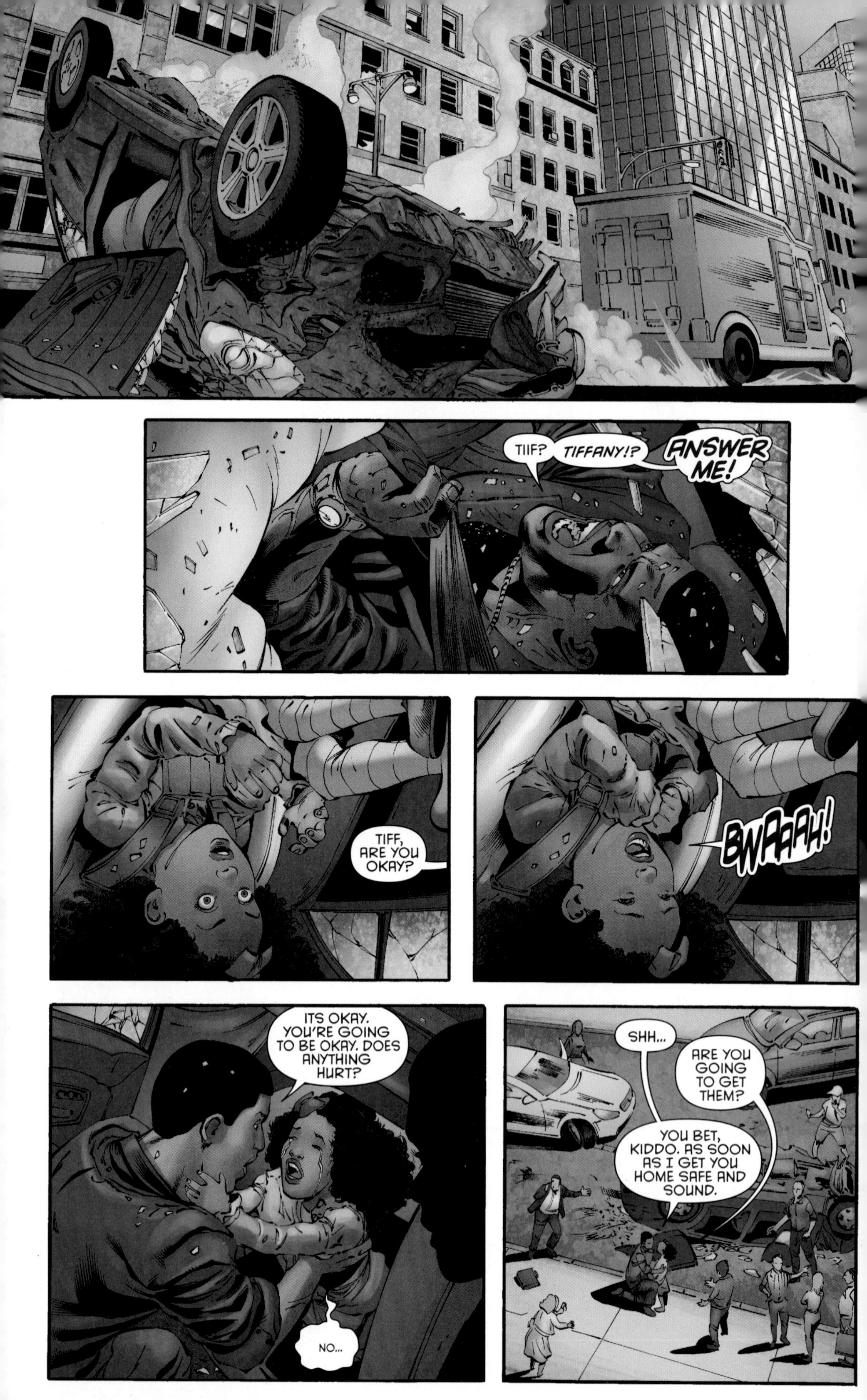
TIIF?
TIFFANY!?
ANSWER ME!
TIFF, ARE YOU OKAY?
BWAAAH!
ITS OKAY. YOU'RE GOING TO BE OKAY. DOES ANYTHING HURT?
NO...
SHH...
ARE YOU GOING TO GET THEM?
YOU BET, KIDDO. AS SOON AS I GET YOU HOME SAFE AND SOUND.

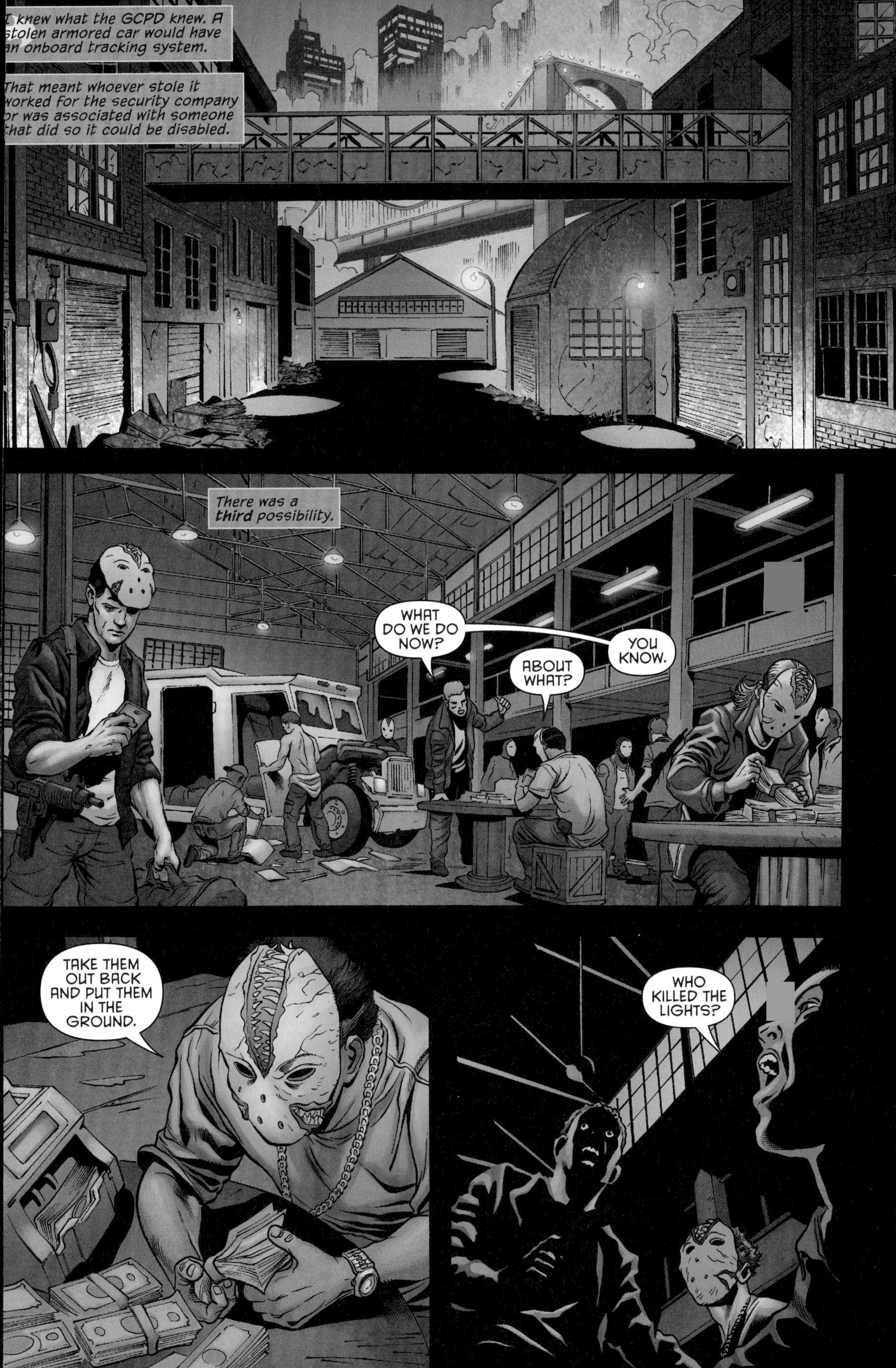
I knew what the GCPD knew. A stolen armored car would have an onboard tracking system.
That meant whoever stole it worked for the security company or was associated with someone that did so it could be disabled.
There was a **third** possibility.
WHAT DO WE DO NOW?
YOU KNOW.
ABOUT WHAT?
TAKE THEM OUT BACK AND PUT THEM IN THE GROUND.
WHO KILLED THE LIGHTS?

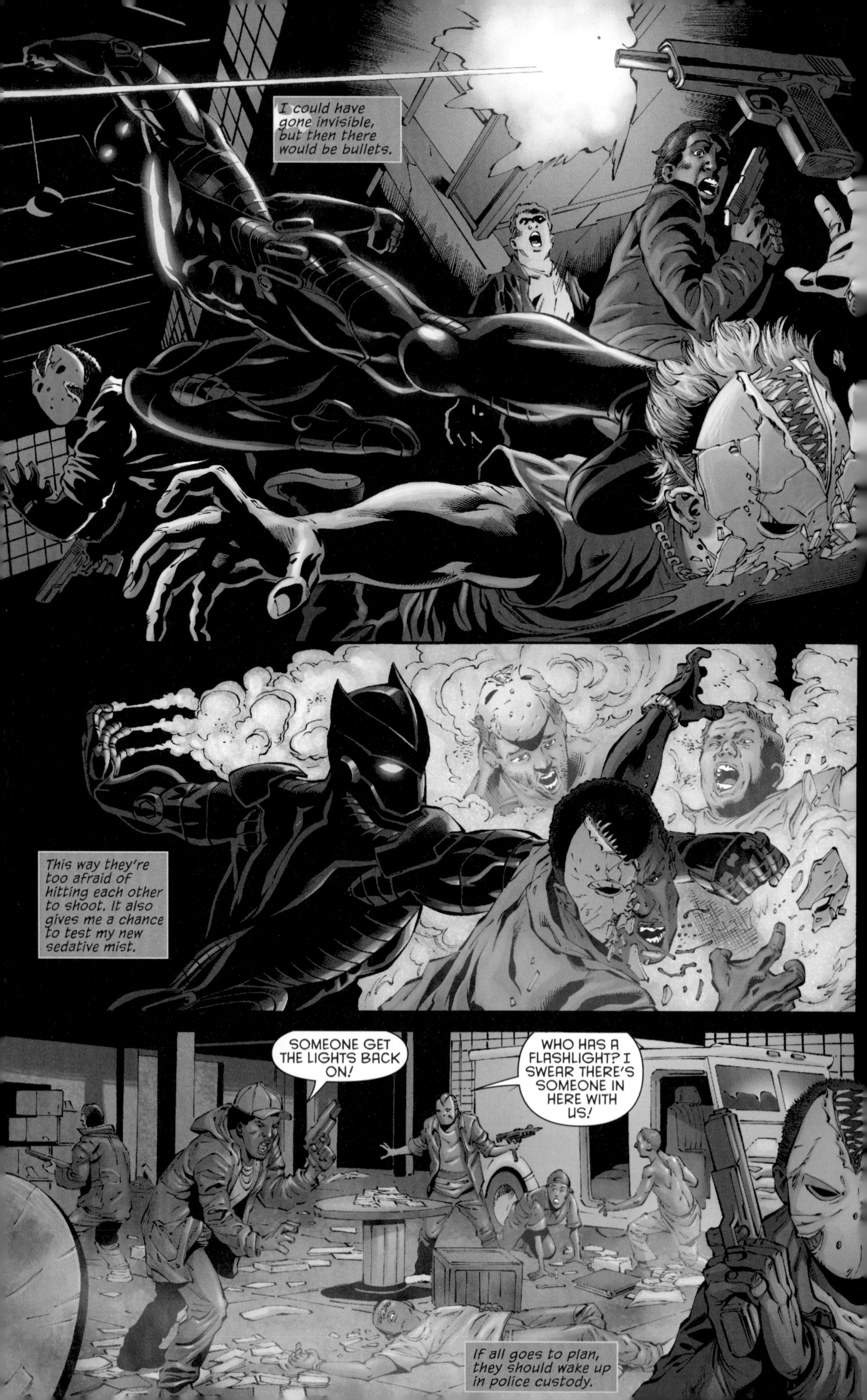
I could have gone invisible, but then there would be bullets.
This way they're too afraid of hitting each other to shoot. It also gives me a chance to test my new sedative mist.
SOMEONE GET THE LIGHTS BACK ON!
WHO HAS A FLASHLIGHT? I SWEAR THERE'S SOMEONE IN HERE WITH US!
If all goes to plan, they should wake up in police custody.

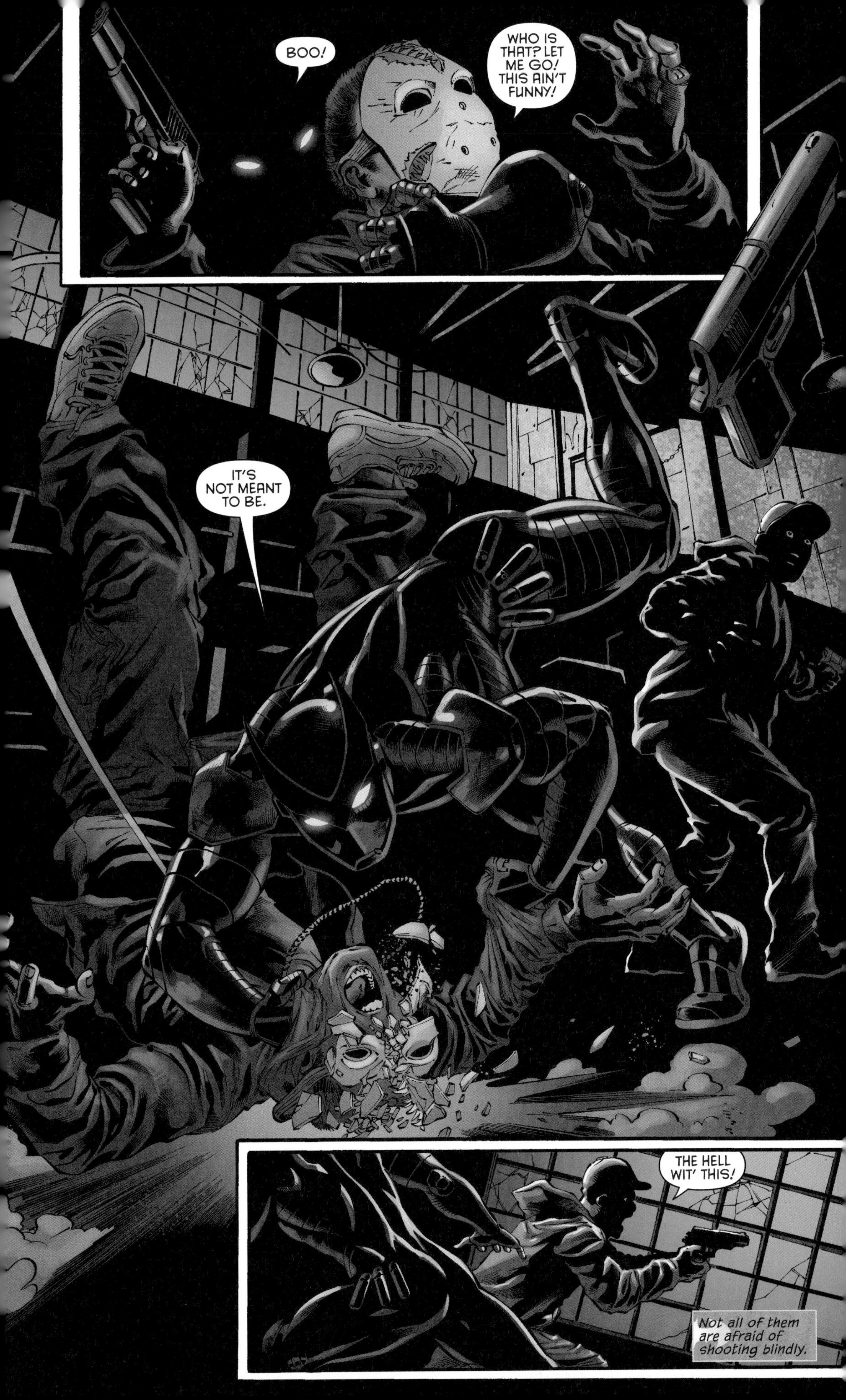
BOO!
WHO IS THAT? LET ME GO! THIS AIN'T FUNNY!
IT'S NOT MEANT TO BE.
THE HELL WIT' THIS!
Not all of them are afraid of shooting blindly.

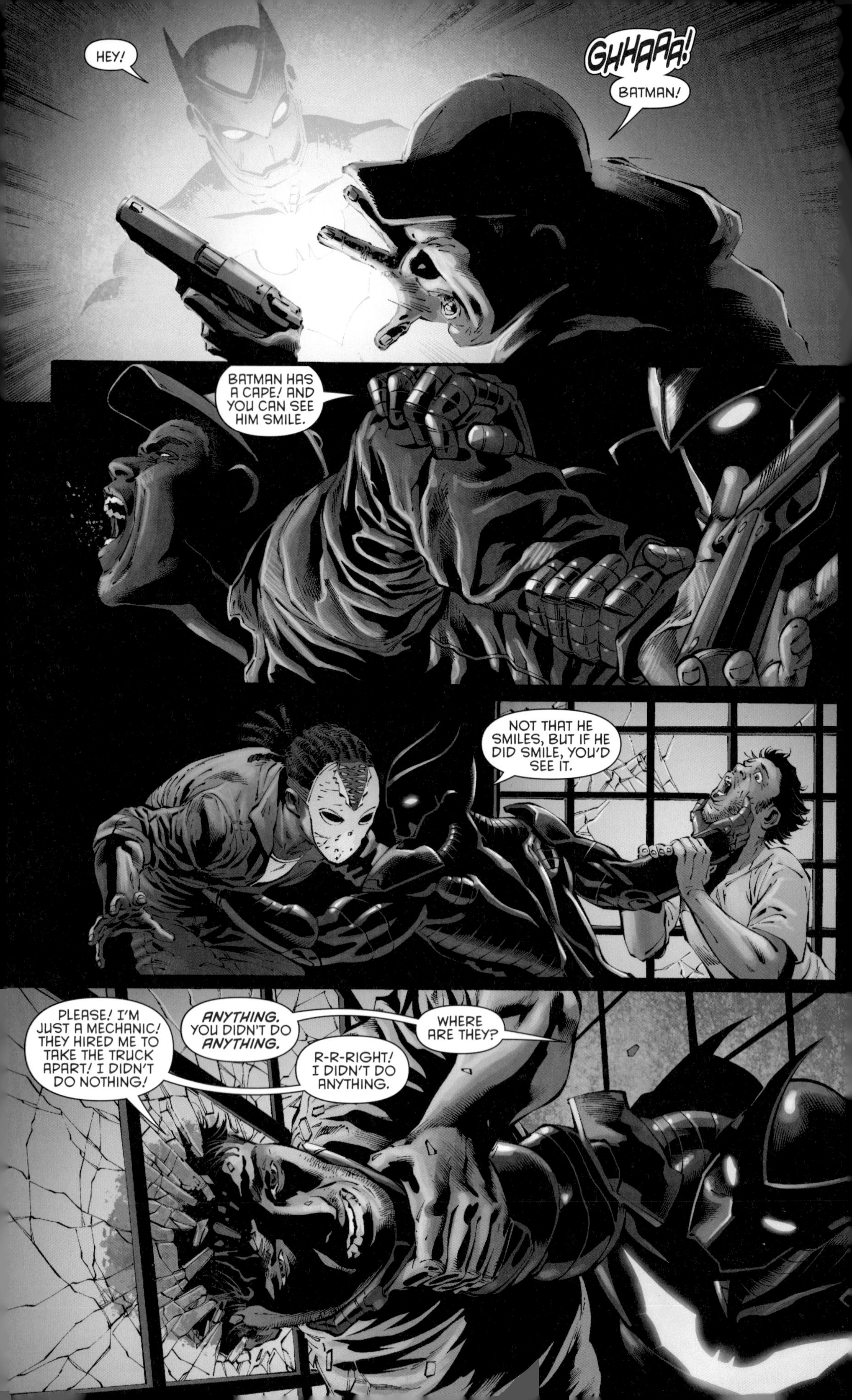
HEY!
GHHAAA!
BATMAN!
BATMAN HAS A CAPE! AND YOU CAN SEE HIM SMILE.
NOT THAT HE SMILES, BUT IF HE DID SMILE, YOU'D SEE IT.
PLEASE! I'M JUST A MECHANIC! THEY HIRED ME TO TAKE THE TRUCK APART! I DIDN'T DO NOTHING!
ANYTHING. YOU DIDN'T DO ANYTHING.
WHERE ARE THEY?
R-R-RIGHT! I DIDN'T DO ANYTHING.

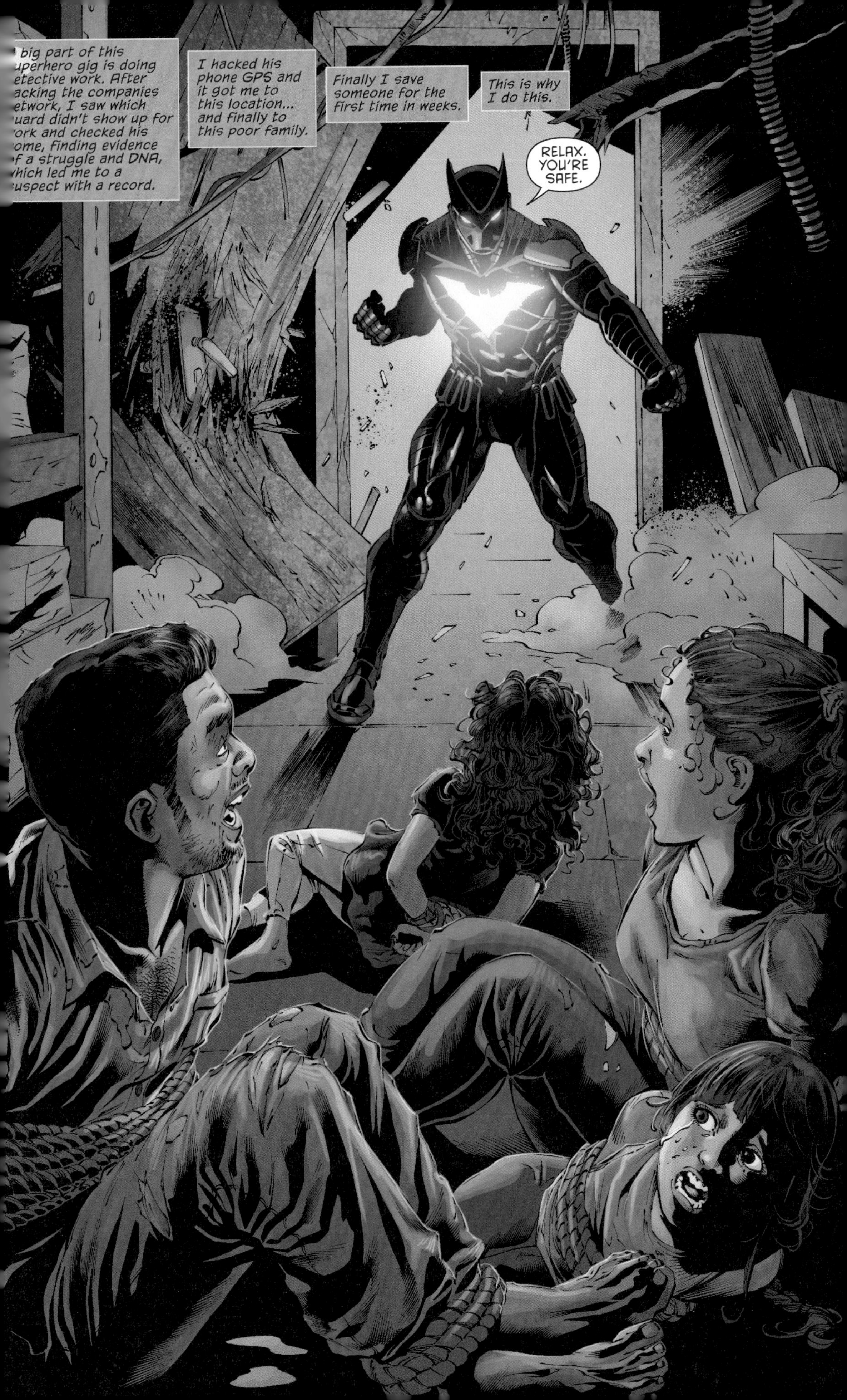
big part of this uperhero gig is doing etective work. After acking the companies etwork, I saw which uard didn't show up for ork and checked his ome, finding evidence f a struggle and DNA, which led me to a uspect with a record.
I hacked his phone GPS and it got me to this location... and finally to this poor family.
Finally I save someone for the first time in weeks.
This is why I do this.
RELAX. YOU'RE SAFE.

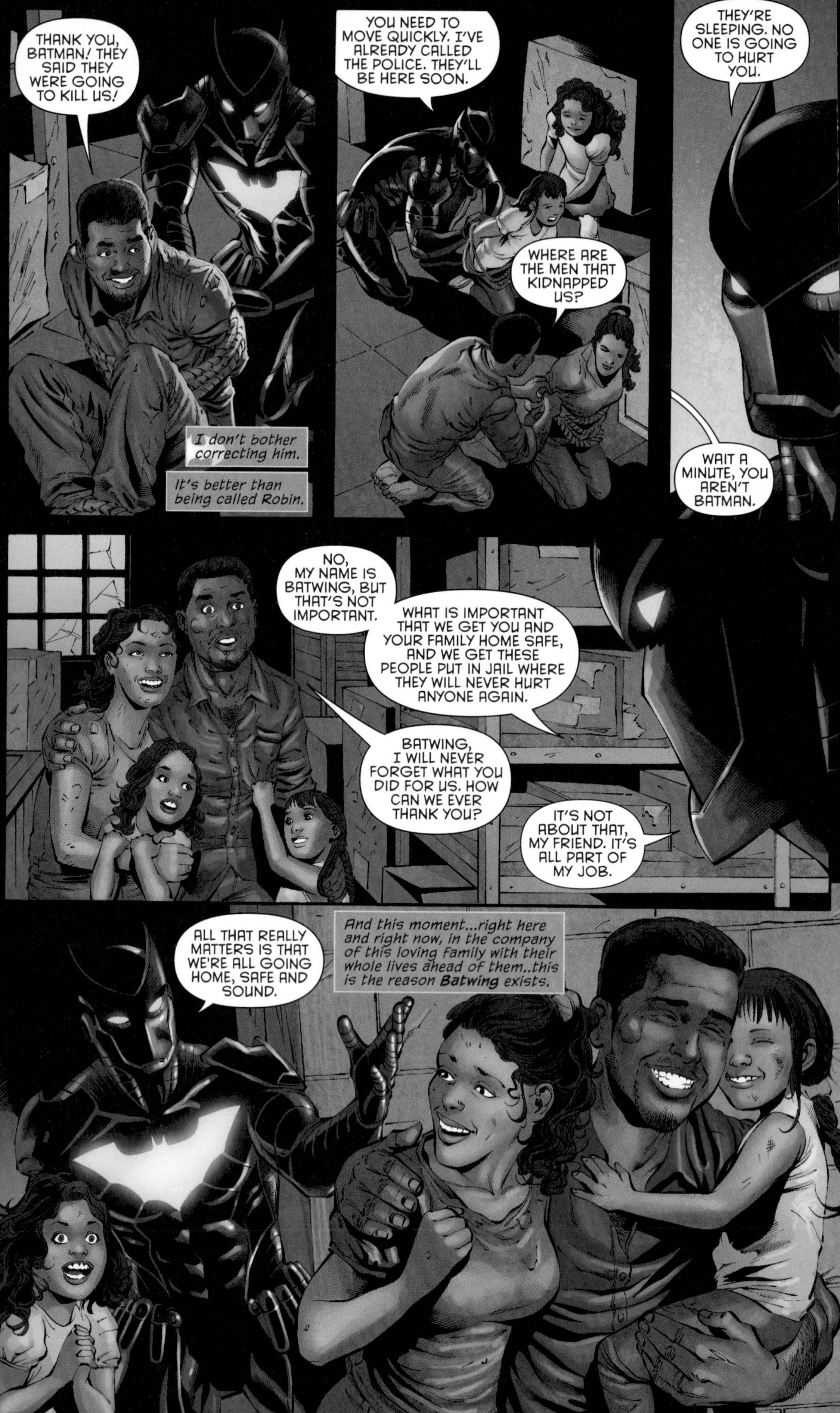

THANK YOU, BATMAN! THEY SAID THEY WERE GOING TO KILL US!
I don't bother correcting him.
It's better than being called Robin.
YOU NEED TO MOVE QUICKLY. I'VE ALREADY CALLED THE POLICE. THEY'LL BE HERE SOON.
WHERE ARE THE MEN THAT KIDNAPPED US?
THEY'RE SLEEPING. NO ONE IS GOING TO HURT YOU.
WAIT A MINUTE, YOU AREN'T BATMAN.
NO, MY NAME IS BATWING, BUT THAT'S NOT IMPORTANT.
WHAT IS IMPORTANT THAT WE GET YOU AND YOUR FAMILY HOME SAFE, AND WE GET THESE PEOPLE PUT IN JAIL WHERE THEY WILL NEVER HURT ANYONE AGAIN.
BATWING, I WILL NEVER FORGET WHAT YOU DID FOR US. HOW CAN WE EVER THANK YOU?
IT'S NOT ABOUT THAT, MY FRIEND. IT'S ALL PART OF MY JOB.
ALL THAT REALLY MATTERS IS THAT WE'RE ALL GOING HOME, SAFE AND SOUND.
And this moment...right here and right now, in the company of this loving family with their whole lives ahead of them..this is the reason Batwing exists.

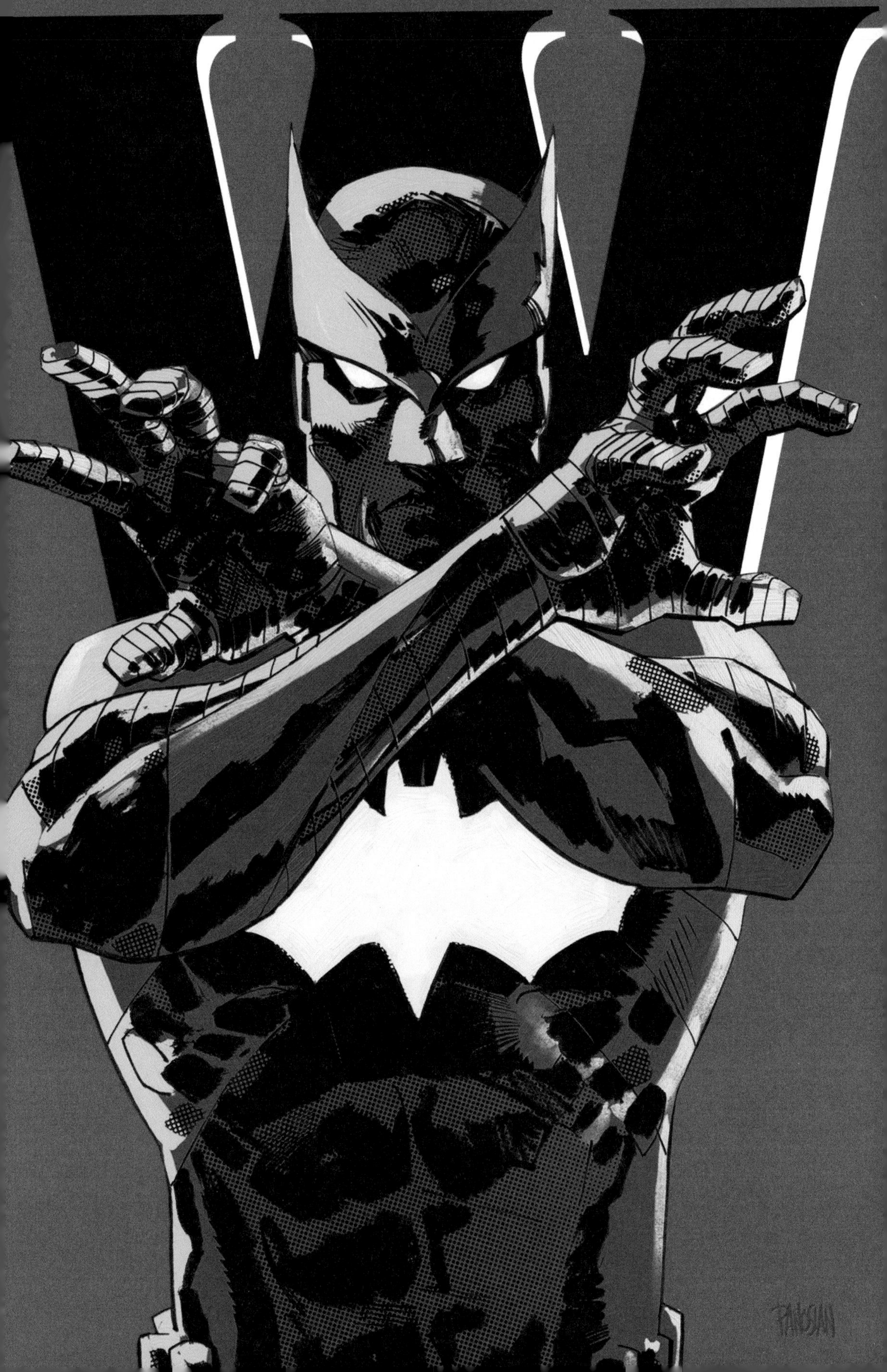
PANOSIAN

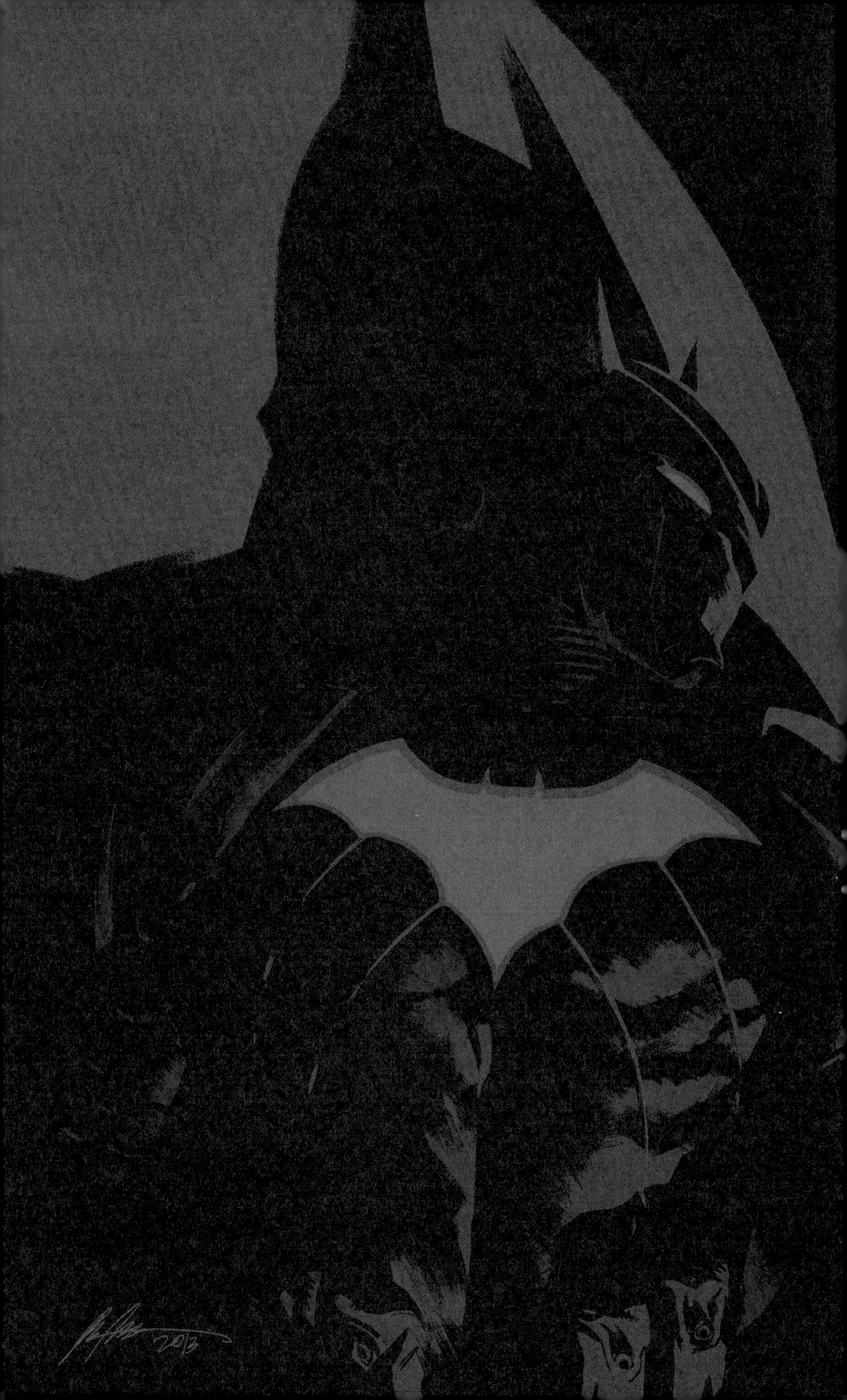

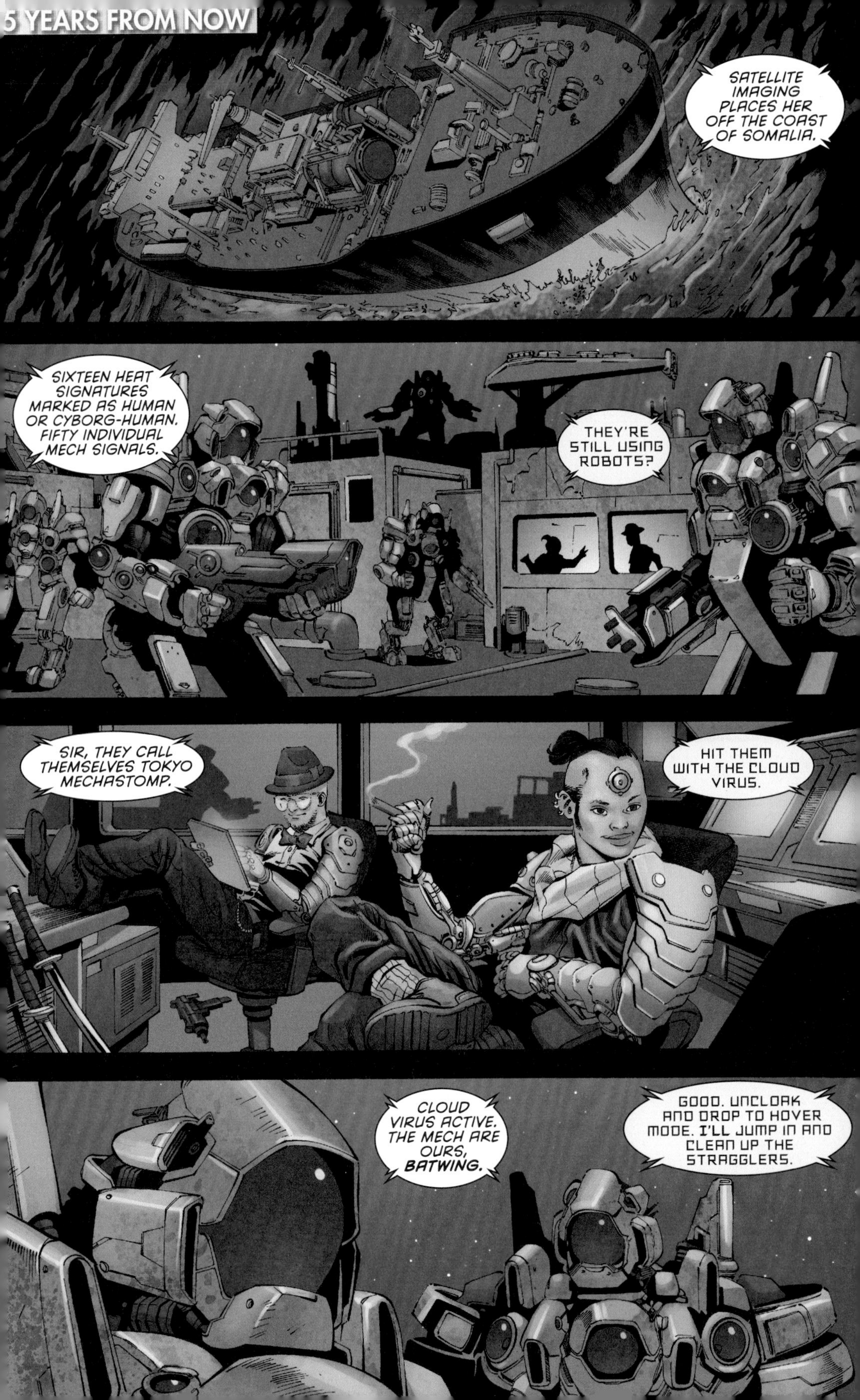
5 YEARS FROM NOW
SATELLITE IMAGING PLACES HER OFF THE COAST OF SOMALIA.
SIXTEEN HEAT SIGNATURES MARKED AS HUMAN OR CYBORG-HUMAN. FIFTY INDIVIDUAL MECH SIGNALS.
THEY'RE STILL USING ROBOTS?
SIR, THEY CALL THEMSELVES TOKYO MECHASTOMP.
HIT THEM WITH THE CLOUD VIRUS.
CLOUD VIRUS ACTIVE. THE MECH ARE OURS, BATWING.
GOOD. UNCLOAK AND DROP TO HOVER MODE. I'LL JUMP IN AND CLEAN UP THE STRAGGLERS.

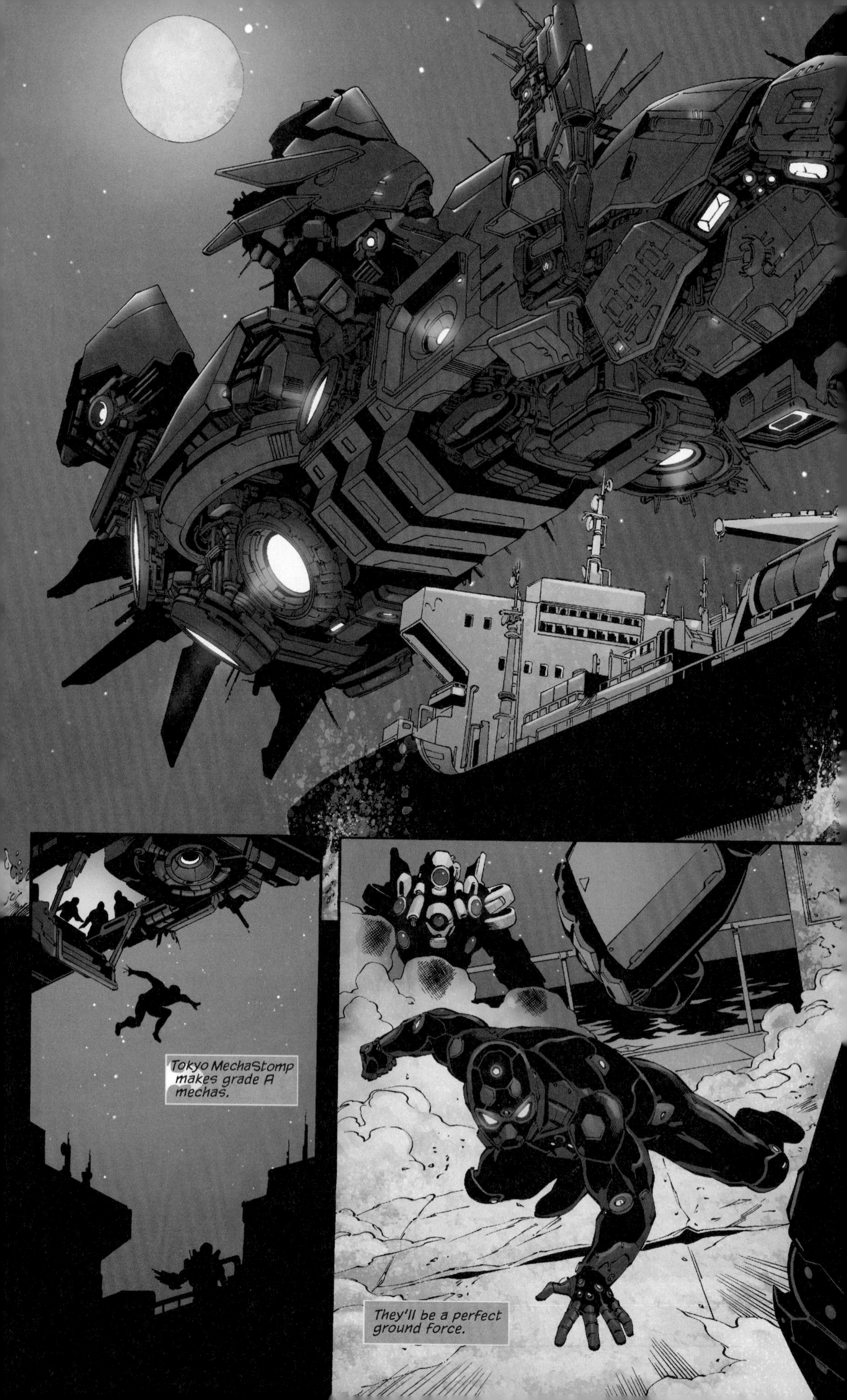
Tokyo MechaStomp makes grade A mechas.
They'll be a perfect ground force.

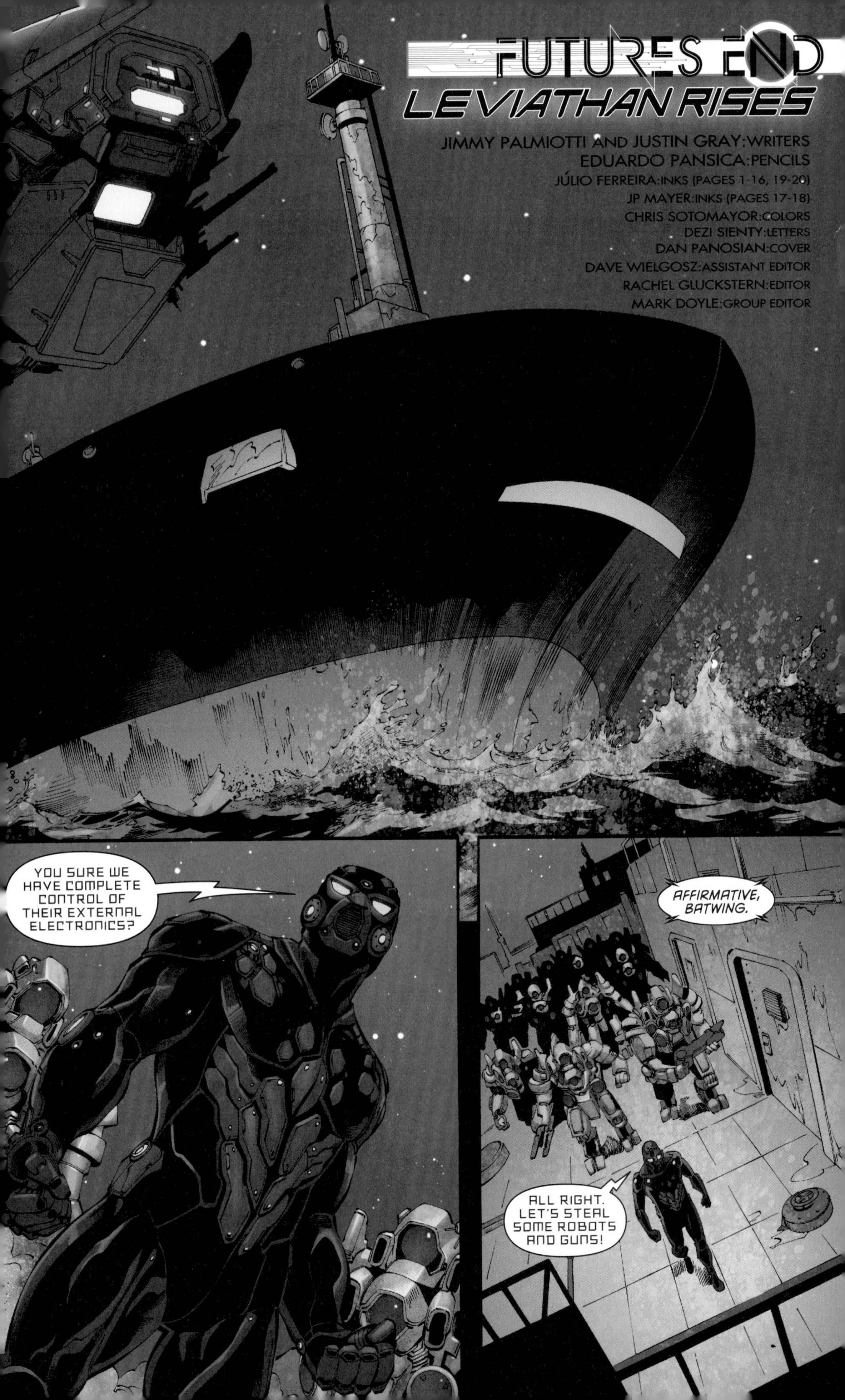
FUTURES END
LEVIATHAN RISES
JIMMY PALMIOTTI AND JUSTIN GRAY:WRITERS
EDUARDO PANSICA:PENCILS
JÚLIO FERREIRA:INKS (PAGES 1-16, 19-20)
JP MAYER:INKS (PAGES 17-18)
CHRIS SOTOMAYOR:COLORS
DEZI SIENTY:LETTERS
DAN PANOSIAN:COVER
DAVE WIELGOSZ:ASSISTANT EDITOR
RACHEL GLUCKSTERN:EDITOR
MARK DOYLE:GROUP EDITOR
YOU SURE WE HAVE COMPLETE CONTROL OF THEIR EXTERNAL ELECTRONICS?
AFFIRMATIVE, BATWING.
ALL RIGHT. LET'S STEAL SOME ROBOTS AND GUNS!

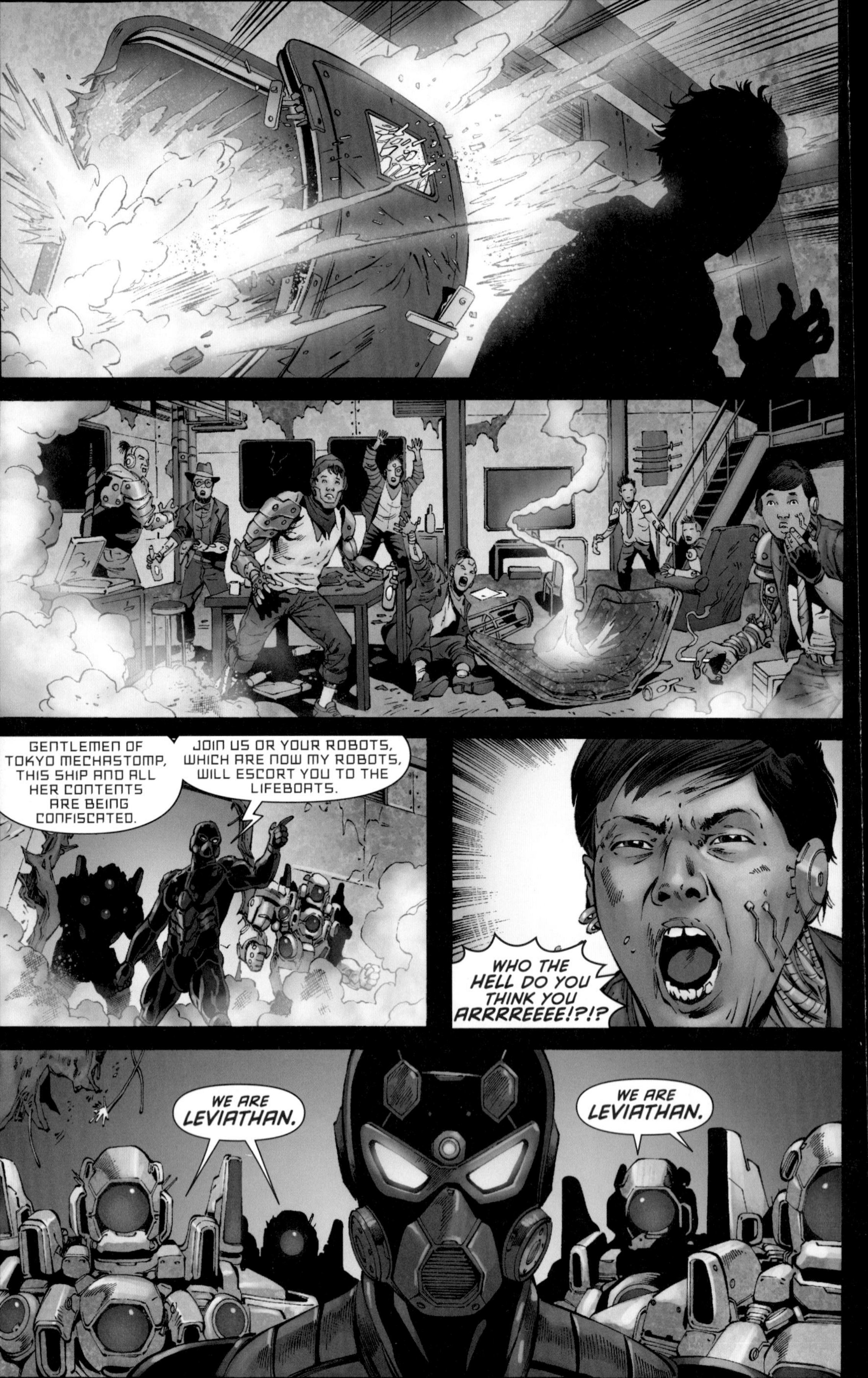
GENTLEMEN OF TOKYO MECHASTOMP, THIS SHIP AND ALL HER CONTENTS ARE BEING CONFISCATED.
JOIN US OR YOUR ROBOTS, WHICH ARE NOW MY ROBOTS, WILL ESCORT YOU TO THE LIFEBOATS.
WHO THE HELL DO YOU THINK YOU ARRRREEEE!?!?
WE ARE LEVIATHAN.
WE ARE LEVIATHAN.

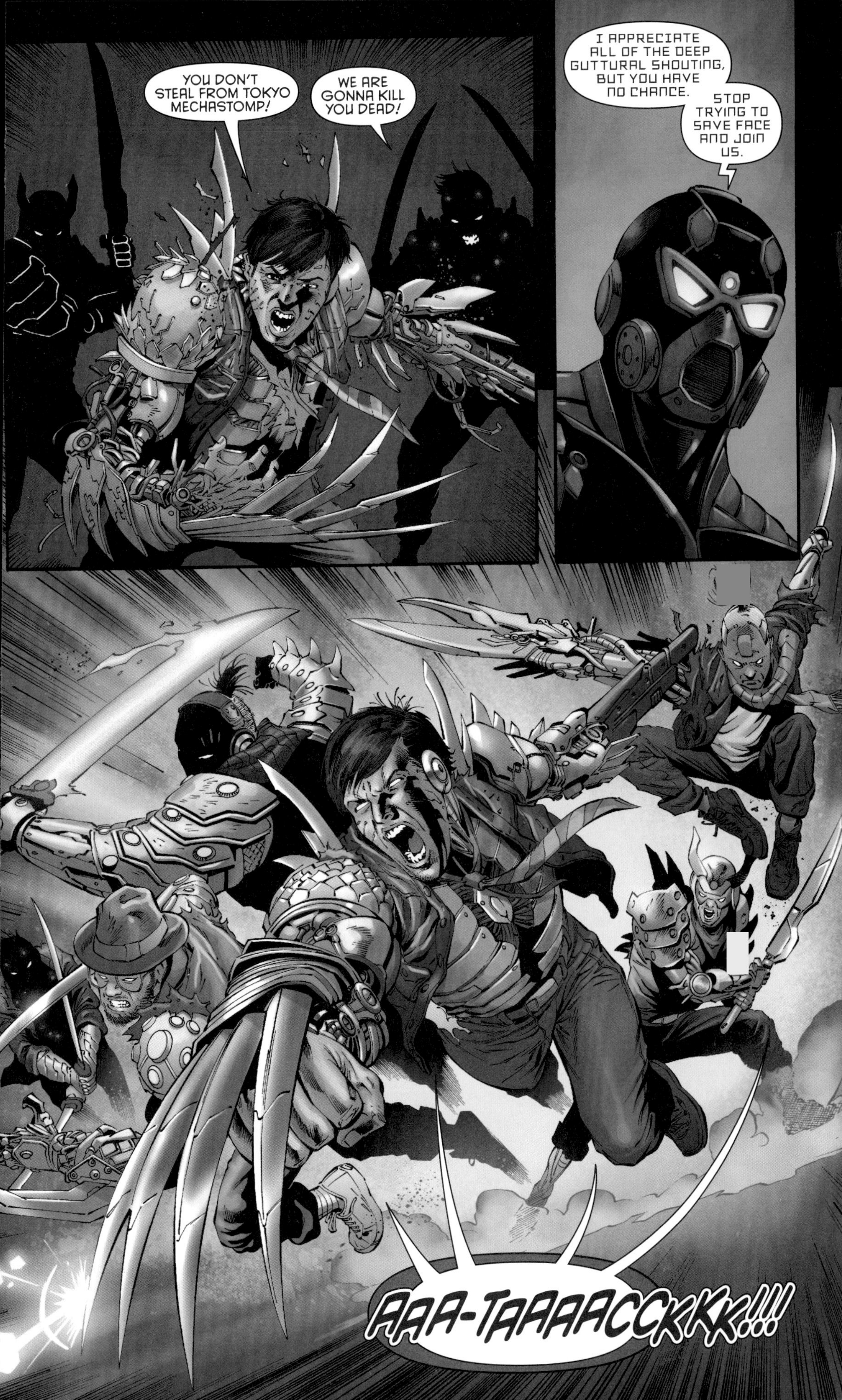
YOU DON'T STEAL FROM TOKYO MECHASTOMP!
WE ARE GONNA KILL YOU DEAD!
I APPRECIATE ALL OF THE DEEP GUTTURAL SHOUTING, BUT YOU HAVE NO CHANCE.
STOP TRYING TO SAVE FACE AND JOIN US.
AAA-TAAAACCKKK!!!

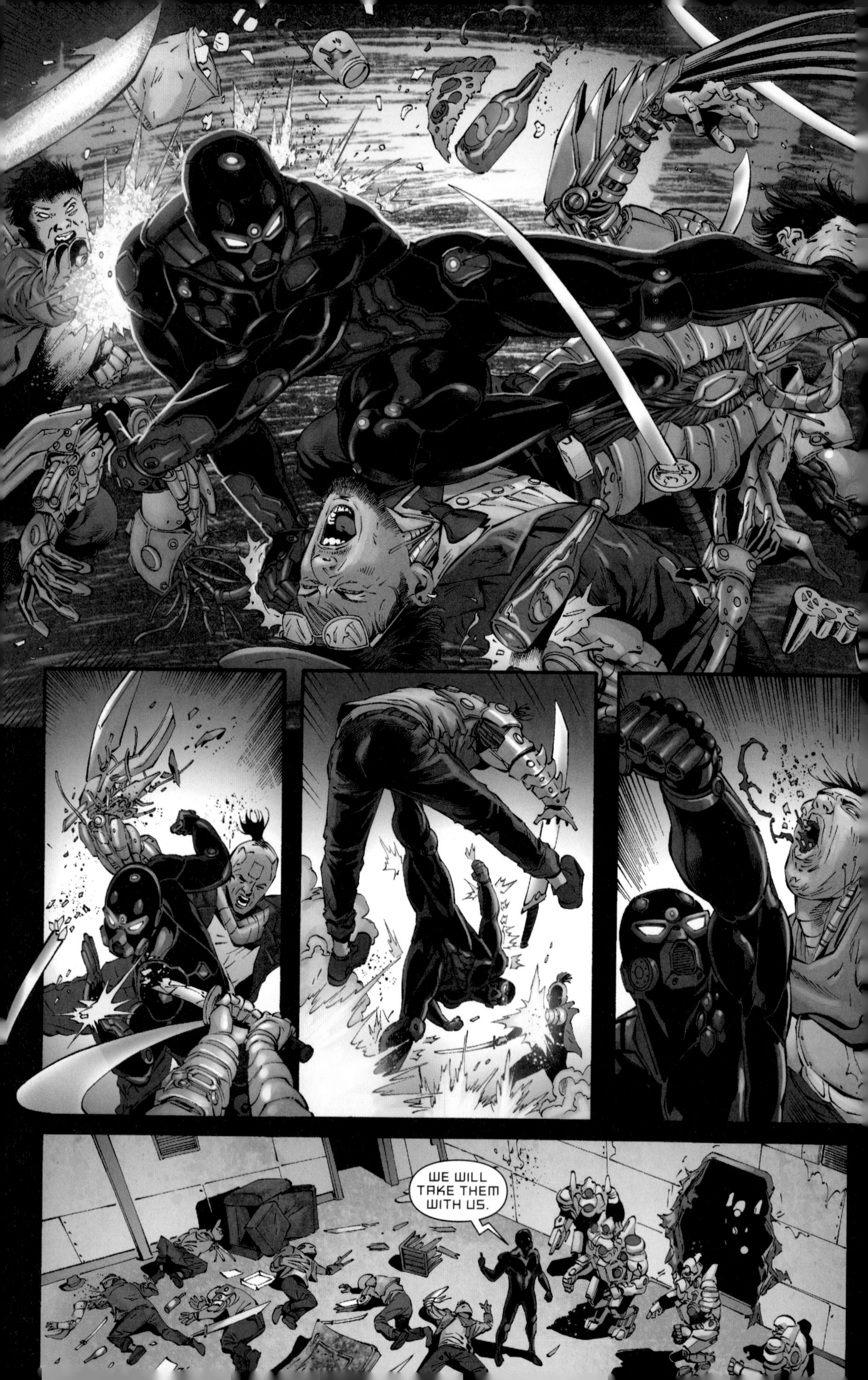
WE WILL TAKE THEM WITH US.

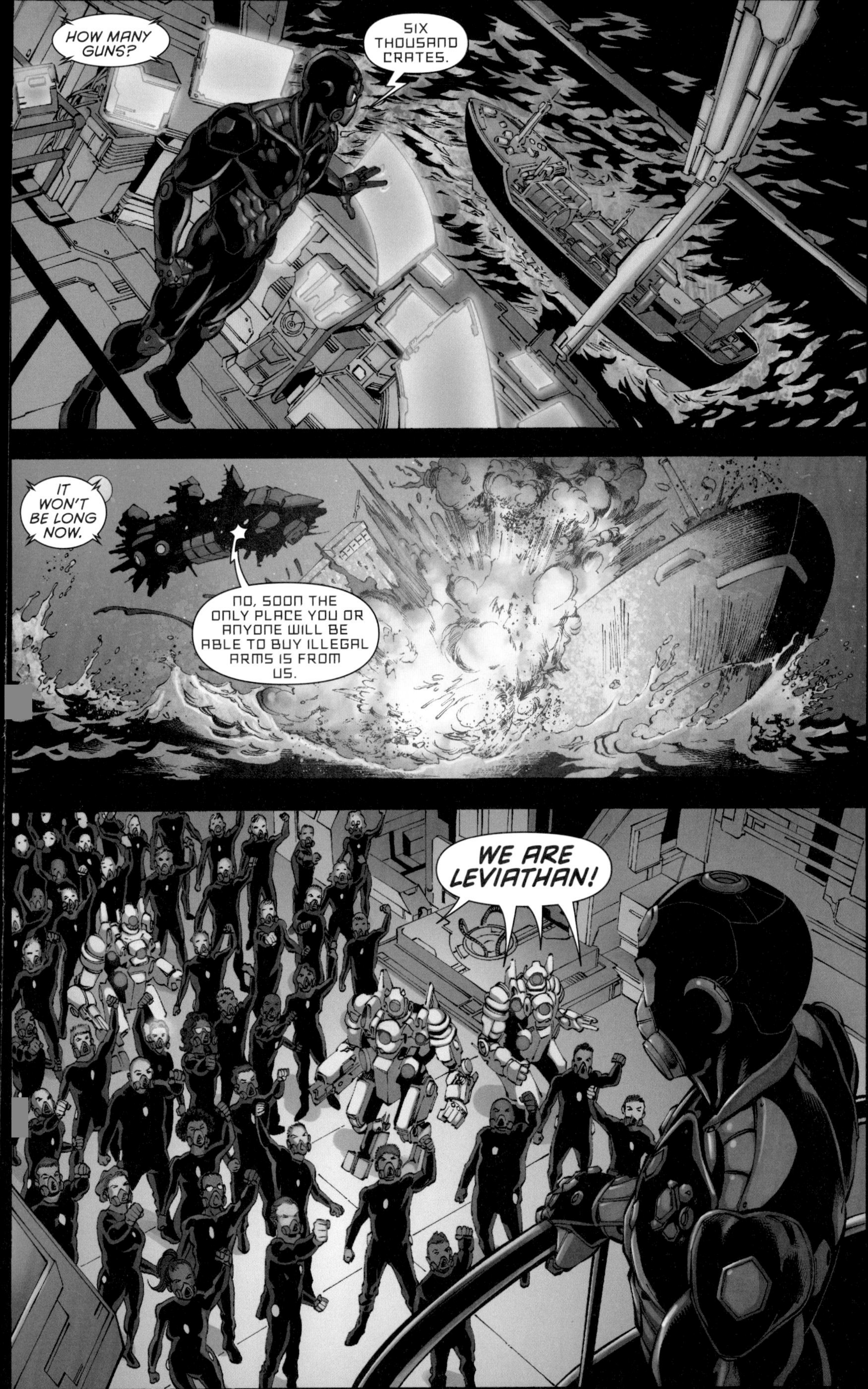
HOW MANY GUNS?
SIX THOUSAND CRATES.
IT WON'T BE LONG NOW.
NO, SOON THE ONLY PLACE YOU OR ANYONE WILL BE ABLE TO BUY ILLEGAL ARMS IS FROM US.
WE ARE LEVIATHAN!

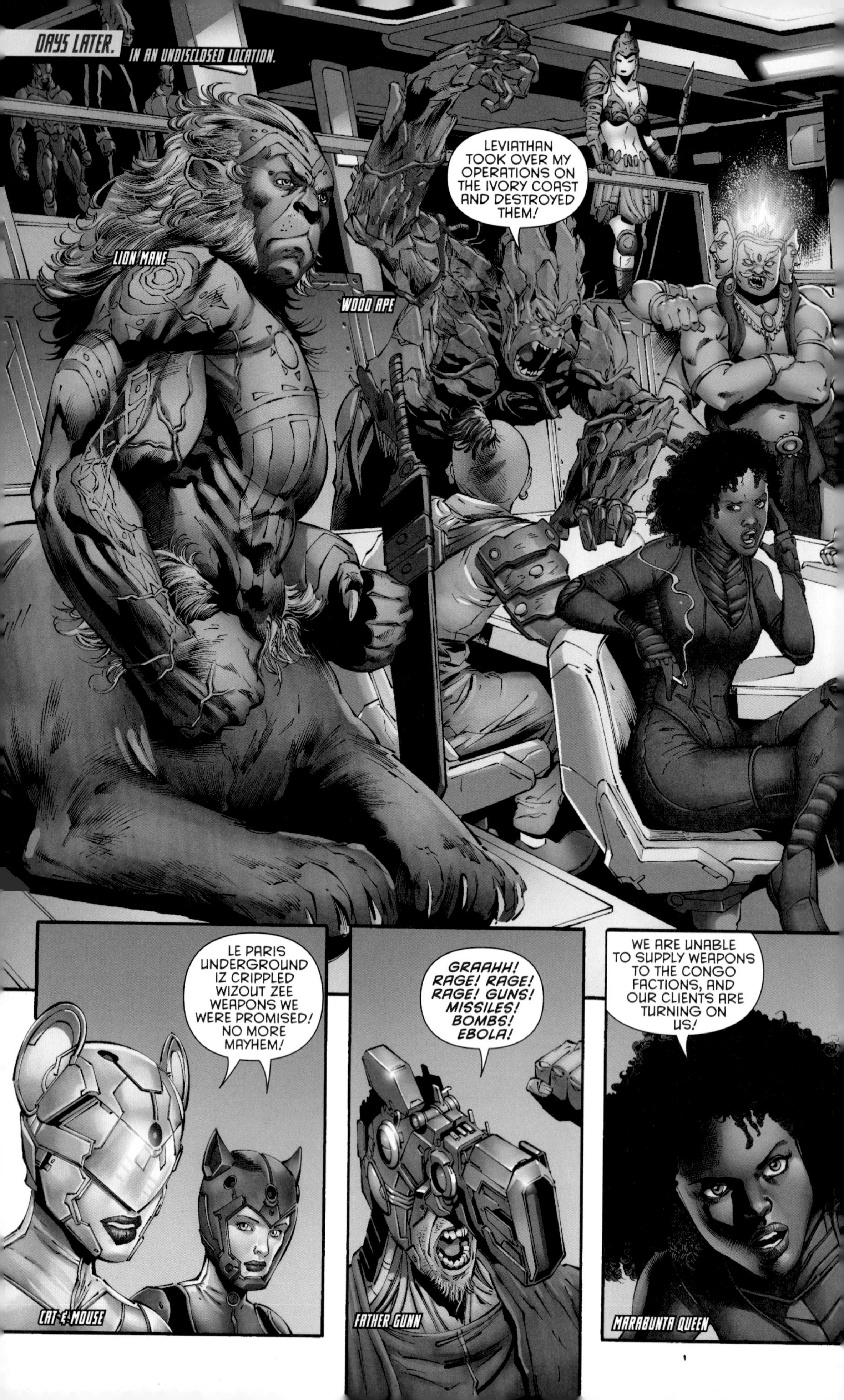
DAYS LATER.
IN AN UNDISCLOSED LOCATION.
LEVIATHAN TOOK OVER MY OPERATIONS ON THE IVORY COAST AND DESTROYED THEM!
LION MANE
WOOD APE
LE PARIS UNDERGROUND IZ CRIPPLED WIZOUT ZEE WEAPONS WE WERE PROMISED! NO MORE MAYHEM!
CAT & MOUSE
GRAAHH! RAGE! RAGE! RAGE! GUNS! MISSILES! BOMBS! EBOLA!
FATHER GUNN
WE ARE UNABLE TO SUPPLY WEAPONS TO THE CONGO FACTIONS, AND OUR CLIENTS ARE TURNING ON US!
MARABUNTA QUEEN

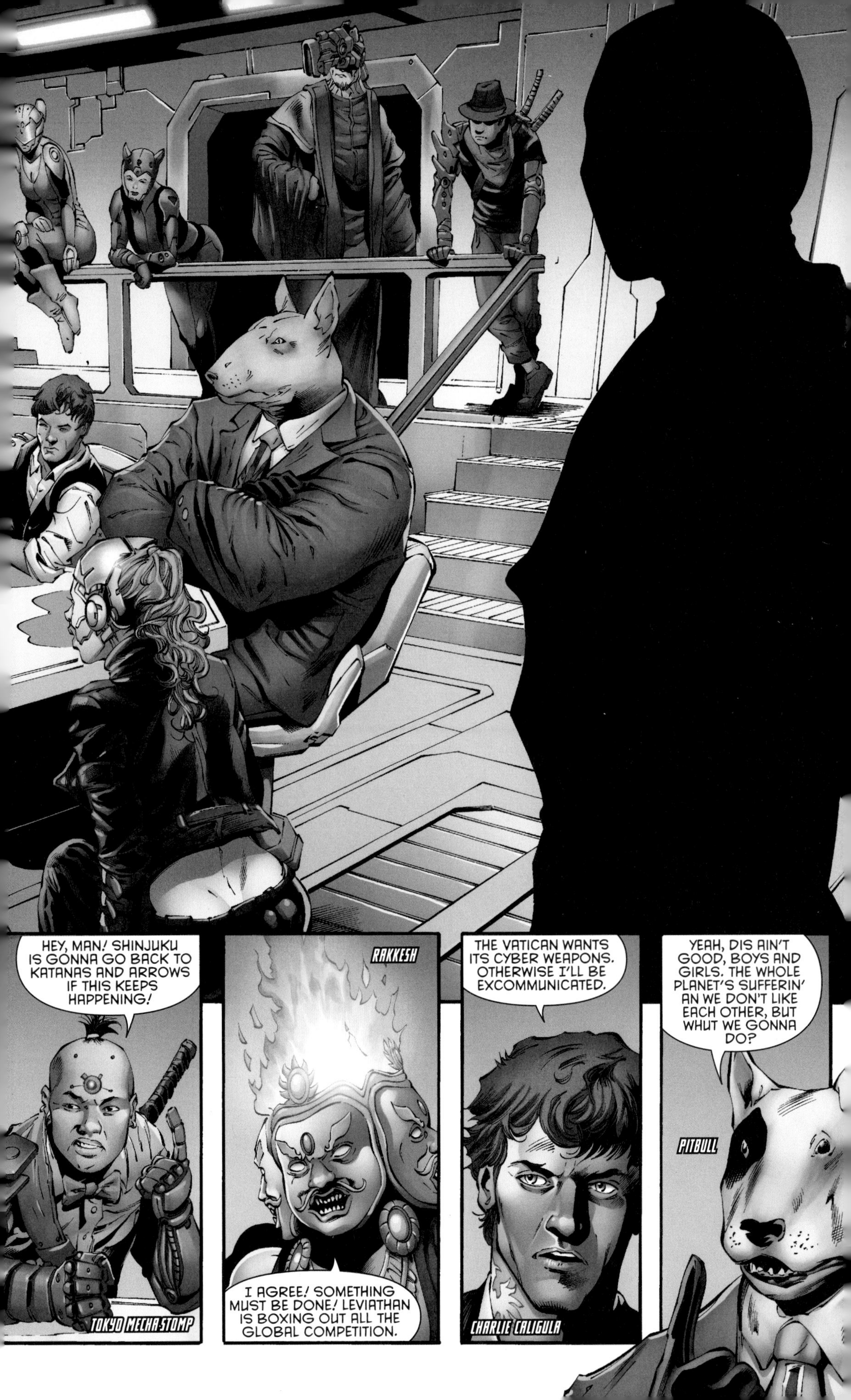
HEY, MAN! SHINJUKU IS GONNA GO BACK TO KATANAS AND ARROWS IF THIS KEEPS HAPPENING!
TOKYO MECHA-STOMP
RAKKESH
I AGREE! SOMETHING MUST BE DONE! LEVIATHAN IS BOXING OUT ALL THE GLOBAL COMPETITION.
THE VATICAN WANTS ITS CYBER WEAPONS. OTHERWISE I'LL BE EXCOMMUNICATED.
CHARLIE CALIGULA
YEAH, DIS AIN'T GOOD, BOYS AND GIRLS. THE WHOLE PLANET'S SUFFERIN' AN WE DON'T LIKE EACH OTHER, BUT WHUT WE GONNA DO?
PITBULL

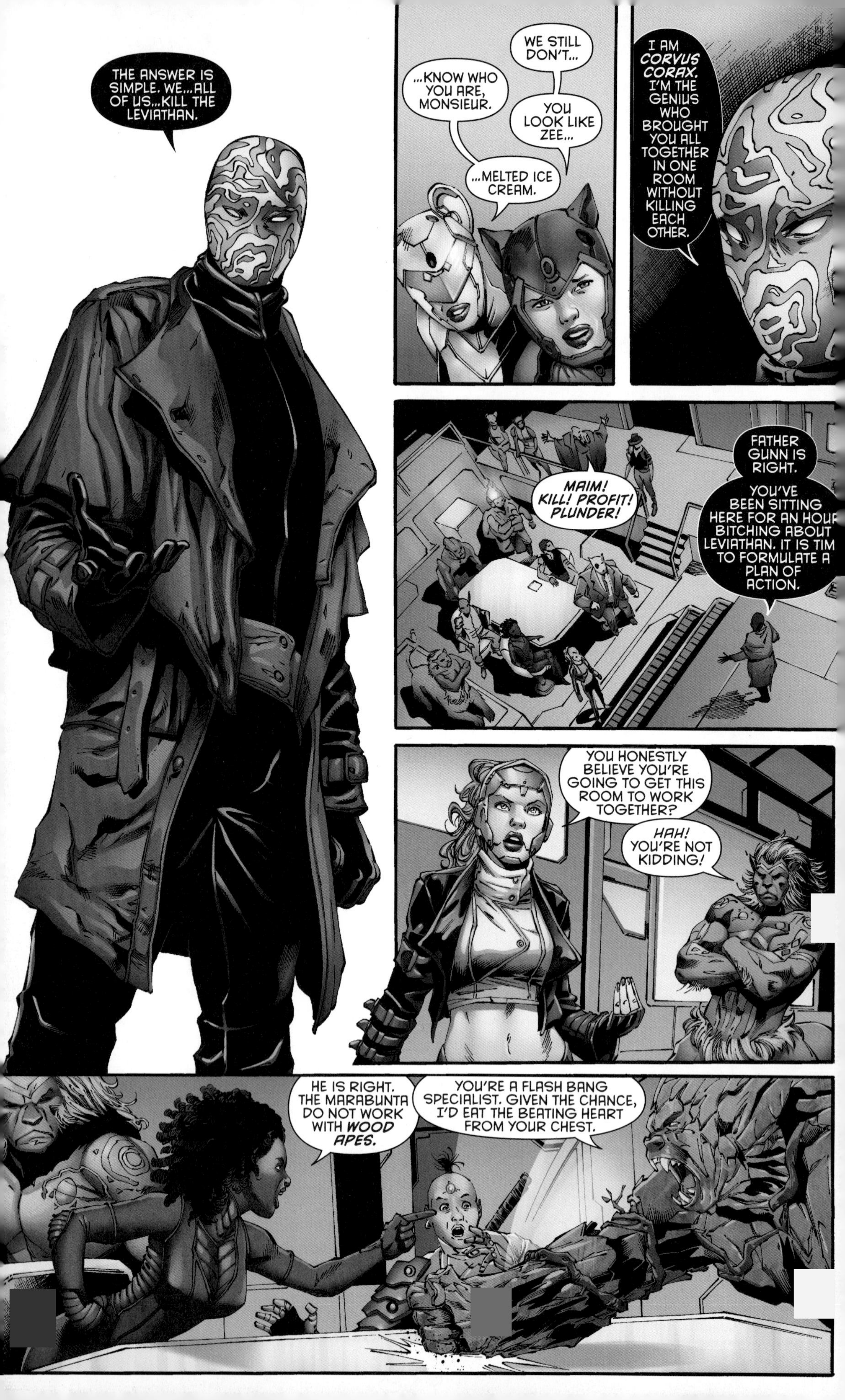

THE ANSWER IS SIMPLE. WE...ALL OF US...KILL THE LEVIATHAN.
WE STILL DON'T...
...KNOW WHO YOU ARE, MONSIEUR.
YOU LOOK LIKE ZEE...
...MELTED ICE CREAM.
I AM *CORVUS CORAX.* I'M THE GENIUS WHO BROUGHT YOU ALL TOGETHER IN ONE ROOM WITHOUT KILLING EACH OTHER.
MAIM! KILL! PROFIT! PLUNDER!
FATHER GUNN IS RIGHT.
YOU'VE BEEN SITTING HERE FOR AN HOU BITCHING ABOUT LEVIATHAN. IT IS TIM TO FORMULATE A PLAN OF ACTION.
YOU HONESTLY BELIEVE YOU'RE GOING TO GET THIS ROOM TO WORK TOGETHER?
HAH! YOU'RE NOT KIDDING*!*
HE IS RIGHT. THE MARABUNTA DO NOT WORK WITH *WOOD APES.*
YOU'RE A FLASH BANG SPECIALIST. GIVEN THE CHANCE, I'D EAT THE BEATING HEART FROM YOUR CHEST.

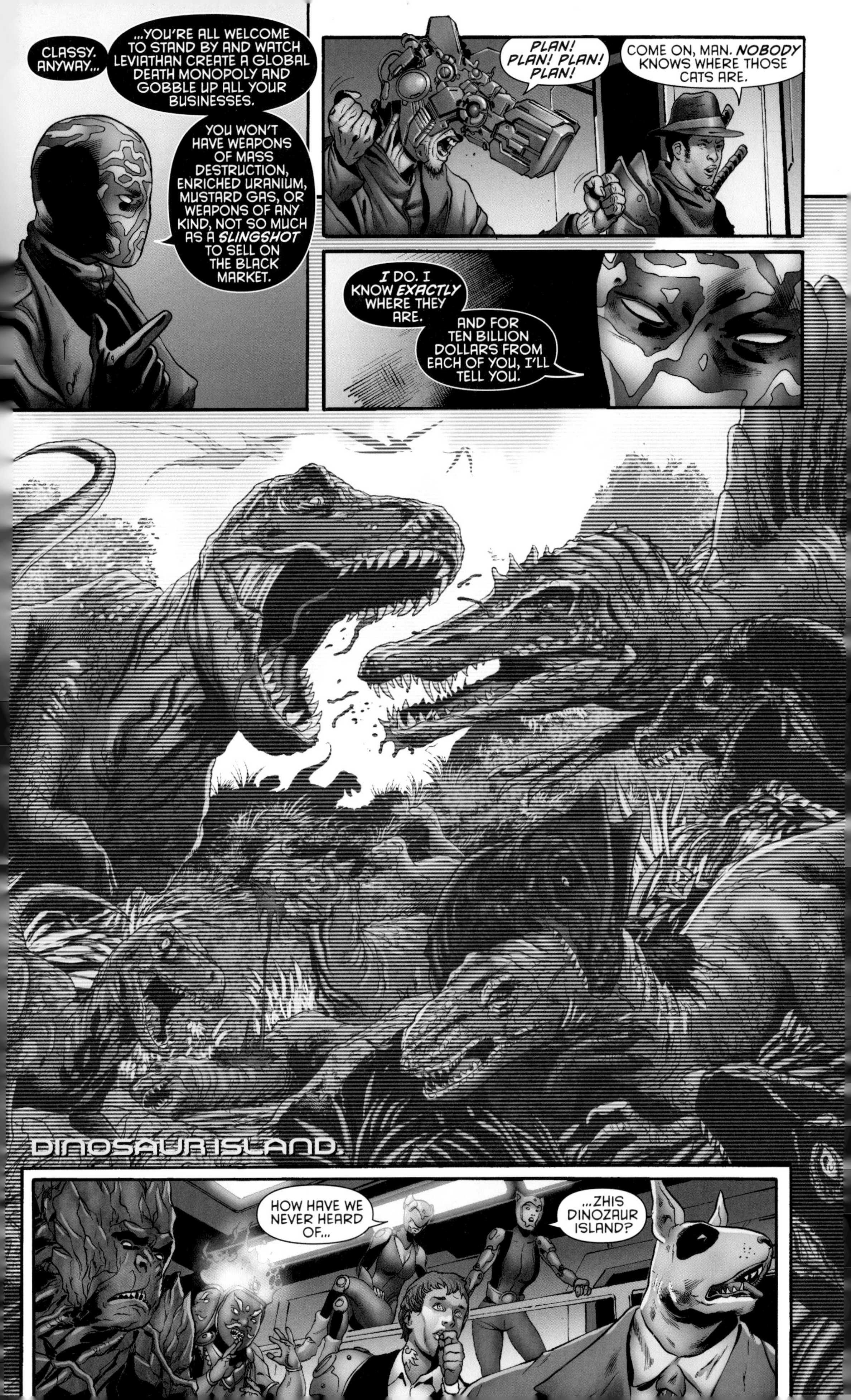
CLASSY. ANYWAY...
...YOU'RE ALL WELCOME TO STAND BY AND WATCH LEVIATHAN CREATE A GLOBAL DEATH MONOPOLY AND GOBBLE UP ALL YOUR BUSINESSES.
YOU WON'T HAVE WEAPONS OF MASS DESTRUCTION, ENRICHED URANIUM, MUSTARD GAS, OR WEAPONS OF ANY KIND, NOT SO MUCH AS A SLINGSHOT TO SELL ON THE BLACK MARKET.
PLAN! PLAN! PLAN! PLAN!
COME ON, MAN. NOBODY KNOWS WHERE THOSE CATS ARE.
I DO. I KNOW EXACTLY WHERE THEY ARE.
AND FOR TEN BILLION DOLLARS FROM EACH OF YOU, I'LL TELL YOU.
DINOSAUR ISLAND.
HOW HAVE WE NEVER HEARD OF...
...ZHIS DINOZAUR ISLAND?

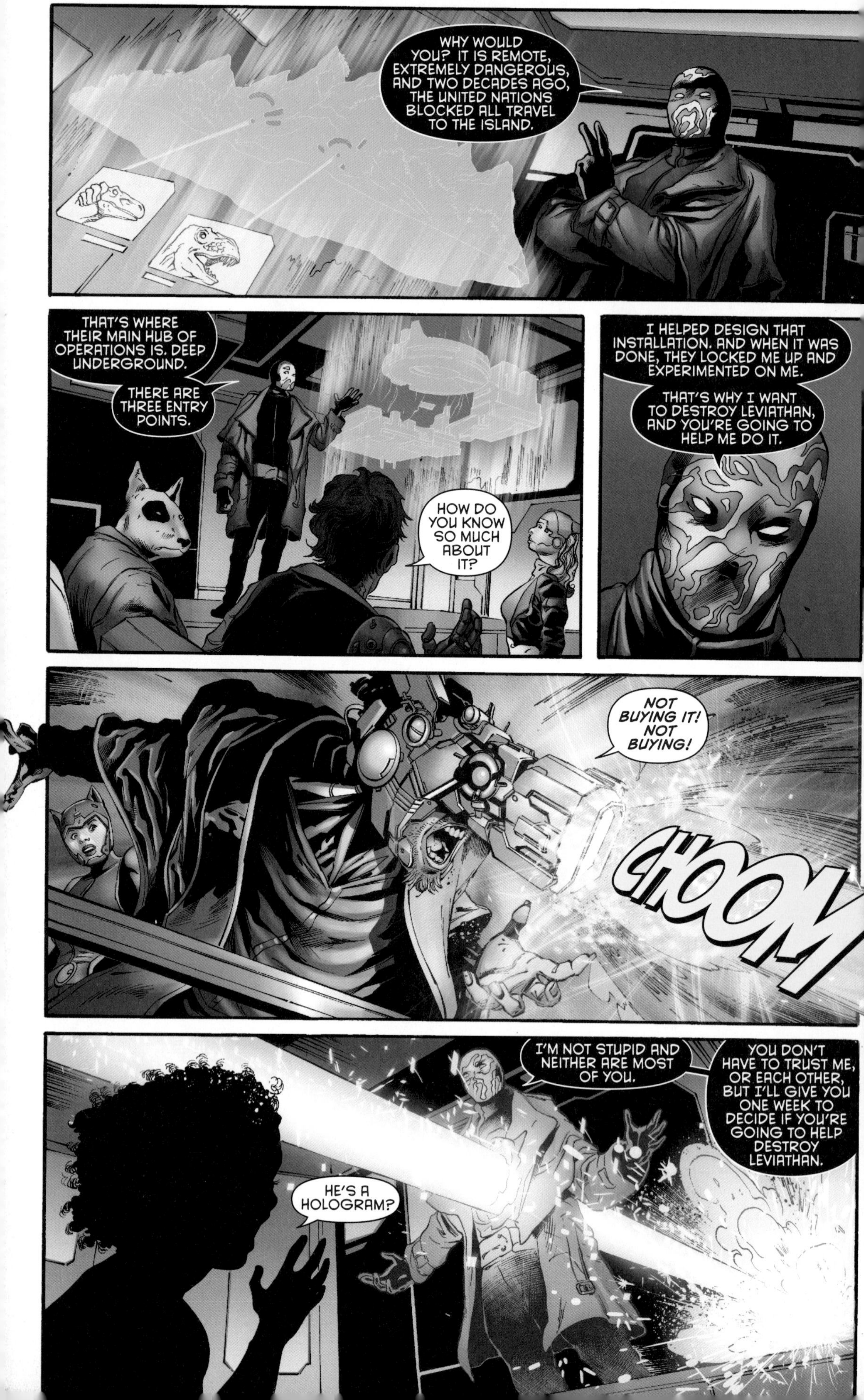
WHY WOULD YOU? IT IS REMOTE, EXTREMELY DANGEROUS, AND TWO DECADES AGO, THE UNITED NATIONS BLOCKED ALL TRAVEL TO THE ISLAND.
THAT'S WHERE THEIR MAIN HUB OF OPERATIONS IS. DEEP UNDERGROUND.
THERE ARE THREE ENTRY POINTS.
HOW DO YOU KNOW SO MUCH ABOUT IT?
I HELPED DESIGN THAT INSTALLATION. AND WHEN IT WAS DONE, THEY LOCKED ME UP AND EXPERIMENTED ON ME.
THAT'S WHY I WANT TO DESTROY LEVIATHAN, AND YOU'RE GOING TO HELP ME DO IT.
NOT BUYING IT! NOT BUYING!
CHOOM
I'M NOT STUPID AND NEITHER ARE MOST OF YOU.
YOU DON'T HAVE TO TRUST ME, OR EACH OTHER, BUT I'LL GIVE YOU ONE WEEK TO DECIDE IF YOU'RE GOING TO HELP DESTROY LEVIATHAN.
HE'S A HOLOGRAM?

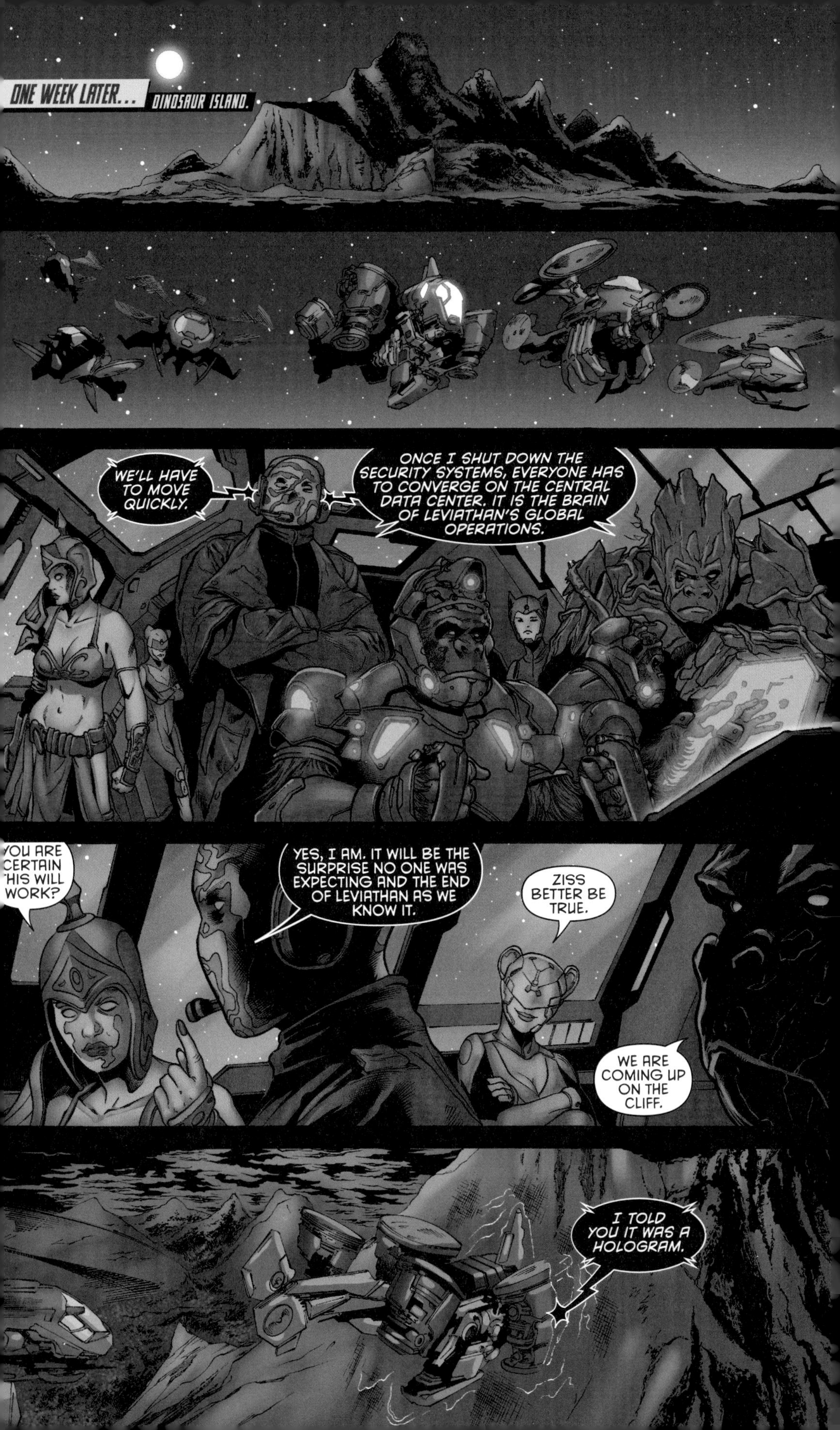

ONE WEEK LATER...
DINOSAUR ISLAND.
WE'LL HAVE TO MOVE QUICKLY.
ONCE I SHUT DOWN THE SECURITY SYSTEMS, EVERYONE HAS TO CONVERGE ON THE CENTRAL DATA CENTER. IT IS THE BRAIN OF LEVIATHAN'S GLOBAL OPERATIONS.
YOU ARE CERTAIN THIS WILL WORK?
YES, I AM. IT WILL BE THE SURPRISE NO ONE WAS EXPECTING AND THE END OF LEVIATHAN AS WE KNOW IT.
ZISS BETTER BE TRUE.
WE ARE COMING UP ON THE CLIFF.
I TOLD YOU IT WAS A HOLOGRAM.

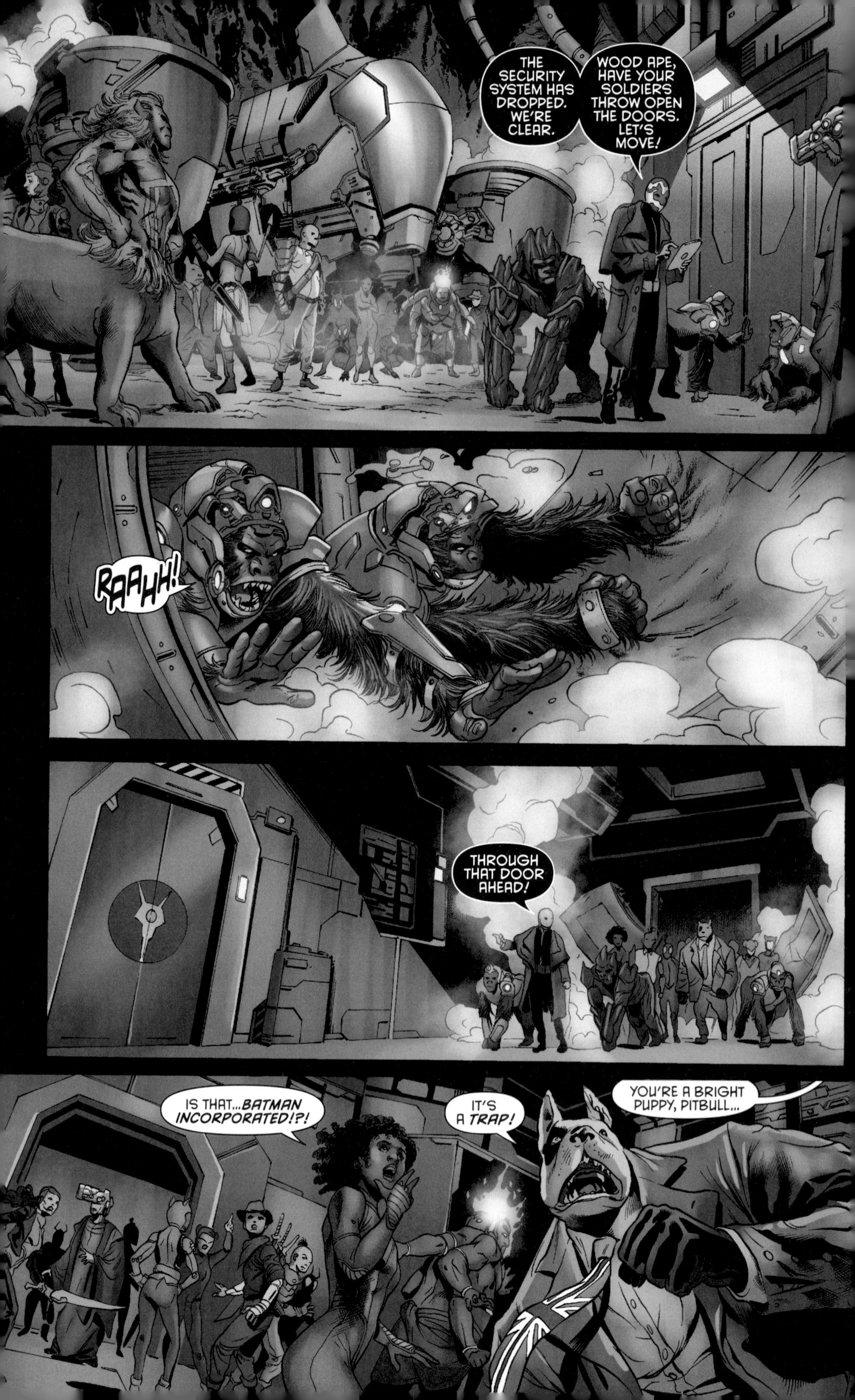
THE SECURITY SYSTEM HAS DROPPED. WE'RE CLEAR.
WOOD APE, HAVE YOUR SOLDIERS THROW OPEN THE DOORS. LET'S MOVE!
RAAHH!
THROUGH THAT DOOR AHEAD!
IS THAT...BATMAN INCORPORATED!?!
IT'S A TRAP!
YOU'RE A BRIGHT PUPPY, PITBULL...

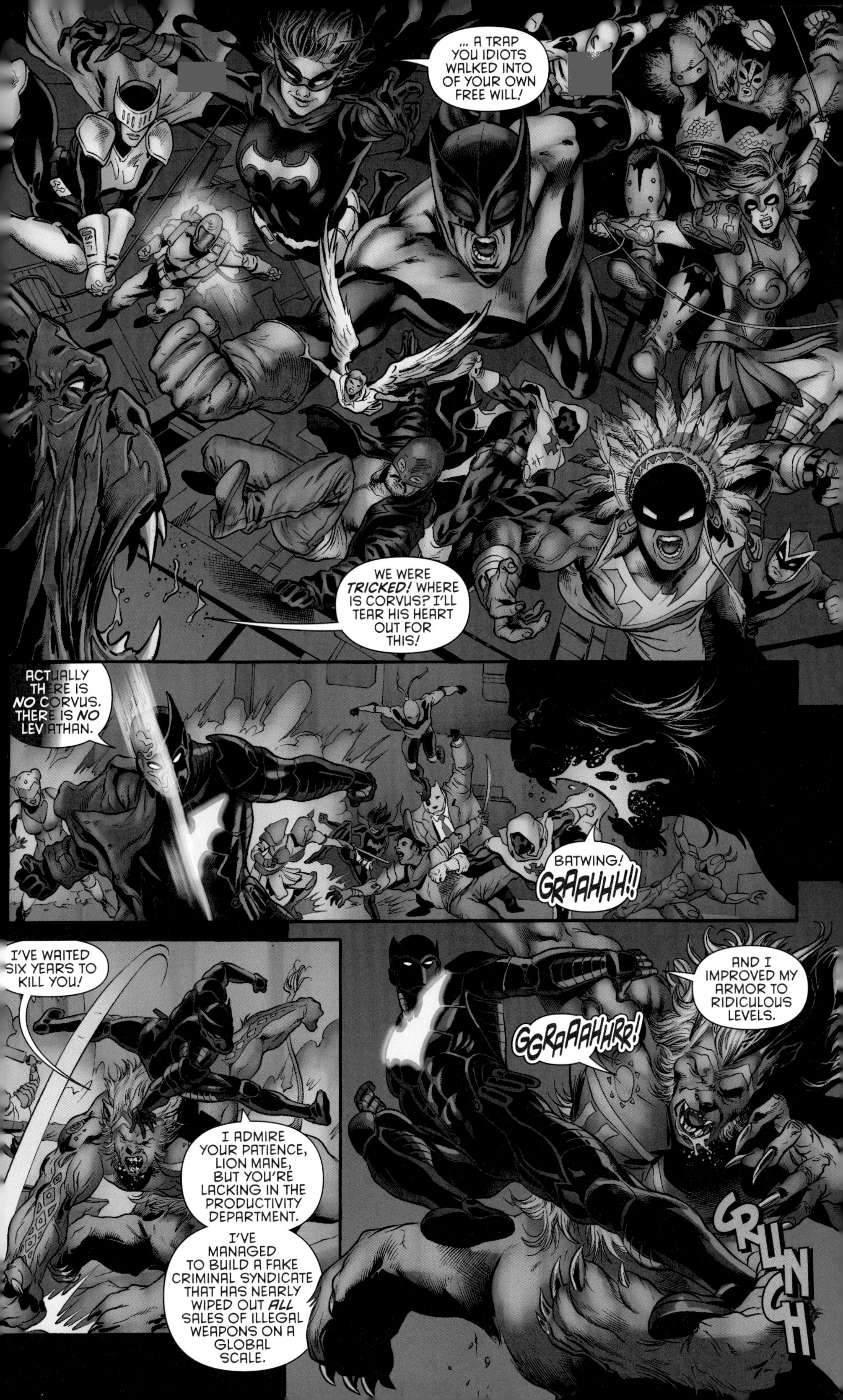
... A TRAP YOU IDIOTS WALKED INTO OF YOUR OWN FREE WILL!
WE WERE *TRICKED!* WHERE IS CORVUS? I'LL TEAR HIS HEART OUT FOR THIS!
ACTUALLY THERE IS *NO* CORVUS. THERE IS *NO* LEVIATHAN.
BATWING!
GRAAHHH!!
I'VE WAITED SIX YEARS TO KILL YOU!
I ADMIRE YOUR PATIENCE, LION MANE, BUT YOU'RE LACKING IN THE PRODUCTIVITY DEPARTMENT.
I'VE MANAGED TO BUILD A FAKE CRIMINAL SYNDICATE THAT HAS NEARLY WIPED OUT *ALL* SALES OF ILLEGAL WEAPONS ON A GLOBAL SCALE.
AND I IMPROVED MY ARMOR TO RIDICULOUS LEVELS.
GGRAAAHHRR!
CRUNCH

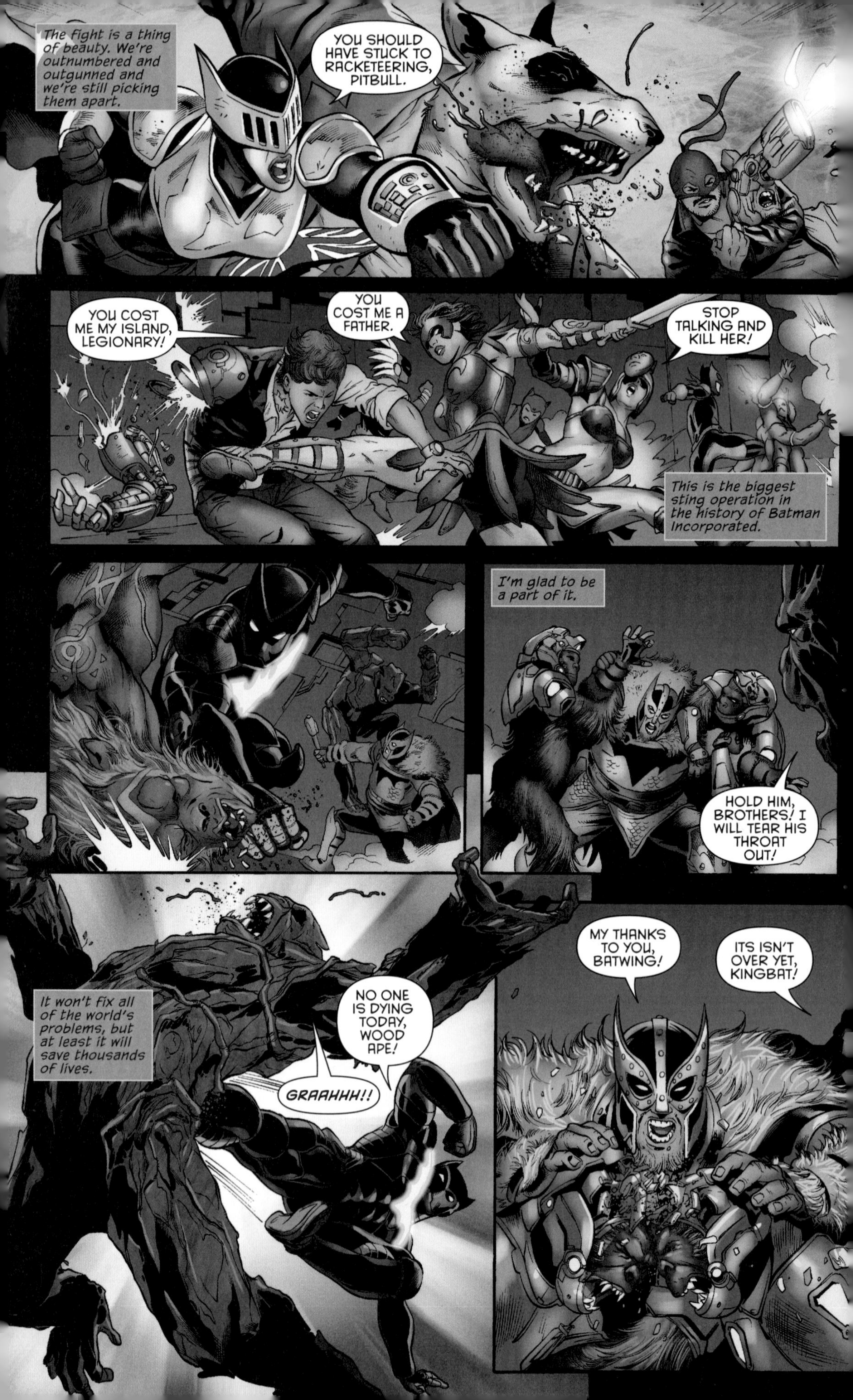
The fight is a thing of beauty. We're outnumbered and outgunned and we're still picking them apart.
YOU SHOULD HAVE STUCK TO RACKETEERING, PITBULL.
YOU COST ME MY ISLAND, LEGIONARY!
YOU COST ME A FATHER.
STOP TALKING AND KILL HER!
This is the biggest sting operation in the history of Batman Incorporated.
I'm glad to be a part of it.
HOLD HIM, BROTHERS! I WILL TEAR HIS THROAT OUT!
It won't fix all of the world's problems, but at least it will save thousands of lives.
NO ONE IS DYING TODAY, WOOD APE!
GRAAHHH!!
MY THANKS TO YOU, BATWING!
ITS ISN'T OVER YET, KINGBAT!

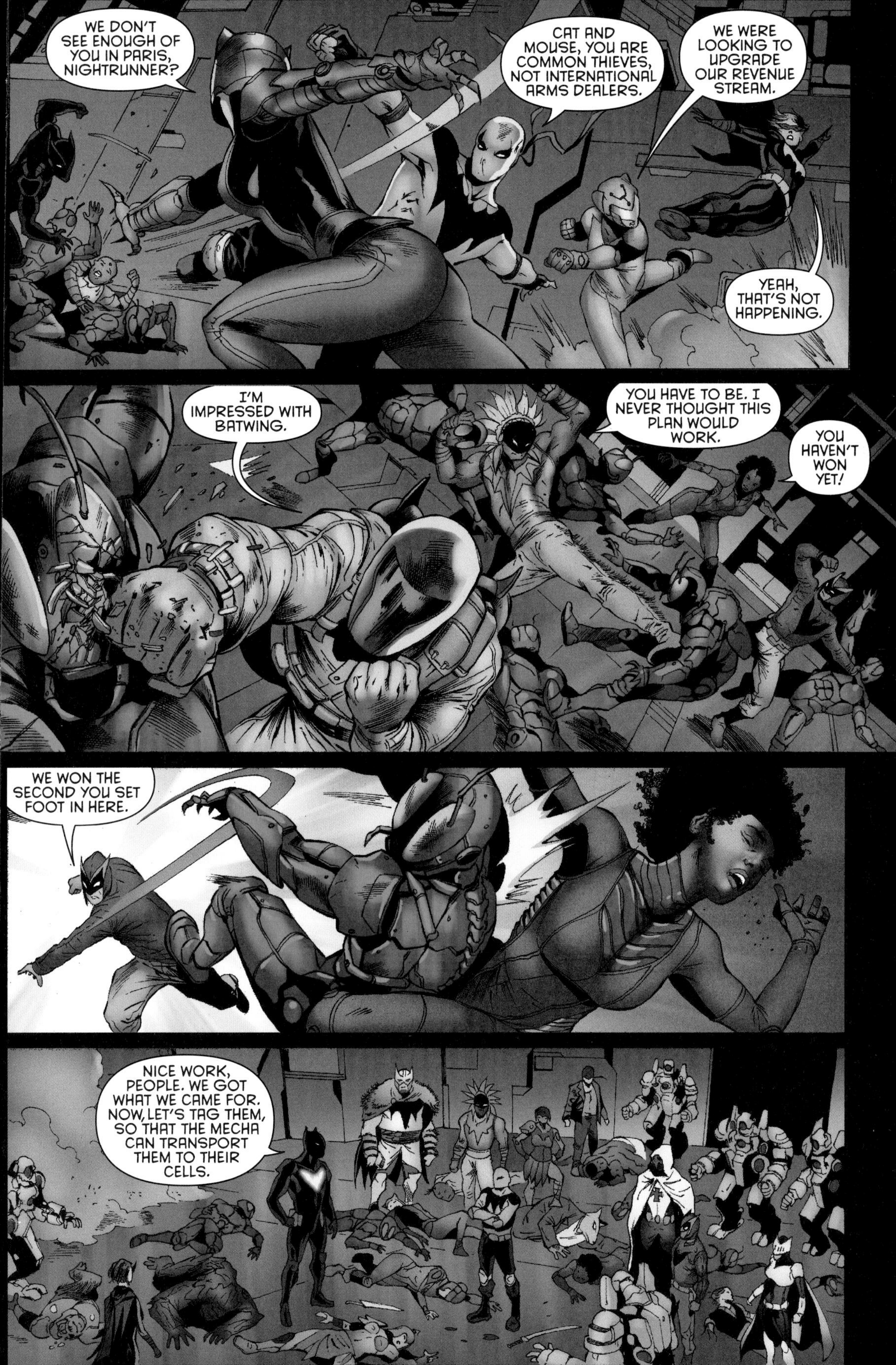
WE DON'T SEE ENOUGH OF YOU IN PARIS, NIGHTRUNNER?
CAT AND MOUSE, YOU ARE COMMON THIEVES, NOT INTERNATIONAL ARMS DEALERS.
WE WERE LOOKING TO UPGRADE OUR REVENUE STREAM.
YEAH, THAT'S NOT HAPPENING.
I'M IMPRESSED WITH BATWING.
YOU HAVE TO BE. I NEVER THOUGHT THIS PLAN WOULD WORK.
YOU HAVEN'T WON YET!
WE WON THE SECOND YOU SET FOOT IN HERE.
NICE WORK, PEOPLE. WE GOT WHAT WE CAME FOR. NOW, LET'S TAG THEM, SO THAT THE MECHA CAN TRANSPORT THEM TO THEIR CELLS.

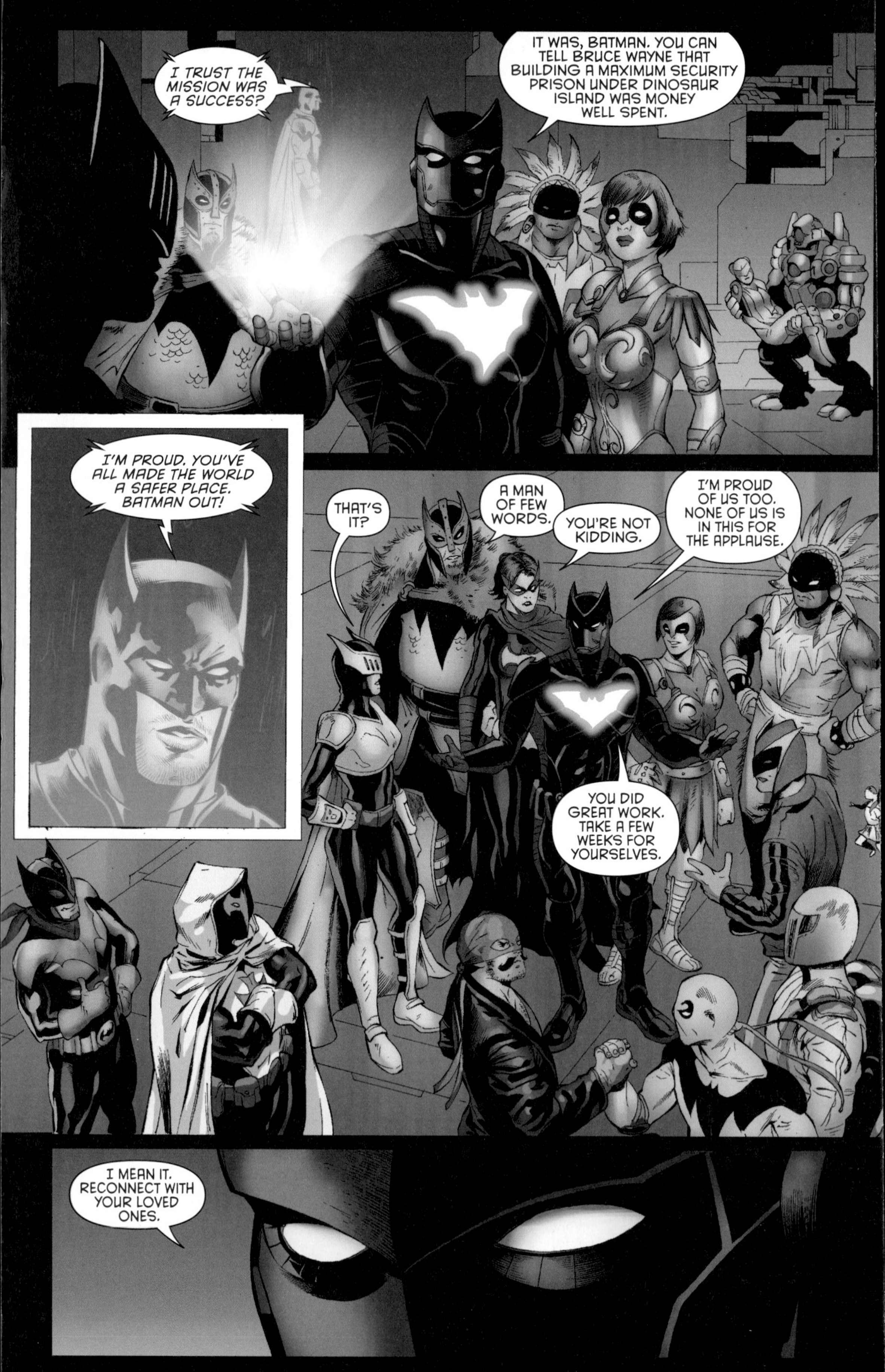
I TRUST THE MISSION WAS A SUCCESS?
IT WAS, BATMAN. YOU CAN TELL BRUCE WAYNE THAT BUILDING A MAXIMUM SECURITY PRISON UNDER DINOSAUR ISLAND WAS MONEY WELL SPENT.
I'M PROUD. YOU'VE ALL MADE THE WORLD A SAFER PLACE. BATMAN OUT!
THAT'S IT?
A MAN OF FEW WORDS.
YOU'RE NOT KIDDING.
I'M PROUD OF US TOO. NONE OF US IS IN THIS FOR THE APPLAUSE.
YOU DID GREAT WORK. TAKE A FEW WEEKS FOR YOURSELVES.
I MEAN IT. RECONNECT WITH YOUR LOVED ONES.

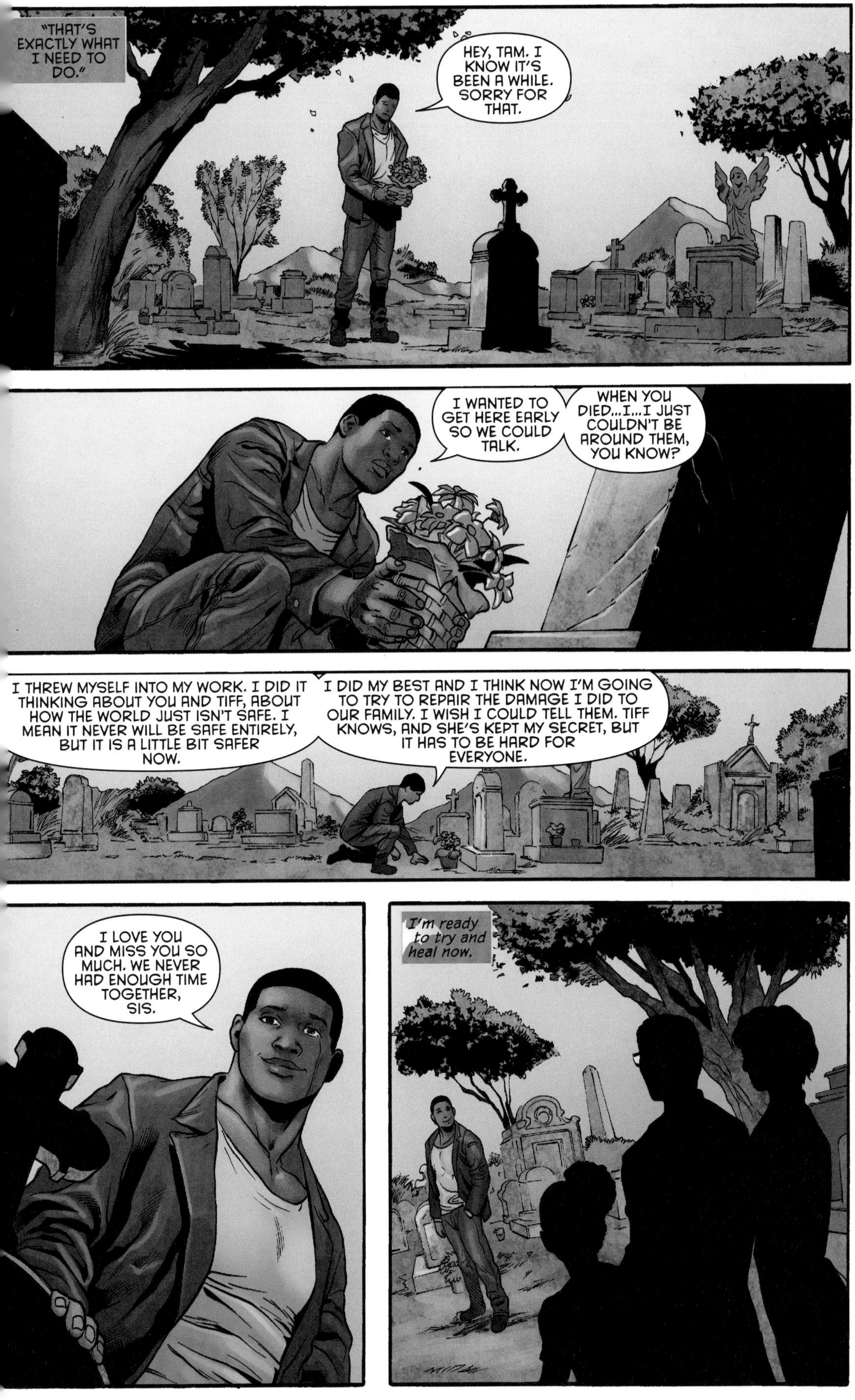
"THAT'S EXACTLY WHAT I NEED TO DO."
HEY, TAM. I KNOW IT'S BEEN A WHILE. SORRY FOR THAT.
I WANTED TO GET HERE EARLY SO WE COULD TALK.
WHEN YOU DIED...I...I JUST COULDN'T BE AROUND THEM, YOU KNOW?
I THREW MYSELF INTO MY WORK. I DID IT THINKING ABOUT YOU AND TIFF, ABOUT HOW THE WORLD JUST ISN'T SAFE. I MEAN IT NEVER WILL BE SAFE ENTIRELY, BUT IT IS A LITTLE BIT SAFER NOW.
I DID MY BEST AND I THINK NOW I'M GOING TO TRY TO REPAIR THE DAMAGE I DID TO OUR FAMILY. I WISH I COULD TELL THEM. TIFF KNOWS, AND SHE'S KEPT MY SECRET, BUT IT HAS TO BE HARD FOR EVERYONE.
I LOVE YOU AND MISS YOU SO MUCH. WE NEVER HAD ENOUGH TIME TOGETHER, SIS.
I'm ready to try and heal now.

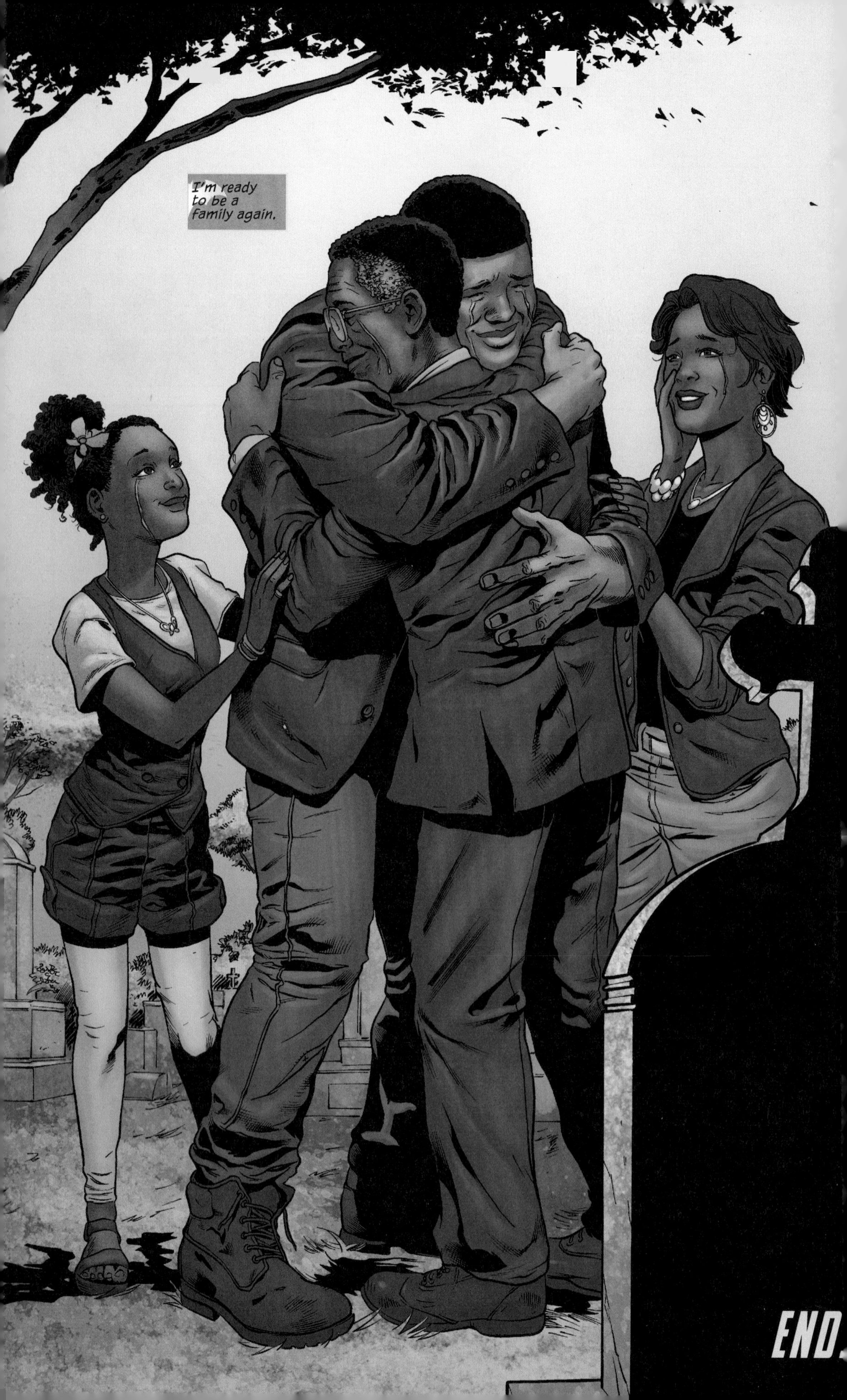
I'm ready to be a family again.
END.